# MEDIEVAL ENGLAND

# MEDIEVAL ENGLAND

EDITED BY

## H W C DAVIS

STUDIO
EDITIONS

London

Reprinted by arrangement with Oxford University Press
Copyright Oxford University Press 1928

This edition published under licence in 1993 by Studio Editions Ltd
Princess House, 50 Eastcastle Street
London W1N 7AP, England

ISBN 1 85891 077 3

Printed in India

# PREFACE

MANY changes and additions have been made in the new edition of the *Companion*; but the plan of the work, as laid down by the original editor, Dr. F. Pierrepont Barnard, has not been modified. Though Dr. Barnard has been prevented by other learned preoccupations from making himself responsible for the revision of the volume, his help and counsel have been freely rendered. The following chapters and sections have been written *de novo* : Ecclesiastical Architecture; The Monks, the Friars, and the Secular Clergy; Handwriting (Chap. XI, § 2); Printed Books (Chap. XI, § 3); Coinage. The rest have been revised and brought to date where there was need.

H. W. C. D.

# CONTENTS

# LIST OF ILLUSTRATIONS

PAGE

A STREET SCENE. Presentation of a book to the Author's Patron, fifteenth century. From the miniature by Jean Fouquet    *Frontispiece*

# ILLUSTRATIONS

# ILLUSTRATIONS xix

PAGE

## XI. LEARNING AND EDUCATION

# I

# ECCLESIASTICAL ARCHITECTURE

And now it is all gone—like an unsubstantial pageant faded ; and between us and the Old English there lies a gulf of mystery which the prose of the historian will never adequately bridge. They cannot come to us, and our imagination can but feebly penetrate to them. Only among the aisles of the cathedral, only as we gaze upon their silent figures sleeping on their tombs, some faint conceptions float before us of what these men were when they were alive.'

## I. *Historical Evolution.*

ARCHITECTURE, like all the arts, has its origin in religion ; its earliest, and still its highest, aim is to mark out and dignify by a permanent memorial a place sanctified by the presence of a spiritual power. It began in the monoliths set up on their wanderings by pastoral peoples ages before the beginnings of agriculture suggested to man the need for permanent shelter for himself and his belongings. And no sooner had the idea occurred to him of protecting his family or his tribe by enclosing walls than he applied it to the sanctuary of his gods and surrounded the sacred site with a stone circle. So, when he made a permanent roof for himself, he made a still more substantial one for his holy places. But the early temples, and all true temples, are first of all the visible witness to the Presence of God and only secondarily a shelter for those who minister or worship at the shrine.

A church, as much as a prehistoric menhir, is a monument set up for a testimony ; and its tower and spire, its size and splendour above any congregational needs of the parish, are evidence of the fact ; these things have their material uses, but before all else they exist to proclaim the Divine Presence at the Altar.

The essential part, the nucleus, of any ecclesiastical building, whether monastery, cathedral, parish church, or private chapel,[1] is therefore the sanctuary in which the high altar stands ; and from it has developed all the rest of the structure, however large and complicated. It is for this essential part that the rector, who holds the principal

[1] *Vide* ' chapel ', *N. E. D.*

endowment of the church, is still personally and directly responsible.

The first Christian church was no doubt a sanctuary simply ; but the earliest type of which any trace remains was an oblong building with an apse at one end as in the Roman basilica ; the altar stood in front of the apse, which enabled those who served it to pass behind it ; and in the apse itself was the chair of the chief celebrant. There was apparently no division of the building into presbytery and nave ; if the building was too wide to be spanned by beams of ordinary length, two rows of pillars were set up parallel to the long sides ; on these were built two lines of thin wall, standing as it were on legs, to carry the beams of a high medial roof ; rows of openings, the clerestory, in these walls threw ample light down into the middle of the church, and below them sloping roofs to the side walls covered the aisles [Figs. 1 and 2].

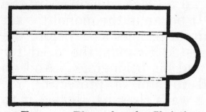

FIG. 1. Plan of early Christian church (S. Agata, Ravenna) with apse, and columns carrying clerestory walls.

There was usually also a *narthex* or large porch at the end remote from the apse ; and the growth in membership and organization of the body is soon reflected in the building by the provision of screens enclosing the space in front of the altar and so reserving it for the officiating clergy. Thus the church was divided into two parts ; one, containing the sanctuary, was called, from the screens (*cancelli*) enclosing it, the chancel ; the other became the nave [Fig. 3]. The foundations of a small Christian church excavated at Silchester show that this, the basilican, plan was introduced into Britain during the Roman occupation ; and as St. Martin's, Canterbury, has Roman work in its walls it is probable that it was originally a basilican church. Brixworth, Northants., and Wing, Bucks., are rare examples of attempts made by early Saxon builders to reproduce the basilican plan ; there were several others in Kent, notably Reculver, of which only foundations or ruins remain. But the native skill was not elsewhere equal to the construction of aisled, apsidal churches ; and, although the Normans reintroduced the apse, it never became a common feature in English architecture. By the time we had acquired the skill to build it we had lost the wish ; for the rectangular chancel, whether copied from Celtic churches or, as is more likely, adopted as being easier to construct, had proved to be the most convenient form.

In the centuries that followed the barbarian inroads and the subsequent Christianization of western Europe the tendency was to emphasize the distinction between nave and chancel, so that in the early Middle Ages, in parish churches particularly, the nave and chancel are separate rectangular buildings communicating by a narrow archway in the dividing wall. This was the plan of most of the early Saxon [1] churches, of which examples remain almost unaltered at Escomb and Bradford-on-Avon—the latter had also porches north and south of the nave, one of which remains.

The rites of the primitive Church at Rome were celebrated in the catacombs where its first preachers were buried ; and it has been held that before the earliest basilicas were built, provincial congregations met in the open air at small shrines raised over the graves of the saints. Certainly relics of the saints were deemed essential to the hallowing of a church, and beneath the chancels of most early churches a crypt was built as a relic-chamber. Examples of seventh-century date remain at Ripon and Hexham, and others of the Saxon period at Repton and Wing ; usually no doubt they were small and crude and have been filled in, as at Brixworth, or rebuilt ; but the crypt remained an important factor in church-planning until the end of the Norman period, when it became the fashion to transfer the relics to shrines in the church above, yet, even in the days of Gothic, crypts were often built as bone-holes, or as chapels, or to raise the level of the chancel floor and so elevate the high altar.

In late Saxon times, after the Danish invasions, a tower is added to the normal church plan. It was usually built at the west end of the nave, sometimes, as at Monkwearmouth, by raising the walls of an existing western porch. Occasionally, however, it was placed between the nave and chancel, where it soon led to a further development in church-planning. It had early become the custom to place side altars in shallow chapels opening out of the nave on either side of the chancel arch, as at Britford, Wilts. ; and the

[1] By Saxon I mean, throughout, of the Anglo-Saxon period.

building of a central tower not only made this practice inconvenient but suggested a better one, which was to build chapels north and south of it, approached by archways in its walls. This introduction of transepts produced the cruciform ground-plan which all through the Middle Ages remained the normal plan for large churches. One of the great contributions of the Normans to English architecture was the plan of a church grouped round a central tower poised upon four open arches.

Fig. 2. RAVENNA: S. AGATA. Interior, showing clerestory walls with windows and roof, carried on columns.

Further development was due mainly to two causes, the provision of space for additional altars and for ceremonial processions. Both causes affected most the monastic churches, and particularly their chancels. Originally the great majority of monks were laymen but gradually more and more took orders, and so incurred the obligation of celebrating a daily mass. Moreover as each altar was dedicated to a saint, the more altars there were in a church the more intercession for those who worshipped in it. Chapels to contain altars were therefore added to the chancel and transepts, and greatly modified the plan of the eastern part of the church ; in the place of the chancel walls rows of arches were set up, leading into aisles having altars at their eastern ends and chapels built out from the north and south walls. These aisles, and those similarly added to nave and transept, provided also a pathway by which the monks in procession could visit in turn each altar in the church and perform the prescribed ritual, part of which was the asperging of the altar with holy water [Fig. 54].

FIG. 3. ROME: S. MARIA IN COSMEDIN. Sixth-century arrangement showing altar in front of apse, and screens enclosing presbytery. (Rebuilt in twelfth century on original plan.)

The desire for a processional path for a similar weekly ceremony in parish churches is mainly responsible for their aisles, though these also gave room for chapels at their eastern ends and moreover enabled worshippers to reach any part of the nave without disturbing those already assembled there.

Ritualistic development in the thirteenth century led to the rebuilding or lengthening of the small chancels of many Saxon and Norman churches in order to provide more space for the choir.

In the later Middle Ages the plan of the parish church

was further modified by the addition of chantry chapels ; in each of these a daily mass was sung for the soul of the founder who had left an endowment for the purpose. In town churches chantry chapels with priests to serve them were often supported by the trade gilds for the benefit of their members both living and dead. To provide these chapels aisles would be added to chancel or nave, or early narrow aisles would be widened [Fig. 53]. It was often specified in the deed of endowment that the chantry priest should instruct the children of the parish and especially of the choir ; for this purpose a room was some-times built above the church porch, which occasionally, as at Northleach, has a fireplace and chimney.

At the Reformation all the altars were dismantled or destroyed, but the empty chapels still show traces of their original purpose in small drains, called piscinae, recessed in the south wall where the sacred vessels were washed after Mass, in square cupboards (*aumbries*) in the north wall where the vessels were locked away, or in niches or brackets on the east wall for the images of saints that guarded the altar [Figs. 46, 47, 48, and 49].

All through the Middle Ages the chancel arch tended to grow wider and higher till at last, in the fifteenth century, churches were often planned without it, and only the great screen served to divide nave and chancel. When the Italian style was revived the basilican plan came again into fashion, and a church became a great hall with an altar on a railed platform at its eastern end. Wren's larger London churches are examples ; they formed the models for the later Nonconformist chapels—Tennyson called the basilica at Trèves, which he visited in 1865, 'the ideal Methodist chapel'. The wheel had come full circle.

Having considered how the parts of the church were disposed so as best to serve the purposes for which they were designed, we have now to examine how the weather was kept out and the light was let in, which, at least in our climate, are the two most important practical functions that any building can serve. This will involve the study of the walls, with their openings, and the roof, with its supports ; and as the walls usually help to support the roof, which in turn governs the form of the doors and windows, the walls and the roof may well be considered together.

The earliest buildings—if we except the conical hut, which was really a tent—were made of timber : four posts were set up at the corners of a rectangle, their tops were connected by beams, and the space enclosed by them was protected from the weather by a thatch-roof resting on the beams and by wattle walls inserted between the posts ; openings in the walls were made by setting up smaller posts supporting a lintel. We have lately been made familiar with this primitive post and lintel construction in the thousands of army huts set up in all parts of the country.

As man's characteristic instinct to strive with Time developed, he sought to give permanence to his buildings by making them of stone ; but he employed the new material in the fashion of the old, substituting columns of stone for the posts, and lintels of stone for the beams. This is the primitive style, seen at its simplest in Stonehenge and at its highest development in the Parthenon ; its essential feature is the flat ceiling which exerts a vertical pressure on its supports. Egypt taught the world the science of it, which is mainly concerned with the supporting column.

The column, to fulfil perfectly its weight-bearing function, must have three parts, the shaft, the base, and the capital. The shaft, to appear stable, must taper from the base upwards ; it is usually fluted, to emphasize the line of pressure and to avoid the flat appearance of a plain column in a strong light ; it is circular because that form offers least obstruction. The base is square, for an outspreading foot gives an appearance of strength. The capital is a single stone, rounded and tapered below to fit the narrowing shaft, broad and square above to support the wide, rectangular lintel between which and the capital itself is usually a thin, projecting, tile-like stone called the abacus, the purpose of which is to widen the area of support and to emphasize the distinction between the weight and the weight-carrier.

The Greeks adopted from Egypt and perfected the system of column and lintel, which indeed was capable of only a limited development because columns can never carry a high superstructure. Buildings of two and even three stories were erected by placing lighter columns on the tops of stouter, e.g. the Ionic and Corinthian Orders above the Doric. The Romans employed these in their earlier buildings, but were soon compelled to devise a system by which loftier structures could be raised and wider spans bridged than was possible by means of lintels—above all, a system in which smaller materials could be substituted for the great lengths of stone essential to the primitive style.

They solved the problem by employing the arch in place of the lintel,[1] and their use of it makes them the master-builders of the world : all later styles are but modifications of their system.

Like the wheel and the ship, the arch, both round and pointed, is a prehistoric invention ; Swift might have used it in support of his argument that the greatest inventions are the products of ages of ignorance. But, as an Arab proverb says, the arch never sleeps : it strives ceaselessly to flatten out like a bent spring, and its stones can be kept in position only so long as its ends are prevented from spreading ; its first employers never learned how to do this securely except by constructing arches underground, where complete abutment was provided by the surrounding earth. It was here that Rome found her model, in the arch of the great sewer built, as is supposed, in the time of the Etruscan dynasty. The new achievement was to construct arches in the air as well as in the earth, and the Romans accomplished it by discovering first that the thrust of one arch may be met and neutralized by that of another, and secondly that an arch can safely bear any weight upon it so long as a greater weight is opposed to its thrust. Both these principles were afterwards more clearly understood by the Gothic architects; but the only practical lessons Rome left her successors to learn were the economical use of material, and the advantage of the pointed arch over the semicircular form.

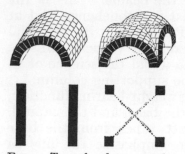

Fig. 4.  Tunnel and cross-vaults.

The vault of the Cloaca Maxima furnished the model for the simplest of all arched roofs, the tunnel or barrel vault—

---

[1] Stone, from its granular composition, is naturally fitted to resist *compression* in the arch ; while the fibrous nature of wood makes it most suitable for the *tension* of the lintel.

which is simply a continuous arch. But this, though simple, is not a convenient form of roof above ground, for it requires abutment along its whole length, and it is difficult to construct openings in its sides. When, however, two barrel vaults intersect at right angles, the square area that is common to both is roofed by four curved sections of the two tunnels, supported by four arches and their own mutual pressure. The drawings [Fig. 4] will complete the explanation. The lines of pressure where the sections meet are called groins, and a stone roof so formed is called a groined vault, or, since the groins cross one another diagonally, a cross-vault. Any square building may be roofed by this means, and any rectangular building by division into squares with piers at the angles to support the arches of the cross-vault.

The discovery of the groined vault is the greatest of all architectural inventions, and an elementary knowledge of its principles is essential to any intelligent appreciation of architecture. For the mediaeval ideal was always to ceil a building with stone, not only to make it homogeneous in appearance but to protect it from fire.

FIG. 5. Timber centering placed upon the supports of an arch to hold the stones in position until their ring is complete.

No Roman examples remain in Britain, and there are no Saxon vaults above ground, but the Saxons used both groined and barrel vaults of crude workmanship to roof their crypts. They also employed the Roman arch to bridge the openings in their walls for doorways and windows, and of these many examples are left. Before an arch is built a framework, called centering, must be constructed of timber to support the stones until the ring is complete and their mutual pressure has locked them securely together. Saxon resources could seldom provide the centering needed for great arches, and so their doorways and chancel arches are usually small. Their largest windows are those in the belfries, and these are formed by means of two small arches meeting in the middle of the window on a long impost stone, which is carried by a shaft or baluster standing in the centre of the sill [Fig. 6]. All other windows are very small, and are usually distinguished from those of later periods by having their glass set back from both the inner and outer faces of the wall. A few windows have triangular heads formed by pairs of long stones set gable-wise ; many small ones have heads formed by chopping a semicircle out of a single stone.

FIG. 6.  ST. MICHAEL'S TOWER,  OXFORD  (c. 1071).  Saxon type, of rough rubble with 'long and short' quoins at the angles, small openings splayed externally, and double windows with baluster shafts in the upper story.  (The high doorway communicated with the ramparts of the city.)

Yet some large Saxon arches do exist, e. g. at Wing, Barnack, and Wittering, and they are so much nearer the Roman model than the later Romanesque work that one is tempted to believe them the work of Italian craftsmen—there is documentary evidence that the early Saxon bishops imported foreign masons. It may be, however, that when they were constructed there was enough Roman work yet remaining to provide models ; it is less likely that the modern theory of Romano-British survival is sound, that the traditions of Roman craftsmanship survived the English Conquest.

Attempts have been made to distinguish the style of the seventh and eighth centuries from that of the period following the Danish inroads, when Cnut is recorded to have rebuilt the destroyed churches ; but the question is so obscure and the number of buildings involved so small that it cannot be discussed in a short, general essay. It may be said, however, that churches with Saxon towers (resembling those of Germany) are almost all of the later period, and that the use of Roman materials commonly marks work of the earlier date.

But though their intercourse with Italy and France, and, later, with Germany, provided the English with models of Romanesque architecture in the early attempts made in those countries to build on Roman principles, a great number, perhaps the majority, of their churches, like Greenstead, Essex, were built of timber in the primitive post and lintel fashion. And even their use of stone suggests the work of men more familiar with the older material; they liked to get it in long blocks and to set them up vertically, both at the angles of the building [1] and also in narrow strips projecting slightly from the face of the wall and dividing it into panels. It is true that flat 'pilasters' are found in Roman walling, and were also afterwards copied by the Normans

FIG. 7. NORMAN WINDOW, SANDFORD (*c.* 1100). Showing nook-shafts in the jambs with cushion caps and square abaci, and bold roll or torus moulding of the dripstone.

FIG. 8. ARCH CONSTRUCTION. Mediaeval method, economizing centering and using small stones easily lifted into position. The origin of the compound pier is seen in the cluster of shafts supporting the rings (orders) of the arch.

in their flat buttresses: but in any case they represent ultimately the posts of timber buildings [Figs. 6 and 40].

Meanwhile in France the Normans, newly converted and therefore zealous Christians, had begun with characteristic energy to develop their own school of Romanesque architecture, based on French models; even before the Conquest Norman masons had built the Confessor's church at Westminster (on the plan of Jumièges or, perhaps, of St. Martin's at Tours), which was as fine a building as any in Normandy and set the type for much of the new construction

---

[1] Where freestone was scarce 'long and short work' is sometimes found on the quoins of Norman towers, e. g. Cholsey, Berks.; though the more usual Norman plan was to avoid the difficulty by building round towers.

in England. For in the century following the Conquest all the greater, and most of the smaller, Saxon churches were rebuilt in the Norman manner, and many more were built where none had previously existed.

Norman Romanesque was superior to Saxon because it used the arch more boldly, to span wider openings and to provide vaulted roofs in all parts of a building, and also because it was a more intelligent attempt to develop the principles of Roman construction, and not merely to imitate Roman work.

FIG. 9. IFFLEY CHURCH, WEST FRONT (c. 1160). Showing arches built in orders, some continuous and some stopped upon shafts with cushion caps having square abaci.

The spacious doorways and lofty arches of Norman churches were made possible by a device which rendered unnecessary the massive centering used in Roman construction ; the arch was built in successive rings one upon another, and thus centering was needed only for the first and smallest ring ; when this had been constructed it served as a support for a second and heavier one, and this for a third. Each ring or order of the arch usually springs from a small shaft set in the jamb of the archway ; the caps of these shafts, with their square, tile-like abaci having the lower edge 'chamfered' or sliced obliquely off, are very characteristic of the style, as is the chevron or zigzag ornament that usually runs round the curve of the arch [Fig. 9].

The great arches of the nave arcades are also built up in orders, but their piers are usually cylindrical ; in the next period, more logically, the pier becomes compound, each member of it corresponding to an order in the arch it carries. Norman piers, and often the walls also, were built with a core of rough, uncoursed rubble with a casing of faced stone which, in early work, had very wide joints—the mortar being sometimes an inch or more in thickness.

The earliest Norman vaults were groined and small, but the builders soon hit upon a plan that enabled them to increase the size without adding to the cost of centering ; this was to construct arches in place of the groins, so producing a skeleton framework of a cross-vault, each section or 'web' of which could be filled in separately, the same centering being used for each in succession and then carried on to the next bay, where the process was repeated. The aisles of all our Norman cathedrals were vaulted in stone in this way : their width being equal to the distance between the nave piers, they could be divided into squares for the purpose ; the square central towers and chancels of many parish churches were similarly vaulted ; but to cover the nave with a stone roof was a more difficult problem. Its bays were much larger than those of the aisles and moreover were oblong ; and therefore its transverse arches, being much wider than the others, rose far above them and made the sections of the vault dangerously steep—for the height of a semicircular arch is always half its span ; moreover the thrusts of a great round arch need heavy abutment, which was difficult to provide at the top of the nave walls [Figs. 10 and 12].

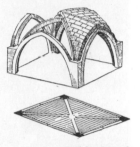

FIG. 10. Ribbed vault showing how skeleton arches are constructed and the webs between them successfully filled in. Note how the pointed form allows arches of varying span to be brought to the same level.

The French architects solved the problem early in the twelfth century by using pointed arches to build the nave vault ; for the height of a pointed arch is independent of its span and so narrow arches can be built high and wide arches low to meet at the same level. In France, therefore, most of the churches are vaulted throughout ; but in England, by the time the new invention reached us, the builders had usually ceiled the nave with timber ; and although later architects have in some places, as at Winchester, added a vault, Durham is the only cathedral nave which possesses a nave vault of Norman date, and many have timber ceilings to this day.

The difficulties of the mason were the opportunity of the carpenter ; the open-timbered roofs of our parish churches are so fine that we can scarcely regret that they were never vaulted. The safest, most durable, and probably the oldest type is the tie-beam roof, in which long transverse beams rest on the side walls and carry upright posts, single (king-post) or in pairs (queen-post), which support the ridge-piece and rafters [Figs. 12, 45, and 58]. But beams of the necessary length and stoutness are comparatively rare and expensive, and so trussed roofs were devised in which smaller timber could be used. To obtain a roof of greater span than was possible with ordinary tie-beams the builders of the Perpendicular period invented the hammer-beam, a short beam projecting from the wall and supported by a strut beneath and carrying a post which in turn supported the rafters

FIG. 11. VAULT-RIBS IN OXFORD CATHEDRAL. The rearmost show the mouldings of the twelfth century, the foremost those of the fourteenth, and the ribs springing from the central column those of the thirteenth. Compare the square Norman abacus with the rounded Gothic, and the more logical compound pier with the cylindrical pillar.

[Fig. 74]. Early roofs, particularly those of the thirteenth century, being tiled, were of high pitch in order that the rain might run rapidly off. In the fifteenth century lead was commonly used, and so the roofs were flatter. Lowering the pitch of the aisle roof allowed a clerestory to be added or enlarged, which was often done in the fifteenth century.

Before the end of the twelfth century the pointed arch supplanted the round in all new buildings. Vaults were now subdivided into smaller sections by intermediate arches ;

so they became lighter both in appearance and in fact. Then it was realized that as all the thrusts of a vault are concentrated at its angles, abutment is needed only at those points. Buttresses were therefore built against the walls

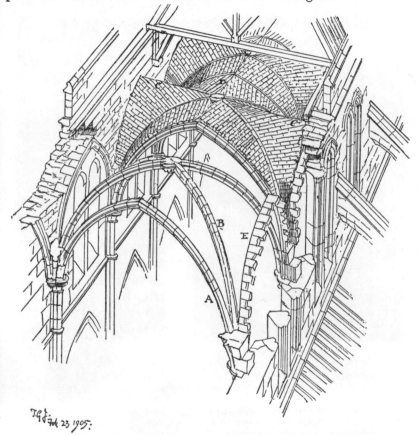

FIG. 12. SKELETON OF HIGH VAULT, with flying buttresses over the aisle roof, supporting the clerestory walls against the thrusts of the vault arches and the tie-beams of the timber roof. The row of arches (the triforium or blindstory), the tops of which are seen below the clerestory windows, opens into the space between the aisle vault and its lean-to roof. Note the parapet and gutter, and the structural purpose of the boss.

to receive the thrusts of the arches within. They could not be built against a nave wall when an aisle was in the way, and so the aisle buttress was carried high above the aisle roof to support a stout bar of stone called a flying buttress which leant like a prop against the top of the nave wall and prevented it from being pushed out by the arches of the high vault.  This system of building with pointed arches supported by buttresses is known as Gothic.  In Norman work the so-called buttress is really only a pilaster,

FIG. 13.  THIRTEENTH-CENTURY DOORWAY, MILTON (c. 1240), showing deeply cut mouldings giving dark lines of shadow, caps with stiff-stalked foliage and rounded abaci much undercut, and bases with upper and lower roll.  (Note the ground-course base-moulding or plinth protecting the foundations of the wall from wet; this is Perpendicular work and suggests that the doorway has been reinserted in a later wall.)

FIG. 14.  PIER OF CHANCEL ARCH, ELSFIELD (c. 1200), showing typical transitional capital with square abacus and volute, water-holding base [Fig. 15], and square plinth with a spur of foliage filling the angle.

the real abutment being provided by the massive thickness of the wall [Fig. 44].

In the last quarter of the twelfth century, sometimes called the *Transition Period*, when the pointed arch had established itself in the vault, the round arch was still commonly used in the doorways. These often had shafts in the jambs as in Norman times, but the capitals, though

FIG. 15. Base of shaft, Stanton Harcourt, with water-holding hollow (c. 1200).

FIG. 16. Transitional string-course (c. 1200), with keel-moulding.

Exterior.                    Interior.

FIG. 17. LANCET WINDOW (c. 1220), with deep interior splay to allow light to spread, chamfered hood mould or dripstone above, and keeled string-course below.

they kept the square abacus, had lost the cushion shape and were ornamented with foliage; a knob of curled leaf-age at the corners of the abacus is as characteristic of the time as the water-holding base or the dog-tooth ornament and keel-moulding which is found on the arches [Figs. 14, 15, 16, and 58].

FIG. 18. NAVE ARCADE, EATON BRAY, BEDFORDSHIRE (*c.* 1220), with deep hollows and bold rolls in the mouldings, tri-lobed stiff-stalked foliage, undercut abacus, and ' water-holding ' base. (Cf. the fourteenth-century mouldings on the chancel arch, and note how the members of the compound pier correspond to the orders of the arch.)

The windows are tall and narrow and usually have pointed heads. This is the shape that gave the name

*Lancet* to the work of the next half-century, which has also been absurdly called the Early English style.[1] Its most easily recognized details are the deeply cut mouldings that outline the arches with contrasting light and shadow, and the stiff-stalked foliage of the bell-shaped capitals on which the square abacus has given place to a circular, muffin-shaped stone with its lower edge much undercut. The deep hollow so produced is repeated in the base of the shaft, but

Bottesford.      Sandwich.      Cowley.

Temple Church.      Carlisle, 1.      Carlisle, 2.

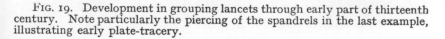

FIG. 19. Development in grouping lancets through early part of thirteenth century. Note particularly the piercing of the spandrels in the last example, illustrating early plate-tracery.

as in that position it collected dust the ' water-holding ' base soon went out of fashion; it marks the time of Richard I and John. The bold contrasts at which the thirteenth-century artists aimed in their mouldings were also attained by the use of dark marble for shafts and caps in the richer buildings. Henceforward development, though it can be traced in all the details, is most striking in the arrangement of the windows. Almost as soon as lancets were introduced it became the practice to group them in threes in the gable-

[1] Absurdly, because its evolution was a task common to the builders of Western Europe, led by those of France.

ends of buildings—a tall one in the middle, with a lower one on either side. A little projecting ridge or dripstone ran round the head of each to throw the wet off the glass ; and when a pair or a triplet of lancets were set close together it would be simpler to put a single arched dripstone over them, so bringing them into one composition ; this, however, would leave an ugly blank space between the heads of the lancets and the enclosing arch. A little circular window, such as the Normans had occasionally used, inserted in this spandrel would obviously improve the composition both artistically and practically ; and before the middle of the thirteenth century many groups of lancets with little circular or quatrefoiled openings above them had been designed both here and in France [Fig. 19].

FIG. 20. 'Mask' or 'Buckle' corbel terminating the drip-stone or hood mould of a lancet window. Dog-tooth ornament above.

During the next century, covered by the reigns of the first three Edwards, the process was carried much farther and produced what is called from its elaborate windows the *Decorated* stage. It occurred to some builder somewhere, or perhaps to several independently, that instead of grouping openings of different shapes it would be simpler to construct a single large arched opening and to insert in it a framework of stone bars, straight and curved, forming lancet lights in the lower part and circles, trefoils, quatre-foils, and other figures in the upper [Figs. 21, 22, 23, and 24].

Such a framework is called tracery, and now that vaulting difficulties had been overcome and the scientific buttressing of arches understood the development of tracery became the great feature of Gothic.

In the reign of the first Edward its forms were of simple geometrical construction, but throughout the first half of the fourteenth century its curves grew more and more complicated until at last, particularly in France, the bars were tortured into patterns resembling twisted tongues of flame ; this stage is therefore called *Flamboyant*. In England flowing tracery was abandoned before it reached this exaggerated development. A decorated window is an unmistakable product of its age, and so too are the ball-flower and the four-leaved flower that were the favourite

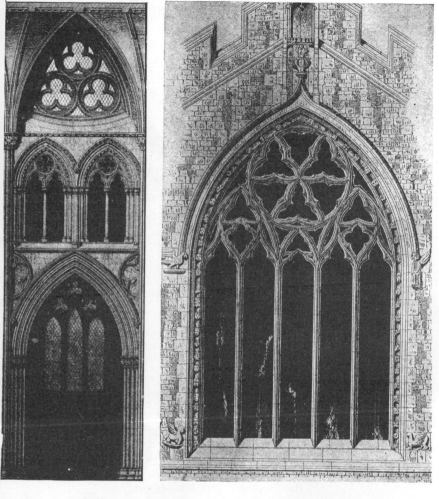

FIG. 21. Three stories in Lichfield Cathedral, with geometrical tracery of the late thirteenth century formed of bars inserted in the window arches.

FIG. 22. Wellingborough. Window with decorated tracery, ball-flower and four-leaved flower in the hollow moulding, and dripstone with ogee curve and foliaged finial. Early fourteenth century.

ornament in the hollows of the contemporary mouldings, which were wider and shallower than those of the lancet stage. Stiff-stalked foliage had gone out of fashion, and its place was taken, when the requisite skill was available, by naturalistic carvings imitated from the leaves of the oak, maple, ivy, and vine, which, though beautiful in themselves, had not the power of the earlier foliage to express support

FIG. 23. Decorated window, Higham Ferrers, Northants (*c.*1330), with reticulated tracery and ogee arch, fourteenth-century buttress, and trefoil-headed priest's door.

FIG. 24. St. Ouen, Rouen. Flamboyant tracery. Late fourteenth century.

FIG. 25. Ball-Flower and Four-leaved Flower of the Decorated period (*c.* 1300).

of the abacus. The plain moulded capital, which could be turned in a lathe, was by far the commoner form. On the other hand the bosses of Edwardian vaults are almost invariably carved with naturalistic foliage, for vaults, with their growing network of ribs, required highly skilled craftsmen. The boss had become a very important feature, decorative and constructional ; it solved the problem of ribs meeting and crossing one another ; and it provided points on which the eye could rest in the maze of interlacing arches. Buttresses, built in stages, weighted with pinnacles, and often enriched with canopied statuary, also contribute alike to the beauty and the stability of fourteenth-century buildings [Figs. 27 and 28].

Even before the Black Death came to put a stop to all building there were signs of a reaction against the wild, undisciplined designs of later Decorated tracery. Side by side with architecture the art of glass-colouring had been

FIG. 26. Bradninch, Devon. Naturalistic carving, forming a wreath round the capital. Note the broad curves of the mouldings and the lack of prominence in the abacus.

making progress ; and possibly the glazier made his protest against the grotesque shapes he was expected to include in his pictorial designs : a shield of arms might fill a quatre-foil, but how could the figure of a saint be contorted to occupy a scimitar-shaped aperture ? [Fig. 24].

At any rate, in the remodelling of the cathedral choir of Gloucester in the second quarter of the fourteenth century curved tracery gave place to rectilinear, and Gothic archi-tecture entered on its last, the *Perpendicular* stage, which, on the resumption of building after the Black Death, became everywhere the fashion [Figs. 30 and 31].

Windows increased still further in size, for the introduction at this time of fan-tracery vaulting, which exerted very little thrust, and the increase in depth of the buttresses, made it possible to convert the wall-area practically into sheets of glass. To strengthen these great windows against wind-pressure and to divide them into compartments suitable for pictorial glazing the mullions were carried up in vertical lines from the sill to the arch and were crossed and stayed by horizontal bars, or transoms, at regular intervals. So was produced the Perpendicular type of window which Ruskin compared to a gridiron, but which, like the gridiron, was perfectly adapted to the use it was intended to serve [Figs. 31 and 37].

Light and more light was the great gift of the Perpendicular builders, and even on the mouldings of their arches they abolished shadows by means of broad and shallow surfaces. The most characteristic are a wide shallow hollow [Fig. 33] called the casement, because it usually runs round the window-frame, and a broad wavy [Fig. 32] surface, like the curves of an open book, which runs

FIG. 27. Fourteenth-century buttress nearly square on plan.

FIG. 28. Fourteenth-century buttress, oblong on plan, depth being greater than width.

FIG. 29. Decorated mouldings (c. 1320) showing the characteristic quarter circle, convex and concave.

round the arches. These are obtusely pointed, so that the head of the window resembles a low, slightly curved triangle; indeed, in many windows the arch has once more given place to the lintel, for the heads are rectangular [Fig. 37]. So, too, is the carved foliage; but of this there is little, for the capitals are usually so small that there is little room for leafage upon them. Sometimes the transoms of windows or the tops of screens are decorated with a row of diamond-shaped leaves called Tudor flower—though it was in use long before the Tudors [Fig. 34].

The arches of the doors are even flatter and wider in proportion than those of the windows; shafts in the jambs become less usual; where they are found they stand, like the nave piers, on tall angular bases, which are a certain mark of Perpendicular work. The archway is set in a square frame, called a label, and the spandrels between it and the door-head are filled with shields or with sunk quatrefoils.

FIG. 30. YELVERTOFT CHURCH (*c.* 1500), showing Perpendicular window with wide, depressed, four-centred arch, rectilinear tracery, deep, thin, buttresses, and the profuse panelling of wall surface characteristic of fifteenth-century work.

The label itself often rests on heads or busts bearing shields carved with the arms of the builder [Fig. 35].

The Dissolution and the Reformation put a stop to church-building for more than a century, the builders being employed in pulling down the finest churches and in raising great houses for the new owners of the monastic estates. But the existing churches from time to time needed repair and were

FIG. 31. CANTERBURY NAVE. Perpendicular windows with rectilinear tracery and transoms producing oblong panels for pictorial glazing. Note the high bases to the piers, the angular mouldings, and the numerous ribs and bosses in the vault.

then patched up in the style of the new manor house. So we often find a long, flat-headed, mullioned window, without tracery, inserted in the days of Elizabeth and James I ; if of the earlier date it will probably have cusps in the heads of the lights ; Jacobean windows have simply a plain elliptical curve [Figs. 38 and 45].

In Italy the pointed arch never completely supplanted the round ; the pointed vault, poised on its pinnacled buttresses, which was the supreme achievement of northern Gothic, did not command the unqualified admiration of Italian architects. Their ideal was to make a still nobler use of the arch by developing the Roman cross-vault ; to apply the last great invention of Graeco-Roman engineers, that of the perfect Arch or Dome, with which Justinian's architect had roofed the church of St. Sophia. The Norman builders had often used a semi-dome to ceil an apsidal chancel or chapel, but with the advent of the pointed arch the apse went out of use in England and with it the idea of domed roofing. In the fifteenth century the English invention of fan-vaulting

[Fig. 55] solved anew the essential problem of the dome, how to support it upon a square: so in roofing, as in planning, the circle was complete; but by this time the Italians had already turned from Gothic to Roman models, and we abandoned our native style to imitate them just at the moment when our own system of vaulting was developing towards the dome. The consequence was that ecclesiastical architecture in England remained in a state of suspended animation for more than a hundred years, until Wren, inspired by Brunelleschi's dome at Florence, the firstfruits of the Renaissance, and Michelangelo's at St. Peter's, its supreme achievement, produced his design for St. Paul's.

For a century our architects have been content feebly to repeat the accomplishments of their predecessors. No great art was ever so achieved, and there will be no development in architecture until they return to the point where the Tudor builders left it when the blight of the Reformation fell upon them.

FIG. 32. Double ogee, fifteenth century.

FIG. 33. Fifteenth - century hollow moulding.

FIG. 34. Tudor Flower.

FIG. 35. FIFTEENTH-CENTURY DOORWAY, Merton College Chapel, A. D. 1424, showing square frame or label with sunk panels in the spandrels, casement hollow between the suites of mouldings, tall bases and angular caps to the thin shafts, and plinth or basement mouldings to the walls. Note the Perpendicular panelling of the door, reproducing the tracery of the windows.

FIG. 36. Church Hand-borough, Oxon. Fifteenth-century capital with Perpendicular mouldings, angular, shallow, and markedly concave. N.B.—A shaft or a mullion with concave faces is invariably Perpendicular. Notice the merging of the abacus into the mouldings of the capital.

FIG. 37. Saltfleetby, Lincolnshire. Square-headed fifteenth-century window with Perpendicular tracery and transom, and label (i. e. rectangular drip-stone) above.

## 2. *The Parish Church.*

The parish was originally the estate over which the lord of the manor had jurisdiction. He built and maintained the earliest church ; and the priest who served it was his private chaplain. This explains why the English clergy have always been solicitous for the rights of property, why the parish living is usually in the gift of the squire, and why the bishop, having once instituted a parish priest, can do little or nothing to control him. By the twelfth century the bishops had succeeded in establishing their right to insist, before consecrating a parish church, on the provision of a permanent freehold endowment for the priest, who should have the cure of souls in the parish and be responsible for it to the bishop of the diocese.

Having been originally the lord's land the churchyard therefore usually adjoins the manor-house or the farm that may now represent it. Almost invariably the level of the ground inside the graveyard wall is higher than that outside ; for as the dead were commonly buried without coffins they soon returned to their dust and made room, like Yorick, for new-comers. So the modern level may be five or six feet above the sill of the church door.

The graveyard itself is often older than the church that stands in it; for even if this had no timbered predecessor the churchyard cross almost certainly had—the wooden cross set up by the early missionaries[1]

[1] Or by the monks of some early local monastery.

as a sign for their converts. Round this the Christian
cemetery grew ; and when in time a church was built it was
set on the north of the area, that its shadow might fall clear
of the graves. That is why the church is never central in an
old churchyard, while the cross usually is.

The outside of the church should first be carefully
examined. Sometimes a trace of long-and-short work
in the jamb of a doorway or on the angle of an aisle,
or a narrow, projecting strip of it on the face of a wall,

FIG. 38. NORTH HINKSEY CHURCH, BERKS.,
showing cross in centre of churchyard and church on north. Note break
in roof-line suggesting that a Norman central tower once existed, and
Jacobean windows inserted in chancel walls.

may be all that is left to indicate the Saxon origin of
the building. Often a wide pilaster buttress, or a line of
heavy string-course broken by later windows, or a corbel-table
of carved stones under the eaves, shows that a wall is of
Norman date, though all its doors and windows are later
insertions. Or a pair of short, shallow buttresses at the
angles of the chancel may suggest that the upper part of
the wall has been rebuilt on a thirteenth-century base.
These are all clues to be followed up inside the building.
For example, a plain tub-shaped font, in a church showing long-and-short work, will usually be Saxon also ;

Norman traces outside will suggest examination of the jambs of the chancel arch, which often remain unaltered, though the arch itself has been rebuilt [cf. Fig. 53] ; or when, as often happens, the eastern arches of the nave are different from the others the explanation may be that a transept has been absorbed by a later aisle or that a Norman central tower has fallen and been removed. This again will usually have left traces on the external line of the roof [Fig. 38]. So the evidence of a thirteenth-century

FIG. 39.  THE CHANCEL, WITTENHAM, BERKS.
The windows show from east to west the forms of fourteenth, thirteenth, twelfth, fourteenth, sixteenth, and seventeenth centuries respectively and tell of successive alterations and additions to the original Norman building.

coupled-buttress may be corroborated by the presence inside of a double piscina.

Similarly inside the church an attempt should be made to find the oldest work and so the core of the building. Thus above the nave arches there may be small blocked windows the sills of which they cut. These must clearly be earlier than the arches ; if the latter are Norman the windows will be the clerestory of the original Saxon nave ; if, as is more common, the arches are of the thirteenth century the windows will probably be Norman, and in that case a deep respond [Fig. 46], being a part of the original wall through

which the arches were cut, should be looked for at the eastern
and western ends of the arcade. A deep respond always
suggests that an aisleless nave preceded the existing plan.

Again, if the windows of an aisle do not march with the
nave arches it is probable that the aisle has been widened.
Or if its doorway is more than one bay from the west end
it is certain that the building has been lengthened westward.
Very often a Norman doorway
will be found in a wall of which
the windows and other details
are later : this means that the
aisle has been added to an
earlier nave by cutting arches
through its walls, its doorway
being rebuilt into the new
wall of the aisle. In such a
case there will sometimes be
a crypt under the aisle to receive the bones dug up in the
strip of churchyard on which
the aisle was built. More frequently there will be traces of
a rough, blocked archway in
the aisle wall ; since services
had to be continued while the
work was going on, the new
wall was built and roofed before the old one was touched :
then, when the aisle was complete, the nave wall was pierced
with arches and the rubbish
and scaffolding was got out

FIG. 40. The north arcade,
Bibury, Gloucestershire. The remains of pilaster strips, and the
traces of a small clerestory window
splayed outwardly, show that the
wall through which the twelfth-
century arches are cut was originally
the external north wall of the Saxon
church.

through an archway left for the purpose. An example of
such a ' masons' hole' may be seen in the photograph of
Iffley [Fig. 44]. So when the buttresses of a western tower are
visible inside a church we may know that the tower was built
clear of the nave, the walls of which were then lengthened
westwards to join up with it. In such a case there will be
a 'straight joint' at the junction, i. e. the stones of the wall
will not be bonded into those of the tower.

Readers who are fortunate enough to live in or near one
of the counties surveyed by the Royal Commission on

Historical Monuments will find in their reports the best of all training in the art of reading the history of a building in its architectural details.

As for some unknown reason the church usually stands north of the village the south door was the one commonly used, and it is often larger and more elaborate than that

FIG. 41. Norman corbel-table, St. Peter's, Oxford. Norman walls were made to overhang the top so that the drippings from the eaves might fall clear of their face. In Gothic the wall carries a parapet and gutter from which the water discharges through spouts, often grotesquely carved and then called gargoyles.

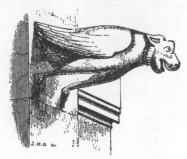

FIG. 42.   Gargoyle, Merton College, Oxford.

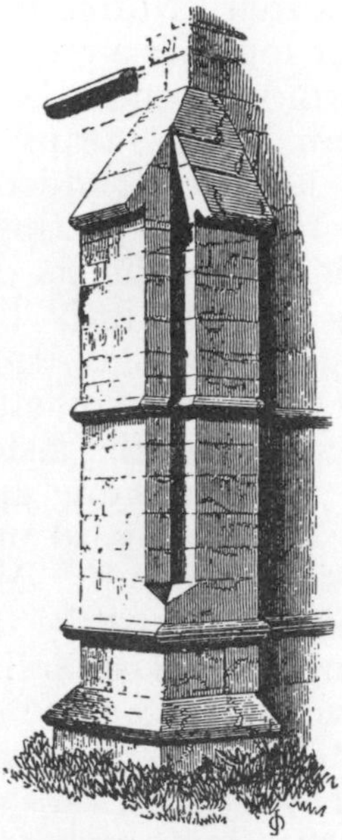

FIG. 43. Irthlingborough. A pair of thirteenth-century buttresses, low, broad, and of slight projection. Later buttresses are deeper and narrower, built in stages, and usually set singly.

on the north, and is protected by a porch. The public notices still posted here remind us that the porch was the usual place for much civil business in the mediaeval parish. The coroner sat here and not in the local public-house ; here executors sometimes made public payment of legacies ; marriage banns were published here in the presence of the parties ; the 'I will' was said and the ring given by 'hosbonds at the chirche dore' ; those who broke their vows did penance appropriately at the place where they took them ; here too the baptismal service was begun, so that the south door was sometimes called the Christening-door.  Usually the porch had stone seats and a stoup for holy water ; altars seem to have existed in a few porches.

FIG. 44.  The Chancel, Iffley, Oxon.  A S T U D Y I N   B U T T R E S S E S.   The flat strip south is Norman and marks the east end of the twelfth-century chancel ; the angle buttress with shaft is early thirteenth century, contemporary with the lancet windows ; the deep buttresses south were added in the fourteenth century and those at the east are modern.

Note the little Norman window in the thirteenth-century gable, which must have been reinserted when the chancel was lengthened, the traces of a masons' hole under the south window, and the Norman corbel-table now carrying the later parapet of the tower.

Above the porch was often a room approached by a newel stair inside the church.  This served various purposes—as a relic chamber, as a room for the sacristan or for the priest who celebrated morrow-mass for travellers who were up before dawn, and almost always as a school ; every one has heard of the ' pedant that keeps a school in a church ' ; he had a contemporary who willed that his body should be buried ' in the lower end of the church, at the stayre foot that goeth up to my schole '.

The western bay of the church was the baptistery ; it was clear of benches, even when these existed elsewhere in the church, and the font stood in the centre of it.  Fonts usually bear in their mouldings and other ornaments unmistakable signs of their date—some have Norman shafts and chevrons, some the dog-tooth and foliage of the thirteenth century, some the ball-flower of the fourteenth, some reproduce on their panelled faces the tracery of the fourteenth and fifteenth centuries.  But a few are perfectly plain cylinders of stone without any mouldings to indicate their date ; these are almost always early Gothic, though some may be Saxon.  An old font always bears the marks of the staple by which its lid was fastened down ; for superstitious uses of the christening water led in the thirteenth century to an order that all fonts should be kept locked.

The north door is now usually blocked, but was in constant use in the Middle Ages, both for the weekly procession and at funerals and christenings ; the west door was used more rarely, e.g. at the great procession on Palm Sunday.

Originally aisles and nave were clear of all seats except a few stone benches round the walls and the nave piers : people came to church to adore the Visible Presence and not to hear sermons ; the references to seats in the earliest Churchwardens' Accounts suggest that they were originally provided for women only.  Pulpits hardly existed in parish churches until the fifteenth century, and even then the fashion was local.  Gloucestershire, for example, has many fifteenth-century pulpits, while Oxfordshire has very few. Over Winchendon, in Buckinghamshire, has the earliest example, of the fourteenth century, while Cassington, near Oxford, has the earliest pews, of the thirteenth.  But neither pews nor pulpits were common until the sixteenth century. Jacobean pulpits of oak, carved with round-arched panels in the Roman manner, are very numerous, and are often accompanied by an hour-glass stand ; contemporary with them are the high box-pews in which the weary could sleep away the ' world-without-end-hour '—like Hogarth's

' Sleeping Congregation ', acting on the text of the preacher,
' Come unto me . . . and I will give you rest '.

This free floor-space in the mediaeval nave was put
to many secular uses ; it was the scene of trial by ordeal
in early times ; county courts sometimes were held in it ;
and if the lord of the manor had no house in the parish he
too would hold his court here. It was also the repository
for many articles of public property : the regimental colours
still found in some parish churches remind us that the arms
which every parish had to provide were stored in the nave,
with the parish coffin, used like a hearse to carry villagers
to the grave, the great fire-hook, with which a burning
cottage was pulled down, half the parish dragging on
its long chain, the ducking-stool for the correction of
scolds, the whip of the official who drove out the dogs
and the tongs with which he disposed of the truculent ones,
the buzzleder, or official spiked staff that formed the warrant
of the sheriff's officer, and the great chest in which the wills of
the villagers were stored—for, as a rubric in the prayer-book
reminds us, it was part of the priest's duty to see that a
sick parishioner duly made his will.

In Romanesque architecture the nave, with its numerous
secular associations, was shut off from the chancel by a
wall pierced with a narrow arch ; but the introduction of the
loftier pointed form led to the general use of screens. These
at first were of stone, as at Balking, Berkshire, but Stanton
Harcourt, near Oxford, has a thirteenth-century example of
oak, and there are a few of fourteenth-century date. In the
fifteenth century, which was the golden age of woodcarving,
the screen became the most striking feature of the church ;
a platform, called the rood loft, was built on the top of it,
approached by a winding stair, which, when built in the pier
of a central tower, often weakened the whole structure.
Though the lofts were destroyed at the Reformation the
stairs with the doorways usually remain ; sometimes, too, a
piscina above the chancel arch marks the site of the altar
that once stood on the rood loft. On its parapet stood the
great crucifix or rood from which it took its name, with
figures of St. John and our Lady on either side. These were
veiled during Lent and were decorated with greenery at
festivals. The term organ-loft, and the modern practice of
placing the organ above the chancel arch, remind us that

the rood loft was originally used to accommodate the organ and the soloists of the choir.

The altars at the eastern ends of the aisles had screens of their own, called parcloses, which shut them off from the nave and the rest of the aisle ; traces of these may often be seen in the eastern capitals of the nave arcade, which were cut to receive their beams.

FIG. 45. EARLY FIFTEENTH-CENTURY ROOD.
SCREEN AND LOFT, Cotes-by-Stow, with foot of rood in middle.
Note also contemporary pulpit, plain tub-shaped font, probably Saxon, stoup at south door, inserted Jacobean window, and tie-beam carrying king- and queen-posts. (A king-post is a single upright standing on the middle of a tie-beam to support the rafters ; queen-posts stand in pairs.)

Standing on the site of these altars one usually observes a hole called a squint cut through the pier of the chancel arch, giving sight of the high altar in the chancel. No completely satisfactory explanation of its purpose has yet been offered, though various guesses have been made.

The separation of the sanctuary from the choir by a line of rails dates from Laud's time, and was rendered necessary by the desecration of the chancel—his order prescribes rails 'near one yard in height, so thick with pillars that dogs may not get in'; the baluster-shaped rails are of the early part of the seventeenth century, the corkscrew forms of the latter half. But the sanctuary was always raised above the level of the chancel, and often its roof is distinguished by a rich ceiling or canopy over the altar; sometimes the eastern bay of the nave roof over the rood is similarly ornamented.

FIG. 46. SQUINTS AT HASELEY, OXON., giving sight of the high altar from the chantry chapel in the aisle. The blocked squint looked on an earlier altar and tells that the chancel has been lengthened eastward. Note the bracket for an image and the remains of the reredos above the site of the chantry altar. Cf. Fig. 49. The half-column or respond is backed by a part of the original nave wall.

The altar itself was a stone slab, about five feet by three, resting on a stone base much lower than the modern table,[1] the reredos of which often cuts off part of the east window. It was marked with five crosses for the Five Wounds, and usually contained relics sealed up in it. Near it, in the south wall, was a drain, the piscina, at which the priest washed his hands and the sacred vessels. In the thirteenth century the arch of the piscina contained two drains, but afterwards

---

[1] Like the early compositors' case—for the average stature was some inches shorter than the modern. Stone coffins, armour, and even Elizabethan clothing, are all too small for average men nowadays. Early sword-hilts and gauntlets will not admit a modern hand.

FiG. 47. PISCINA, North Aisle, Cumnor, Berks., of the four-teenth century, with single drain for the ablutions of the priest's fingers and the rinsings of the chalice.

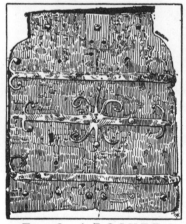

FIG. 48. A LOCKER in Drayton Church, Berks., to con-tain the eucharistic vessels and the chrismatory or box contain-ing vials for the three kinds of holy oil, the oil of catechumens, the oil for the sick, and the holy chrism. The door is original, with thirteenth-century ironwork.

the ablution of the vessels was drunk by the priest, and one drain only was used. There are rare examples of cisterns in some chancels. Above the drain was the credence, the shelf on which the flagons were placed. And on the other side of the altar, or sometimes in the east wall, were the lockers in which the vessels were kept when not in use. Their doors seldom remain, but their hinges and the sockets of their locks may generally be noted [Figs. 47 and 48].

In the south wall of the sanctuary are seats (usually three) for the celebrant and his assistants. Farther west in the corner near the chancel arch may be a small, low window fitted with a grating and a shutter but, originally, without glass ; sometimes there is a stone seat or a reading desk at its side. The purpose of such ' low-side' windows, which are also found occasionally in the north wall and even in the aisles, is uncertain. The most absurd of the numerous theories is the popular one that they were used to give sight of the altar to per-sons, particularly lepers, outside the church ; but it is hardly ever possible to see the altar through one of them ; and lepers were rigidly segregated into commu-nities of their own for which lazar houses with chapels were built and endowed. The ex-planation which covers most cases is that the sacring bell was rung at the opening in churches which had no sanctus-bell turret ; in many churches this turret may be seen above the chancel arch and in some—e.g. Idbury, Oxfordshire [Fig. 51]—the bell itself remains. Archbishop Peckham in 1281 ordered that ' In elevatione Corporis Domini pulsetur campana *in uno latere* ut populares . . . seu in agris seu in domibus flectant genua ' ; and it seems probable that his order refers to the use of the low-side window. The bell may have hung from the hook that is sometimes found in the ceiling of the recess ; and the seat would have served for the sacristan who rang it [Fig. 50].

Before the thirteenth century there was neither cross nor candle on the altar ; then, with the defining of the doctrine of transubstantiation, came new ritual and the use of an altar cross with a candle on either side. In the fifteenth century the figure was added to the simple cross. In early crucifixes the head is erect, not drooping on one shoulder ; there is therefore no basis for the theory that chancels were sometimes built intentionally out of exact line with the nave to symbolize the drooping head on the cross. The effect was doubtless due to a slight error in laying out the lines of work.

In the north wall of the chancel here is often a large ornamented recess called the Easter Sepulchre, because in it the Host was laid away

FIG. 49. ENSTONE, OXON. Reredos of altar in chantry chapel, fifteenth century. Note mullions carried to head of arch, brackets and canopies for images, and casement moulding round jambs and head of window.

on Good Friday evening, to be watched night and day and brought forth again with high festival on Easter morning. In both walls may be found the hooks from which the Lenten Veil was suspended in front of the altar from the first Sunday in Lent until Thursday in Holy Week. At Chieveley in Berkshire there is a small beam across the sanctuary from which the veil was hung.

Other long narrow recesses, more rarely found, were intended to hold the staves of banners used in the ceremonial

Fig. 50.    L O W - S I D E   W I N D O W , Wigginton, Oxon., formed by a transom in the south-west window of chancel; now glazed, but originally fitted with a shutter. The seat was perhaps used by the sacristan, who rang a bell at the opening.  The ball-flowers in the moulding of the canopy give the date *c.* 1300.

processions.   There are good examples at Earls Barton and Gamlingay and Broadwell [Fig. 52].

At the consecrating of a church, carried out by the bishop with elaborate ceremonial, the walls were anointed in twelve places within and without the building.   These spots were marked with consecration crosses six inches to a foot in length, carved or painted or, as at Uffington, made of latten and fitted into a matrix, like a memorial brass. They should not be confused with the small crosses, crudely formed of dots, on the jambs of doorways, which may possibly have been cut as tokens by persons having a vow.

Other shallow scratchings, roughly geometrical, sometimes found on the squared stonework, are believed to be masons' marks—not connected with the modern mystery of Freemasons, but simply the 'sign manual' of the individual mason who shaped the stone and marked it so that responsibility might be fixed if the work was not true. There is a good series of masons' marks on the Norman work at Peterborough. Almost always on the south wall there are one or more dials, circles with a few radii scratched on quoin or jamb, having a hole in the centre for the iron pin, the shadow of which marked the canonical hours of daylight and guided the sacristan in ringing the bell for the several services of the day.

Fig. 51. IDBURY, OXON. Sanctus bell in its niche above chancel roof.

Of all the beauty that has perished from our parish churches that which would be most missed by their builders is the glory of colour that once made them resplendent. The walls that now show rough rubble like the interior of a stable were originally coated with plaster painted with scenes from sacred history or with the figures of the saints ; over the chancel arch was the great Doom, showing the resurrection of the dead, the angels escorting the blessed to heaven and the devils gleefully dragging the wicked to the mouth of hell; facing the main doorway St. Christopher forded a stream, carrying the Infant Christ ; another picture showed Michael weighing a soul in his balance, with our Lady standing by in prayer and a demon trying to drag down the other scale. There were saints in the splay of the

windows, and others in the coloured glass, each easily
recognized by an appropriate emblem—St. Catherine by
her wheel, St. Anne by the book from which she taught our
Lady, St. Laurence with his gridiron, St. Andrew with his
saltire cross. There was, be-
sides, the beauty of mediaeval
armory, the shields and badges
that proclaimed the benefactors
of the parish and were as well
known as the emblems of the
saints themselves. Then all
the mouldings were outlined in
colour, all the foliage was green
or gold, and even the woodwork
of screen and roof was coloured
in harmony.

Of all this only the faintest
traces are left, and they can
give no idea of the original
beauty : for the colour-scheme
was designed as a whole ; and
where, as at Fairford, the glass is
left, its effect is spoilt because
the wall-paintings have given
place to whitewash. Most of the
paintings that still exist belong
to the fifteenth century ; but at
Stowell, near Northleach, are
traces of figures in the civil costume of the twelfth century, and
at Newington, near Banbury,
there are some fine but little-
known examples of early Decorated date. Those at Hayles in
Gloucestershire are even earlier,
but are mainly heraldic, showing
a decorative pattern composed

FIG. 52. BROADWELL,
OXON. Recess for banner-
staves carried in the Sunday procession.

of the shields of Edward I and his great barons. Here the
floor-tiles were designed in harmony with the colour-scheme
of the walls ; and this was probably the general custom.

'Who increaseth knowledge increaseth also sorrow' :
the delight that comes from archaeological learning is

often tempered by the realization of how much beauty has gone beyond recall. So that the student who has learned to know and love our ancient churches must often repeat to himself the comment of Dr. Johnson when speaking of the ruins of Oseney, ' Sir, I viewed it with indignation '. But the worst destruction is that which obliterates landmarks by substituting new work for old on the plea of restoration ; that is still going on, and will continue so long as ignorant incumbents have power to tamper with national monuments. Meanwhile Mr. Hardy has provided us with a suitable form of prayer to be used in time of danger to the churches :

From restorations of Thy
    fane,
  From smoothings of Thy
    sward,
From zealous churchmen's
    pick and plane,
  Deliver us, Good Lord.

FIG. 53. LEDBURY, HERE-FORD. Showing Norman corbel-table, clerestory windows, and line of aisle-roof, telling that the wall has been heightened, the roof raised, and the aisle widened. Note also the impost and shafts of a vanished Norman arch in the foreground.

### 3. *Monastic Buildings.*

The spoliation of the monasteries robbed the monks not only of their lands but of their characters ; and though they have since found many defenders the ground of defence has usually been ill taken on the practical services they rendered to the nation. It is no doubt true that our civilization, such as it is, is largely based on the labours of religious communities ; but only Victorian utilitarianism could have supposed that a monk regarded labour for material needs as equivalent to prayer for spiritual vision. The essential purpose of his existence was not work but worship; like Mary he chose the better part, which is not that of material improvement but of reducing material demands.

A monastery, then, was primarily a great church in which prayer and praise were continually offered by a body of men vowed to this service, who, in the intervals between their devotions, ate, slept, and worked in the church precincts. The buildings that served them for these purposes, though substantially built, were of the simplest character, and were grouped round a square, one side of which was formed by the church nave, and part of another by the wall of the transept. Since the church rose high above its out-buildings it was usually set to the north of them, where it screened them from the northerly winds without inter-cepting the sunshine. The opposite side of the square was formed by the refectory or frater and the kitchen, built under a single long roof, with an undercroft or store-room below them, and communicating by means of a hatch in the end wall of the refectory.

If we did not know it from the Rules we might deduce from the generally small size of the kitchens that the popular notions of monastic good cheer are silly inventions, like the stories of subterranean passages running from one monastery to another with which trippers delight to be deluded. The profusion boasted of by Brakelond was spread before the guests, not the brethren; the great kitchen at Glastonbury [Fig. 63] was not that of the monks' frater but was built to enable the abbot to fulfil the secular duty which devolved on the greater monasteries of entertaining the sovereign and the high officials of the realm when their business called them into the district. At one end of the frater was the high table with a crucifix or picture, the *maiestas*, above it, and near the other end was a pulpit from which a monk read to the brethren while they ate. The *calefactorium*, where the single fire of the monastery burned from All Saints' Day to Easter, was commonly at one end of the south side; it was a small room to which a monk, chilled with sitting in the open cloister, might retire for a short time to warm himself.

Continuing the line of the transept on the eastern side of the quadrangle were the Chapter-house, the abbot's

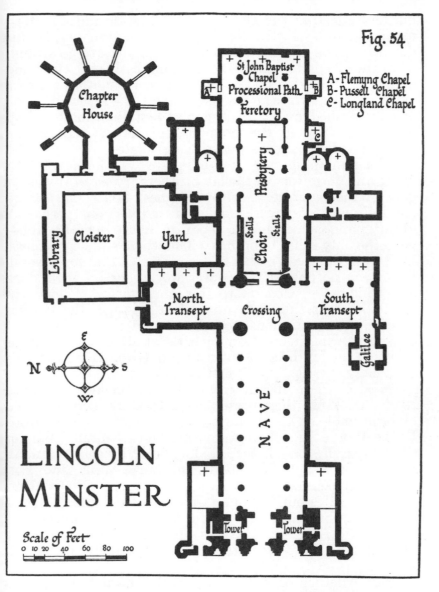

Fig. 54

A- Flemyng Chapel
B- Pussell Chapel
C- Longland Chapel

Chapter House

St John Baptist Chapel
Processional Path
Feretory

Presbytery

Library

Cloister

Yard

Stalls

Choir

Stalls

North Transept

Crossing

South Transept

Galilee

NAVE

LINCOLN MINSTER

Scale of Feet
0  10 20  40  60  80  100

Tower

Tower

parlour, and the offices of those who managed the affairs of the monastery. In the chapter-house the brethren met daily after breakfast to hear the reading of that part of the martyrology connected with the day, to recite the appropriate prayers, to confess any breaches of discipline and do public penance for them, and to hear from the abbot any matters affecting the community.  The dormitory of the monks was above this block ; from it a stairway, leading down into the transept, enabled the monks to go straight from their beds to matins in the church shortly after midnight.  At the other end of the dormitory another stairway led down to a latrine (*domus necessaria*), the sewer of which, usually flushed by the diversion of a stream, may perhaps have given rise to the popular legends of underground communications and secret treasure vaults.

The remaining side of the square was formed by the frater and dormitory of the lay brothers ; west of it was the gate of the monastery, with the guest house (*hospitium*). An infirmary for sick monks, a *scriptorium*, perhaps a library, and sometimes a separate house for the abbot, were the only other buildings.  The whole site was enclosed by a wall, but even if this had not existed the monks would have seen nothing of the outer world, for all their doors and windows opened on to the inner garth.  Round this on all its four sides ran an arched passage, the cloister, fitted with a continuous stone bench and also with movable desks and windscreens, forming little 'studies', called carrels, in which the brethren might read and write.  Here, too, they took daily exercise, ' walking the studious cloister pale '.

Most of the monastic churches that survive—comparatively few—owe their preservation to their having served, or been made at the Reformation to serve, as cathedrals. In the Middle Ages there were thirteen cathedrals—Bangor, Chichester, Exeter, Hereford, Lichfield, Lincoln, Llandaff, London, St. Asaph, St. Davids, Salisbury, Wells, and York —that were served as now by secular canons who lived not in communities but in houses grouped round the Cathedral Close.   Eight cathedrals were attached to monasteries, Canterbury, Carlisle, Durham, Ely, Norwich, Rochester, Winchester, Worcester, the bishops of these being also abbots.

But whether or not a cathedral was also a monastic church, it existed to serve a similar purpose ; and therefore cathedral and minster were built on the same plan.  That purpose was not to provide accommodation for congregational worship ; a mediaeval church was not planned with the needs of the general public in view.

It existed first of all to contain altars where the Presence

Fig. 55.  THE CLOISTERS, GLOUCESTER, c. 1400, showing the Lavatorium with its long trough at which the mcnks washed.

of God might continually dwell and where ' day by day for ever prayer and praise should rise to Him, where day by day should ever be renewed the holy mystery of the change of the creatures of Bread and Wine into the Body and Blood of Christ '. The first object of the builder was to provide for the residential choir of priests, whether secular or monastic. The east end of the nave, the central crossing, and the western bays of the chancel were therefore screened off and fitted with stalls on three sides, leaving a broad area in the middle for the great lectern and an open space round the high altar ; the transepts and the choir aisles and the eastern ends of the nave aisles were occupied by chapels, each with its altar dedicated to a saint ; and in the thirteenth century a specially important chapel dedicated to our Lady was added, usually by lengthening the church eastward. The only part of the building available for public worship was therefore the western bays of the nave and of its aisles ; the altar for the laity stood against the screen that separated the priests' part of the nave from the people's.

A stall, as the etymology of the word implies, was a standing place ; but, since the choir had often to stand for an hour or more at a stretch, the stalls were provided with tip-up seats, each having beneath it a little ledge called a misericord, too high and too small for a seat but enabling an old or tired man to relieve his legs of a part of the weight. The carving on our old misericords is usually more curious than edifying.

The two doorways leading from the church into the cloister, often wrongly called the abbot's and monks' doors, were used in the Sunday procession round the church and its precincts. The officiating priest asperged the high altar and then, followed by the choir, passed round the ambulatory or aisle surrounding the high altar, the transepts, and the lady chapel, asperging each altar in turn ; next, passing out into the cloister by the eastern door, the procession visited and asperged the chapter-house, dormitory, frater, &c., returning to the church by the western doorway and so, after the nave altars had been asperged, re-entering the choir through the screens.

All the great churches possessed relics of the saints which attracted pilgrims and their offerings, and which were therefore laid out on the altars that they might be viewed at certain regular times. But as some pilgrims, then as now, came rather with the idea of what they could take away, each chapel was protected by a screen or grille through which the visitors peeped as they passed in order round the ambulatory. Near the principal shrine there was also a watching chamber from which a watch might be kept on the relics set out upon it and on the offerings laid before it. Traces of all these things may be found by those who know how to look for them in our minster churches.

## Books for reference.

JACKSON, Sir T. G., *Reason in Architecture*, 1906.
GARBETT, *Principles of Design in Architecture*, 9th ed., 1906.
STATHAM, *Architecture for General Readers*, 1895.
PARKER, J. H., *Glossary of Terms used in Architecture*, 1845.
—— *Introduction to the Study of Gothic Architecture*, 13th ed., 1900.
RICKMAN, T., & PARKER, J. H., *An Attempt to discriminate the Styles of English Architecture*, 7th ed., 1881
BLOXAM, M H., *Principles of Gothic Ecclesiastical Architecture*, 2 vols., 11th ed., 1862.
—— *Companion to Gothic Architecture*, 11th ed., 1862.
BOND, F., *Gothic Architecture in England*, 1905.
—— *Introduction to English Church Architecture*, 2 vols., 1913.
THOMPSON, A. HAMILTON, *The Ground Plan of the English Parish Church*, 1911.
—— *The Historical Growth of the English Parish Church*, 1911.
—— *English Monasteries*, 1913.
LAMBORN, E. A. G., *The Story of Architecture in Oxford Stone*, 1912.
COX, J. C., & HARVEY, A., *English Church Furniture*, 1907.
GASQUET, F. A. (Cardinal), *English Monastic Life*, 1904.

# II

# DOMESTIC ARCHITECTURE

### 1. *Simple and Defensive Character of Early Domestic Architecture.*

THERE are few people who are not willing to recognize the fact that an Englishman's house is his castle : and there are equally few who recognize that in early times, conversely, an Englishman's castle was his house. Such was, however, the case, and it is difficult to draw a hard and fast line between military and domestic architecture. In early times, and indeed through all the centuries down to the days of the Tudors, one of the first requisites of a dwelling was adequate means of defence against attack. The necessity for precaution varied according to circumstances ; according to the district, and to the importance of the owner of the house. Near the Scottish border, where forays were of frequent occurrence, all houses of any importance were strongly fortified, and very curious structures they were. What are known as *pele towers* [Fig. 56] consisted of little besides a single tower standing within a small irregular enclosure. Very many houses in the North of England retain the ancient pele buried among later additions : it being the nucleus round which the more modern buildings have gathered. The tower contained some five stages ; the basement was occupied by the cattle in times of trouble ; the floor above was a store, and here was the entrance door, reached by a ladder. From this floor started the circular stone staircase which led to the upper floors, the first of which contained the hall or common-room. In many cases each stage contained only the one room, but in later examples small separate sleeping chambers were contrived in the enormously thick walls. The roof was generally flat, and served as a look-out. This primitive type of dwelling lingered on till quite late in some parts of the Lowlands of Scotland, and dwellings with no more elaborate accommodation than this were still built in those districts at a time when such vast and splendid mansions as Burghley House and Holdenby were being reared in England.

These quaint pele towers are mentioned because they show in a striking manner the kind of accommodation which satisfied the better class of people during the period when men's efforts were directed almost as much to the preser-

FIG. 56. YANWITH PELE, WESTMORLAND
fourteenth century.

vation as to the enjoyment of life. But the particular form of the towers is a local survival. They provide the necessary rooms one over the other, in order to minimize the extent of wall liable to close attack. Where danger was more remote the requisite rooms were placed alongside of one another. An interesting example of the vertical arrangement is still to be seen, far away from the Scottish border, at Castleton in Derbyshire, where the small twelfth-century keep of the castle still remains perched high up above the precipitous gorge into which the well-known Peak cavern opens. From this side it is inaccessible ; on another the ground falls abruptly away to a valley, while across the steep tongue of land which intervenes between the gorge and the valley is drawn the enclosing wall of the castle. It was in this keep that the domestic part of the establishment was lodged, on three or four floors of one room each.

Three or four rooms were all that were required in the century succeeding the Conquest, and these rooms (arranged in the majority of cases horizontally) always bore the same relation to each other. This relation was maintained for five centuries, and the vast palace of Audley End, built in the reign of James I, was but an elaboration of the few apartments which satisfied the domestic wants of our Norman kings. The root-idea underlying both is the same. The most important of the rooms was the hall, and its importance can hardly be exaggerated. It was the common living-room of the house, and such it continued to be for century after century, until, with the progress of ideas, and the subdivision of space into more and more chambers for special uses, its old character changed. It became an entrance hall : a great vestibule instead of a great living-room. It ceased to be the centre of the domestic system, and house-planning was regarded from a different point of view. The supreme importance of the hall is indicated by the fact that it became synonymous with the house itself ; the chief residence of a village was called the Hall, a name which has survived down to the present day.

Attached to the hall were two other rooms, the kitchen and—to use the expressive term of later years—the parlour. The former was always known as the kitchen, but the latter was first termed the *solar* or *sollere*, and was the private chamber of the lord : in later times the principal room devoted to the use of the family, as distinguished from the servants, was called the *parlour*, and is so named on most house plans of Queen Elizabeth's time. The idea that underlay the arrangements of all houses was therefore extremely simple : the hall in the middle ; at one end the kitchen, or servants' quarters ; at the other end the solar, or family quarters. In early times there was a very scanty subdivision of rooms, and the servants' end was more elaborated than the master's, although more for his benefit than

for theirs.  So early as the reign of King Henry III we hear
of a larder, a sewery, and a cellar, forming part of the kitchen
department ;  but these rooms were introduced for the lord's
convenience, not for his servants' ; and it may be taken for
granted that quite down to recent times, if inconvenience
had to be suffered, it fell upon the servants rather than
upon the master.   Still the greatest personages in the
land were content with arrangements which would be
intolerable in the present day.   There must have been
cases of overcrowding which would have scandalized modern
ideas.   Indeed, we know from the minstrel's lays which
have survived that it was customary for the whole household, except the lord and lady, not only to eat in the hall,
but to use it as a sleeping apartment.   If room could
not be found in the hall, guests were quite content to sleep
in the stables, or indeed anywhere under cover ; and it was
no particular mark of inferiority, nor in any way an unusual
proceeding, for Ivanhoe, when he visited his father's house
in disguise, to take his night's rest in the stable.   Nor need
we sympathize overmuch with Don Quixote when he was
relegated to the loft of the inn for his repose.  *Autres temps,
autres mœurs*.  Although the lord had his solar, or private
room, it was certainly no more than he wanted, for it
served for all purposes not public.   It was at once bedroom
and audience-chamber.   Edward I and his queen were sitting on their bed, attended by the ladies of the court, when
they were nearly killed by lightning in the year 1287.   Nevertheless, limited as the accommodation was, it was considered enough for the purpose during the three centuries
that followed the Conquest.

Yanwith Pele [Fig. 56] is actually the tower of a fourteenth-century house containing accommodation arranged
round a courtyard ; but it gives a fair idea of what a pele
tower is like.   It consists of three stories, the ordinary
number being five.   The square-headed windows are insertions of the sixteenth century.   Yanwith is a good example
of the way in which an early house was planned : exhibiting
the customary relation of the hall, kitchen, and solar, which
in this instance was placed in the tower.

Although the rooms already mentioned constituted the
main part of the house, namely, the hall, the solar, and
the kitchen, they were not always on the same level.   The

solar appears always to have been an upper chamber, and was approached, unless the hall also was on an upper floor, by steps of wood or stone which led sometimes direct from the hall and sometimes from the court outside.  The space beneath the solar, and also beneath the hall when the two were on the same level, was used as cellars or stores, and was usually approached from outside.  These arrangements were extremely simple, extremely rough, and one would suppose extremely uncomfortable ;  and it is in the expansion of these rooms, in adding more and more for the family, and more and more for the servants and the service of the family, that the growth of English domestic architecture consists ;  but down to the end of the reign of James I the hall divided the family apartments from those of the servants, and was the common ground upon which the household met, particularly at meal-times.

The solar usually had a fireplace with a flue ;  but the hall was generally warmed by a fire on a central hearth, the smoke finding its way out through a lantern on the roof.  This custom was not finally superseded until Elizabeth's reign, since a palace which was built at Richmond for Henry VII about the year 1500 had the same arrangement.  In the return of the Commissioners of Parliament made in 1649, they expressly mention, when describing the great hall, that it had ' in the midst a brick hearth for a charcoal fire, having a large lanthorn in the roof of the hall fitted for that purpose, turretted and covered with lead '.  At Penshurst, in Kent, the lantern still remains in the roof of the great hall.   When there was no opportunity for the smoke to escape through the roof, as was the case with the keep of a castle, where the hall had two or three floors over it, a fireplace was provided ;  and the chimneys which enclosed the flues of such fireplaces, or those of the solars, are to be seen on a number of early houses.  Among them may be instanced a house at Christchurch, Hampshire ;  the Jews' house at Lincoln, where the base remains ;  and the manor-house at Boothby Pagnell, in Lincolnshire, all of the twelfth century.

Although the component parts of houses were much the same in all cases, yet these parts were differently arranged to meet local or personal needs, so that no two houses are exactly alike.  Not very many early examples have survived, and of those that do remain a great number have been

incorporated with modern buildings, or have been altered
from their original arrangements. It is only through the
light thrown by contemporary records, and by such remains
as are to be found up and down the country, that the original
apartments can be pieced together ; and there is no building to which the curious inquirer can go, and there see clearly
before his eyes the actual rooms and doors and windows in
the relation to each other which they had when built five
or six centuries ago. Perhaps the most perfect example
left of a great hall of the twelfth century is that at Oakham

FIG. 57. OAKHAM CASTLE: EXTERIOR (about 1180).

Castle [Figs. 57 and 58]. It is 65 feet long by 43 feet wide, and
might easily be mistaken by a casual visitor for a church,
for the roof is carried on two rows of pillars and arches, which
thus divide the building into what look like a nave and two
aisles. Nor is this the only resemblance : for the pillars
have bases upon which they stand, and capitals which support the arches, just in the manner of churches. The windows in the side walls are small, according to the custom
of the time, and there is a little east window ; but it is too
high up for a church, and there is nothing to suggest a chancel. There is no fireplace, therefore the inference is that
there was a fire on the floor, and a lantern on the roof. The

resemblance of this domestic hall to a church is a fact of great significance, for it tends to show, and in a striking way, that there was no essential difference between ecclesiastical and domestic architecture—a fact which is not so generally grasped as it ought to be. Architecture was at that time a science of construction, and problems of similar nature were solved in similar ways, whether they occurred in a church or in a house. Architectural treatment was not then a means of displaying the learning, or the ignorance, of the designer : it was the ordinary method of expression adopted as a matter of course. In the hall at Oakham a large space had to be covered, and recourse was had to the usual expedient of dividing the width into three parts by means of pillars carrying a wall, so that the roof might be formed of three short spans instead of one long one. The wall was carried on the pillars by means of arches, not because they looked well or lent mystery to the view by impeding it, but because that was the best method of construction known to the builders. Had they been able to cover the space with one large roof without using intermediate support, no doubt they would have done so. The difference in architectural treatment between ecclesiastical and domestic buildings will be found not so much in the detail as in the general disposition consequent upon the different purposes to be fulfilled. A door, an arch, or a window might be taken from either and placed in the other without the slightest incongruity in appearance, unless it might arise from the window having a transom, or horizontal cross-bar, which very seldom occurs in church windows before the Perpendicular period. But a house with two stories, and a fireplace in the upper one, would be a composite structure that could never be mistaken for a church. At the same time, while the detail of particular features would be alike in both buildings, it is also true that more richness and elaboration were bestowed upon the church than upon the house. As houses developed in complexity the distinction naturally increased, and by the time of the great house-building era of Elizabeth's days, a domestic style had established itself which was widely different from that associated with churches : but even then masons were not so much alive as the modern amateur could wish to the difference which ought to exist between church-work

FIG. 58. OAKHAM CASTLE HALL: INTERIOR.

and house-work, and churches which were 'restored' in the early part of the seventeenth century often have a curiously domestic look.

From the thirteenth century onwards there were many fine houses built of wood and plaster in certain districts, particularly in the Western counties, from Cheshire to Herefordshire, and some of the most picturesque remains which we possess are to be seen in that part of England. But naturally it is not among these that we must seek for examples of the fortified mansion, but rather in localities where stone was to be found. Of the latter class Aydon Castle, in Northumberland, is a good specimen [Fig. 59], as is Little

FIG. 59. AYDON CASTLE, NORTHUMBERLAND.

Wenham, in Suffolk, which is remarkable for affording an early instance of the use of brick. Of the two plans of Aydon Castle [Fig. 60] the upper floor indicates the extent of the house ; the additional walls that appear on the ground-plan are those which enclosed the courtyards. In this example the kitchens and servants' offices are on the ground-floor ; the hall and family rooms are on the upper floor. The hall, which is the large central apartment, was approached by an outside staircase that led in the usual manner into the *screens* (see p. 60) at the end of the hall. At Stokesay Castle, in Shropshire, the main fortifications are of stone, while the existing gatehouse, built in Elizabethan times, when defence was no longer of importance, is of timberwork.

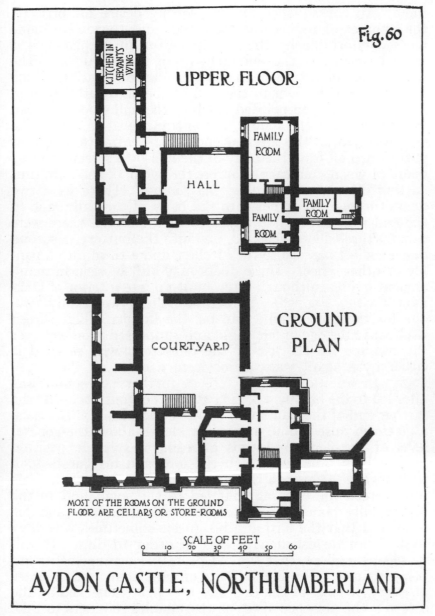

Fig. 60

UPPER FLOOR

KITCHEN IN SERVANTS' WING

FAMILY ROOM

HALL

FAMILY ROOM

FAMILY ROOM

COURTYARD

GROUND PLAN

MOST OF THE ROOMS ON THE GROUND FLOOR ARE CELLARS OR STORE-ROOMS

SCALE OF FEET
0    10    20    30    40    50    60

AYDON CASTLE, NORTHUMBERLAND

2. *The Fourteenth-Century House.*

During the twelfth and thirteenth centuries no great advance seems to have been made in the arrangement of dwellings, but in the fourteenth much was done to improve them.  In consequence of the growing desire for privacy, the number of rooms was increased, and they were made more comfortable by the multiplication of fireplaces, and more cheerful by the enlargement of the windows.  The hall gradually assumed that particular disposition which characterized it down to the end of the sixteenth century. It has already been pointed out how the hall stood between the kitchen and the solar.  The entrance was in one of the side walls, near the kitchen end ; this entrance was now partitioned off from the body of the hall by a screen, usually made of wood, and carried across the width of the hall, thus cutting off a passage, called *the screens*.  There were two doors through the screen into the body of the hall ; and in the end wall of the hall adjacent to the screen there were usually three doors, that led, one into the buttery, a second down a short passage to the kitchen, and a third into a pantry or other office.  These doors may still be seen in many ancient houses, although often built up (see interior of Oakham Castle, Fig. 58).  Sometimes there were only two, one for the buttery and one for the kitchen.  The screen itself was nine or ten feet high, and supported a gallery over the passage for the use of the minstrels, who reached it either by a small staircase or from a room on the upper floor.  In addition to the screen, further protection was afforded to the hall by a porch outside the front door.  At the farther end of the hall, away from the screen, was the dais, a platform raised some five or six inches above the general level of the floor, and thus affording a suitable position for the high table, at which the lord and his guests took their meals.   Through the end wall at the back of the dais was pierced the opening that led to the solar, and to the other family rooms.  Fireplaces were still rare in halls, and it is on record that the lord and his guests sometimes withdrew to a room furnished with one in order to dine.  It will be seen, therefore, that the old primitive arrangements are being refined.  The fierce blasts of wind that used to enter at every opening of the door are now partly checked by the screen ;  the presence of which also enables retainers to take their ale at the buttery, and to reach the kitchen without actually passing through the hall.  But the latter is still a somewhat dismal apartment : scantily lighted, and that by windows high up in the wall, and chilly from want of a fireplace, or, if not chilly, smoky from want of a flue. In subsequent years these defects were remedied : a fireplace was introduced into one of the side walls, and a bay window was placed at the end of the dais, with the sill brought down sufficiently low to enable the occupants to look out. But hitherto there had been no great desire for a prospect, inasmuch as the hall was enclosed within a wall of defence. At Sutton Courtenay, in Berkshire, there is at the upper end of the hall a small low side-window beneath the ordinary window. This may be the first indication of a desire to obtain an outlook from the dais.

Those who are familiar with the halls of colleges will no doubt have felt the description of the hall of a fourteenth-century house to be no new thing. Indeed, there is no better way of realizing the appearance and arrangement of an ancient hall than by inspecting those of the colleges of Oxford and Cambridge. There can be seen the hall, the screens, and in some cases the buttery too, occupying the same relation to each other, and answering the same purposes, as they did in large houses of five centuries ago.

In addition to the rooms required for actual domestic use, some of the larger houses had a chapel incorporated with them ; but this was a comparatively infrequent feature, not being an essential item, as were the hall, the solar, and the kitchen. Naturally, the number of rooms varied with the size of the household and the wealth of the owner ; and these early homes range from the inconsiderable houses of Woodcroft and Northborough in Northamptonshire to the castles of Raby in Durham and Broughton in Oxfordshire : but all were as yet small compared with the vast edifices of Elizabeth's time. All, however, were more or less fortified, according to the district and the importance of the owner. In the extreme north of England houses followed the old fortalice type to a much later date than elsewhere. In more peaceful regions the smaller personages could trust themselves to less defensible houses than could their great neighbours. Thus throughout the country we get some mixture of types, and it is impossible to say that by a certain year such features were universally dropped, or such others universally adopted : but always and everywhere the houses had the same root-idea of hall, solar, and kitchen. The external treatment, too, varied according to the locality.

The earlier houses which have survived are of stone, but it should be remembered that wood played a large part in the construction of all buildings : that many of the rooms of important houses, and even of castles, were built of wood. These have all perished, and in what remains in stone we see only a portion of the original structure.

One of the commonest means of adding to the security of a house in flat districts was to surround it with a moat, and most houses of any consequence were so surrounded. In many cases the moats have almost if not entirely disappeared, their presence being indicated only by a depression in the ground ; but in a few instances they still remain, and continue to wash the walls of the dwellings they protected. In hilly districts they were not necessary, as a precipitous situation served the builder's turn in this respect. Another means of defence adopted was to build the house round a courtyard, for by the end of the fourteenth century the number of rooms had increased to such an extent as to enable this to be done. The old range of buildings with which we are now familiar—the hall, the solar (or, as it may now be called, 'the parlour'), and the kitchen—was supplemented by other rooms, arranged in two wings returning at right angles to it, and thus forming three sides of a court. The fourth was closed by a wall, or occupied by a further range of buildings, having in the middle the gatehouse. Round the whole went the moat. The outer walls were still so constructed as to diminish, as far as possible, facilities for hostile entry. The windows were few, and no larger than was absolutely requisite. Projecting towers or turrets were placed at the corners, and sometimes also half-way along each side, furnished with loopholes for the bowmen or embrasures for cannon. Where the hall came, the windows of which were probably larger, the moat was wider, to give additional security. The only means of ingress was through the gateway, access to which was gained by a drawbridge over the moat. This entrance and its approaches were commanded by flanking towers, and its narrow passage was closed at each end by ponderous gates, and often by a portcullis in addition. Though not castles in the sense of being military strongholds, many of the precautions of a castle were adopted in these fortified manor-houses, and life within them must have been dull, and hedged about

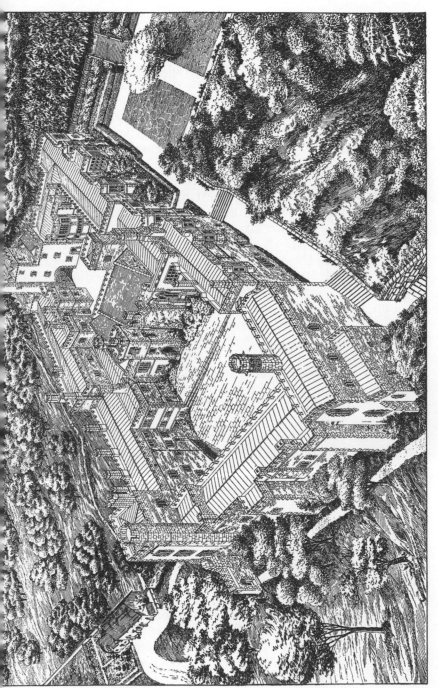

Fig. 61. HADDON HALL.

with endless restrictions.   No wonder that when the time came to cast restraint aside, the whole country blossomed out into buildings that vied with each other in the cheerfulness of their aspect and the freedom of their surroundings.

In hilly country the conditions of the site did not always permit of so regular a disposition as was possible on level land.   At Haddon Hall [Figs. 61, 62], for instance, the entrance tower is at one corner of the building, instead of being midway in the front ; and there is no attempt to observe straightness of line or regularity of disposition.   Haddon is perhaps the best example left to us of an ancient house : as it was when the family gave it up as a place of residence a hundred and fifty years ago, so it remains to-day.   The very depressions in the kitchen table made by the mincing-knife are there still.   Nor has the building been altered to keep pace with the times since the days when the tide of fashion set strongly in the direction of modern ideas. There is not a sash-window in the whole place.   Yet up to the end of the sixteenth century it had been altered to suit the changing requirements of its inmates ; generation after generation had pulled down or added to the work of its fathers, so as to make itself more comfortable, until the most extensive operations of all were undertaken by Dorothy Vernon and her husband in the closing years of the sixteenth century ; and hardly anything has been done since.

Haddon consists of two courts, and possessed them before the end of the fourteenth century.   The outer walls are sparsely furnished with windows, and the hall, which required more light than other rooms, was placed in the block that separates the two courts, thus enabling it to derive its light from one or both of them.   The kitchen, which comes up to an outside wall, suffers accordingly : its windows are so small that even at midday it is only dimly lighted ; the neighbouring offices are even darker. The family side of the house is far more cheerful.   It looks towards the south, and was greatly improved in Elizabeth's reign, when large windows were the fashion.   But the arrangements which satisfied the wants of the Vernons and the Manners down to the seventeenth century were found to be incompatible with the comfort that became indispensable in the eighteenth ; the place ceased to be

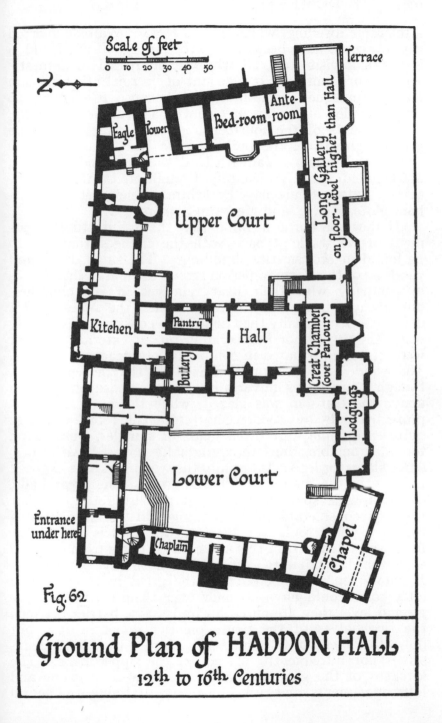

Scale of feet

0 10 20 30 40 50

N

Eagle Tower

Bed-room

Ante-room

Terrace

Long Gallery on floor-level higher than Hall

Upper Court

Kitchen

Pantry

Hall

Great Chamber (over Parlour)

Buttery

Lodgings

Lower Court

Entrance under here

Chaplain

Chapel

Fig. 62

# Ground Plan of HADDON HALL
## 12th to 16th Centuries

a tolerable dwelling, which indeed Horace Walpole averred it never could have been, and so the family left it.  Haddon is worth a visit from all who are interested in domestic architecture, not only on account of its romantic situation and picturesque appearance, but because it conveys so vivid an idea of the arrangement of a mediaeval dwelling. Other houses of the fourteenth century which show the gradual growth of the buildings are Raby Castle, in the county of Durham ; Yanwith Hall, Westmorland [Fig. 56] ; Markenfield Hall, Yorkshire ; Broughton Castle, Oxfordshire ; Sutton Courtenay, Berkshire ; Penshurst and Ightham Mote, Kent ; and Meare in Somerset.

It must be borne in mind that the architectural treatment of houses kept pace with the changes that are to be found in ecclesiastical buildings.  The small doors and windows of the Norman period strove to enlarge themselves in company with their near relatives in the churches, but always they were confronted with the necessity for defence.  Occasionally they defied this constraint, especially when they were not immediately on an external wall, or were in homes situated in comparatively peaceful districts. The windows began to be glazed in the better houses, though by no means universally.  In many cases the portion above the transom was glazed, while the lower half was protected only by wooden shutters.  The roofs, which in quite early time were often made of shingles, were found too inflammable, and were gradually covered with tiles, stone slates, or lead.  Internally the woodwork was exposed to view in the manner of church roofs.  The great halls, often of wide span, had roofs of much elaboration that required considerable skill and ingenuity in the framing together.  The roof over Westminster Hall is one of the finest specimens left of this class, but it dates from a period somewhat later than the time at which we have yet arrived. It should be remembered that the great halls with their lofty roofs could have no floor over them : when on the ground level they presented an impassable barrier between the two halves of the house on the upper story ; but down to the end of the fourteenth century they were themselves not infrequently placed on the upper floor.  The kitchens of the greater establishments were spacious and lofty apartments, and built in a substantial and ornamental

Fig. 63.   ABBOT'S KITCHEN, GLASTONBURY.

manner, which is something of a surprise and even shock to our modern ideas. The great kitchen of Glastonbury Abbey is a large building of stone, beautifully vaulted, and crowned with a lantern [see Fig. 63]. But no doubt this treatment arose primarily from the desire, not for a handsome kitchen, but for a fireproof structure. The abbot's kitchen at Durham is equally fine, if not finer. It is of octagonal shape, thirty-six feet across, and is vaulted in a simple but highly ingenious way. It contained four large fireplaces as well as ovens—for it must be remembered that the abbeys in those days were not only great residential establishments but also hotels. In this connexion, again, nothing will convey a better idea of the work that went on in the kitchen of a mediaeval house than a visit to that of a large college, such as Christ Church at Oxford or Trinity at Cambridge. It is true that at Glastonbury, Durham, and Raby Castle the magnificence of kitchens reached its high-water mark, but even in smaller establishments, such as Stanton Harcourt, in Oxfordshire, it was a commodious apartment, and as time went on it was supplemented by numerous smaller rooms for special purposes, which will be mentioned hereafter.

### 3.  *The Fifteenth-Century House.*

During the fifteenth century the ideas which we have traced as underlying the arrangement of houses were very much developed. Hitherto defence had been one of the most important factors in determining the plan and the general treatment. It had led to the adoption of a court-yard, small in extent, and of which two or perhaps three sides were occupied by buildings. This court was now to be developed in size and regularity of plan, but always founded on the original idea of a hall placed between the kitchen and the parlour. Attention began to be paid to the grouping and arrangement, not only from motives of convenience and security, but also from regard to external appearance. The struggle between the old over-mastering desire for safety and the new desire for elegance and cheerfulness was carried on all through this century and well into the next, but throughout this period the old desire continued to affect the results. Elegance and cheerfulness, however, asserted themselves, and produced

such creations as the great hall at Kenilworth Castle, and
the Buck Hall at Cowdray, in Sussex : large and lofty
apartments with abundance of light admitted through
windows of beautiful design. These castles and mansions
were still difficult of access for those who had not the privilege of entrance, for there was yet the moat to cross and
the gatehouse to traverse ; and it was in the gatehouses
that some of the last relics of the old defensive appliances
lingered. They were a curious mixture of the old and of
the new. In them appeared sinister openings of the old
cross-œuillet form from which the arrow could fly, or of
circular shape from which the cannon-ball could speed
on a heavier but hardly longer flight. With these were
mingled devices and ornamentation ; and while the
stranger waited for the drawbridge to fall and the portcullis
to creak slowly upwards, his eye could wander over the
armorial insignia which taught him the family history of
the personage he came to see. The very plan of some of
the houses shows how considerations of appearance mingled
with those of defence. There are examples in which a
strict symmetry of outline and of grouping is observed,
projecting turrets being introduced at intervals that
depended as much upon the designer's sense of proportion
as upon the dictates of military science. Of this mode
of building Hurstmonceux, in Sussex, is a splendid illustration. Another smaller but interesting instance is to be
seen in the ruins of Kirby Muxloe, in Leicestershire. The
moat remains, enclosing a rectangular space which is
bounded by the remnants of the walls of the house.
The ground and first floors of the gatehouse remain,
and one corner tower is standing to its full height. The
date is probably about 1460, and the builder must have
been the William, Lord Hastings, who was executed by
Richard III. It is quite clear that there was a tower at
each angle of the building, and a projection in the centre of
each front, thus giving a symmetrical plan. The central
projection on one front formed the gateway, but how the
others were utilized there is nothing to show. Both the
gateway and the corner tower are strictly symmetrical in
themselves, except for the position of a door or a window ;
projections which correspond with each other being carefully made equal. This is quite different from the haphazard

FIG. 64.  OXBURGH HALL:  GATEHOUSE.

arrangement of Haddon, for instance, and is a significan
fact, for the time was rapidly approaching when Englisl
architecture was to feel the touch of Italian influences
which brought, among other things, a regard for symmetry
amounting sometimes to affectation.  At Kirby Muxlo
there is still a real desire for defence.  The drawbridge an

the portcullis indicate this, as also do the embrasures, set low
for the better serving of the cannon. Such windows as
remain are sparingly introduced into outer walls, especially
on the ground-floor ; they are less restricted on the upper
one. Yet level with the top of the drawbridge when it

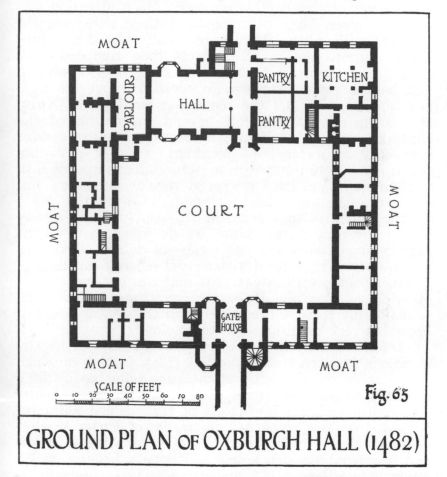

**GROUND PLAN OF OXBURGH HALL (1482)**

was raised, and looking straight upon the direct approach,
are two-light windows of fair height and width. The mixture
is curious, for the defensive arrangements are genuine. The
possibility of having to repel an attack was evidently
contemplated, while at the same time the size of the windows
was such as to afford the assailant an opportunity for
a telling counter-stroke. In connexion with the gateway

are the usual chambers for those in charge, and each room here, as well as in the corner tower (which also is provided with embrasures on the ground-floor), is supplied with a latrine in an attached building. The arrangement of these conveniences in connexion with mediaeval buildings is a matter of considerable interest. Much attention was bestowed upon their planning, and they were supplied with great liberality. They were usually placed in a projecting turret, and in all respects they complied with sanitary requirements far better than their successors in Elizabethan times, which were sometimes cut off from any outside wall. Of the remaining buildings at Kirby Muxloe there is nothing left beyond the outline of the enclosing wall. It is certain that the projecting towers were connected by a range of buildings of lower elevation, which must have resulted in a picturesque composition of straight roofs and lofty towers at regular intervals ; but where the hall was placed, or what rooms went to make up the buildings that enclosed the courtyard, is merely matter for conjecture. What we do know, however, is that combined with the old means of defence there was a large courtyard planned with a strict regard to symmetry. Another point worth attention is that this house was built of brick, as also was Hurstmonceux : and brick, which seems hardly to have been used until this century, was to become a very usual material to employ.[1]

Another brick house of about the same date as Kirby Muxloe is Oxburgh Hall, in Norfolk [Figs. 64, 65], of which considerably more is left ; at the same time, having been used continuously as a habitation, it has undergone many alterations, and has lost much of the genuine antiquity possessed by the untouched fragments of Kirby Muxloe. Oxburgh also is built round a courtyard within a moat, and is entered through a fine and lofty gatehouse, which retains some defensive contrivances. This gatehouse is at the bottom of the plan. Immediately opposite to it is the hall with its porch, screens, and bay-windows. To the left of the hall are the family rooms, and to the right are the servants' rooms, the kitchen being in the right-hand top

[1] Under the guidance of Mr. C. R. Peers, of the Board of Works, the remains at Kirby Muxloe have now been uncovered and displayed, to the great advantage of archaeological research.

corner. The small rooms which complete the quadrangle were used for various inferior purposes. The entrance-porch of the hall is not exactly opposite to the gatehouse. Symmetry of design was to be more generally adopted in the next century ; and although it seems to have been observed at Kirby Muxloe, it was not yet universally accepted as a maxim of house-planning. The exterior treatment at Oxburgh is also freer than in earlier buildings ; windows occur plentifully in the outside walls, though they are yet small, seldom exceeding three lights in width ; they still have pointed heads, but the curves are much flatter than in former times.

#### 4. *The Tudor House.*

We have now come to the Tudor period. Ecclesiastical architecture was passing through its gorgeous sunset at King's College Chapel, Cambridge, St. George's Chapel, Windsor, and Henry VII's Chapel at Westminster. Its forms were still applied to domestic architecture, but the differences of treatment were growing more marked, and the use of brick for houses emphasized them. Windows in churches had increased to a size far beyond the needs or the possibilities of domestic architecture. The small Tudor flat-pointed window had no place in a church. Chimneys, which were essentially a domestic feature, were no longer subjected to a treatment analogous to that applied to a pinnacle ; they became independent structures, upon which extraordinary pains were bestowed. Every flue was separate, and was formed of cut and moulded brickwork of surprising and intricate pattern. No country can produce such magnificent specimens of design in brick as our English chimneys of the end of the fifteenth century and the opening years of the sixteenth, and they are almost invariably decorated in a fashion derived from Gothic sources, and not from the new source of inspiration, Italy.

The sixteenth century witnessed in English architecture the first stages of that change from Gothic inspiration to Classic, which affected the whole of Europe. It began with the tomb erected by Henry VIII over his father's body in the splendid chapel reared at Westminster by the deceased monarch. This tomb was designed by an Italian, Piero Torrigiano, and it set the fashion, to a certain extent, for many subsequent tombs ; but its influence hardly went farther. From independent sources came bits of detail in the same spirit, appearing here and there amid work which was thoroughly English in character. But the new fashion was confined to minutiae, and even in such isolated pieces of design as the chantries in cathedrals and large churches it went only skin-deep, and left the framework of the body still Gothic. When one-third of the century had passed, there came the dissolution of the monasteries, and the

Fig. 66.   COMPTON WINYATES.

end of ecclesiastical architecture for the time being ; and what development there was in architecture must henceforward be sought for in houses. Of these there was no lack : Henry VIII's reign saw many new ones, but Elizabeth's vastly more. There probably never was, until our own day, so much building done in fifty years as during the reign of Elizabeth : and it is in the sixteenth century that domestic architecture really developed, and produced so many examples as to enable us to study them with tolerable completeness.

All through the first half of the century the old desire for defence survived, and houses were surrounded by moats.

The ancient simple arrangements of plan were still adhered
to.   The hall was the centre of domestic life.   At right
angles from it ran the blocks containing on the one hand the

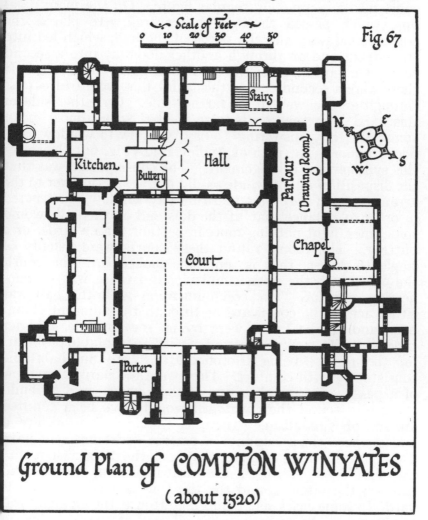

Ground Plan of COMPTON WINYATES
(about 1520)

kitchen and its dependencies, on the other hand the parlour
and its supplementary rooms, thus forming three sides of a
court, the square of which was completed by the gatehouse,
flanked right and left with a room or two, which were
occupied by the porter, and by the falconers and other
outdoor servants [Figs. 66, 67, Compton Winyates].   The

court-plan survived throughout the century, but the increasing desire for symmetry, which was one of the outcomes of the Italian influence, soon began to fashion the court into a completely regular figure. On the main axial line, which passed through the centre, were placed the entrance gateway and the porch of the hall, which led into the screens and on through another doorway into a second court or a garden, after the moat had gone out of use. If there were a second court, this axial line would also pass through an archway in its farther side. On either side of this axial line, the courts were treated with almost exact symmetry, bay answering to bay, window to window, and door to door. The plan of Audley End [Fig. 69] illustrates this symmetrical arrangement. The consequence was that the disposition of the windows did not always answer to the arrangement of the rooms, and a fine bay-window, constructed in order to balance that at the dais end of the hall, would sometimes light nothing more important than a larder or a buttery. The rooms round these courts were usually of single thickness, that is, one side looked into the court, the other into the open country ; and there was no connecting corridor. The communication with the hall was either across the courtyard or through the adjacent chambers, and as the latter were by no means wide, in later times the owners were confronted with an insoluble problem ; for the rooms, being thoroughfares, were uninhabitable consistently with comfort. They were too narrow to allow of a passage being taken out of their width, and to build a corridor round the courtyard would have been counted an act of vandalism. There is in Northamptonshire a house where the occupants of certain bedrooms still have the choice of three unusual routes to the breakfast-room ; the first leads through the drawing-room, the second through the kitchen, and the third across the open courtyard. In some cases, as at Burghley House, the architectural treatment of the courtyard has allowed of a corridor being constructed round it without serious detriment to the effect, but in many cases this has not been possible, and in consequence the houses have been found intolerable and have been abandoned.

But considerations of this kind did not enter into the social ideas of the sixteenth century. The rooms sur-

Fig. 68. AUDLEY END.

rounding the quadrangles, divided into groups of three or four, made admirable lodgings for a guest and his retinue, and each group had its door into the adjacent court. Although these groups were self-contained, there was a certain number of rooms that were common to the whole of the family and guests, of which the chief were the hall (now always on the ground-floor), the great chamber, and the long gallery. The last two were always upstairs, the former being the successor of the solar in its character of audience-chamber, and the latter being a product of the times, of which the origin is obscure. Certain it is that there was no such room in the fortified houses of the fifteenth century, built though they may have been round a courtyard. Possibly there was something of the kind in the original Hampton Court Palace, which dates from 1515 to 1540. But the long gallery first became general in Elizabeth's reign, and it developed to an extent quite astonishing. In some of the large houses it was as much as 180 or 200 feet long, and not infrequently the house was expressly contrived so as to obtain a gallery of great length. An unwieldy apartment of this kind could only be upstairs. It was usually placed on the first floor, but often on the second. One of the uses for which these long galleries were built was the performance of music. An inscription on the chimney-piece of the gallery at Apethorpe in Northamptonshire makes this clear. Another use, according to Sir Henry Wootton, was the taking of 'gentle exercise'. In order to reach these important upper rooms, good staircases were required. In old days 'newel' staircases were all that was necessary. These are to be found in the earliest mediaeval houses, and were for centuries the only method of ascending from one floor to another. They may still be climbed in many an old church tower, and obviously were merely utilitarian, and destitute of any ornamental intention. In England they seldom exceeded four feet in width, although in France they were developed, in the time of Francis I, into grand features, and are, indeed, distinctive of French architecture of that period. The smaller variety continued in use in England until well into the sixteenth century, the latest example being probably that in the market-house at Rothwell, built about 1578. But quite suddenly, apparently, and without any noteworthy inter-

mediate step, they were superseded by the broad straight
flights of stairs which characterize Elizabethan houses,
where, in place of the continuous circular ascent, broken only
at intervals by an insignificant halting-place, we find straight

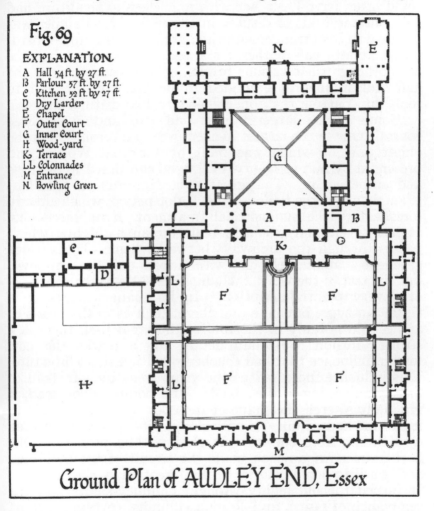

Fig. 69

EXPLANATION

A Hall 54 ft. by 27 ft.
B Parlour 57 ft. by 27 ft.
C Kitchen 32 ft. by 27 ft.
D Dry Larder
E Chapel
F Outer Court
G Inner Court
H Wood-yard
K Terrace
LL Colonnades
M Entrance
N Bowling Green

Ground Plan of AUDLEY END, Essex

flights of not more than six or seven steps, and then a
spacious landing. More often than not, these fine staircases are in wood rather than in stone, and on the decoration
of the woodwork all the fancy of the Elizabethan workman
was expended [see Fig. 70]. There was always at least
one great staircase, and often there were three or four,

all required by the exigencies of the planning, which arose quite as much from the desire to possess a splendid and symmetrical house as from the need for obtaining the requisite accommodation ; for the wants of the inmates could often have been met with much less expenditure had not considerations of display intervened. The designer was prodigal in his arrangements, and staircases had to be introduced at intervals, either for appearance' sake, to balance each other in their various towers, or of necessity, since the hall still frequently extended in height from ground to roof, thus cutting the upper floor into two distinct halves.

Some of the larger houses had two and even three courts. One of the largest of them was Hampton Court, the oldest part of which was built by Cardinal Wolsey and presented by him to Henry VIII, who continued to increase and embellish it. This great palace affords an excellent example of a large house of the Tudor period, which already foreshadows the symmetrical treatment of its successors. It has several large courts built on an axial line which passes through the archways between them. The various gatehouses are embellished with turrets and bay-windows, but the rest of the work, including the sides of the courts, is of a very plain description. In its main features it is Gothic in type, but here and there, such as in the heads of arches and notably in the roof of the great hall, there is a strong infusion of Italian detail, which marks the new foreign influence that had touched our English architecture. This influence increased as the years went by. Instead of merely appearing in the spandrel of a pointed door-head, it gradually altered the shape of the doorway itself : gave to it a round arch, flanked it with classic pilasters, and crowned it with a classic cornice. It changed the profiles of the horizontal strings which made the circuit of the building ; and gave to what was a Gothic creation a classic form. It turned the old highly wrought chimney-shafts into the semblance of Greek and Roman columns, carrying a short length of entablature by way of chimney-cap. Yet in spite of all this foreign detail, the body of the house was English : notwithstanding the trammels of symmetry, its plan remained unchanged.

Its windows were a development of the English type, but with heads square instead of pointed, and with mullions

and transoms much increased in number. The old windows
of two or three lights gave place to windows of four, five,
and six ; instead of being two tiers high, they became
three or even four. The area of glass was more than
doubled, and its increase alarmed Bacon, who found it

FIG. 70. STAIRCASE AT CREWE HALL.

difficult to get away from sun or cold. The windows were
glazed, and no longer closed only with a shutter. A special
development was the bay-window. Already in the fifteenth
century such windows had been introduced, but they were
small in size and only one story high ; towards the end of
the sixteenth, however, they had developed into features
which often dominated the architecture, and many a

building owes its distinctive character to the bay-windows that embellish it. They are sometimes adjuncts of one or two stories, crowned with a rich parapet : but occasionally they reach the whole height of the house, and all the architectural members which make the circuit of the walls also go round the bays, thus converting them from adjuncts into integral parts of the structure.

The courtyards at Hampton Court may have been adopted from motives of security, for it was a moated house ; but those of the large Elizabethan houses were survivals, and were retained partly from sentiment, partly for architectural effect. One of these great houses must have been an extraordinary sight. Burghley House, as we now see it, is large, and has been compared to a village : but it was not half so large as were Holdenby and Audley End [Figs. 68, 69] in their prime. Holdenby was approached on the axial line by a 'large, long, straight, fair way', as Lord Burghley called it, going the length of 'the green'. This road led to the gatehouse, which gave access to a green court surrounded by a wall pierced with a great arch on either side. Upon a terrace formed by a short flight of steps stood the front of the house, with its entrance in the centre. Through this a second court was reached, on the opposite side of which, still on the main axis, was the porch of the hall. Traversing the screens, another door gave access to yet another court, containing the kitchens, and out of this a central archway led into the gardens. It was a palace rather than a house, and was no doubt built on so vast a scale in order to accommodate the queen on her progresses.

The plan of Audley End [Fig. 69] shows the enormous extent of one of the great houses of the early seventeenth century. It is quite symmetrical in disposition, except for the excrescence on the left, which contained the kitchen. The hall occupies the middle of the block between the two large courts, and one of the wings at the upper end contained the chapel. There are six staircases in the first court, four in the second, and two adjacent to the wings at the upper end, twelve in all. The only part left of this vast mansion is the lower front and the two wings of the second court ; but what is left forms a large house.

There was another type of mansion besides that built

round the old-fashioned court. This had a long straight body with a wing at right angles to it at each end, and a projecting porch in the middle, giving a kind of m shape, or, where the porch did not project, an H shape. It has been supposed that the E shape was adopted out of compliment to Elizabeth. This may be so, but the conjecture is not borne out by a study of the evolution of the house-planning of the period ; although the architect, or surveyor, John Thorpe, did design himself a house in the shape of his initials I T, which was never built ; and Sir Thomas Tresham actually built two small houses embodying the idea of the Trinity, and of the Passion of Christ, the former being an equilateral triangle and the latter a Greek cross. Among the smaller houses the H plan was very common, and they often had a courtyard enclosed by a wall, both in front and at the back ; the one entered through a gate-house on the centre-line, the other having a central archway in the wall. Of this type there are plenty of examples left in out-of-the-way villages, where a quaint archway in a forecourt leads directly up to the house door, which itself is in the centre of a symmetrical structure.

We thus see that the old type of house, built round a court and surrounded by a moat, was continued till quite late ; in time the moat was omitted, and the courtyard, which was formerly planned in a somewhat haphazard way, was reduced to strict order and symmetry ; its insignificant lights were multiplied indefinitely, and it was embellished with bay-windows and with stair-turrets ; its doorways were enlarged ; its porch was decorated with classic pilasters. But it was essentially the same house, with its hall in the middle, and its kitchen and its parlour on either side : the dais was there, and the hall screen with its gallery above : from the screens ran passages to the kitchen, the buttery, and sometimes the larder ; just as things had been a hundred or two hundred years earlier. But the buildings flanking the hall were greatly increased and subdivided. The kitchen was supplemented by a scullery, a 'pastry', where the ovens were, a surveying place, a spicery, a bolting-house, and several other rooms of a like nature. A 'hall for hynds' also appears on contemporary plans. The family apartments now included the parlour, the winter parlour, the great chamber, the

gallery, the chapel, and a vast number of ' lodgings ', as they
were called, rooms which could serve as bedrooms or as
sitting-rooms for guests.    Many of the largest of these
houses have either been pulled down or abandoned to
decay.    Others have been greatly curtailed in size, or so
altered to suit modern requirements as to have lost much
of their ancient character.    But as instances of the courtyard plan may be cited Burghley House and Kirby Hall,
both in Northamptonshire ;   Blickling Hall in Norfolk,

FIG. 71.   CHASTLETON.

Knole in Kent, and Hoghton Tower in Lancashire :    as
examples of the H plan, Hatfield House, Montacute in
Somerset, and Doddington in Lincolnshire.    Smaller houses
are to be seen at Fountains Hall, Yorkshire, Cold Ashton in
Gloucestershire, and Chastleton in Oxfordshire [Figs. 71, 72],
which is an instance of a house built round a very small
court.    It is, however, of great interest, as it has undergone
but little alteration and actually retains that rare feature
the dais.    These are but a few out of many that might be
named :    and every county possesses in a greater or less
degree examples illustrating work of the Elizabethan period.
They are not always, perhaps not often, complete or

untouched specimens ; but characteristics that may be
lacking in some will be found present in others, and there is

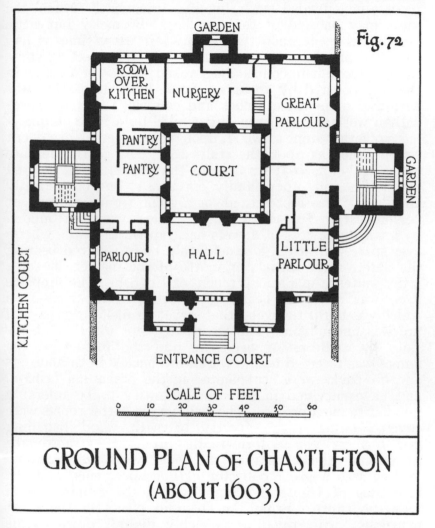

Fig. 72

GROUND PLAN of CHASTLETON
(ABOUT 1603)

always something to show how the Elizabethan architect
did his work.

Inside, the same influences were at work which had
changed the exterior. There were much the same features
as formerly, but they were differently embellished, and
the general result was one of greatly increased enrichment. The development of the staircase has been already

mentioned : how from a plain circular flight of steps, of which the only purpose was to give access to the upper floors, it became crowded with fanciful ornament. Much the same may be said of the fireplace. Formerly but little design was spent upon this feature ; in early times it had consisted of a hearth on the floor, with a projecting stone canopy above it to collect the smoke ; or else of a recess in the wall covered by an arch. Some little decoration was bestowed upon these arches and canopies ; but in Elizabethan work the arch was surrounded by a huge chimneypiece of either stone or wood, upon which as much ornament was lavished as upon the staircases. The central feature was usually the coat of arms of the owner, supplemented by badges and other family emblems ; but occasionally an allegory was represented, or a scene from scripture, or personifications of the virtues. These were surrounded by intricate devices of flowers or strap-work, while, whereever space permitted, a panel would be introduced bearing the date, or the initials or motto of the master, or some pithy sentence in Latin, French, or English. The fireplace itself was merely a hearth-stone lying in the recess, on which was burnt the wood that served as fuel, for a sea-coal fire was uncommon. The wood was kept together at the sides by andirons or fire-dogs, and the impact of the flames was received upon an iron fire-back. Both andirons and fire-backs were ornamented in the prevailing fashion, and have survived in sufficient quantity to be tolerably familiar to most people. The walls of the better rooms were covered either with tapestry or with wood panelling [see Fig. 73]. The former was often of extraordinary richness in the houses of the more wealthy. Cardinal Wolsey was a great collector of fine specimens, and the tapestries of Hampton Court excited the admiration of foreign visitors. From the splendid pieces in the great mansions ' with royal arras richly dight ', down to the ' smirched worm-eaten tapestry ' of the ale-house, there were many gradations of excellence, and an infinite variety of subjects, in which gods and goddesses, saints, martyrs, and prophets, huntsmen, fishermen, Roman emperors, and a host of other personages played their parts ; for the characters of mythology, as well as of sacred and secular history, seemed equally real to the men and women of

Fig. 73. WOOD PANELLING FROM CHURCH FARM, CLARE, SUFFOLK,
now in the Victoria and Albert Museum.

Elizabeth's days. The hall at Wollaton Hall, Nottingham-shire [Fig. 74], is a fine example of the interior treatment of an Elizabethan room. There is the stone screen, the large fireplace, and the panelling on the walls. The roof is of the open-timber type, but it has the peculiarity that it supports the floor of a room above. The windows, owing to the fact that the hall is surrounded by other rooms on every side, are at an unusual height from the floor.

The ceilings of Elizabeth's time were decorated in a manner peculiar to England. It was derived from the panelled ceilings of the early Tudor period, which were formed of wooden ribs arranged in rectangular patterns. These ribs were subsequently constructed in plaster, and, owing to the pliant nature of that material, soon became diverted from their original straight forms into all kinds of geometrical and interlacing designs. Like Alph, the sacred river, they meandered with a mazy motion over the whole surface of the ceiling ; often emphasized, where they crossed, with delicately modelled foliage, and enclosing in their course panels of different shapes wherein, once more, the arms of the owner were emblazoned. The diversity of pattern and of treatment is marvellous, and it would be difficult to point to two designs exactly alike in different houses. No doubt there were repetitions, for the craftsmen seem to have worked from stock designs ; but either the duplicates have vanished in the destruction that has overtaken many of these houses, or the detail was varied in the various cases. The effect of an Elizabethan room was therefore exceedingly rich ; the walls were handsomely covered, and the great chimney-piece was a centre of decoration ; the ceiling was elaborately adorned, and the windows were filled with glass of quaint and intricate pattern, or of glowing colours amid which the ' pomp of heraldry ' was again displayed. Everything was done to set forth the estate and dignity of the owner. The triumph of peace was complete ; it was no longer necessary to take thought of defence ; it was no longer needful to stay the fancy of the designer from a sense that, in the ever-present risk of destruc-tion by attack, expenditure upon ornament was a waste of resources. The ingenuity formerly lavished on contri-vances for ensuring safety was now expended on decora-tion. Houses were built for comfort, convenience, and display, and they had at length entered upon that phase of development which allies them far more closely to the twentieth century than to the thirteenth.

FIG. 74. WOLLATON HALL, NOTTS. (1580–8).

## 5. *Town-Houses.*

The development of domestic architecture in early times, and indeed down to the reign of James I, has necessarily to be traced by an examination of houses in the country, since there it is that examples are to be found. Of town-houses during the Middle Ages but little can be told with certainty, for they have practically all been swept away in the course of the improvements which have taken place from time to time in towns both large and small. Most of them were built of wood and were liable to be destroyed in such conflagrations as the Great Fire of London in 1666. Indeed, two earlier fires of London are on record which caused vast damage ; one took place in the year 1189, and the other in 1212. In consequence of these disasters it was made compulsory to build the party walls between houses of stone 3 feet thick and 16 feet high. But as to the remainder of the buildings no restrictions appear to have been imposed, and the superstructures were still built of wood, as in former times. In spite of the wholesale destruction which has overtaken mediaeval town-houses, there still remain ancient examples in towns like York, Chester, Shrewsbury, and Coventry, as well as in sleepy old market-towns up and down the country. But these examples are more frequently of the time of Elizabeth and James than of earlier centuries. Nevertheless, making allowance for the particular character of the work due to its later date, they convey some idea of what town-houses of the Middle Ages were like. It is almost impossible to reconstruct their plans, for the very few mediaeval examples that have survived have been completely altered as to the interior. We can gather, however, that the basements were vaulted chambers, partly above ground, and that over them were probably two stories of rooms. In a few instances there may have been shops on the ground-floor, as in the case of the Butchers' Row in Shrewsbury ; but it would seem that merchandise was more frequently sold at fairs than over the counter of a shop. Although mostly built of wood, some few were of stone, and were in the nature of landmarks, owing to their greater durability. In stone houses the fronts were vertical, but in wooden houses, particularly when it became in later times customary to have three or four stories, each story was made to project beyond that below, until the two sides of the narrow streets nearly met at the top.

There is a stone house-front of the twelfth century at Lincoln, known as the Jew's House, and there are three

FIG. 75. THE GEORGE INN, GLASTONBURY.

or four good fifteenth-century fronts elsewhere, notably those of the George Inn at Glastonbury [see Fig. 75] and the Angel at Grantham. But these houses, although they show how the fronts were treated, throw but little light on the internal arrangements.

It seems clear that the restricted space available in the heart of a town caused the houses to be crowded together, and gave no great frontage to them. But in the outskirts, where ground was less valuable, and sometimes even in thickly populated streets, houses of important citizens or the premises of wealthy companies were built on the same lines as those adopted in the more ample spaces of the country. There was a courtyard, and the hall, kitchens, and family rooms were arranged in the usual relation to each other, although it was often necessary, owing to lack of ground, to make all the windows face into the court.

There are plenty of examples remaining of town-houses of the seventeenth and eighteenth centuries; for earlier periods information has largely to be sought in documents and surveys. But even the fairly numerous surveys of Elizabeth's time do not throw much light on the subject at that period. John Thorpe, the well-known surveyor of the time, has left a few plans of London houses, but these were of considerable size and give little help in regard to ordinary tenements. The state of things in the Middle Ages is largely a matter of conjecture, which the researches of students have, so far, not converted into certainty. There can be little doubt, however, that ordinary houses, picturesque enough in appearance, were but miserable homes, judged by even the most lenient standards of to-day; and the destructive fires from which not London alone but many provincial towns suffered, brought about much-needed improvements which, but for such drastic remedies, might have been indefinitely postponed.

### Books for reference.

Turner & Parker, *Domestic Architecture in England*, 4 vols. (from the Conquest to Henry VIII), 1877.

Dolman, *An Analysis of Ancient Domestic Architecture in Great Britain*, 2 vols., 1864.

Pugin, *Specimens of Gothic Architecture in England*, 2 vols. (Gothic and Tudor), 1821.

Pugin, *Examples of Gothic Architecture in England*, 3 vols. (Gothic and Tudor), 1831.

Nash, *Mansions of England*, 4 vols., folio (Tudor and Elizabethan), 1839–49. Reprinted in 4to, 1869.

Habershon, *Ancient Half-timbered Edifices of England*, 1836.

Richardson, *Architectural Remains of the Reigns of Elizabeth and James I*, 1840.

—— *Specimens of the Architecture of the Reigns of Elizabeth and James I*, 1837.

—— *Studies from Old English Mansions*, 1841–8.

Shaw, *Details of Elizabethan Architecture*, 1834.

Gotch, *Early Renaissance Architecture in England* (1500–1625), 1901.

—— *Architecture of the Renaissance in England* (1560–1635), 1891–4.

—— *The Growth of the English House* (1100–1800), 1909.

Addy, *The Evolution of the English House*, 1905.

# III

# WAR

## § 1. MILITARY ARCHITECTURE

THE maxim *si vis pacem, para bellum* has led all civilized nations to provide against invasion by means of walls or fortresses impassable to an enemy. The Saxons were not a civilized people ; a state of war was to them habitual ; they neither expected nor wished to dwell in peace, and their fortifications were merely of that rudimentary kind which would prevent them from surprise by a sudden attack. The defensible Roman sites, London excepted, were not occupied by them until the walls had fallen into ruin. Their *burhs*, of which we hear a good deal during the Danish wars, were rather natural strongholds than fortified posts ; and their only attempt to improve upon the natural defences of hill or river was to add a fence or hedge, perhaps on an earthen rampart, on the least protected sides. Thus the Anglo-Saxon Chronicle tells us that in 547 Bamburgh was enclosed by a hedge ; an interpolation adds that a wall was afterwards built, but this was probably of post-Conquest date ; the verb 'to timber', commonly used of fortification, is itself evidence that a stockade was the usual defence. It is only late in the Saxon period that we hear even of ditches as military works. Of Towcester alone it is recorded (921) that it was 'encompassed with a wall of stone', though even here it is probable that Edward the Elder merely restored the Roman wall as his sister did that of Chester. It is true that entries in Domesday Book refer to certain houses in many towns the tenants of which were charged with the repair of the city wall ; but 'wall' here means any kind of rampart. Certainly no Saxon town but Exeter, which held out for eighteen days, was strong enough to make any serious resistance to William's storm.

The science of fortification came back into England with the Normans ; there would indeed, as Ordericus Vitalis noted (p. 117), have been no Norman Conquest if the castles once attributed to the Saxons had really existed. The first reference to 'castles' in the Chronicle does not occur until the eve of the Conquest—which began not in 1066 but in the settlement of the Confessor's Norman friends on English estates. Two highly significant facts are to be noted in these early references : the castles have Norman names and Norman lords—Richard's Castle, Robert's Castle, Pentecost Castle ; and they are designed not for national defence but as places of refuge for an unpopular lord to secure him against native revolt. Thus we are told that the Godwins returned in force from exile in 1052, and 'when Archbishop Robert and the Frenchmen heard that, they took their horses and went, some west to Pentecost's Castle,[1] some north to Robert's Castle'.[2] These early examples were merely the advance guard of the great host which in the next generation was to establish a Norman garrison in every important lordship in England.

It is significant, again, that William's first act when he set foot on English soil was to build a castle at Hastings, as the Chronicle and the Bayeux Tapestry alike record. Had the battle gone against him he would have taken refuge here until relieved by ships from home. As he almost invariably repeated this performance in newly invaded territory it is important to consider his work at Hastings as the type of fortress with which all England was soon to become familiar. Several pictures in the Bayeux Tapestry, study of the site, and consideration of the time taken to construct it show that it was not at all the kind of castle pictured by novel readers, but rather that associated with the ancient game called 'I'm the king of the castle'.[3] It was simply a great mound with a wooden stockade round its flattened summit, standing in a levelled courtyard or 'bailey' and formed of the soil dug from the deep moat which encircled it and from that obtained by levelling the surrounding area. An outer ditch, with a fenced bank on its counterscarp or inner bank, enclosed the whole. Within this fence, in the bailey, were wooden sheds to shelter the garrison and their horses ; and upon the mound itself, protected by moat and stockade,

---

[1] In Herefordshire.  [2] Probably Clavering in Essex.
[3] Played, perhaps, by 'me and my aunts' in the hayfield : one child stands on a heap and the others try to pull him down.

stood the timbered tower of their leader, overlooking both the bailey and the surrounding country.

An inclined plane of timber, half bridge, half ladder, thrown across the inner moat, gave access to the mound from the bailey ; the drawbridge over the outer ditch was defended by a wooden tower on the counterscarp ; and in large castles there were sometimes other towers on the line of the *palum*, or outer stockade.  These were termed *bretasches*, a name sometimes given also to the lord's tower on the *motte* or mound, though the more usual term for this was *turris*, for which *keep* was afterwards

FIG. 76.   WILLIAM'S CASTLE AT HASTINGS, October 1066, showing the pioneers digging the ditch, throwing the earth up on the mount and compacting it with blows, the stockade being set up on the summit, and the wooden tower, probably brought over from Normandy in sections, fitted together in readiness to be carried up to the platform within the palisade.

substituted.  The motte was commonly placed at one end of the bailey, with the outer moat at its foot, so that in the last extremity the owner might escape into the open country beyond ; where, as at Windsor and Arundel, it is centrally placed, the bailey has probably been duplicated or enlarged at a later period.  Such a fortress could be thrown up, as Hastings castle was, in a few days ; and yet, in the absence of siege artillery, would be impregnable as long as the stores of the defenders lasted—we may be sure that a sufficient part of the plunder secured by William's foragers was used to provision his new castle.

In the years immediately following the battle of Hastings, as the English chronicler mournfully informs us, the Normans ' built castles wide throughout the nation ' ;

in 1067 alone and in a single short campaign William himself is recorded to have founded castles at York, Nottingham, Lincoln, 'and everywhere in those parts', viz. Cambridge, Huntingdon, Stamford, Leicester, and Warwick at least. Meanwhile his barons, and particularly his brother Odo, were doing the same elsewhere. At York a second castle, the mound of which still survives, was built in 1069 and was completed in a single week. By no possibility could material, transport, and skilled labour have been forthcoming to build with such speed in masonry. It remains a marvel how stone was quarried, squared,

FIG. 77. SKETCH OF AN EARLY NORMAN CASTLE (Dinant) from the Bayeux Tapestry, showing the moated hillock with palisade enclosing the wooden tower on its flattened summit, and the ladder-bridge, guarded at either end, by which it was approached from the bailey.

and transported for the vast and numerous ecclesiastical buildings of the age. Obviously these early Norman castles were of the Hastings type pictured in the Tapestry, thrown up by the unskilled, forced labour of Saxon peasants working under Norman direction, as the Chronicle records that the adulterine castles were, in the evil days of Stephen. Most of them, even at this day, show no sign of masonry; there is merely the great hillock, natural or artificial, standing in its ditched enclosure, all its timbered work long perished. This absence of stonework led our older antiquaries to suppose that many mounds were Saxon, and to confuse them with the *burhs* fortified against the Danes. But a *burg* was a city, not a citadel; and its defensive ramparts were designed to safeguard a whole population against a surprise attack. The castle, on the other hand, was essentially a lord's stronghold and permanent residence, and was thus a much smaller, and a much stronger, work. Moreover the moated hillock is peculiar to the Norman dominions, and is found, for

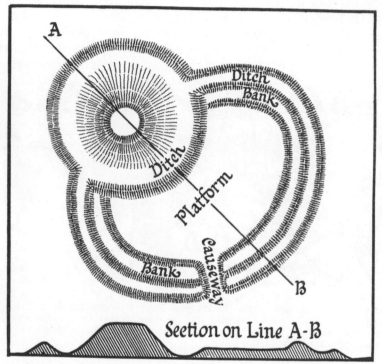

FIG. 78. PLAN AND ELEVATION OF A MOTTE AND BAILEY showing the moated mound on which stood a tower within a stockade (see Fig. 77); and the base-court, platform, or bailey, encircled by an outer moat and a bank for a palisade.

example, in Wales and Ireland, where the Saxons had never set foot. Its name, *motte*, too, is a purely Norman word.

The sites chosen for the castles built in towns also indicate clearly both the race that made them and their motive in doing so. The mound stands a little aloof from the town, usually astride its wall or even just outside it, and always cut off from it by *palum* and ditch. Such a position is not best chosen for the defence of the town as a whole, but it is precisely that which would be selected by a builder who had to guard against attacks from within the town as well as from without it ; for, in either event, the castle could be assaulted only on one side. A native lord who had nothing to fear from his people would have built his castle where it would best serve the common interest—in the centre of the town or on the highest site. But the mound and bailey are never found where they could be attacked by the townsmen on several sides at once. If any castle at all was built by a Saxon thegn it was Dover, where Harold is known to have constructed some defensive works ; but it is remarkable that, though Harold was familiar with the castles of Normandy, and fought at Hastings in Norman equipment, there is no motte in Dover castle.

So much space has been devoted to the early earthwork castle, partly because a good deal of misconception still prevails, but even more because it contains the germs of all later developments in mediaeval fortification. The great Edwardian castles were achieved not *per saltum*, but by slow evolution from the Norman motte and palum.

The obvious method of attack on a timbered fortress is by fire ; obviously, too, the outer stockade, and particularly its gate and bridge, would be first assaulted. As soon, therefore, as labour and material could be obtained the palum would be replaced by a wall of masonry, built on the earthen rampart; the drawbridge would be defended by a stone gate-house ; and towers of stone would be substituted for the timber bretasches. The sheds and stables of the garrison were built against the inner side of the containing wall, now usually termed the *castellum*, and their roofs perhaps served as a platform for the defenders— for the fertile Norman mind delighted in the principle of killing two birds with one stone : thus it is recorded that Robert d'Oilli founded Oxford castle in 1071 and built a chapel in it in 1074 ; the tower attached to that chapel still stands on the bailey wall overlooking the entrance from the west, and there can be little doubt that it is a part of the stone castellum with which in 1074 d'Oilli replaced the palisade of his bailey of 1071. So, at Earls Barton, Judith, niece of the Conqueror, seems to have drawn the line of her castellum so as to include upon it the tower of the neighbouring Saxon church, thus using in the defence of her bailey what might otherwise have become a menace to it. In some castles nothing more was done, and some, indeed, retained their timber works as long as they were occupied ; in very few was any further advance made until the time of Henry II.

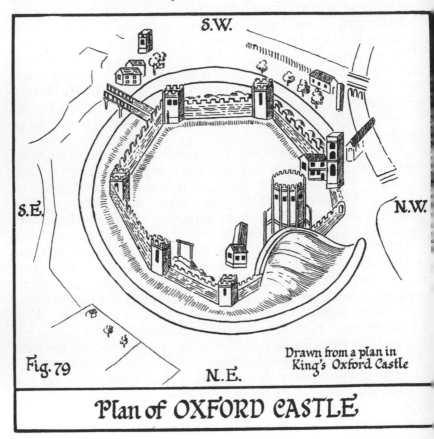

S.W.

S.E.

N.W.

Fig. 79

Drawn from a plan in King's Oxford Castle

N.E.

## Plan of OXFORD CASTLE

In the majority of castles the next step was similarly to reconstruct the palisade on the motte in stonework, to rebuild the timber hall with masonry, and to replace the ladder-bridge by an arch and steps of stone. The circular or polygonal fortress thus built as an inner and last defence surrounding the lord's own dwelling is called a shell-keep. Those at Carisbrooke and Lincoln were built before 1154, and Oxford had an early many-sided one of which pictures still exist. Tonbridge, Farnham, Lewes, and Totnes are

FIG. 80. THE GREAT TOWER, NEWCASTLE.
A typical square keep, built by Henry II, showing entrance on
second floor, approached by an open outer stair commanded by
a fore-building (cf. the later barbican, e.g. Fig. 107). All openings
in the basement walls are modern. Note the few and small
original openings, the single large window being in a buttress on
the least exposed face.

other examples. But the greater lords borrowed from
France the idea of a massive square tower several stories
high with walls of enormous thickness—12 to 20 feet—
so that communicating passages could be made in them,
strengthened by flat buttresses and loopholed for archery

on each side of their upper stories. The basement had neither door nor loophole in its craggy wall, and was used as a store-room approached only by a trap-door in the floor above. The single entrance was on this floor, commonly the hall of the castle, and was reached by a ladder or an open stair. The second story served as a private retreat for the lord and his family, an oratory and sleeping chambers being sometimes hollowed out in its walls ; and the battlemented roof was a kitchen in time of peace and the centre of defensive operations in war ; the fireplaces, with ovens, sometimes found on the roof, would be used both for cooking and for heating missiles.

Two examples were built in England during the Conqueror's lifetime, the White Tower and Colchester Keep, with their chapels and party-walls the largest and most elaborate of all. Bridgenorth Keep was built in 1102 ; but the great majority of square keeps are due to the military and political genius of Henry II. Hedingham, Rochester, Newcastle, and Norwich are among the most famous.

The solid square keep was both stronger and more commodious than the open shell-keep, and was therefore preferred by those who had the resources to build it. But such a ponderous structure could not safely be founded on the made-up earth of the motte [1] ; it was therefore usually built on the level ground of the bailey ; but in many instances a new site was chosen for it, and the motte and bailey were abandoned. This was done, for example, at Montgomery, where the 'vulture's nest' of the Earl of Shrewsbury was built a mile away from Earl Roger's earthwork fortress.

Late in the twelfth century the cylindrical keep, also a French invention, came into England. It had three important advantages over the rectangular form : it presented no angles to be shattered by an oblique shot ; its loopholes gave a wider field of fire to the defence ; and its stones, with their radiating joints, could be much less easily dislodged than the parallel-jointed masonry of the square-faced tower. Moreover the scaffolding round a

---

[1] There are, however, a few examples of square keeps built on the motte late in the twelfth century when the earth had thoroughly settled ; when the hillock was a natural one no subsidence was to be feared.

...ed so as to form a spiral ...erial can be wheeled at an ...Conisborough, our finest ...Plantagenet, who died in ...talus, the sloping face of ...e bore and battering-ram ...he wall but also served as a

FIG. 81. THE KEEP, CONIS-BOROUGH, built by Hamelyn Plantagenet, brother of Henry II, *c.* 1200. The cylindrical form gets rid of 'dead angles' (the areas along a diagonal line which cannot be commanded by loopholes in either face of a square tower) and enables the defenders' missiles to search every part of the surrounding area and so check mining operations. Note the talus or sloping base from which stones dropped from the battlements would glance off and damage the enemy, and the enormous solid buttresses which bore turrets at their summits.

...the castle of Coucy before the middle of the thirteenth century. In England ideas were already changing at that date, and so we have but few towers of this form, and fewer still of the polygonal type that was contemporary with it in France.

The solid keep, square or round, was so strong as to be almost independent of its outworks; even if the enemy forced its moat and curtain-wall they could do little harm to its impregnable basement. But, on the other hand, its strength was that of mere inertia, like the carapace of the tortoise or, at best, the spiny ball of the porcupine; it had no sally-ports for a counter-offensive, and its accommodation was too limited for a garrison large enough for any but purely defensive tactics. A hostile army could not hope to reduce it, but they could easily mask it and pass it by without any check to their progress or any serious danger to their lines of communication.

By the middle of the thirteenth century, therefore, the keep had gone out of fashion, though the building of shell-keeps was not entirely abandoned. But castles were ceasing to be private strongholds and were becoming national institutions, factors in the royal strategy. They had therefore to be planned to serve as bases for offensive operations and so to accommodate forces large enough to

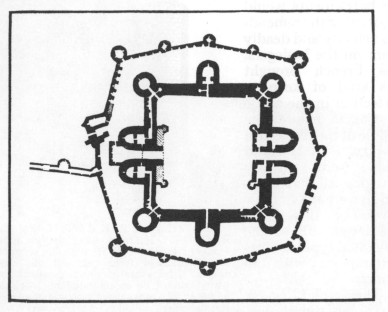

FIG. 82. PLAN OF BEAUMARIS CASTLE.

make effective excursions; they must be burhs rather than mottes, communal, not manorial, fortresses. This meant that the attention of the architect was diverted from the centre to the circumference. His problem, if he had known it, was that of the Neolithic tribesmen who designed the hill-camps that gave security to a whole tribe; and, unconsciously, he solved it on the same principles.

First, like them, but unlike the Norman builder who drew the line of his oval bailey irrespective of contours, he realized that the nature of the site must govern the shape of his defensive enclosure. So the walls of Kidwelly, *c.* 1250, form a semicircle resting on the river; Conway and

Carnarvon took the shapes of the promontories upon which they were built; and Caerphilly that of its island.

Secondly, the thirteenth-century castle-planner, this time unlike the keep-builders, realized that posts must be provided so that the whole of the garrison could be simultaneously engaged in the defence, and that the inner part of his fortress should be not merely a refuge if the outer fell but an active means of support to prevent its doing so. He therefore built his defences on a concentric plan, each wall higher than the one outside it, so that the archers, like the tribesmen on their concentric earthen ramparts,

FIG. 83. BEAUMARIS CASTLE: ELEVATION showing the flanking towers in both the outer curtain and the inner shell-keep, enabling the defenders to shoot parallel to the walls and so protect their faces; the successive lines of archery-posts one above another; and the arrangement of the towers by which each could be separately held even if one or more were captured.

or like a company with its front rank kneeling, could fire simultaneously over the heads of their comrades. At Carnarvon three rows of archers could thus concentrate their aim on any point attacked. If the besiegers penetrated the outer ring they would then find themselves exposed to the concentrated fire of the inner lines, penned in a narrow space broken up by cross-walls and enfiladed by loopholes in towers projecting from the face of the second line of defence.

The third resemblance between the thirteenth-century castle and the prehistoric hill-fort was in the importance attached to the outworks defending its entrance; just as the designer of the one was careful to narrow the approaches and to provide false turnings down which an enemy might rush to destruction in a cul-de-sac, so the builder of the other planned an outer barbican, double gates, and a narrow, angled passage between high walls, before his entrance arch.

The concentric plan was probably brought home by the Crusaders, who had learned to appreciate it in their attacks on Saracen fortresses. Its influence in England is first seen in attempts to remodel existing castles, the most successful of which transformed the Conqueror's Tower of London into the concentric fortress that we now see. Of castles built *de novo* on the new plan Edward I's Welsh

Fig. 84. WALMGATE BAR, YORK, showing a gate in the city wall with bartizans (hanging turrets) at the angles, approached from an outer barbican by a narrow passage between high, battlemented walls, in which an enemy could be trapped and annihilated. Note the development of the idea first seen in the fore-building of Newcastle (Fig. 80).

fortresses are the most famous, Beaumaris, finished by his son, being the most complete and instructive example.

But the same genius that brought the castle to its highest perfection in England was responsible also for the conditions that caused its decay. The central executive grew so strong and efficient under the English Justinian that no feudal lord could hope to wield independent power by entrenching himself in a castle ; the king's commercial policy stimulated the rise of a merchant class and developed the growth of towns ; as these grew in importance the manorial fortress waned, and the new principles of fortification had hardly been fully exemplified in the castle before they were applied to the city walls, which henceforward were to be the principal care of the military engineer.

So in all the stretches of city walls that yet remain we see the flanking towers or bastions which were invented to enfilade the concentric castle wall, and the traces of complicated entrance-works, though in all but Bootham Gate at York the barbican no longer blocks the way.

The development of explosive artillery, and the power of the central exchequer virtually to monopolize it, pre-

FIG. 85. B O D I A M  C A S T L E, showing flanking towers in the curtain-wall, gate-house with machicolated parapet, and barbican tower standing in the middle of the causeway across the moat, with drawbridges before and behind it.

vented any revival of castle-building. Moreover an era of peace and material progress had induced ideas of comfort and convenience that made fortress life intolerable and led to new conceptions of domestic arrangements. So the later 'castles', though numerous, are rather defensive dwellings than fortresses. They may have towers, but their windows will be traceried openings, lighting domestic apartments, not arrow-slits in the walls of guard-rooms and retainers' halls.

Bodiam, built in 1386, preserves the features of a century earlier; but Bodiam was situated in the part of England where a foreign foe last set foot; it was built, as its licence states, 'in defence of the adjacent country against the king's enemies', viz. the French, who had several times landed on the low shore and sacked Winchelsea and Rye.

Camber, not far away, built by Henry VIII, brings us to the last stage of castle-building, when the ancient idea of 'fortresses' was giving place to the modern one of 'forts': instead of the lofty tower that would have offered an easy mark to cannon it has the solid squat bastion which is nothing but a gun-emplacement; it is not so much a castle as a battery.

A few matters of detail may be touched upon in conclusion. Every mediaeval castle had its well, usually situated in the foundations of the keep; in the later towers a shaft in the thickness of the wall, carried up from the basement to the summit, allowed water to be drawn up to any floor; at Conisborough an emergency supply was kept in cisterns fitted into the buttresses. Fireplaces, also, and *garderobes* (latrines) were hollowed out in the walls, having vents in their outer face; Bishop Rede's castle at Amberley shows some good examples. Dovecotes, and even lofts for carrier pigeons, were occasionally provided in towers. Every keep had its oratory, if not its chapel.

Parapets of walls and towers were embattled or loop-holed from the first; but this would not serve against an enemy who had managed to reach the foot of the wall. The earliest Norman towers therefore had doorways in the parapet from which a hinged platform fell down like the tailboard of a cart, enabling some of the garrison to step out upon it and drop missiles perpendicularly. As this exposed them to the aim of the besiegers, a covered scaffold of timber, called a *hourde* (cf. hoarding), having openings in its floor, was substituted for the platform. This again could be set on fire by flaming arrows, and so an overhanging gallery of stone replaced the timber scaffold; the slits in its floor, through which stones or lime could be dropped, were called machicolations—from *coulis*, a groove, and *mâcher*, to crush; the device was probably invented by the Saracens to economize timber, and was first made fashionable by Richard's use of it at Chateau Gaillard. But in England machicolated parapets are common only in gate-houses.

The hearse or portcullis (*porte-coulis*) was, as readers of *Marmion* know, a heavy grating that slid up and down in grooves in the jambs of the gateway and could be used to close it instantly in an emergency ; the grooves usually remain, though the portcullis may be gone ; and often in the chamber above the gate may be seen the stout beam from which it hung and traces of the pulley by which it was raised.

It may be of interest to add that the numerous small, quadrangular moats of which traces are marked on the Ordnance Map were never the sites of castles.  The Surveyors of the Royal Commission on Historical Monuments refer to them as Homestead Moats, and tell us that the makers of the majority of them were 'members of the wealthy middle class that arose at the end of the twelfth century and in the thirteenth century, whose demand for land was met by sub-infeudation by the larger landowners impoverished in consequence of the Barons' Wars.  The owners of the new manors thus created required security for their possessions in disturbed times, and therefore defended their homesteads with moats. . . . The earth from the moat was thrown inside and spread over the island thus formed, on which was built the house with its barns and cattlesheds.'

## Books for reference.

OMAN, *A History of the Art of War in the Middle Ages,* 1898.
CLARK, *Mediaeval Military Architecture in England,* 1884.
ARMITAGE, *The Early Norman Castles of Great Britain,* 1912.
MORRIS and JORDAN, *Local History and Antiquities,* 1910.
ROUND, *The Castles of the Conquest,* Archaeologia, vol. lviii.
VIOLLET-LE-DUC, *Military Architecture,* translated by Macdermott, 2nd ed., 1879.
—— *Annals of a Fortress,* translated by Bucknall, 1875.
   (These two last books must be used with caution, as they contain doubtful matter.)
HAMILTON THOMPSON, *Military Architecture in England during the Middle Ages,* 1912.
F. M. STENTON, *The Development of the Castle in England and Wales,* 1910.
Eng. Hist. Review, vols. xix, xxi.

## § 2. THE ART OF WAR

### 1. *From the Anglo-Saxon Conquest to the Battle of Hastings.*

IN the things that belong to war, no less than in the things that belong to peace, there is a complete break in British history at the Anglo-Saxon conquest. All our modern institutions go back in a continuous line to the days of the half-mythical Hengist and Cerdic, and then comes a great gap. In military institutions most of all is this the case : the Roman left many legacies of arms and armour, and even of fortification, to the Frank and the Visigoth, but the Angle and the Saxon inherited little or nothing from him. Dwelling far from the Rhine, at the very back of Germany, they were much less imbued with any tincture of Roman civilization than the Teutonic races of the South and East. Goths, Gepidae, Lombards, and Burgundians had learnt in the fifth century to wear armour, to fight on horseback, and to use a considerable variety of weapons. But the Old English, at their coming to Britain, were still a nation of foot-soldiers, and were seldom provided with any defensive armour save the shield. Even as late as the eleventh century, representations of men in armour are very rare in Anglo-Saxon manuscripts. However, we know that helm and mail-shirt (*byrne*) existed from the earliest time of the settlement in Britain. Bede mentions them as being worn by kings and other great ones : and the *Beowulf* repeatedly speaks of the ' war net woven by the smith ', the ' hard and hand-locked byrnie ', and the ' white (i.e. polished) helm '. The head-piece was sometimes of metal, sometimes merely of leather, stretched across an iron foundation, or having a framework of iron or bronze placed over it [Fig. 144] : it was often adorned with the figure of a wild boar by way of amulet, and hence was called the boar-helm. But the majority of the Old English went forth to war in their tunics and felt caps alone, without any defensive armour save a shield of linden-wood, strengthened at the centre by a projecting iron boss, and at the edge by an iron rim [Fig. 144]. Of weapons of offence the spear seems to have been by far the most common, and 'spear-wight' is a frequent synonym for the warrior [Figs. 136–9]. The sword was not so universally employed : when found in early English graves it is a straight cut-and-thrust weapon, about three feet in length, and generally destitute of cross-piece or guard [Figs. 133, 134]. The axe was much less common : when we come upon it, we find a light weapon with a very curved head, suitable for casting no less than for hewing [Fig. 141]. The dagger was better known than either axe or sword, and was usually the second weapon of the Anglo-Saxon spearman. It was a large two-edged stabbing-knife, some fifteen inches long. This was the *seax*, which in popular etymology was supposed to have given the Saxons their name. Bows [Fig. 143], javelins, and slings were known, but not much used : our ancestors were given to close fighting, not to 'long-bowls' and skirmishing tactics.

The most important part of the military strength of one of the Heptarchic kingdoms consisted of the king's sworn companions, the *comites* of Tacitus, the *gesiths* of the old law-books. These were personal retainers of the early 'alderman' or prince, who had vowed to be his 'men', and to follow him in peace and war. They had surrendered their freedom to him, and sworn to obey him in all things : on the other hand, he maintained them, gave them their arms and raiment, parted the plunder with them, and endowed them with land after a successful conquest of British soil. To aid the *gesiths*, the whole levy of the country-side was called out when necessary ; for *fyrd-faru*, the going out to war, was one of the three primary duties of the Anglo-Saxon subject. But this rude assembly, hastily equipped with improvised arms, was but the shaft of the weapon of which the *comitatus* formed the iron head.

During the four centuries in which they were occupied in expelling their Celtic neighbours, or fighting among themselves, the English seem to have made little progress in their military institutions. No desperate need came upon them, and they kept up their ancient war customs long after their kinsmen on the continent had begun to

modify them.  Their wars were spasmodic and inconclusive :
a victorious campaign did not mean the permanent union
of the conquered with the conquering state, but only that
the king of one did homage to the king of the other as long
as he was compelled to do so.  The holding down of the
vanquished would only have been possible if the conqueror
had kept a standing army, and had learnt how to build
fortresses among the newly subdued districts.  Neither of
these ideas had come to the Old English : both *gesiths*
and *fyrd* went home after a victory, and fortification was
almost unknown.  The nation dwelt in open towns and
villages, and had not even learnt how to patch up the
ancient walls of such places as had a Roman origin.  That
is why we just as often find the sees of Saxon bishops
founded in obscure villages like Wells, Lichfield, Sidna-
cester, or Ramsbury, as in old Roman sites like London,
York, or Canterbury.

The objectless strife of the Heptarchic kingdoms was
still in full swing, and Wessex, under Ecgberht, had just
supplanted Mercia as the temporarily dominant state,
when a new and all-important factor appeared in English
politics.  The *Vikings* (men of the *viks* or creeks) from
Denmark and Norway had first shown themselves on the
English coast at the end of the eighth century : but about
830 they began to appear in vastly increased numbers,
and became a pressing danger to all the Anglo-Saxon
realms.  They were war-bands of professional pirates, led
by chiefs elected for their skill and courage.  At first they
came merely to sack peaceful seaports, and to plunder the
treasuries of wealthy monasteries, their desire being to
pillage rather than to fight.  But their first successes soon
emboldened them to sail forth in much larger numbers, and
to try more dangerous feats than the hasty harrying of
the shore.  From the first the Vikings showed a great
superiority as a fighting force to the English who came out
against them.  The latter, though they had once been
bold seamen themselves, had for many years lost their
original aptitude for the sea : in the annals of the Hep-
tarchy naval expeditions are very rare, and none of the
kingdoms that were in existence in 830–50 had any fleet
to oppose to this new enemy.  The Vikings came and went
unhindered, retiring to their ships [Fig. 233] when they

found themselves hopelessly outnumbered, and disappearing into the ocean. Against the force which generally came out to meet them—the hasty levies of a single shire—they were as a rule successful, for they were professional soldiers contending with rustics fresh from the plough, and were far better furnished with arms and armour than the raw and undisciplined masses of the *fyrd*. A course of almost unbroken victory led to the rapid growth of the Viking bands : in the second generation they began to raid far inland, and to fortify for themselves permanent camps on convenient islands or headlands. A little later their confidence grew so great that they took in hand the actual conquest of England. In 867 they stormed York, slew the last two kings of Northumbria, and firmly established themselves north of the Humber. Mercia fell into their hands a little later, and they would probably have mastered Wessex also but for the military reforms of King Alfred, the saviour of England.

That great monarch was no sooner seated on the throne (871) than he began to build a permanent war-fleet to oppose the invaders even before they could get to land. Before this scheme could be completed he had to fight hard against those of the Danes who were already seated in England. The decisive battle of Ethandun forced the Viking host to capitulate, accept Christianity, and remove northward out of Wessex (878). During the next fourteen years Alfred was busily engaged in reorganizing the military strength of his realm. He constructed a large fleet of war-vessels of a size and speed exceeding those of the enemy. He built strong *burhs*, or fortified places, in the chief strategical spots of Wessex, allotting to each of them a region the warriors of which were to supply the garrison and keep the works in repair. The burhs appear to have been as a rule mere earthwork and palisading, for masonry had hardly begun to be utilized for fortification. Though we know that Alfred patched up the broken Roman walls of London in 886, and that his daughter Æthelflæd a few years later (907) did the same at Chester, yet such instances were very rare. But shipbuilding and systematic fortification were not the king's only devices. He carried out a great scheme for strengthening his field army by adding to it as many fully-equipped warriors as he could contrive.

This was done by taking into strict military dependence on the king, after the manner of the *comitatus* of the early ages, all the larger landed proprietors of the kingdom. Every holder of five *hides* of land, whatever his birth and status, was to be made 'of *thegn-right* worthy', i. e. to take up both the privileges and the military duties of a member of the king's war-band.  For the word *thegn* of late had superseded the earlier term of *gesith* as the appellation of those who had become the king's men and joined his following.  The thegns, whether men of ancient noble blood or newly ennobled *ceorls*, had to serve in complete armour, with iron helm and mail-shirt, like the Vikings whom they had to oppose.  They had to follow their lord whenever he took the field, which in the days of Alfred and his immediate successors was very often.  For example, during the years 892–6 almost continuous campaigning was in progress, while the attack of Hasting, the greatest of the Viking chiefs, was being beaten off from Wessex. The enlarged thegnhood formed the core of Alfred's army, but it was strengthened by the *fyrd*, which was made more useful by dividing it into two halves, of which one went out to war while the other remained behind to till the land.

Alfred's descendants, Edward the Elder and Æthelstan, carried on his system, and turned it to use for attacking the Danes who had settled in England, as well as for beating off their raids on Wessex.  Edward was especially noted for his development of the use of *burhs* : he built great numbers of them, first along his own frontier, and then in the Danish districts which he subdued one after the other.  These strongholds, with their garrisons of military settlers, proved too much for the enemy, who seldom succeeded in capturing them, or in shaking off the English supremacy when it had once been established. They often rebelled, and sometimes launched a desperate attack on Wessex, but such operations only resulted in a tremendous retaliatory raid by the English, who swept a whole region clear and left new *burhs* to hold it down. Now that they had farms to be burnt and cattle to be plundered, the Vikings no longer possessed their old superiority over the English in the matter of mobility. They were obliged to take the defensive, and had no longer the movable base depending on their ships which had been the strength of their ancestors. At last the men of the Danelaw came to the conclusion that submission might pay better than resistance. The decisive battle of Brunanburh (937) in which King Æthelstan defeated a great confederacy of English-Danes, Scots, and Vikings from Ireland and the north, finally settled the fate of England. The surviving Scandinavian settlers submitted, and though they gave trouble once and again to Æthelstan's successors, became in a single generation very good Englishmen.

The Danish wars thus left their mark on the country in the development of the *burhs*, in the enlargement of the thegnhood, and generally in the creation of a certain tendency towards feudalism. To protect themselves in that century of storm and stress the smaller freemen had begun to commend themselves to the thegns, just as the thegns were forced to put themselves in direct dependence on the king. By the middle of the tenth century and the time of King Edgar the 'lordless man' had become an anomaly, on whom the law looked askance.

The short tenure of power by the Danish dynasty of Cnut, which followed the fall of Æthelred the Redeless, left one permanent mark on the military institutions of England. It was Cnut who first conceived the idea of a standing army. When the rest of his host returned to Denmark in 1015 he kept about him several thousand picked mercenaries, whom he called his *huscarls* or military household. They were, of course (like the Anglo-Saxon *gesiths* of five centuries before), only one more development of the old Teutonic *comitatus* of the primitive king. But they were more permanently embodied, received a definite pay, and were organized into a fixed number of 'ships' crews'. Unlike the thegnhood they were not scattered about on their lands, but were always concentrated under the king's hand, so as to be ready for instant service. It seems to have been Cnut's household troops who made popular in England the great two-handed Danish axe with heavy head and five-foot shaft [Fig. 142]. It was their special weapon, just as it was that of the Viking bodyguard of the Eastern emperors at Constantinople, the famous corps of the 'Varangians' whose institution dates not long after that of Cnut's housecarls.

When the Danish dynasty passed away Edward the

Confessor continued to maintain under arms a body of professional fighting men. But, with his usual unwisdom, he allowed his great earls to do the same : Godwine, Leofric, and Siward also kept their halls full of housecarls, admirable aids in lawful war, but tempting tools for rebellion. It was their existence which made so natural the civil troubles of the Confessor's reign.

The Anglo-Danish system of war, the characteristic feature of which was the formation of infantry in compact masses armed with spear, axe, and shield, was brought to a sudden end by the first great battle in English history of which we have a full account, the great fight of Hastings. Then for the first time the old national tactics were tried against the new methods that had grown up on the continent, where the strength of armies now consisted in their array of mailed horsemen, and the infantry had become a subsidiary arm, mainly consisting of archers and slingers used for the mere opening of the combat. Edward the Confessor's Norman favourite, Ralph, Earl of Hereford, had tried to teach the English thegns horsemanship, but had failed : his levies fled when opposed to the Welsh, *quia Anglos contra morem in equis pugnare iussit* (1055). It was to be disastrous to the land that its fighting men were so reluctant to learn ; for eleven years later the presence of a few thousand cavalry on Harold's side would undoubtedly have changed the event of Hastings.

At that decisive fight the English king drew up his host in a dense mass along the brow of a steep hill-side, throwing up for the protection of the front line a rough defence, a ditch and a hasty fence of stakes and wattled boughs, hewn from the great forest of the Andredesweald which lay just at his back. He trusted in this manner to beat back the charge of the Norman horse, the efficiency of which he had learnt to respect, since he himself had served a campaign with Duke William a few years back. In the centre were his housecarls with their axes, around the two royal standards of the Dragon and the Fighting Man : on each side were the levies of the shires, in which the well-equipped men [Figs. 144 and 147] were outnumbered by the unarmoured rustics bearing a motley equipment of spears, axes, clubs, and swords.

Duke William, on the other hand, advanced up the

hill-side in a looser array : first came a line of archers [Fig. 145] and crossbowmen, then another of infantry with spear and shield, in the third the flower of the host, the feudal horse [Fig. 146] of Normandy and the mounted mercenaries gathered from all parts of Europe for the great enterprise.

The incidents of the battle are related in the ordinary histories : the military lesson taught at Hastings was that the purely defensive system of the Anglo-Danish infantry was insufficient to resist cavalry and archers skilfully combined by a capable general. William won because he was able to use two sorts of tactics against an enemy who had only one : a passive defensive by an army without good missile weapons is hopeless against an adversary who employs the combination of missiles and of cavalry charges. And he was able to reap the fruits of his victory because, as Ordericus Vitalis tells us, ' the fortresses which the Gauls call *castella* had been very few in the provinces of England ; and on this account the English, although warlike and daring, had nevertheless shown themselves too feeble to resist their enemies'.

## 2. *From the Norman Conquest to the Accession of Edward I.*

The Norman Conquest brought about a complete change in the military organization of England. For the mailed axeman fighting on foot, and the ditch and palisades of the *burh,* there were substituted the feudal horseman and the baronial castle. William the Conqueror and his sons called out the footmen of the *fyrd* on more than one occasion, but it was not the chief strength of their hosts, and indeed they generally used it only when the baronage and knighthood was for some reason or other not to be trusted. The cavalry, which during this period formed the really important part of the armed forces of the Crown, was raised on a principle new in England though familiar enough on the continent. William divided four-fifths of the soil of England among the military adventurers who had followed him : on each of the new landholders there was imposed the duty of producing a certain fixed number of knights at the king's call : the quota varied from a single ' shield ' up to many scores. The assessment was made very roughly, but at the bottom of it there seems to have lain the Old English notion that a five-hide unit should produce a fully armed fighting man. But the church and many of the lay holders were let off easily, and gave much less than their hidage would have justified. The surviving Anglo-Saxon landholders, who had ' bought

FIG. 86. ATTACKING A TOWN with scaling ladders. (From Bodl. MS. 264. Fourteenth century.)

back their lands ' from the king, had to fall into line with the new-comers, and to take up the duties of knight-service. The tenants-in-chief were allowed to provide their quota of horsemen in whatever way they pleased : some maintained knights in their household, but the majority granted out small estates to sub-tenants on the feudal obligations. As long as the due number of shields was forthcoming the king made no objection. The process of sub-infeudation was tolerably complete by the time of Henry I, and the *vetus feoffamentum*, or old enfeoffment, was technically supposed to end on the day of his death. Later grants of land were said to belong to the *novum feoffamentum*.

For two centuries after the Conquest the military equipment of the knight varied little : an account of his body-armour will be found in the section on Arms and Armour.

All through the time of the Anglo-Norman and early Plantagenet kings the skill of the military architect was developing with great rapidity, while the machinery of

FIG. 87. ATTACKING A TOWN. Siege artillery old and new: one of the earliest cannons between a cross-bow and a catapult. (From Bodl. MS. 264. Fourteenth century.)

siege-craft was very little improved. The ascendancy which the defensive had gained over the offensive was maintained till the invention of gunpowder in the fourteenth century. When castles or towns fell it was generally by famine. The cheapest way to deal with a rebel was not to waste time or lives by trying to storm his stronghold, but to block up its exits, and starve him out. The period 1066–1300 was essentially one of sieges, not of great battles in the open. Rufus and Henry I when dealing with their restless barons, Stephen when contending with Matilda, Henry II when warring against rebels at home and foreign enemies abroad, conducted countless leaguers, but in their time there were only three great battles, that of Tenchebrai in 1105, Northallerton in 1178, and Lincoln in 1141. Bremûle, Alnwick, and Fornham were little more than cavalry skirmishes.

When, for one reason or another, a siege was pressed hard, and not turned into a mere blockade, the military engines employed were simple. They were the *mangonel*, the *balista*, and the *trébuchet*, which worked respectively by torsion, by tension, and by counterpoise. The mangonel was a machine for throwing heavy stones : it was composed

FIG. 88. ENGINE FOR SHOOT-ING MISSILES.

of two fixed uprights, and a movable beam worked by the twisting of ropes, which, when drawn back and then suddenly released, cast the missile through the air in a high curve. The balista, on the other hand, was essentially a device for shooting great bolts and javelins ; it was like an enormous cross-bow, and cast its missiles point-blank, not with a high trajectory like the mangonel. The trébuchet consisted of a balance with a long beam : one end was loaded with heavy weights, in the other, which was dragged down by force, the missile was placed ; when the weighted end was released, it threw the other end violently into the air, and the missile sped on its way. This device was later than the other two, and did not grow popular till the thirteenth century. Much confusion is caused to the reader of chronicles by the tiresome vagueness of the nomenclature employed by many of the mediaeval writers, who use the names of military machines in the most inexact and confusing manner. When we read of *tormenta, catapults, perrières, slings, biffae, springals,* and so forth, it is often extremely difficult to discover which

of these engines is really meant.   But it is certain that all
belonged to one of the three classes which we have defined
above.

Much more effective than *mangonels* or *trébuchets* were
two other methods of attack, that by the mine and that by
the ' movable tower'.   When a castle was built on soft
ground, and was not protected by a wet ditch, mining was
likely to be successful.   The mine was driven under ground
till the wall was reached : stones were then removed from
the latter, and the breach was underpinned, that is, supported with beams, among which were thrust straw and

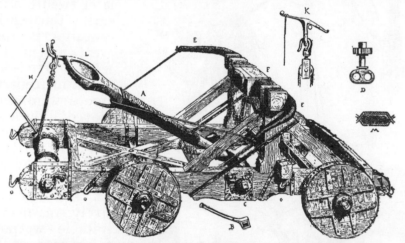

Fig. 89.  S T O N E - T H R O W I N G   E N G I N E.

brushwood.   When this was ignited and the beams were
burnt through, the wall collapsed and a practicable breach
was formed.   Two well-known examples of the successful
use of mining in English history are the capture of Rochester
Castle by King John in 1214, and that of Bedford Castle
by the Justiciar De Burgh in 1224.   The use of the movable
tower (*beffroi, belfragium*) required more skill : it was
a wooden structure several stories high protected from
fire by raw hides or metal plates.   It was moved forward
on rollers till it reached the wall, the ditch, if there was
one, being filled with fascines and so levelled up to the
height of the adjacent ground.   When the tower neared
the rampart a drawbridge was dropped from it on to the
battlements, and the besiegers, who could thus throw

a column against a thin line of defenders, rushed across to overpower the garrison. The best remembered siege in which the place fell before this machine was that of Jerusalem by the Crusaders in 1099 : Richard I employed it at Acre, but it was famine rather than engineering which really reduced that stronghold.

FIG. 90. TRÉBUCHET OR SLINGING MACHINE.

A marked feature of the military history of England in the later twelfth and early thirteenth centuries is the great extent to which professional mercenary troops were employed. The feudal levy, being theoretically liable to serve only for forty days consecutively, was an unsuitable weapon for protracted warfare. Hence came the idea of *scutage*, by which the king offered his vassals the chance of paying a sum of money for every shield (*scutum*) that they were bound to furnish instead of serving in person. The practice was begun by Henry I, but only became common under his grandson Henry II. The money thus obtained, usually two marks (26s. 8d.) per shield, could be spent on hiring mercenaries, who were not only better disciplined and more efficient soldiers, but were prepared to keep the field for any length of time so long as their pay was forthcoming. Most of

FIG. 91   ASSAULT FROM THE SIEGE-TOWER.
From Viollet-le-Duc's *L'Architecture militaire*.

Henry II's foreign wars were fought with their aid : Richard I and John employed them by the thousand. It will be remembered that a special clause in Magna Carta is devoted to the banishment of the foreign men-at-arms and crossbowmen *qui venerunt cum armis et equis ad nocumentum regni*. Henry III was less well provided with such followers, but only because his financial embarrassments rendered him incapable of paying them. We hear of his employing mercenaries at Taillebourg, but Lewes and Evesham were fought out by purely native troops.

Though the feudal horsemen, supplemented by hired professional soldiers, did most of the fighting under the early Plantagenets, it must not be supposed that the national levy, the descendant of the Old English *fyrd*, had been allowed to be forgotten. It was called out for domestic troubles and to repel Welsh and Scottish raids. The sheriff, among his many and varied duties, was charged with that of leading the men of his shire whenever they were summoned. We have valuable information as to their equipment from the two *Assizes of Arms* of Henry II (1181) and Henry III (1252). In the former the richer men, with property worth more than sixteen marks, are bidden to appear with lances, hauberks of mail, and helms ; those with less than sixteen and more than ten marks are to have lances, hauberks, or gambesons, and steel caps, while the poorer classes came unarmoured and with ' swords, knives, and any sort of smaller arms '. In the Assize of Henry III we find an important change, in that all men with more than 40s. and less than 100s. in land, and burgesses with chattels worth more than nine and less than twenty marks, are commanded to take the field with a bow and arrows instead of the lance prescribed by the earlier ordinance. This is the first indication of the rise of archery in England. In the twelfth century crossbowmen were more esteemed than archers, and it had not occurred to Henry II to order any class of his subjects to furnish themselves with the weapon which in later generations was to be the special pride of the island.

### 3. *The Predominance of the Longbow.  1272–1485.*

The appearance of the longbow as a national weapon in the Assize of Arms of 1252 is the dividing line in the military history of mediaeval England. Down to that date the feudal horseman was the chief power in battle, and the art of war in England was but a reflection of that of the continent.  But a new system was about to develop itself, unlike any that had been seen in any other European country, in which the efficiency of infantry armed with missile weapons was to be the main factor.  Simon de Montfort was the last English general who won his victories by the charge of heavy cavalry alone : his great pupil, Edward I, was to be the first who turned the archer to full account.

The bow had always been known in England ; we have even seen it play a notable part in battle at Hastings, but it had never, till the second half of the thirteenth century, been considered a weapon of primary importance.  The first district the archers of which win special notice is South Wales, and it seems likely that from there improved archery spread over the Western Midlands.  In the end of the twelfth century Giraldus Cambrensis praises the ' stiff, large, and strong bows' of the men of Gwent, and tells how the Anglo-Normans could never have conquered Ireland without the aid of the shafts of their Welsh auxiliaries.  Yet the crossbowman plays a much greater part than the archer in the wars of Richard I, John, and Henry III, and we are somewhat surprised when we find the bow prescribed as the natural weapon of the yeomanry in the Assize of Arms of 1252.  Nothing is said of the efficiency of archers at Lewes and Evesham, and it is only when we arrive at the reign of Edward I that we find the bowman coming to the front.  The first note is struck in 1282, when we are told that the army of Llewellyn was beaten at the fight of Orewin Bridge, because the English broke up the firm array of spearmen by pouring in volleys of arrows before the cavalry was allowed to charge.  The same plan was used against the bands of the rebel prince Madoc in 1295.  But the first full account of the scientific use of archery that we get is at Falkirk in 1298.  Wallace had arrayed his Scots in four great masses, ' schiltrons' as the chroniclers call them.  The first attack of the English cavalry upon these solid clumps of pikemen was a complete failure.  Then King Edward drew back his knights, and brought forward his bowmen (most of whom, as we are incidentally told, were Welsh).  He concentrated their discharges on certain parts of the hostile masses, and, when these were riddled with arrows, sent his cavalry into the shaken spots. The charge was completely successful, and the Scots were ridden down and cut to pieces.

This was almost a repetition of the tactics of William the Conqueror at Hastings, where cavalry and archers had been used in much the same way. Yet the victory did not

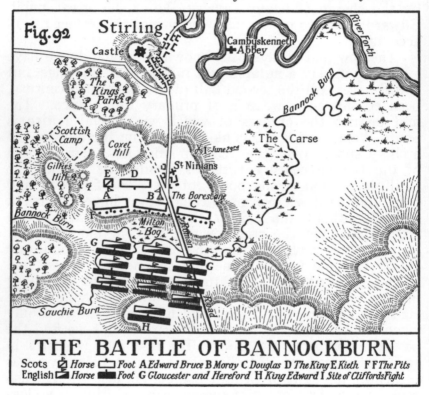

## THE BATTLE OF BANNOCKBURN

Scots ⚑ Horse ▭ Foot  A Edward Bruce B Moray C Douglas D The King E Kieth  F F The Pits
English ◧ Horse ▬ Foot  G Gloucester and Hereford  H King Edward  I Site of Cliffords Fight

make such an impression on English commanders as might have been expected. Edward II at Bannockburn (1314) did not copy his great father's tactics, but tried to break up Bruce's host by a mere frontal attack of cavalry. The Scottish pikemen, well posted behind a marshy burn, and with their front protected by small pitfalls, 'pottes' as Barbour calls them, kept the English knighthood at bay without much difficulty, and finally hurled them back across the water with great loss. Edward had brought many archers to the field, but did not know how to use them. 'He put them behind the knights, instead of on their flanks,' wrote Baker of Swinbrooke, ' and bade them fire over their heads : hence they hit some few Scots in the breast, but struck many more of their own friends in the back.' At one moment of the battle some of the bowmen on the English left did push to the front ; but Bruce ordered them to be charged in flank by a small cavalry reserve which he had set aside, and they were

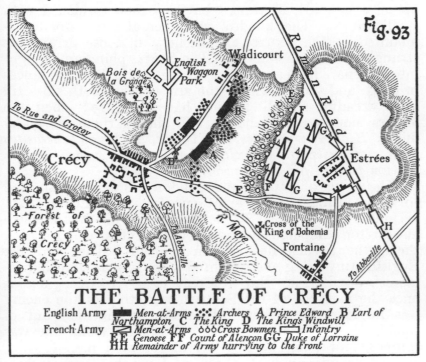

**THE BATTLE OF CRÉCY**

English Army ▬ *Men-at-Arms* ⋮⋮⋮ *Archers* A *Prince Edward* B *Earl of Northampton* C *The King* D *The King's Windmill*
French Army ▭ *Men-at-Arms* ○○○*Cross Bowmen* ▭ *Infantry*
EE *Genoese* FF *Count of Alençon* GG *Duke of Lorraine*
HH *Remainder of Army hurrying to the Front*

ridden down or scattered for want of protection from the knights.

The lesson which Edward II had failed to learn from Falkirk had not been lost on more capable men. The reign of Edward III opens with two astounding victories for the archer : the first was that of Dupplin (1332), won by Edward Balliol and his English auxiliaries over the partisans of David Bruce. The invaders of Scotland dismounted their men-at-arms and formed them in a solid mass, while arraying their bowmen in thin crescent-shaped wings on either hand. The Scots, attacking in massive columns, were shot down so rapidly by the concentric rain of shafts, that they broke and fled before they had succeeded in overwhelming Balliol's small body of dismounted cavalry. Halidon Hill (1333) was an exact reproduction of Dupplin on a larger scale : most of the victors of the former fight were present, and we cannot doubt that it was they who induced the young Edward III to copy the successful tactics of the preceding year. The English were drawn up on a hill-side, in three 'battles' each furnished with small wings. The knights and men-at-arms stood dismounted in the centre, the archery in loose array was strung out on either flank. The Scots, plunging straight into the snare in heavy masses, were checked by the lances in front, and shot down by the arrows from both sides till after dreadful slaughter they had to retire : then the victors mounted their horses and chased them for many miles. *Hic didicit a Scotis*, says Baker, *Anglorum generositas dextrarios reservare venationi hostium, et contra morem suorum patrum pedes pugnare*.

The tactics of Dupplin and Halidon Hill were transported to the continent with great success when Edward III became involved in his French wars. In his first Flemish and Breton campaigns he did not get the chance of applying them, the French declining a pitched battle, and the English army being overweighted with German and Netherlandish auxiliaries. But at Crécy (1346) we recognize at once the methods of the Scottish war, though the enemy was no longer composed of masses of pikemen but of squadrons of feudal horsemen. Edward's front line was composed of two 'battles' of dismounted men-at-arms, each 1,200 strong with three or four thousand archers arrayed on its wings. The bowmen stood in equal divisions on the flanks of the knights, somewhat thrown forward, so that the dismounted cavalry were, as Froissart remarks, *au fond de la bataille*. The French army had not foreseen a fight that day, and came quite unexpectedly upon the English host. King Philip VI tried to hold his vassals back, and to draw up some sort of order of battle. But the rash and undisciplined French baronage pressed forward so heedlessly that an engagement became inevitable. A line of Genoese mercenary crossbowmen was first thrown out, but the archers shot them down almost before they had got into range with their clumsy weapons.  Then the French *noblesse* charged : to their surprise they found that they could hardly reach the English line : the archers slew horses and men in such numbers that a bank of dead and wounded was built up in front of them, and the whole mass was brought to a standstill.  More squadrons came pushing up from the rear, and in spite of the carnage the French several times got to handstrokes with the English dismounted men-at-arms.  But they failed to break through them, and meanwhile the storm of arrows was always beating upon their flanks.  After fifteen or sixteen fruitless onsets the ranks of the assailants were so thinned and their spirit so broken that they melted away to the rear, leaving 1,500 barons and knights and 10,000 meaner men dead in front of the English line.

This astonishing victory made a deep impression all over the continent, and marked the commencement of that ascendancy of the English infantry in war which was to last for a full century.  For the next four generations the tactics first seen at Dupplin Moor dominated Western Europe : the English armies were invariably arrayed with clumps of dismounted men-at-arms in the centre, and with lines of archers on the wings.  They tried to choose a favourable position, with clear ground in front and obstacles to cover their flanks, and then waited to be attacked.  As long as their enemies were obliging enough to deliver frontal assaults upon them, they never failed to gain the victory.

Poitiers (1356) resembled Crécy in many of its details, but had its own peculiar features.  John of France, remembering the slaughter of horses in the earlier battle, dismounted his knights and bade them attack the English position on foot ; but he sent forward a forlorn hope of a few hundred cavalry, who were to try to break into the weakest spot of the Black Prince's front.  This advance guard of mounted men was easily shot down : the columns of mailed knights on foot, however, succeeded in struggling up to the line and getting to hand-to-hand fighting.  But they could not break through.  The two leading columns had been driven off the field, when the French king with his reserve advanced for a last effort.  When he was halfway up the slope, the Prince of Wales massed his wearied troops, bade them quit their line of hedge, and charged downhill. He also sent off a small detachment to make a circuit to the right and fall upon the king's flank. This sudden assault was successful : dispirited by the repulse of their main body, the French third line gave way, and when threatened by the demonstration against their flank, broke and fled. King John, refusing to turn back, was captured together with his son Philip and his most faithful retainers.

Thus the English system of tactics proved as successful against dismounted men-at-arms at Poitiers as it had against mounted squadrons at Crécy. If any further confirmation of its excellence was required, the Black Prince's victory at Navarette (1367) over the numerous light horse of Henry of Castile was sufficient evidence. Aljubarrota (1385), a success won by the Portuguese over the Spaniards and French, may also be mentioned. The victor was assisted by English auxiliaries and adopted English methods, closely copying the arrangements of Poitiers.

If Edward III was ultimately unsuccessful in his attack on France it was not owing to any fault in his tactics, but purely because the enemy made up his mind to refuse pitched battles, and wearied out the English by scattered raids and long sieges. The next century was to show that the system of Dupplin Moor and Crécy was as effective as ever under the proper conditions.

The equipment of the knights who fought under Edward III is described in the Section on Arms and Armour. Plate armour was now superseding chain-mail, but the increased protection it gave to the body was won at the cost of a notable addition of weight ; the knight of 1350, with his elaborate double sheathing, of plate laid above the original mail, had lost the power of rapid and easy movement which the knight of 1250 had still possessed. He tired sooner, could not walk far or long when he dismounted, and when he had lost his footing found it difficult to rise again. But fashion persisted in adding extra pieces to his panoply, and the development of the longbow with its penetrating shaft tempted the armourer to make the plate ever thicker and heavier. By the fifteenth century its weight had become so overwhelming that a man-at-arms once overthrown was quite at the mercy of his enemy, and that combatants were not unfrequently exhausted by a short fight to such an extent that they were actually stifled in their armour, and died without having received any mortal wound.

Contemporary with the invention of plate armour there arose a new power which was to revolutionize all the old ideas : this was gunpowder. Its origin is obscure,

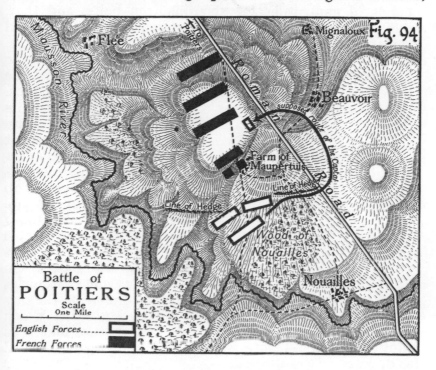

but goes back at least to the second decade of the four-teenth century. The first powder was ill made and irregular in its effect : the earliest cannon were small, clumsily built, and hard to work. But with all their faults they revolutionized the relations of the offensive and the defensive. Cannon could batter down walls of a solidity which would have laughed to scorn all manner of mangonels and catapults. The most perfect fortresses of the elder age, even the famous triple walls of Constantinople itself, proved helpless before the new invention. Its beginnings, however, were modest. The first certain picture of a cannon occurs in the Mildmete MS. in Christ Church library, where it is represented as a bottle-shaped machine shooting out bolts, not balls. It is dated 1326. This being so we have no reason to doubt the statement that cannon of a primitive sort, ' crakys of war ' the chronicler calls them, were used at Edward III's siege of Berwick in 1333. And it is certain that in 1338 the French fleet which attacked Southampton was provided with a *pot de fer* and three pounds of gunpowder for shooting iron bolts, and that, later in the same year, *pouldres et canons* were employed against the English castle of Puy Guilhem in Aquitaine. The first official mention of their use on this side of the Channel is in 1344, when the king directed one Thomas de Roldeston, his chief engineer, to make powder for his guns.

FIG. 95. HOOPED CANNON, fifteenth century (Cotton MS. Julius, E. iv).

One of Roldeston's accounts shows that he had to pay eighteenpence a pound for saltpetre and eightpence for sulphur, so that powder was a very costly compound in those days. But its use spread rapidly : in 1346–7 Edward had a considerable battering train of siege guns at the leaguer of Calais. On the other hand, it is very doubtful that, as some chronicles assert, he had guns at Crécy, for the cannon of the day were too heavy and clumsy for the forced marches which he had been executing just before that battle, and it is many years later before we find them employed for field (as opposed to siege) work.

The art of metal-casting was in its infancy in the fourteenth century, and the first molten guns, small though they were, were so liable to flaws and airholes, which made them burst after a little use, that for a time they were unpopular. Instead, bars of approved quality were welded together around a wooden core, and then clamped by four or five iron hoops to keep them still more solidly compacted. When the core was withdrawn, a practicable gun was the result. But the hooped guns were hardly less dangerous than the cast, for after a time the welding gave way at some point, and an unlucky discharge resolved the

engine into its component parts, and sent them flying in
all directions.  It was an accident of this kind which slew
James II of Scotland at the siege of Roxburgh (1460).

As years went on and both gun-founders and powder-
makers grew more skilful, the advantage of the offensive
over the defensive grew more and more marked, and
famine ceased to be the besieger's best weapon.  After
a time the besieged also took to using cannon, to oppose
the enemy's fire, search his trenches, and beat down his
palisades.  But the older type of fortress did not easily
lend itself to the use of artillery, for the ramparts were
generally too narrow, and where they were not, the constant
recoil of the pieces was found to shake the masonry.  Sometimes the defender's cannon had to be withdrawn because
it was doing as much damage to the walls as was that of
the besieger.  Artillery, in fact, ultimately forced military
engineers to take in hand the general reconstruction of
strongholds, and to cease putting all their trust in high
walls of hewn stone.  But this development came much
later than the times with which we are now dealing.  There
was so little civil war in England between 1320 and 1460
that the need for reconstruction did not make itself felt.

The reigns of Richard II and Henry IV make a practical
break in the history of the great continental wars of
England, though we must not forget episodes like John of
Gaunt's expedition to Castile (1385), or Clarence's presence
with English auxiliaries at the battle of St. Cloud (1411).
But when the second act of the Hundred Years' War
commenced, with Henry V's siege of Harfleur, we find that
the tactics of English and French alike had altered little
during the forty years of comparative peace that had gone
by.  The French had learnt nothing in their civil wars
nor in their Flemish campaigns, and Homildon Hill and
Shrewsbury had only confirmed the English in their confidence in the longbow.  Agincourt, therefore, reads like
a mere repetition of Poitiers.  Henry V, like the Black
Prince, took up the best position he could find, covered
with woods on both flanks, and arrayed his men in three
corps, each composed of a central mass of dismounted
men-at-arms with wings of archers.  He only improved on
his great-uncle's arrangements by giving his archers iron-
shod stakes, which they arranged in front of themselves,

as *chevaux de frise*, to keep off cavalry.  The Constable of France (like King John at Poitiers) formed three heavy lines of dismounted men-at-arms, and sent on in front of them a forlorn hope of picked knights on horseback.  The main difference between the two fights lay in the fact that at Poitiers the two armies had between them a scrubby hill-side, and at Agincourt newly ploughed fields sodden with ten days of rain.  At the second battle, as at the first,

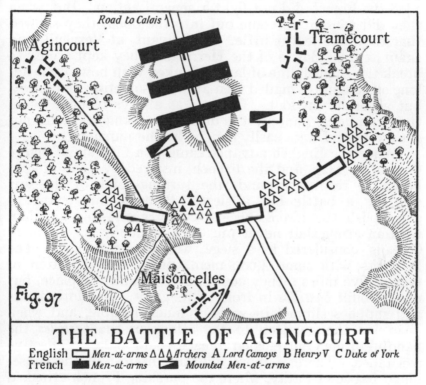

**THE BATTLE OF AGINCOURT**

English ☐ *Men-at-arms* △△△ *Archers* A *Lord Camoys* B *Henry V* C *Duke of York*
French ■ *Men-at-arms* ◣ *Mounted Men-at-arms*

the French mounted men were shot down long before they could close.  But when the masses of men-at-arms on foot came up, they were so riddled with arrows, so embogged in the deep mud, and so tired by walking a mile in their heavy armour, that they came to a complete standstill in front of King Henry's line.  The English, in spite of their inferior numbers, saw the enemy reduced to such helplessness that they were emboldened to charge.  The result was an easy victory : the French lines were hurled one on another in complete helplessness : men fell in heaps and were stifled as they lay. The English archers flung down their bows and beat upon the armour of the crowded knights with swords and mallets 'like smiths hammering upon anvils', till all who stayed behind had been overthrown and the rest had fled.

No battle of such importance as Agincourt was fought during the rest of the war, which became for the next ten years mainly an affair of sieges. Even to deliver Rouen in 1418 the French did not fight a general action. But when they did consent to come out into the open, they showed that they had learnt little. At Cravant, at Verneuil, and again at the 'Battle of the Herrings', they kept trying to break the English line of lances flanked with bows by headlong onslaughts of mailed men-at-arms, sometimes mounted, but generally on foot. Defeat was always bloody, for in their cumbrous panoply the dismounted knights could not get away, and were easily caught by the pursuer.

When the English advance came to a final stand before Orleans in 1429, and the French, inspired by Joan of Arc, began to recover ground, the turning-point of the war was not a battle but a siege. Bedford was trying to accomplish the impossible, to conquer a whole kingdom with an army that never mustered 15,000 or 20,000 men. Orleans, considered as a siege, was almost farcical. The besiegers, with some 4,000 men, tried to cover a front of four or five miles : they could not surround the place, but merely built *bastilles* in front of its gates. Reinforcements and supplies slipped in without much trouble, and when Joan led the garrison to the attack of the *bastilles* the handful of men entrenched in each could make no effective resistance. There is more military interest in the subsequent battle of Patay, where the pursuing French attacked the retreating English 'before they could form a line, or the archers could fix their stakes'. They rushed in, caught the invaders in disorder, and routed them. From this moment the annals of the war, instead of consisting of a long list of French fortresses beleaguered and taken by the English, become an equally weary chronicle of English garrisons surrounded and slowly reduced by the French. The only pitched battles were fought in the very last years of the war. At Formigny (1450) the English army, advancing to the relief of Caen, was faced by a covering force, and took up a position in which it waited to be attacked. Bow and lance were holding their own, when a fresh French corps appeared from a different direction, and fell upon the flank and rear of the English. The thin line of archers and men-at-arms, ranged along a hedgeside, could not protect itself by forming a new front : it was rolled up, enveloped, and absolutely cut to pieces. The English tactics in fact were only certain of success if the flanks were absolutely safe, which at Formigny they were not, and if the enemy confined himself to frontal attacks.

Castillon, the last battle of the Hundred Years' War, differs in character from all the rest, in that the English attacked an entrenched position, instead of assuming the defensive in their usual style. The French had fortified themselves behind earthworks, on which they had planted much artillery. The aged Lord Talbot, a veteran of thirty years' service, threw away his previous reputation for capable generalship by assailing the enemy's almost impregnable lines with a frontal attack. His men-at-arms dismounted and dashed at the earthworks, but were blown to pieces by the fire of the cannon, and recoiled in disorder ; the French then sallied out upon the archers and completed the rout.

The armies with which the latter half of the Hundred Years' War were fought were raised by a method which had first appeared under Edward I, and became normal under Edward III. Instead of issuing *Commissions of Array* to raise shire-levies, as he had done in his earlier years, that monarch regularly, in his later campaigns, procured his men by *Indenture*. By this system the king bargained with his knights and nobles, or even with professional mercenary captains, that they should enlist for his service contingents of volunteers. The number of soldiers to be procured was stated, as also the time for which the hire was made, and the rate at which the king was to pay. A typical indenture may be quoted as an example : on September 30, 1360, Edward III bargains with Thomas, Earl of Kent, that the latter shall raise sixty men-at-arms (of whom ten are to be knights) and 120 bowmen, all properly equipped and provided with horses. The term of hire is for three months, the rate is to be ' the accustomed wages of war ', and the sum is to be paid to the earl beforehand, that he may have ready money for fitting out the contingent. Such agreements were of course quite distinct from a vassal's ordinary feudal obligations : they were private bargains which he made for his own profit.

Many English knights and nobles loved the military life so well that they remained overseas at the head of their companies for very long periods, and practically became professional soldiers. Similarly, a class of the same sort was developed to fill the ranks : the pay of a man-at-arms or an archer was high, considering the purchasing power of money in those days. The former received (1346) a shilling a day, the latter sixpence if he brought a horse, threepence if he was on foot. This, with the chance of plunder and ransom-money, was a very tempting maintenance for a man of the fourteenth or fifteenth century. It was at the head of such bands, skilled veterans with a keen eye for booty, that John of Gaunt, Henry V, or the Duke of Bedford, carried out their French campaigns. One of the most notable results of the final expulsion of the English from Normandy and Aquitaine in 1451-3 was that thousands of these professional mercenaries, accustomed for years to nothing but war, were cast adrift without employment. Their presence was not the least important of the conditions which made the outbreak of the Wars of the Roses possible, and even probable. The idle hands were there, and the mischief was not long in coming.

The armies which fought for York or Lancaster had as their core the military households of the nobles, largely composed of the disbanded veterans from the French war, and the retainers gathered under the evil system of ' Livery and Maintenance '. This was a device by which great lords invited their smaller neighbours to put themselves under their protection, to wear their ' livery '—i. e. their badge, the Bear and Ragged Staff of Neville, or the Stafford Knot, or the Holland Cresset—and to be ' maintained ', i. e. championed, by them in their quarrels and lawsuits. In return the receiver of the livery undertook to turn out in arms at his patron's call. Wealthy knights and squires who could put a couple of hundred retainers into the field did not think it beneath their dignity to accept the badge of a great earl like Warwick or Northumberland. It was not unknown for even a baron to place himself under the protection of one of the greater magnates.    Both the Yorkists and the Lancastrians used to supplement their bands of partisans by issuing commissions of array to call out the shire-levies.    But the troops thus obtained were far less useful to them than their own liveried retainers, since the greater part of the nation would gladly have been neutral, and did not like to be forced to take a side, with the chance of discovering that it was the weaker one. Nothing can be more typical of public feeling than the fact that no town chose to stand a siege during the whole war.    Whatever the temper of the citizens, they used to open their gates to any leader who appeared before them with a sufficient force.    Even London, which passed as being a Yorkist stronghold, was ready to capitulate without a blow after the second battle of St. Albans.

The battles of the Wars of the Roses were fought on the old system of English tactics.    Each party arrayed itself in three 'battles', consisting of a central body of dismounted men-at-arms and billmen, with wings of archers.    The army which was on the defensive seized a hill-side or a hedgerow and held it : the opposing troops strove to turn them out.    The fights were usually bloody, because of the great force of excellent archery, and because the heavy armour of the man-at-arms made it impossible for him to fly with speed if his party was routed.    The second battle of St. Albans, Towton, Barnet, and Tewkesbury were all first-class battles of this simple kind. Northampton was complicated by the fact that the Lancastrians had entrenched themselves and garnished their lines with cannon : but a severe rain-storm just before the engagement flooded their works, and drenched their powder, so that they got no profit from their precaution. At Edgecote the Yorkists had hardly any archers with them, and owed their defeat to the preponderant arrow-flight of the northern rebels.    The first battle of St. Albans was little more than a scuffle on a large scale down the High Street of a small town.

The one new feature presented by the battles of the Wars of the Roses is that cannon were frequently employed in them : a new feature in English engagements.    But it cannot be said that the artillery made much difference in the fate of the day. At Northampton it was drowned out by rain : at Barnet both sides shot at each other all night without any effective result. At Tewkesbury it seems to have been a little more serviceable. But only at the obscure fight of Lose-Coat Field (1470) does it seem to have settled the fate of the day : there the Lincolnshire rebels, marching to surprise King Edward's camp, found him already arrayed to meet them, and were scattered by one general salvo of his guns. The smaller firearms are also heard of for the first time in this war. Warwick, at the second battle of St. Albans, had some Burgundian ' hand-gun men' [Fig. 175], but they did him little service ; a storm, which beat in their faces and blew out their matches, seems to have utterly nonplussed them. Nor do we hear any good of a similar body of mercenaries, lent by Charles the Bold to Edward IV for his expedition to conquer England in 1471. The fact was that the long-bow was still too effective to fear the competition of the clumsy tubes, mounted on wooden staves and fired by matches, which were the progenitors of the musket.

In sieges, however, firearms made their mark during the Wars of the Roses. Cannon made short work of the old fastnesses. The best remembered sieges are those of Bamburgh and Dunstanburgh (1465), when Warwick's artillery easily battered down the massive walls of the Percy strongholds. The only fortresses which made very long defences were those unusually favoured by natural position, and placed in remote corners. Jasper Tudor long held out in Harlech, and Oxford in St. Michael's Mount : both were difficult to get at with the short-ranged artillery of that day, and it is possible that, owing to their inaccessibility, they were only blockaded and not battered. But unfortunately details are wanting.

### 4. *The Growth of Firearms and the Decline of the Longbow. 1485–1602.*

The Wars of the Roses had, for a whole generation, kept England practically out of continental politics. The attempts of Edward IV to intervene in them had come to a most inglorious end. As a natural consequence we find that while beyond the Channel the military art was going through a complete transformation, and assuming a more modern character, in England it remained unchanged. The cautious policy of Henry VII protracted this state of affairs into the beginning of the sixteenth century. Abroad every monarch was beginning to raise a standing army. The arquebus was rapidly superseding the cross-bow and all other missile weapons. The pike of the Swiss and the *Lanzknechts* was at the height of its reputation : the man-at-arms was relinquishing the habit of dismounting for battle, which had been the rule since Poitiers, and was once more charging on horseback. But in England things went on in the old style of Crécy and Agincourt, and no changes were to be seen till the sixteenth century was well advanced.

The military importance of Henry VII's reign consists rather in what he undid than in what he accomplished. His great feat was the abolition of the evil custom of Livery and Maintenance. The 'household men' and badged retainers, who made rebellion so easy, were an abomination to him. He made the giving of liveries and the making of private treaties and agreements penal. Even his most faithful servant the Earl of Oxford, the victor of Bosworth, was heavily fined for having too many servants wearing the silver mullet of the De Veres. In military organization Henry went back to the modes of Edward III, and raised his armies mainly by commissions of array to the counties, but partly by the indenture system.

From the tactical point of view his reign forms but a continuation on a small scale of the Wars of the Roses. In the forms of battle, the use of arms and armour, and the arraying of troops, we see little change. We still find the men-at-arms dismounting to fight, and the archery ranging themselves on the wings. It is worth noting that at Stoke Field, where the Earl of Lincoln brought a number of German mercenaries to the fray, bow and bill prevailed easily over pike and hand-gun. The *Lanzknechts* of Martin Schwartz were shot down by the archery no less than the Irish javelin-men of Fitzgerald. Blackheath Field, on the other hand, shows another point of interest : Lord Audley and the Cornishmen were routed, not for want of archery, but for want of artillery. It is said that after the fight observers noted that the rebels' bows averaged several inches more in length than those of the men of the home counties who had come out in the king's behalf. But the thundering discharges of the royal train of cannon, to which the Cornish had nothing to oppose, settled the day. The fight may fairly be compared to Edward IV's victory at Lose-Coat Field. The English armies were seldom seen on the continent during Henry VII's reign : in the one important expedition, that of Lord Morley to Flanders in 1491, the archers are said to have acquitted themselves well against the French, whose entrenched camp by Dixmude they succeeded in capturing.

The only visible change was in armour : this had grown heavier than ever, and from about 1490 to 1530

FIG. 98. BRONZE CANNON (contemp. picture of Henry VIII's defence of Portsmouth : Brit. Mus.).

was at its most ponderous stage ; it had become absolutely impossible for a knight once overthrown to get on his legs again, and a very short fight in such cumbrous panoply sufficed to tire out the strongest man. The fact was that the armourers were engaged in a vain attempt to cope with the penetrating power of firearms, and had not yet confessed themselves beaten. It was only in the middle of the sixteenth century that men began to see that the contest must be given up, and that the practical thing to do was to risk the balls, and win back some degree of mobility by discarding as much as possible of the armour. By 1530 it had reached the stage when it not only cumbered its wearer, but prevented him from doing much harm to his adversaries.

The reign of Henry VIII contrasts with that of his father in that all the new influences in the military art began to cross the Channel. The knights once more took to fighting habitually on horseback, which they had not done since Bannockburn. The pictures of the king's victory at Guinegate (the 'Battle of the Spurs'), painted by his command, show his men-at-arms riding forward in orderly squadrons of a deep formation. Henry was a patron of firearms, not only of cannon but of the smaller weapons also. He took great interest in his foundry, where large bronze pieces, much more effective than the hooped guns of the previous century, were cast. His founders, Peter of Cöln and Peter Baude, even made for him shells, then a new invention : they are described as 'hollow shot of

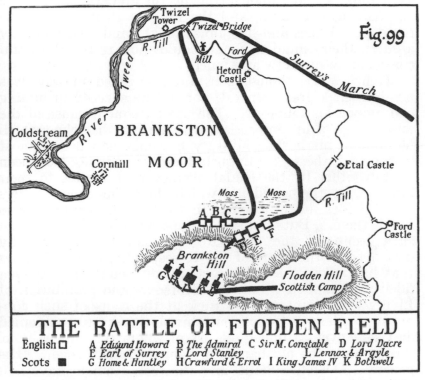

**Fig. 99**

THE BATTLE OF FLODDEN FIELD

English □   A Edmund Howard   B The Admiral   C Sir M. Constable   D Lord Dacre
            E Earl of Surrey    F Lord Stanley                       L Lennox & Argyle
Scots ■     G Home & Huntley   H Crawfurd & Errol   I King James IV   K Bothwell

iron filled with fireworks and fitted with a match, which broke into small pieces, whereof any hitting a man did kill or spoil him' (1543). In the second half of his reign Henry often hired Germans and other mercenaries armed with *calivers* and arquebuses, and seems to have induced his own subjects to begin to employ these weapons.

But the bow was still the main arm of the English infantry : it still had an enormous advantage in rapidity of discharge over any sort of firearm, which quite compensated for its somewhat inferior penetrating power.

Flodden Field was its last great victory : there the enemy was the same as at the old fights of Dupplin Moor and Halidon Hill, the heavy masses of the Scottish pikemen. James IV, like so many of his predecessors in the command of a Scottish host, made at Flodden the mistake of coming down from his position and making a fierce frontal attack on Surrey's army. In different parts of the field the fortunes of the day varied : but its main crisis was settled, as at Falkirk and Halidon Hill, by the archery shaking the Scottish main column, and the knights then getting into the gaps. James and his nobles fought and died valiantly around their standard, but could not resist the fatal combination of arrow and lance.

Henry VIII, though constantly engaged in war, was not himself a great general, nor did he succeed in finding one among his followers. The most frequent cause of the miscarriage of his enterprises was the bad discipline which he kept in his hosts. Military mutinies had been almost unknown hitherto in English history : armies had been kept together by the feudal obedience of vassals to their lords, or by the confidence which the professional soldiers raised under indentures felt in the veteran captains who hired them. But Henry's troops were inspired by no such feelings : the old baronage had been practically destroyed in the Wars of the Roses, and the new families that had taken their places could not count on any such fidelity from their retainers. Moreover the prohibition of Livery and Maintenance struck at the roots of such connexions. Henry's troops were shire-levies, hastily embodied and sent oversea under officers of whom they knew little, quite unlike the old bands of Agincourt or Verneuil. His generals, Dorset, Suffolk, and the rest, seem to have had little control over them. Both the campaign of 1512 round St. Sebastian and that of 1523 in Artois and Picardy came to a summary end owing to the army ' going on strike ', seizing shipping, and returning home. Henry himself was able to secure obedience by employing his usual drastic methods, but none of his lieutenants could do the like. Hence came many disgraceful scenes of indiscipline. This was enough, without other co-operating causes, to account for many of his military fiascos.

One of the facts which strikes us most forcibly in con-

sidering Henry's career is that it was well for England that
he did not copy his continental contemporaries in raising
a standing army. The Tudor despotism was bad enough
as things stood, but if the king had been provided with
a large permanent force of mercenaries there would have
been no check on his tyranny. Fortunately his unsound
finance proved sufficient to prevent any such idea from
being put into practice. Obliged to depend for military
force on shire-levies and volunteers engaged for short
periods, he had to take public opinion into consideration.
There was a danger, as the 'Pilgrimage of Grace' showed,
that if he pressed matters too far he might find the whole
country in arms, and have no force to defend him save
his handful of 'Gentlemen-pensioners' and Yeomen of the
Guard. Hence he was compelled to humour the nation in
a fashion that must often have been galling to him.

It is perhaps worth noting that Henry was the first
English sovereign who prescribed a fixed uniform for his
army. In early reigns the wearing of the red St. George's
cross as a distinguishing mark had been considered sufficient. But in his ordinance of 1543 the king commanded
that the whole of his infantry should be furnished with
blue coats trimmed with red, and parti-coloured breeches,
of which one leg was to be red and one blue. The red
cross was to be retained, and no one was to wear any other
badge belonging to any captain or commander. Over their
blue coats the billmen and archers generally wore a plain
back-and-breast piece, or occasionally a leather 'jack'.
The headgear consisted partly of the round steel cap usual
in the previous generation, partly of the *morion*, a pointed
cap with a broad brim, somewhat peaked in front and
behind.

There is little to note in the reigns of Edward VI and
Mary, in which the military practices of the time of their
father were simply continued. We seemed to trace an
ever-growing use of firearms, both great and small, but the
bow was still the main weapon of the infantry. At Pinkie,
the last great battle with the pikemen of Scotland, the
men-at-arms charged the hostile columns and were beaten
off, but artillery was then brought up and set to play upon
the heavy masses with fatal effect. When it had shaken
them the cavalry charged again, this time with complete

success and murderous result. We hear less of the archery than at Flodden, the last battle of the old type. Indeed, Pinkie reminds us more of Marignano, the great continental battle (1515) in which Francis I had beaten the famous pikemen of Switzerland by combining cavalry charges and salvoes of artillery.

One token of the fact that we are leaving the Middle Ages and approaching modern military phraseology is that during the reign of Mary we find the first use of the word 'regiment' in its present sense. The English contingent sent to the aid of the Spaniards in the campaign of St. Quentin is officially called 'a regiment of 1,000 horse and 4,000 foot'. These troops consisted of 500 'lances' (fully equipped men-at-arms), 500 'demi-lances' (light horse), and 40 'bands' of foot-soldiers, each consisting of 100 men under a captain, lieutenant, and 'ancient' (ensign, of which 'ancient' is probably only a corrupt form).

Down to Mary's reign the shire-levy had been theoretically under the command of the sheriff, as in early Norman and Plantagenet days, though actually raised by commissions of array for each county. Now a new officer, the 'Lord-Lieutenant', was created to take complete charge of the military affairs of the county, the sheriff becoming a purely civil magistrate. The new arrangement lasted down to the nineteenth century.

In Elizabeth's long reign the last traces of the old English tactics of the Middle Ages disappear, and in things military the nation falls into line with the practice of the continent. The main feature of the time is the complete decay of the longbow. In 1558 it was still the principal weapon of the infantry, in 1597 its use was officially prohibited. All through the early years of the reign it is still to the fore : in the siege of Leith (1559–60) and in the first campaigns in France and Holland we hear much of it. But the arquebusier and 'caliver-man' were already arrayed alongside of the archer, as readers of the famous *Ballad of Lord Willoughby* will remember. In Leicester's army in the Netherlands (1585) the archers were in a minority : in the great host raised against the Spanish Armada the wealthier counties gave their contingents almost entirely in men furnished with firearms ; it was only in some of the midland shires that the bowmen out-numbered the arquebusiers. As early as Elizabeth's second year (1559) it is worth noting that the picked trained-bands of London had all carried firearms, though the general levy did not. Archery was dying a natural death in the last fifteen years of the century, to the accompaniment of a furious controversy in print between professional soldiers, in which Sir Roger Williams was the main advocate of the arquebus and Sir John Smyth the defender of the old national weapon. Finally, in 1597, the Council took the last step, by ordering the Lords-Lieutenant no longer to accept as properly equipped any member of the county militia who came furnished with bow and arrows alone.

The controversy of Smyth and Williams on the relative merits of bow and arquebus is very amusing reading. Smyth insists on the superior rapidity of discharge of the archer, who (as he thinks) can ' loose off' about six times as fast as the man with a gun. He thinks that the latter is bad at hitting the mark, owing to the weight of his weapon, and liable to get muddled with the complicated manage-ment of match, powder-horn, bullets, wads, and ramrod. He had seen flurried musketeers forget to insert any bullet at all, or put no wad above the bullet, so that the latter rolled out of the muzzle when inclined a little downward. Powder was damped in rain, or on the other hand the soldier got his match too near his powder-horn and blew himself up ! Altogether he would prefer to have a hundred good archers than three hundred arquebusiers. Williams replies that the defects above named only apply to raw soldiers ; trained men shoot fast and accurately, and do not make the clumsy mistakes of which Smyth speaks. He thinks that the archer is much more at the mercy of wind and weather than the musketeer. Rain loosens his cord and unsprings his bow ; while a few days of cold or damp bivouacs so weaken his strength that only a few men in a score will retain their full vigour and ' shoot strong shoots '. On the other hand the arquebus of a tired or weak man goes off perfectly well, if only he has kept his powder dry. Williams is also great on the moral effect of firearms : the smoke and fire are much more encouraging to one's own side and terrifying to the enemy than the silent fall of the arrow. However the merits of the controversy lay, the advocate of firearms was practically victorious, and the old national weapon was relegated to the lumber-room.

The cavalry, all through Elizabeth's reign, were gradually shedding some of their ponderous armour. By 1600, as pointed out in the Section on Arms and Armour, it was much lightened. Even the *tassets* were not always worn : Sir Philip Sidney's mortal wound at Zutphen is put down to the fact that he had refused to don them on the fatal morning. In fact, the horseman's armour was now intended to protect him from lance and sword, but did not purport to stop a musket ball, though some still fondly dreamed of ' pistol-proof' suits.

For military service within the kingdom Elizabeth relied on the shire-levies, now regularly called *militia*. They were frequently mustered for inspection of arms, and seem to have been fairly efficient. For the suppression of the ' Rising in the North' (1569) as many as 20,000 were embodied, and for protection against the Armada not less than 60,000 were called out under the Lords-Lieutenant (1588). For service in Ireland and on the continent another method was adopted : ' colonels' were authorized to raise ' regiments', and if volunteers were insufficient men were ' pressed' from the shires to complete the *cadres*. The custom (as those who remember the dealings of Sir John Falstaff in Shakespeare will guess) was one which led to abuses. Each village tried to get its local ne'er-do-weels and loafers taken by the recruiting office, with the result that the material of a ' pressed' regiment left much to be desired. Discipline seems to have often been in the same unsatisfactory state that we have noted in the reign of Henry VIII, and for the same reasons. It was perhaps at its worst in the unfortunate ' Journey of Portugal' in 1589.

The permanently embodied regiments wore uniforms, but there was no general dress for the whole army. We hear of corps in blue, red, white, and ' motley or any other sad green colour or russet'. The corps were at first very large : 2,000 or 3,000 strong, after the model of the Spanish *tercios*. But by the end of the reign the more manageable number of 1,200 or 1,500 was commoner. These bodies were divided into ' companies' (the earlier ' bands ') from

100 to 150 strong : each was under a captain, and carried its own flag. The infantry was arrayed in a central mass of pikemen and halberdiers ('halberd' has superseded the older term 'bill'), with musketeers and caliver-men on the wings. Archers were still to be found mixed with the 'shot' during the first thirty years of the reign. When armies closed, the musketeers retired for cover behind the pikemen, with whom lay the final decision of battle. Cavalry always worked on the wings, and the 'demi-lance' with his light armour was more common than the fully-armed 'lance'. Many horsemen had begun to use pistols, like the German *Reiters*, a fact which did not add to their efficiency, as it tended to distract their attention from the all-importance of shock and impact in cavalry affairs.

Artillery, always growing in efficiency, was regularly used in battle no less than in sieges. But its slowness of discharge and its short range still prevented it from playing a decisive part in the majority of engagements. The calibres and patterns of gun were now very numerous and complicated, ranging from 'cannon' and 'demi-cannon' downwards, through sakers, culverins, &c., to small wall-pieces, some of which were breach-loaders of a primitive type. But in England, though the teaching of the great sieges of the Dutch War of Independence was known to our professional soldiers, it was not much applied. The parsimonious Elizabeth was equally loath to spend money on stone and mortar and on powder and shot, and England could show little to compare with the great fortresses of the continent. It was not till the war of Charles I with his Parliament that the military art in all its branches reaches a new and interesting stage, and that period lies beyond the scope of this volume.

## *Books for reference.*

CLARK, *Mediaeval Military Architecture in England*, 1884.
ARMITAGE, Mrs., *Early Norman Castles*, 1912.
HAMILTON THOMPSON, *Military Architecture in England during the Middle Ages*, 1912.
ROUND, J. H., *Geoffrey de Mandeville*, 1892.
VIOLLET-LE-DUC, *Military Architecture*, translated by Macdermott, edited by Parker, 2nd edition, 1879.
——— *Annals of a Fortress*, translated by Bucknall, 1875.
   These two last books must be used with caution, as they contain doubtful matter.
(See also the list on p. 193.)

# IV

## COSTUME, CIVIL

### I. *Anglo-Saxon Period.*

FROM illustrated records we gather that the royal habit consisted of a plain tunic girded round the waist, a mantle

FIG. 100. King Edgar (Cott. MS. Vesp. A. viii).

FIG. 101. Anglo-Saxon Lady (from a tenth-century Benedictional).

or short cloak fastened on the right shoulder by a *fibula*, the legs being clad in hose or long stockings, drawn up over short breeches, and swathed below the knee with bandages : this is the ' cross-gartering' still found in use in England in the seventeenth century, and worn at the present day by the peasants of the Apennines, and in the modified form of the Indian puttee by British soldiers [Fig. 100]. Great ladies wore a long gown with wide hanging sleeves, a super-tunic reaching down to the knees and usually girded with a swathe of cloth, a large mantle thrown over the left shoulder, and, if married or 'religious', the invariable coverchief or hood [Fig. 101]. Shirts and shifts of linen, with a long gown for women and a short, belted tunic for men, with shoes, and hat or cap, and cloaks for bad weather, were the ordinary dress for free persons. Slaves went pollheaded and barefoot.

The civil costume of the Danes was of white linen, red, blue, or natural-coloured woollen cloth, and furred mantles, similar in fact to that of the Anglo-Saxons, like whom the Danes wore long hair in which they took great pride.

## 2. *Norman and Plantagenet Periods.*

The habit of the kings of the Norman dynasty differs little from those of earlier times, the tunic and mantle being worn with slight variations of shape, and the wide-sleeved gown known as the *dalmatic* [Fig. 102] making its appearance in the time of Henry I; thenceforward the regal habiliments have remained almost unchanged until the present day.

The monumental effigies at Fontevrault of Henry II and of his son Cœur de Lion [Fig. 103] have special value as showing the regal costume of the time, which reached to the feet and was brilliant in its decorations. A similar fashion may be seen in the effigies of the queens of Henry II [Fig. 104] and of John, interred in the same abbey church, and of Richard I's queen, Berengaria, now in the cathedral of Le Mans. The figure of King John at Worcester, the earliest contemporary monumental effigy of an English monarch in this country, is shown in the usual royal vestments, but they are somewhat shorter, in the mode then established. Only slight modifications in the now accepted regal habits are observable in the effigies of Henry III, Edward II, Edward III, Richard II, Henry IV, and Henry VII.

After the Conquest the costume of the nobility rapidly increased in extravagance, with the introduction of fur-lined mantles, and upper and under tunics. Sleeves, hair and beard all reached to a great length in the time of Rufus. Peak-toed boots and caps of the Phrygian form were worn, and the general costliness of dress justly excited the anger of the monkish historians. The ladies of the time wore tight gowns with very long sleeves pendent from the wrists, and often tied up into knots, long trailing skirts, and silk-broidered hair [Fig. 105]. The dress of the middle classes consisted of long and short tunics, mantles, *chausses*, or swathings, and short boots. The husbandmen favoured much the same garb, but of the plainest character; they

FIG. 102. Effigy of King John (Worcester Cathedral).

FIG. 103. Effigy of Richard I (Fontevrault Abbey).

FIG. 104. Effigy of Eleanor, Q. of Henry II (Fontevrault Abbey).

wore flat-brimmed hats, or close-fitting round or flat skull-caps, and often went barefoot.

The general civil costume of men in the upper classes during the thirteenth century consisted of an under-tunic with tight, buttoned sleeves, a short upper-tunic, or *garde-cors*, sometimes spoken of as a *ciclaton* or *cyclas*, gown, hood, and mantle of rich stuff, short boots or shoes, with long toes, and gloves. Fur was much used for linings. The hood, or a variety of it, a white coif tied under the chin, was a constant feature of men's dress. The costume of a youth is given in Fig. 106.   He wears a tunic, gathered in at the waist, apparently by a girdle ; a tippet over the shoulders, hosen, and rather high boots.   The new-fashioned clothes were now shaped to the body, not cut by simple gore and length as before.

The costume of ladies of the upper classes during the same period consisted of a close gown, super-tunic, and

FIG. 105.   Lady of Norman Period (Cott. MS. Nero, C. iv).

FIG. 106.   Civil Costume, c. 1200 (Sloane MS. 1975).

mantle of great fullness ; and the gorget, or wimple, was generally worn by married gentlewomen or nuns.   The hair was confined in a variety of ways by head-dresses, which usually included a caul or net, and was covered with the veil ; the whole presenting a ' confection ' of great elegance, which is well exemplified by the effigy in Westminster Abbey of Aveline, Countess of Lancaster [Fig. 107].   Of simpler form and detail, and plainer materials, were the habits of less exalted ladies.   The wimple was at first never worn without the veil ; in the fourteenth century it is frequently seen alone, or the head-dress is formed by pinning up the veil on either side of the face.   The lower orders of both sexes wore tunics, or smocks, and plain gowns and mantles of various coarse cloths, known as *russet, birrus, cordetum,* and *sarcilis.*

With the accession of Edward I in 1272 came an abatement in the richness of male apparel, and it is probable that, save on the day of his coronation, the great monarch was never in his lifetime so gorgeously clothed as he was

FIG. 107. Effigy of Aveline, Countess of Lanc., *d.* 1273 (Westminster Abbey).

FIG. 108. Civil Costume, *temp.* Ed. ii (Royal MS. 14, E. iii).

FIG. 109. Brass of Lady Northwode, *c.* 1330 (Minster, Isle of Sheppey).

when he was placed in his coffin. The plainness of the king's habit was naturally followed by the courtiers, but the simple dress shown in the conventional effigy of Queen Eleanor at Westminster by no means illustrates that of the ladies of her time, who were much rebuked, alike by the priest and by the satirist, for their pride and extravagance, for their kirtles or their gowns, 'lacis moult estreitement,' their naked necks and horned head-dresses. Extravagant costumes were avoided in funeral monuments.

After the death of Edward I, though regal state-robes remained unaltered, extravagance reached to a great height in the garments of his successor and of the nobility. New fopperies were introduced from France or were invented by unworthy favourites like the profligate Gaveston, or the Despensers, and were eagerly adopted by the king and the

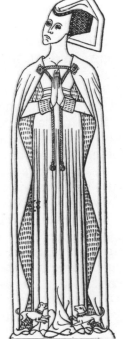

FIG. 110. Effigy of Blanche de la Tour, daughter of Edward III, *d.* 1340 (Westminster Abbey).

FIG. 111. Brass of Lady Curson, 1471 (Belaugh, Norfolk).

FIG. 112. Effigy of William of Hatfield, second son of Edward III (York Minster).

courtiers; and although the financial condition of the country was not consonant with a like display among the middle and lower classes, a luxurious fashion was now set in England which became still more ostentatious and eccentric in the following reign. The ordinary dress of the commonalty at this time is shown in Fig. 108. The costume of the ladies of the time of Edward II underwent no particular change : the wimple continued, but many varieties of head-dress were introduced [e. g. Fig. 109]. It is during this reign that we see the rise of a special habit for legal dignitaries, the semi-clerical character of which betrays its origin : the lawyer was ceasing to be necessarily a churchman.

The extravagance in the civil costume of the nobility, that originated, as we have seen, in the court of Edward II, rapidly increased and spread during the reign of Edward III [Fig. 110]. The long gowns, plain hoods, and tunics of male attire now gave place to the short, tight-fitting, often richly embroidered coat, buttoned down the front, with sleeves also closely buttoned from the elbow to the wrist, and garnished with long pendent slips, called tippets, that hung from the shoulder. The 'gay cote graceless' was girt round the waist by the *baudric* (belt), from which the *anelace* (poniard) and *gypcière* (hanging purse) were suspended. A mantle, forming a cape on the breast, was thrown back over the left shoulder, and hung in long folds behind, all the edges being *slittered* or *dagged*. In the absence of the mantle, a hood, or *capuchon*, of which there were many shapes, was in use : it was often buttoned close up to the chin in front, and had a long *liripipe* or streamer hanging behind. Hosen were worn, and short, sharp-pointed boots or shoes, elegantly diapered with Gothic patterns. In this, as in other reigns, sumptuary laws were passed with the object of regulating luxury in dress according to the rank or wealth of the wearer, but then, as always, were treated with absolute disregard. During the long reign of Edward III the costume of the ladies also underwent considerable changes. Their garments were always of great richness, and one variety blended with another to such an extent that it is not easy to disentangle them. Long tight-sleeved gowns appear, often embroidered with armorial bearings, and having long pendent streamers hanging from the upper arm, as in the dress of men. We find also shorter kirtles, the tight sleeves of which were extended so as to cover the backs of the hands, combined with a close upper tunic. Another notable and later costume was composed of the kirtle with its girdle, the sideless garment known as the *cotehardi*, and the mantle fastened across the chest with cords, habits that endured for nearly two hundred years [Figs. 110 and 111]. The head-dresses were of great variety, the main characteristic being that the hair was braided and somewhat closely dressed with kerchiefs and frets of gold network. The ancient wimple was gradually passing away, and, after 1377, in harmony with the fopperies of Richard II's time, various extravagant kinds of head-gear appeared. The male dress of the lower orders consisted of short tunics, hoods, and hosen, the female dress of kirtles and upper tunics. Mourn-

FIG. 114. Hat of Nobleman, fourteenth century (Add. MSS. 12,228).

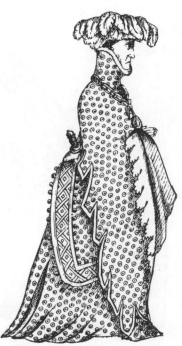

FIG. 115. Hat of Gentleman, fourteenth century (Royal MS. 15, D. i).

FIG. 113. Knight in Civil Costume, *temp*. Rich. II (Harl. MS. 1319).

ing habits in the form of long black mantles were introduced early in the reign of Edward III.

Luxury and extravagance in dress reached a climax during the reign of Richard II : the example set by the king and the court was imitated by all classes to such an extent that contemporary writers declared that it was impossible to distinguish rank from rank or rich from poor. The rhyming literature of the period may now be added to the evidence of the monuments and the MSS., and the pages of Chaucer vividly describe the dresses of all classes. The king of course outshone the courtiers in his coats embroidered with precious stones and various devices. His portrait in Westminster Abbey shows him in a robe decorated with his initial and roses, and in the Wilton House diptych his mantle is embroidered all over with his badge of the White Hart.

Certain garments, such as the *jupon* and *cote-hardi*, were worn alike in civil and in military costume, and this involves

FIG. 116. Gentleman in Civil Costume, early fifteenth century (Royal MS. 15, D. iii).

FIG. 118. Brass of lady of Clopton family, *c.* 1435 (Long Melford, Suffolk).

FIG. 117. Richard III when Duke of Gloucester (Royal MS. 15, E. iv).

a certain amount of overlapping of the two branches of the whole subject of costume, and causes in both cases a continual difficulty in presenting an absolutely consecutive picture.

It is clearly to be gathered that the nobility and upper classes continued to wear the short *jupon*, often party-coloured, with narrow waist-belt and tight sleeves, as well as the new-fashioned looser body-garment with full-hanging, slittered sleeves, one variety of which had skirts reaching to the ground [Fig. 112]. Beneath these was the under-tunic, with its long tight sleeves and cuffs spreading over the backs of the hands. The hosen were not in pairs, but party-coloured like the *jupons*, and at one time the long toes of fashionable shoes were fastened to the knees by light chains. Over all the men of rank wore in full dress a great full-sleeved gown, trailing on the ground, with a high collar fitting tight under

FIG. 119. From effigy of Lady de Thorpe, *c.* 1420 (Ashwell Thorpe, Norfolk).

FIG. 120. Horned head-dress, fifteenth century (Royal MS. 15, E. xlvii).

FIG. 121. Heart-shaped head-dress, fifteenth century (Froissart, Harl. MS. 4379–80).

FIG. 122. Turban head-dress, fifteenth century (Harl. MS. 2278).

FIG. 123. Steeple-cap, fifteenth century (Froissart, Harl. MS. 4379–80).

the chin and covering the ears [Fig. 113]. In fact, from the back view it was not easy to distinguish a man thus clad from a woman. Every edge of this garment was deeply *slittered* or cut into fantastic shapes, called 'cut-work'. Riders on horseback wore hoods, and 'cut-work', close, or loose caps, turned up all round and ornamented with a single feather in front [Fig. 114]. The most characteristic caps of this time were those supposed to have been formed out of the hood whose back-piece was bound round the head, with a broad piece gathered into the top, the full neck-piece being divided into strips in fan-fashion, with the edges *slittered* or jagged, such divided pieces either falling about in any direction, or carefully laid together on one side, while the long *liripipe* hung from the band and reached almost to the ground. This queer and characteristic head-gear is very

FIG. 124. CIVIL AND MILITARY COSTUME of the fifteenth century. Scene at a joust from Cotton MS. Nero, D. ix.

typical of the period, and long found favour [Fig. 115]. Similar forms of this costume were in use by all classes, the long *pokes*, or bag-pipe shaped sleeves, and short *jupons* being the distinguishing peculiarities of the time. The dress of the women of the upper classes was no less splendid and fantastic. It comprised the kirtle, with its narrow girdle for the *gypcière*, the plain or fur-faced *cote-hardi*, and the mantle embroidered with heraldry, mottoes, or devices.

The gathering of the hair into enriched cauls, over which was worn a chaplet, a coronet, or a veil, was the precursor of the more splendid tiring of like character that appears in the early years of the fifteenth century.

### 3.  *Period of York and Lancaster.*

With regard to civil dress from the beginning of the fifteenth century, many changes took place during the hundred

FIG. 125.  CIVIL AND MILITARY COSTUME of the fifteenth century.  Another scene from Cotton MS. Nero, D. ix.

years now to be touched upon.  In spite of sumptuary edicts regulating the length of gowns and sleeves, and the quantities of material to be used, the habits of men in the upper classes abated but little in their excess.  Sweeping fur-trimmed gowns, with long hanging sleeves, and capacious tippets with super-abundance of cloth, and the peculiar *slittered* caps, continued in vogue.  *Baudrics* of bells, worn transversely from the shoulder to the knee [Fig. 116], and gay girdles are notable items of festival apparel in the time of Henry IV and Henry V. The reign of Henry VI brought with it a mixed costume, in which were included very short tight jackets, pleated down the back, and girded round the waist, where the dagger hung in front, and having sleeves very full at the shoulders [Fig. 117]. We find also a long low-necked gown, with full hanging sleeves; tight hosen; square-toed shoes, or very long

Fig. 126. FIFTEENTH-CENTURY DRESS. Dames of Warling at the Court of the King of France. From Cotton MS. Nero, D. ix.

sharp-toed boots and shoes [Fig. 117]. The head-gear comprised the *bycocket*[1] with its feather in front, small close caps with short pendent bands, tasselled or fringed, and with a feather behind; and steeple-shaped or sugar-loaf felt hats, with brims flat, or turned up in various ways,

[1] The *bycocket* was perhaps identical with the ‘cap of maintenance’: the question has been discussed in *Archaeologia*, xlvii. 279. *Abacot* is a corrupt form which originated in the inclusion in the word of the article ‘a’.

and upright side-feathers. Towards the end of the century a simpler style of male attire began to be affected, and the short gowns and sober apparel of the middle classes in the reign of Henry VII had their origin in the last years of Edward IV. The wardrobe accounts of Richard III indicate how great a love of fine clothing pervaded the mind of this restless and ambitious spirit.

With regard to the habits of women during the fifteenth century, the kirtle with its girdle, the *cote-hardi*, and the long mantle or surcoat fastened with cords across the chest —*la surcote ouverte*—continued in favour [Fig. 111], the latter lasting indeed until far into the sixteenth century. But in the time of Henry VI full gowns with long and capacious sleeves, and open turned-over collars, sometimes showing the square-cut undervest, with very short, tightly girded waists, came into fashion [Fig. 118]. With the former costume the extravagant head-dresses continued. The hair was arranged in cauls to a great width on either side of the face, and surmounted by a coronet, or a chaplet, with precisely the same details as the military orles (cf. Fig. 162); over this a veil was cast, but hung down behind only, like a curtain [Fig. 119]. Another head-gear consisted of a light arrangement formed by a kerchief, often of transparent material, disposed so as to resemble a pair of square wings, supported apparently on a wire foundation [Fig. 111]. This was the delicate 'butterfly head-dress', which became fashionable about 1470 and prevailed for some twenty years. In other varieties of this time the tiring has less projection at the sides, but is elevated in the form of two thick horns [Fig. 120]. In the reign of Henry VI these forked coiffures became yet higher. Some took a heart-shape [Fig. 121], and full turbans of Italian fashion were also in use, the hair in some cases flowing through them and hanging down the back [Fig. 122]. The last-named head-dresses, and others, were worn with the short-waisted gowns which continued long after the middle of the fifteenth century. In the reign of Edward IV gowns were confined at the waist with broad bands, and gold chains were worn round the neck; the tall steeple-cap [Figs. 123 and 124] with long gauze veil flowing almost to the ground came in, and lasted with slight variations until the death of Edward IV—a graceful and picturesque costume. The steeple-cap, with modifications, survives in the holiday attire of some of the Norman peasantry. With the middle and lower orders hoods or kerchiefs were worn in the place of the dainty eccentricities of the upper classes. During the reign of Henry VII moderation in apparel, so long absent, is again discernible, but the extravagance still displayed at the funerals of the nobility and gentry led to the promulgation of his edict regulating expenditure on mourning. At the close of the fifteenth century the ancient wimple was reintroduced for aged gentlewomen, who often ended their lives in convents, where it was worn.

## 4. *Tudor Period.*

As to the civil habits during the Tudor period, there need be the less compunction in compressing a great deal into a small space, because we have now come into the light of day, and the surviving works of immortal painters have placed the originals before us with the perfection of art. The reproductions of the portraits of kings and queens, noble men and fair dames of the sixteenth century, have made their costumes almost as familiar to us as our own. Who is not well acquainted, for instance, with the appearance of Henry VII in his simple furred gown and square cap, as shown in his painted portraits, as well as in his bronze effigy in the Abbey; and with that of his comely queen, wearing the familiar pedimental headdress? Equally well known is the truculent personality of Henry VIII, standing wide, with his short hair, flat cap, black and gold embroidered shirt, puffed and slashed velvet, silk, or satin *hose-stocks*, coloured cloth hose—stocks and hose being now separated for the first time—and slashed broad-toed shoes, his burly body habited in embroidered crimson doublet with full sleeves, and velvet jerkin, heavy with gold and small lace, full of cut-work, and with or without sleeves attached by *points* or by buttons. When to this dress is added the *frock* of cloth of gold or silver, or one of the numerous varieties of gowns, the gorgeous figure is sufficiently complete; and so many portraits remain of the king that a great part of his wardrobe is quite familiar to us. The genius of Holbein has similarly made us acquainted with the costume of the king's six wives, and that of

Edward VI, both in painted pictures and in the priceless drawings in the Royal collection at Windsor, known as 'Holbein's Heads'. Queen Mary with her beautiful embroidered gown, jewelled petticoat, small hood, ruff, and *pomander* is well shown by De Heere's fine portrait in the possession of the Society of Antiquaries ; and as to Queen Elizabeth, in her great ruff, vast *fardingale*, the prototype of the crinoline, deep peaked and jewelled *stomacher* and ropes of pearls, what need to dwell on a costume that has been depicted a thousand times. We know from these sources that the queen's wardrobe was enormous and fantastic. But without such faithful evidence one might have been slow to believe that, even in that age of far-fetched conceits, any one would have worn, for instance, a dress embroidered all over with representations of human eyes and ears.[1]

The habits of the nobility and upper classes in the time of Henry VII had little of the simplicity affected by the king, though the garments were much the same [Fig. 127], consisting of shirt, breche, pettycote, doublet, long cote, stomacher, hosen, socks, and shoes. With this went a square cap, or, later, a very wide-brimmed hat, with drooping party-coloured plumes, worn on one side over a gold coif or caul that confined the long flowing hair. Sometimes we see the hat slung at the back. A specimen of female costume at this time is given in Fig. 128. Among the middle classes, the sober male apparel, originating as already mentioned in the last years of Edward IV, continued during the reign of Henry VII, when it comprised a plain coat, pleated down the front, a waist-belt for dagger and purse, hosen and shoes, a close hat with a gold band and, hanging over the shoulders, a long tippet.

The costume of the nobles and upper classes in Henry VIII's time followed that of the king in both form and richness, and has been in like manner fully illustrated. The fine portrait by Holbein, or Streetes, at Hampton Court of the Earl of Surrey [Fig. 129] is an excellent example, and shows him arrayed in scarlet of different depths. He wears a flat cap from which droops a single feather, white shirt,

---

[1] This conceit has reference to the old saying, repeated by Erasmus in his *Adagia* from Lucian and Aristotle : ' Many are the eyes and ears of princes '. Two circles composed of eyes and ears appear on the reverse type of a well-known jetton of Henry IV of France, dated 1609, with the legend, *servat vigilantia regna.*

*pinched* and laced and embroidered with black, a short doublet open in front, a full jerkin with very wide puffed and slashed sleeves, full *hose-stocks*, and hose and small banded and jewelled shoes. Sleeves, both for men and for women, were now separate articles of dress, and were of different colours and materials from the rest of the body-clothing; they were *trussed* at the shoulders by points. The

FIG. 127. Civil Costume, *temp*. Hen. VII (Harl. MS. 4939).

FIG. 128. Female Costume, *temp*. Hen. VII (Harl. MS. 4425).

waistcoat is first mentioned at the end of this reign: it was sleeved, and worn under the doublet. The ancient hood is now quite gone, and the flat hats were cut and slashed, and edged or laden with feathers as worn on the close-helmets of the time. Men of the middle classes wore plain doublets, low, narrow-brimmed hats, puffed *stocks*, and hose. In the time of Edward VI and Mary the small, flat, round bonnet continued in general use; it lingered long with apprentices, and was spoken of as 'the city flat cap'. It still survives at Christ's Hospital, and in the 'muffin cap' of the parish schoolboy. The stuffed *upper-stocks* of the middle of the century developed during the reign of Elizabeth into the large paned and slashed *bombasted trunkhose*; the doublet lost its skirts, and the body of it, by lengthening and quilting, was brought to the peascod shape, the whole, including the full divided sleeves, which showed the embroidered shirt, being richly laced and slashed. Hose

FIG. 129. Portrait of Thomas, Earl of Surrey, by Holbein, or Streetes, *temp.* Henry VIII (at Hampton Court).

FIG. 130. Portrait of Lord Russell of Thornhaugh, *temp.* Eliz. (at Woburn Abbey).

drawn up over the knee, a wide ruff, a brimmed and slightly conical hat, and a short cloak completed the dress [Fig. 130]. This costume continued, with slight modifications, until the reign of James I. Simple doublets, and *trunks*, or full breeches, of cloth, frieze, and canvas, were worn by the lower orders.

The ladies of the courts of Henry VIII and Elizabeth naturally followed the modes of the sovereigns. In the former reign the old-fashioned pedimental head-dress lingered, the paned lappets being at first pinned up at the sides and then modified into a smarter shape, and finally cut off; small French hoods, decorated with goldsmiths' work, and little bonnets of velvet, close hoods or cloth caps being worn by the middle and lower orders, with plain gowns and puffed sleeves. In the time of Elizabeth much ridicule was cast upon the vagaries of ladies' dress:

FIG. 131. Brass of Anne Reid, 1577 (St. Margaret's, Norwich).

FIG. 132. Brass of Matilda Grene, widow, 1462 (Green's Norton, Northants.).

on their laced and starched ruffs, *supportasses*, hoods, caps, kerchiefs, painted fans, ear-rings, and dyed hair; on their costly gowns, kirtles, scented gloves, corked shoes, velvet masks, looking-glasses, gold chains, and pomanders. This Italianate costume is found as the type of 'Vanity' in Emblem Books of the age. Some approach to moderation in dress is discernible in the middle of the reign; perhaps in consequence of the queen's commands respecting excess in apparel. The costume of the women of the middle classes, with its plain French hood, ruff, and gown with a little puffing at the shoulders, could hardly be simpler. As with the military so with the civil costume of the sixteenth century, the monumental effigies, no less than the painted pictures, supply an inexhaustible source of information [Fig. 131].

Margaret, Countess of Richmond, mother of the king, in 1492 issued an ordinance for her own household, regulating with great detail the mourning costume for each estate of women. Of these habiliments the pleated *barbe*, the surcoat, and the hood are the most important; they were of old standing, and are constantly shown in their varieties on monumental effigies, from the fourteenth until after the middle of the sixteenth century [Fig. 132]; the black hood *à calèche* and black gown and mantle taking their places before the end of it.

*Books for reference.*

See list on p. 193.

# V

# COSTUME, MILITARY

## 1. *Anglo-Saxon Period.*

ON the departure of the Romans, about the beginning of the fifth century, the Romanized Britons were in a higher state of civilization than their conquerors, the pagan Jutes, Saxons, and Angles, who, having raided the country during the fourth century, now obtained the mastery of Kent, and ultimately of the greater part of the island. We find from Old-English graves that straight-bladed, double- or single-edged iron swords [Figs. 133 to 135] suspended from leather waist-belts, single-edged knives, and iron-headed, seven-foot spears [Figs. 136–40] were the weapons of offence of these warlike intruders, and round, wooden and hide-covered targets,[1] with large convex iron umbos, those of defence [Fig. 144]. The two-handed axe [Fig. 142], reintroduced by the Danes, the stone hammer, the sling, and the bow and arrow [Fig. 143] were used by light-armed men of lower status. Helmets of leather, bronze, iron, or wood, with occasional crests of boars on the ridge, protected the head, the hair of which was worn long. The mail-shirt, short-sleeved and short-skirted body armour, is depicted in illuminations as though it consisted of rings placed close together and flat upon a tunic [Fig. 147]. This is only one mode of representing interlinked chain-mail among many used by artists from the thirteenth to the fifteenth centuries to indicate this same defence [Figs. 148–51]. For the armour, costume, manners and customs of the later Anglo-Saxons after their conversion there is evidence in their illuminated MSS. [Figs. 100, 101, and 144]. These MSS., however, must be used with caution. Many of them are copied from Frankish or late Roman originals and therefore are unreliable evidence for Anglo-Saxon armour and costume.

[1] Often of linden wood because of its lightness (cf. Skeat's *Piers Plowman*, ii. 28).

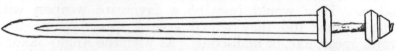

Fig. 133. Anglo-Saxon sword (Fairford graves, Gloucestershire).

Fig. 134. Anglo-Saxon sword with bronze mountings of sheath (Anglo-Saxon cemetery, Wilbraham, Cambridgeshire).

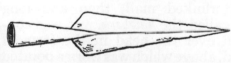

Fig. 135. Norwegian sword (Hewitt's *Ancient Armour*, 1855, i. 33).

Fig. 136. Anglo-Saxon leaf-shaped spear-head (Fairford graves).

Fig. 137. Anglo-Saxon ogee-shaped spear-head (found near Bredon Hill, Worcestershire).

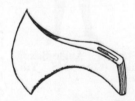

Fig. 138. Anglo-Saxon barbed spear-head (found at Sibertswold Down, Kent).

Fig. 139. Anglo-Saxon four-sided spear-head (Fairford graves).

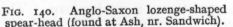

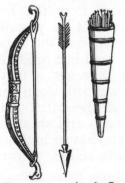

Fig. 140. Anglo-Saxon lozenge-shaped spear-head (found at Ash, nr. Sandwich).

Fig. 141. Anglo-Saxon taper axe-head (Anglo-Saxon cemetery at Ozingell).

Fig. 142. Norwegian axe (Gokstad grave-mounds).

Fig. 143. Anglo-Saxon bow, arrow and quiver (Cotton MS. Tib. C. vi).

The armour and costume of the Danish settlers in England developed generally in their new country into greater splendour than was affected by the Anglo-Saxons of the tenth century. The new-comers were expert bowmen, and famous for their skill in the use of the axe. Many of their swords were made in France, and had richly ornamented hilts, and their most prized helmets came from Poitou. They would inscribe a favourite weapon with *runes* ; often too they would give a special name to a sword, spear, axe, or mail-coat. As with the Anglo-Saxons, slingers played an important part in the Danish host. The shields of the Danes were circular, and painted with red and black and white and yellow, and even adorned with gold.

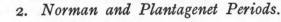

FIG. 144. Anglo-Saxon soldier (Cott. MS. Tib. C. vi).

## 2. *Norman and Plantagenet Periods.*

The priceless monument known as the Bayeux Tapestry exhibits with great precision the armour of the end of the eleventh century [Figs. 145–7]. The principal bodily defence under the Norman dynasty was the ringed tunic of interlinked mail, then and long after called the *hawberk*. It was continued over the head in the form of a hood, above which was worn a pointed helmet with a nasal and sometimes a neck-guard. This *hawberk* was the improved successor of the *guð-byrne*, or battle-shirt, of later Anglo-Saxon times. It perhaps came to us from the East,[1] and had its origin in remote antiquity. It is possible that some of the varieties of representation in the Tapestry and in illuminated MSS. indicate not mail but quilted defences. In the twelfth century *chausses* (breeches) of mail began to be used. The hair of the English was still worn very long, the Normans being distinguished in the stitch-work of the Tapestry by their close-shaven faces and short hair, which makes their heads look as though shaven high up at the back. Their shields were of the kite shape, a form derived from the Frankish and

[1] Sir Charles Oman doubts this. Layard, however, it is said, found the two specimens of it now at the British Museum in the ruins of Nineveh.

Byzantine shield, and in some cases were decorated with fanciful devices. The principal weapons used on both sides at Hastings were the broad-bladed sword, the mace, the seven-foot spear or lance ; the English alone used the two-handed Danish axe, a weapon that could cut off a horse's head or a man's leg at a single blow [Figs. 142, 147]. Like the Danes, the Normans were expert bowmen, and their archery contributed largely to the victory at Hastings [Fig. 145]. There were also men with axes and slingers in the opposing hosts at that battle. The armour and weapons of this time continued with little change till the close of the twelfth century, when the cross-bow and

FIG. 145. Norman archer, 1066 (Bayeux Tapestry).

FIG. 146. Norman horse-man, 1066 (Bayeux Tapestry).

FIG. 147. English axe-man, 1066 (Bayeux Tapestry).

quarrel appeared and remained in use until its final extinction by firearms. The trigger of the cross-bow was the distant ancestor of the elaborate mechanisms of the seventeenth-century firelocks.

We know from seals, sculptures, and illuminated MSS. that the usual military harness of a gentleman in the last years of the twelfth century consisted of a *gambeson* or quilted body-garment of leather or linen stuffed with wool, tow, or rags, and above it a long-sleeved hawberk with its attached hood drawn over the head and covering the mouth [cf. Fig. 148]. Under the hawberk or the gambeson was worn a small plate, known as the *plastron de fer*, to protect the chest. The mail sleeves ended in mittens with separate receptacles for the thumbs, and with a hole in the palm through which the hands could be passed so that the mittens might hang from the wrists when the bare hand had to be used. The hawberk was kept in place by straps interlaced in the mail round the brows and the wrists [cf. Fig. 148], the head being further protected by a

FIG. 148.    From effigy of Wm. Marshall, Earl of Pembroke, *d.* 1231.

FIG. 149.    From Gt. Seal of John.

skull-cap of iron worn under the hood, which usually had a flapped opening tied or buckled up over the ear [Fig. 148], and a thick woollen coif was worn to relieve the pressure of the mail hood and cap. Mail *chausses* were worn on the legs, tightened by straps below the knees [cf. Figs. 156, 159]; the heels were furnished with prick-spurs, and a surcoat reaching to just below the knee was confined round the waist by a strap (*cingulum*). A long and heavy sword was suspended from a broad transverse belt, in its turn supported behind by an attachment to the *cingulum*, and usually fastened to the scabbard in later times in a very curious and complicated way. On the left arm the knight bore a great *heater-shaped* shield, curved more or less to cover and protect the body, fastened to the arm by *enarmes*, or leather loops, and suspended by a *guige* (strap) that passed over the right shoulder [cf. Figs. 149 and 151]. Occasionally the *martel de fer*, a combined hammer and pick, was carried, in conjunction with a circular targe, and was used with great efficacy for breaking up the coats of mail and other defences, and thus making fatal openings for sword and lance. It is noteworthy that, almost through-out the twelfth century, the skirts of the tunic, long or short, appear below the hawberk, and not above it: the first and second seals of Cœur de Lion exhibit examples [Fig. 151]. The latter also gives an early instance of the cylindrical flat-topped helm, with the usual wooden or leather fan-cresting of the period. The seal of John [Fig. 149] shows him completely clad in mail, with a hood covering the mouth and drawn up to a rounded iron head-piece, and with a tunic, or, as it had now become, a surcoat, worn over the hawberk. This important change was of widespread intro-duction in the first years of the thirteenth century, and was intended, not so much to modify the heat of the sun's rays on the mail in Eastern climes, though that was one of its uses, as to protect the hawberk from wet and rust, to 'were hitte fro the wete', in damp northern regions. The twelfth-century head-piece, at first pointed or cone-shaped, with a nasal [Figs. 145–7], was changed later into a flat or round-topped iron cap, with a band below the chin, as may be seen in one of the earliest of the effigies in the Temple Church, that formerly attributed to Geoffrey de Man-deville, who died in 1144 [Fig. 150]. Finally, the flat-topped cylindrical helm, with a hinged *aventaille*, made its appearance about 1250, and lasted till the

FIG. 150.  From an effigy in the Temple Church.

FIG. 151.  From second Gt. Seal of Richard I.

end of the century. The helm was put on over the mail hood just before entering the fight. Prick-spurs [e. g. Figs. 149, 151] were worn until the middle of the fourteenth century, though the rowel was known in the thirteenth, and is seen, for example, on the second seal of Henry III and on the Botiler slab of 1285.

With the close of the twelfth and the opening of the

thirteenth century we enter upon a new and wide field of inquiry, and information regarding armour and costume may be best derived, first from the monumental effigies, to which later on the brasses must be added: the stone texts and brazen records which adorn English churches in such profusion, and illustrate the history of our subject with

a fullness unexampled elsewhere in Europe. These authorities are supplemented by the Great Seals of the kings, by the signets of minor personages, and by the precise and detailed and dated evidence of the illuminated MSS. Such will be the copious sources of information until the time of Henry VIII, when the pencil of Holbein and his successors place the living originals before us.

The ring mail-coat of the twelfth century endured not only throughout the thirteenth, but lingered for about twenty years into the fourteenth, the first changes being

FIG. 152. Brass of Sir John de Creke, c. 1325 (Westley Waterless, Cambridgeshire).

FIG. 153. Brass of Ralph, Lord Stafford, 1347 (Elsing, Norfolk).

the introduction of the separate mail-hood [Fig. 152], of small pieces of plate or *cuir-bouilli* at the knees and elbows, of slight modifications in form and addition in length to the surcoat, and such alterations in the details of the sword-belt as fashion dictated. It may be noted that the knee, being the most exposed part of a horseman, was the first portion of the body to receive plate. The *ailettes*, a picturesque addition to the harness of this period, appear to have been mere flimsy additions in *cuir-bouilli*, or parchment on wire frames, for the display of heraldry. They were painted with armorials, and the numerous examples on continental brasses clearly show that they had no significance whatever as items of defence. The cross-legged attitude of many effigies of the last half of the thirteenth century and the first half of the four-

teenth was a peculiar convention of English sculpture, and bore no reference whatever to the Crusades.

The most conspicuous garment of the knight in the thirteenth and fourteenth centuries is of course the surcoat, which in later times was usually embroidered or painted with the wearer's arms. As has already been stated, the surcoat, at first falling only to the knees [Fig. 149], became longer in the latter years of the thirteenth century, and at the end of the century reached such a length that men called upon

FIG. 154. Brass of John Cray, Esq., *c.* 1390 (Chinnor, Oxon.).

FIG. 155. Brass of Sir Geo. Felbrigge, 1400 (Playford, Suffolk).

suddenly to fight on foot sometimes got their legs entangled in its ample folds, and fell an easy prey to the enemy. The skirt was accordingly evenly reduced all round [Fig. 153], but even this amount of drapery was found to be an inconvenience. A new and strange garment was therefore formed by cutting away the whole of the front of the surcoat up to the middle of the thighs, slitting it up the sides to the hips, taking it in at the body, and lacing it on the right side [Fig. 152]. Thus was formed

N

the *military cyclas*,[1] which appears to have been a purely English invention. It did not long find favour ; the useless, flapping hinder part was an incumbrance, and it does not appear on more than twenty monumental effigies between 1321 and 1346. As early as 1340 this tail was cut off the cyclas [Fig. 153]; next the full skirt disappeared, and what remained of the surcoat was fitted tightly to the body, the lower edges of the garment thus formed were 'quainted' or dagged, it was laced up at the side, and the *jupon* made its appearance [Figs. 154, 155]. These six stages are remarkable features in the gradual change of fashion in the surcoat from long and loose to short and tight within two hundred years.

The military costume of the fourteenth century is, in point of artistic grace, more attractive to the student of armour than that of any other period. The growing desire for more splendid and less cumbrous defences led to the employment of several varieties of lighter armour, among which were the peculiar armour known as ' banded ' mail [Fig. 152], the construction of which has baffled antiquaries, *pourpoint*, studded or bezanted defence [Fig. 156], *jazerine*, scales, and *cuir-bouilli*. The use of these protections, combined with plate, brought about in the course of a hundred years the gradual extinction of mail, save as an auxiliary to plate, and produced a wonderful and interesting variety in armour. Of these fascinating panoplies, unfortunately, only a score of helms and helmets and a few isolated pieces of plate have survived to our day : a *coute* (elbow-cop), a *poleyn* (knee-cop), a cuff of a gauntlet, perchance a fragment of *jazerine* or a portion of a *camail*. The brass [Fig. 152] of Sir John de Creke (*c.* 1325) shows him in a quilted *gambeson*, over which is a short-sleeved hawberk of banded mail, with the upper arm strengthened by half-plates or *demi-brassarts* ; over the mail in succession are a *habergeon* of some stuff, with a scalloped edge, a *haketon* of either *pourpoint* or studded defence, and a *cyclas*. Over the mail-hood, which is apparently, as in the old style, continuous with the hawberk, a fluted bascinet, with an ogee top (a rare form) and an ornamental coronal or *prente*, is worn. The forearm is further protected by *vambraces* or *avant-bras*, and lion-faced disks and *coudes* defend the

[1] Rock, *Textile Fabrics*, p. 27.

shoulders and elbows respectively. He has mail *chausses*, reinforced with *demi-jambes* (greaves) ; while *genouillères* or *poleyns* defend the knees, and *demi-sollerets* the outer sides of the feet. A small shield is borne on the left arm, and rowelled spurs are now usually worn, to avoid inflicting dangerous wounds on horses. This is an elaborate and highly curious military costume of many items, and it well exemplifies the rapidity with which the time-honoured panoply of the thirteenth century gave way before the exigencies of extravagant fashion and the advancing require-ments of military men. No doubt the man also wore beneath the four body-garments at least the leather *cuire*, the *cuera* of the Spaniards, to keep off the pressure of the plate. In their hurry for change the knights rushed from one extreme to another. The sword-belts, the changes and details of which throughout the Middle Ages are alone sufficient to form a volume of much artistic interest, were now in a similar state of transition ; they were generally attached to the scabbards by metal *lockets*. The beautiful alabaster effigy of John of Eltham (1334), in Westminster Abbey, exhibits him in armour much more advanced than that of Creke. He wears the *hawberk, haketon,* and *cyclas,* but no *gambeson* or *habergeon,* and has old-fashioned prick-spurs. His bascinet is fitted with its *camail,* and the transverse sword-belt has progressed in style. A few years later the *miséricorde* [Fig. 154] was introduced, and from this time forward it is never lost sight of as an essential weapon of a knight. This was a long, narrow-bladed dagger used to slip between or under the plates of armour, or through the *ocularia* (vizor-holes). The effigy of Sir John de Lyons (1346) at Warkworth, in Northamptonshire, shows slight further changes ; a *gambeson,* a sleeved *haketon,* and a *cyclas* are worn. It is at this time that the *cyclas* vanishes, as explained above, by the simple process of cutting the back skirt level with the front. The skirted *jupon* thus formed is well illustrated in the small figures of Lord Stafford [Fig. 153] and of Lord Hastings on the brass of Sir Hugh de Hastings (1347) at Elsing, in Norfolk. From this tight-fitting and short-skirted transitional body-garment to the *jupon* proper was but a step ; and no doubt all the three docked forms of the surcoat, the *cyclas,* the tailless *cyclas* (or skirted *jupon*), and the *jupon*, were worn on the glorious field of Crécy in 1346. The shield, carried by knights from time immemorial and displayed on their recumbent effigies, ceased to appear soon after the middle of the century, and occurs last in the brass of William de Aldeburgh (*c.* 1360). The *jupon*, which had its origin in civil dress, is first seen as a military garment about 1340, overlapping, in the usual way, for a few years the disappearing *cyclas* and skirted *jupon*. Specially associated with it is the *baudric* or horizontal belt worn across the hips [Fig. 154]. This was no longer sustained at the back by the ancient subsidiary *cingulum* or waist-belt, which now passes away with the longer surcoats it girded, but apparently was looped up with hooks at the back or sewn to the *jupon*. As a civil belt it was in being as early as 1335, the *anelace*, a heavy, broad-bladed, sharp-pointed, double-edged knife, about two feet long in all, which appears frequently in the brasses of civilians, being slung from it; in its military capacity it supported the sword, which was fastened close up to it, and the *miséricorde*. The change was not popular, and the transverse belts held their ground until the middle of the century, when the girdler's art reached its culminating point. Like the surcoat and the *cyclas*, the *jupon* had its

FIG. 156. From brass of Sir Miles Stapleton, 1364 (formerly of Ingham, Norfolk).

slight accidents of shape, finally taking the typical form well shown by the latten effigy (1376) of the Black Prince at Canterbury, and by hundreds of routine alabaster and stone effigies and brasses, of the last quarter of the fourteenth century and the first quarter of the fifteenth, throughout the kingdom [Fig. 154]. During this half-century the knightly equipment consisted of a pointed bascinet with an attached *camail*; articulated plates on the shoulders; *arrière-bras* and *avant-bras* (or *rerebraces* and *vambraces*) of plate, for the upper and lower arms respectively; and cuffed gauntlets, with *gadlings* on the knuckles; while *cuisses, jambes*, and articulated *sollerets*, all of plate, protected the legs and feet, which were furnished with rowelled spurs.

The body was clad in a mail hawberk, of which a small portion appeared below the *quainted* edge of the *jupon*, the latter often being embellished with the arms of the wearer on back and front. The emblazoned *jupon* was in fact the forerunner of the military *tabard*. Over all was clasped the elaborate baudric, with its manifold variety of decorations, sustaining the sword and *miséricorde*. This was a beautiful and graceful equipment, but the delicacy of the details is only to be realized by a close study of effigies and illuminated MSS. [Figs. 154, 155]. During the fourteenth century the helm [Fig. 157] was worn in battle and tourney over the Assyrian-like *bascinet* and *camail*, when the latter headpiece was not furnished with a vizor. It is clear from the moderate arch of its bottom curve, and from seals and illuminations, that this fourteenth-century helm did not rest on the shoulders, as did later fifteenth-century helms, but was probably wadded inside so that it might fit closely to the bascinet. It was secured to the front of the cuirass by a chain, and may have been also fastened to the back of the cuirass by a strap. Bascinets with a beak-shaped vizor appeared in the last quarter of the century, and some half-dozen actual examples have been preserved [Fig. 158].

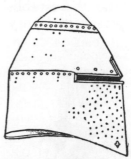

FIG. 157. Tilting helm of Sir Richard Pembridge, *d.* 1375 (Exhib. Archaeol. Institute, 1880).

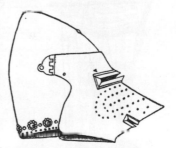

FIG. 158. Bascinet with pointed vizor, *c.* 1400 (Exhib. Archaeol. Institute, 1880).

In military equipment there was a steady continuance of the change which, starting from the accession of Edward II in 1327, had settled into the *camail* and *bascinet* type as shown in the effigy of the Black Prince [cf. Figs. 153-6]. The *camail* was merely the surviving lower half of the mail coif. The cord which secured the *camail* to the *bascinet* ran, for safety, in a groove in the latter. This is clearly expressed in the Felbrigge brass [Fig. 155]. A loose *jupon*, introduced from Burgundy, was frequently worn,

but does not appear in monumental effigies. It is here
to be noted that, in the literature of the day, old terms for
defences of mail were frequently used in speaking of portions
of armour of plate or of *cuir-bouilli* (then much employed),
and that fashions in armour constantly overlapped.

### 3. *Period of York and Lancaster.*

After the establishment of the House of Lancaster, in
the person of Henry IV, in 1399, the gradual swallowing

FIG. 159. Brass of ...
D'Eresby, *c.* 1410 (Spilsby, Lincs.).

FIG. 160. Brass of
Sir John Lyale, *c.* 1420
(Thruxton, Hants).

FIG. 161. Brass of
Sir John Barnard, 1451
(Isleham, Cambs.).

up of mail by plate continued ; and within ten years of
the beginning of the fifteenth century the *camail* had been
reinforced by a high gorget of plate [Fig. 159], of the same
form as the old mail protection, of which latter a few links
at first appeared below the edge of the new steel defence.
Extended articulated shoulder-pieces often with distinct
*pallets* [Fig. 160], now defend the *vif de l'auberc*—known

in later times as the *défaut de la cuirasse*—at the armpits, and mail appears only below the *taces* which, with the breastplate and back-piece, a true 'pair of plates', have taken the place of the *jupon*, and now protect the body. The *taces* were overlapping hip-bands, generally hinged on the left side and buckled on the right, overlapping upwards. The horizontal *baudric* is now clean gone, and a narrow transverse belt sustains the sword and *miséricorde* [Fig. 160]. A few years later the tassets have increased in number, and mail is no longer visible. The man is now 'locked up in steel', and the change from mail to plate in a hundred years has been complete and remarkable. During the reign of Henry V the decorated *orle* or wreath for diminishing the pressure of the helm is to be observed round the *bascinets* [Fig. 162], and small *tuilles* begin to appear, hung in front from the lowest *tace* [Fig. 163]. These were the forerunners of the larger *tuilles* or *tassets* [Figs. 164–6] which were well established, together with the *cuirasse à emboîtement*, when Henry VI had been twenty years on the throne. The larger hanging *tuilles* took the place of the lowest hoop of the taces, and by falling closer to the thigh prevented a weapon from getting under the taces. The *cuirasse à emboîtement* was formed of two portions, which respectively covered the chest and the midriff; the lower half, known as the *demi-*

FIG. 162. From effigy of Sir Robert Goushill, *c.* 1425 (Hoveringham, Notts.).

FIG. 163. From brass of Roger Elmbrygge, Esq., *c.* 1435 (Beddington, Surrey).

*placcate*, overlapped the upper, and was connected with it by a strap or a sliding rivet, so that the body could be bent with comparative ease. The gilt latten effigy at Warwick of Richard Beauchamp, Earl of Warwick, who died in 1439 [Figs. 164, 165], with its reinforced shoulder-guards—it was the period *par excellence* of reinforcements—and great left elbow-piece, is an admirable illustration. The *bascinets* of this time, which gradually approached in form to the close *armets* [Fig. 167], and in a less degree

to the *salades* [Fig. 168] or open helmets of the middle of
the century, rarely had vizors; and the earlier ones were
decorated at the apex by a single feather stuck in a tube.
The form of the helms, with their *panaches* or *pennaches*
[Fig. 170], crests, wreaths, and mantlings [Fig. 169], is
well ascertained from those shown beneath the heads of
effigies and brasses. Later fifteenth-century helms were

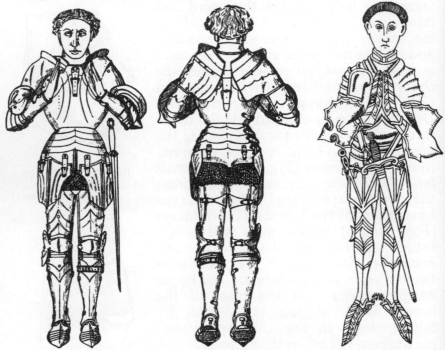

FIGS. 164 and 165. Effigy of Richard Beauchamp,
Earl of Warwick, *d.* 1439. Date of armour, *c.* 1450
(St. Mary's, Warwick).

FIG. 166. Brass of
Thos. Peyton, Esq.,
1484 (Isleham, Cambs.).

deeply curved at the bottom, so as to fit closely down
to the shoulders, and were firmly fixed to both chest
and back. The head could move inside them, and as
they did not touch it there was less vibration from blows
[Fig. 171]. For knights, archers, and other soldiers alike
*jazerine* continued in use for lighter adjuncts of armour,
as also did *brigandine*, which was its reverse in construction,
having the metal splints inside instead of outside the
material. In the latter part of the century the quilted *jack*

appeared, often stuffed with mail. This was the legitimate ancestor of the Elizabethan *jack* with steel plates sewn into it : the ' stiel cotte ' of the Musters of Armada times. An interesting point in the consideration of armour is the accuracy with which the smallest details of the actual remains, naturally increasing in number as we come later, are corroborated by historical evidence and faithful monu-

FIG. 167. Helmet, *c.* 1450–80 (Exhib. Arch. Inst., 1880).

FIG. 168. Salade and Bavier, *c.* 1450–90 (Exhib. Arch. Inst., 1880).

FIG. 169. From brass of Sir Nicholas Dagworth, 1401 (Blickling, Norfolk).

FIG. 170. From brass of Lord Ferrers of Chartley, *c.* 1412 (Merevale, Warwickshire).

ments in village churches.[1] It is evident that *tilting* armour began to be differentiated from *hosting* array soon after the beginning of the fifteenth century. During the reign of Edward IV the high plate gorget [Fig. 159] gave way to the moderate standard of mail [Fig. 173] or of plate [Fig. 169], and the vizored *salade*, with its *mentonnière*, or more properly *bavier* [Fig. 168] came in. The Yorkist Collar of Suns and Roses, with the pendent badges of

[1] e.g. the fine series of windows at Long Melford. Vide *Trans. Royal Hist. Soc.*, xvi. 178.

the different royal houses such as York, March, and later Beaufort and Tudor, now appeared beside the official Lancastrian Collar of SS. [Fig. 161], which had its unknown origin when Henry of Lancaster was a boy. Again pressing forward, we shortly meet with representations of an oft-quoted garment, the tabard (already spoken of as a descendant of the military jupon), with its fourfold picture of arms on front, back, and flap-sleeves. It first appeared late in the reign of Henry V, the sleeves or wings being then mere 'flappers', but is rarely seen in monuments before the end of the fifteenth century. The standards[1] of mail [Fig. 173], globular breastplates [Figs. 166, 173], great channelled shoulder-guards [Figs. 166, 173], and reinforcing pieces [Figs. 161, 164–6], upright neck-guards [Fig. 174], very large elbow-pieces [Figs. 161, 164–6], long pointed tassets or tuilles and sollerets [Fig. 166], vizored armets, the lower part of which opened out on hinges [Fig. 167], and salades with baviers[3] fixed to the breastplate [Fig. 168], long-necked spurs,[4] and ponderous swords hung directly in

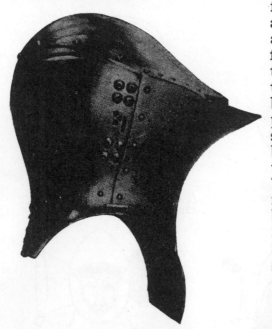

FIG. 171. TILTING HELM,[2] late fifteenth century (at Haughton Castle, Northumberland).

---

[1] A very early example of a mail standard (1341) is shown in *Archaeologia*, xviii (1814) : effigy of Louis, Count of Clermont.

[2] See, too, *Proc. Soc. Ant.* 1912–13, pp. 163 et seq. ; ibid., p. 16, fig. 2 (first half of the fifteenth century) ; ibid., xviii. 74 (second half of the fifteenth century).

[3] See an interesting note on this in Douce's *Illustrations of Shakespeare*, pp. 269–73.

[4] Necessitated by the use of horse armour. The *flanchards* (iron vallance)

front [Fig. 166], are characteristic features of armour of the middle and latter part of the century.

Almost concurrent with the rise and course of the change from mail to plate was the origin and gradually increasing employment of gunpowder. The explosive itself, and its manner of use, derived indirectly from the Greek Fire of the twelfth and thirteenth centuries ; and the later heavy plate was designed not only for the tournament, but also as a protection against the ' newfangled bullets ' rather than against pikes, bills, or arrows. A ball from a hand-gun was found to drive mail into the body, thus making

FIG. 172. From brass of Roger Elmbrygge, Esq., c. 1435 (Bedding-ton, Surrey).

FIG. 173. From brass of Rich. Quatremayne, c. 1460 (Thame, Oxon.).

FIG. 174. From brass of John Den-gayn, c. 1460 (Quy, Cambs.).

a bad wound. The first recorded mention of cannon is in 1326, and the use both of powder and of cannons is well established by documentary evidence of the second quarter of the fourteenth century. Side by side, therefore, with the increase of plate arose cannon which cast *quarrels* and stone balls and at the end of the fifteenth century the hand-guns [Fig. 175] began, little by little, to win the upper hand and break up the magnificent suits of steel which the armourers had conceived with so much skill. The new weapons slowly changed the art of war, and eventually, after the lapse of two hundred years, caused armour to be entirely abandoned save as a glistering item of parade. In the meantime the heavy suits, unaffected by the new artillery, for they were now designed for tilting not for warfare, reached their climax of perfection, the armourers along the horse's sides kept the rider's heels at a distance from the animal's flanks.

being encouraged in their efforts during the early years of the sixteenth century by the friendly rivalry of three chivalrous and sumptuous monarchs, Henry VIII, Maximilian, and Francis I. Heavy armour, in its turn, then gradually declined.

### 4. *Tudor Period.*

The military equipment of the last years of the fifteenth century and the first of the sixteenth had not quite the refine-

FIG. 175. Hand-gun man, fifteenth century (Burney MS. 169, fo. 127).

ment of its immediate forerunner, yet it would be difficult to criticize adversely the magnificent fluted suits of the time. The *tuilles* are now shorter, and mail reappears, after the absence of a century, in the form of a skirt worn under the *tuilles* [Fig. 176]. Apart from the beauty of the fluted breastplates, the flexible gauntlets, and other pieces, attention must be called to the workmanship of the close-helmets, with their plain, cable, or serrated combs, and complicated so-called *bellows-vizors* — real masterpieces of the pure working of iron with hammer and anvil which have never been surpassed [Fig. 177]. Doubtless the glory of armour of this period centres in the tilting suits, of which such magnificent examples are preserved at Vienna. Very fine suits, however, together with specimens of the jousting lance, may be seen in the Tower ; some of them the actual equipment of Henry VIII. The adaptation of armour to the fashion of the puffed suits of this period marks the special *dégringolade* of the ancient art, though some forms of armour had already, centuries before, followed those of civil dress. Military costume of every grade is well shown in the pictures at Hampton Court illustrating the Field of the Cloth of Gold and the events connected with that prodigal display. Important characteristics of the armour of Henry VIII's time are the salient *lamboys*, fluted steel skirts or *bases*, suspended from the waist, with some-

FIG. 176. Suit of fluted armour, *temp*. Henry VIII (Meyrick Collection).

FIG. 177. Fluted close-helmet, *c.* 1510–25 (Museum of Artillery, Woolwich).

FIG. 178. Bases or Lamboys, *temp*. Henry VIII (in the Tower).

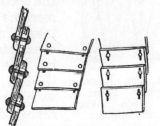

FIG. 179. Sliding rivets profile, front and back, sixteenth century (in the Tower).

times a semicircular space left in front and behind for wear on horseback [Fig. 178]. These partially took the place of the *tuilles*, but were used only to a limited extent. Their place, as well as that of the *tuilles*, was taken by the series of over-lapping plates, playing freely on rivets one over the other,

[Fig. 179]. The pike was introduced into England during this reign, and the disuse of armour in warfare was now steadily progressing throughout Europe, the general tendency being for plate armour not to extend below the knees, save in the suits for the tournament.    The halberdiers wore full-feathered flat hats and corslets, and guarded the colours, while, after the enemy had been broken by archery, ' shot ',

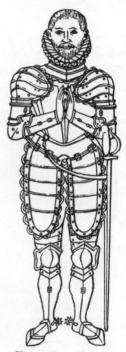

cavalry, or pikes, the black-billmen, with their murderous weapons, did ' the slaughter or execution of the battle '. The Elizabethan breastplate *par excellence* took the form of the peascod doublet of civil dress, with its *tapul*, or ridge down the centre[1] [Figs. 180; 130].    The old vizored *salades* have quite passed away, as have also in their turn the fluted close-helmets, with the bellows-vizors of Henry VIII's time.    The close-helmets that gradually succeed exhibit the comb which becomes such a conspicuous feature in the *burgonet* with its *buffe* or chin-piece [Fig. 181], and other head-pieces with their *cinquecento* decorations [Figs. 182, 183], just after the middle of the sixteenth century.    The high-combed *morions* [Fig. 182] were worn by pike-men, and the peaked and spiked *cabassets* [Fig. 183] by musketeers, because the formation of the brims of

Fig. 180. Brass of Humphrey Brewster, Esq., 1593 (Wrentham, Suffolk).

the latter did not impede the sight. Those worn by officers were often of elaborate *repoussé* work, and engraved with Renaissance details.    Such were the head-pieces specially associated, as many a picture shows, with the ' spacious times of great Elizabeth '. *Morions* and *cabassets* of both kinds for common soldiers were made either plain or with large *repoussé* fleurs-de-lis of German and Italian fashion on the sides.    With the combed close-helmets of this period must be mentioned the powerful and beautiful suits of tilting

[1] It has been suggested that this form was believed to cause bullets to glance off.

armour, of the style shown in Jacobi's book, made for Leicester, Hatton, Sir Henry Lee, and other royal favourites. Reflexions of such suits of harness, *armure de parade*, are to be seen on monumental effigies of the time [Fig. 180]. *Carabines, petronels, arquebuses*, corslets (i.e. breast- and back-plates), and bandoliers belong to this period; while the sleeveless and waistless buff jerkin, afterwards the famous buff coat of the Civil War, came into general use for pikemen, arquebusiers, musketeers (whose longer, heavier weapon was superseding the ar juebus), and *targiters*, early in the last quarter of the sixteenth century. The last-named were light infantry of the Spanish type, carrying only a sword

FIG. 181. Burgonet with Buffe, *c.* 1515–30 (Exhib. Arch. Inst., 1880).　　FIG. 182. Morion, *temp.* Elizabeth (Exhib. Arch. Inst., 1880).　　FIG. 183. Cabasset, *temp*. Elizabeth (Exhib. Arch. Inst., 1880).

and target, and without armour. Their targets being shot-proof, they received the enemy's fire, and before he could reload attacked at close quarters, getting also if possible inside the guard of the pikemen.

From this point we can only refer generally to such portions of armour as still survived.[1] We may note that arquebusiers of the Civil War period wore a striking form of helmet, to the *umbril*, or peak, of which was fixed a triple bar, a light form of vizor [Fig. 185]. By statutes of 1672 and 1673 horsemen were ordered to wear breastplate, backpiece, and pot-helmet [Fig. 186], and to carry a sword and pistols; musketeers were to have a musket, bandoliers, and

[1] The final discarding of armour may be read of in Firth's *Cromwell's Army*. See, too, the article by Julian Corbett, ' Firearms and Armour ', *Longman's Magazine*, 1899, p 157, referred to by Firth, p. 121, n. 5.

sword ; and pikemen, back, breast, pot, pike, and sword.
In the time of William III the lately embodied carbineers
wore breast- and back-pieces and iron skull-caps (the ' privy
cap of fence ' of the time of Henri Quatre), sewn into the
crown of their felt hats. The sublime periwig is constantly
represented in statues and pictures of the early years of
the eighteenth century as worn with the cuirass (akin to

FIG. 185. Pot-helmet, temp.
Great Civil War (Meyrick Collection).

FIG. 184. Effigy of
Sir Denner Strutt,
1641 (Warley, Essex).

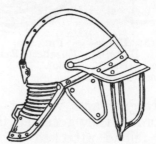

FIG. 186. Lobster - tailed
Burgonet, *temp*. Great Civil
War (Exhib. Arch. Inst., 1880).

the Roman *lorica*), which had come to be a mere convention
of the pseudo-classic sculpture of the time. The effigy
(1707) of Sir Cloudesley Shovel in Westminster Abbey is
a typical example. The plate gorget, then a mere flat collar,
continued to be worn over the buff coat during and after
the Civil Wars. It remained in ever-decreasing dimensions
until the present day, now assuming the form of a small
lunated-shaped brass plate, the badge of certain favoured
cavalry regiments and the last remnant in legitimate
descent of the ancient warlike panoply of the Middle Ages.

## Books for reference.

### (Chapters IV and V.)

FAIRHOLT, *Costume in England*, 3rd edition by Dillon, 2 vols. (Bohn Series), 1885.
—— *Satirical Songs and Poems on Costume.* Percy Society, 1849.
PLANCHÉ, *History of British Costume*, 3rd edition (Bohn Series), 1893.
—— *Cyclopaedia of Costume*, 2 vols., 1879.
DEMAY, *Le Costume au moyen-âge d'après les sceaux*, Paris, 1880.
*Sketch-Book of Willard de Honnecourt*: A. Darcel, Paris, 1858; also by R. Willis, 1859.
SHAW, *Dresses and Decorations of the Middle Ages*, 2 vols., 1843.
LUARD, *History of the Dress of the British Soldier*, 1852.
SCOTT, SIBBALD, *The British Army : its Origin, Progress, and Equipment*, 3 vols., 1860–80.
FORTESCUE, *History of the British Army*, 2 vols., 1899.
HEWITT, *Ancient Armour and Weapons in Europe*, 3 vols., 1855.
DEMMIN, *An Illustrated History of Arms and Armour*, translated by Black (Bohn Series), 1877.
MEYRICK, *Ancient Armour in Europe*, 2 vols., 1830.
DE COSSON & BURGES, ' Ancient Helmets and Examples of Mail ', *Archaeological Journal*, 1881.
FFOULKES, C. J., *Armour and Weapons*, 1909.
—— *The Armourer and his Craft*, 1912.
LAKING, SIR GUY, *Arms and Armour*, 5 vols., 1920–2.
BURTON, *The Book of the Sword*, 1883.
HAINES, *A Manual of Monumental Brasses*, 2 vols., 1861.
DRUITT, *Costume as Illustrated by Monumental Brasses*, 1906.
BOUTELL, *Monumental Brasses and Slabs*, 1847.
—— *The Monumental Brasses of England*, 1849.
STOTHARD, *Monumental Effigies of Great Britain*, 1817.
HOLLIS, T. & G., *Monumental Effigies of Great Britain*, 1840–2.
HARTSHORNE, C. H., *Sepulchral Monuments*, 1840.
—— ALBERT, *Monumental Effigies in Northamptonshire*, 1875.
—— —— ' The Sword-belts of the Middle Ages ', *Archaeological Journal*.
COTMAN, *Engravings of Sepulchral Brasses in Norfolk and Suffolk*, 2 vols., 1839.
FRANKLIN HUDSON, *The Brasses of Northamptonshire*, 1853
WALLER, *A Series of Monumental Brasses*, 1842–64.
MACKLIN, *Monumental Brasses*, 1892; also *The Brasses of England*, 1907.
BLOXAM, *Companion to Gothic Ecclesiastical Architecture : Ecclesiastical Vestments*, 11th edition, 1882.
MACALISTER, *Ecclesiastical Vestments*, 1896.
DILLON, *An Almain Armourer's Album*, 1905.
ENLART, C., *Le Costume* (vol. iii of his *Manuel d'Archéologie Française*), Paris, 1916.

FIG. 187. ARMOUR AND HERALDRY: middle of thirteenth century (Cambridge MS. Ee. 3. 59), showing for armour Helms, Helmets, Maces, Pommels, Surcoats, Saddles, Housings, the Panache, and Battle-axe.

# VI
## HERALDRY
### 1. *Origin of Armory.*

THE use of heraldic insignia is only one of the many manifestations of symbolism which we find prevalent in all periods and among all races. The same instinct of individual

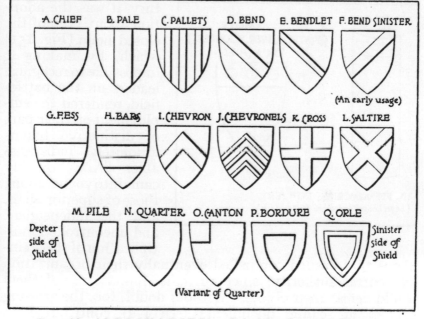

FIG. 188. 'ORDINARIES' or Primitive Armorial Bearings.

display or of social and military expedience that prompts the tattoo of a savage and the totem of his tribe, and in a higher environment is exemplified in the personal devices assigned by classical art and literature to the heroes of the Trojan War, or in the eagle of Rome and the ensigned shields of her cohorts, lies also at the root of that special and minutely organized system of pictorial language, the mediaeval ' armory' of Western Europe. In the list of purchases for the Tournament of Windsor Park in 1278 *blazona* is the term used for a shield. *Blazon*, which is a word of uncertain derivation, was used first of a shield, then of the bearings on it, then of the description of the bearings. It was in France, probably the original home of the tournament, that coat-armour was first subjected to scientific regulation; consequently most of the technical terms of heraldry are of French origin, and it was from France that it was imported into England as a science, though as yet at an immature stage. But whatever influence natural impulse or passing fashion may have exerted in the promotion of this form of symbolism prior to the thirteenth century, it was the adoption about 1180 of the closed helm [Fig. 151] which, by making it impossible to recognize leaders on the battlefield, rendered the employment on their part of distinctive tokens absolutely indispensable. 'Arms' quickly came into vogue among those of superior birth, and the independent and uncontrolled multiplication of these em-

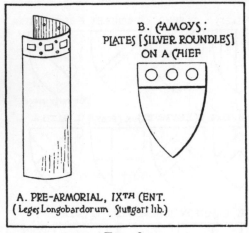

B. CAMOYS: PLATES [SILVER ROUNDLES] ON A CHIEF

A. PRE-ARMORIAL, IX^TH CENT. ( Leges Longobardorum Stuttgart lib.)

FIG. 189.

blems that ensued compelled eventually their organization by central authority, since an indiscriminate use of them would defeat their object. Without doubt, too, the growing custom of sealing documents (see § 2) contributed to induce regularity in bearings, as also did the establishment of inherited surnames about the same period (see Canting Arms, p. 223).

Considerations of convenience, and the feelings of pride and veneration which attached to symbols associated with the exploits of ancestors or relatives, combined to fix heraldic insignia mainly on a hereditary and family basis, into which nevertheless there also entered to a considerable extent the element of connexion by tenure; while, to avoid confusion even within these limits, coats were further distinguished as regards seniority and degrees either of kinship or of matrimonial or feudal alliance, by marks of cadency or by differences respectively. It may be that the Crusades, bringing together as they did large numbers of the upper classes of Europe, assisted the tendency to organization by illustrating its necessity with striking clearness ; the tournaments also, which in England became the mode in and after the thirteenth century, and which originally were open only to the armigerous of four generations standing (see under Paternal Arms, § 3), doubtless helped towards the same end : and distinction acquired in the Holy Land or in the joust aided in the conversion of temporary or personal into permanent and hereditary insignia. Indeed, instances exist in which, on the introduction of armory, a personal device previously used by an individual was directly, or in some modified manner, made to serve as the armorial bearing of his family. Naturally, universal fixity of custom did not immediately come into operation, and we find cases before 1300 not only of the canon of he-

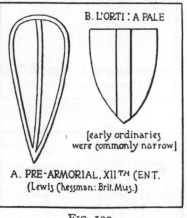

FIG. 190.

redity in coats being disregarded, but of the same person using different coats at different times, many of which appear later as subsidiary quarterings. In the *Dictionarius*, too, of John Garland, written at some time after 1218, is a passage which seems to show that the capricious and unrestricted assumption of undifferentiated armorial devices had not disappeared in the first quarter of the thirteenth century : ' The shield-makers [of Paris] serve the towns throughout France and England, and sell to knights [*militibus*] shields . . . on which are painted lions and fleurs-de-lys.' This appears to indicate that, side by side with the rise of individualism in armory and its gradual organization, we have the continued existence of the state of things illustrated a generation earlier in the *Itinerary of Richard I*, where, in the description of the king's advance from Ascalon in 1192, we read that shields were adorned, seemingly wholesale, with 'fiery red prowling lions or golden flying dragons', thus showing little general advance in the Third Crusade beyond the fashions of the Bayeux Tapestry. In the political poem 'Versus de Guerra Regis Iohannis' 'shields of various colours' are mentioned as being used at the Fair of Lincoln in 1217, and, though not certain, it is likely that these were heraldic. The explanation doubtless is that fixed and organized armory began with the most prominent leaders in war, and took time to work downwards to the mass of those of gentle blood. Still, in the thirteenth century irregularity was exceptional, and at the opening of the fourteenth century the hereditary principle may be regarded as completely established.

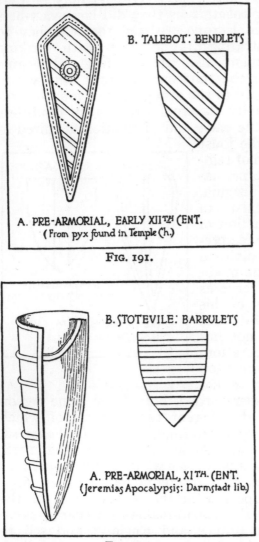

B. TALEBOT: BENDLETS

A. PRE-ARMORIAL, EARLY XII TH CENT.
(From pyx found in Temple Ch.)

FIG. 191.

B. STOTEVILE: BARRULETS

A. PRE-ARMORIAL, XI TH. CENT.
(Jeremias Apocalypsis: Darmstadt lib.)

FIG. 192.

The chief peculiarity, then, of mediaeval armory, as compared with earlier or other symbolical usages, is that the former, owing to the above causes, was subjected to an organization with definite and detailed rules, enforced ultimately by official control, that it was mainly heritable in character, and that it became the badge of a specific social position. Its mainspring is to be found, not simply in the love of symbolism, which is instinctive, but in the need for its widespread employment in the most serious of human activities, war, and therefore for its reduction to a set system.

'Arms' were so called from their being originally depicted upon the most conspicuous portion of the defensive armour, the shield. To assist in the leading of larger bodies in war, and for recognition at a distance, they were

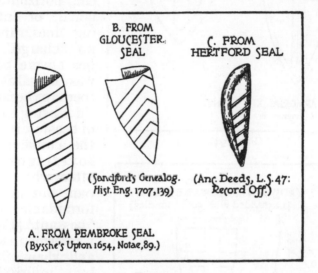

Fig. 193.

in addition displayed on banners. After 1200, when, owing to improvement in armour, the shield began to diminish in size, it became the practice to embroider them upon the various styles of surcoat worn at successive periods till the fifteenth century [e.g. Figs. 153, 155; hence arose the phrases 'coat of arms' and 'coat-armour'. Devices on war-shields were painted flat and unshaded, and sometimes were embossed in relief on *cuir-bouilli*. The characteristic of the earliest armorial bearings is simplicity and boldness of design and strong contrast of colours. Thus they well fulfilled their primary purpose of readily indicating, even in the dust, confusion, and excitement of battle, the identity of the bearer.

A large proportion of these primitive coats is composed of figures formed by various arrangements of straight lines, known in heraldic language, from their frequent appearance, as the 'Ordinaries' [Fig. 188, A–Q]. Many, however, of the oldest armorial shields are merely bi-coloured 'fields' divided into two or more compartments by vertical, horizontal, diagonal, or intersecting lines, and bear no 'charge'. If a beast were borne, it was usually a lion (perhaps because, besides being the 'king of beasts', it was also the emblem of the sovereign), which often, when not rampant but in the less formidable posture of 'passant' [Fig. 230], was termed a leopard, and when it lost size by multiplication, beyond three at any rate, a *lioncel*. Objects obviously emblematical explain themselves, and the admission into armory of animals, and many other charges that subsequently appeared, is intelligible enough : but there is more uncertainty about the meaning of the ordinaries and certain other of the early devices, the symbolic purport of which is not evident, which cannot well, except quite occasionally, be 'canting' signs (see § 3), and which are not sufficiently decorative to justify

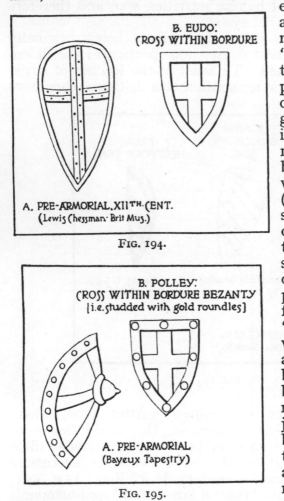

B. EUDO:
CROSS WITHIN BORDURE

A. PRE-ARMORIAL, XIITH. CENT.
(Lewis Chessman. Brit Mus.)

FIG. 194.

B. POLLEY:
CROSS WITHIN BORDURE BEZANTY
[i.e. studded with gold roundles]

A. PRE-ARMORIAL
(Bayeux Tapestry)

FIG. 195.

their being looked upon as purely ornamental. It has therefore been thought that most of the ordinaries were not arbitrary abstract inventions of geometrical permutation and combination, but that they had a concrete

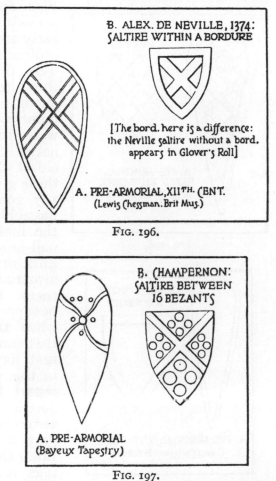

B. ALEX. DE NEVILLE, 1374:
SALTIRE WITHIN A BORDURE

[The bord. here is a difference:
the Neville saltire without a bord.
appears in Glover's Roll]

A. PRE-ARMORIAL, XII TH. CENT.
(Lewis Chessman. Brit Mus.)

FIG. 196.

B. CHAMPERNON:
SALTIRE BETWEEN
16 BEZANTS

A. PRE-ARMORIAL
(Bayeux Tapestry)

FIG. 197.

origin in the structural requirements of the more primitive and larger pre-armorial shield; and that when shields became smaller and probably less clumsily made, these constructional aids were no longer necessary, and remained only as dummy survivals (after the wont of obsolete things) which were utilized, however, for armorial purposes. As Freeman put it, 'The real necessities of one age become the mere tradition of a later'. Wood as a rule formed the principal element in the composition of the mediaeval service-shield, and the boards, leather-covered or not, that constituted the body of it, were in pre-armorial times strengthened by wooden or iron clamps, strips, and crossbars, and by studs, nails, or rims of metal. Such stays and knobs are seen upon representations of shields anterior to the age of systematized armory, and it was not unnatural that they should have been, as we know they were, gilded or silvered, or fancifully painted another colour than that of the rest of the shield, as was often the case with the later non-armorial shields in armorial times : somewhat as the frame-timbers of houses and as studded and iron-bound doors were treated. It is the old story of decorated construction, which is universal.

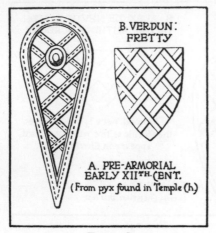

B. VERDUN :
FRETTY

A. PRE-ARMORIAL
EARLY XII TH. CENT.
(From pyx found in Temple (h)

FIG. 198.

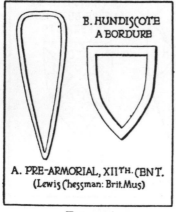

B. HUNDISCOTE
A BORDURE

A. PRE-ARMORIAL, XII TH. CENT.
(Lewis Chessman: Brit. Mus)

FIG. 199.

Figs. 190–8 show braced pre-armorial shields by the side of early armorial shields bearing ordinaries, which originally were drawn narrower than they afterwards became when, owing to the increase in the number of coats, diminutives were multiplied and ordinaries charged. Among the oldest charges too are found those given in Figs. 189, 195, 197, 200–3, all of which may possibly have originated in the highly important metal nail-heads, rivets, boss-nuts, and cramps of the pre-armorial shield shown beside them. It must not, of course, be supposed that such charges, when they appear in coats that came into being after the first days of armory, arose in this way : without doubt (apart from the element of heredity or connexion) some symbolical reference or mere play upon words then dictated the choice of the bearings (see § 3). Sometimes charges apparently were suggested by artistic forms that had been wrought out for other purposes and were pressed into the service of armory. Particularly does this seem to have occurred in the case of many of the numerous designs of the cross, the popularity of which was possibly enhanced by the Crusades ; but the prototypes of some shapes are to be found in the metal braces referred to above [e.g. Figs. 194–7].

To revert to the Ordinaries, the *bend sinister* indicates early usage, for as time went on there arose a mistaken notion that it was a sign of illegitimacy, an error, referred to by Petra-Sancta in 1638, which probably originated in the fact that the debruisement of a coat by a bendlet sinister became one of the marks of bastardy in the later Middle Ages ; though how early that fashion appeared is uncertain. The *canton* was at first only another term for a *quarter*, but in later days was drawn smaller than its full share, probably in the first instance to clear it from other bearings when they became more numerous or complicated. As to the charge known as the *bezant* [Fig. 195], this was a natural term to apply to the gold roundel as the want of English gold money occasioned the circulation of that coin here, and it was therefore a familiar object. It appears in the earliest Roll of Arms, that is, 'Glover's Roll', *c.* 1240–5.

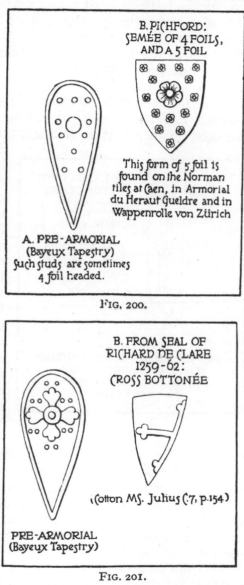

**B. PICHFORD:** SEMÉE OF 4 FOILS, AND A 5 FOIL

This form of 5 foil is found on the Norman tiles at Caen, in Armorial du Heraut Gueldre and in Wappenrolle von Zürich

A. PRE-ARMORIAL (Bayeux Tapestry) Such studs are sometimes 4 foil headed.

FIG. 200.

B. FROM SEAL OF RICHARD DE CLARE 1259–62: CROSS BOTTONÉE

(Cotton MS. Julius C.7, p.154)

PRE-ARMORIAL (Bayeux Tapestry)

FIG. 201.

## 2. *Early Armory: Sources of Evidence.*

Among the earliest quite trustworthy armorial evidences are those found on seals, which came gradually into general use after the Norman Conquest, at a time when there was a perpetual shifting of landed property, and comparatively few of the laity at least could write. How the custom had spread downwards by the end of Stephen's reign may be seen from the sneer of the Justiciar, Richard de Lucy, recorded in the Chronicle of Battle Abbey : ' In old times it was not the fashion for every knightling (*militulus*) to have a seal, which befits only princes and great men.' This is borne out by a grant of Geoffrey de Mandeville, second Earl of Essex (*d.* 1165), in which occurs the passage, ' Istam cartam feci signari sigillo dapiferi mei . . .

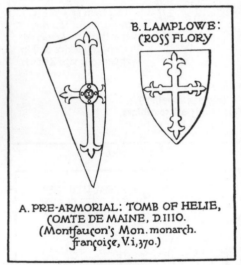

B. LAMPLOWE: (ROSS FLORY

A. PRE-ARMORIAL: TOMB OF HELIE, (OMTE DE MAINE, D.1110. (Montfauçon's Mon. monarch. françoise, V.i,370.)

FIG. 202.

donec sim miles et habeam sigillum, et tunc eam firmabo proprio sigillo '. By Henry III's time, however, if not before, a seal had become an essential part of a deed, and seals themselves had become largely armorial. Thus, whereas before the rise of heraldry in the twelfth century devices on seals had been arbitrary, the inscription alone denoting the possessor, the application to them of armory and their widespread use were contemporaneous move-ments. Necessarily persons not entitled to armorial bearings, yeomen, merchants, and the like, continued to use unheraldic seals. Indeed, the affixing of seals in lieu of signatures continued, perhaps because the forgery of a seal was more difficult than that of an autograph, long after the art of writing had become relatively common, and survives in the conventional seals still placed on many legal instruments. King John could write, but he did not sign, he sealed Magna Carta ; and the first royal sign-manual of which a specimen exists in England is that of Richard II. After about 1520 the combination of seal and signature, which often appears before that date, became the almost universal practice, though it was not till 1677–8 that signatures alone were made legally necessary in deeds concerning real property, and heraldic seals did not even then disappear from them at once. Thus the witness of seals extends over something like 600 years.

Since armorial seals would not be extensively used in legal transactions until armory was fairly organized, they are not the oldest evidences, but their heraldic importance is obvious, for the devices thereon must be those claimed, and accepted as borne, at the time of impression, seeing that they are the acknowledged representatives, as it were,

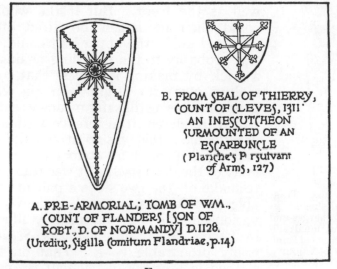

B. FROM SEAL OF THIERRY,
COUNT OF CLEVES, 1311·
AN INESCUTCHEON
SURMOUNTED OF AN
ESCARBUNCLE
(Planche's P rsuivant
of Arms, 127)

A. PRE-ARMORIAL; TOMB OF WM.,
COUNT OF FLANDERS [SON OF
ROBT., D. OF NORMANDY] D.1128.
(Uredius, Sigilla comitum Flandriae, p.14)

Fig. 203.

of the bearer. Moreover, as a rule, the owner's name, and sometimes that of his father, is inscribed round the margin. The frequent breaking, or recasting, by the heir of the metal die of his predecessor still further narrows the limits of identification. Metal dies were generally made of brass, latten, bronze, or lead, occasionally of silver, more rarely of steel or gold. Jet, porcelain, horn, bone, ivory, and stone were also used. Impressions of seals were taken in beeswax, brown, red, green, yellow, black, or white: the first four being the commonest. In shape, before the thirteenth century, they were generally a pointed oval, the *vesica*, which had a religious origin, and when afterwards the seals of laymen commonly assumed a circular form, ecclesiastics for the most part adhered to the pointed ellipse. The impress was made either *plaqué* (or *en placard*), that is, on the face of the document, or was suspended to the deed by a parchment label or a silk cord. Various methods were adopted to lessen the facility of fraudulent removal from one document to another. A common device for preventing a seal *plaqué* from being detached was to make cross cuts in the parchment, turn back the tongues thus formed, and press the wax on the spot so that it was forced through the orifice and appeared on the back of the deed as well as the front. But if the whole seal could then no longer be lifted off with a heated knife, the upper half could, and it was probably to the guarding against such a trick by making it useless that countersealing owes its origin. In the case of pendent seals a still safer means was devised which rendered transference wellnigh impracticable : this was to attach the seal or seals to a pendulous strip cut out of the body of the deed itself. It was thus possible to make on the two sides a pair of inseparable impressions, as with a coin. These various methods are admirably illustrated in Lecoy de la Marche's *Les Sceaux*, an easily procurable book. That on the inscribed face of the instrument is known as the seal or the obverse of the seal, that on the back as the counter-seal or the reverse of the seal, the two being regarded as constituting together a single seal. Another term for the obverse was ' the authentic ', and for the reverse the *Secretum* or ' privy-seal '. The latter came into use apparently after about 1170. Both were usually the same shape and size, but often the counter-seal, which almost invariably bore a different design, was smaller. The *Secretum* was not necessarily used only as a counterseal. The severe punishment of abjuration of the realm is on record as having been inflicted for counterfeiting the seal of another person ; and when a matrix was lost the

FIG. 204. Transitional shield : armorial charges and constructional radiated boss. (Tomb of Geof. of Anjou(?), *d.* 1151, father of Henry II: Le Mans Museum.) Cf. shield of unidentified effigy in Temple Church.

owner gave public notice of the fact, and sometimes repudiated it, lest the finder, or the thief, might turn it to his own purposes. The seal of a dead man was placed in a box, or purse, closed under the seals of three 'honest persons', and in due course was defaced, as we have said, by his heirs or executors. The care bestowed on the safeguarding of seals adds to the authenticity of their evidence.

A seal might be either official or personal. The former furnishes proof of arms attached to a public office, secular or ecclesiastic, and such also would be the ' Common

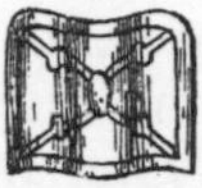

FIG. 208. Non-armorial, late fifteenth century: h a n d - t a r g e t (Monbijou Palace Museum, Berlin).

FIG. 205. Non-armorial, close of thirteenth century (Add. MSS. 11639, f. 520).

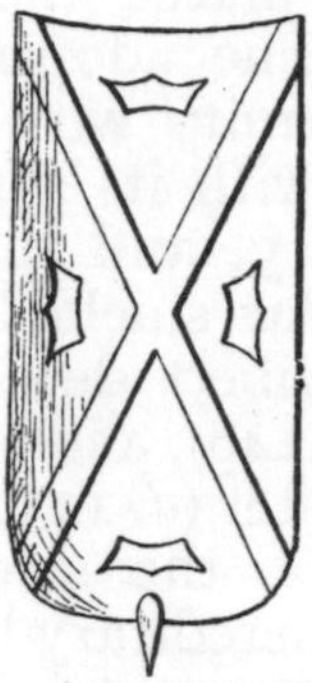

FIG. 206. Non-armorial, fifteenth century: archer's pavois, apparently with sight-holes and handholes, for shooting kneeling (Arsenal of Berlin).

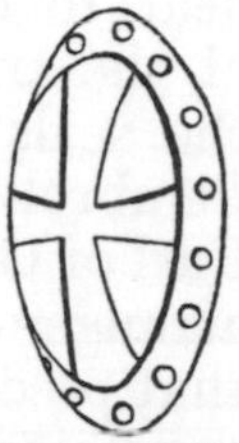

FIG. 207. Non-armorial, sixteenth century: foot-soldier's shield (from the Weisskunig).

FIG. 209. Non-armorial, sixteenth century: hand-buckler (Triumphs of the E m p. Maximilian, Pl. 37).

*Note.*—These five figures show ancient pre-armorial methods of strengthening still in use in later non-armorial shields.

Seal ' of a corporate body or of a religious house. The latter would show the personal coat, or the badge, or both, of its possessor. Official arms naturally came into existence only for business purposes. Among official seals it is to be noted that the first Great Seal of Richard I (c. 1189), the first in which a king of England is represented with the closed helm, is also the first which displays on the shield an armorial bearing [Fig. 210]. It is a lion rampant sinister, which seems to be facing a second lion that is invisible, owing to the shield being in profile ; the couple forming the position termed combatant, or counter-rampant.

This is confirmed by two contemporary writers. William Brito, in his Latin poem *Philippis*, makes William des Barres say of Richard, who was then count of Poitou. ' I recognize the gaping jaws of the lions on his shield ' ; and in the *Itinerary of Richard I* we read that at the interview between the king and Isaac, Emperor of Cyprus, in 1191, the saddle of the former was decorated with ' a pair of golden lioncels facing one another open-jawed, one forepaw of each extended towards the other [beast] as though to rend it '. To his second seal, struck in 1198, he added the third lion, but placed the animals passant gardant as now [Fig. 151]. The adoption of a triad of lions may have been in conformity with the taste for the mystic number three, which, with its square nine, was so dear to heraldry, and to which the shape of the triangular shield lent itself. From the seals of Gilbert de Clare, first Earl of Pembroke (*d.* 1148), and of Gilbert de Clare, Earl of Gloucester (*d.* 1230), we see how one arrangement of the strengthening bands that preceded hereditary bearings may have suggested a later coat. It is in Stephen's reign that the first beginnings of armorials are seen. The Pembroke seal [Fig. 193, A] shows the long Norman kite-shield, with the gabled top of that period, stiffened by bars which follow the direction of the gable, thus forming a succession of chevrons, or rather chevronels, as they came to be called later ; and in a seal [Fig. 193, C], *c.* 1138-48, of another Gilbert de Clare, first Earl of Hertford (*d.* 1152), five narrow gabled ribs are indicated on the shield. Bars were a natural and not uncommon contrivance for binding together a large shield, but from the coincidence of this form of clamp appearing on the shields of two contemporaneous members of the same family in the infancy of heraldry, it seems probable that we have here a very early instance of the practical appliance being put to the symbolical use which was in time wholly to supersede it. The Gloucester seal which we reproduce [Fig. 193, B] is subsequent to the general adoption of armory, and shows the familiar, and by that time well established, Clare coat of three chevrons. It may be mentioned that the helmets

FIG. 210. From First Seal of Richard I.

on the Pembroke and Hertford seals are open, while the helm on the Gloucester shield is closed. The 103 seals appended to the duplicates of the letter of the barons of England to Boniface VIII in 1301, objecting to his intervention in the English claim to the overlordship of Scotland, are a valuable body of evidence as to the arms of the leading men of the kingdom at that date. There are only nineteen counter-seals : this may give an idea of how far countersealing was then prevalent. Two copies of this document are preserved in the Record Office. In the British Museum, too, there is a large collection of early seals. An early *Sigillum* and *Contra Sigillum* or *Secretum* is that used by Peter de Mauley, fourth Baron Mulgrave, in signing the above letter to the Pope [Fig. 211]. Actually this was the seal of his father, as the legend on the seal will show. The field of the shield and housings are diapered with scrollwork. An interesting specimen of a matrix is the silver seal of Thomas de Prayers, *c.* Edward II [Fig. 212]. The loop of the handle works a screw which projects the centre of the matrix, so that an impression may be taken with or without the surrounding legend ' *Sigillum* ', &c. ; further, the centre may be screwed off, when a smaller matrix appears for counter-sealing. This last seemingly is the coat of his mother, who was a Verdun [Fig. 198]. The star shows the point where the screw-motion ends, and also which side to turn uppermost when impressing.

Of great value, though not altogether so trustworthy as that of seals, is the testimony of monuments, stone, metal, wooden, or glass. These being sentimental, not legal, in their origin, were of less practical importance, and mistakes in their case might more easily escape immediate notice, and were more likely to be allowed to remain uncorrected. An early incised slab exhibiting armorial evidence is that (*c.* 1285) of Sir John le Botiler. He bore three covered cups, two of which are repeated on the plate skull-cap worn over his mail-coif [Fig. 213], a foreshadowing of the later crest. The name and charge arose from the office of king's butler long held by his family. A later slab, displaying considerably more heraldry, is the semi-effigial monument (1346) of Sir John Daubygne [Fig. 214]; and a brass which furnishes a profusion of information as to kinship and alliances is that (1391) of Lady

Willoughby de Eresby [Fig. 215]. These three monuments illustrate the growing custom of placing armorial records on tombs. The gilding, white metal, and coloured resins and enamels that were employed in the armorials of many brasses have rarely survived the wear and tear of time ; for although found on walls and altar-tombs, brasses were usually laid down in pavement-slabs as a substitute for the more expensive and obstructive stone monuments in effigy or in relief, and so were subjected to the friction of thoroughfare. The expansion and contraction of the metal would also contribute to the loss of the colouring matter. But where armorial windows have escaped demolition, the hues of the coats are often preserved for us ; though, owing to certain difficulties connected with glass-painting, and the changes and fading they undergo in course of time, these are not always accurate. As a sample of a window record we may instance that (*c.* 1485) to the wife of John Peyton of Suffolk [Fig. 216], in which her costume tells us

FIG. 211.    Seals of De Mauley, *Baron's Letter*, 1301.

both the name of her husband and her own maiden name ; for, as is not uncommon before 1500, the coat-armour of her family is depicted on her kirtle and that of her husband on her mantle, symbolizing her estate as a *feme covert* and protected, i. e. a married woman. After the above date the impaled arrangement, borrowed from the shield, is more usual, the *baron's* (husband's) arms being on the dexter, the *feme's* on the sinister side of the mantle [Fig. 217]. Fig. 218 shows an impaled arrangement by which the arms of the *feme* are displayed on her mantle, and those of the *baron* on its turned-back lining. When the arms are on the mantle only, or are the same on both mantle and kirtle, they are those of the lady's house.

Other, though less prolific, sources of evidence are found in illuminated MSS. as early as Henry III's time, and in altar-cloths and priestly vestments, upon which the arms of patrons were frequently embroidered : on the border of the Syon cope (*c.* 1300) [Fig. 330], now in the South Kensington Museum, some sixty coats are worked in colours ; while the stole that belongs to the same set of robes is adorned with forty-six, and the maniple with eighteen. Here may be noted the collection of arms (*temp.* Hen. V to Hen. VII) carved on the roof of the cloisters at Canterbury Cathedral, and the stall-plates, prior to 1500, of the Knights of the Garter in St. George's Chapel, Windsor.

FIG. 212. Seals of Thomas de Prayers *Archaeologia*, xxix. 405.

Of the highest value, too, are the Rolls of Arms and similar armorial collections which contain lists of the bearings of the royal family, the nobility, and other gentry. Some of these were schedules of the arms of persons present at particular sieges, tournaments, &c. ; some were general catalogues of coats in use, to which class belong the first three of the Rolls about to be described. 'Glover's Roll ', perhaps the earliest of all, takes us back to 1240–5 and contains 218 coats. The original is lost, and we have only a copy made in 1586 by Robert Glover, Somerset Herald. This does not give drawings of the coats, merely blazes them, but in so doing supplies the tinctures, which seals do not till long after the invention of the dot and line method [Fig. 219], a contrivance in use on the continent as early as 1600, but, so far as is known, first adopted in

England in 1654, when it appears in Bysshe's edition of Upton (see § 3). Where pigments have been applied to monuments of stone and wood they have often, like those on brasses, become obliterated through destruction or decay. Some Rolls, however, do provide coloured drawings, as in the case of 'Charles's Roll', a fifteenth-century copy of a Roll of *c.* 1280–95. Since, although not contemporary, this is an early transcript, we may take it as a specimen.

FIG. 213. Sir John le Botiler, *c.* 1285 (slab, St. Bride's, Glamorgan).

FIG. 214. Sir John Daubyngne, 1346 (slab, Brize Norton, Oxon.).

It is composed of four membranes of vellum, about a foot wide, sewn together so as to form one long slip of $8\frac{1}{2}$ feet. The 486 shields, each superscribed with the bearer's name, are arranged nine abreast in fifty-four rows. This Roll derives its name from its owner, Nicholas Charles, who was Lancaster Herald in the reign of James I. Another, known as 'St. George's Roll', containing 677 coats, is a transcript made in 1607 by Charles from an old Roll (then in the possession of Sir Richard St. George, Norroy), also of about 1280–95. This will supply a representation of 'tricking',

that is, sketching arms in outline and indicating the colours
by letters, which was practised as far back as the fifteenth
century [Fig. 220]. In tricking, where the same charge
occurred more than once on a shield, often only the first
was drawn, the places of the rest being marked by the

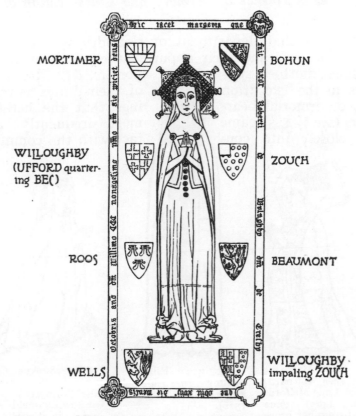

MORTIMER

BOHUN

WILLOUGHBY
(UFFORD quarter-
ing BE())

ZOUCH

ROOS

BEAUMONT

WELLS

WILLOUGHBY
impaling ZOUCH

FIG. 215. Margaret, daughter of William, Baron Zouch, and
wife of Robert, Baron Willoughby de Eresby, 1391 (brass, Spilsby,
Lincolnshire).

figures 2, 3, &c. One of the most interesting Rolls is the
famous *Le Siège de Karlaverok*, a Roll of Arms and Chronicle
combined. It is a metrical account, in the debased Anglo-
French of the time, of the siege of the castle of Carlaverock,
on the Solway, by Edward I in July 1300, and gives the
blazons of 106 bannerets and knights who mustered on
the occasion. The earliest series of contemporary dated
drawings of shields of arms will be found in the *Historia*

*Minor* of Matthew Paris, who died about 1259. An account of a number of both published and unpublished Rolls will be found in *The Genealogist* for 1881. Some have been printed since.

### 3. *The Accidence of Armory and Classification of Coats.*

Armory is that department of Heraldry which relates to coats of arms and their appurtenances, such as crests, mantlings, mottoes, sup- porters, &c. ; but since it was in the execution of their duties as regu- lators of armorial bear- ings that the heraldic officers (see §§ 4, 5) came most frequently and most closely into con- tact with the commun-

FIG. 216. Margaret Peyton [*née* Barnard] (window, Long Melford, Suffolk, *c.* 1485). Face restored from her brass at Isleham, Cambridge-shire.

FIG. 217. Elizabeth Shelley [*née* Michel-grove] (brass, Clapham, 1526).

FIG. 218. Anne Coun-tess of Stafford [*née* Ne-ville] (formerly in North window,LichfieldCathe-dral, 1480. See Dingley, *Hist. from Marble*, II. ccclxiii).

ity, and since many of their other functions gradually fell into disuse and oblivion, Heraldry and Armory have in vulgar parlance practically become convertible terms : or rather the former has in its application been narrowed down to the latter, while the latter, unfortunately, is in some danger of fading into an archaism. The scope of this Section, which is concerned in the main with Heraldry in its connexion with History, does not admit of or necessi-tate our entering into the details of what is known as the

Accidence, or Grammar, of Armory: the vast mass of rules and provisions, extending from broad principles to minute and complicated refinements, that constitutes the science of blazonry. This is readily accessible in a host of works, large and small, elementary and advanced. A list of some of the most useful and easily procurable of these is given later.

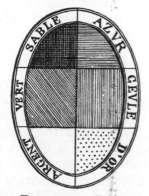

FIG. 219. Tincture points and lines (Bysshe's *Upton*, 1654, but originally from the *Armorial Chart of the Duchy of Brabant*, by Langrius, 1600).

It is clear from the descriptions of the coats in the oldest Rolls that a code of accepted custom, the variations in which are but slight, regulated the practice of blazonry 150 years before the first extant treatise on the subject was written in this country, and nearly 250 years before the incorporation of the College of Arms in 1483. The earliest heraldic works known to have been produced in England were the *Tractatus de Armis* of *Iohannes de Bado Aureo* ('John of Guildford', a pseudonym: *Bado* is for *Vado*) and the *De Studio Militari* of Nicholas Upton, who was possibly the author of both. The former was composed at the suggestion of the 'Good Queen Anne', first wife of Richard II, and was finished at some time after her death in 1394; the latter, dedicated to the 'Good Duke Humphrey' of Gloucester, the Maecenas of the age, was completed probably before August 1436; neither was printed till 1654. These are in Latin. The first book printed in England that deals with armory, *The Boke of St.*

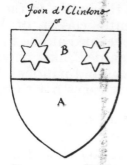

FIG. 220. Trick of Arms: A = argent, B = azure (*St. George's Roll*).

*Albans*, is in English, and appeared in 1486. The authorship of the armorial portion, which is based in part upon Upton, is uncertain. The fact that one of the earliest productions of the English press was a treatise on armory testifies to the importance and popularity of the subject. Among the heraldic MSS. in the possession of the writer is an early sixteenth-century translation by John Blount of the *De Studio Militari*.

A fundamental principle, imperative for the practical purposes of armory and therefore jealously guarded by both the officials and the bearers of coat-armour, was that no two persons should use the same arms ; and that this yet unwritten law was early recognized and enforced is manifest, among other proofs, from the extreme rarity of repeated coats among the many hundreds contained in the Rolls, and from the cases of contested coats that occur ; while, on the other hand, the small number of these cases affords additional evidence to the same effect. Mention is made in the Carlaverock Roll of a disputed coat, when, 'many, man and woman, marvelled' that two persons should bear the same ; and a judicial combat over a coat is recorded a few years later, in 1312. These controversies naturally arose on the occasion of military expeditions, when the similarity or the irregular assumption of coats would be readily detected ; and the action taken by the Crown in the fifteenth century (see § 5) for the regulation of armorial bearings was due, not to a sentimental regard for the rights of private possession or to a sense of moral outrage at the unwarranted use of coat-armour, but to sheer military necessity. Owing, indeed, to intercourse in the battle, in the crusade, and in the tourney, among the gentle classes of Western Europe, the laws of armory developed at one time to some extent a tendency to become regarded like chivalry and knighthood, not merely as local and national, but as catholic and European ; though this seems not to have applied to countries between which a third nation intervened, as convenience in war was less likely to be affected. Thus, that the bearing of the same arms or the same device, even by a foreigner, was upon occasion viewed with resentment, can be seen, for instance, in the angry words that passed between Sir John Chandos and the Marshal of Clermont on the day before the battle of Poitiers ; or in an episode of that period where a Frenchman challenged to combat a Genoese for displaying the same charge as himself, the head of an ox, the Italian escaping from his dangerous situation by protesting that the head on his shield was only that of a cow.

Coats, when classified according to their nature and origin, fall fairly conveniently into ten divisions, with a little unavoidable overlapping here and there. The first

four are 'Public', the rest 'Private Arms'. (1) Arms of
Dominion are those attached to dominions, and are borne
by sovereigns as such on their escutcheons, flags, seals, &c.
They are not family coats. (2) Arms of Pretension (i. e.
*claim*) are those of dominions not actually possessed by the
bearer, but to which he lays claim. Thus Edward III, who at
first quartered the fleurs-de-lis of France as Arms of Alliance,
in token of his maternal descent, after the lions of England,
on laying claim to the French crown shifted them to the
senior position, France being considered the more ancient
and more important kingdom, and bore them as Arms of
Pretension. They continued to be borne by the English
sovereigns until 1801. It may be noted that Richard II
sometimes bore England quartering France instead of the
reverse. To this class, or to Augmentations, may be referred
the arms of an heiress's family borne (after her father's
death and if there be issue) expectantly, on behalf of the
children, by her husband 'in pretence', i. e. on a smaller
shield in the centre of his own, the former indicating the
claim. This was not a common mediaeval practice, but
is found as far back as the fifteenth century. (3) Arms
of Community are those of corporate bodies, such as cities,
universities, religious houses, societies, and the like. They
are often derived from the coats of founders, benefactors,
or former members of distinction [e. g. Fig. 221]. Under
this heading may come the arms of sees borne by their
bishops : a bishop being a 'corporation sole', as opposed
to a 'corporation aggregate'. (4) Arms of Office or Official
Dignity are those connected with official appointments.
They can be borne alone, or impaled with the personal arms
of the occupant, the dexter, or more honourable, half of
the shield being given to the coat of office as perpetual.
Such are those of the Kings of Arms [Fig. 222] ; and
those of bishoprics may be placed either under Class 3
or here. A bishop is considered as wedded to his see
(*maritus ecclesiae*), and his personal coat may be impaled
with that of the diocese, but to the sinister. Although this
arrangement appears in the '3d Parliament Roll' of 1515,
and is found indeed as early as 1396 (see § 2), it was a fashion
uncommon before the Reformation, but is in accordance
with an old occasional custom of placing the wife's arms
first if she were of higher rank or greater estate. When

a bishop dies *eius ecclesia dicitur viduata*. In his will, dated 1464, Archbishop Boothe leaves 'my mitre and pastoral staff to the cathedral church of York, *sponsae meae*'. A peculiarity of the personal arms of bishops in the days of celibacy before the Reformation was that they need not be debruised with marks of cadency, because ecclesiastics could not have legal issue. (5) Paternal Arms are those that descend from the first possessor to his posterity. By heraldic tradition perfect 'nobility' (*gentlehood*) was only acquired after inherited arms had been borne for four generations (cf. p. 197). This was in accordance with the formula *quia sanguis non purgatur usque ad quartum*. Supposing an *Atavus*, or great-great-great-grandfather, had 'obteined cote-armor by his desert', the first to inherit

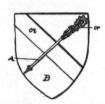

the coat would be his son, the *Abavus*, in whom the arms were said to be 'begun', and who was regarded as a 'gentleman of coat-armour', as was his son, the *Proavus*, in whom the arms 'grew'; in the next generation the arms were 'completed' in the *Avus*, who thus became a 'gentleman of blood', as was his son, the *Pater*; while the *Filius* of the last was the first 'gentleman of blood perfect', who, if he could reckon five armigerous descents on his mother's side

FIG. 221. Arms of the Monastery of St. Agatha, being those of Scrope of Bolton differenced with a crozier.

as well, was also a 'gentleman of ancestry'. These exacting qualifications, if they were ever rigidly insisted upon, which may be more than doubted, became relaxed as time went on. (6) Arms of Alliance are derived from 'heiresses', i.e. females of armigerous houses, who, owing to the extinction of the males, represent their families. (*a*) These arms (see under 2) may be quartered by those borne of an heiress mother, and thenceforward transmitted as a quartering to descendants, whereby is perpetuated the memory of many old families that have failed in the male line. (*b*) In former times the paternal coat was sometimes placed after, or discarded for, that of an armigerous heiress who brought in as a wife a great property or was 'of more eminent nobility', and the same might be done in the case of a mother's coat on the same grounds : a course which tended to obscure family history. (7) Arms of Concession or Augmentation were those granted by the sovereign, or other feudal superior, in commemoration of an exploit, or to indicate a connexion of some nature, or of 'meer grace'. To the first belongs the addition by Henry VIII of a composition suggested by the royal arms of Scotland to be borne *in medio bende* on the coat of Thomas Howard, Earl of Surrey, as a memorial of his victory of Flodden Field [Fig. 223, A] : to the second the granting by Henry VIII of a chief, bearing a selection from the royal arms of England, to Thomas Manners, first Earl of Rutland, to mark his descent from Henry's grand-aunt, Ann Plantagenet, sister of Edward IV [Fig. 223, B] ; to the third the concession by Richard II to Thomas Mowbray, first Duke of Norfolk, of the right to impale the (mythical) coat of Edward the Confessor, the king's patron saint, with his own [Fig. 223, C]. Augmentations were also borne on cantons, or might be quartered before the paternal coat. The term 'special concession' was applied to Augmentations which contained charges from the royal arms, and could therefore be granted only by the sovereign. These, when impaled, or marshalled, took precedence of the paternal coat, or they might supersede the latter.

FIG. 222. Sir Wm. Segar, Garter, 1603–33 (Guillim, 1724, VI. i. 419).

Among Augmentations is to be included the Red Hand, or badge of Ulster, borne as a charge on a canton, or on an inescutcheon, by all baronets except those of Scotland. (8) Arms of Succession or Adoption (*a*) were those that, in the absence of heirs by blood, accrued by entail, will, or donation during the life of the donor, to strangers. Succession to property passing in this way has often been made conditional on the assumption of the arms, and usually the name, of the donor. These arms were borne either in place of, or (if the donor so willed it) quartered before those of the 'adopted successor' : unless the latter were of a more ancient family, in which case, according to the armorists, he was not bound to assume coat or name, 'and yet might enjoy the property'. It was, however, maintained by some that so long as a single male heir by blood existed (monks and attainted persons not excepted), personal coats could not be alienated, no matter what happened to the property, the bearer having only a life interest, not absolute possession. But a case of the grant of arms by one inheritor to another in 1391 is recorded in *The Topographer*, ii. 192. The royal sanction was supposed to be necessary to alienation. (*b*) There was another class of Arms of Succession, unconnected with any question of blood or adoption. These were attached to lordships or estates, from holder to holder of which they passed. They were also termed Arms of Tenure or Feudal Arms, and many ancient 'collateral' shields and early quarterings were coats of such lordships, not of family alliances. In some instances,

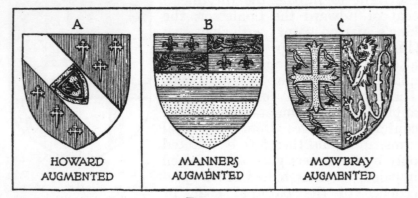

FIG. 223.

before the days of marshalling, family arms were discarded in their favour. (9) Arms of Patronage were of two kinds. (*a*) Those assumed, usually as additions to their paternal arms, by lords of manors, patrons of benefices, &c., to betoken their rights as such ; to which probably in numerous instances the castles, wool-combs, mill-rinds, wheels, hunting-horns, arrows, &c., that appear as charges owe their introduction into armory, though some such may indicate the terms of a tenure and so come under (*b*), those granted by the sovereign, or other immediate feudal superior, to holders of land in fee under them : often in consideration of the performance of a particular duty, as castle-ward, stewardship, &c. Frequently in these cases the overlord's coat, differenced, was borne [Fig. 224, A–D ] ; or some ordinary or charge was taken from his shield and added to the paternal arms of the tenant, thus forming what was known as a 'composed coat'; e.g. Hardres of Kent held the manor of Hardres by knight service of Tunbridge Castle, a seignory of the Clares, Earls of Gloucester, and 'debruised' the Hardres lion with a chevron [Fig. 225] from the Clare coat [Fig. 193, B]. Again, in some instances the bearings of a tenant appear to have been suggested by the sword, knife, helmet, bow, arrow, spur, ring, cup, horn, &c., of his overlord, which in many early tenures (c. 1050–1300) were delivered by him to the tenant and held by the latter and his descendants as evidence of the grant. At Trinity College, Cambridge, a deed of 1135 is still preserved to which the knife of the grantor is appended in

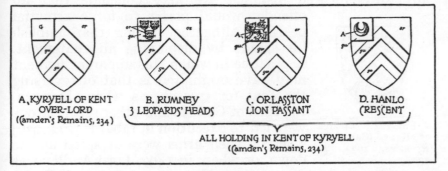

A. KYRYELL OF KENT
OVER-LORD
(Camden's Remains, 234)

B. RUMNEY
3 LEOPARDS' HEADS

C. ORLASSTON
LION PASSANT

D. HANLO
CRESCENT

ALL HOLDING IN KENT OF KYRYELL
(Camden's Remains, 234)

FIG. 224.

lieu of a seal, and this is not an isolated instance. One of the best-known cases is that of the rangership of Bernwood Forest, Bucks., held by a horn, which was represented on the coat of arms of the descendant of Nigel, the original grantee: *Argent, a fess gules between two crescents in chief and a horn in base vert.* 'Nigel's horn' is engraved in vol. iii of *Archaeologia.* (10) Arms of Religion. Ecclesiastics and Knights of Religious Orders at times left their paternal arms and took others made up of sacred objects, such as mitres, keys, or figures of saints. To this division is also to be relegated the so-called coat of Edward the Confessor assumed by Richard II. These arms, when marshalled, took precedence of all others.

Two other classes of arms enumerated by the old armorists are : (11) Arms of Assumption or Conquest. There was a theory that the bearings of a person who fled, leaving his shield or his banner on the field, or who was vanquished in fight, whether in war or in 'lists of combat', could be assumed and borne in a sinister quarter, or otherwise added in whole or in part to his own arms, by the victor, *iure gentium*. (12) Arms of Abatement. 'Abatements' or 'rebatings' were a series of marks of disgrace to be borne on the scutcheon for 'ungentle' acts, such as boasting, slaying a prisoner, cowardice, drunkenness, debauchery, discourtesy to women, treachery, and so forth. It is extremely doubtful whether the former of these two supposed laws of armory was ever actually in operation, and the only examples adduced appear to have been really cases of augmentation ; while as to the latter, in the absence of any authenticated instance, we may conclude that an

FIG. 225. Hardres of Kent (Camden's *Remains*, 1674, p. 232).

offender would prefer to forgo armorial bearings altogether rather than publish his shame by displaying an abatement. A practice in which this apparent figment may have originated is that of reversing the coat for treason, as when, in 1323, the Earl of Carlisle and other rebel barons were led to execution in tabards [Fig. 226] whereon their arms were depicted upside down, or when, in 1497, Lord Audley was drawn from Newgate to Tower Hill, for heading, in a paper tabard painted with his arms reversed and torn. This was the manner in which a traitor's shield was said to be rebated. According to the mediaeval jurists, it was a survival from 'the old form of hanging traitors by the feet'. When, however, a knight was 'disgraded' he was regarded as dead in chivalry, and this inversion of the coat of arms was in consonance with the ordinary procedure at funerals, by which the herald of a defunct nobleman, as his representative, wore his late master's tabard inverted. That this symbolic custom is as old as the first days of armory may be seen from the reversed shields drawn by Matthew Paris in the margins of his *Historia Minor* when he records the death of the owners. An example, as late as 1630, is to be seen on a tombstone at Domfront, in Normandy. The reversal of the coat of arms formed part of the sentence of Sir Ralph Grey, who was degraded from knighthood (see § 6) in 1464, and the

Earl of Carlisle also had been so degraded. Indeed, the displaying of the culprit's shield 'with the heels of the arms upwards' commonly formed part of the ceremony of degradation from knighthood.

In connexion with the origin of coats attention must be paid to Canting, or Allusive, Arms (*arma cantantia, armes parlantes*), arms that tell their tale without words, *non verbis sed* REBUS : 'the ancient silent names.' These have been prompted by the name [Figs. 216 and 217], office [Fig. 213], personal peculiarity, deeds, abode, &c., of the first bearer, or of his overlord. They are very natural and convenient, and therefore exceedingly common, and form to a great extent the basis of early armory ; probably far more so even than we know, for many allusions must have become unrecognizable owing to their ephemeral character, to linguistic changes, or to alterations in the names of the bearers. The arms of Thomas *Salle* (1422) were two *sal*amanders *sal*iant in *sal*tire. It will be seen that some of the arms discussed under the above ten divisions were obviously canting arms.

FIG. 226. Sir William Brugge, 1st Garter King-of-Arms, *d.* 1449 (MS. Ashmole 764).

The coat was often a surer indication of consanguinity than the surname, the latter being frequently taken from, or dropped for, that of an estate, while the arms were retained. For instance, the Lyllings of Yorkshire, who were Lucys by blood, had by Richard I's time relinquished the name of Lucy and taken that of Lylling, East Lylling being their *caput baroniae*; but they kept the canting Lucy coat of three luces [Fig. 216, where Barnard impales Lucy on the kirtle].

## 4. *Heraldic Officers.*

Heralds existed long before the rise of armorial bearings. They acted as messengers of war, peace, or courtesy ; and, among other duties, superintended trials by wager and numbered the slain in battle. But a considerable stimulus was given after 1300 to the employment of these officials by the

spread of the use of coat-armour, for, being closely bound up
with military arrangements, its direction naturally fell to
them. During the age of chivalry not only the sovereign,
but also many of the magnates of the realm, maintained
in their establishments heraldic officers, whose appointment, it is said, had to be approved by the royal heralds.
Theoretically, it seems that dukes, marquises, earls, and
viscounts were allowed one herald and one pursuivant ;
barons and bannerets a pursuivant only ; though whether
any such hard-and-fast rule ever obtained in actual practice may be doubted. We know that Sir John Chandos,
banneret, kept his herald (*temp*. Edw. III), but this probably was in his capacity of Constable of Aquitaine. As with
some of the king's heraldic attendants, these were frequently
designated by the name, or a badge, or other token of the
house they served. Such were ' Hereford herald ' of Humphrey de Bohun, Earl of Hereford (*temp*. Edw. III), ' Eagle-
vert pursuivant ' of Richard Nevill, Earl of Salisbury (*temp*.
Hen. VI), from the Monthermer coat, and ' Esperance pursuivant ' of the Duke of Northumberland (*temp*. Edw. IV),
from one of the Percy warcries (cf. Shakes. *Hen. IV*,
Act v. ii. 97). Wolsey kept a herald in his train, but in his
time only two of the nobility did so : the custom was then
dying out, and became extinct before the reign of Elizabeth.
Private heralds are said to have had authority to grant, on
behalf of their lords, Arms of Patronage and differences.

As their older title of 'Ancient' (*veteranus*) implies, heralds
were often veteran retainers, who in their experiences in
the battle-field, at the tournament, and on ceremonial occasions, had acquired a knowledge of matters armorial. Being
sometimes otherwise uneducated men, it is possible that
not a few of the fabulous and fantastic excrescences
which defaced and afterwards discredited their science (the
ascribing, for example, of coats of arms and ' gentility ' to
classical, Biblical, and mythical personages, and the explain-
ing of colours, charges, &c., by allegorical or chivalrous fic-
tions) are due to the twofold object on their part of exalting
their calling and of flattering the vanity of their patrons. As
with other crafts, too, ' mystery ' meant ' protection ' from
competition. All this was derided by Fransus in his *Insignium
et Armorum Explicatio* as early as 1588. Still, we owe to
them copies of many of the early Rolls of Arms, and to

one of the more cultivated among them the Chronicle Roll *Le Siège de Karlaverok* ; and the historical poem *Le Prince Noir* was undoubtedly written by the herald of Sir John Chandos. Monstrelet, too, tells us that in compiling his *Chronicles* he made particular inquiries from kings-of-arms, heralds, and pursuivants, of their recollections ; and Froissart says much the same. All these three grades of heraldic officials appear in existence as far back as the reign of Henry III ; the superior title ' king-of-arms ' (i. e. of armorial emblems), or its obsolete equivalent ' king of heralds ', being in England confined to heralds in the royal employ [Fig. 226]. In the Middle Ages the appellation ' king ' was given in France to several officers who performed special functions about the household of the sovereign. Such were the *Roy de Ribauldes*, whose duties were somewhat those of a combined chief of police and magistrate within the royal precincts ; and the *Roy de Merciers*, who acted as inspector of the wares, weights, and measures of the traders that attended the court. Similarly, in England, we find letters patent granted in the reign of Richard II, and ratified by Henry VI, confirming the powers and privileges of a ' King of the Minstrels ', who appears frequently in our history before and after those times. So too the Minstrels of France were incorporated by charter under a king in 1330. The title of ' King-of-Heralds ', or ' King-of-Arms ', was an analogous usage ; further accentuated, however, by the fact that, as the ' image of his master ', he was crowned and consecrated, and wore the coat of arms of the monarch whose proxy he was.

Edward III appointed two provincial kings-of-arms, ' Norroy ' and perhaps ' Surroy ', with armorial jurisdiction north and south of Trent respectively ; and there are traces of some such arrangement still earlier, under Edward I. ' Clarenceux ' came into existence in the person of the herald of Lionel, Duke of Clarence, third son of Edward III, and Henry V created the herald of his brother, Thomas Duke of Clarence, a king-of-arms with the style of Clarenceux and with the office of Surroy, which, however, as a title, if it ever existed, had already become extinct. In 1420, at the siege of Rouen, the king's heralds held their first regular chapter, and drew up a code of procedure for their own guidance. The same king nominated a herald for the order of the Garter, and permanently annexed to that post a new and distinct one of Principal King-of-arms ' over all the servants of arms in England'. Many special royal heraldic officials, variously named, appear and disappear in other reigns till as late as Elizabeth inclusive : examples of which are ' Agincourt king-of-arms ' (Henry V, in commemoration of the victory) ; ' March king-of-arms ' (Edward IV, from his earlier title, a practice then common with the sovereign) ; ' Falcon herald ' (Edward IV, from one of his badges) ; ' Blanch Sanglier pursuivant' (Richard III, from his badge of the White Boar) ; but in 1605–6 the nomenclature of the heralds of the court finally settled down into what it is now.

In 1483 a further stage of organization was reached when Richard III granted a charter by which twelve of the most approved of the officers of arms of the Crown were formed into a corporation, and endowed with ' a right faire and stately house ' in London, thus instituting what came to be known as the Heralds' College or College of Arms. Garter, Principal King-of-arms, was appointed its head ; under him were the two provincial kings-of-arms, Clarenceux and Norroy, and several heralds and pursuivants, each with his own appellation. The whole College was subject to the Earl Marshal, as President of the Court of Chivalry (see § 6), and the nomination, with the royal assent, of the officials passed into his hands. At the fall of Richard III the members of the College were turned out of their house, and after some seventy years of vicissitudes and temporary shifts for a home, they acquired Derby House from Queen Mary I. This was destroyed by the great fire of 1666, but the records were saved, and the College, as we see it now, was rebuilt on the same site from the designs of Wren.

The chief functions and rights of ' Garter ' were to arrange ceremonials of embassies, to determine precedence, to grant armorial bearings to, and order the funerals of peers, the two archbishops, the Bishop of Winchester (as prelate of the Garter), and Knights of the Garter ; in addition to which he exercised jurisdiction concurrent with, but not independent of, the provincial kings in the conferring of coat-armour. Certain of these privileges, however, were a matter of controversy between him and his brother kings.

The duties and powers of a provincial king-of-arms within his province, or of a herald or a pursuivant acting as his deputy, were to investigate and record the arms, crest, cognizances (badges), 'antient words' (either *cris de guerre* or mottoes), and descent of every gentleman below the baronage, of whatever estate or degree, except Knights of the Garter; to prohibit any one from bearing another's arms, or those to which he had otherwise no right, or such as were not true armory (i. e. violated the rules of blazon), and from altering his arms without licence; to forbid (a regulation often disregarded) any merchant or other to put a merchant-mark (the prototype of the modern trade-mark) on a shield, the latter belonging exclusively to gentlemen of coat-armour; on receipt of the customary fee, to confirm arms to gentlemen ignorant of their coats, or to give arms to ungentle persons who were fit and deserving; to allow no coats of arms, flags, helms, crests, or anything pertaining to achievements, to be set up in churches at funerals of gentry below the peerage without his permission, and on such occasions to record the armorial insignia, the age, dates, and other information as to the death, burial, marriage, and issue of the deceased. Authority was also given him to enter all castles, houses, or churches, and demolish or deface any armorials there displayed which might not be in accordance with the laws of arms, whether on walls, windows, plate, jewellery, documents, flags, or tombs; and he had the disposing of tournaments and combats.

The heralds of the College acted as assistants or as deputies for the kings-of-arms. They are now all distinguished by names taken from places, which first appear with any degree of certainty as titles of officers of arms of the sovereign in the reigns indicated in the following list, though some were not continuous; but all have been so since the third year of James I. Several of them occur earlier as titles of the heralds of princes or other grandees. 'Windsor herald' (Edward III, perhaps so entitled because prior to the time of Henry V he served as herald of the Order of the Garter at Windsor); 'Chester herald' (Richard II, from the then newly-created principality of Chester); 'Lancaster herald' (Henry IV, from his duchy, or perhaps as old as Edward III's time); 'York herald' (Edward IV, from his duchy); 'Somerset herald' (Henry VII, in honour of his mother's family, cf. 'Portcullis' below); 'Richmond herald' (Henry VII, from his earldom). One of the obligations of the heralds

was the instruction of the pursuivants. Under Henry IV
Lancaster was promoted to a kingship, but reduced to herald
again by Edward IV.

The pursuivants (lit. 'followers') were probationary
heralds. In the age of Chivalry the proper period of their
novitiate was seven years, the usual duration of 'appren-
ticeships' in trades and professions. They are named from
badges : 'Rougecroix' (Henry V, from St. George's Cross,
the badge of England) ; 'Bluemantle' (variously given as
dating from Edward III or Henry V, and as so called from
the tincture of the field of the coat of France, or from the
colour of the mantle of the French king, or from that of
the robes of the Order of the Garter) ; 'Rougedragon'
(Henry VII, from the badge of Wales which was displayed
on one of the three standards borne by him in the Bosworth
campaign) ; 'Portcullis' (Henry VII, a Beaufort badge).
The royal blood he derived from his mother, the Countess
of Richmond, a great-granddaughter of Edward III in
the Beaufort line, strengthened his claim to the throne :
as the Portcullis was to the door or the barriers of a gateway,
so this descent was, and thus the accompanying motto put
it, an *altera securitas*.

The person of an officer of arms was sacrosanct : to
offer violence to him was 'no lesse than sacriledge'. The
scutcheon at his girdle, or, from the fifteenth century
onward, his tabard, was his passport.

## 5. *The Visitations.*

As early as 1333 the Crown, to prevent bloodshed, had
interposed between claimants to the same coat, stayed
combat, and referred the question to judgement ; and in 1386
there was legislation on the subject (see § 6). Henry V,
when preparing for his French campaign of 1417, went a
step farther, and on June 2 of that year issued a proclamation that no man should bear arms without proving by
what ancestral right or by whose gift he bore them, and
claims were to be submitted to officers appointed for the
purpose. Persons who had borne coat-armour at Agincourt alone were excepted, as a particular mark of favour : the
fact of their having been present on that occasion as armigerous being regarded as sufficient title to arms. How far
the edict was carried out is uncertain, and in any case it

applied to only the four counties of Hants, Wilts., Dorset, and Sussex, and to a special occasion. In the fourteenth and fifteenth centuries grants of arms were sometimes made direct from the Crown, occasionally through the Chancellor under the Great Seal.

'Visitations', which may be described as heraldic Circuits in pursuance of the functions of the officers of arms (see § 4), are said, though on doubtful authority, to have been made in the reigns of Edward IV and Henry VII ; but a systematic enforcement of armorial regulations throughout the kingdom under royal commission was undertaken in the periodical Visitations which began in 1528-9 and continued till 1686 at intervals of about thirty years. This space of time, virtually a generation, was selected as being 'within memory', and within which living testimony was procurable and documents were unlikely to have got lost or destroyed. One cause of the measure was that the rising mercantile class and other of the 'meaner people' were inclined to assume without right or warrant the emblems of gentility. The Visitations, in fact, were social rather than military in their origin, for armorial bearings were, in the sixteenth century, fast ceasing to be a necessary, or even an important, factor in military array, though for purposes of display they were still prominent in the field. The dissolution of the monasteries, too, in 1536-9 probably enhanced the necessity for their continuance, since the genealogies of the landed and gentle class had been commonly recorded for purposes connected with ecclesiastical law and Church property, and deposited for security, in the religious houses.

The Visitations disappeared with the last Stuart king. According to the kings-of-arms this was due to the ' continued disturbances of the State which had kept many of the gentry from their seats ' ; but other reasons may be found. There had grown up a feeling on the part of some of the gentlefolk that the interference of the heralds was inquisitorial. Again, the older armigerous families of established position considered that they needed no official recognition, and, conversely, objected to the recognition of newly-risen families, holding that it discounted the value of heraldic sanction; and as time went on this feeling was intensified by the somewhat promiscuous grants of arms to the latter by the later sixteenth-

and seventeenth-century heralds. There is evidence that the purchase of gentility from the heralds was resented by the county gentry and repudiated by juries as early as the time of Henry VIII. The growth, moreover, of an upper-middle class with commercially acquired wealth, often far greater than that of the minor gentry, had tended to obliterate the hitherto obvious dividing line, largely of feudal origin, between gentle and simple : and this consideration is said to have influenced William III in refusing to issue a commission for another Visitation. Thus one of the causes of the establishment of the visitations ultimately became one of the causes of their cessation : in attempting to bar the social aspirations of the *nouveau riche* heraldry was swamped by him. Other factors assisted to the same end. The Great Civil War and the Revolution of 1688 had produced in a measure a new line of social cleavage, vertical rather than horizontal, whereby class distinctions had become to some extent obscured by the more vital considerations aroused in the struggle for and against civil and religious freedom. Again, the College of Arms had fallen into temporary disrepute owing to dissensions among the officials, mainly arising from personal jealousies and from disputes about their mutual privileges and fees ; and the improvements in the keeping of parish registers after the Restoration offered a substitute for the genealogical records of the heralds. The entries, indeed, in the later Visitation Books show that a considerable proportion of the ancient gentry ignored the summons of the kings-of-arms ; some ' look'd on this matter as a trick to get money '.

The process pursued in the Visitations, which, in order to find the country gentlemen at home, were never taken during the sitting of Parliament, and always between March and September, when country roads were least bad, was as follows. Commissions were issued by the Crown under the Broad (Great) Seal to the provincial kings-of-arms requiring them, or their deputies, to visit their provinces and summon all persons below the baronage, that used coat-armour or styled themselves esquires or gentlemen, to attend and prove their right thereto, or, if more convenient, to receive the heralds at their houses. Circular letters were sent by the Earl Marshal to the lords lieutenant of each shire to direct the high constables or bailiffs of the hundreds and mayors of towns to aid the heralds by furnishing lists of the gentry, or reputed gentry, resident in their hundreds. The arms and descents submitted were accepted and recorded, or 'respited for proof', or 'disallowed'. The ancient prescriptive right to bear arms was recognized by the Heralds' College as late as the Gartership of Sir William Dugdale (1677–86), a user of about a hundred years, or three generations, being regarded as sufficient authority. New families might apply for and, if suitable, receive grants of arms. Usurpers of armorial bearings or of the title of esquire or dignity of gentleman were forced to 'disclaim' by signing a declaration that they were not gentlemen, or they were 'disclaimed' at the Assizes or Quarter Sessions, and the local officials were forbidden so to address them. They were further made 'infamous' by having their names and false pretensions proclaimed by the public crier and posted up in the market-place nearest to their homes. Occasionally the heralds appear to have been content merely to forbid by letter to a usurper the use of arms, and refrained from inflicting any public disgrace. But while impostors were in this way weeded out, there is no doubt that, rather than pay the heralds' fees, heads of families of unquestionable armorial position frequently disclaimed : an act which would not injure them locally, where their true estate was well known. Many such simply disregarded the summons of the heralds. On the other hand, to be held up to open derision as a spurious claimant to 'gentleness' was a real rebuff to the *novus homo* who aspired to rise in social position as he had risen in fortune. In order to counteract the practice of disclaiming on the part of armigerous persons, the heralds were directed never to disclaim any such on account of inability to pay the fees, and the Visitation Books contain many allusions to pedigrees and arms entered gratuitously. The registration of *descents* by the visiting heralds was not confined to those of gentlemen of coat-armour.

Nowadays, when the term 'gentleman' is loosely used, with partly a moral and ethical, partly a professional, educational, and financial, and with or without an ancestral connotation, it is essential for a right understanding of our subject to divest the idea of all later aggregations, and to appreciate the importance attached, prior to the eighteenth century, to the title as indicating simply a definite status.

That, in fact, was formerly the only meaning of the word ; for the community was divided into two classes, *nobiles* or gentle-folk, embracing all grades from untitled gentry upwards inclusive, and *ignobiles*, or ungentle, those below, and the right to bear coat-armour was the distinguishing mark of the *nobilis* : a condition of society that obtained in Germany and Russia till our own day. The subdivision into Major and Minor nobility, the former taking in all above knight, and such special degrees as ' Excellent' and ' Princely' accorded to those above viscount, are comparatively unimportant, and indeed irrelevant, niceties of distinction that do not in the least affect the main classification: between *nobilis* and *ignobilis* there was a great gulf fixed, it was the only social gulf, and it could only be passed by acquiring the right to bear arms.

It was a proviso of the Earl Marshal that arms should not be granted ' to any vyle or dishonest [*unhonoured*] occupation', and there are instances of kings-of-arms being fined and even imprisoned for disregarding this order. The Visitation records made by the heralds were preserved in the College of Arms, and in questions of genealogy were and still are admitted as evidence in courts of law. The officers of Arms on their Visitations were empowered to impose fines, but we do not know that they did so. They could also cite before the Earl Marshal's Court those who refused to appear, which would entail on the recalcitrants trouble and expense at least (see § 6). A monopoly of armorial business of what kind soever was given to each king-of-arms within his own province : no painter, glazier, or other artificer was to meddle with heraldic subjects without his sanction.

### 6.  *The Court of Chivalry.*

Closely allied with the College of Arms was the Court of Chivalry (*curia militaris*, or Court of Honour), of which the former was in some respects a subordinate department. Originally the Court of Chivalry was presided over by the two great military officers of the State, the Lord High Constable and the Lord Marshal as his deputy, and had cognizance of combats in which questions of treason, coat-armour, and honour were involved, also of tournaments, and chivalry generally. Previous to 1386 the Marshal, in his judicial capacity, acted only as indispensable coadjutor of the

Constable, but he was then empowered to sit as president, with or without the Constable, ' except in matters touching life and member ', when a Constable was appointed *pro illa vice* ; and thenceforward his style was always Earl Marshal. His was the only earldom by office then remaining in England. He had authority to summon the officers of arms to assist him in cases relating to honour, coat-armour, and pedigree : for such interests, at first touching comparatively few, had become widely diffused, and special juridical machinery for dealing with them had become necessary. In consequence the Court of Chivalry came commonly to be termed also the Earl Marshal's Court, more especially after the regular succession of Constables ceased.

There is an instinctive tendency on the part of special tribunals to extend their jurisdiction, and only four years later than the above changes, owing to complaints of encroachment by the Earl Marshal's Court on the ordinary courts, a restricting statute was passed by Richard II, which provides us with a clear definition of its legal limits, though not of its heraldic powers. As regards the former, its purview was confined to ' causes and quarrels touching the honor of Gentlemen and the integritie of their coate-armors (which ought to be no lesse deere unto them than their owne lives), whereof the [common] lawes of this Realme do give no remedie nor action ' ; and for the decision of which the Court of Chivalry had the power to grant combat. Some sixty or seventy years later its position is thus defined by the Judges : ' The Constable and Marshal have a law by themselves, and the common law takes cognizance of it and concurs ' ; very much as it concurred in ecclesiastical law.

The Marshalship was in early times on the whole, but not regularly, hereditary. The tenure was in some cases for life, or *durante bene placito*, or merely for a limited period ; while now and again the office was placed in commission. It was not till 1672 that it became the permanent heritage of the Howards, and in 1677 of the Dukes of Norfolk. The hereditary High Constableship was abolished as a standing office by Henry VIII in 1521, and thenceforward temporary Constables were appointed for particular occasions, as at coronations, and when a court of chivalry was held to superintend a trial by combat.

In the Middle Ages, when the circulation of money was imperfect, rent largely paid in kind, and transport indifferent, the sovereign like other great landowners, in order to live upon the produce of scattered demesne manors, and for purposes of superintendence, was in frequent movement about the country ; and the Earl Marshal, as one of the great officers of the royal household, accompanied the king in his peregrinations. The High Steward, the King's Coroner, and the Earl Marshal exercised a peculiar jurisdiction for a radius of twelve miles round the court wherever it might happen to be stationed for the time being ; hence the Court of Chivalry was usually held within the ' verge ' (*circle*), as the circumference of that radius was technically called. When the court was in residence at Westminster the Earl Marshal sat in the Painted Chamber ; or in later times at his own house in the Strand, or in the Hall of the College of Arms. In time of war, however, it being the Marshal's duty to ' order battles ' and lead the vanguard, the Court of Chivalry followed the army. When needful, peers and judges were invited to aid in its judgements, and, besides the heraldic officials, the Marshal was also assisted by a Doctor of Civil Law, who ' resolved doubts ', the Law of Arms ' being in most part directed by the Civil Law ', the procedure of which was followed in the Court of Chivalry. Its prison was the Marshalsea. One of the prerogatives claimed by the Court was that its officers were amenable to it alone, and it also possessed the right of arraigning before it persons who acted as heralds without authority. A case for the Court of Chivalry had to be one for which no relief could be obtained at common law. No damages could be awarded by it, and proceedings in it were not by jury, but by witnesses or by combat.

Although the Court of Chivalry could order and arrange for a dispute to be decided by combat (a procedure granted only to the armigerous, and for the conduct of which there were fixed rules), still it often peaceably settled differences which otherwise would have been put to the arbitrament of the duel. Typical suits tried in this court between 1312 and 1732, and which were not referred to combat, may be summed up as follows : (1) *A* accuses *B* of unwarrantably using the same arms as *A*, for which offence there ' lay a combat, even as for those things which are most sacred '.

*B* (or *A*, as it may be) proves his superior right to them by descent and they are confirmed to him, the other being forbidden to bear them. The head of a house could even call on the Court to enforce the bearing of a difference by a cadet. (2) An action is brought at common law for calling traitor, and the common law judges rule that, combat being the proper test, it is a case not for them but for the Marshal's Court. (3) *C*, a gentleman, is cited for striking *D*, whom he knows to be also a gentleman, and, as such, unfit to have such disgrace done him. *C* is bound over to admit his fault and to maintain *D*'s reputation against any injurious comment that may result from the insult; *D*, having drawn his sword at the time of the assault, leaves the court without a stain on his gentlehood. (4) *E* summons *F* for calling him a 'base, lying fellow', &c. Defendant pleads that *E* is no gentleman, and therefore not capable of redress in this court. Investigation shows that he is, since the arms of his family are recorded in the archives of the College of Arms, and his pedigree is proved. *F* presumably is punished, but the judgement is not stated. (5) *G* challenges *H*, a baronet, as not fulfilling the conditions required [in those days, 1623] for that title, especially as regards 'gentry'. *H* wins his cause. The same defendant was also proceeded against for quartering with his own arms others to which he had no right. (6) *J* charges *K* with having slanderously alleged that *J* ran away in battle. *K* is cast in damages, fined, and committed to prison till he has made payment. (7) *L* complains that *M*, with intent to provoke a duel, has proclaimed that *L* is baseborn and no gentleman, whereas he is a 'gentleman of ancestry' (see § 3). The judgement is not on record. (8) *N*, a gentleman, arraigns *N*, who bears the same name but is a merchant, for using the former's coat of arms, though not related. The prosecutor gains his suit; yet, despite this, the defendant's family seem to have persisted in using the coat. This, however, was in the seventeenth century, when the Court was losing its hold. (9) The Earl Marshal proceeds against the executors of *X* for displaying at his funeral arms not legally his. This suit, which took place in 1732, after the Visitations had ceased for more than a generation, was an unsuccessful attempt to resuscitate the Court. The prosecution was treated with ridicule, and although fines were imposed it was found impossible to exact them.

The severest punishment administered by the Court of Chivalry was 'solemn disgradation' from knighthood, which apparently was inflicted with great reluctance, for only some half-dozen instances are known. It was not necessarily decreed or conducted by this Court, which, however, carried out the ceremony in the case of Sir Francis Michell, in 1621. He had been accused by the Commons before the Lords, and convicted, of official corruption, and the Lord Chief Justice, on behalf of the Upper House, pronounced sentence of degradation and directed the Earl Marshal's Court to execute the penalty. The officers of the College of Arms were ordered by the Earl Marshal to attend at Westminster in their tabards. The culprit was placed on a scaffold erected in the King's Bench Court, wearing the emblems of knighthood, his belt, gilded sword, and gilt spurs, many of the peers being present as spectators. A herald then read the sentence which deprived him of the title of knight. That done, his belt was cut and the sword fell to the ground, his spurs were hacked from his heels and flung away to right and left, his sword was broken over his head and the fragments treated in the same way : thenceforth he was to be reputed 'an infamous, errant knave'. This was in the main the regular ceremonial on such occasions, and that similar ceremonies date from as far back as 1242 we learn from Matthew Paris. Michell was further adjudged incapable of employment, fined £1,000, and confined to his own house during the royal pleasure.

The fourteenth and fifteenth centuries saw the Court of Chivalry at its best and strongest. The insight given by the Hundred Years' War into the privileged position of the aristocracy in France doubtless contributed to a demand on the part of the quality in England for the maintenance of a court that dealt with questions in which points of honour were concerned ; with mere personal affronts, with duels rendered unavoidable in quarrels which 'for want of witnesses could not be decided otherwise', and with distinctions of rank wherewith armorial rights and regulations were closely interwoven. During the social tension, also, among the upper classes that prevailed throughout the Wars of the Roses the demand continued ; but after they ceased the Court of Chivalry tended to sink more and more into the position of an heraldic office, and by 1600 it was steadily becoming an anachronism. Its revival by Charles I for arbitrary purposes ultimately only assisted its decline, and in the following century it fell, says Blackstone, ' into contempt and disuse '. The causes of its decay were to a great extent the same as those that brought the Visitations to a close, to which may be added the constant overriding of its proceedings by the Court' of King's Bench, to which there had always been an appeal from the Earl Marshal : the common law was ever jealous of the civil law.

It is easy to smile at the Court of Honour in its later days, when it had done its work and outlived its use : but for many generations it was in England the localized expression of that high moral code and that self-restraint inculcated by mediaeval chivalry in matters of conduct outside indictable crime and with which the ordinary law of a land cannot successfully interfere. That code was undoubtedly in a great measure based on Christian teaching, but was probably more operative on the knightly mind through its presentment in the form of *noblesse oblige*. The mere existence of a court of this nature must have acted as a check ; and the urging, in a relatively rough stage of social development, of such precepts among the ' Nine Virtues of Chivalry ' as to be merciful to all, to do no harm to the poor, to show hospitality especially to strangers, to protect maid or widow from insult, not only refined the higher classes to whom they were directly addressed, but doubtless percolated downwards and affected in some degree the lower strata of society by the example of their betters ; while in such as enjoined the keeping of a promise to foe no less than friend, or forbade the slaying of a prisoner or killing in cold blood, we may see the foundations of International Law and the germ of the Geneva Convention.

## 7. *Summary.*

The history of English armory falls into two periods. The earlier is that in which the armorial shield was in actual use in warfare, and, roughly speaking, ranges from 1150 to 1500. As body-armour improved, the general tendency was for the shield gradually to diminish in size, till the large three-foot shield, or thereabouts, which covered the whole trunk of the solely mail-clad knight of the opening years of heraldry [Fig. 227], shrank to the small heater-shaped shield of some eighteen inches long, or less, that served his partly plate-encased descendant as little more than a buckler, or stroke-warder [Fig. 228]. The discarding of the shield by mounted men began as early as the latter half of the fourteenth century, when plate was gradually asserting its entire predominance over mail ; and on the whole its diminution proceeded *pari passu* with its growing disuse, till by the end of the fifteenth century it had virtually disappeared as a weapon.   So far

FIG. 227.   William Long-sword, Earl of Salisbury ; *d.* 1226 (effigy, Salisbury Cathedral).

FIG. 228. . . . Bacon (brass, *c.* 1320, Gorleston, Suffolk). Legs restored from FitzRalph brass of same date and pattern.

as is known, the Aldeburgh brass of 1360, at Aldborough, Yorkshire, is the last in which a shield appears as part of the equipment ; the Wantone brass of 1347, at Wimbish, Essex, is the first in which the effigy bears no shield.   By ordinary foot-soldiers it was retained much later, but they, as non-armigerous, do not concern us here.   During the first 150 years (1150–1300) of this period heraldry may be said to have been in process of formation as an exact science ; from 1300 to 1500 may be regarded as its golden age, the zenith being reached in the reigns of Edward III and Richard II.

With the final disappearance of the shield as an implement of war, about 1500, began the decadence of armory ; both the shield and its bearings survived in their genealogical and decorative uses alone. In the days of the service-shield any alterations in its form naturally were prompted by practical considerations of defensive utility, and when in those days it was applied to ornamental purposes, as a rule it was represented in the shape used at the time ; yet even then there was an inclination to adapt its outlines to architectural and aesthetic fashions, more particularly after 1400 when the shield was dropping out of use. Subsequently to 1500, however, its configuration became

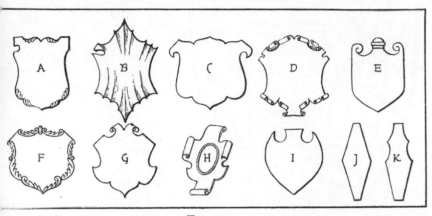

FIG. 229.

entirely arbitrary, and was dictated not merely by the prevailing character of contemporaneous art, but, within that limit, often was further distorted by the fancy or the caprice of the individual artist. Again, the shield, so long as it was borne in battle, obviously was of more consequence than the charge : the latter therefore was forced to conform in figure or in posture to the contour of the former ; but when it fell into desuetude actuality of contour vanished from the purely decorative escutcheon. All manner of impossible and fantastic types appear [Fig. 229, A–H]. Some of these were suggested by their architectural environment. Others were due to a new practice, which arose after the abandonment of the war-shield had rendered accuracy in its representation of less moment and its conventionalization permissible ; that of drawing first the charges and then the outline of the scutcheon to fit them. This method had one merit : it reduced to a minimum the amount of unoccupied field, and therein incidentally obeyed a traditional rule of mediaeval armory ; though the obedience was of an inverse nature, for it was the need for conspicuousness that had compelled a large and bold depiction of the charge upon the war-shield, and the bearing was fitted to the field, not the field to the bearing. Through the various stages of the classical revival the conformation of shields continued to follow architecture, and occasionally we find identical reproductions of Greek [Fig. 229, I] and Roman models [Fig. 229, J, K]. The sources of the examples given in Fig. 229 are: A, the Barnard wood-carvings at Abington Hall, Northants., 1485–1508 ; B, the monument of Abbot Ramryge, at St. Albans, 1529 ; C, the arms of Anne Bullen, from *MS. Coll. of Arms*, i. 2, fol. 13; D, the Great Seal of Katherine Parr, *Archaeologia*, v. 232 ; E, a stone carving of the arms of Edward VI over the entrance at Penshurst

FIG. 230. From effigy of John of Eltham, brother of Edward III, 1336 (Westminster Abbey).

Place, Kent ; F, the Great Seal of Edward VI, 1547 ; G, the achievement of Elizabeth, Harl. MS. 6096 ; H, Leigh's *Accedence of Armorie*, 1562, fol. 16 b, apparently a *cartouche*, or oval shield, on a bracket ; I, cf. the 'shields of the Amazons', Petit, *Dissertatio de Amazonibus*, Amst. 1687, p. 180 et seq. ; J, K, Bolton's *Elements of Armorie*, 1610, p. 147: cf. Smith's *Dictionary of Greek and Roman Antiquities*, 1890, ii. 80.

Although broad-based shields were not unfrequently employed in war contemporaneously with pointed shields between 1200 and 1500, still one striking normal difference in the decorative escutcheons of the sixteenth and succeeding centuries is the usual widening of the base, a tendency to which had set in from about 1450 onwards. This alteration was introduced for greater convenience in quartering a number of coats, a custom uncommon before 1500 ; numerous quarterings moreover would make a shield too indistinct and confusing for military use. Later, the canon of filling the field came to be disregarded, and charges decreased in their proportions relatively to the size of shields, the shapes of which remained fanciful. This new phase of armorial and artistic deterioration had already set in under the later Tudors, but proceeded from bad to worse in and after the following century. To this was added the further fault of multiplying and crowding charges to confusion.

FIG. 231. *Vide* Talbot Banners, *Catalogue Heraldic Exhib., Soc. Antiq.*, 1894, Plates xxv, xxvi.

Curiously enough, as shields became unreal and conventional, animals charged upon them tended to become unconventional and quasi-natural. This sacrifice of dramatic to literal truth was by no means an improvement from an emblematic point of view, for by being naturalized in appearance they lost in symbolical force. Thus there was a debasement not only in the shields but also in the bearings. The conventional armorial lion, for instance, of the Middle Ages symbolizes in its perfected type all the peculiar features and powers of the beast, which to that end are grotesquely exaggerated, in order that its presentment may be as terrific as possible. Its majesty, ferocity, agility, and rampageousness are intentionally portrayed with extreme and grim extravagance. Its inevitable activity is indicated by the sinuous leanness of a body scarcely thicker than the many-tufted tail with which it was supposed to lash its fury, to cover up its tracks, and to describe around itself a charmed circle in the sand as a ring-fence to enclose its prey ; while being 'armed and langued', that is, having its teeth and tongue and eagle-like claws depicted, of a different colour from the rest, those aggressive and ravening members are brought into special prominence. And, apparently, common sense was not shocked; presumably because a lion was rarely seen in England. [Figs. 230 and 231. A particularly beautiful lion, from a French MS. of *c.* 1350, is given by Viollet-le-Duc in his *Mobilier Français* (v. 175).] The same change from conventionalization to realism affected also inanimate charges, a case of which is shown in Fig. 232, A–D, which illustrate the *manche*, D marking a return to the unconventionalized form of the actual sleeve in which the bearing originated.

The substitution of the concrete for the abstract dealt a further blow at genuine symbolism. As an example of this may be adduced the picture, rather than arms, granted in 1605 to the Gardeners' Company of London. Two centuries before, a spade, or a rake, would have sufficed; but here we have a landscape, embellished with flowers, and in the foreground a man digging. The eighteenth and the first half of the nineteenth century saw armory at its worst. In the motley collection of objects, heraldic and pictorial, that crowd the coat devised for Lord Nelson are jumbled together four ordinaries and a cross flory, blazing bombs, a seascape, a palm-tree, a shipwreck, a ruined battery, and an inscription. A rich and varied store of debased heraldry is to be found throughout the whole series of English book-plates, which did not come into vogue till armorial decay had set in.

It requires some effort of the imagination for us fully to realize to how great an extent heraldry in its numerous branches, aspects, and applications, in one way or another according to the age, entered directly or indirectly into the lives of our forefathers prior to the eighteenth century. Its importance was unquestioned and unquestionable, its significance intense. In battle and in duel, in pageant and in joust; on armour, weapons, shields, and flags; on housings, harness, equipages, and tents; in the crest, the badge, the device, the livery, and the *cri de guerre*; in architecture, whether military, ecclesiastical, or domestic, without doors or within; on the gate-house of the castle, on the chimney-hood of the hall; on wall or in window of manor-house and church; on roof-beam or on ceiling, on pavement and on tomb; on tapestry, on furniture, on panel, and on plate; on the clothing of both sexes, and on the vestments of the priest; on jewellery, on bindings, in illuminations, and in seals ; in the class-barrier fixed at table by the 'Salt', and in many an ale-house sign ; in the figure-heads and names, and on the gunwales, masts, and sails of ships [e.g. Fig. 235], at the Visitations of the officers of arms, and at the gorgeous heraldic funerals of the gentry ; in the armorial allusions in which early literature abounds (one of the indications that a knowledge of heraldry formed no small part of the education of gentle men and women), and in the political songs of the people where great men's badges did duty for their names ; at every turn and in every guise it met the eye or ear. The yeoman, who served as hobilar, archer, or billman, and who, as ungentle, bore no coat on service

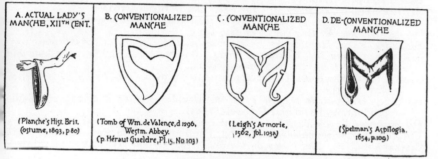

FIG. 232.

(though, like the dalesmen of the Lake District, he may have displayed one in his home), read his place in camp and field by the bearings on the banner or the pennon of the commander in whose train he fought, in all likelihood the only language he could spell. And long after armory ceased to be a factor in military array, its social and genealogical import remained vigorous. To the diverse sentiments of the jealous gentleman of ancient lineage, of the new-created gentle, of the aspirant to gentlehood, and of the rejected of the heralds who had been 'disclaymed to be noe gent', it appealed as a very real thing full of precious meaning. Coat-armour was the *preuve de noblesse* of the possessor, it was the hallmark coveted by the parvenu.

## Books for reference.

PLANCHÉ, *The Pursuivant of Arms*, last edition, 1873 (critical and historical : an important book).

BOUTELL, *Heraldry, Historical and Popular*, 3rd edition, 1864 (general).

—— *English Heraldry*, 6th edition, 1899 (elementary).

WOODWARD, *Heraldry, British and Foreign*, new and enlarged edition, 2 vols., 1896 (general).

—— *Ecclesiastical Heraldry, British and Foreign*, 1894.

GUILLIM, *Display of Heraldry*, 6th edition, 1724 (a classic, but contains much that is exploded).

EDMONDSON, *Complete Body of Heraldry*, 2 vols., 1780 (still valuable for references).

BEDFORD, *The Blazon of Episcopacy* (England and Wales only), 1897.

PARKER, *Glossary of Terms used in Heraldry*, new edition by H. Gough, 1894.

ELVIN, *A Dictionary of Heraldry*, 1889. (Useful for technical terms.)

EVE, *Decorative Heraldry*, 1897 (artistic)

ST. JOHN HOPE, *Heraldry for Craftsmen and Designers*, 1913.

—— *The Stall-Plates of the Knights of the Garter, 1348–1485*, 1901.

—— *A Grammar of English Heraldry*, 1913.

BALFOUR, PAUL, *Heraldry in Relation to Scottish History and Art*, 1900.

STEVENSON, *Heraldry in Scotland*, 1914. (' A recension ' of SETON'S *Law and Practice of Heraldry in Scotland*, 1863.)

GREENSTREET and RUSSELL, ' Reference List of the Rolls of Arms ' (*Genealogist*, vol. v, 1881).

BOUTON, *Armorial de 1334 à 1372 par Gueldre Héraut d'Armes*, Facsimile reproduction, Paris and Brussels, 1881.

*Die Wappenrolle von Zürich* (14th cent.), Facsimile reproduction, Zürich, 1860.

VIRGIL SOLIS, *Wappenbüchlein* (1555), Facsimile reproduction, Munich, 1886.

GRAZEBROOK, G., *The Dates of Variously-shaped Shields*, privately printed, 1890.

—— *The Earl Marshal's Court in England*, privately printed, 1895.

NOBLE, *A History of the College of Arms*, 1805.

W. DE GRAY BIRCH, *Seals*, 1907.

DE RAADT, *Sceaux Armoriés*, Brussels, 1898–1903.

SCHLUMBERGER and BLANCHET, *Collections sigillographiques*, Paris, 1914.

CHASSANT and DELBARRE, *Dictionnaire de Sigillographie*, 1860 (an excellent little manual).

MOULE, *Bibliotheca Heraldica*, 1822 (an exhaustive analytical bibliography down to that date).

GATFIELD, *Guide to Books and MSS. relating to English and Foreign Heraldry*, 1892. (A great collection, but ill arranged.)

BOARD OF EDUCATION, *Classed Catalogue of Books on Heraldry*, 1901. (Needs bringing down to date.)

PAPWORTH, *Ordinary of British Armorials*, 1874.

BURKE, *General Armory*.

N.B.—Of the last two books each is the complement of the other : the former gives coats and names, the latter names and coats.

# VII

# SHIPPING

## 1. *Shipping before the Norman Conquest.*

IF we leave aside such vessels as may have been used
by the ancient Britons, as well as the fleet, whatever its
character, that Caesar describes as assisting the Veneti
against him, we may refer the beginning of the English navy
to the institution of the *Classis Britannica,* or *Classiarii
Britannici* (according to the respective readings of French
and English antiquaries) by the Roman Caesars to ensure
the command of the Channel and the North Sea and the
protection of the limiting shores. Historically therefore, in
heirship if not in institutions, we may regard our navy as
directly descended from that of Rome ; like it a supreme
factor in the forging of an empire, and only exceeding its
forerunner in the extent of its sway. The exact date of
the formation of the British division of the Roman fleet is
unknown, but it is supposed to have been created by
Claudius at the time of, or shortly after, his invasion of
Britain in A.D. 43. We know that, later, its ports were
*Bononia* (Boulogne)—the head-quarters—*Dubris* (Dover),
*Rutupiae* (Richborough), *Portus Lemanis* (Hythe), and other
places, and that at a still later period it grew so large that
it was divided into twelve sections attached to additional
stations extending down the Channel on the Gallic shore.
It is, perhaps, hardly a flight of antiquarian fancy to see in
the stations on the ' Saxon Shore ', rather than in Teutonic
institutions, the germ of the combination afterwards famous
as the Cinque Ports, a germ stimulated into growth by
strategic position, tradition of naval warfare, and habit of
seafaring life. All our knowledge of the *Classis Britannica*
has been gained from funeral inscriptions, and from them
we learn that there were corporations of carpenters, caulkers,
sail-makers, and others at *Regnum* (Chichester) in connexion
with it. Of the ships we can only surmise that they were

of the Mediterranean galley type with such modifications as experience showed to be necessary in a wilder sea than the Mediterranean ; but it is possible that certain local forms and peculiarities are survivals from this forgotten source. The name of one ship, *Triremis Radians*, is preserved in an inscription, and should be mentioned as the earliest name of a British ship that has come down to us. The *Classis Britannica* affords us the earliest example of the influence of sea-power in the history of these islands, since by controlling it Carausius was enabled, in A.D. 286, to declare himself Emperor of Britain, and he and his successor Allectus retained their independence as long as they held the command of the Channel.

The Roman galley with its one mast and sail, large, heavily built, beaked for ramming, and essentially depending on human muscle for motive power, died out without establishing itself, being an extraneous product brought by foreigners and going with them. It was different with its successor, common in the main to Anglo-Saxons, Danes, and Normans, who may be considered together as the Scandinavian group. The Scandinavian ship, a galley of course, but sufficiently well designed, stable, and weatherly to be used also as a real sailing-ship, possessing characteristics to which ship designers have returned to-day, became naturalized here with its inventors, and remained for centuries the model of the northern war-ship until changes in naval arms and tactics modified shipbuilding—distinctly for the worse. However, it must always be remembered that, side by side with these military ships described and illustrated in histories, there was invariably the plodding cargo-ship constructed not for speed but for profit, tub-shaped, round-bowed, and flat-bottomed, unobtrusive, but in the end the only foundation on which military navies can be built up. The galleys bulk largely in Roman history, but behind them were merchantmen of 250 tons ; the Northmen were traders before they were ravagers, and in the Anglo-Saxon laws we find customs and commercial regulations, including a primitive insurance system, which imply the existence of a relatively large trade. The turn of the cargo-ship came in the fourteenth and fifteenth centuries, when, by the revolution due to the introduction of artillery, consequent tactical necessities, larger crews and longer voyages, with the additional stores needed, it ousted the galley model and remained in possession until the present century.

The figure given here of what is known as the Gokstad ship [Fig. 233] found in a burial-mound, the grave of some forgotten chief, in Southern Norway in 1880, and assigned to the ninth century, will illustrate generally the qualities of the vessels in use for many centuries until military developments, especially the gradual use of cargo-vessels in warfare, led to larger and heavier ships of higher freeboard. This Viking ship, clincher-built, caulked with hair and iron-fastened, was 66 feet long on the keel and 78 feet over all, with 15½ feet extreme breadth, and the

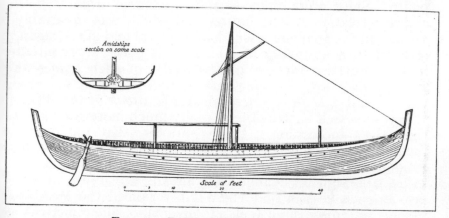

FIG. 233. THE GOKSTAD SHIP.

reader will notice the beautiful proportions, the sharp entry and run fore and aft, the great sheer, or rise, at stem and stern, and the general combination of lightness, strength, and grace. All the Scandinavian ships conformed to this model, although classified under many different names; swiftness, except in the *knerrir*, or cargo-carriers, being the chief aim of the builders. Ships were usually from 50 to 150 feet, or more, in length; one belonging to Cnut the Great is known to have been of at least 300 feet. They had from twelve to thirty-five 'rooms' or seats for the rowers, and the larger vessels were decked, with cabins below and a raised platform aft. Externally they were painted white, blue, red, or any combination of colours, with the warriors' shields, also of different colours, ranged round the gunwales, both to save space and to serve as a protection. Both ends of the vessel were alike, so that it could be steered from either by the paddle used everywhere until the invention of the rudder. Standards and pennants are spoken of in the Sagas, and there was one mast with a square sail of woollen stuff, white, or in coloured stripes of blue, red, and green. There are references to fighting-tops on the masts, but they were probably a late introduction. As the two-armed iron anchor was certainly used by the Romans, as it is shown in the Bayeux Tapestry, and as the Northmen learnt the use of the sail from the Romans, they may be supposed to have copied the anchor, at first stockless, but there is no positive evidence on the point. Ships were named, and the name usually bore a direct relation to the figure-head which was invariably present in the shape of a wooden, or metal and gilt, dragon, or head of an animal or of a bird. The poetic sense latent in the Northern races expressed itself in such names as *Deer of the Surf*, *Sea-king's Deer*, and *Horse of the Sea*, while a sail was sometimes called *The Cloak of the Wind*. It was in vessels such as these, really much more seaworthy than their successors in later centuries, that the Anglo-Saxons came to England, that the Danes invaded the Anglo-Saxons, and that William I crushed both, although in his time signs of change were already apparent ; it was also in such vessels that the Vikings ranged the Mediterranean, and discovered Iceland, Greenland, and America.

Anglo-Saxon continental commerce extended from the North German ports to the Bay of Biscay. It was not carried wholly in English ships, but the existence of a regular system of port dues implies a trade of some magnitude. From the time of the complete settlement shipbuilding had probably been retrograding, and the only instance known to us of any improvement is in the ' long ships ', designed and built by Alfred, pulling sixty oars, and described as being swifter and steadier than the Danish. The Jutes, Saxons, and Angles had never been so bold a race of seamen as the Danes, and the settlement of the latter was needed to stimulate commerce and navigation. It seems probable that, as a whole, the navies of the Anglo-Saxon and Danish kings were based on a more or less permanent state organization, and were larger than those of the continental powers, whose fleets, outside the Mediterranean, hardly existed in a specialized form. But English superiority in this respect was not necessarily due to greater political sagacity, but to political and geographical needs which automatically enforced certain consequences.

It is unnecessary to notice here the continual maritime battles the Anglo-Saxons fought, usually to their loss, with their opponents ; or to do more than mention the extra-ordinary legends associated with Edgar (A.D. 959–75), who is said to have asserted the sovereignty of the British seas, and to have had from 3,600 to 4,800 ships, numbers which imply at least 180,000 to 240,000 seamen and soldiers. More authentic is Æthelred's levy, in 1008, of a vessel, or an equivalent payment in money, from every 310 hides of land, the earliest precedent for the legality of ship-money.

### 2. *The Cinque Ports.*

Whatever may have been the cause of his remissness, Harold's loss of the command of the Channel, and his neglect of the elementary strategic principle of attacking the enemy on his own coasts, cost him crown and life. The greater part of Harold's fleet seems to have been carried away by his sons, and the course of events indicates that for some years the Conqueror had practically no English navy. In such circumstances the association known as the Cinque Ports—of Dover, Romney, Sandwich, Hastings, Hythe, and other places—came into prominence, and although accustomed to render especial service to the Crown before the Conquest, now, by the habit of comparative discipline, co-ordinated effort, and comradeship, became for two centuries the backbone of English fleets, and sometimes with its own strength alone successfully maintained an equal maritime struggle with France. The Cinque Ports fleet was the analogue of the Channel Squadron of to-day, always mobilized or ready for mobilization.

One result of the Conquest was that the Channel, from being a field of combat between opposing races, became a waterway uniting two portions of the same empire ; under our Angevin kings the small kingdom of France was ringed round by English possessions or independent feudatories, nor had the French king direct or indirect control over one foot of seaboard until Philip Augustus seized Normandy in 1204. Therefore the services of the Cinque

Ports were chiefly rendered during the thirteenth and fourteenth centuries ; previous to that era their prosperity and loyalty were fostered by charters and privileges accorded by successive monarchs, and their efficiency perfected by training in crushing piracy (an occupation in those early centuries merely a branch of trade), in supplying naval contingents for Scottish and Welsh wars, in transporting troops, and other duties.  When their full strength was called upon they were required to furnish fifty-seven ships and some 1,300 men for fifteen days at their own expense, and for any longer period at the expense of the Crown. The Portsmen played a most important part during the reign of John, to whom, with the exception of one short interval, they remained faithful during the entire reign, and it was mainly owing to their support that he was able to retain his crown.  In 1217 the Cinque Ports justified the exemptions and privileges that had aroused the jealousy of other coast towns by winning the first decisive sea-battle in English history.  A single land-victory may decide a campaign, but rarely a war ; the results of a sea-victory are frequently more far-reaching and may mean the ruin or the salvation of a nation.  In this instance the immediate consequence of the engagement off the South Foreland, on August 24, 1217, was to complete the advantage which the English had gained by the Battle of Lincoln and to ensure the retirement of the French invader. Within less than three weeks—on September 11—Lewis of France, his communications destroyed, signed a peace and left England.  Seldom in history can cause and effect be so clearly connected.

The Cinque Ports fleet was sometimes called ' The Royal Navy of the Cinque Ports ', but during the whole period of its existence there was always available, side by side with it, a force, more or less strong, of royal ships and galleys and the whole strength of the kingdom in merchant vessels.  It was of these latter, if we exclude the reign of Henry V, that the bulk of the fleets consisted to the time of Henry VIII ; only one-thirtieth of the ships collected by Edward III for the reduction of Calais belonged to the Crown, and probably ordinary fleets were often without any royal vessels at all.  As the royal ships belonged exclusively to the king, and had to be maintained from the royal revenues, it was to his interest to use, as much as possible, the Cinque Ports and merchantmen, since the latter only required some temporary additions to convert them into fighting ships.  The steady growth of commerce, due to successful war and the extension of English dominion through four centuries, tended to the increase of merchant-men available and to a diminution of the importance of the Cinque Ports.  An ordinance of Henry II in 1181 forbidding the sale of English ships to foreigners implies not only a recognition of the value of a native marine but also that shipbuilding was a flourishing industry.  The creation of a great Crown navy by Henry V, the beginning of a new era, the increase in the size and cost of ships, and the physical changes caused by the sea to the injury of the Ports, ended in the destruction of their national utility.  The days when ' they were enfranchised that they might be a guard and a wall between us and foreigners ' were over ; a Cinque Ports squadron was in commission from September 1444 until April 1445, which must be almost or quite the last instance of the employment of the Ports in their associated capacity.  At the head of both the civil and military busi-ness of the Five Ports was the Warden, at first always the governor of Dover Castle, afterwards usually a courtier, and now commonly a politician.  But in the Middle Ages both his duties and his privileges were very real, rendering him an important personage, and frequently leading to friction with the Lord Admiral with whom he was often in conflict.

### 3.  *Shipping from William I to Henry V.*

It will be convenient to consider here as a whole the technical details of shipping between the Conquest and the reign of Henry V, when begins the development of the modern ship.  Besides the spur of growing commerce and its corollary, the fact, true in all ages, that the larger a merchantman the cheaper relatively it is to work, the most important stimulus to advancement was derived from the southern races during the Crusades.  From the dawn of human progress until the rediscovery of America the Mediterranean was the centre of maritime advance ; the art of building, improvements in rigging and sailing, increase in size, the application of tactics to the formation and handling of fleets in action, maritime codes, signalling, and other details, all had their origin there.   While England was using 50 and 100 ton vessels, Barcelona, Venice, and Genoa were building three-decked ships capable of carrying hundreds of tons of cargo and hundreds of passengers ;  in such circumstances the Crusades, by bringing the Northerners into contact with more civilized races, necessarily tended to advancement, although the effect was not immediate since England had not then any use for large ships.  English ships, however, must frequently have been larger than is usually supposed, if it be true that there were 300 or 400 persons on board the *Blanche Nef* when she was lost with Henry I's son William in 1120 ;  and in 1170 a chronicler records the loss of another vessel with 400 people in her.

The chief alteration in the military navy, following the Conquest, was the gradual introduction of the cargo-ship into the fighting squadrons instead of leaving battles to be fought out, as before, between the long-ships.   The introduction of the sailing-ship of high freeboard was the knell of the rowing ship, which was also racially distasteful to men of Northern origin when they were called upon to do the work of slaves for pay instead of plunder.  Galley could board galley, but could hardly board the loftier sailing-vessel which, before it carried artillery, it could at most try to ram and sink while exposed to a plunging fire :  added to this, events tended more and more to send fleets or ships to sea in winter, a duty for which the galley was utterly unfit, while the fighting proportion of the crews grew too large for the limited space afforded by a rowing vessel. Therefore, after the reign of Edward I, galleys fell steadily out of use until, by the end of the fourteenth century, they had disappeared except for special purposes.   Often the number of men in the crew of a galley of this period shows that it must have depended chiefly on sail-power, although the name remained, as it remained as late as the eighteenth century, to describe a particular build capable of using sweeps on occasion.   Moreover, English sovereigns often lessened their expenses by allowing merchants to hire men-of-war in time of peace, a usual proceeding down to the reign of Elizabeth, and no sane merchant would freight a galley unless expense was no object.

By the reign of John *cogs* [1] and ' great ships ' were in use,

---

[1] The *cog* was a cargo-ship, broadly built with blunt prow and stern.

besides many others doubtless presenting only variations in size or detail. The barge, a favourite Norman build, being the enlarged Viking long-ship, sometimes with two decks, using oar and sail, and brought over by the Conqueror, was adopted here and was probably the model of the semi-fighting, semi-cargo ship which, under various names, made up the bulk of the fighting fleets. There was no accurate method of measuring tonnage, which was simply calculated by the number of tuns of Bordeaux wine a ship carried when laden, but by 1214 ships of 80 and 100 of such tuns were not uncommon, and we hear, under Edward III, of 200 tuns and upwards. A ship found in 1823 in an old channel of the river Rother at the west end of the Isle of Oxney, buried in nineteen feet of deposit, belongs perhaps to this period. Apparently a merchantman, she was assigned by the antiquaries of 1823 to the reign of Edward I, and is supposed to have been lost in the great storm of 1287, when old Winchelsea was destroyed and the course of the Rother changed. She was built of oak and single-masted, round-bowed and flat-floored with no keel, and had one cabin forward and two aft. That she was open amidships when found does not prove that no deck, either permanent or temporary, originally existed. She was caulked with moss, which points to great antiquity, and her boats, of which the remains were found near, were caulked with hair. Altogether, except in her greater depth, she resembles the modern Thames barge which, with the Newcastle ' keel ', is probably a survival of Plantagenet shipping. The rigging of these vessels was simpler than that of to-day, because they had only one mast with one square sail, but the names and things in use were much the same. Forestays and mainstays took the place of shrouds which, with rattlins, were brought into use in the fourteenth century, the modern backstay dating from the late sixteenth or early seventeenth century. The yard was fitted with braces, and the sail, usually coloured and sometimes decorated with armorial bearings, had brails and reefs, while additional canvas was provided in the shape of one or more bonnets which laced on to the foot of the sail. The hull was painted red or other colours, and was sometimes ornamented with heraldic badges or designs in gilt. Sheets, cranelines and bowlines, trusses, collars, racks, davits, halliards, bolt-ropes, seizings, hawsers, shivers, pulleys, spikes (handspikes), ribands, hatches, foothooks, buoys, and windlasses, were used then as now. Some form of pump or baler ('wynding-balie'), worked by means of the windlass, was used to free the ship of water; the bowsprit did not come into fashion until the fifteenth century, but is sometimes seen in a rudimentary form with the forestay made fast to it. The modern rudder was introduced towards the end of the thirteenth century; it appears in an English MS. of about 1300, and on the seal of the town of Damme in 1309. From the fact that it is shown in Northern MSS., seals, and coins earlier than in those of South French or Italian provenance.

FIG. 234. THE EVOLUTION OF THE FORECASTLE
THROUGH 400 YEARS.

it may be presumed to be a Northern, perhaps a Flemish, invention.

If we may judge of the appearance of ships from the illuminations in MSS., the high Norman stem and stern posts were still in use during the greater part of the period under consideration. The necessities of warfare, the need for more space and a position of greater advantage than the deck, led to the introduction of 'castles', temporary structures of wood in the bow and stern, which could be put in place during a cruise and afterwards removed. A fighting-top was also slung or fixed at some point along the mast. The gradual evolution of the temporary castle into the later forecastle and poop can be followed with sufficient precision from the MSS. available [Fig. 234]. At first we have a skeleton structure of beams, lashed to the stem and gunwale, supporting a lofty platform; then the stem is bent outwards and the platform lowered and brought over it ; next the platform becomes a permanent part of the projecting stem which is widened out into a geometrical shape—square or pentagonal—and juts out far beyond the cutwater. As this would make the ship pitch heavily and take water on board in tons, a further step was either to lengthen the keel and body of the hull to bring it under the forecastle, or to bring this inboard. Both processes, but chiefly the latter, operated to effect the change towards the modern type, leaving the beakhead of the fifteenth, sixteenth, and seventeenth centuries as a survival of the obsolete Norman prow. The development of the poop was more direct, since it was brought altogether inboard at an earlier date. To fill in the body of the forecastle and poop with cabins, afterwards to increase the number of these cabins by having two or three decks of them in the structures fore and aft, was a natural proceeding as crews increased and voyages became longer.

### 4. *Mediaeval Warfare, Tactics, and Organization.*

Among the Mediterranean sea-powers treatises on tactics and the art of naval warfare had been in use for centuries, but in the North methods of fighting were still primitive. Owing to the limited range of offensive weapons the object of commanders was to come to hand-grips without delay. The battle of 1217 is the earliest instance that we can trace of any appreciation of tactics ; there, the English worked to windward and fell, in superior force, on the weathermost French ships, obeying the tactical axiom of concentrating on that part of the enemy's fleet which can least easily be assisted, a maxim acted upon by Howard in July 1588, by Monck in June 1666, and by Nelson at the Nile. How little any such principles were understood in 1217 may be appreciated from the fact that the French commander, a fighter of long and varied experience under both crowns, did not dream of the English purpose, but thought that they were bent on attacking Calais in his absence. Actual fighting was of a simple character ; as the vessels closed the archers plied their bows, and then boarding was attempted, and for this purpose grappling irons were an essential portion of equipment. Fighting was done by the knights and soldiers, the office of the seamen being only to handle the ship ; the conquered were usually thrown overboard unless valuable for ransom. Stones and javelins were hurled from the tops, and Greek Fire was known in England in the reign of Richard I, although there is no recorded instance of its use on board English or French ships. Heavy engines for throwing stones were fixed on deck, and such things as quicklime thrown from windward to blind the enemy ; there were three cannon on board the *Christopher* in 1338, but the use of artillery did not practically affect tactics or shipbuilding during the fourteenth century. As fireships (of course of Mediterranean and classical origin) were used by the Flemings in 1304 they may be presumed to have been known to the English.

Ships and men for the fleets were obtained by impressment, the practical exercise by the sovereign of his right to the goods and services of all his subjects, nor, at this period, did it bear hardly upon those liable to it. The men were paid threepence a day, and, towards the end of the fourteenth or beginning of the fifteenth century, a ' reward ' of sixpence a week ; in view of the value of money this was a very high rate, higher than they had ever received before. Eventually the specialization of the fighting ship and their growing political power freed owners from the burden, while the men, being helpless, continued exposed to a demand systematically exercised under conditions arbitrarily fixed by force to their disadvantage. One result of the impressment system was that there was never any continuous command of the Channel other than that which the Cinque Ports could maintain. At each outbreak of war ships and men were pressed, and dismissed at its close, or as soon as the sea was cleared of the enemy ; thus the work had to be done over again every time. From a petition *temp.* Richard II we learn that in the flourishing times of Edward III there were 150 merchantmen fit for the line of battle—to borrow a later phrase—and, whatever the imperfections of the system, it did not prevent England from maintaining a consistent maritime superiority. The whole of the Hundred Years' War, a war not of defence but of conquest, was only possible as the result of controlling the Channel, just as in later centuries the Elizabethan war with Spain was fought out in the Netherlands, on the Spanish coasts, and in the West Indies, and the wars with Louis XIV and Napoleon on the continent, as the consequence of sea ascendency over a wider area. Merchantmen hired by the Crown received 3s. 4d. a ton per quarter, but owners had frequently some difficulty in obtaining payment. It was probably due to this difficulty that, in 1347, taxes on merchandise known as tunnage and poundage were levied specifically for naval purposes ; from the reign of Henry V it became customary to grant these duties for the life of the monarch, who was expected to maintain the navy from them.

There were three ship's officers, a rector, or master, at sixpence a day, a constable, and a steersman, all in command of the seamen only. Down to 1296 fleets were directed by officers called 'governors', or 'keepers', or 'justices', &c., but in March of that year William de Leybourne is styled Admiral, the earliest French date for the title being 1244, though it was of earlier use still in the Mediterranean. It is of Sicilian origin and is derived from the Arab *emir* ; the first naval commander to whom it is applied is George of Antioch (d. *c.* 1150), the lieutenant of Roger the Great, the first Norman king of Sicily. An Admiralty Court having jurisdiction in maritime causes, hitherto decided by the ordinary law courts, was constituted about 1350. The institution of this court was coincident with, and perhaps the consequence of, the first real claim of an English sovereign to be 'lord of the English sea and of the passage of the sea', but the claim was one of legal jurisdiction rather than of political supremacy as in the seventeenth century. A famous commercial code of the period issued by Richard I, and known as the Laws of Oléron, was only a recompilation of maritime customs and practices which had taken form in classical antiquity ; but the ordinances made in 1190 on discipline and punishments in the fleet may be considered the first 'articles of war' of our navy. The framers of the Norwegian code of 940 had the honour of humanizing the brutal law by which all wrecks and their cargoes belonged to the lord of the littoral or the Crown ; the example was followed by Richard in 1190 and then by Philip Augustus.

The English archives teem with complaints of, and attempts to remedy, the piracy which was constant for many centuries, and of which the profitable continuance proves the existence of a relatively large commerce. Privateering was not recognized by the issue of letters of marque until the reign of Henry III, and no doubt both before and after that period much that the victims called piracy the victors called privateering. Before the adoption of the system of letters of marque it was open to any private individual to fit out a ship to go cruising, and of course with no check but that of a complicated international protest on its operations; these would be limited only by its capacity for attack. When the Crown had a share in the privateer's profits it was to the interest of the sovereign to put down unauthorized endeavours, but it was not until 1585 that persons fitting out privateers had to give surety in the Admiralty Court not to injure neutrals or allies.

Besides being fancifully painted, a mediaeval ship was also decorated with the banners and pennons of the captain, the knights serving on board, and the especial banner of the owner or of the town to which it belonged. The Bayeux Tapestry, anterior to the period of heraldic bearings, shows two-, three-, four-, or five-pointed pennons in blue and yellow, or red and blue, some having a St. George's cross, and others a yellow cross. Many early cognizances were religious in signification; but when heraldic bearings became hereditary, towards the end of the thirteenth century, coats of arms grew purely secular in construction. The St. George's Cross is said to have been made the national badge by Richard I, but must have been in general use long before his reign. Equivalent to the present ' H.M.S. ' were the words ' of Westminster ', ' of the Tower ', and ' of Greenwich ', added to the ship's name, the second being used in the fourteenth and fifteenth centuries, and the third in the early sixteenth century. Even in the late seventeenth century the expression ' of Whitehall ' was sometimes used to designate a man-of-war. Abroad ships' names were almost invariably religious in form, the vessel being placed under the protection of a saint; here, the custom never took more than partial hold, and they were more often secular. In the sixteenth century many men-of-war names were derived from the royal badges and arms, e.g. *Antelope, Bull, Dragon, Sun, Rose in Sun, Falcon in Fetterlock, Golden Lion*; others were figurative, as the

*Mary Rose* in honour of Mary Tudor, sister of Henry VIII, the *Katherine Pomegranate* and *Katherine Plesaunce* after Katherine of Aragon (whose device was the pomegranate of Granada), and the *Elizabeth Jonas* which Elizabeth herself named as indicating her escape from her sister Mary.

The navy was under the direct control of the king, but from the reign of John we find an official called the Clerk, or Keeper, of the King's Ships, who attended to the duties of ordinary civil administration. The post existed in a modified form, in which the holder was called Clerk of the Acts, until the suppression of the Navy Board, to which he acted as secretary, in 1832. The royal ships were kept in the southern ports, especially Rye, Winchelsea, and Portsmouth ; at the last place there was in 1212 a kind of dock, or enclosed space, to receive the ships, as well as storehouses for their belongings. The earliest lighthouses, or 'nightflares', in Britain were the two erected by the Romans on the east and west cliffs at Dover. There must have been many lights kept up by religious houses during the 350 years following the Conquest. We hear of a light at Winchelsea in 1261, on the Ecrehou reefs in 1309, and at St. Catherine's (Isle of Wight), 1314, and Spurn Head, 1427. At St. Catherine's a part of the old light-tower still remains.

### 5. *Henry V and the Fifteenth-Century Navy.*

The fifteenth century is remarkable for the advance of shipbuilding, both in the size of vessels and in a corresponding addition in masts and sails. By the close of the century we can see a distinct approximation to the modern type [Fig. 235]. This was probably due to the fact that the navy of Henry V included a number of large Genoese ships, captured while in the French service, which provided a new model for English shipwrights. Moreover, the commercial prosperity of the first half of the century resulted in a larger seaborne trade, therefore the trading classes were ready to adopt improvements for which they could now find use. In 1439 and 1451, respectively, there were at least thirty-six and fifty merchant ships of 100 tons and upwards, including ten of 300 tons and upwards, numbers which compare favourably with the first half of the reign of Elizabeth ; and some principal ports, as Newcastle, Yarmouth, and Bristol, are absent from the lists from which these figures are taken. Two of the Dartmouth ships were of 400 tons each, the *Grâce-Dieu* of Hull was as big, and in 1460 William Canynge of Bristol possessed a fleet which contained one vessel of 400, one of 500, and another of 900 tons. Besides the trade with the opposite continental coasts, there had been, even in the preceding century, a considerable Icelandic and Baltic trade, and by 1422 English vessels were sailing to the Mediterranean, while a large passenger service with Spain existed for the conveyance of pilgrims desiring to visit the shrine of St. James at Compostella. The earliest sailing directions we possess are assigned to the reign of Edward IV, and include the coasts of Spain and Portugal.

FIG. 235. SHIP OF THE FIF-TEENTH CENTURY (Life of Richard, Earl of Warwick; Cott. MS. Julius, E. iv).

We find in the reign of Henry V the first approach to the powerful standing navy of later centuries ; he was also the first king completely to discard the galley and to build great sailing-ships of from 400 to 800 tons. Such a size necessarily required more sail area, and two masts, or even three and four by the end of the century, were common. The former single mast, the Low Latin *medianus*, was moved forward by the South French and Mediterranean races and became the *mât de misaine* (Ital. *mezzana*), or foremast, but the North French, English, and Northern races generally, moved it aft and called it the mizen mast. As it was impossible to build such vessels—depending solely on sail propulsion, and loaded with tophamper in the shape of forecastle and poop which were now solid, permanent structures—on galley lines which would have afforded no stability, the broad, deep cargo-ship became, subject to modifications, the model of the next three centuries. Moreover, the introduction of artillery placed on deck further enforced, if it did not originate, the change, since the long, narrow, shallow galley could never carry broadside guns, and in fact even in the broad cargo-ship their presence necessitated the ' tumbling home ', or transverse narrowing in of the upper works, so characteristic of the old ship, and was the immediate cause in this and many other ways of the specialization of the man-of-war. It was, however, only the final acceptance of a change that had been long progressing in the substitution in warfare of the ship of high freeboard for the narrower and faster one depending on human muscle for movement. Henry V possessed the finest navy in the world, and undoubtedly intended that it should continue so, but national feeling was not ripe for the support of a strong navy in time of peace, and the destruction that commenced within a week of his death soon annihilated it. During the reign of Henry VI such fleets as were sent to sea were of armed merchantmen procured by contract, and, although Edward IV took some steps towards reconstituting a Crown navy, it was not until Henry VII occupied the throne that the work was regularly carried on. He inherited from his predecessors six ships; but all of these were discarded before the end of his reign.

## 6. *The Navy under the Tudors.*

We are quite ignorant of the intermediate steps, but the inventories of the ships of Henry VII show that they possessed three and four masts, with topmasts as separate spars although fixed, and in one instance a top-gallant mast. Each mast had its corresponding sail, and there was now a spritsail on the bowsprit, and poop and forecastle were lofty and roomy structures. Possibly there were no intermediate steps, and the ships of Henry VII may be in direct descent from the Mediterranean models captured by Henry V, but the biggest ship of Henry VII, the *Regent*, of 600 tons, was built by his order on the lines of the French vessel in which he came over to Milford Haven in 1485. Two of his ships, the *Sweepstake* and the *Mary Fortune* (both built in 1497), were furnished with oars as well as masts and sails. Portholes, probably circular openings with no form of portlid, were introduced in the second half of the century, and rows of cannon laid on wooden beds armed the upper deck and the two or three tiers of forecastle and poop. The heaviest guns were *serpentines*, breechloading so far as the powder charge was concerned, and using a leaden, stone, or iron ball of from four to six ounces, or firing iron ' dice ', pieces of iron an inch and a half square. There were also guns of smaller calibre, known as *murderers*, *stone-guns*, and *hand-guns*. But all the old equipment of bows and arrows, javelins, &c., was still carried, with good reason, since the heavy gun of the period could only be loaded and fired twice in an hour.[1]

Two great steps towards the maintenance of a navy were taken by Henry VII. One was that he began the bounty system (in which he had been preceded by Venice, Genoa, Portugal, and Spain), by which builders of new ships were allowed a deduction from the customs of the first voyage as a reward for their enterprise. At first an uncertain amount, it became, in the sixteenth century, a regular allowance of five shillings a ton on vessels of 100 tons and upwards, and, down to the reign of Charles I, to which it continued, of five shillings on vessels of 200 tons or more. Henry also founded our first permanent dockyard. Earlier kings had possessed storehouses, and the mediaeval dock was simply a mud and brushwood fence round a ship hauled up on the mud above high-water mark ; Henry V had, as well as storehouses, some sort of workshops at Southampton, that place and the river Hamble flowing into the Solent being the naval head-quarters during his reign. Henry VII not only founded Portsmouth Yard, but built there, in 1495, at a cost of £193 0s. 6¾d., the first dry dock known in England. Whether it was the product of native ingenuity or copied from a foreign model is unknown ; it was constructed of wood, only the dockhead being of stone, and when a ship was inside, the space between and outside the gates was filled in with gravel.

The first English Navigation Act, itself later by a century than one enacted in Aragon, was due to Richard II. Both this, and another passed under Edward IV, had little effect, but Henry VII made a more serious effort to encourage English shipping by protective legislation. An Act of the

[1] See Goldingham, ' Navy under Henry VII ', in the *English Historical Review*, xxxiii. 472 ff.

first year of his reign was framed on the same lines as the famous measure of 1651, in that wines and other articles were to be imported only in ships owned by English subjects, and for 'the most part' manned by native crews. The only change in administration to be noticed during this century is the institution of the office, probably copied from Spain, of Lord Admiral in 1406. Theoretically the Lord Admiral governed the navy during peace and led it in war ; in reality, during the fifteenth century, it was a mere court

FIG. 236. R O W - B A R G E (from a MS. at Magdalene College, Cambridge).

office filled by relatives of the sovereign or by powerful nobles who had no practical relation with the navy.

Heretofore the navy had played a part of utility rather than of necessity, of offence as an auxiliary of the army rather than an independent factor in warfare, but during the reign of Henry VIII external circumstances were compelling change. Not merely had France become an organised kingdom, but the union with Brittany in 1491 had given it control of ocean ports and command of a race of fine seamen, with the result that the French kings were already organizing a navy with a better prospect of success than had yet existed. Again, on the continent, the era of

the professional soldier was beginning, and the nucleus of
a standing army was to be found in all the greater of the
western states, while Spain, in addition to its army and
the naval growth due to its transatlantic commerce, controlled the maritime power of the Low Countries. Neither
inclination nor necessity had hitherto disposed Englishmen
to permit the formation of a permanent military force, yet
the militia levies were no match for trained veterans,
especially since improvements in artillery and musketry

FIG. 237. THE 'HENRY GRACE A DIEU'
(from a MS. at Magdalene College, Cambridge).

had impaired the value of the English archer. Moreover,
the discoveries of Spain and Portugal, the great apparent,
but really illusory, maritime strength of the former power,
and the attempts of England herself in northerly latitudes,
all turned men's minds to the question of sea-power with
a wider understanding of its possibilities than had been
grasped before. Although all these causes were at work in
increasing the importance of the navy, they would have
failed perhaps in effect but for that natural genius for the
sea, the inheritance of the race, which enabled the men of
the sixteenth century to appreciate and use the weapon
Henry's sagacity prepared for them, nor was it of slight

consequence that the king himself happened to delight in the sea and ships and took a daily interest in matters relating to them. During Henry's reign at least eighty-five vessels, great and small, and thirteen row-barges of twenty tons each, were added to the navy, while his father had been content with five ships. There had been nothing like it before, except in the reign of Henry V, who had made a similar—relatively greater—increase, but in that instance the effort died out with the man to whose initiative it was

FIG. 238.  THE 'TIGER', 1546 (Anthony's MS., Add. MS. 22047).

owing.  Henry V was too soon, but when the man again arrived the moment had also come, and the seed then sown has flourished into a mighty tree.

Of the eighty-five ships, twenty-six were bought from Italian or Hanseatic owners, and thirteen were prizes, so that forty-six were built in the thirty-eight years of the reign.  In building there was a great advance, as may be seen from a comparison of the *Mary Rose* and the *Tiger*, belonging respectively to the beginning and the end of the reign.  The *Mary Rose* differs little, if at all, from vessels of the preceding century; the *Tiger* [Fig. 238] is a flush-decked ship with no superstructures, built probably on finer lines, heavily armed on a gun-deck (that is to say, on a deck below the upper deck), and looking a better sea-boat than many later vessels. Possibly not a few of these improvements were due to Henry himself, as the Spanish ambassador wrote to the Emperor in 1541 that the King was building according to a model of which he was the inventor, but the great shipwright of the time was James Baker, whose memory lived long among naval men as the first to adapt English ships to carry heavy guns. But it will be

FIG. 239. THE 'ANNE GALLANT', 1546 (Anthony's MS., Add. MS. 22047).

seen from the illustration of the *Anne Gallant* [Fig. 239], of the same date as the *Tiger* and three of her sisters, that the old fashion of lofty forecastle and poop was still in favour, and it survived the improved model, becoming exaggerated in comparison with that of the reign of Henry VIII. It was now growing usual to build vessels carvel-fashion—with the planks laid edge to edge—as being stronger than the clincher-built ships used from very early times. Decoration was obtained chiefly by banners and streamers, the latter of great length. In 1514 the flags for the *Great Harry* were painted by Vincent Vulpe, an Italian ; one of these a streamer displaying a dragon 45 yards long. Red, green, yellow, or white cloths were hung round the large basket-shaped tops, and painted wooden shields were ranged along the sides. As well as being carved and gilt the hulls were painted various colours, including ash, or timber, colour which became more common under Elizabeth, and finally developed into the yellow regulation coat above water of the ships of the late seventeenth and eighteenth centuries.

Edward IV had provided 'jackets', which may have been some sort of uniform, for the men, and the custom was continued by Henry VII, and extended by his son during the first years of his reign when he had a full treasury. Clothes supplied by Henry VIII were in white and green, the Tudor colours, and made of cloth for the sailors, and of satin and damask for the officers. In connexion with the question of uniform, it may be mentioned that a contemporary painting of the destruction of the French *Cordelière* in 1512 shows her men in red doublets.

The galley at no time formed so important an item in English fleets as it did in the navies of the Mediterranean powers. Obviously, this low-built craft was less suited to the vicissitudes of the ocean than to inland seas. Indeed, off our coasts it was only in a calm, when early sailing-ships were somewhat helpless, that the galley could operate with effect even in the Channel, and there a calm could not be depended upon to last. Still, we read of its being regularly used at home during the Norman and Plantagenet periods for purposes of harbour and coastal defence against enemies or pirates, and for the carrying out of such duties as in late days were performed by the 'revenue-cutter'; also by both English and French for short-distance raids on the adjacent seaboards when suitable weather could be reckoned on.

The galley, too, owing to its limited storage accommodation, could not remain long at sea, and that consideration would assist in confining its serviceableness to a great extent to the shorter distances of enclosed waters. Again, in the early days of powder, its gun-power was limited to stem and stern cannon, more particularly to the former: it had normally no broadside artillery, and subsequent attempts to introduce this were not permanently successful. It could carry only light guns, and the shock of the discharge of even these was apt to damage the hull of such lightly constructed boats.

The chief manœuvring value of the galley lay in its

independence of wind, its chief fighting value lay in its ram, and these two advantages made it a dangerous foe till sailing-ships came to be handled more quickly. In the end our Elizabethan seamen boasted that they could regard galleys with contempt. The galley could not be used for laying alongside and boarding a hostile vessel owing to its oars, which, in this way, served as a hindrance to itself and a protection to the enemy, much as the 'tumbling-home' of sailing-ships made the gap between the bulwarks of opposing craft too wide to be jumped. Boarding from its narrow bows, in turn, could only be made 'in column against line' as it were, and the projection of the beak, or 'spur', intensified this disadvantage. There was a further drawback to its being utilized for storming purposes. The bulk of the available space in a galley was required for the numerous oarsmen, and when to this was added that needed for other non-combatants such as mariners and artificers, a strong contingent of the latter being especially necessary on so comparatively fragile a vessel, it is clear that only a restricted number of fighting-men could be carried. One of the risks run by the galley was that of being caught while turning, which, owing to its length, took time, and cut down amidships by one of the heavier sailing-craft. This would shiver its oarage, smash into its low, frail free-board, and mean utter destruction. The galley continued to be useful for harbour defence until we find the last one left in Elizabeth's navy employed as a guardship at Thames-mouth and finally suffering the degradation of serving as a tug for supply-ships.

The *Galie Subtile* here shown [Fig. 240] was built in 1544, was of 200 tons burden, and carried 250 mariners (the number of soldiers drafted on is not stated) and three brass guns in the bows. In one account twenty-eight other guns of iron are mentioned as part of her equipment, but they do not appear in our drawing and must have been of very small calibre. Indeed, as we see, she is described as having only eight gunners. She presented a gay appearance. Her hull was painted in three colours horizontally disposed : yellow at the top, below that timber-colour, and the bottom dark brown ; the beak was yellow, including the point, then timber-colour, and below that scarlet. The awning at the bows was yellow ; the canopy at the stern was yellow outside, decorated with the Royal Arms and St. George's cross, and scarlet inside ; while the dragon's head was green and its tongue scarlet. The big gun in the bows was steel blue, the two smaller ones above it were green. The conventional shields along the gunwale, a dummy ornamental survival of the actual shields of Viking days, displayed variously a St. George's cross ; France and England quarterly ; *azure, a single lys or* ; or blue charged with H or R (for *Henricus* and *Rex*) in gold. The mast was scarlet,

FIG. 240. THE 'GALIE SUBTILE' (from a MS. at Magdalene College, Cambridge).

the yard timber-colour, the top white and yellow (the latter shows the darker), and the sweeps were white and scarlet. The flags on the hull, reckoning from the bows, were : (1) the Tudor livery colours of white and green, or *Barry argent and vert* ; (2) St. George, with a white fly ; (3) azure with a single gold lys, for France, and a gold ♄ for Henry in the fly ; (4) St. George, with white fly and a yellow border to the red cross ; (5) as no. 1 ; (6) as no. 4 ; (7) blue, with R H in yellow ; (8) the Royal Arms, which are partly repeated on the fly ; (9) St. George, with a fly of the Tudor colours. The streamers from the top and yard-arm bear St. George's cross with yellow border and

Tudor fly. The jolly-boat has a yellow gunwale, timber-coloured sides, and brown bottom. The master on the quarter-deck is in white with a red cross on his breast, and the crew wear pink jackets. This drawing is from the Pepysian Library in Magdalene College, Cambridge.

More enduring than Henry's experiments in shipbuilding, which, in some respects, hardly outlived him, were his improvements in armament. Hitherto vessels had carried serpentines weighing some 250 lb., and firing balls that could have had no effect whatever against a ship's sides, but the king introduced on shipboard heavy guns, from the

FIG. 241. A MERCHANTMAN of the year 1519.

land service, weighing 2,000 and 3,000 lb. ; the results were seen in the Elizabethan war when the Spanish ships were hopelessly outmatched in the weight of metal thrown in a broadside, and the heavy armament, in proportion to tonnage, of English men-of-war became a tradition continuing almost to the present day. Guns were now frequently mounted on wheeled carriages and were elevated or depressed by *quoins* (wedges), and some light pieces were carried in the tops, as is the custom now. Sometimes serpentines were placed, two or three or more together, on a frame, answering to the modern quick-firer ; cross-bar shot and inflammable mixtures, shot from cross-bows, to set an enemy's sails on fire, were in use. The ideal fighting ship is one which possesses high speed combined with the greatest power of offence and greatest capacity for resistance, qualities which naval constructors of the present day are vainly trying to obtain in conjunction, for one or the other has more or less to be sacrificed.   Shipbuilding in the sixteenth century, and for long afterwards, was a purely empirical art, but we see in Henry's ships the first consistent attempt with these objects in view.   Whether he obtained speed we do not know ; the defensive capacity,

FIG. 242.   A CARRACK (from Royal MS. 20 E. ix).

the stoutness of the sides, must have been as great as that of any probable antagonist ; the high offensive power was certainly attained.

Besides reorganizing and improving the combatant branch, Henry VIII re-created the administration.   Doubtless experience had shown the insufficiency of the one Clerk of the Ships, and several times during the reign additional but temporary help had been provided.   In 1546 the duties of the mediaeval officer were divided among a Treasurer, Comptroller, and Surveyor, the Clerk still remaining, but in a subordinate capacity.   The organization thus established by Henry has been altered and enlarged, but remains to-day the same in principle as framed by him. The king also drew up the first English set of regulations for the guidance of fleets at sea, some such orders being necessary now that navies were doing something more than merely transporting troops, or fighting an action and returning home ; these instructions dealt with the relative positions of ships in action, boarding, the use of flags, councils of war, and the duties of officers. Portsmouth dockyard was enlarged, and Woolwich and Deptford yards were founded in 1512 and 1517 ; shipwrights were obtained by impressment, and received from twopence to sixpence a day in addition to food and lodging. Soldiers were still carried on board ship, but seamen were now fighters as well ; their pay was 5s. a month, but in 1546 was raised to 6s. 8d., being still relatively less than in the preceding century, and officers received the same pay as the men, with the addition of a certain number of ' dead pays ' (v. Glossary), value 5s. each, according to rank. The sailors were allowed a gallon of beer a day, and, except when necessity compelled, water was not carried by men-of-war until the middle of the seventeenth century, and even then a money allowance was given when it was used instead of beer. It will be seen from this brief outline that Henry VIII re-fashioned the navy in three directions—shipbuilding, armament, and administration. He may be said to have created it, since from his reign it has been recognized as the especial national arm, and it is scarcely an exaggeration to say that the Spanish war at the end of the century was won by him, for Elizabeth never showed any real understanding of sea-power, and but for Henry's legacy of ships, of organization, and, above all, of the tradition of action by sea, if she moved at all in that direction would probably have moved too late.

The reigns of Edward VI and Mary call for little remark beyond a note that the often-repeated statement that they neglected the navy is incorrect. Edward VI was particularly interested in it ; and if, for various reasons, it remained nearly stationary or even somewhat decreased in strength, it still could compare not unfavourably with that of the first fifteen years of the reign of Elizabeth. In 1550 the Regency proceeded to carry out another reform purposed by Henry VIII, by forming a Victualling Department to take the place of the many individual agents who had

hitherto acted independently.   The question of the acknowledgement of English supremacy of the narrow seas, indicated by striking flag and lowering topsail, again comes
into prominence during these two reigns ; it was enforced
against Flemings and other nations, sometimes at the
cannon's mouth, but the matter was very tenderly treated
with France, nor was the claim ever admitted by that
power.

A marked feature of the reign of Elizabeth is the increase
in merchant shipping.   The bounty on new ships was now
always 5s. a ton, but the growth of commerce, the stimulus
of warfare, and a larger ocean trade encouraged shipbuilding to an extent hitherto unknown.   As fleets were
composed mostly of armed merchantmen, with a nucleus
of royal ships which undertook all the real fighting, it was
important that the government should know how many
vessels were available.   Therefore there are several returns
of the number of ships of 100 tons and upwards which
enable us to measure the maritime strength of the kingdom.
As the differentiation of the man-of-war from the merchantman only commenced with the use of artillery on shipboard,
and was hardly strongly marked as yet, such vessels were
able, theoretically, to take their place in the fighting line,
although in practice the desire of masters and owners to
save their ships from injury or destruction rendered them
of little value in actual warfare.   But for trading voyages
merchantmen were, and always had been, armed on the
same principle, if in a lighter fashion, as men-of-war, since
they depended on themselves for safety against pirates and
other enemies.   The earliest return remaining is of 1560,
and, although incomplete, shows 76 ships of 100 tons and
upwards ; the next surviving one of 1577, also incomplete,
gives 135, and the next, of 1582, is 177, figures which show
a steady growth ; and it is an instructive commentary on
them that in 1580 Philip's ambassador here wrote to his
master that the whole of the trade between England and
Spain was carried on in English ships.   Increase of shipping
necessarily encouraged seafaring life, and legislation was
directed to the same end.   To assist the fisheries, the
nursery of seamen, was an obvious method, and an Act of
1548, which ordered fish to be eaten on two days a week
under pecuniary penalties, was now renewed and enforced ;

other privileges were granted to fishing vessels and the
Navigation Acts were more rigidly applied.   A return of
1582 shows that there were upwards of 16,000 seamen,
fishermen, and masters of ships available at that time.
Except in 1588, when some 10,000 or 12,000 seamen were
in pay, none of the Elizabethan fleets required more than
from 2,000 to 6,000 men, so that the resources of the
kingdom in this respect were more than equal to the
demands made upon them.   The prospect of plunder
attracted men to the fleets without much necessity for
impressment, but pay was raised to 10s. a month in 1585.
In 1582 and 1602 scales of pay for officers were drawn up
in place of the 'dead pays' (v. Glossary) and rewards
allotted to them under Henry VIII.

   The rights of the seamen to prize money remained very
indefinite during the centuries under review.   In early
times, when there was little distinction between warfare
and piracy, no doubt the captors kept whatever they took,
but as the power of the Crown grew stronger the sovereign
claimed all or part of the prize.   John allotted prize money,
but not, apparently, on any other principle than his own
decision as to the amount to be given ; Henry III appears
not to have expected more than a share.   In the contract-
fleets of the reign of Henry VI the whole proceeds were
granted to owners, officers, and crews ;  and in the agreement which Henry VIII made with Sir Edward Howard in
1512 the king reserved to himself half the profits of captures
and all the ordnance taken.   By a very old custom, of
which the origin was lost in antiquity, the men were entitled
to pillage for themselves on the upper deck of a prize, as
soon as she was taken, without being called to account ;
and each of the superior officers was allowed an especial
perquisite, e. g. the captain, the personal belongings of the
other captain ;  the master, the best cable ;  the gunner,
a piece of ordnance, &c.   Edward VI gave £100 to the
crew of a man-of-war that took a French galley, in which,
of course, there would be little or nothing to plunder.
During the reign of Elizabeth it was common for privateers
to be sent to sea on a joint-stock principle, the proceeds
of captures being divided into thirds, of which one went
to the owners of the ship, one to the victuallers, and one to
the officers and men, the last being in lieu of wages.   Eliza-

beth promised as little as she could, and usually sought
means to evade her engagements, but in the Cadiz voyage
of 1596 the men were to be granted, over and above their
wages, a third of the value of all prizes and merchandise,
except treasure or jewels, which she reserved to herself.
In Elizabeth's reign also the question of the Right of Search
and of the seizure of contraband of war came into prominence, and led to difficulties with neutral powers, although
both claims had been exercised from the thirteenth century
and perhaps earlier.   An Order in Council of 1589 for the
first time clearly defined contraband, making the term
include all articles necessary for the equipment of ships
used in warfare by land or sea, and foodstuffs.

During the last months of Mary's reign the dockyards
were working energetically, and the same activity continued, for a time, after Elizabeth's accession.   But an
analysis of the navy list of her reign shows that, exclusive
of rebuildings and prizes, only twenty-nine vessels of 100
tons and upwards were added to the navy between 1558
and 1603, notwithstanding eighteen years of warfare and
the fact that fleets were now acting thousands of miles from
home.   The earlier of the big ships built under Elizabeth
were large vessels of the type favoured in the middle of the
century—short, broad, and with lofty superstructures ;  in
later years vessels of from 200 to 400 tons were preferred,
and even in the larger ones the tophamper was greatly
diminished.   Three large ships, of from 800 to 1,000 tons
each, were built in 1559 and 1560, and one of them was
the first *Victory* in the English navy.   Unfortunately no
drawing of her exists, but she doubtless resembled, on
a larger scale, the illustration here given of an Elizabethan
man-of-war of the first half of the reign [Fig. 243], had the
same lofty poop, ponderous beakhead, and probably a much
higher forecastle ;  from an incidental reference in Hakluyt
we know that her waist, the lowest part of the vessel, was
twenty feet above the water-line.   About the middle of the
reign, when Sir John Hawkyns became chief of the naval
administration, ships were constructed on finer lines than
hitherto, longer in proportion to their breadth, and sat
lower in the water, and were therefore much more weatherly
than their predecessors.   Even with these improvements
the total length, including the great rake, or overhang,

of the stem and beakhead forward and the stern-post aft, was little more than three, or three and a half, times the beam. The galley had a length of seven or eight times her beam, thus approximating in proportions to the modern steamer. Externally ships were painted black and white, or green and white, or red, or timber-colour ; figure-heads, usually a dragon or a lion (probably taken from the supporters of the royal arms), were in use ; carved figures of men and beasts, brackets, and gilding, decorated both the outside and the inside ; cabins were painted and upholstered in green and white, and the royal arms in gold and colours were on the stern. Many improvements were introduced. Topmasts were now raised or lowered instead of being fixed, sheathing by means of a layer of tar and hair covered by thin planking became usual, but lead sheathing, copied from the Spanish navy, had been used here in the reign of Edward VI ; chain pumps and a patent log, very much like one now employed, were other inventions. Ingenuity was further turned to maritime matters with the result that centreboard boats, paddlewheels, diving-dresses, submarine boats, unsinkable ships, and the elevating screw for ship guns were all described in more or less detail. The large ships had two decks, an upper one and a gundeck underneath ; about 1590 a third, called a false orlop, or platform, and laid in the hold to carry cabins and stores, was brought in ; this deck, 'the orlop' distinctively of the seventeenth and eighteenth centuries, did not at first run the whole length of the ship. Pillars to support the decks, and riders to strengthen the sides, were other additions.

A ship was divided transversely, on both upper and lower decks, at the terminations of the forecastle and poop by 'cobridge heads', i.e. bulkheads, strong barricades of timber pierced for musketry and armed with small guns pointing fore and aft. These were fortresses to which the crew might retire and still defend themselves if the ship was boarded. Gravel ballast was used, and the quantity necessary in such crank ships left little room for stores, one reason for the disease prevalent at sea, and the failure of so many of the Elizabethan enterprises due to a too early return home from want of provisions. Moreover, a large portion of the space left in the hold after the ballast was in place was taken up by the cooking galley, a solid structure

of bricks and mortar built upon it. With their cables,
ammunition, and sea stores on board, men-of-war could
seldom carry provisions for more than three or four weeks,
so that a fleet of victuallers attended every expedition.

Among the dockyards, Portsmouth sank in importance
owing to the want of skilled labour and the expensive
necessity of sending from London all the stores required

FIG. 243. ELIZABETHAN MAN-OF-WAR
Rawlinson MSS., Bodleian.

except timber. Chatham took its place, for although ships
were moored in the Medway and victualling stores were
lodged at Rochester in 1550, it was not until 1565–70 that
wharves and storehouses were built. But as no dry dock
was constructed at Chatham during this reign, and as that
at Portsmouth was allowed to go to ruin, Woolwich and
Deptford were the most important yards for building and
repairs, while most of the seaworthy ships were laid up
in the Medway ; they were moored between Upnor and

Rochester, and, from 1585, protected at night by a chain drawn across the river from the first-named place, where a fort also existed. One of the chief shipwrights, Peter Pett, belonged to a family which produced a continuous line of builders from the reign of Henry VIII to that of Mary II ; another, Mathew Baker, son of the James Baker previously mentioned, devised, in 1582, the first rule for the measurement of tonnage, which had hitherto been a matter of estimation and comparison.

The flag shown on the ensign staff of the ship from the Rawlinson MSS. [Fig. 243] is the Tudor green and white, a common flag during the sixteenth century ; the St. George's Cross was the national flag, but only men-of-war were permitted to wear it in the main-top. Falcons, lions, and other badges were also used on flags, and the Cadiz fleet of 1596 was divided into four squadrons, each distinguished by its flag of crimson, white, blue, and orange-tawny, this being the first indication of the later fleet divisions of the red, white, and blue. In action the men on deck were hidden by waistcloths of painted canvas running round the bulwarks, as shown in the drawing of the *Black Piness* [Fig. 244], or protected by large wooden mantlets running on wheels.

One more important feature of the reign of Elizabeth remains to be noticed—the growth of a science of naval strategy, the natural corollary of fleet action as a principal instead of a subservient arm. The new position taken by the navy brought into the service men who in the preceding centuries would have been commanders in French wars, and who now brought to bear in a fresh field the genius for warfare that had made the English feudal army one of the finest in Europe. Although great soldiers like Edward III and Henry V, and such a naval statesman as Henry VIII, had little to learn as to the use of sea-power within the limits marked out by their political aims, the eighteen years of conflict with Spain show a progressive and more general understanding of the laws governing naval war. Drake's West Indian raid of 1585-6, utterly wrong in principle, is succeeded by the same leader's magnificent attack on the Peninsular coast in 1587, a cruise conducted entirely in accordance with modern maxims and on which his fame must mainly rest. In 1588 the proposed ruinous division of the English force into three widely separated fleets is altered to concentration, and the desire of the seamen to fight the Armada in Spanish waters was only baffled by Elizabeth's vacillation. In 1589 there is again the attack on the Spanish coast, the right course, although badly carried out and a failure in results, and, as a consequence, Elizabeth, whose sole idea was to use the navy commercially to return a profit in prizes, ceased fleet operations in sufficient force for five years. In 1595 she was again tempted by the prospect of West Indian plunder, but in 1596, 1597, and afterwards she followed the better system of striking at the heart instead of the limbs. Through all

FIG. 244. THE 'BLACK PINESS', in which Sir Philip Sidney's body was carried to England (from the copper-plate by Derick Theodor de Brijon, 1587. Brit. Mus. C. 21, f. 13).

these years there is to be traced the controversy between the class represented by the queen, diffident, ignorant, and satisfied with a timid local defence, or with capturing merchantmen, and the more advanced, who regarded the navy essentially in the same light as we do now. These latter included writers like Ralegh, Essex, and Monson, many of whose views, based on their own experience and classical comparison, are as sound as though they had had our advantage of three more centuries of gigantic naval struggle from which to reason.

## *Books for reference.*

ADAIR, ' English Galleys in the Sixteenth Century ', *Eng. Hist. Rev.* xxxv (1920), pp. 497–512.

CLARKE & THURSFIELD, *The Navy and the Nation,* 1897.

CLOWES & OTHERS, *A History of the Royal Navy,* 1897, &c.

COLOMB, *Naval Warfare : its Ruling Principles and Practice historically treated,* 1891.

CORBETT, *Drake and the Tudor Navy.* 2 vols., 1897.

HADOW, *Sir Walter Raleigh : Selections from his Writings,* 1917.

HERVEY, *The Naval History of Great Britain from the Earliest Times to the Rising of Parliament in 1779.* 5 vols., 1779.

JAMES, *The Naval History of Great Britain.* 6 vols., 1822.

JONES, *The British Merchant Service,* 1898.

LAUGHTON, *Studies in Naval History,* 1887.

LESLIE, *Old Sea Wings, Ways, and Words in the Days of Oak and Hemp,* 1890.

MAHAN, *The Influence of Sea Power on History,* 1890.

NAVY RECORDS SOCIETY, Publications of the.

NICOLAS, *A History of the Royal Navy.* 2 vols., 1847.

OPPENHEIM, *A History of the Administration of the Royal Navy from 1509 to 1660,* 1896.

ROBINSON, *The British Fleet,* 1896.

WILLIAMSON, *Maritime Enterprise 1485–1558,* 1913.

# VIII

## TOWN LIFE

### 1. *Old-English Towns before 1066.*

THE word *town* at the present day calls up several ideas, chief above all being that of a collection of houses and streets, with families living close together, as distinguished from the open country. We talk of cities, towns, and boroughs as separate, and yet in a general sense we may apply the term *town* to any one of them, especially in the adjectival form, as town clerk, town life, or in the phrases 'town and gown', 'we go to town'. We have market-towns, large and small towns, towns that are or have been walled and towns that never had a wall, seaport towns, cathedral towns, university and county towns. Here, then, we have an organization of wide extent, adaptable to the manifold forms of collective life, and changing with the growth of ages, a great engine of social civilization and government. It is much the same in other old European countries. To find the underlying principle and unit which has expanded in England so variously and with much difference of local custom, we must go back to the period when the Anglo-Saxons came into Britain. There is much that is obscure in the early history of the people and their towns, but some things we may discern; and we should remember that at the end of six hundred years of Old-English and Danish rule we shall find an advanced stage of progress on which the Norman Conquest entered.

Our early English forefathers settled in Britain as they gradually conquered it after the departure of the Romans, mainly as an agricultural people, shunning the great cities, the centres of commercial luxury, and the fortresses which had protected and regulated the life of the Romano-British population. They seem at first to have destroyed the towns they took; but, conquering the land only step by step, some important places did not fall into their hands till later years, when they had learnt to understand better the value of fortified towns and civil life; these, abandoned for a while, were rebuilt, and formed homes for the new institutions that were to grow up within them. Thus Bath, Gloucester, and Cirencester, cities of the Roman period, were not taken till 577, when the Anglo-Saxons had occupied parts of the island over a hundred and fifty years. The history of London, York, Chester, Colchester, Exeter, Lincoln, and of other cities also stretches back to Roman times.

If we inquire, What is a town? what causes it to be established? we find that we must not think of towns as all formed on one pattern, nor must we imagine those of our English and Danish forefathers as resembling the towns of the present day. The six hundred years during which England was a-making before the Norman trod these shores saw many changes and much progress in the character and civilization of the people, but their qualities of independence and love of the soil remained throughout. Men had to live as well as fight; as the land was gained it was allotted to the free house-father, or to the free family, in holdings of 120 acres (a hide) each; the leader with his men, the family whose several members were united by ties of kinship, laboured hard in peace as in war. While fighting raged in one district, in another the ox would be toiling at the plough, the sound of the axe would be heard in the woods, or the ring of the anvil as the warrior forged his sword. Ranks and classes of social order were fixed, the king, the thegn, the ceorl; petty kingdoms were set up and fell; the Welsh were driven to the western half of the island; Christianity was reintroduced to the land by Augustine, bringing milder manners among the heathen English with some arts and commerce in its train. Nearly two hundred years later, when the Welsh were even yet not done with, the Danes, strong and sturdy kindred to the English races, landed, and began their long contest for possession and supremacy in England; at first merely plundering, they successively conquered and settled large tracts, from which they kept up endless fighting for over a century and a half. Shortly after the peaceful reign of Edgar, the Danes and Northmen from over the seas again began a series of invasions, ravaging the land and burning cities, till at last the country submitted to them, and Swegen became king over all England. The great struggle ended when his son Cnut was elected

king and married Emma, the widow of the English Æthelred. But even during the Danish wars, as in the earlier
ages, some parts of the land had quiet, and progress was
made in spite of all the political unrest.

The congregation of men together in dwellings for the
purpose of protection, or for constant necessities of buying
and selling among themselves, or to supply others, seem to
have been the chief causes that have formed the core of
towns ; the two first indeed might and did happen together.
Recalling the bald outline of the first six centuries of English
story, we should expect to find few native settlements of
this kind in the earliest ages, while with the increase of trade
and commerce they would become more numerous. From
the pages of the Anglo-Saxon Chronicle may be gathered a
fairly long list of towns and cities existing, or built at various
times, during the Old-English period, and the names of
many more are found in other English documents and in
Domesday Book. Little, however, is known of the details
of daily life within them : we can but judge from a few
descriptive terms of their difference in importance and
status. A *burh* (afterwards *borough* or *bury*) was a fortified
place or stronghold ; it may have been a castle or a
strong dwelling for soldiers, surrounded by earthworks and
stockades [Fig. 78], which in later years men learnt to
supersede by a stone wall ; defence against the foe was its
main object. The protection afforded by a burh and the
supplies necessary for the garrison brought countrymen
together, and in some cases this formed the beginning of
a town. A *tun* (our word *town*) originally was the enclosure
round a house with its yard, or round a farm or an estate ;
and the word came to mean a collection of men and houses
within a boundary, and more particularly a village community. This sense the word kept long after the Norman
Conquest ; Chaucer's ' povre persoun of a toun ' is the
incumbent of a country parish. When a burh was built
in or perhaps near this tun the latter became a borough or
fortified town, but at first even a burh was not always
walled. Bamburgh (the old capital of Bernicia) is said to
have been enclosed by a hedge or stockade.

The tuns, large or small, scattered over the land as it
was gained, at distances of time, would vary in development
according to locality and necessity. In some cases a family

group dwelling together would call it their *ham* or home, as Godmundingham the home of the Godmund family, Nottingham the home of the Snotingas. Many a tun remained a village, or if extensive might have several hamlets planted within it, without ever becoming a town in the modern sense ; a church might later be built, and the tun became a parish. The country parish of Ardley, in Hertfordshire, bears on its record book the name ' The Towne Book ' to this day.

In process of time the English began to rebuild and reoccupy the fortified Roman towns hitherto neglected. Such a station they called *ceaster* (from the Latin *castrum*), and thus new life was given to Chester, Rochester, Colchester, Manchester, Gloucester, and other towns. The Danish wars gave a great impulse to the building of strong places. In East Anglia, Ipswich and Norwich were burnt by the invaders, and much damage was suffered at their hands by other English cities, especially by London and Canterbury in 851, and by York in 867. King Alfred built a fort at Athelney and repaired London ; his son Edward the Elder and daughter Æthelflæd, Lady of the Mercians, spent several years in fortifying numerous towns and castles on their frontiers as defences against the Danes, while on the other hand they had taken from the enemy fortified towns, such as Colchester and Huntingdon, Derby and Leicester. Edward is said to have brought English and Danes to live together in Nottingham, which is a token of the way in which the two peoples might sit down side by side when their differences were quieted. Relics of the settlement by the Danes still exist in the names given to their towns and villages, as in Lincolnshire and Yorkshire we find Kettilby, Somerby, Danby, Whitby, Grimsby, and the like. Derby, too, has the Norse ending : *by*, meaning habitation, village, or town, being the Danish equivalent for the English tun. In Mid-England they appear to have associated five, sometimes seven, strong towns or *burhs* together in their resistance to the English—Lincoln, Leicester, Stamford, Nottingham, and Derby, with York and Chester—these were taken from them by Æthelflæd and her brother.

*Wic* signified a dwelling or country house of a king, bishop, or family community ; it also denoted street or market-place, whence we may conclude that a town grew up round the dwelling which had greater needs than the capacities of its allotted land or small self-supporting village could supply. Later a church might be erected, or a burh might be built. Painswick and Warwick (Wæringa Wic) are examples. *Wic* also meant creek or bay, and has this meaning in the names of many towns along the coast, especially in East Anglia, which must have grown up around the anchorages or stations resorted to by the early invaders of this island ; such are Ipswich, Norwich, and Berwick. The word occurs too in Nantwich, Droitwich, and other places in Cheshire and Worcestershire, where the bays or salt-pans gather men together for the industry of salt evaporation.

The market, whither men came frequently to exchange or sell their country produce and the various articles of daily life, would be held on many a central spot among the agricultural tuns as convenience required, becoming fixed by custom and in due time regulated by law. Hence arose the simple market-town, like Eye (Suffolk) and Berkeley (Gloucestershire) named in Domesday. There were possibilities of expansion in each kind of town according to its needs and circumstances.

Of fairs we have scarcely any record in England before the Norman Conquest. Dr. Cunningham considers that the Danes and Northmen were then the leading merchants. The evidences of Anglo-Saxon commerce in France and Italy, the great trade in salt fish (due to the frequent fasts enjoined by the Church) along the northern seas, and the growing enterprise of English merchants, stimulated by the hardy Northern blood, combine to make it likely that the beginnings of some of these annual marts existed, and, maybe, occasioned in some cases the growth of a town.

Further, in connexion with a few towns before the Conquest we find a *port* (*portus*). Northampton, burnt by Swegen in 1010, is called a port ; there are Bridport, Langport, Stockport, and Dudley Port ; and two or three places in the Midlands were, and still are, called Portstreet. A Roman lawyer defined a *portus* as an ' enclosed place, strengthened, into which merchandise may be brought and thence taken away ' ; and by a law of Edward the Elder no one was to buy ' out of port ', for the security and honesty of buyer and seller. His son Æthelstan repeated the law with a variation, adding 'that every marketing be within port', and that money was to be minted within port. The port, therefore, seems to have been an enclosure on land, it might or might not be settled near some water-way which afforded a haven. These laws show that there must have been increasing commerce, and provision made at least in some English towns for the harbouring and supervision of valuable wares while under sale. A law of Æthelred nearly a century later provides for the safety of merchant ships coming 'within port', which accords with the usual association of the word with a haven on a river or the sea-coast. Portceaster (now Porchester) seems to have been originally a Roman military station or camp near the haven (which also gave its name to Portsmouth), adopted and revived by the English.

To build a monastery for the Christian English, the members of which would cultivate the arts of agriculture under its rules of holy life, was to plant a self-centred community of another sort. Not so shut up as to exclude all relations with the world around it, the monastery in the course of years, for one reason or another, attracted other dwellers to its neighbourhood, tenants perhaps on lands belonging to the convent, bound by ties resembling those of men to their lord in other settlements, with their own needs and life subordinate to the more powerful superior. In such a manner grew up several towns. Among the early English examples was Abingdon (Berks.) ; at Shaftesbury, the origin of which may have been military, there was a nunnery planted by King Alfred.

In the account of Bury St. Edmunds in Domesday Book are some passages which show this growth round a monastery. The record compares its condition twenty or thirty years before, in the time of Edward the Confessor, with that at the date of the survey : ' In the town where the glorious king and martyr St. Edmund lies buried, in the time of King Edward, Baldwin the abbot held for the sus-tenance of the monks 118 men ; and they can sell and give their land ; and under them 52 *bordarii* (i.e. cottagers), from whom the abbot can have help ; [there are] 54 freemen poor enough, 43 living upon alms, each of them has one *bordarius*. There are now two mills and two store ponds or fish-ponds. This town was then worth ten pounds, now twenty. . . . It now contains a greater circuit of land, which was then ploughed and sown, where one with another there are thirty priests, deacons, and clerks ; twenty-eight nuns and poor brethren, who pray daily for the king and all Christian people ; eighty (less five) bakers, brewers, tailors, launders, shoemakers, parmenters, cooks, porters, serving-men, and these all minister to the saint and abbot and brethren. Besides whom there are thirteen upon the land of the reeve [representing the king] who have their dwellings in the same town, and under them five *bordarii* ; now there are 34 persons owing military service, taking French and English together, and under them twenty-two *bordarii*.   In the whole there are now 342 dwellings in the demesne of the land of St. Edmund, which was arable in the time of King Edward.'

Another organization that might grow up in some of the old English towns under religious and social influence was a gild or association of certain persons for brotherhood, mutual benefit, and burial, paying fees towards a common fund.   There may have been many of these organized and acting without any written agreement.   There are documents of that kind which prove the existence of four such societies.   One Orky granted a hall in memory of himself and his wife to a gild worshipping at St. Peter's Church, Abbotsbury (Dorset), and the ordinances by which he and his fellow gildsmen bound themselves are set forth.   The contributions were to be in money or in wax for the church, and in loaves, wheat, and wood ; the steward was to arrange the feast and to give notice of burials ; good behaviour was to be enforced.   The last clause but one ends with the words, ' Now we have faith, through God's assistance, that the aforesaid ordinance, if we rightly maintain it, shall be to the benefit of us all.'   Another gild, at Exeter, was to hold meetings three times a year ; a third (of somewhat later date) was connected with St. Peter's monastery, near the same city, and combined for religious purposes about a dozen associations or gild-ships at Woodbury, Colyton, Bideford, Sidmouth, Exmouth, and other places.   A fourth was a gild of thegns at Cambridge, which included also *cnihts*, perhaps armed retainers in the service of the thegns. All these records, except that of the Woodbury-Exeter gild, are of the first half of the eleventh century.   There were several gilds of *cnihts* existing even earlier ; in the ninth century mention is found of one at Canterbury. In the reign of Edward the Confessor the *cnihts* of Winchester had a hall in which they used ' to drink their gild ' ; and in London the same king gave a charter to a *cnihten-gild,* which claimed to be as old as Cnut. This brotherhood came to an end in 1125, when some of their descendants were burgesses of London. Very little is known of the object of the gilds of *cnihts* ; it was probably good-fellowship among the men, who not only served their superiors as military companions, but appear to have been burgesses of standing, like the *burh-thegns* referred to in other places.

When we come to the days of Edward the Confessor, in the eleventh century, we find that there was at least one chief town in every county ; some counties had two or three of the head rank. These were all borough towns or county towns. In such a town the land belonged to many lords ; it had not grown up on the tun or holding of one lord, but contained the town houses of several great lords or thegns, who, besides, held land elsewhere within the county. Frequently the king also owned land and houses there. The great man had to keep his burghers or fighting men ready somewhere, they could not all dwell in the strongholds ; he might live in the country himself, and possess property in two or three other places, but he had houses in the head town where these men could live and pursue their avocations while at peace. His men, the burghers (some of whom may by this time have become lesser thegns), followed him to battle when called upon, and served him in the duties of keeping up the walls and bridges ; in combination with the burghers of other lords they may have gradually acquired a society and privileges regarding trade and property of their own. To belong to one of the old set, holding a burgage house from father to son, was accounted a distinction among one's fellows in the town. Thus out of the Old-English military system was growing up step by step one series of important towns, the burgesses of which were later to be regarded rather as men of peace than of war. These *burhs* have certain characteristics and privileges in common : (*a*) a special law court (*burhmot*) to settle disputes arising in the borough ; (*b*) a market which is protected by the king's peace ; (*c*) a mint, at which the king's coin is struck and stamped with the name of the borough.  Some of them have further (*d*) the privilege of compounding with the king in a lump annual payment ( *firma burgi*) for all rents and other dues which the borough population owe to him.

## 2.   *Town Government.   1066–1485.*

When William the Conqueror had established himself in England, and began to take reckoning of the land and the people by the Great Survey, he found a large part of the population settled in towns and boroughs under a system of local government.   Their inhabitants were bound to perform certain duties towards their country and their king ; town-dwellers also gained advantages to themselves, especially concerning trade and intercourse—advantages which varied according to their locality or opportunity.   Under the old laws the inhabitants met in a borough-moot or port-moot at regular intervals, two or three times a year, to settle local business.   There was besides a reeve as chief officer, whose original function was to collect, on behalf of the king, tolls or dues which were paid by the trading citizens for all kinds of licences and privileges.   In many old towns he was called the Port-reeve.   London and Canterbury had port-reeves.   Oxford has her Port Meadow still ; no doubt her head officer was once a port-reeve.   As time went on, other duties could be laid on him ; it was convenient to require the head-man, who was responsible for local dues, to collect also that portion which fell upon his fellow townsmen of the general taxes, levied for military expeditions and purposes other than local, such as the Dane-geld.   Thus the port-reeve in a town or borough, like the shire-reeve or sheriff in a county, became of great importance in the government of the land, because through him, as through the sheriff, the king obtained his revenues.   On the other hand, being the head of the port-moot, he presided over local justice, and the townsmen had in him a chief to represent them ; if they desired new privileges or redress of grievances, he was the medium of communication with the sovereign. If the town were not a borough, it yet would have a reeve or a provost.   Though after the Conquest much

was changed, as new needs and new officers grew up
under the Norman lords, the basis of the local government
was left, and was used by William. In many places the
Old-English titles remained till quite modern times : there
was a port-reeve in Tavistock, Devon, as late as 1886 ; and
Rotherham (Yorkshire) was governed by two greaves (the
Old-English *gerefa*, reeve), acting latterly with feoffees, till
1871, when, under a charter of incorporation, the town
appointed a mayor instead.

Some of the Norman lords who had received fiefs and
towns in England, on settling their French tenants in
a borough side by side with the English, introduced also
the customs of the French *bourg*, or borough, of Breteuil
in Normandy, which seem to have spread in time to
the English tenants. This was done especially at Hereford and Shrewsbury, while at Rhuddlan a new borough
was founded with these customs before 1086. Some
members of certain great families, from one generation
to another, when founding new towns, or confirming the
privileges of old ones, granted the laws of Breteuil in
their charters, or referred to Hereford or Shrewsbury as
exemplars ; these places are to be traced particularly on
the Welsh borders, in Wales, and (a few) in Ireland, besides
others to be found scattered in England, as Bideford, Lichfield, and Preston (Lancashire). In the twelfth, thirteenth,
and fourteenth centuries numerous towns, already grown
or growing into full life, obtained from the Crown or from
their chief lord sanction and recognition of their rights and
privileges ; later towns modelled their rules on those of
other cities formerly so acknowledged, and the charters
thus granted (and paid for) became the standard of their
liberties. A great many boroughs took London as their
pattern ; some of the oldest of these were Oxford, Winchester, and Bristol, and each again in turn served as
example to many others. Dublin and Waterford, which
copied their customs from Bristol, became the two chief
mother-towns in Ireland. Hereford was the chief mother-
town for Welsh boroughs. Many of these charters referred
to older grants now lost, which were confirmed in them ;
sometimes they also added fresh rights. Thus grew little by
little over the land the same general law regarding the towns
as parts of the state, leaving varieties of local constitution

which accorded with the origin of each place and the development of local usage. The process has continued throughout history; some towns have decayed, like Tavistock, which cannot afford the luxury of a mayor and corporation; others were planted, like Winchelsea, or have sprung up rapidly in recent days, like Middlesbrough, or again have jogged quietly along for centuries, the nucleus of a common religious and agricultural life, till quickened into larger growth by modern discoveries, like Rotherham. Since the beginning of the thirteenth century the typical idea of an embodied town has been a *communa*, consisting of citizens ruled by elected officers, a mayor and aldermen. The common council came into definite existence somewhat later. *Civitas* signified the same thing, an individual community, whence we have *citizens*, a word more freely applied than *city*, which in England is limited to places of special eminence, such as cathedral towns and some recent corporations. Their ancient seals bear witness to their titles, as that of Lynn, *sigillum communitatis Lennie*; Coventry, *sigillum comunitatis ville de coventre*, and so with Bideford, Grimsby, and others; Norwich, the county city, has *Sigillum comune civitalis norwici*; Thetford, *sigillum commune burgencium de Theford*.

Who were the townsmen who formed the body politic of the chartered town? This is a complicated question, much discussed, but some indications are clear. In the earliest documents after the Conquest it is always the 'burgesses' to whom the privileges are secured, who must attend the moot, and whose duties and powers are set down. Several examples of véry early *custumals*, or bodies of ordinances, exist, as those for Preston, Newcastle-on-Tyne, Winchester, and of later date for Hereford and Worcester, which show that the burgesses had become endowed with certain peculiar legal privileges. Originally every burgess probably held land or a house of some sort (*burgage*) within the town, with a strip or strips of land for cultivation just outside the town on one side; and on another side had the right of pasturing his cattle on the common land belonging to the town. It was the burgesses who paid certain customs to the Crown, and rents for their burgages (all which, compounded for, made the *firma burgi*), and who imposed tolls on traders coming into the town. In a 'port' the burgesses were the successors of the portmen, whom the port-reeve had summoned to the Portman-moot or Port-moot. At Gloucester in the fourteenth century a burgess was made

FIG. 245. Letters patent from K. Henry III granting the site of the present Town Hall of Oxford in 1228 (Oxford City Documents).

a portman. Here it seems that the name had survived, attached to a special office. Roughly speaking, the burgesses appear to have stood in the place of the garrison men who in the early settlements had dwelt, as we have seen, in the burh houses ; some may have retained their holdings in the arable fields, but others turned to trade; or all, the personal duties of defence had generally become commuted for substitutes or for money. The number of burgesses would be limited by the space at their disposal. The position passed from father to son, but others who desired to share the burgesses' privileges might pay for admission among them. In this way, though many might come and go, and there might be other dwellers, rich and poor, a special and permanent body of enrolled men formed the heart of each town and carried on its local government.

There are some twelfth-century charters which granted the burgesses the right to elect a Reeve, an officer who gave place in many towns during the Angevin period to the Mayor as chief magistrate; the name, apparently from *maior*, was introduced by the Norman-French.

FIG. 246.   Mace and Seals of the Corporation of Burford.

We know when the office of mayor began in England, since the older boroughs were careful to keep lists of their officials year by year.   London, which had a portreeve under William I, elected her first mayor about 1193; King's Lynn in 1204, Bristol in 1217; Gloucester had one as early as 1220 (though the office was not 'created' there till

1483), Oxford before 1200, Rye in 1304. The citizens did
not always require a charter to give them leave to elect
Gloucester and Rye chose their mayors before they were
chartered. It was only by degrees, however, that the
towns appointed mayors ; the title was not adopted in some
places till as late as the days of Elizabeth and James I.

Aldermen (and alderman is a thoroughly English word for
a chief or magistrate) are found next in dignity to the mayor
in most corporations. In towns which were divided into
wards an alderman presided over each ward ; in some places
jurats, or sworn assistants to the mayor, were appointed
and it is believed that in towns possessing a merchant gild
the alderman at the head of the gild sooner or later took
his part in the municipal government. The early history of
these borough senators is obscure ; their number of course
varied as well as their duties. Towards the end of the
fifteenth century town councils were generally elected in
addition to the mayor and aldermen. Norwich, which
belonged to the king's demesne, appointed a provost under
the charter of Richard I (1194), but after about thirty years
this rule was changed ; four bailiffs, one over each division
or leet of the town—originally hamlets—were elected by
the burgesses in 1223, and the joint government by the
bailiffs and commonalty lasted till 1403, when the people
desired further liberty and expansion, and, purchasing a new
charter, were united under a mayor with two sheriffs. The
steps by which the twenty-four men of the leets, who were
chosen by the people in order to elect the bailiffs, became
a recognized court and made ordinances for the profit of
the town, and finally reappeared as the twenty-four of the
mayor's council, are most instructive in showing the gradual
growth of one organization out of the other, and should be
studied in Mrs. Green's interesting work on *Town Life in
the Fifteenth Century*.

Many towns owe their origin not to a *burh*, but rather
to the *tun* or the *ham*, which after the Conquest was given
as the whole or part of a *manor*, large or small, into the
hands of a greater or of a lesser lord. Some lords endowed
their tenants with the rights of burgesses, while reserving
certain claims as evidence of their lordship. Such boroughs
often showed feeble life, and in many cases did not attain
a mayor ; they had a reeve or borough-reeve, as at Ma

chester, or a bailiff, as at Chippenham. At Birmingham there was a high bailiff and a low bailiff. The lord of the manor had rights to certain tolls and dues ; the bailiff originally was his officer to collect these, and to represent him at the local court that, regularly attended by the tenants of the manor, governed its affairs. This court, which had dealt with many rights and needs as they arose, probably became known after the thirteenth century by distinct names relative to its different jurisdictions. As the Court Leet (or *law-day*), which was held frequently, it was a court of local criminal procedure, and annually chose its administrative officers. The Court Leet was thus a feature in both manor and borough, and it is interesting to find public order in a town with burgesses maintained for centuries upon this universal organ of local government. Though Manchester had burgesses with a charter as early as 1301, this was granted by the then lord of the manor, and she was subject to manorial jurisdiction, decreasing in later times, till 1845, when the last lord sold the manor and his rights to the town, which had already received a royal charter in 1838. Birmingham, too, was known as a borough, with its *foreign* (i.e. group of dwellers ' without ' the borough limits), as early as the thirteenth century ; for 150 years (1392–1545) the burgesses maintained a flourishing social gild, whose hall became the Town Hall; but Birmingham did not obtain its royal charter, with right to elect a mayor, till 1838. A free municipal government grew up in such places in conjunction with, and finally overshadowing, that of the manor.

The practice of making laws or by-laws by the inhabitants (from Scandinavian *by*, a habitation, village, or town) has of ancient time belonged to all local organizations, especially to towns, manors, and gilds. They were written and carefully kept as a body of liberties or customs to be appealed to for the settlement of disputes, and if necessary were amended at meetings of the members. The early customs were not usually detailed in the charters—the case of Manchester seems to be exceptional—but their existence was understood. Some of these town custumals, customaries, or ordinances, happily preserved from destruction, supply many interesting points in early municipal history otherwise unattainable ; it is to be regretted that so few

are actually known.   Among them the city of Winchester
is fortunate in possessing a small parchment roll written in
the fourteenth century, entitled, ' Þese ben þe olde vsages

FIG. 247.   THE TOWER OF LONDON in the fifteenth century
Royal MS. 16 F. ii.

of þe Cite of Wynchestre, þat haueþ be y-vsed in þe tyme
of oure elderne '.   Here we find enumerated the ' meyre ',
and the four and twenty sworn men of the heads of the
city, who are the mayor's council ; the two bailiffs, who

act as constables ; the four serjeants, who are to fulfil the
behests of the mayor and bailiffs ; and two coroners, sworn
on behalf of the king. The city possesses ' a seal commune
and an authentyk' (see p. 291) with which the charters
granted by the town are sealed, carefully kept in one box
enclosed in another with two locks. There are aldermen

FIG. 248. WALLED TOWN, fifteenth century (from Hours of
H. Beauchamp, Duke of Warwick).

who have specified duties regarding the charters or title-
deeds of town property, and the distraining for rents ; and
there is a town clerk, who registers non-freemen marketing
in the town, &c. Blankets, quilts, and burel cloth were
chief industries of the place ; strict regulations governed
those who might make these articles, laid down their size,
and fixed what tax must be paid to the town for each
house where they were made. The sale of wool and hides
was also dealt with, Winchester being one of the staple
towns for wools. A great many of the ' vsages' are market
regulations stating the customs to be paid on each kind of

ware and the times to be kept ; another seems to treat
of the method of sale at the fair ; others show what tolls
are to be taken at the town gates for every cart-load or
horse-load of goods entering, and detail other dues, all
of which would go towards the *firma* of the town. Six
men are to be specially chosen to gather and account for
the king's taxes and money for the common needs of the
town. Winchester being an important city had its own
courts of justice, and the rest of the ' vsages ' deal with
legal proceedings and the holding of property.

The ordinances of Worcester, written down in 1467, give
an interesting picture of the activities of an old and busy
town of weavers at this period. The good citizens were
careful to have their acts publicly read and proclaimed at
their annual Michaelmas meeting, that all might understand, and the bailiffs, high and low, two aldermen, and
two chamberlains were bound to see them carried out. The
Town Council had an upper chamber of twenty-four men,
called the ' Great Clothing ' (evidently known by their
superior livery, which they were to renew once in three
years) ; and another of forty-eight commoners, chosen from
the commons of the city. Their deliberations in council
were to be kept private ; no holes or windows might be
made through which to peer into the hall. Many laws are
directed towards keeping the peace within and without :
to avoid frays with the followers of great men the inhabitants might not wear other ' signs ' (badges) or liveries than
those of the king or of their craft ; they must not draw
weapon against one another by misrule, although each
should keep a ' defensable wepyn ' at home. The manner
of becoming a burgess and how that class was gradually
extending outside the original circle of the town are shown,
with the privileges and liberties so dearly prized. In the
great gild-house was not only the hall where the Town
Council met for the affairs of the city, the commonalty
annually chose their officers, and the election of burgesses
to go to Parliament was openly made, but there were rooms
which could be hired weekly by certain burgesses in which
to house their goods. Part of the market, too, was held
in the ' yelde-hall ', as it was called, and a bell rang out
to warn folks of the hours at and during which different
business might be transacted. Labourers had to stand for

hire at the Grass Cross at five o'clock on summer, six o'clock on winter, mornings. Citizens who had committed small offences were privileged to be imprisoned in a room under the gild-hall instead of in the common gaol. Bells were much used in Worcester. The Town Council were summoned by a special clang from the great bell of the parish of St. Andrew; and the Bow-bell, usually rung at nine o'clock, is to be continued 'for grete ease of the seid cite', the parish clerk to have his fee therefor. Sanitary regulations are made: pigs may not go at large, and the water must be kept clean near Severn bridge; fire-hooks and buckets are provided against fire. The bridge and the quay are to be kept repaired, also the city gates; and if any part of the walls fall into ruin the stones must not be carried away, but the chamberlains must have it repaired as far as available means 'may stretch'. Among the trades, butchers may not be cooks; and he who sells ale to be taken away must have a sign at his door, while those bakers who bake horse-bread shall not keep a hostelry.[1] There must have been several craft gilds in the city; except the tilers, they are not separately named, but collectively it is required that the five pageants which it is their duty to bring out yearly to the worship of God and the city shall 'not be to seek', and that the crafts shall duly sustain them and their lights and torches, besides all, 'in their best arraye harnesid', taking part with their cressets in the great city Watch on St. John's Eve.

Robert Ricart, town clerk of Bristol in 1479 and following years, compiled a chronicle history of his city, part iv of which sets forth 'the laudable costume; of this worshipfull Towne' relating to the election and duties of the mayor and other officers. Here we may see the sheriff and the councillors, honourably apparelled, going to the new mayor's house to fetch him to the gild-hall in his scarlet gown, those who have been mayors wearing scarlet cloaks and black hoods; others have their cloaks borne after them by servants. The proceedings go on with courteous formality. After his farewell speech at the high dais, before all the commons, the old mayor hands a book (presumably the Bible) to the new mayor, who lays his hand upon it, while

---

[1] Horse-bread made of coarse grain was commonly in use for feeding horses till the last century.

the town clerk, standing up, reads the oath of office, which he swears to keep, kissing the book. The old mayor then delivers to him the king's sword—emblem of his duty to the king—his hat, and the casket containing the seals of the city, and they change places. This done, the whole company take home, first, the new mayor, and then the ex-mayor, ' with trompetts and clareners, in as joyful, honourable, and solempne wise as can be devised ' ; some of the council dine with one, some with the other, after which all assemble at the High Cross, in the centre of the town, and walk to service at St. Michael's Church, finishing up with ' cake-brede and wyne ' at the new mayor's. The worthy Ricart shows, in order of date, what the mayor has to do from his election till Christmas, ending with the proclamations to keep peace during the holidays, and that no one should go a-mumming, close-visaged (masked), after curfew without a light in his hands. Here these customs close.

### 3. *Gilds and Crafts.*

Closely connected with the life in towns from early times were the spontaneous societies among fellow men called gilds. Men could band together in a gild for many objects : for social purposes, for religious worship, for help in sickness and burial, for the performance of some definite task, for the increase of trade and commerce, for the betterment of individual crafts. The germ of the gild was simple, the feeling of brotherhood and neighbourliness, and the impulse to mutual help among private men and women ; for this reason there was little hindrance to its creation in any parish, village, or small town, as well as in the largest. Unless the gilds grew rich and important they were let alone by the governing powers ; they filled up gaps in the social fabric not provided for by the systems of agricultural life or of military defence, but harmonizing with the efforts of the Church. If they desired to devote the rent of land or houses to purposes of education or religion they had to obtain leave from the Crown ; but where their effect was to produce wealth they were adopted and encouraged by authority, and strongly influenced the progress of the municipal government of many places.

*Social-religious gilds.* Gilds naturally fall into two

classes, the social-religious and the trade gilds, the latter being of two kinds, merchant gilds and gilds of crafts. Although there were social-religious gilds before the Conquest (see p. 287, Orky's gild), little further is known of them till about the beginning of the thirteenth century, from which time they began to be formed here and there in towns ; there may have been many at this period, but a large number of the notices that exist being undated, we are left in doubt. From the fourteenth to the sixteenth centuries these societies and fraternities abounded, and several of them were set up not long before the Reformation. No doubt some had a short life ; the members might die or remove, or fail in paying their contributions ; the brotherhood might have finished their special work and, unnoticed, cease to exist. But they were so numerous and collectively so important, being spread all over the land, and were so much feared as wealthy agencies supporting superstitious uses, that in the last year of Henry VIII and the first year of Edward VI two Acts were passed which suppressed them all, and appropriated their property to the Crown. A very few escaped, such as the gild of the Holy Ghost at Basingstoke, because it was an educational foundation ; one or two at Cambridge which originated Corpus Christi College ; and Lench's Trust at Birmingham, a charity. The trading gilds, brotherhoods of crafts and 'mysteries', had so much in common with them, on their religious side, that they were included in the inquiry which preceded the Acts ; but they escaped the same fate because their character as mercantile and trade companies was clear.

It was the merchant and craft gilds that touched most closely the organization and working of town life ; it will, however, help us to understand them if we see what was the general character of the gild. All gilds were organized societies, made rules and appointed officers, and were careful of their accounts. Lynn in Norfolk, in the fourteenth century a flourishing commercial and seaport town, was then full of small gilds, besides owning a powerful gild merchant. The statutes of the gild of St. Edmund at Lynn say that there shall be four meetings a year ('four dayes of spekyngges tokedere for here comune profyte' is the phrase of St. Katherine's gild in the same town), one the 'general' day for annual business ; to this every brother and sister

who is summoned must come under pain of a penny, unless
he make proper excuse ; he must come in time, and 'if he
sit him down and grumble' he must pay another penny.
Most gild meetings were called 'mornspeech', i.e. talk in
the morning. New members find sureties and pay 5s. and
certain house-fees to the gild-house. The officers are an
alderman, two stewards and a dean (all chosen yearly), and
a clerk to say mass. At the 'mornspeech' no one must
speak maliciously or disparagingly to his brother or sister,
or be rebel of his tongue against the alderman ; and no
one may disclose to strangers the affairs discussed. The
stewards, who have the care of the property of the gild,
must give sureties and render an account at the yearly
meeting. Part of this property was a buttery or store of
ale, 'a chambre where the ale lyeth in', which no one
might enter without leave of the officer, and from which
the alderman was allowed two gallons, the stewards one
gallon apiece, the dean and the clerk a pottle (half a gallon)
each, for every night while the 'drink' lasted during the
season of the general mornspeech. It was not in all cases
that the 'drinking togeder' extended over more than one
night. Proper behaviour and etiquette at this feast was
enforced. No one may appear there before the alderman
and the gild brothers and sisters in tabard nor cloak, bare
leg nor bare foot ; he must not make a noise either at drink
or at mornspeech ; if he disobeys the dean when he tells
him to be still, he must receive the rod (? be whipped) or
pay a fine ; and on no account may he sleep, nor keep the
ale-cup standing. After the alderman rises no one but the
officer may stay in the house. When a brother or a sister
die, the dean brings candles to the dirge, summoning all
the brotherhood to attend ; each offers a farthing at the
church for the dead man's soul, and gives a farthing in
alms ; afterwards fifteen masses are to be paid for out of
the gild property, from which also the wax-candles are
provided. The dean and the clerk are paid by the year.
Finally, it was the duty of the alderman and the gild to
try to reconcile those members who had quarrelled and
would go to law ; if they did not succeed, the quarrelsome
member might do as he list, but must pay the gild a good
round fine. In other Norfolk gilds the annual mornspeech
is to be held after 'the drinking', which lasts several days ;

some of the fines are to be paid in wax 'to the light',
i.e. for the gild's candles in the church; the property of
the gild in the stewards' hands is to be accounted for with
the increase, showing that the money or goods were to be
put to use and profit. Some gilds bought cows or oxen
and let them out. A sick member who could not come to
the 'general day' was to have meat and drink sent to
him; and the giving of help to poor brethren, and to those
who had suffered loss by sea, by fire, or by 'the sending
of God', is a frequent ordinance. Nearly all such gilds had
some provision for prayers, masses for the dead, and candles
for their services in the church to which they attached
themselves; in a few these purposes seemed to supply the
chief motive of their foundation, but the greater number
dealt with social life, including religious observances as
a usual element.

Details differ according to local custom, and the names
of officers occasionally vary; in some places, too, fuller
provision is made for the objects named above. For
example, at Lincoln in several gilds the chief officers are
called Gracemen and Wardens; the poor receive gifts of
bread at the burial of a gild brother, besides six cups of
ale at the gild's feast, and a number are fed annually; the
money of the gild is put out to use among the members,
and the increase thereof brought in twice a year; a deserving brother or sister who cannot earn his living is to be
helped by loan or gift. During the gild feast the clerk was
to read out the ordinances that all might know them.
Lastly, the Lincoln men must have desired to encourage
foreign pilgrimages: four gilds provide a penny from each
member as help to a brother or a sister who goes to the
Holy Land, a halfpenny or more to one who goes to
St. James of (Compostella in) Galicia, or to Rome. The
brethren shall accompany him as far as the gates of the
city, and shall welcome him on his return, when he would
doubtless be readmitted to his gild with great honour. At
Lincoln, too, was that gild founded by brethren and sistren
specifically of 'the rank of common and middling folks',
who would rather not have any of such rank as mayor or
bailiff among them, 'unless he is found to be of humble,
good, and honest conversation'.

Briefly, then, the gild was an association of men and

women who paid certain fees, agreed to worship in a given church, chose an alderman to rule them, and stewards (or wardens) to take care of their money and put it to use. They met yearly to elect new officers, to admit new brethren, and to receive account of their money, some of which was spent upon wax-lights for the church, torches for burial, help to sick, poor, or other unfortunate brethren, and ale at the yearly festival ; besides this, they had other regular meetings for business. They required good behaviour and proper manners both at feasts and at meetings, and obedience to their officers ; brawlers and thieves were to be expelled, new brethren must be of good reputation and character. If there were a dispute between members, it was the duty of the brotherhood to try to ' bring them at one ' ; their officers must use all their skill to make the peace by means of arbitration. And this self-governing company made for their own regulation a body of ordinances or by-laws, to which they might add from time to time if needful.

These general features and ideas pervaded the gilds of this country, and their constitution was so elastic and free that expansion or adaptation was easy. Various good works were undertaken : forty gilds at Bodmin, ' for the glory of God and the good of man ', helped to rebuild the church there in 1469–72. Several gilds in East Anglia undertook the reparation of churches ; gilds at Coventry, Maidstone, and York provided hostels and beds for poor pilgrims and for strangers ; and Ludlow had its ancient gild of Palmers. Gilds in Birmingham and Essex contributed to the repair of roads and bridges ; another, in Worcester, repaired the walls and bridge of that city. A free school, or a schoolmaster, was maintained by gilds at Worcester, Ludlow, and Bristol. There were also gilds of ringers of church bells.

*Craft Gilds.* In the town, also, men who followed the same occupation united expressly for the protection of their trade, and to form regulations concerning their work, their apprentices and servants, and the hours to be kept, against bad workmanship, and for a hundred matters which concerned themselves. With a similar constitution they generally included some of the customs of the simple social gild. Two gilds in Lincoln, the fullers and the tailors,

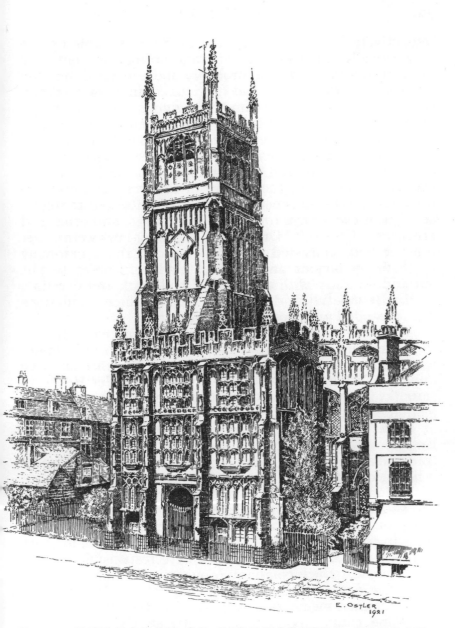

FIG. 249. THE PORCH OF CIRENCESTER CHURCH,
the upper stories of which were used as a Guildhall by woolmen.

respectively founded in 1297 and 1328, are notable for the exceptionally small number of trade ordinances contained in their by-laws, though probably more existed but are unrecorded ; their social and religious ordinances, however, closely resemble those of non-trading gilds. The governing officers of the crafts varied slightly in name and number. They usually consisted of a master and two or four wardens ; in some companies assistants were added. The wardens acted as searchers and treasurers ; their duties were to examine and oversee the quality of the work and material produced by the gildsmen and their servants, and to render account of *quarterages* (members' fees), fines, and other gild property. The Craft ' Ordinary ', as the by-laws were some-times called, consisted of rules, besides those enforcing brotherly behaviour and charity, made ' in order to put out and do away with all kinds of bad work and deceits ', as the Bristol fullers declared in 1406. These regulations were amended and increased as need arose.

Weavers and bakers had their gilds from early times ; the bakers in Coventry from 1208. The weavers in Notting-ham, York, Oxford, Huntingdon, and Winchester were important enough to obtain royal charters under Henry II (1160) ; in many places they were paying for royal pro-tection as early as 1130 ; and if, as seems possible, some of them were formed by foreigners who had settled in English towns at and after the Conquest, bringing their trade with them, the sanction of the Crown would give a necessary authority. Some later crafts, as for instance the tailors of Exeter in 1466, started with royal patents, and thereby were almost independent of the city ; but the usual authority that controlled the numerous crafts which arose in towns about the fourteenth century was the court of the mayor and aldermen, who were responsible for the king's peace. Each company brought its ordinances to be allowed and registered, its officers annually to be sworn in, and sometimes members and apprentices for enrolment. In the same court, too, disputes between companies were settled by arbitration. In 1428 the town clerk of York records how there had been a long strife betwixt the marshals (farriers) and smiths of the city, each party alleging that the other encroached upon their craft and drew away part of their living ; ' thus they were many dayes and yerres in variance, and ayther craft trubled other, and yerely tuke and held distresse of other, so ferre furth that many yerys mayors and the chamber was hugely vexed with them'. At last the mayor induced them to submit their 'points' to four arbitrators, chosen by him from other companies, an arrangement which happily ended in a full 'accordement' declared before the mayor. The changes of trade and fashion caused many a dispute between gilds of kindred occupations, as the cappers and the hatmakers, the plasterers and the tilers, the skinners and the vestmakers, &c. ; and this became a serious matter when, as in York, Beverley, Coventry, Chester, and Dublin, the city depended on the contributions and support of the gilds for its annual show of miracle plays.

FIG. 250. MONEY-BOX of the Oxford Cordwainers' Company.

In the fifteenth century there were in York about sixty craft gilds, in Bristol twenty-six. In 1390 Beverley had thirty-eight ; in Norwich, Newcastle-on-Tyne, Coventry, Winchester —wherever busy artisans congregated — they were numerous. In the matter of food, bakers and brewers had to conform to the assize of bread and of ale (i.e. fixed regulations under an ancient statute in accordance with the price of grain), by which the mayor periodically set the prices ; crafts of the bakers and the butchers must have been found in nearly every town. Even in a university town like Oxford, where the weavers' company, which had existed from the time of Henry I, had died out by 1323, the cordwainers (shoemakers), a fraternity nearly as old, lived on till the beginning of the seventeenth century ; and there were besides glovers, barbers, cooks, mercers, and tailors, the last of which, incorporated in 1569, continued with much reputation till a century ago. Some of these companies, such as the bakers of Bristol and the mercers of York, grew rich, built themselves halls, and entertained great men, who were not ashamed to become members. Owing to changes in the methods of trade and various other causes these gilds and companies died away; they had fulfilled a useful part during many ages, but by the end of the eighteenth century the few left in country towns were almost forgotten. Only in London, where about eighty companies still exist, does the shadow of their former activity remain to remind us of what once were the safeguards of honest work and well-regulated trade, and the sustainers of the charitable spirit among the artisan class in our towns; only in London the Lord Mayor's show survives as the last relic of the bravery formerly displayed by the crafts in civic processions on Midsummer Eve, in the pageants and plays on the day of Corpus Christi, or in the Riding of St. George's Gild at Norwich. In London, too, one great institution, the Trinity House of Deptford, owing its origin to a gild, probably of shipmen, still exercises its historic functions over sea-craft and seamanship.

*Gilds Merchant.* The form of gild which most affected the prosperity of towns after the Conquest was the gild merchant, in which the burgesses who were traders united together and obtained certain privileges from the king in favour of their commerce. The towns of Northern France may have possessed such gilds at the time, and it is possible that the Norman-French brought this application of the idea with them. One of the principal provisions in the charters granted to many towns from the reign of Henry I to that of John (some gilds were granted later) was that the burgesses should have a *gilda mercatoria,* ' a gild merchant with their *hanse* '. The typical constitution of this gild, with, of course, special variations, was that of the gilds before described. At the head was an alderman (not a mayor), and two or four wardens or stewards, elected by the gildsmen. The members paid entrance fees and regular dues, besides finding sureties; they held mornspeeches, made their own ordinances, and kept their yearly feast or ' drinking '. The provisions as to civil behaviour, charity,

E. Ostler.
1921.

Fig 251. HOUSE IN CHIPPING CAMPDEN built by William Greville, wool-merchant, who, on his brass in the church, is called *Flos Mercatorum*.

and help were also included among their laws. The principal
objects of the members of a merchant gild were to nourish
and monopolize trade, to attract it to themselves within
the town to the exclusion of those not qualified, and outside
and beyond the town to obtain freedom from the universal
tolls and dues. The *hanse* seems to have been the entrance
fee, or the annual payment, sometimes it may have signified
the toll paid by non-gildsmen ; as at commencement it was
a chief source of their common fund, the right to enforce
it was naturally named in the charter. The gild merchant
was established in the infancy of trade, before the days of
the gilds of separate crafts, and craftsmen were freely
admitted. In Leicester, where the rolls of members exist
from 1196, men of about forty different occupations were
included in the first roll. At Ipswich all the free burgesses
were to form the gild under the alderman and four assistants
(1200), quite a separate organization from that of the
original town. Women and strangers might be admitted
to the gild, though not to the rights of burgesses. As
a great many of the burgesses were in trade, the same men
often belonged to both the borough and the gild, the mayor
of the town and the alderman of the gild being not infrequently one and the same person. A flourishing gild added
to the wealth and reputation of the town ; its ordinances
dealt with the food supply, the wool trade, and other traffic
in which the burgesses were interested.

The gild made regulations for securing honest dealing,
for the examination of goods with regard to quality and
measurement, and into the details of dyes and processes ;
they tested weights and presented criminal cases before the
mayor. Sometimes the gild, which might keep a separate
purse, lent money to the town, as at Leicester in 1239.
As affairs increased, the gild officers required more help ;
at Leicester in 1225 a body of twenty-four sworn gildsmen
were appointed, who formed a standing council ' to serve
the alderman in town business '. A similar institution
probably gave rise later to the Common or Town Council
in several places. The gild was obliged to possess a hall
for meetings and other business ; and since doubtless many
of the same burgesses served both gild and borough, it was
found convenient to transact the administration of the
borough there also ; thus in not a few municipalities the

Gild Hall became the Town Hall. (The gild-hall used by
the town authorities did not always belong to a merchant
gild ; in Ludlow and several other places they occupied
the hall of a social gild.) In this way, about the thirteenth
century, the gild of merchants, with its newer methods and
its business-like habits in keeping accounts, was gradually
growing into union with the governing functions of the town,
and its laws were combining with and forming the laws of

FIG. 252.   OLD  TOWN  HALL,  LEOMINSTER.

the town, as we see in the cases of Winchester, Worcester,
Preston, and Berwick-upon-Tweed. In Gloucester the gild
was kept distinct from the borough till the middle of the
sixteenth century. These bodies accordingly formed an
important element in the growth of industrial towns from
the end of the eleventh century ; their separate identity
died away principally in the fourteenth century, but in
various ways their influence lasted long and left its mark
behind. It must always be remembered that there is great
diversity in the history of towns ; they rose and fell at

varying dates ; each one has its life-story, founded on its
peculiar circumstances ; and this principle applies also to
the study of the life of the merchant gild.

### 4. *Markets and Fairs.*

From ancient times the countrymen and others who
brought their produce to be sold in the boroughs and towns
had to pay various dues to the king or to the local lord,
for leave to enter the walls, for leave to stand in a fixed
spot or particular street where buyers would know where
to find them, rents for stalls, and fines should they break
the rules of the market. These together made a considerable sum at the end of the year, and the rights of a market
became in some places a valuable property, especially after

FIG. 253. The old Oxford Town Hall
or *Domus Conversorum* (from Ingram's
*Memorials*).

the Conquest, when new
tolls were introduced ; as
that on passing through
a forest, crossing a bridge,
entering a town, and so on,
so much a load should be
paid, according to the class
of ware. In King Alfred's
time, Æthelred of Mercia
and his wife Æthelflæd,
wishing to help the church
in Worcester, where they had built a burh, granted to the
bishop half their market rights, i. e. the profits which would
have come to them ' both in market and in street ' ; and
Alfred's son, King Edward the Elder, granted the tolls of
the ' town's cheaping ' in Taunton to the see of Winchester.
*Cheaping* was Old-English for buying or bargaining, from
*ceapian*, to bargain or trade ; *cheap-stowe* meant a market-
place, and the root *cheap* appears in such names as Chep-
stowe, Chipping Norton, Chipping Sudbury, &c., as well as
in the word *ceap-mann*, a chapman, bargainer, or merchant.
Some of the selling and bargaining was done in an open
street, where the vendors were accustomed to stand ; hence
' Cheapside ' is the name of a well-known street in London.
In 1319 the market standings in Oxford were held along
a considerable part of High Street and Cornmarket Street,
and the same state of things would be found in many
towns.

Domesday Book mentions markets in about fifty towns,

and it is known that others existed which are not included therein. Some had then been set up quite recently, and in succeeding centuries, as population increased and new towns were settled, markets were freely granted. A market might not be set up in any place : if it were too near one already established it would interfere with the trade of the earlier market ; inquiry had to be made whether a new one would injure the rights of the king or of others. A famous lawyer of the thirteenth century considered that the distance between markets should be not less than a little over six miles, an interval which would allow time for the walk to market in the morning, for the sale of wares in the middle of the day, and for the market folk to get home by daylight, the last being an important consideration on account of the numerous robbers.

Sunday marketing was forbidden among both Danes and English as early as 906, and the prohibition was repeated several times before the Conquest. None the less that day, which must have been a convenient one to those whose week was filled with toil—the churchyard being handy for setting down their baskets—long continued to be so used in many places. But slowly the Church prevailed against early law and custom. Bishops imposed fines for breaking ' the holiday rest ' ; towards 1201 Eustace, Abbot of Flay, went about preaching that no one should sell in the market on Sundays ; in 1285 a statute was passed forbidding fairs and markets to be held in churchyards ; and at length, in 1448, Henry VI forbade the holding of fairs and markets on Sundays : no wares were to be shown, ' necessary victual only except '. The old laws were careful to protect the roads and ways about the city ; within three miles round ' no man ought to stop or hinder another . . . if he comes in the city's peace ' ; ' the roads from city to city, from borough to borough, by which men go to market and to their other business, are under the law of the county '. Once established, a market might not be removed, nor its day be changed, except for great need : uncertainty was fatal to prosperous trade. Markets, being a necessity to country towns as well as to boroughs and cities, increased in number in spite of tolls and imposts by which the owners, lords of manors, abbots, bishops, and royal officers attempted to swell their profits, even sometimes to the king's loss of his dues. During a great inquiry made throughout the country at the beginning of Edward I's reign, numerous complaints were brought as to exactions and frauds connected with markets, and an Act was afterwards passed for the correction of such abuses. Within the thirteenth century the market law became settled, and has remained almost unchanged till modern times.

And as among a company assembled for bargain and sale disputes were certain to arise as to weight, measure, or quality of stuff, in every market it was provided that there should be a court composed of merchants, held by the mayor or the steward of the Court Leet in the Tolbooth or some other convenient spot. This was the court of *Pie-powder*, or *pieds poudrés*, 'dusty feet', so called because the chapmen or merchants came straight in, without ceremony, to have their differences adjusted on the day on which they happened, and to have offenders punished without delay. When held at a fair, the court would sit so long as the fair lasted. The Tolbooth itself was an adjunct of market law, being originally a hut or booth set apart for the payment of tolls and dues, where goods were weighed and the court sat; if, later, a permanent building were erected, it might become a prison or a town-hall. For bread, wine, and ale the prices had to be fixed once a week by the mayor or bailiff, according to a regular scale, so that in this respect there was no opportunity for haggling; but there might be room for fraud in the quality and in the weight. In the 'Usages of Winchester', before quoted (p. 296), rules are laid down as to the sale of fish and poultry. They shall not be bought wholesale before nine in the morning; a board on which fish is shown for sale pays rent a farthing a day; every cart-load of fish on the board pays a halfpenny; tolls are paid besides for cart-loads, horse-loads, and man-loads of fish brought in by non-burgesses—salmon, lampreys, and herrings sold in Lent, for each kind a special toll. Butchers pay for their stalls, and merchants of unslaughtered goats, sheep, and swine are registered. Bakers in the town are well looked after. They must keep the assize with good bread of full weight; those from outside who sell their bread in the High Street pay more rent than those who stand in the other streets, and every baker must put his seal upon his loaves. For cheese and butter, grease and 'smear' (fat or ointment) brought into the city, so much a stone is to be paid as toll.

So also, in the ordinances of Berwick-upon-Tweed and of Worcester, rules for the sale of supplies in market are carefully made to hinder those who would take wrongful advantage, and to ensure fair dealing to all.

A market draws in from the immediate neighbourhood the trade for supplying daily wants at frequent intervals, such as once, twice, or thrice a week ; a fair, held annually or biennially, gave opportunity to merchants travelling from a distance to sell goods from other parts of the realm or from abroad. The origin of fairs is traced to tribal customs and religious festivals. A holy shrine would attract people from afar to share in its special benefits ; meeting strangers there from distant counties, they would combine profit with spiritual weal, the merchants would open their wares, the better-off would buy their pepper, ginger, sugar, and other rare stores, their silks and linen, and the yearly holy day or holiday, regularly anticipated, became a fair or mart. In a dispute in the reign of King John as to a fair held at Shillingford, the Abbot of Abingdon claimed that the abbey possessed the fair free from tolls to the king because the assembly was in order to keep the wake or saint's festival, though buying and selling went on there. Various other local reasons, such as good roads or the neighbourhood of waterways, would help to determine the seat of a fair. They were, like the markets, in olden times often held in churchyards, where booths were made out of the boughs of trees. About 1183 the tenants of Boldon, in Durham, were bound to erect such lodges or booths at the fairs of St. Cuthbert ; at Hereford certain tenants had to cut rods or wattle in the neighbouring wood for making enclosures at the fair. With the fair still more than with the market, a concourse of people buying and selling must be controlled by authority ; peace and protection must be paid for ; and it was soon realized that fairs were profitable to those who possessed the rights of enforcing these advantages. Some fairs were granted for charitable purposes. Stourbridge fair, near Cambridge, one of the most famous in the Middle Ages, originated in a grant by King John for the maintenance of a hospital for lepers, though it afterwards became the property of the burgesses of Cambridge. Another, at Burley, in Rutland, was granted to aid the restoration of that town, which had been burnt. As commerce increased abroad and at home, fresh opportunities were sought by merchants for the sale, and by town populations for the acquisition, of numberless new and useful stores and objects which they had no other chance of procuring; and accordingly it is found that numerous grants of the right to hold a fair were made by the Crown from the twelfth century onwards. Henry I granted several to great churches and priories, which afterwards became important fairs. Thus he granted to Canterbury a fair of five days; to St. Andrew's, Rochester, the gift of ' all customs and liberties, and the entire toll of the two days' fair on the feast of St. Paulinus '; to Winchester Cathedral a ıair of eight days' at St. Giles's Church on the eastern hill, with the king's rents and rights, including those given by William II. Others were granted during the reign of Henry I to ecclesiastical bodies at Malmesbury, St. Albans, Bath, and Ramsey, to the monastery of Tavistock, and to St. Frideswide's Priory, Oxford, the last to extend over seven days in July. During the seventy-four years from the first year of King John to the last of Henry III, about 2,000 fairs with their rights were granted, of which but a few were in Wales, Ireland, and France.

The owner ' proclaimed ' the opening of the fair; his proclamation included orders to keep the peace, to maintain honest dealing, and restrain vagabonds; it also gave notice of the Pie-powder Court. While a fair was being held no business was allowed in the market, and shops were closed; ' the town courts (as in Oxford during St. Frideswide's fair) were closed in favour of the Pie-powder Court . . . and the keys of the city gates were given over by the mayor to the prior '; the fair enjoyed a monopoly of trade and law for the time. At Westminster, Ely, and Winchester the same rules are recorded. Some fairs became especially famous, such as those of St. Giles at Winchester, Boston, Stourbridge (near Cambridge), and St. Bartholomew's in Smithfield, founded by Rahere for his priory church in 1133. This might be because the commodities were reputed better than those offered elsewhere, or because some special article was procurable, or because the amusements provided by the wayfaring showmen were noted above all others. For centuries Nottingham was still celebrated for its goose fair; Birmingham fair for onions and gingerbread; Barnet for its horse fair, whither ponies were brought even from Wales and Yorkshire; and

ENTREE ROYALLE DE LA REYNE MERE DV ROY TRES CHRESTIEN DANS LA VILLE DE LONDRE

FIG. 254. A LONDON STREET. Pageant at the entrance of Marie de Medici, the mother of Henrietta Maria, into London, October 1638. By P. de la Serre.

St. Bartholomew's (once a great cloth fair) and Greenwich for their plays, shows, and various amusements.

Fairs, like other institutions, waxed and waned. Some that were flourishing in former days had decayed by Stuart times, while others lived on because they were a convenience, indeed almost a necessity to country life ; the squires and farmers of the country-side, the house-wives in villages and towns, counted on a yearly visit to the nearest fair for laying in their stores of articles not to be bought at ordinary times in market or shop. Since the introduction of railways and of other improved means of communication, fairs have rapidly declined. The business which gave them life having departed, they degenerated : in many places they have been suppressed, and the survivors appear to be gradually dying out. In 1792 at least 1,600 fairs were annually held in England and Wales ; by 1888 the number was reduced to 1,144 ; and of those which remain it seems that it is not so much the business as the pleasure side, the attraction of shows and of sociability, that chiefly keeps them alive.

## Books for reference.

1. MAITLAND, Township and Borough, 1898.
   —— Domesday and Beyond, 1897, § 9, ' The Boroughs '.
   GROSS, The Gild Merchant, 1890, vol. i, Appendix B.
   KEMBLE, The Saxons in England, 1849, vol. ii, Appendix C.
   W. CUNNINGHAM, Growth of English History and Commerce, 3rd edition, 1896, vol. i.
   R. L. POOLE, Historical Atlas of Modern Europe, Map 17 by Jas. Tait.
   HUGHES, T. H., and LAMBORN, E. A. G., Towns and Town Planning, 1922.
   TOUT, ' Mediaeval Town Planning ', in The Town-Planning Review, vol. viii, No. 1, April 1919.
2. Miss M. BATESON in English Historical Review, 1900–1, ' The Laws of Breteuil '.
   STUBBS, Constitutional History, 1878, chaps. v, § 44 ; xi, § 131 ; xv, §§ 211, 212 ; xxi, §§ 807–11.
   BALLARD, Domesday Boroughs (1904) ; and British Borough Charters (1913).
   BATESON, Cambridge Gilds (1903); and Borough Customs (2 vols., 1904–6).
   Mrs. J. R. GREEN, Town Life in the Fifteenth Century, 1894, vol. i, chaps. ii, iv, vii, xiv.
   TOULMIN SMITH, English Gilds, 1870, Part III.
3. W. CUNNINGHAM, op. cit., vol. i, Book III, chap. iv.
   TOULMIN SMITH, English Gilds.
   GROSS, The Gild Merchant (1890), vol. i, chaps. i–v.
   Records of Leicester, edited by Miss M. Bateson, 1899, Introduction.
4. Report by C. I. ELTON and COSTELLOE on ' Markets and Fairs ' appended to First Report of Royal Commission, 1889.
   W. CUNNINGHAM, op. cit., vol. i, pp. 180–2, 240.
   HENRY MORLEY, Memoirs of Bartholomew Fair, 1874.
   KEMBLE, Saxons in England, vol. ii, pp. 328, 332.

# IX

# COUNTRY LIFE

## 1. *Before Domesday.*

A SECTION which is called 'Country Life' needs must be wide, and perhaps somewhat straggling, as is the country itself when contrasted with the town. The whole extent cannot be traversed ; some paths must be followed, while others are left untrodden, and we cannot pursue any of them very far without encountering a mass of difficulties caused in great measure by the changes which time brings about in the meaning of technical terms, and by the variations of custom and phrase in different parts of England. Yet for the present our purpose is rather to avoid difficult and exceptional cases, and to understand technical terms in the sense which they bear in the more familiar scenes of our history. We seek specimens, not curiosities, and these we shall endeavour to classify by their best known names.

If we look backwards from the Conquest into Anglo-Saxon times we find already existing the division of the country into *shires* and *hundreds* and *tuns* or *vills* (townships) ; we come across the institution of the *manor* (though the name itself is Norman), and many of the elements of feudalism ; we also meet with the terms *folkland, bocland* (bookland), and *lænland* (leased land). Let us try to get some ideas as to these by way of beginning.

Some of the shires corresponded to the old tribal kingdoms ; such were Sussex, Essex, Norfolk, Suffolk, the old dominions of the South Saxons, the East Saxons, the North and South Anglian folk. Others were of later creation, such as the mass of midland counties carved out of Mercia. Yet, however formed, each shire had its *shire moot*, or court, which was held twice a year. The *sheriff* (the king's officer) presided, and with him sat the *bishop* and the *ealdorman* ; it was attended by the landowners, twelve chosen representatives from each hundred, and the reeve and four men from each township which was unrepresented by its lord or his steward. It dealt with civil, criminal, and ecclesiastical cases, though, when William I severed the spiritual and temporal courts, the last-named branch of jurisdiction was withdrawn to the bishops' courts. When Henry II instituted the travelling justices, the shire moot was called together to meet them. With the disputed origin of the *hundred* or the *wapentake*, as the corresponding division in the northern shires was called, we are not concerned. Hundreds differed in size; the name, apparently first given to an association of persons for purposes of defence and police, was transferred to the district where they dwelt. As with the shire, the most visible sign of union in the hundred was the *hundred moot*, presided over by the hundred's ealdor, and attended by those who held land in it, and (like the shire court) by representatives of some townships. Its jurisdiction was civil and criminal, and an appeal lay from it to the shire court.

The smallest territorial division was that of the *township* or *vill*, the ancestor of the civil parish of our own day. The inhabitants of the vill were not bound by any very close ties. They may have been in earliest times connected by blood; they may have represented the old village community, the association of free men holding land in common, which existed among our Anglo-Saxon forefathers in their home on the continent, and was perhaps transplanted by them into England. Though the idea that the land belonged to the vill and not to each dweller in it had passed away, there remained the practice of ploughing together, each villager finding his share of oxen for the plough-team. This was some sort of bond; the possession of common land for grazing was another; the habit of sending men to the hundred court a third; and by the time of Domesday, the fact that the vill was the smallest subdivision called on to testify to the commissioners was yet another tie. We know, however, that vills differed very greatly in size, and we must be on our guard against thinking that they had much sense of corporate existence. In some there may have been a township court even from early days, but it is certain that a great many had no court at all.

When we turn from the divisions of the land to the ownership of it, we find that the idea that the land is the possession of the people is at an early date replaced by the idea that the land is the king's. By degrees the title *Rex Angliae* supplants that of *Rex Anglorum*. We must not be misled by the term 'folkland'. This is not land of the folk, but land held by folk-right; it is opposed to bookland, which is land held by a charter or book granted by the king. What these charters or books conferred were privileges: either immunities from performing certain duties, such as providing the king with food and lodging on his travels, doing military service for him, or repairing bridges and highways; or else rights to take the profits of jurisdiction, the fines inflicted for thefts, assaults, or other offences. For example, when land is declared by 'book' to be free from thief-taking, it does not mean that thieves were to go unpunished in that district: clearly no landholder would desire that his property should be made a sanctuary for evil-doers. What is meant is that the fines for theft in that district, which hitherto went to the king, now went to some one else—to the person to whom the land had been booked.

These charters or books granting rights over land were at first principally bestowed on the Church, but there was no reason why such books should not be bestowed upon thegns as well as on bishops and abbots. Further still, bishops and abbots themselves found that they had something to grant. Thus, supposing that a bishop or an abbot held land by book from the king on conditions which freed him from all obligations save those of the *trinoda necessitas* —that threefold duty of repairing fortifications and bridges and of service with the *fyrd* or national levy—there were many rights and privileges which would be left in his hands. These he could grant out in his turn. It is certain that even before the Conquest it was a practice of the Church to grant part of the land, which was 'booked' to it from the king, on lease (*læn*) perhaps for two or three lives, to persons whose duty it was to discharge the 'law of riding', including all military service, and to pay church-scot and other tolls due to the Church. These persons are generally described as the 'knight', the 'soldier', the 'true and faithful man' *of the Church*.

Here, then, before the days of the Normans, we have many of the characteristics of feudal England. We have an edifice of at least four stories. Between the king and the

cultivator are the holders of bookland, who in their turn
are making grants of land on lease.  If these leases are not
always held on condition of doing military service, yet
military service is rendered for some of them.  Further, where
by the 'books' grants of jurisdiction have been made, the
lord of the land has his own court.  At the basis of the system
are the small cultivators, free and unfree, who till acre-
strips in the open fields of the village community, and pay
rent, usually in kind and labour, to a manorial lord.

## 2.  *Manors and Servile Tenants.*

Domesday reveals manors of all sorts and sizes, inhabited
by many or by few persons.  Take, for example, the Archbishop of Canterbury's great manor of Harrow, with land
for seventy teams of oxen, and the Westminster manor of
Cowley, with land for but one team, and only two villeins
on it.  Can any description be said to be 'typical' where
we have such wide differences ?  Again, are we to describe
the manor of Domesday, or that of the twelfth or thirteenth
century ?  Are we to take one from the rich and populous
east, or from the poor and thin west ?  How are we to look
at it ?  An economist will wish to see how the manor was
administered from within, under what conditions the folk
on it lived, how the land was tilled, and so forth ; a lawyer
will concern himself with the legal rights and status of the
tenants ; the lord of the manor will be interested in what
may be got from it for himself ; the royal officials will
think of it as a unit for taxation : they will want to know
how much it should pay, and who is responsible for the
payment.  The usual form of entry in Domesday was
somewhat in this fashion.  In M (place-name), A (man's
name) holds *a* (so many) hides subject to payment of geld.
There is land for *b* teams : there are in the demesne *c* teams.
Then follows the catalogue of villeins and other servile
tenants with their teams, and further particulars about
pasture, wood, stock, horses, pigs, sheep.  Mills, saltpits,
fishponds are also mentioned ; and the entry usually concludes with *valuit T. R. E.*, so much, i.e. the annual value
in the time of King Edward the Confessor, and *valet*, its
worth at the time of the Survey.

It is impossible in the space at our command to embark
upon a discussion of even a tenth of the questions which

an entry seemingly so simple as this raises. But a few
words must be said, though even these will be tentative :
the problems of Domesday, if not insoluble, are certainly
not yet solved.

First, as to the hide ; this was the unit of rating. We
may take it that at the time of the Conquest the hide was
reckoned at 120 acres. This was the amount of arable land
which in the remote past was assumed to be necessary for the
support of one family. In modern eyes it seems an absurdly
large amount, but we must remember that the systems of
farming were extremely poor. They were either the two-
field or the three-field system ; that is to say, the land was
either alternately under crop or left fallow in the former ;
or in the latter cropping and fallowing came in a rotation
of three. With an energetic cultivator this would mean
two-thirds under crop and one-third fallow ; but it might
be the other way about. Thus the acreage of a hide under
crop in any one year would be sixty acres with the same
amount fallow, or eighty acres, with forty acres fallow.
Further, the yield of land was very poor. An agricultural
reformer of the thirteenth century, Walter of Henley,
expected to get only ten bushels to the acre in return for
two ; we shall not be far wrong if, in the eleventh century,
we take six bushels as an average return ; and this will
not all go for bread : much was used in brewing. Further,
when the family bond was stronger, the numbers inhabiting
one tenement were larger. Married brothers, with their
wives and children, may have dwelt together and shared
an inheritance.

Yet, though we may assign 120 acres on an average to
the hide, this was often an assumption. Measures were
vague : there is a fondness for round numbers ; the hide is
the measure of assessment. So many hides will be reckoned
to the county, or to the hundred, or to the vill, and the
geld gathered on this basis, without any pains being taken
to be sure that so many hides of 120 acres each lie there.
Hence we find some counties rated high and some low.
Leicester is heavily rated, Devonshire sparingly. Apparently
land and tillage in the first county were much more valuable
than in the second, and more could be paid. Sometimes
Domesday expressly says that though a manor contains five
hides, it is rated at three. The king has granted an immunity

to two hides. They pay no geld. This is what is called *beneficial hidation*.

This must suffice for the hide, or, as it is called in the returns of some counties, the *carucate*. We may, however, notice two subdivisions, the *virgate* or *yard land*, which was a quarter-hide, and the *bovate*, an eighth of a carucate. Here indeed we come on a topic which can be only mentioned, not pursued, the connexion between measures of land and natural units. The acre is a fair day's ploughing ; the hide or carucate, the amount of land a team (*caruca*) will plough in that portion of the year given to ploughing. The team of oxen is eight, hence one-eighth of a carucate— the *ploughgang*—is the *oxgang* or *bovate*, the land for one ox ; though of course one ox never ploughed alone. It also becomes plain to us that, as it is rare for the villein to possess more than two oxen, and quite usual for the *bordar* or *cottar* to have no oxen at all, the servile tenants will have to unite to do their ploughing. There will be a regular routine for all ; no experiments will be possible. There is no chance for the man with ideas under the system of open field farming.

The usual manor will contain land of three kinds, arable land, pasture land, and waste or common land, which may be either forest or down land, or both, where cattle and pigs may be turned out to get food while the pasture land is growing its hay crop, and where the tenants will get wood and turf for firing. This is a natural division, but besides there was an artificial division ; there was *demesne land* and *tenants' land*. The first was land which was worked for the lord's private benefit, the second was what the free and unfree tenants of the manor were allowed to till for themselves. The unfree tenants are often collectively spoken of as *villeins*, hence the term ' land held in villeinage '. Yet, to speak strictly, the villeins were but one unfree class out of a number. Domesday speaks of *coliberti* (*gebúras*, boors), *cotarii* and *bordarii* (cottars), *villani* (villeins), and we may gather that their position stands in the order given ; the *colibertus* is the worst off, the villein the best, or perhaps we should say, the least ill off. But no hard-and-fast division can be made according to the amount of land they hold, or by the oxen they possess, or by the duties they pay. Generally speaking, we may think of the villein with a virgate of land, the *bordarius* with less, the others with little or none ; or again, we may picture the villein with two oxen, and the rest with none ; but exceptions are frequent. We find cottars with four or five acres and bordars with oxen. The precise amount of their servitude cannot be fixed ; they are more free than the slave proper, in that they have some rights. Yet they are unfree. Domesday contrasts them with the *sokemen*, the *liberi tenentes*. But in what are they unfree ? They are bound to perform certain services for their lord ; they work on his demesne land. These services are divided into ' week-work ' (so many days each week) and ' boon-work ' (certain extra days at the busy seasons of harvest and ploughing). Besides these, there are other duties and tributes, carrying or carting, dues of fowls, eggs, and so on. Often they cannot sell their oxen ' out of the manor ', or marry a daughter without their lord's leave. Yet should we press closely the degree of unfreedom the line is again blurred. Exceptions and apparent contradictions are common. We must, however, remember two things. First, that economic freedom and legal freedom need not be the same ; for example, a man who is *legally* free may undertake to perform tasks which we commonly regard as the work of an unfree man ; he may, for instance, accept land from a manorial lord on condition of doing ' villein ' services ; on the other hand, a man legally unfree may have been excused his villein services. ' Freedom ' in each of the cases will depend on the point of view. Secondly, we may bear in mind that as we advance from Domesday to the thirteenth century, Roman law has an increasing influence with our lawyers, and Roman law treats the serf as a chattel, a thing without rights. Thus, in the theory of the royal courts of law villeins are likely to find their position becoming more and more servile, while in the practice of the time it is perhaps becoming more and more free.

The typical manor then was mainly cultivated by unfree labour. The land called the *demesne* might be a piece severed from the land held in villeinage, or it might be intermixed with it. But the lord depended on his villeins for the tillage of the demesne. His estate was rich not merely if it was wide in acreage, but if it was also well stocked with men. Consequently no small part of the right management of an estate lay in making the villeins punctually discharge their work. This was the task of the bailiff, who directed the ploughing, sowing, and reaping, gave out the seed, watched the harvest gathered, and looked after stock and horses. At first we may picture the manor going on almost entirely without interchange of money. Payments are made 'in kind' or in labour. It is, as economists say, under a natural economy. By degrees, as money becomes more plentiful, the use of it creeps into country districts. Then begins the practice of *commutation of service*. Villeins offer to pay money instead of their services ; the lord agrees to take the money. How fast this process spread is difficult to say. We know that while in Henry I's day the exchequer took much of its payments in kind, by Henry II's time money was usually paid ; but the king, though the greatest of manorial lords, cannot be taken as a type. He was in advance of the rest. But by the time of the Black Death (1348), it appears as if commutation of service had become fairly common, and after that time it went on with increasing rapidity.[1]

This practice of commutation of service is of very great consequence. It is the first step in the gradual substitution of the free labourer for the servile tenant. To the later progress of this change we shall return ; in the meanwhile we may note three things: (1) commutation was a matter of agreement between lord and villein ; (2) a new period begins in rural history when a money economy takes the place of the old natural economy, when money has become common enough to take the place of payments in service or in kind, since as soon as payments are made in money a man enjoys a larger measure of freedom : he may be no better off in material comfort, but he is to a far greater extent master of his own time ; and (3) the fact that lords were willing to accept money instead of services shows that there was in existence a considerable number of labourers who could be hired. Had it not been so, the lords would not have found labourers to cultivate their demesne land, and the money paid to them would not have been an acceptable substitute for the commuted services. The

[1] The extent to which commutation had gone in 1348 is discussed by T. W. Page, *The End of Villeinage in England* (New York, 1900), on a statistical basis.

practice of commutation led to the growth of a class of
*copyholders*, or enfranchised villeins, who were so called
because their title-deed was a copy of the entry in the
manor court-roll which recorded their bargain with the lord.

### 3. *Feudal Tenures.*

Leaving these lowly persons, the unfree tenants, let us
turn our attention to the lords of the manors. We know
that the Conquest was a shrewd blow to the Anglo-Saxon
landowners. Much land was confiscated; many small
owners who had been free sank into a servile position. The
land was mostly in Norman hands. Yet though William I
had rewarded his followers with wide estates, for his own
safety he had not allowed these estates to be concentrated,
save in the special cases of the palatine earldoms. Even
these were soon reduced in number. Bishop Odo's possessions in Kent were forfeited; so were Robert de Belesme's
in Shropshire. Robert of Mortain might hold near 800
manors, but they were in twenty different counties. Herein
is the explanation of the apparent restlessness that marks
the great barons, and the court too, for the king was the
greatest of all landowners. They roam with a train of
followers from one estate to another; there is a great
bustle of preparation; a few days' stay consumes the produce stored up during the year; then they go on to their
next manor, and the country-side sinks back into its accustomed quiet. It is not till money becomes so plentiful that
produce can be sold and the price paid to the landowner,
that the king can manage to settle down, or that the lords
can afford to make prolonged stays with the court. Till
that time hunger will keep them incessantly on the road.

Under the feudal system there was a great variety of
tenures. A man might hold his land direct from the king,
in which case he was a *tenant-in-chief*, or he might hold it
from some intermediate lord; he would then be a *mesne
tenant*, and the lord from whom he held was his *mesne lord*.
A careful distinction must be drawn between tenure by
*Knight-Service* and *Socage Tenure*. Tenure by knight-
service was, as the name shows, essentially military. The
tenant of a knight's fee (land liable for the service of
one knight) had to follow his lord in the field for forty
days in the year at his own expense. In an age when

fighting was thought to be the only profession for a
gentleman, tenure by knight-service was naturally reckoned
more dignified and more aristocratic than tenure by free
socage, which called for the performance of peaceful
services or the payment of money. When a man who
held a knight's fee did not take up his 'knighthood' he
could be fined. This *Distraint of Knighthood* was used by

FIG. 255. Knocking down acorns for swine. Treading grapes.[1]

FIG. 256. Harrowing, sowing, and digging.[1]

Charles I's advisers as a means of raising money. It was
singularly unjust, as apart from the fact that feudal customs
had fallen into disuse with the lapse of time, and for
a century and a half obligatory knighthood had ceased to
be enforced, the fine fell on a comparatively poor class.
The normal revenue (£20) of the knight's fee which had been
thought adequate to support knightly rank in Edward I's
day, was certainly not enough in the reign of Charles I.
Money had fallen in purchasing power ; an annual revenue
of £20 had become a very small one.

[1] From the Barnard wood-carvings at Abington Hall, Northants (1485–1508).

There were other tenures of a rarer and more quaint
character.  Tenure by *Grand Serjeanty* involved the performance of special service to the king, such as holding the
post of the king's butler, his marshal, his chamberlain, or
his champion.  *Petit Serjeanty* was a tenure by which the
tenant had to render each year some small service, or to
give his lord a bow, a sword, or a lance, or, it might be,

FIG. 257.   Reaping and binding.[1]

FIG. 258.   Weeding and picking flowers (?).[1]

hounds, sparrow-hawks, herrings, gloves, a pair of scarlet
hose, a steel needle, a pound of cummin seed.  Many other
examples, equally quaint, may be found written in Blount's
*Ancient Tenures*.  *Frankalmoign* (free alms) was the tenure
on which members of religious houses sometimes held their
land : here the usual condition was the performance of
certain services for the welfare of the donor's soul.  These
nominal rents were intended merely to perpetuate the
recognition of lordship : we may find a parallel in the
practice of closing college gates once a year at Cambridge

[1] Barnard wood-carvings, Abington Hall.

in order to prevent the establishment of any right of way through the courts.

If we turn to the question of payments due from the land, we must first of all remember that until Henry II's day all taxation fell upon land. The king was entitled to the *three feudal aids* from his tenants in chivalry : to knight his son, to provide a dowry for his daughter, or to pay a ransom for himself should he fall into the hands of his enemy. The old Danegeld reappeared under the name of *hidage* (2s. on the hide) in Henry II's day, and *carucage* under Richard I and John. Henry II, to make his army more durable and more useful than the feudal levy, gave to the sub-tenants the option of commuting their military

FIG. 259. Performing monkey (Abington Hall).

service for a payment of varying amount which was assessed on the knight's fee. This payment was known as *scutage*. Feudal lords gathered a revenue from the profits of *wardships* of the minors under them, and had also a right to *heriots* and *reliefs*. In theory the lord was supposed to provide his ' man ' with a horse ; when the man died this had nominally to be returned : hence grew the practice of taking a *heriot* in the shape of the best beast from the dead man's estate. The *relief* was a payment made by the incoming heir before he became seised of his estate, that is to say, got possession of it. Thus the ' heriot ' and ' relief ' were primitive forms of death duties.

Since the power and wealth of each great landowner depended upon those under him duly discharging their services and dues, it became a matter of great interest to prevent any diminution of those services and dues, such as, for example, would occur if the tenant alienated too much of his land, or if the land became split up into such small pieces that the tenants were too poor to discharge their duties. Hence came the practice of *entail*, dating in its earliest form from Anglo-Saxon days, but revived and strengthened by Edward I's statute, the Second of Westminster, *De Donis Conditionalibus* (1285), which kept estates together by forbidding the owner of entailed lands to dispose of them against the terms of the entail. A similar object was kept in view in the Third Statute of Westminster, *Quia Emptores* (1290), which provided (*a*) that the owner of land which was not entailed might sell or give it away as he pleased, and (*b*) that the land thus alienated

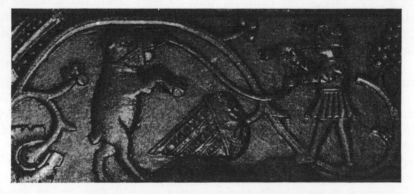

FIG. 260. Dancing bear (Abington Hall).

should be held by the recipient from the ' chief lord ', that is, the lord of the alienor. This stopped the practice of *sub infeudation*, that is to say, the creation of smaller intermediate feudal holdings, and protected the superior lord against having so much of his original grant regranted away that his services and dues were endangered. Further, as the superior lord took much profit at a time when his tenant died and the land passed to the heir, he would resent land passing into the hand of a corporation such as the Church, for this never died, and there would be no fines of re-entry. Hence the Statute of *Mortmain* (1279) enacted that if any person either sold or gave land to any religious body, the land should be forfeited. The effect of this statute was considerably mitigated by the practice, which mediaeval kings found very profitable, of granting licences

to alienate lands in mortmain. All these measures strengthened the position of the superior lords, and most of all the
supreme landowner, the king.

### 4. *The Black Death.*

The quiet annals of the country-side were rudely broken
into by the Black Death. This appalling pestilence destroyed near one-half of the population, and it was no whit
less fatal in the country than in the towns. We can easily
understand that agriculture would be paralysed when half
the workers lay stricken ; we shall be prepared for the
scarcity of food that followed ; we can well believe that
the harvest lay rotting in the fields with none to gather it.
Scarcity, nay even famine, had indeed been no unknown
thing in English rural life ; rather, it had been all too
common ; but the Black Death brought with it a chain of
results peculiarly its own.

The first consequence was a sharp rise in prices ; then,
since the former ' living wage ' no longer afforded a living,
there followed a rise in wages. This placed the landowners
in a difficult position. Those who had accepted commutation of service, who had agreed to take money instead of
work from their villeins, found that the money they received
no longer represented the work they had lost. They had
commuted when the wage of the hired labourer was low ;
now that it was high their money would not go so far ;
they could not pay for enough hired work to replace the
villein services which they had lost. The first remedy
which occurred to the landowners, and therefore to the
Crown and Parliament who represented mainly the land-
owning class, was to return to the old state of things, to
' put back the clock by legislation '. The successive Statutes
of Labourers ordered that men were not to ask or take
higher prices or higher wages. If prices did not rise, there
would be no need for higher wages ; and though it may
seem strange to us that Parliament should claim to fix
prices, there was nothing strange about it to fourteenth-
century eyes. Merchant and craft gilds regulated prices of
commodities in the towns ; why should not Parliament do
the same in the country ? However, Parliament's action,
in spite of the ferocious penalties imposed and rigorous
inquisitions by the Justices appointed under the Statutes

of Labourers, came to nothing ; the rise in prices went on, and with it the rise of wages. The landowners were left confronted with a diminished revenue, a scarcity of labour, and the problem which is familiar in English agriculture, of how to make two ends meet.

Various attempts were made to solve it. The first was to cast the burden of finding labour on an intermediary. Landowners began to let land at a rent, and as the tenants, in many cases the old villeins, had no money to find stock, the landowner himself provided stock and seed, for which the tenant had to return an equivalent at the end of his term. These *stock and land leases* give us the beginning of the modern farmer. Hitherto there had been but two persons on the land, lord and labourer. Henceforward a go-between becomes more common, till we get the familiar triple division of landlord, farmer, and labourer.

This was a sensible plan, but it could not prove a complete remedy. All labourers, whether free or servile, were naturally anxious to profit by the higher wages which were offered by many, in defiance of the Statutes of Labourers. It was easy to run away from a lord who offered only the legal rate, or who desired to maintain the old plan of taking services instead of commutation, and though the law provided plenty of penalties, certainly in no way wanting in ferocity, yet to put men in prison did not mend matters. ' Men in prison reap no fields.' Where serfs did not escape singly, they became mutinous collectively. The discontent of those to whom freedom seemed over-slow in coming culminated in the Peasant Revolt of 1381. When order was again restored after an outburst of burnings, robberies, murders, and executions, the legal position of the villeins remained as it had been. Practically, however, they had won an almost complete victory. Serfdom fell rapidly into desuetude ; wages remained at their higher level ; labour continued to be more expensive. Hence a new policy was urgently called for.

### 5. *The Growth of Sheep-Farming.*

The problem was how to do with less labour. Sheep-farming instead of arable farming offered a solution ; and as the woollen manufacture was growing rapidly in England in the end of the fourteenth century and throughout the fifteenth, while there was also a ready market for wool in Flanders, this was a very profitable solution for the lords. Yet this sheep-farming brought hardships on the labourers. To keep sheep it was necessary to throw together large tracts of ground and to enclose them with hedges. Hence the lords began first to enclose the common land that had hitherto pastured alike the cattle of both lord and villager ; and the villager soon found himself pinched for pasture land for his few beasts. Further, the lords wished to enclose their demesne lands. Where these lay separate from the land held in villeinage no hardship followed. But the demesne often lay intermixed with the villeins' land. Under the two and three field systems, land was not held in a block. Each tenant held a number of scattered acre or half-acre strips. This curious plan was the outcome of necessity and equity. When one of the two or three great fields lay fallow, it was plain that if a tenant held all his land in that field he would be poorly off for food during the year of fallowing. Of necessity he must hold some land in each field. But further, these great fields differed in fertility, one part from another. Hence in common fairness the land was split into smaller strips, so that all might share alike ; and the acre or half-acre was a convenient day or half-day's ploughing. Thus the arable land of England was mostly ' open field ', a mass of strips, scattered among various holders, each strip separated off by nothing but a balk of unploughed ground. Where the demesne land lay scattered among the land held in villeinage in open field, it was clear that to enclose it was necessary either to re-allot, or to drive off the villein tenants altogether. This last plan was too tempting to be resisted. Consequently, the lords set themselves to get rid of what villeins remained, and to use all the land of the manor for sheep. This process of depopulation went on vigorously. The Tudors legislated against it, but even in Elizabeth's day it was not entirely stopped.

The results of this were slow in revealing themselves in their completeness, yet when revealed they were little short of an agrarian revolution. It is true that by the better methods of farming that can be employed when the land is enclosed, enough corn was raised to provide for home needs ; but the new staple of rural England was sheep-

farming, and not corn-growing. Parliament was greatly
alarmed lest the rural population might dwindle. The
villein tenants had indeed won their freedom, but they had
lost their holdings. It was a Pyrrhic victory. Some found
employment on the sheep farms ; some went to the towns ;
many eked out their earnings on the land by working at the
loom and setting the women of their households to spin.
Here we may mark the beginning of the alliance between
agriculture and weaving, an alliance which prospered so
abundantly that an eighteenth-century writer could describe
the spinning wheel as ' the great sheet anchor' of the
cottager, which was only broken when machinery and
steam power literally beat the hand worker out of the field
into the factory-room.

Meagre as our sketch has been, the remainder of our
rural history must be treated even more scantily. The
seventeenth century was a time of political unrest, but of
agrarian quietude. The rush of enclosure and depopulation
was stayed ; it is only towards the last days of the century
that we notice the great landed families beginning to marry
money in the city, and the new moneyed men beginning
to buy estates. This did something to sway the landed
interest from Toryism to Whiggery, though only for a time.
To hold land became the hall-mark of a gentleman ; to have
a wide estate made a man of consequence among political
jobbers. It is not without point that the third of our
Georges is ' Farmer George ', for in his day there was a new
era of prosperity for the farmer. The great manufacturing
towns springing up, according to the old country gentleman's ideas, with the unwholesome rapidity of toadstools,
yet disclosed to him, toadlike, a hidden jewel. Those who
dwelt therein must eat : they called for much corn and
much meat. Hence prices rose and rents followed them.
Agricultural reformers came to teach better methods :
Townshend, Bakewell, Colling, showed what may be done
with root crops, and the better breeding of sheep and
beasts. Arthur Young belaboured the dull, old-fashioned
cultivator with good advice. He improved him out of all
knowledge, nay, often out of existence altogether. In the
nineteenth century some of Arthur Young's ideals were,
we know, realized, with large farms worked on scientific
methods ; and old-world ways, and small yeomen farmers

banished to agrarian rubbish heaps. Yet somehow the promised prosperity seems to have been mislaid in the process of change. The ideals are not so golden as they appeared in the glow of Arthur Young's eloquence.

## 6. *Games.*

An account of country life can hardly be complete without some mention, even the shortest, of games and sport. Early games are of great variety, but all alike must be dismissed cursorily. Football, which is heard of as early as the time of Edward III, was exceedingly popular, but not always approved by peaceable citizens. This was natural, as it was often played in the streets, ' breaking men's windows and committing other great enormities '. Davenant, in 1634, declares it ' not very civille ' in the narrow roads of London, and the Kingston tradesmen put up their shutters when it was played. An even severer judgement is that of Sir T. Elyot (*c.* 1530), who declares football to be ' nothinge but beastely furie and exstreme violence '. The kindred game of *hurling* (a rudimentary Rugby game) in one form required two or three miles of country, and the goals were often ponds, in which ball and players plunged together, ' scrambling and scratching '. *Campball*, another variety, was described as a ' friendlie fyghte ', and perhaps James I was not wrong when he condemned football as ' meeter for lameing than making able '. But in this as in other respects, James was a degenerate Scot. *Stoolball*, a game for girls—Herrick played it with Lucia for sugar-cakes and wine—has given us cricket. *Pall Mall* was a fashionable game in the seventeenth century. Cotgrave tells us that it was played in an alley, and the object was to strike a round boxball with a mallet through a high arch of iron. *Cambuc* is described by Strutt as a sort of golf, but was more probably hockey ; anyhow, Edward III found it wise to forbid it as a waste of time. The lower orders indulged in many varieties of bowls and quoits, in games of skittles named *kayles, closh, loggats, Dutch pins*, and others. Since none below the rank of gentleman could tilt at a tournament, the populace mimicked their sport by running at the *Quintain*. This familiar engine had many forms, sometimes rewarding an unskilful striker with a clout on the back, sometimes with a dusting of meal, sometimes with a sousing of water. A fourteenth-century picture shows three boys engaged in attacking a water-butt who have taken the preliminary precaution of removing their clothes. Other outdoor games popular with rustics in the sixteenth century were Prisoner's Base and Barley-break (otherwise called Last-in-hell); these had the advantage of being games in which both sexes could join. The most fashionable of all ball-games was *tennis*, which established itself in the course of the sixteenth century, having been apparently borrowed from France. Then, as now, it was a game played in an enclosed oblong court, specially built for the purpose; for this reason the game was too expensive to be taken up by the many.

Royal persons, who mostly played tennis themselves, were often discouraging towards popular games. They described them as unthrifty, and urged that arrow shooting was more profitable. No doubt it was duller. The Tudor sovereigns were more lenient. Henry VIII was a great athlete, skilled in leaping and casting the bar, and a noted wrestler, though Francis I proved a better, and threw him. Elizabeth smiled on manly games, but since the players insisted on playing on Sundays, as they always had done, the Puritans were shocked. Games in fact went from bad to worse; from being 'unthrifty' they became 'snares of the devil'. Yet in spite of preachers the love of games did not die out, and they continued, as they always had done, to exercise a strong influence on English life and character.

### 7. *Hunting and Hawking.*

Not much need be said of the hunting of deer, which was carried on either 'at force' (in the open country) or in a park where the cross-bow was used to shoot the quarry, and greyhounds were employed to course the wounded. Elizabeth saw sixteen bucks slain at Cowdray in this fashion. But it is worth notice that in Shakespeare's day, and even later, the fox was looked down upon. The author of the *Noble Arte of Venerye* (1576) classes the fox with 'badgerd and such like vermine', and held 'small pastime of hunting them especially within the ground'. Humphrey of Gloucester is a fox, and to be slain anyhow, 'Be it by gins or snares or subtlety'; and Oliver St. John, speaking against Strafford, says, 'It was never accounted either cruelty or foul play to knock foxes or wolves on the head.'    He, however, was a Parliamentarian and a man who was rarely known to smile, so perhaps cannot be taken as a sound authority on sport.

Hawking, a sport now so little known, had in its day an enormous vogue.    Perhaps it was most popular in Elizabeth's reign.    Shakespeare was a keen falconer, and knew all about it : see *Taming of the Shrew*, IV. i. 191.    It is those survivals in ordinary phrase of what may with justice be termed the language of hawking which chiefly recall the sport to our minds.    No more than a few examples can be given.    We have ' mews', the place where hawks were ' mewed' or kept when moulting.    Then when the royal mews were turned into the royal stables, the word took its later familiar meaning.    We have the ' pitch', to which the falcon *toured* (soared) ;    the ' stoop', with which she descended on her quarry ;    the ' lure', which tempted her back ;    the ' haggard', the hawk captured and reclaimed from the wild state, as opposed to the ' eyas', which had been trained from a nestling.    Though the short-winged hawk was more popular in France, the long-winged hawk, generically a *falcon*, whether peregrine, merlin, or hobby, was chiefly favoured in England.    The ' astringer' (one who flew goshawks or short-winged hawks) and the ' falconer' worked quite differently :    the first flew his hawk in wooded and cramped country, since the bird pursues the game ;    the second, in the open, as the falcon rises above and ' stoops'.    The best of the sport was to be got by flying at the heron ;    but ' flying at the brook', where mallards were the quarry, or flying at partridges, was popular.

Hawking is often mentioned in our laws.    Under the Normans the right of keeping hawks was restricted to the upper classes, but in the Forest Charter every free man might have an eyrie in his own woods.    To steal a hawk was felony ;    and the Bishop of Ely once excommunicated a thief who took one from the cloisters of Bermondsey.    Any one who destroyed falcon's eggs might be imprisoned for a year.    The *Boke of St. Albans*, in 1486, gives an interesting but fanciful catalogue of the hawks proper for various persons, beginning with an eagle for an emperor, and coming down to the ' sparrow-hawk for a priest, the musket (male sparrow-hawk) for a holy-water clerk, the kestrel for a knave'. By Elizabeth's days at latest any restrictions on the kind of hawk kept had vanished.

Between the falconer and the man with a newfangled weapon called a ' caliver ' or ' hand-gonne ' there was no love lost. ' A health to all that shot and miss'd ' was the falconer's toast. Unfortunately the percentage of missers gradually became less, and the army of fowlers larger, till the sport of falconry wellnigh decayed altogether.

Falconry indeed has seen a revival, but two other ancient English sports have of necessity disappeared—wolf-hunting and boar-hunting. The tale that wolves were extirpated in England by the annual tribute of 300 wolf-skins which Constantine of Wales was bound to render to Edgar is untrue. The Norman kings certainly kept wolf-hunters, and wolf-hunting tenures are common enough in their day, though the tenures may well have survived the wolves. Thomas Engaine held lands in Pitchley on condition of finding dogs at his own cost for the destruction of wolves and foxes, 43 Edw. III ; and Robert Plumpton held wolf-hunt land in Nottingham for the winding of a horn and chasing the wolves in Sherwood Forest, 5 Hen. VI. Wolves became extinct in England about the time of Henry VII, but in Scotland they lasted till the seventeenth century, while in Ireland they were common enough at that time for the Irish Council to offer substantial rewards for their destruction ; £6 for a bitch-wolf, £5 for a dog-wolf, and 40s. for a cub. The last wolves seem to have been destroyed in the Wicklow hills about the middle of the eighteenth century.

Wolf-hunting was a necessity ; boar-hunting was much more looked on as a sport. Kings from Edward the Confessor downwards took part in it. The boar was the ' proper prey' of the mastiff. He was chased with relays of hounds until he turned, when the hunters ran in on foot with sword or spear, the latter branching out into several forks to hold the boar from breaking through. There were wild boars in Chartley, Savernake, and the county of Durham till Henry VII's reign ; and James I was regaled at Whalley with what he was informed was a ' wild boar pye ', but perhaps the British Solomon was deceived by a common pork pie.

Not much need be said of the bears which vanished

Dancing Bear        Performing Dog

Playing Bowls

Hawking        Playing Chess

Hunting the Stag

Cock-fighting        Fencing

FIG. 261.

Shoeing a Horse

A Wheelbarrow

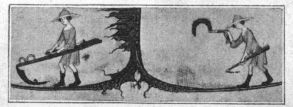

Reaping & Mowing

Ploughing

Digging

Netting Birds

A Windmill

A Wagon

Fig. 262.

before historic times ; of the wild cattle, now represented by the herds at Chillingham, Cadzow, and Chartley ; of the beavers of the Teifi, for which Giraldus Cambrensis is the authority ; of the wild cat, now almost extinct in our islands ; of the bustard pursued on the Sussex downs, in the middle of the eighteenth century, with dogs and bludgeons. Such of these as still remain owe their existence to the spirit which leads many men now to preserve rare and curious denizens of our island instead of destroying them. Were they left to take their chance, they would soon follow the wolf and the wild boar into the catalogue of the extinct.

The difference between our ideas of what constitutes ' sport ' and those of our remoter ancestors may be measured by the fact that, popular as hunting was, baiting was even more so. And its popularity lasted long. We may follow it through the centuries. FitzStephen in the twelfth century tells of bulls, bears, boars, and even horses being baited. Henry VIII enjoyed the sport ; Elizabeth commanded ' the bulls, the bears, and the ape to be baited in the tiltyard ' ; Abraham Slender says it was ' meat and drink ' to him to see Sackerson loose or take him by the chain. Pepys and Evelyn, in Charles II's day, witnessed ' bear-fighting ' orgies in the Paris Garden, or the ' Old Bear Garden ' at Southwark. Cock-fighting ran even a longer course. It was much practised in schools on Shrove Tuesday ; the scholars set on the cocks, and the pedagogues saw fair play. As the cocks were not, until comparatively late times, armed with steel spurs, the ' sport ' was less cruel and destructive than it afterwards became. Cocks were, however, subject to another outrage, that of being made a ' cock-shy ', when they were pelted with stones. In the Scilly Islands, after the cock-shying was over, the boys claimed a right to wind up the entertainment by throwing stones at dwelling-house doors. They might be bought off with money or pancakes ; but much damage was done, and the Scilly islanders seemed to have endured this preposterous tyranny somewhat meekly.

### Books for reference.

The list of authorities which follows makes no pretence to be complete. It is only intended to name a few of the better known and most interesting books. A student may with advantage look at such things as the Domesday Book, and the mass of grants, charters, and land-books ; but to learn what is to be learnt from them, he must refer to the writings of those who have made special studies of these ancient documents.

MAITLAND's *Domesday Book and Beyond* (1897), ROUND's *Feudal England* (1895), VINOGRADOFF's *Villeinage in England* (1892), and SEEBOHM's *Village Community* (1890) may be selected out of a very large number of books of this nature.

THOROLD ROGERS's *History of Agriculture and Prices* (1866–87) gives a mass of information, though the writer's conclusions, embodied also in *Six Centuries of Work and Wages* (1890), are not always generally accepted.

JESSOPP's *Coming of the Friars* (1890) and POWELL's *Rising in East Anglia* (1896) tell the story of the Black Death and the Peasant Revolt in East Anglia.

DAVENPORT, F. G., *The Economic Development of a Norfolk Manor, 1086–1565* (1906), gives valuable illustrations of the process by which the villein became the copyholder. The same subject is more generally treated by E. P. Cheyney in *The Disappearance of English Serfdom* (*Eng. Hist. Rev.* 1900, pp. 20–37).

JOHNSON, A. H., *The Disappearance of the Small Landowner* (1909), is a useful study of the effect of Enclosures at different periods.

TREVELYAN's *England in the Age of Wyclif* (1899) gives a fuller account of the troubles of 1381.

The management of a thirteenth-century estate is displayed in WALTER OF HENLEY's *Husbandry* (Royal Hist. Soc., 1890).

FITZHERBERT, *Boke of Husbandry* (1534), and *Surveyinge* (1539), treat of agricultural implements and methods in the sixteenth century.

ASHLEY's *Economic History* (1888–94) and CUNNINGHAM's *Growth of English Industry and Commerce* (3rd ed., 1896) both treat fully the developments of English farming and the inter-connexion between it and the woollen industry.

Various chapters in TRAILL's *Social England* (1894–7) bear on country life at all periods.

In the matter of sports, STRUTT's *Sports and Pastimes* (ed. Cox, 1903) is a recognized authority.

GOVETT's *The King's Book of Sports* (1890) has a great deal of interesting information, and the Introductions to the various volumes in the *Badminton Library* give us a good account of early games.

For Hunting and Hawking we have *The Boke of St. Albans*, commonly attributed to DAME JULIANA BERNERS (1486 : ed. Blades, 1881), TURBERVILLE's *Booke of Falconrie* (1611), and BERT's *Treatise of Hawkes and Hawking* (1619).

A most interesting and vivid series of pictures of English sports in Shakespeare's day is to be found in MADDEN's *Diary of Master William Silence* (1890). See too *Shakespeare's England* (Oxford, 1917), vol. ii, c. 27. HARTING's *British Animals Extinct within Historic Times* (1880) also bears on the same subject.

For curious forms of tenure THOMAS BLUNT, *Fragmenta Antiquitatis or Ancient Tenures of Land* (1679 ; re-edited by Hazlitt, 1874), is still useful.

GROSS, C., *The Gild Merchant*, 2 vols., 1890.

FURLEY, J. S., *City Government of Winchester*, 1923.

# X

# THE MONKS, THE FRIARS, AND THE SECULAR CLERGY

## § 1. MONASTICISM

### 1. *Egyptian Monasticism.*

MONASTICISM had its origin in the deserts of Egypt, to which men fled from the cities to pursue an ideal of absolute renunciation and self-surrender. About 305, after twenty years of solitude, the hermit St. Anthony organized a system of life in Northern Egypt for the many disciples who sought his guidance. Vast numbers assembled in large settlements, where they continued to live very much as hermits ; the dominating spirit was intense individualism, and they sought to rival one another in extreme asceticism. In Southern Egypt St. Pachomius founded the first monastery in which the brethren lived a common life, dividing their day between the services of the Church, the reading of the Bible, and labour for their self-supporting community. About 315 St. Pachomius wrote the first monastic Rule, and before his death in 346 he was the supreme head of nine monasteries of men and one of women which constituted the first monastic Order.

From Egypt monasticism spread to Palestine, Syria, and to the Greek-speaking lands. St. Basil spent a year in visiting the monks of Egypt and Syria before he founded a monastery near Neocaesarea in Pontus about 360. He asserted the superiority of community life over that of hermits living in association, and advanced beyond the ideal of St. Pachomius, for he intended that his monks should do good to their fellow men. He founded orphanages for children of both sexes close to the monastery, and allowed boys who were not destined to be monks to be admitted into the monastery for their education.

Before the middle of the fourth century monasticism was introduced from Egypt into Western Europe through Italy. Thence it spread to Gaul and the Celtic lands, in which the earliest monasteries were mission stations. In Ireland in the sixth century several great monasteries were founded for more than a thousand monks ; and about

563 the Irish monk St. Columba founded the famous monastery of Iona from which Christianity was introduced first into Scotland and afterwards into Northumbria.

## 2. *Origin of Benedictinism.*

At the end of the fifth century monastic life in Italy and France was in decay ; the monks had attempted to emulate the extreme asceticism of eastern monasticism and had failed. The real founder of western monasticism was St. Benedict. He was born at Nursia, not far from Spoleto in Umbria, and was sent when a youth to study in the schools of Rome. Disgusted with the licentious life of the city, he determined, about the year 500, to become a monk, and fled from Rome. For three years he lived as a hermit in a cave at Subiaco in the Sabine Hills. Then, when many disciples gathered round him, he built twelve monasteries in the neighbourhood, in each of which he put twelve monks with abbots of his choice.

Owing to the persecution of a wicked priest St. Benedict left Subiaco with a few monks, and about 525 he founded a new monastery at Monte Cassino, half-way between Rome and Naples. For the monks of Monte Cassino he wrote a little Rule for beginners in the school of the service of God. It was the fruit of ripe experience and knowledge ; he had studied the history of Egyptian monasticism, and was acquainted with eastern and western Rules, and owed more to St. Basil than to any other monastic legislator. He dealt with the spiritual life of the monk, the *Opus Dei*, or the daily services of the Church, the organization of the monastery, the duties of the abbot and other officers, the reception of novices and guests. But he left the abbot a large discretion in regard to the diet and dress of the monks, the training of the novices, the number and duties of the officers. He introduced the vow of stability, by which the monk bound himself for life to the monastery in which he made his profession, but he made no attempt to found an Order by uniting monasteries under a central government.

## 3. *Benedictine Houses in Anglo-Saxon England.*

When Monte Cassino was burnt by the Lombards in 581, the monks fled to Rome to live in a monastery attached to the Lateran Basilica, and they took with them the copy of the Rule written by St. Benedict himself. About 594 Pope Gregory the Great completed his work on the life and miracles of St. Benedict in which he praised the Rule for its marvellous discretion and lucidity.

FIG. 263. ST. BENEDICT OF NURSIA (Brit. Mus. MS. Arundel 155, fo. 133).

St. Augustine was prior of the monastery of St. Andrew on the Coelian Hill when Pope Gregory the Great sent him as abbot with about forty monks on his mission to England. After his consecration as Archbishop of the English, St. Augustine continued to live the common life with monks and priests in a building hard by the church which he rebuilt as the cathedral church of Canterbury. Outside the walls of the city he founded a house for monks, which was afterwards known as St. Augustine's monastery. This was probably the first Benedictine house outside Italy; for the Rule of St. Benedict was unknown in France until after the death of St. Columban in 615. In other monasteries which were founded by Roman missionaries in East Anglia and elsewhere the Rule of St. Benedict was regarded as the model for monastic life; but as monasteries were mission centres in which monks and priests lived together there was much diversity in its observance. The monastic customs of the Scots missionaries were observed at Lindisfarne and other monasteries until St. Wilfrid introduced the Rule of St. Benedict into Northumbria about 661.

The Northumbrian thegn Benedict Biscop had been a monk in the islands of the Lérins off the coast of Provence and abbot of the monastery of St. Peter and St. Paul at Canterbury, and had also visited Rome several times before he returned to Northumbria and founded Monkwearmouth (674) and Jarrow (680). He taught the Rule of St. Benedict and gave his monks Customs chosen from those of seventeen monasteries which he had visited on his journeys. He brought masons and glaziers from France to Wearmouth and sent to Rome and France for books, pictures, sculptures, vestments, and vessels for the service of the altar. Bede spent his life in the monasteries of Monkwearmouth and Jarrow, and wrote in them the Ecclesiastical History of the English people with that wonderful simplicity and candour which entitle him to rank with the greatest of mediaeval historians.

From the first beginnings of monasticism women had steadily shown their desire for a common life in the service of God. The necessity for providing them with suitable priests to celebrate mass and to hear confessions led to the institution of ' double' monasteries. These were nunneries to which a small community of priests was attached, and sometimes lay brothers for manual labour, but the buildings for the men were separate from those of the women. In the seventh and eighth centuries several great English houses for women were double, among them Whitby, Hartlepool, Ely, Sheppey, Barking, Wimborne, and Repton.

Even in the early years of the eighth century many of the monasteries were monastic only in name, and the Danish invasions and conquests proved fatal to their existence.

### 4.  *Benedict of Aniane.*

In France the Rule of St. Benedict had been gradually adopted, spreading from monastery to monastery and from one diocese to another.   But, as in England, there was great diversity of observance, and in the eighth century monastic discipline was in urgent need of the revival which became the lifework of Witiza, afterwards known as Benedict of Aniane.

As a young man he was in the service of Pippin and of Charles the Great, but after a narrow escape from drowning he renounced the world and entered the monastery of St. Seine near Dijon, where he learnt the Benedictine Rule and adopted the name of Benedict.  Looking upon the Rule as only the beginning of a religious life, he sought to emulate the asceticism of eastern monks.   In less than three years he left St. Seine with a few companions to found a monastery on his own estate in a narrow valley of Languedoc beside the stream of the Aniane.   They built a dwelling close to the little church of St. Saturninus, and laboured with their own hands in great poverty and under stern discipline. Gradually their fame spread abroad, and a crowd of disciples gathered round Benedict.   After two or three years he and his monks built a larger church, dedicated to St. Mary, just beyond the valley.   This, too, was a humble building thatched with straw ;   the altar vessels were of wood, glass, or tin, for he then rejected silver ;   he also forbade the use of silk chasubles.   Aniane soon became a model for other monasteries.

But the revival of monastic life in Languedoc attracted the notice of Charles the Great, and Benedict came under the influence of the artistic renaissance of which the Frankish court was the centre.   There was no instruction either in the Rule or in the life of St. Benedict about the character of the church or its ornaments ;   and Benedict of Aniane now accepted the tradition of Rome and of other monastic churches that nothing was too splendid for the worship of God.  In 782, by the command of Charles the Great and with the help of dukes and counts, Benedict began to build a vast and splendid church and cloisters with many pillars of marble in the arcades. The vessels of the church were of the finest workmanship. The seven-branched candlestick with its knops, its bowls and flowers, was designed to be like that which Bezaleel made for the Tabernacle ; seven lamps hung above the altar of the Trinity, and a hoop of silver lamps was in the choir. There was a multitude of service books, costly vestments, and silver chalices. The monastic buildings were vast, and as the monks still grew too numerous for them Benedict founded priories dependent on the mother house.

Benedict's biographer, Ardo, who was himself a monk at Aniane, told how he went to other monasteries to find monks who could explain whatever he did not understand in the Rule of St. Benedict, and above all he questioned those who had been to Monte Cassino. He collected the texts of the Rules of eastern and western monasticism for his great work, the *Codex Regularum*. Louis the Pious gave Benedict authority to reform the monasteries of his kingdom of Aquitaine, and throughout the empire after he succeeded Charles the Great as emperor in 814 ; he then built the monastery of Inde, a few miles from his palace at Aix-la-Chapelle, for Benedict and his monks. In 817 a great council of abbots and monks was summoned to Aix-la-Chapelle by Louis. They met in the palace on July 10, and sat for many days while Benedict expounded the Rule. When the resolutions which he had drafted were approved by the assembly, the emperor confirmed them under the title of the 'Capitula of 817', and made them binding on all the monasteries of the empire. When the Rule was not clear or altogether silent, Benedict supplemented it by his teaching ; he added an Order of Service for the ecclesiastical year which was probably written at Monte Cassino in the eighth century, and he adopted with trifling differences a document known as the *Ordo qualiter*, its full title being ' Ordo in monasterio qualiter a fratribus religiose ac studiose conversari vel domino militari oportet', which was written by an unknown Benedictine monk either in Italy or in Provence, and which gives a clear account of the monastic day with its round of services, reading and manual labour, and the detailed procedure of the daily chapter.

Ardo wrote that all monasteries were brought to such uniformity that they might have been under one master in one place. But Benedict died in 822, and it is very doubtful whether his reforms were observed in the troubled years of the rebellion of the sons of Louis the Pious which led to the disruption of the empire and of the invasions of Northmen, Saracens, and Hungarians. A hundred years later his conception of a congregation of monasteries and his Customs with their underlying spirit of uniformity became the basis of the Cluniac reform.

## 5. *Cluny*.

It is probable that the Customs of Benedict continued to be observed in some of the twelve monasteries to which he had sent abbots and monks. There is a tradition that monastic discipline was maintained at St. Savin near Poitiers, after it had declined in most monasteries. When Count Badilo had restored St. Martin at Autun about 870 the Abbot of St. Savin sent eighteen of his monks, and with their help other monasteries were restored and reformed. Among them was Baume-les-Messieurs, some miles north-east of Lons-le-Saunier in the Jura. William, Duke of Aquitaine, heard much of the fame of Baume from knights of his household, who were often kindly welcomed by the monks. In 910 he gave his vill of Cluny with the chapel of St. Mary and St. Peter and all other appurtenances, chapels, serfs of either sex, vineyards, fields, meadows, woods, waters, and wastes to Berno, Abbot of Baume, for the maintenance of a community of monks who should live a regular life according to the Rule of St. Benedict. In his charter the duke set forth his ideal for the community. 'With a full heart and mind the monks shall build an exceeding pleasant place, so far as they can and know how. We will also that in our time and those of our successors, works of mercy shall be shown daily to the poor and needy, to travellers and pilgrims so far as the opportunity and ability of the place shall allow.'

The founder died before even the church was finished, and other friends helped Abbot Odo to build the monastery. The fame of Cluny rapidly spread abroad, and lands, property, and privileges of every kind were granted to the house. From the first it enjoyed the protection of the

Papacy ; Gregory V (996–9) forbade any bishop to exercise any function within the monastery except by invitation ; John XIX (1024–33) forbade any bishop to put the monastery under an interdict or to excommunicate any of the monks wheresoever they might be. This exemption from episcopal jurisdiction was extended to all Cluniac monasteries in all lands. Kings and princes, dukes, counts, and bishops, appealed to the abbots of Cluny to send monks to new foundations and to restore monasteries which had fallen into disorder and decay ; many Benedictine monasteries, like Fleury, adopted the Customs of Cluny for their own use, but remained independent and in their turn reformed other monasteries. From Burgundy the Cluniacs spread into Aquitaine and thence across the Loire ; into Auvergne, the valley of the Rhone, Switzerland ; Provence, Languedoc, Gascony, Castile, Navarre, and Aragon. Under Abbot Hugh they passed on into Normandy and other provinces in the north of France.

The Customs which the monks of Baume brought to Cluny were those of Benedict of Aniane, and as need arose the abbots added to them or changed them. Early in the second half of the eleventh century a monk named Bernard wrote a most complete and detailed account of the occurrences of everyday life in the monastery ; he studied the earlier written Customs and learnt much more from the teaching of Abbot Hugh, who ruled Cluny from 1049 to 1109.

Through Benedict of Aniane the Cluniacs inherited the tradition of splendour in the worship of God. Their first church was much enlarged or in great part rebuilt during the rule of Abbot Majolus, and Abbot Odilo adorned it with beautiful ornaments, costly hangings, altar-cloths, vestments, banners, hoops of lights and lamps, gospel-books with covers of gold or silver, studded with gems, and gold and silver reliquaries. A special building was given up to the goldsmiths, the setters of precious stones, and the glass workers. Abbot Odilo renewed all the monastic buildings, and brought marble columns for the cloister, from quarries in the Alps, up the river Durance and along the Rhone and the Saône. When Peter Damiani stayed at Cluny for eight days in 1063, the monk who was with him marvelled at the aisled church with its many altars, the relics of the saints, and the costly treasures ; the immense and beautiful cloister which seemed to invite monks to dwell there, the dormitory with three lights always burning, the refectory with its paintings, the other stone buildings ranged around the cloister, and the bounteous water supply. He praised the strict lives of the monks, their alms to the poor, their hospitality to all.

The first abbots of Cluny derived the conception of an order or federation of monasteries, united under one ruler, from Benedict of Aniane, and they gave it a remarkable development. They aimed at a common observance of the Rule of St. Benedict, which meant in practice the adoption of the Customs of Cluny. New monasteries were founded, not as abbeys but as priories dependent on the mother house, and the prior was nominated by the abbot. In 1060 the heads of all Cluniac monasteries, with the exception of eleven important affiliated abbeys, were reduced to the rank of priors. Abbot Hugh was the supreme head of two hundred monasteries, and of these many, including La Charité-sur-Loire, had a number of dependent priories. The Abbot of Cluny had the same authority over all Cluniac monks as over those of the mother house ; they made their profession to him alone, either at Cluny or when he came to visit their houses, and he could transfer them from one monastery to another.

### 6. *Cluniac Influence in Anglo-Saxon England.*

The first influence of Cluny on England was indirect. In the middle of the tenth century there was a brilliant revival of monastic life under the influence of St. Dunstan, St. Ethelwold, and St. Oswald, who sought the help of reformers in other lands. English monks were sent to learn the customs of monastic life in the famous monastery of Fleury near Orleans, which was known as St. Benoît-sur-Loire since 655, when one of the monks went to Monte Cassino and brought away the body of St. Benedict while that monastery was lying deserted and in ruins after its destruction by the Lombards. Fleury had been reformed by Odo, Abbot of Cluny, in 930, and the English monks brought back the Customs of Benedict of Aniane, which had been adopted at Cluny, viz. the Capitula of 817 and the *Ordo qualiter*.

About forty monasteries for men in Wessex, the Fenland, and the Severn valley were founded or restored during the reign of Edgar. Almost all the nunneries, with the notable exception of Barking, were in Wessex, viz. Wilton, St. Mary's at Winchester, Romsey, Wherwell, and Amesbury ; none of them was 'double', but they were served by a body of secular chaplains, who had a share in the property of the house. The Rule of St. Benedict was followed everywhere, and St. Ethelwold, Bishop of Winchester, translated it into English for secular men who turned to monastic life and knew no Latin. He compiled Customs, known as the Regularis Concordia, to supplement the Rule, and these were adopted for universal observance at a synodal council of bishops, abbots, and abbesses at Winchester. The Regularis Concordia prescribed the order of service throughout the year and gave instructions for the arrangement of the monastic day ; in many points it was in substantial agreement with the earliest Customs written expressly for Cluny and with other Customs of Cluniac origin. Great new churches were built for the

FIG. 264. ST. ETHELBURGA OF BARKING, Wells Cathedral, West front. (Photo by Phillips, Wells.)

monks, and their ornaments were splendid and costly, for, like St. Dunstan, St. Ethelwold was a skilled craftsman and goldsmith. Magnificent manuscripts were written and illuminated in the cathedral monastery of Winchester. A keen interest in the study of history was shown in the vigorous continuations of the Anglo-Saxon Chronicle, at Abingdon, Worcester, and Canterbury,[1] and in the series of ecclesiastical biographies which are the chief sources for the reigns of Edgar and his sons. But the frequent and terrible ravages of the Danes from 980 to 1016 proved fatal to this brilliant revival. When Cnut restored peace the older generation had passed away. In the judgement of William of Malmesbury, 'zeal for letters and religion had grown cold many years before the coming of the Normans'.

## 7. *Effects of Norman Conquest.*

In the first half of the eleventh century there was a strong revival of monastic life in Normandy. One of the most strenuous of the Cluniac abbots, William of St. Bénigne at Dijon, came north to reform Fécamp in 1001, and owing to his influence many new monasteries were founded. Although they remained independent of Cluny, Cluniac Customs were adopted and observed at Mont St. Michel, St. Ouen, Jumièges, St. Wandrille, Lire, and other houses. When St. Evroul was refounded in 1050, Cluniac Customs were introduced from Jumièges, and soon after 1059 the abbot sent a young monk to study the way of life at Cluny, and Abbot Hugh the Great sent one of his own monks to instruct the monks of St. Evroul in the Customs. In 1066 there was a singular contrast between the vigorous life of the Norman monasteries and the apathy of those in England.

With Lanfranc's help William the Conqueror chose men of learning and religion from the Norman monasteries to succeed English abbots. Paul of St. Albans came from Caen, Scotland of St. Augustine's, Canterbury, and Serlo of Gloucester from Mont St. Michel, Ingulf of Crowland from St. Wandrille, Walter of Evesham from Cérisy, his successor Robert from Jumièges. From Jumièges, too,

---

[1] The so-called Peterborough Chronicle is merely, up to the middle of the reign of Henry I, a Peterborough recension of a Canterbury Chronicle.

Godfrey came to Malmesbury, Theodwin to Ely, Athelelm and Reginald to Abingdon. The three first Norman abbots of Westminster came in succession from Jumièges, Bernay, and Bec. In the course of the twelfth century Evesham, Abingdon, Glastonbury, and Ramsey had Cluniac monks as abbots.

Archbishop Lanfranc had been prior of Bec for twenty-five years and abbot of Caen for seven years before William the Conqueror appointed him to the see of Canterbury in 1070. He found that the monks of his cathedral monastery differed little in their lives from secular canons except that they kept their vows of chastity; they hunted and hawked and diced and indulged in the pleasures of the table. He introduced changes very gradually, for, in the words of William of Malmesbury, ' he knew the art of arts, that is he was exceeding skilled in the governing of souls'. In 1077 he sent for Henry, a monk of Bec, to be prior of Canterbury, and for his guidance he wrote the monastic Constitutions or Customs of Canterbury. So far as they relate to the daily life and administration of the monastery these Constitutions are a much-abridged version of the Customs of Bernard of Cluny with trifling additions, but Lanfranc made some changes in the order of service throughout the year, especially in the celebration of festivals. The Customs of Canterbury were gradually adopted at St. Albans, Westminster, St. Augustine's, Canterbury, and in other monasteries.

Many new monasteries were founded in the reigns of William the Conqueror and his sons. William had vowed a monastery to God before the battle of Hastings; the high altar of the church was set on the spot where Harold's standard fell, and the first monks came from Marmoutier on the Loire, the great monastery which had been built in honour of St. Martin of Tours. When the Norman lords received their lands in England they showed the same zeal as in Normandy in founding monasteries to the glory of God and for the safety of their souls, and they were generous in adding to the endowments of English and Norman monasteries. Some like Malvern, Shrewsbury, St. Werburgh's, Chester, and St. John's, Colchester, were independent foundations, others were dependent priories which are sometimes called cells. During the rule of Abbot Paul

(1077–93) the priories of Wallingford, Tynemouth, Belvoir, Binham, and Hertford were given to St. Albans. Gloucester and Tewkesbury were enriched with grants of lands and churches in Wales, the gifts of Norman lords in the Marches. From Winchcombe in Gloucestershire Prior Aldwyn set out on a mission to revive monastic life in Northumbria, and at Evesham two of the monks were stirred to accompany him ; with the help of the Bishop of Durham they rebuilt the monasteries of Jarrow and Wearmouth.

Norman monasteries had dependent priories in England ; Boxgrove was given to Lessay, Hayling to Jumièges, Arundel to Séez. Monasteries on the pilgrim routes through France to Rome and the Holy Land were endowed with churches and lands. To St. Florent de Saumur in Anjou belonged cells at Sele, Monmouth, Sporle, and Andover ; to Marmoutier the cells of Holy Trinity, York, Allerton Mauleverer, and Newport Pagnell. About 1110 Ansgot de Burwell founded Burwell Priory in Lincolnshire for the house of La Sauve Majeure near Bordeaux, which he had visited on his way home from a pilgrimage to St. James of Compostella. The first Cluniac monastery in England was founded by William de Warenne, who with his wife Gundrada had visited Cluny in the course of a pilgrimage to Rome. Abbot Hugh was away from Cluny at the time of their visit, but they sent and begged for three or four monks, to whom they would give the stone church of St. Pancras which they had built below their castle at Lewes, and had endowed with as much land, animals, and other necessaries as would support twelve monks. Abbot Hugh hesitated to send monks overseas to a strange and distant land ; but at last he yielded, after he had seen William de Warenne's foundation charter and William the Conqueror's confirmation. He dispatched Prior Lanzo and three monks to Lewes in 1077. Lanzo ruled Lewes for thirty years, and, in the judgement of William of Malmesbury, no monastery excelled it in the good lives of the monks, in hospitality to guests, and in charity to all. Lewes had dependent priories at Castle Acre in Norfolk, Prittlewell and Stanesgate in Essex, Farleigh in Wiltshire, Monks Horton in Kent, and Clifford in Herefordshire ; and Thetford, which was directly dependent on Cluny, received the first twelve monks and their prior from Lewes. At the request of other

Norman lords Cluniac monks from the great priory of La Charité-sur-Loire came to Much Wenlock in Shropshire, St. Andrew's outside Northampton, Daventry, and Pontefract. In 1082 a London citizen, Alwin Child, took the first steps towards founding Bermondsey Priory and enrolled other benefactors ; and the first four monks from La Charité arrived in 1088. In the course of the twelfth century the Cluniac houses in England increased to thirty-eight, but some of these were very small priories. A yearly payment in recognition of subjection was due to the mother house which had supplied the priory with its first inmates. On several occasions in the thirteenth century, when Cluny was in financial difficulties, the popes gave to the abbot the power of levying special subsidies, which was a source of the great embarrassment of the English houses, already strained to pay heavy taxes to the Crown.

The abbots of Cluny sometimes came to England, and there were occasional general chapters, as at Cluny in 1132, but it was not until 1200 that Hugh V, who had been abbot of Reading, instituted a yearly general chapter at Cluny to be attended by all the priors of the Order whether they were directly dependent on the mother house or not. He then surrendered some of the autocracy of Cluny. The Order was divided into provinces, and in each province one or two *camerarii* were appointed to make visitations on behalf of the Abbot of Cluny and give their reports at the General Chapter. The English monasteries, with Paisley and its three dependent priories in Scotland, constituted one province. But the duty of yearly attendance at the General Chapter was so unpopular that it was frequently evaded. Early in the fourteenth century it was limited to the heads of priories directly dependent on Cluny, and during the wars with France it could not be enforced. The yearly payments which were due to the mother house in token of subjection ceased. On account of the liability to these payments and the centralized system of government from Cluny, the English houses were affected by the legislation against alien priories, and towards the end of the fourteenth century they took out certificates of denization from the Crown and freed themselves altogether from their dependence on Cluny.

Cluniac influence on English monasticism cannot be

measured merely by the number of priories. The conception of independence of the Church in England which was so characteristic of the Norman kings was unfavourable to the spread of an Order which was autocratically ruled by a head residing in the south of Burgundy. Henry I was so much attracted by Cluny that he was reckoned among the chief benefactors who helped to build the great new church. He chose Cluniac monks from Lewes for the monastery which he refounded at Reading. But Reading was always an independent house. In the same way when King Stephen founded Faversham and took twelve monks with a prior from Bermondsey, he negotiated with the Abbot of Cluny and the Prior of La Charité for its complete independence.

### 8. *The Cistercian Revival.*

The end of the eleventh century saw the rise of several new monastic Orders in different parts of France. These were the Orders of Cîteaux, Fontevrault, Tiron, Savigny, Grandmont, and the Chartreuse. They had their origin in a wave of asceticism, and the early success of some of them was due to the influence of popular preachers. They show a strong reaction against the ideals of Cluny and in the direction of the Italian school of monasticism which was represented by Peter Damiani.

The monastery of Cîteaux owed its foundation to dissensions at Molesme, in the north-west of the duchy of Burgundy. Molesme had been founded in 1075 for a band of thirteen hermits who had chosen Robert, then Prior of Provins, as their teacher of monastic life. Men of noble birth entered Molesme, and their kinsfolk endowed it with rich possessions. Abbot Robert and some of the brethren strove in vain to uphold the first ideal of poverty and manual labour ; when he urged his monks to renounce gifts of churches and tithes, the opposition replied, ' So long as the Cluniacs and the monks of Marmoutier have retained these things, we will not give them up, nor will we be condemned by our brethren far and wide as rash discoverers of new things.' In 1098 Abbot Robert, Prior Alberic, and the sub-prior, Stephen Harding the Englishman, went with four other monks to the papal legate, Hugh, Archbishop of Lyons ; they asked for permission to found a monastery in which they could order their lives wholly according to the Rule of St. Benedict, with which they believed the Customs of Molesme to be at variance. They had chosen Cîteaux, a desolate marshy spot about fifteen miles south-east of Dijon, and had the approval of Odo Duke of Burgundy and the Viscount of Beaune. When the legate sanctioned their departure, twenty-two monks left Molesme and settled at Cîteaux on March 21, 1098. The Viscount of Beaune gave them the chapel of the district with the land around it ; the Duke of Burgundy, who was a kinsman of Abbot Robert, helped them to finish a two-storied wooden building for their refectory and dormitory and made them so large a grant of land and cattle that he was reckoned as their founder. The jealous monks of Molesme appealed to Urban II for the recall of Abbot Robert, and late in 1097 he was compelled to return ; Alberic was elected Abbot of Cîteaux, and was succeeded by Stephen Harding in 1109. The new community had a hard struggle for existence, and at first failed to attract men, but in 1112 St. Bernard, then a very young man, left his home at St. Seine a few miles north-west of Dijon and arrived at Cîteaux with thirty companions. The development of the Cistercian Order was assured. Within the next three years Stephen Harding had sent out twelve monks with an abbot at their head to each of the first four daughter houses, La Ferté, Pontigny, Clairvaux, and Morimond. The Cistercians resolved to keep the Rule of St. Benedict in the letter without the snare of using discretion, and to abandon everything which they did not find either in the Rule or in the Life of St. Benedict. Orderic Vitalis was justified in describing them as innovators ; for in their determination to keep the Rule as the Jews kept the law of Moses, they rejected much of the tradition of monastic observance which Benedict of Aniane had derived from early commentaries. Within the first few years they compiled their *Liber Usuum,* which bears so close a resemblance in structure to Cluniac Customs that we may suppose they brought a copy of the Customs with them from Molesme ; in its details, however, the *Liber Usuum* reflects an absolute contrast with the Customs of Cluny, e.g. in the shortening of services and insistence on manual labour, and in the simplicity of the vestments and ornaments which it prescribes. In their desire to avoid pride and the corruption of poverty, 'keeper of virtues', the Cistercians used altar-cloths of linen, crucifixes of painted wood, one iron candlestick, no costly vestments but only chasubles of fustian or linen, nothing to attract a host of sightseers as at Cluny. There was the most rigorous simplicity in all the details of daily life, beds, diet, and dress, and probably to avoid the expense of the dye they chose a white habit in contrast with the black of Benedictine usage. Although the first Cistercians refused gifts of churches, tithes, and villeins, they accepted vineyards, meadows, woods, fisheries, and mills, horses, and cattle. They decided to have lay brothers as well as hired servants to help with the manual labour. Lay brothers lived alone at the 'granges', not more than a day's journey from the monastery, because the Rule enjoined that monks should live in a cloister. Here they diverged widely from the practice of the Cluniacs, who sent monks to take charge of their 'obediences' during the week with lay brothers under them. They chose sites remote from towns and forbade the reception of the Duke of Burgundy and other princes in their cloister on feast-days. But they were bound by the Rule of St. Benedict to show hospitality to all guests, rich and poor alike, and as the duchy of Burgundy has been called the cross-roads of Europe in the Middle Ages, the fame of Cîteaux and its daughter houses was rapidly spread abroad.

The problem of framing regulations which would maintain Cistercian principles in the new monasteries was solved in the *Carta Caritatis*, which was confirmed by Pope Calixtus II in 1119. In this constitution of the Cistercian Order it was agreed that the Rule should be observed everywhere as at Cîteaux, and that the Customs and Service Books of all Cistercian houses should be uniform. A system of visitation was devised by which the Abbot of Cîteaux visited the daughter houses at least once a year, and as each monastery became a mother house it acquired the same responsibility for its daughter houses. The visitation of the mother house of Cîteaux was entrusted to the four abbots of her first daughter houses. All the abbots were bound to assemble at the yearly general chapter, which was held at Cîteaux in September to discuss the observance of the Rule and the keeping of peace among themselves. At the General Chapter new statutes were made and promulgated as difficulties arose. Each house had autonomy, elected its abbot, and recruited its own novices. Like the Cluniacs the Cistercians were exempt from episcopal visitation. In 1152 the Order had spread so rapidly that there were three hundred and thirty houses scattered over France, Germany, Italy, Spain, and England.

### 9. *Orders of Fontevrault, Savigny, Tiron, Grandmont, La Chatreuse.*

The preaching of St. Bernard, Abbot of Clairvaux, contributed greatly to the success of the Cistercian Order ; and the Orders of Fontevrault, Savigny, and Tiron owed even their origin to popular preachers. The Breton Robert of Arbrissel studied in the schools of Paris and was summoned by the Bishop of Rennes to help him as arch-priest in reforming abuses in the diocese ; there he made enemies and withdrew to live for a time with some disciples at La Roe near Angers. Urban II, when preaching the crusade in France, heard a sermon at Angers from Robert of Arbrissel, and bade him give his life to preaching. Accordingly Robert spent the next four years as a wandering preacher in Anjou, Touraine, and Poitou, in company with two of his disciples, Bernard of Ponthieu and Vitalis of Mortain. Men and women of all ranks were attracted by Robert, and left their homes to follow him ; the throng became so great that he realized the need of a home and the discipline of a regular life for his community. He determined to found a monastery for a large number of women to which he would attach a small community of priests and lay brothers for their service. In 1101 he settled them in the forest of Fontevrault in Anjou. The cloister and buildings for the women were remote from those of the men ; the great church of St. Mary was that of the nuns to which the priests came only to celebrate mass and to hear confessions, for the monks had their separate oratory. Both monks and nuns kept the Rule of St. Benedict, and Robert added statutes to define the relations between them. Already in 1105 Fontevrault had five daughter houses, and when Robert died in 1119, the Order had spread over western France. By his advice a woman was

chosen to succeed him as head of the Order and Abbess of
Fontevrault, and the duty of visiting the other houses
devolved upon her.

When Robert founded Fontevrault he left the charge
of the throng of men to his two disciples, Vitalis of Mortain
and Bernard of Tiron.    About 1105 Vitalis of Mortain
founded a monastery in the forest of Savigny in the diocese
of Avranches in Normandy.   He gave the Rule of St. Benedict to his monks and demanded from them severe manual
labour with rigorous fasting ;  he rejected the Customs of
Cluny and of the great Benedictine monasteries.    His
successor Geoffrey insisted on a still more austere life.
Already Savigny had daughter houses ;  Geoffrey visited
them every year and followed the Cistercians in instituting
a general chapter.    Abbot Serlo, the fourth Abbot of
Savigny, had difficulty in enforcing discipline, and at his
request in 1147 the Cistercian General Chapter agreed to
incorporate the thirty monasteries of Savigny into their
Order ;  they were regarded as of the filiation of Clairvaux,
and Savigny was put next after the first four daughter
houses of Cîteaux.

With the help of the Bishop of Chartres and the Comte
de Perche Bernard founded a monastery at Tiron.   He had
been abbot of the Benedictine monastery of St. Cyprien
at Poitiers, and had left it with some of his brethren
because he disliked the idea of subjection to Cluny.   He
was not hostile to the older tradition of monastic observance, and among the novices who flocked to Tiron were
sculptors, painters, and goldsmiths, as well as masons,
workers in wood and metal who were lavish of their skill
in the service of the community.   In the middle of the
twelfth century there were eleven abbeys and more than
a hundred priories of the Order of Tiron in France, England,
and Scotland.   The founder instituted a yearly general
chapter as at Cîteaux, but in some respects he followed
the government of the Order of Cluny, for the heads of
houses were nominated by Tiron.

Yet another Order was founded in the early years of
the twelfth century in the diocese of Limoges.   St. Stephen
lived the life of a hermit, and when disciples gathered
around him he founded the monastery of Muret.   He
gave his monks the Rule of St. Benedict, and added his

own Rule to enforce simplicity of life and seclusion from the world, and to guard against wealth and the acquisition of property at any distance. Shortly after his death in 1125 the community removed to Grandmont from which the Order took its name, and in the twelfth century it spread into many dioceses of France as well as into England and Spain.

In the early years of Molesme, a young canon of Rheims, by name Bruno, came with six companions in search of a life of solitude. But after a short stay they went on their journey southwards and found the Bishop of Grenoble, who gave them a home among the mountains near his cathedral city. There in 1084 they founded the monastery of La Chartreuse, which gave its name to the Carthusian Order. The monks were isolated from the world as well as from one another, and lived in two-roomed houses (each with a little garden) built around the great cloister ; there they ate, slept, said their services, and worked except on Sundays and a certain number of feast-days, when they went to the great church for all services, listened to a sermon in the chapter-house, took a common meal in the refectory, and conversed with their fellows afterwards. They kept the Rule of St. Benedict. The written Customs of the Carthusians were compiled under Guigo, Prior of the Grande Chartreuse, who died in 1137. The number prescribed for each monastery was thirteen monks and sixteen lay brothers ; the latter were responsible for the secular business of the house and lived apart from the monks. The austere life of silence did not attract men, and the Order spread slowly ; in 1151 there were fourteen charterhouses, in 1258 fifty-six.

## 10. *Regular Canons.*

Revivals of monasticism had a strong influence on the clergy. Bishops attempted to induce the secular canons who served their cathedral churches to live a common life ; Chrodegang, Bishop of Metz from 742 to 766, drew up a Rule which was in great part derived from that of St. Benedict. In the second half of the eleventh century there was a similar movement which spread gradually in Italy, France, Germany, and England ; communities of priests bound themselves to live a regular life and were known as Regular Canons. There is no precise evidence to show when or where they first accepted the Rule of

St. Augustine, which was adapted from a letter written by the Bishop of Hippo to a convent of nuns in his diocese. The Rule is very brief and touches the spirit of monastic life rather than its détails, but it served the Regular Canons as a principle of unity and gave them a status comparable with that of the sons of St. Benedict. Houses of Augustinian Canons were at first independent units like Benedictine monasteries, and like them were subject to episcopal visitation. The Customs which were compiled in famous houses to supplement the Rule of St. Augustine were gradually adopted in others, in which they were varied as necessity arose; those of St. Victor at Paris were very largely derived from the Customs of Cluny.

FIGS. 265, 266. Seals of the Augustinian Canons of Southwick Priory.

In .1121 St. Norbert founded the Premonstratensian Order of Regular Canons. As he could not reform his fellow canons of the cathedral church of Xanten he left

them, and became a wandering preacher in France and
Flanders, until the Bishop of Laon persuaded him to
settle in the forest of Coucy in a desolate spot called Prémontré. He preached about the country-side and attracted
disciples, and after much perplexity he adopted the Rule
of St. Augustine for his community, and added many
precepts for a strict life. Several monasteries were founded,

FIGS. 267, 267A. Seals of the Augustinian Canons of Merton Priory.

and in 1125 Honorius III confirmed the statutes of the
Order. In 1126 Norbert became Archbishop of Magdeburg.
Shortly afterwards the Premonstratensian abbots met
together, and as they desired, like the Cistercians, to observe
unity in all things, they compiled a Book of Customs,
and took much from the Cistercian *Liber Usuum* and
statutes. The Order was divided into provinces, and two
abbots were annually appointed to visit the houses of each
province and report to the General Chapter, for the
Premonstratensians were exempted by the Pope from
episcopal visitation.

## 11. *Military Orders.*

The military Orders of the Templars and the Hospitallers had their origin at Jerusalem, and owed their influence and power to the Crusades. Hugh de Payens, a knight of Champagne, and eight companions bound themselves by a perpetual vow to defend the kingdom of Jerusalem, and Baldwin II gave them a lodging in his palace close to the site of the Temple. They lived on alms and escorted pilgrims from Jerusalem to the Jordan. Hugh de Payens went home to Europe to seek the approval of the Church and to enlist recruits ; in 1128 he met St. Bernard at the Council of Troyes, and obtained his help in drawing up the Rule of the Templars. Owing to his guidance the Templars adopted the Rule of St. Benedict in the austere spirit of the Cistercians, and, like the Cistercians, they wore a white habit, to which they added a red cross. There were four ranks in the Order: the knights, or heavy cavalry ; the serjeants, or light cavalry ; the farmers, who were entrusted with the administration of property ; and the chaplains.

The Hospitallers were founded about 1092, and in the time of their first Grand Master their aim was the service of the poor and of strangers in a hostelry near the church of the Holy Sepulchre. Under the second Master, Raymond du Puy (1125–57 ?), they became a military order like the Templars, but they adopted the Rule of St. Augustine and wore a black habit with a white cross. Both Orders had great privileges and were endowed with large estates in the east and in all the countries of Europe from which Crusaders went to the Holy Land.

## 12. *The New Orders in England.*

All the new orders of monks and regular canons found a welcome in England in the twelfth century. At the beginning the most popular were the Augustinian Canons. Their first house was the priory of St. Botolph at Colchester. The priests who served that church resolved to join a religious order ; two of them went to France and studied the Rule and Customs of the Augustinians at Chartres and Beauvais, and returned to teach the new way of life to their brethren. The movement spread to other communities of priests or secular canons who became regular canons of St. Augustine. Moreover, in the first half of the twelfth century many new houses of Augustinian Canons were founded ; the majority were in East Anglia, Lincolnshire, and Yorkshire, where their number exceeded those of any other Order. Among their more famous houses in other counties were St. Bartholomew's, Smithfield, Dunstable, Oseney, Cirencester, Bristol, and Lanthony. The rapid growth of their foundations was arrested after the coming of the Cistercians.

In 1128 twelve monks with their Abbot John set out from L'Aumône in the diocese of Chartres which had been founded as a daughter house of Cîteaux by Stephen's brother, Thibaut IV, Count of Blois. They came to settle on land at Waverley, near Farnham, which was given them by William Giffard, Bishop of Winchester, a few weeks before his death. In 1152 Waverley had five daughter houses in the south and midlands, and Garendon and Bordesley had daughters of their own. But the Cistercian settlement in the north was of far greater interest. St. Bernard sent William the Englishman and other monks from Clairvaux to Henry I with a letter in which he requested the king to help his followers to recover the heritage for which Christ had died. Henry received them with favour, and in 1131 Walter Espec granted them land near Helmsley in Yorkshire for the foundation of Rievaulx. The simplicity of the Cistercian life attracted some of the Benedictines of the house of St. Mary at York, dissensions arose about the right way of keeping the Rule of St. Benedict, and in October 1132 thirteen of the monks left their monastery and took refuge with Thurstan, Archbishop of York. After two or three months he gave them a site for a monastery in Skeldale near Ripon, where they spent the winter in great hardship. St. Bernard, to whom they applied for counsel, sent them a monk from Clairvaux as their teacher. For two years they had a most severe struggle with poverty until the Dean of York came to join them and brought both books and money. In thirteen years, between 1136 and 1150, these monks of Fountains founded eight daughter houses in Northumberland, Yorkshire, and Lincolnshire.

The monks of the Order of Savigny received their first home in England from Stephen. Savigny was in his Norman county of Mortain, and in 1123 Ewan of Avranches came

with twelve monks to settle at Tulket near Preston ; four years later Stephen endowed this community with lands at Furness, and they removed thither to build their monastery, which was affiliated as a daughter house to Savigny. Like the Cistercians the monks of Savigny went out to found new monasteries in a spirit of religious knight-errantry, and both at Byland and Jervaulx they showed indomitable determination in the face of great privations and difficulties. When the Abbot of Savigny incorporated his houses in the Order of Cîteaux in 1147, thirteen of them were in England. The Abbot of Furness opposed the union, but was compelled to give way.

The monks of the Order of Tiron found Henry I a kindly benefactor, for he gave them a yearly pension of fifteen marks to pay for their shoes. When he was in Normandy, probably in 1114, he invited Bernard of Tiron to come and see him, and he favoured the monastery of St. Mary of Kemeys in Pembrokeshire, which was founded and given to Tiron by Robert FitzMartin. The abbey of Tiron had also priories at Hamble in Hampshire and Titley in Herefordshire.

The first house of Premonstratensian Canons was founded at Newhouse in Lincolnshire in 1143, and the first canons came from a daughter house of Prémontré at Lisques, near Calais. Eleven houses in the midland and northern counties were founded from Newhouse within fifty years ; the most important was Welbeck, which became the mother of seven daughter houses. In all there were thirty-two English houses of Premonstratensian Canons.

The first English Charterhouse was founded by Henry II about 1173 as a part of his penance for the murder of Thomas Becket. Its success was due to the third prior, Hugh of Avalon, who ruled at Witham for eleven years before he became Bishop of Lincoln. A second Charterhouse was founded a few miles away at Hinton in 1232. The extreme austerity of the Carthusians attracted no other founder until the middle of the fourteenth century. Then the fervour of their devotion and the utter sincerity of their religious life appealed to men who had lost interest in other monastic orders, and seven Charterhouses were founded between 1343 and 1414.

In the reign of John the priories of Grosmont in Eskdale

and Cresswell in Herefordshire were founded and given to
the prior and brethren of the Order of Grandmont, and
a third house was Abberbury in Shropshire.

About 1100 the Hospitallers received lands at Clerken-
well on which they built the Priory of St. John of Jerusalem.
They founded commanderies on their estates throughout
the country, and after the deduction of an allowance for
the maintenance of the small communities who managed
them, the revenues were paid to the head house in London.

Hugh de Payens, the founder of the Templars, came to
London in 1128 to plead for his Order. Their first foundation was outside Holborn Bars, and before he left England
Hugh appointed the head of the English province of
the Order. In the reign of Henry II the head house, known
as the New Temple, was built south of the Strand, and the
Patriarch of Jerusalem consecrated the church in 1185.
The Templars founded preceptories, as cells of their London
house, in many counties of England.

### 13. *The Order of Sempringham.*

In 1131 St. Gilbert of Sempringham founded a purely
English Order which owed much to the model of Fontevrault. It arose out of the practical needs of a small
number of women, for whom St. Gilbert founded a nunnery
against the north wall of the parish church of Sempringham
in Lincolnshire which he served as rector. First he added
lay sisters for household service, and then lay brothers to
work on the land, giving to all a rule of life. The little
community grew in numbers, and in 1139 St. Gilbert
accepted lands for it from his feudal lord, Gilbert of Ghent.
Sempringham Priory with its double church, cloisters, and
other buildings was erected on a new site close to the parish
church, and St. Gilbert was offered more land for new
foundations. He was perplexed by the problem of governing the communities, and in 1147 he set out with some of
his Cistercian friends for the General Chapter at Cîteaux
to ask if the Order would take over the charge of Sempringham and other houses. His request was refused. Pope
Eugenius III was present at the chapter, and laid upon him
the care of his Order. St. Bernard invited him to Clairvaux
and helped him to draw up the Institutes of Sempringham.
During his stay at Clairvaux, St. Gilbert studied the Rules

and Customs of divers monasteries, and heard of Robert of Arbrissel, who had been confronted with the same problem fifty years earlier and had solved it by founding the Order of Fontevrault. St. Bernard was in close touch with Fontevrault, and he obtained from the head house or from one of its priories in Champagne a copy of the Rule of Fontevrault from which St. Gilbert borrowed some of the Institutes of Sempringham. He added priests to serve the community and help him in the work of administration. They had a separate chapel with their own cloister remote from that of the women. The great church belonged to the nuns, and it was divided by a partition wall which was high enough to prevent the men and women from seeing each other, but it did not reach to the roof, so that the women might hear the daily High Mass celebrated at the canons' altar and the sermon preached on feast-days. Like Robert of Arbrissel, Gilbert of Sempringham was Master of the Order ; Robert had chosen a woman as his successor, which led to difficulties with the monks of Fontevrault, but St. Gilbert set up two independent communities of men and women, both owing implicit obedience to the Master, and he strictly defined the relations between them. Stores, money, and books were under the charge of the nuns as at Fontevrault, but the management of property and all buying and selling was assigned to the men. St. Gilbert gave the Rule of St. Benedict to the nuns, lay sisters, and lay brothers, but like St. Norbert he chose the Rule of St. Augustine for his canons, and bound the whole community by strict rules of life and discipline which were largely copied from the *Liber Usuum* and Institutes of the Cistercians. But he chose the Premonstratensian system of visitation, and provided that every year two canons and a lay brother should visit the men and two nuns and a lay sister the women, and that they should report to the General Chapter. After the death of St. Gilbert in 1189 most of the new foundations were for men alone, and of the twenty-six houses of the Order only eleven were double. With the exception of three small single houses all were in Lincolnshire, Yorkshire, and the adjoining counties.

A few years after St. Gilbert had studied the organization of Fontevrault at Clairvaux with the help of St. Bernard, Robert de Beaumont, Earl of Leicester, founded Nun-eaton Priory in Warwickshire as a house of the Order of Fontevrault. From its first foundation Fontevrault had attracted the kings of England, who were generous benefactors. Henry II and Queen Eleanor were lavish in their gifts to this Angevin monastery, and about 1176, with the sanction of Pope Alexander III, Henry increased the possessions of Amesbury and brought nuns from Fontevrault to take the place of Benedictines, whose lives were then reported to be a public scandal.

Throughout the Middle Ages the premier nunneries for women were the great Benedictine houses in the south, St. Mary's, Winchester, Romsey, Wherwell, Wilton, Shaftesbury, and Barking. After the Norman Conquest the chief new Benedictine nunneries were Elstow and Godstow. The majority of new foundations for women were unimportant, though fairly numerous in the eastern counties; of the nunneries in Yorkshire ten were Benedictine and twelve Cistercian; in Lincolnshire there were seven Cistercian nunneries.

## 14. *Hospitality of Monasteries.*

Hospitality was the duty of all monasteries, but it was exercised most freely by the great Benedictine monasteries and some houses of Augustinian Canons. St. Albans, Peterborough, York, and Durham were on the great North road, there were bridges across the Severn at Gloucester, Tewkesbury, Worcester, and Shrewsbury, Bristol was a port, Canterbury and Winchester were near the sea and close to ports which commanded the passages to the continent. Eynsham was near Oxford and showed large hospitality to scholars of the University. Travellers, merchants, and pilgrims were courteously received by the hostellers at the guest house in the outer courtyard, which was often a splendid building with a great hall and chambers attached to it. At the Augustinian monastery of Barnwell, near Cambridge, it was part of the hosteller's duty ' to be careful that perfect cleanliness and propriety should be found in his department, namely to keep clean cloths and clean towels; cups without flaws; spoons of silver; mattresses, blankets, sheets not merely clean but untorn; proper pillows; quilts to cover the beds of full length and width and pleasing to the eyes of those who enter the room;

a proper laver of metal ; a bason clean both inside and out ; in winter a candle and candlesticks ; fire that does not smoke ; writing materials ; clean salt in salt-cellars that have been well scrubbed ; food served in porringers that have been well washed and are unbroken ; the whole Guest House kept clean of spiders-webs and dirt and strewn with rushes under foot ; . . . a sufficient quantity of straw in the beds ; keys and locks to the doors and good bolts on the inside, so as to keep the doors securely locked while the guests are asleep'. The hosteller was bidden to remember that ' by showing cheerful hospitality to guests the reputation of the monastery is increased, friendships are multiplied, animosities are blunted, God is honoured, charity is increased, and a plenteous reward in heaven is promised'. At St. Albans there was stabling for 300 horses, and Abingdon had a special endowment to meet the cost of new shoes for the guests' horses. It was usual to give free hospitality for two days, but the custom was much abused. Queen Isabella left her pack of hounds for two years at Canterbury towards the end of the reign of Edward II. In the fourteenth century, whenever a monastery put forward a plea for the appropriation of the revenue of a parish church, the burden of hospitality was one of the chief reasons.

Poorer folk were entertained in the Almonry near the Gatehouse. This building was in some places a home for poor bedesmen, for Great Malvern had thirty resident poor, in others a hospital for sick poor as at Barnwell, as well as a lodging for poor boys who were taught in the Almonry school. When new clothes and shoes were given out at regular times in the monastery, the old ones were handed to the Almoner for the poor. All that was left from meals in the refectory and the guest-house was reserved for the Almoner ; although the customary portions for monks, their servants, and guests were large, it was impossible for the monasteries to economize by cutting down their allowances of food and drink, because they would be defrauding the poor thereby. Twice a week at St. Augustine's, Canterbury, and at Westminster, the Almoner distributed food to all the poor who came to the ' dole house', and if necessary more bread was provided, so that no one went away without a share. At Barnwell the

Almoner was bidden to endow with a more copious largess pilgrims, palmers, chaplains, beggars, and lepers. It was the duty of the Almoner to find out the sick poor in the neighbourhood, to visit them with his servants, and to take them food and drink.

### 15. *Libraries, Studies, and Schools.*

Some of the great Benedictine monasteries had very large libraries, not reserved only for the use of their own brethren, for books were lent on an adequate security to persons in general. A special room called the *scriptorium* was set apart for the writing of books, and hired writers sometimes supplemented the work of the monks. The *scriptorium* at St. Albans was endowed by Abbot Paul (1077–93). Abbot Simon de Gorham (1167–83) instituted the office of historiographer, which was held by Roger of Wendover until his death in 1236, when he was succeeded by Matthew Paris, the greatest English historian of the Middle Ages, who wrote about foreign and home affairs with remarkable knowledge and interest, and included many original documents. The writing of general history was continued at St. Albans by Rishanger, Trokelowe, Walsingham, and other monks in the fourteenth and fifteenth centuries ; annals, chronicles, and histories of value for some periods from the eleventh century to the fourteenth were written at Canterbury, Durham, Worcester, Winchester, Westminster, Bury St. Edmunds, Peterborough, and Durham.

There is evidence that during the monastic revival in the reigns of Edgar and his sons there were schools in monasteries for boys and youths, whether they were destined to be monks, secular clerks, or laymen. After the Norman Conquest the school for novices within the monastery was no longer open to others. In towns in which Benedictine or Augustinian monasteries were the dominant power, it is probable that they took a strong interest in the grammar school, which was in some way dependent upon them.[1] In some cases the endowment may have been

[1] Very divergent views of the importance of monastic schools are held by different scholars ; cf. G. G. Coulton, ' Monastic Schools in the Middle Ages ', *Contemporary Review*, 1913, pp. 818–35 ; A. F. Leach, *The Schools of Medieval England*, and the criticism by A. G. Little in *E. H. R.*, 1915, pp. 525–9.

provided or supplemented out of an abbot's revenues, in others a founder may have put the monastery in the position of trustees, like a body of governors at the present day. It is most probable that the appointment of the master was made by the abbot or some other official. At Bury St. Edmunds Abbot Samson gave an endowment of five marks towards the payment of the schoolmaster and provided free lodgings in a hostel which was open to rich and poor. There were distinguished scholars among the masters appointed by the abbots of St. Albans. Alexander Neckham (d. 1217) of the University of Paris was one of the most learned men of his age, and he was succeeded by a master from the University of Salerno. It is probable that after the rise of the Universities of Oxford and Cambridge, to which students flocked in great numbers, the standard of education in the grammar schools declined and became more elementary.

## 16. *Financial Difficulties.*

Although the revenues of the monasteries were seriously affected by the Black Death, finance was often a great difficulty in the earlier centuries when the monks kept almost all their estates in their own hands and were dependent on the success of their farming even for their food. Droughts and floods resulted in the failure and destruction of crops, a murrain among sheep brought distress to the Cistercians and Gilbertines, who depended largely on the sale of their wool.

In England as in France the Benedictines and Cluniacs were zealous in building great churches to the glory of God, and in using the arts of sculpture and painting and the crafts of the goldsmith and metal-worker in His service. Although the Cistercians were at first content with humble buildings, in the later years of the twelfth century and in the thirteenth they built larger churches of singular architectural beauty. But in spite of the offerings of travellers and pilgrims the greater part of the cost was with few exceptions a charge on the monastic revenues. In 1237 and 1267 the papal legates, Cardinals Otto and Ottoboni, forbade abbots to pull down old churches on the pretext of building a larger or more beautiful fabric without first securing the consent of the bishop, who was bound to consider carefully whether it was expedient to grant or refuse the licence. There was no system of insurance against damage by fire, though fires were frequent in the Middle Ages, and it was impossible to borrow money at a reasonable rate of interest, for both Jews and Italian merchants were extortionate moneylenders. The costs of litigation in which the monks were frequently involved as landowners and patrons of benefices were enormously high. In the course of the thirteenth century taxation became very heavy, and there is plenty of evidence that it was difficult to find money for payments due to the Crown and to the Papacy. Monasteries speculated in a form of life annuities ; for sums of money paid down they bound themselves to provide food and drink, and sometimes clothes and lodging as well, to individuals for the rest of their lives. The results were often disastrous, and both papal legates and bishops attempted to regulate the practice, but in vain. Some of the monks showed conspicuous skill in the management of estates and in financial administration, like Prior Eastry of Canterbury (1284–1331), who discharged debts of £4,924 18s. 4d. and bought real property with a rental of £87 15s. But the incompetence and extravagance of others sometimes led to so serious a financial crisis that the king intervened to protect a monastery from distraint by creditors, and put it in the hands of special commissioners who collected the revenues, provided for the maintenance of monks and servants and for alms, and set aside the residue for the payment of debt. Financial difficulties and mismanagement were among the chief factors in the decline of the monasteries in the later centuries.

## Books for reference.

### (a) Monasticism, General.

Cambridge Medieval History, vol. i, chap. xviii, ' Monasticism ', by CUTHBERT BUTLER.

BUTLER, C., Benedictine Monachism.

Sancti Benedicti Regula Monachorum, ed. C. Butler.

The Rule of St. Benedict, translated by F. A. GASQUET, 1906.

LUCAS HOLSTENIUS, Codex regularum monasticarum, 1759.

HEIMBUCHER, Die Orden und Congregationen, 1907.

Les Archives de la France monastique, ed. Beaunier et Besse, Introduction.

GRAHAM, R. ' The Relation of Cluny to some other Movements of Monastic Reform ', Journal of Theological Studies, xv. 179–95.

MASON, W. A. P. ' The Beginnings of the Cistercian Order ', Roy. Hist. Soc. Trans., New Series, xix. 169–207.

VACANDARD, Vie de St. Bernard.

The Rule of St. Augustine, Owens' College Essays, ed. Tout and Tait.

BERLIÈRE, L'Ordre monastique, 1921.

(See p. 380.)

**Fig. 269**

PROVINCE
OF
GLASGOW

ANGLIA
MONASTICA
Province of
YORK

Lindisfarne (B)

Alnwick (Pr.C)
Brinkburn (A.C)
Newminster (Ci)
Lanercost (A.C)  Hexham. (A.C)  Tynemouth. (B)
Carlisle (A.C)  Jarrow (B)
Blanchland (Pr.C)  Wearmouth. (B)
Holme Cultram (Ci)  Finchale (B)
Armathwaite (B)  Durham. (B)

Shap (Pr.C)  Guisborough (Gisburn) (A.C)
Egleston (Pr.C)  Basedale (Ci)  Whitby (B)
Marrick (B)  Easby (St.Agatha's) (Pr.C)  Grosmont (Gran)
Coverham (Pr.C)  Mountgrace (Ca)
Jervaulx (Ci)  Rievaulx (Ci)  Rosedale (Ci)
Cartmel (A.C)  Ardern (B)  Byland (Ci)
Conished (A.C)  Fountains (Ci)  Newburgh. (A.C)
Turne (Ci)  Marton (A.C)  Malton (G)  Yeddingham. (B)
Coekersand (Pr.C)  Nun Monkton (B)  Kirkham (A.C)  Bridlington. (A.C)
Sawley (Ci)  Sinningthwaite (Ci)  YORK (St.Mary's (B))  Watton (G)
Whalley (Ci)  Arthington  Healaugh Park (A.C)  St.Andrew's (G)  Nun Keeling (B)
Lytham. (B)  Wilberfoss (B)  Warter (A.C)
Kirkstall (Ci)  Nun Appleton (Ci)  Nunburnholm (B)
Selby (B)  Ellerton (Ci)  Meaux (Ci)
Drax (A.C)  Swyne (Ci)  Kingston-upon-Hull (Ca)
Pontefract (Ci)
Nostell (A.C)
Hampole (Ci)
Monk Bretton. (Cl)

Mattersey (G)
Blyth (B)
Roche (Ci)
Worksop (A.C)
Welbeck (Pr.)  Broadholme (Pr.C)

Newstead (A.C)  Rufford (Ci)
Beauvale (Ca)  Thurgarton. (A.C)
Lenton. (Cl)

Arms of the
See of York

PROVINCE   OF   CANTERBURY

Reference

K.W.

Fig. 270

ANGLIA
MONASTICA
· Province of ·
CANTERBURY

CARDIGAN
BAY

THE

IRISH

SEA

BRISTOL CHANNEL

THE EN

Whalley (Ci)
Penwortham (B)
Burscough (A.C)
Up Holland (B)
Birkenhead (B)
Norton (A.C)
Vale Royal (Ci)
Chester
St Werburgh (B)
St. Mary (BN)
Combermere (Ci)
Trentham (A.C)
Haughmond (A.C)
Lilleshall (A.C)
Shrewsbury
Wenlock
Buildwas (Ci)
Penmon (B)
Basingwerk (Ci)
Conway (Ci)
Valle Crucis (Ci)
Bedgellert (A.C)
Strata Mareella (Ci)
Cwmhir (Ci)
Strata florida (Ci)
Wigmore (A.C)
Leominster (B)
Worcester (B)
Clifford (Cl)
Gt Malvern (B)
Cardigan (B)
St Dogmaels (T)
Brecon. St John (B)
Dore (Ci)
Llanthony (A.C)
Tewkesbury
Gloucester
Flaxley (Ci)
New Llanthony (A.C)
Haverford (A.C)
Whitland (Ci)
Tintern (Ci)
Usk (B)
Neath (Ci)
Caerleon (Ci)
Margam (Ci)
Kingswood (Ci)
Bristol St Augustine (A.C)
Bath
Keynsham (A.C)
Farleigh (Cl)
Hinton (Ca)
Witham (Ca)
Cleeve (Ci)
Glastonbury (B)
Bruton (A.C)
Barnstaple (Ci)
Athelney (B)
Muchelney (B)
Barlynch (A.C)
Shaftesbury (BN)
Hartland (A.C)
Taunton (A.C)
Sherborn (B)
Montacute (Cl)
Cerne
Milton
Dunkeswell (Ci)
ford (Ci)
Launceston (A.C)
Abbotsbury (B)
Bindon (Ci)
Tavistock (B)
Bodmin (A.C)
Buckland (Ci)
Buckfast (Ci)
Torre (Pr.C)
Plympton (A.C)

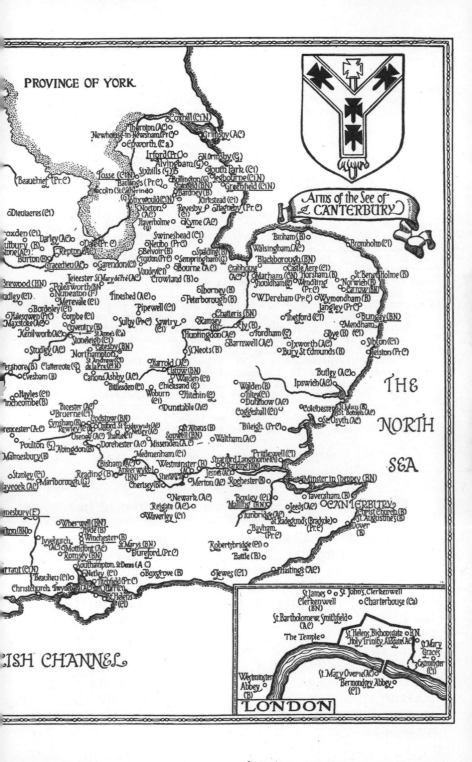

*(b) Monasticism in England.*

DUGDALE, *Monasticon Anglicanum*, edition of 1817–30.

*The Victoria County Histories*, ' Religious Houses '.

HUNT, W., *A History of the English Church, 597–1066*, chaps. x–xii, xvii–xx.

BATESON, M., 'Origin and Early History of Double Monasteries', *Roy. Hist. Soc. Trans.*, New Series, xiii. 137–98.

HAMILTON THOMPSON, A., 'Double Monasteries and the Male Element in Nunneries', Appendix VIII to the *Archbishops' Report on the Ministry of Women*.

*Millénaire de Cluny (Académie de Mâcon*, i. 291–373, ' Les prieurés anglais ').

COOKE, A. M., 'The Settlement of the Cistercians in England ', *Eng. Hist. Rev.* viii. 625–76.

FRERE, W. H., ' The Early History of Canons Regular ', printed in *Fasciculus J. W. Clark dicatus*, pp. 186–216.

CLARK, J. WILLIS, *The Observances in use at the Augustinian Priory at Barnwell*, 1897.

GASQUET, F. A., ' The English Premonstratensians ', *Roy. Hist. Soc. Trans.*, New Series, xvii. 1–22.

—— *Collectanea Anglo-Premonstratensia*, vol. i (Roy. Hist. Soc.), 1901.

—— *English Monastic Life.*

GRAHAM, R., *St. Gilbert of Sempringham and the Gilbertines*; ' The Intellectual Influence of English Monasticism from the Tenth to Twelfth Centuries ', *Roy. Hist. Soc. Trans.*, New Series, xvii. 23–65.

—— *An Essay on English Monasteries* (Historical Association).

JESSOPP, A., *Studies by a Recluse*, 1893.

*Customary of the Monasteries of St. Augustine, Canterbury, and St. Peter, Westminster*, ed. E. M. Thompson (Henry Bradshaw Society).

*Chronica Jocelini de Brakelonde*, ed. Rokewode (Camden Society, 1840) ; also edited by T. Arnold in *Memorials of St. Edmund's Abbey*, vol. i (Rolls Series, 1890).

ECKENSTEIN, *Woman under Monasticism*, 1896.

PEDRICK, *Monastic Seals of the Thirteenth Century.*

## § 2. THE MENDICANT ORDERS

### 1. *The Four Orders.*

The 'Four Orders' so frequently mentioned in mediaeval literature and wills were : (1) the Dominicans or Friars Preachers, often called in France Jacobins from their house in Paris, in England Black Friars or occasionally ' Shod ' Friars ; (2) the Franciscans or Friars Minor or Minorites, called in France Cordeliers, in England Grey Friars or occasionally Barefoot Friars ; (3) the Carmelites, or Order of the Blessed Virgin Mary of Mount Carmel, popularly known as the White Friars ; (4) the Austin Friars or Order of Friars Hermits of St. Augustine, formed by the union of a number of small congregations of hermits. Many smaller Orders, of which the Friars of the Sack were the most important, sprang up during the earlier part of the thirteenth century, but were suppressed by the second Council of Lyons in 1274.

Each of the four Orders had a separate origin and distinct characteristics. In course of time they tended to become more and more assimilated through the exigencies of their work and through conscious or unconscious imitation of each other. They were alike in identifying to a greater or less degree the service of God with the service of man. The idea was a new one, and was first revealed to the mediaeval mind in the Crusades, in which a contemporary chronicler saw a means devised by God to reconcile religion with the world. It was this conception which distinguished the Friars from the Monks, even more than their renunciation of corporate property, and which connects them on the one hand with the Military Orders and the Regular Canons and on the other with the Society of Jesus.

All the four Orders, either from their beginning or early in their career, refused to hold permanent endowments and depended on voluntary contributions. It was necessary that they should live in populous districts where alms were more plentiful, and most of the friaries were founded in towns.

The Dominicans were founded to combat heresy in the south of France, and were at first an offshoot of the Regular Canons. St. Dominic was himself a canon, and not only adopted for his preaching friars the Rule of St. Augustine and the habit of the canons (with some modifications), but based the Constitutions of the new Order on those of the Premonstratensians. It was none the less a new Order which Honorius III confirmed in 1216. The new and essential features were : (1) the Order was centralized and de-localized . the friar was not bound to any particular convent, but had (as friend and foe expressed it) the world for his cloister, and he took an oath of obedience to the head of the whole Order ; he was independent of the parochial and diocesan organization ; (2) the Friars Preachers were the first religious Order to give up manual labour as one of the duties of religious life and to put study in the forefront of their activities. To intellectual work canonical observances had to give way, and 'all the hours in church shall be abbreviated lest the brethren lose devotion and their study be at all impeded'. To secure this object the local prior had authority to grant dispensations from canonical observances whenever it seemed expedient—a practice which gave great elasticity to the institution but led to divisions among the brethren ; (3) the constitution was based on election and representation. All administrative officers, from conventual prior to master-general, were elected by a simple majority of authorized voters. The same principle prevailed in the general chapters in which the legislative power was vested. The General Chapter met every year ; the operative part of it was the Master-General and a small body known as *diffinitores*. Every third year the *diffinitores* were the provincial priors, but for two years out of three representatives of the provinces specially elected for the purpose acted as *diffinitores*. This body not only managed the business of the chapters but could call to account, punish, suspend, and even depose the officers. A general chapter specially called for the election of a new Master included both the provincial priors and the elected representatives. The Dominican organization was gradually adopted with modifications by all the Mendicant Orders ; but the chapters of elected representatives alone (without officers) remained a feature exclusively of the Dominican constitution.

The Dominicans were not at first a Mendicant Order ; they gave up their endowments in 1221 partly in imitation of the Franciscans. But renunciation of property did not have the same meaning for the former that it had for the latter. The Friars Preachers adopted poverty because it would free them from the cares of property, lend force to their arguments, and make their appeal more effective. In the view of St. Francis and his followers the life of poverty— the sacrifice of all material things—was their appeal, their message to the world. The General Constitutions of the Franciscan Order declare that ' God has called us not only for our own salvation but also for the edification of others by example, counsel, and wholesome exhortation '. The life of self-sacrifice was not merely a means of winning souls but an end in itself.

The Franciscan Order began, not as an offshoot of a regular Order of clerks or monks, but as one of the numerous lay fraternities of penitents which sprang up in Italy and Southern France at the end of the twelfth century and beginning of the thirteenth. Most of them were short-lived, and some were branded as heretical. That the Franciscan Order escaped the dangers which beset its youth must be ascribed mainly to the personality of St. Francis—to his humility combined with unswerving faith in his ideals and to his

FIG. 271.

power of drawing all men to him. But St. Francis was not an organizer, and was impressed rather with the evil than with the good of organization. The exercise of authority by one man over others was repugnant to his nature. The relations between the officers and the brethren were expressed in the titles minister, custodian, and guardian, which were deliberately adopted in contrast with those of abbot or master or prior. It was enjoined in the Rule of 1223 that ' those brethren who are ministers and servants of the other brethren, shall visit and admonish their brethren, and shall humbly and charitably correct them, not commanding them anything against their souls and our Rule '. The Rule, however, provided no effective checks on a General Minister who chose to claim arbitrary power, as the famous Brother Elias did, and the Franciscan Order ensured for itself stability and self-government by adopting at a critical time (1239) the main features of the Dominican constitution. At the same time the Order was divided into thirty-two (later thirty-four) provinces, half of which were cismontane, half ultramontane. From this period also the preponderance of the lay element, which had distinguished the Franciscan Order, ceased, and lay brothers were excluded from offices.

## 2. *Foundations and Organization in England.*

At the General Chapter at Bologna May 30, 1221, the Dominican Order was divided into provinces, and missions were organized to two new countries, Hungary and England, which were forthwith erected into provinces. The provinces were eight in number—Spain, Provence, France, Lombardy, Rome, Germany, Hungary, and England. These were subsequently increased by additions and divisions to eighteen.

The English province included England, Wales, Scotland, and Ireland.[1]

The Dominican mission to England consisted of the provincial prior, Gilbert ' de Fraxineto ' (probably a Provençal), and twelve brethren. Reaching England in the train of Peter des Roches, Bishop of Winchester, about the time of the death of St. Dominic (August 6, 1221), they proceeded to Canterbury, where Gilbert preached before the Archbishop Stephen Langton and secured his support for the Order. Passing through London (August 10) they arrived at Oxford

---

[1] The vicariate of Ireland from the middle of the thirteenth century held provincial chapters and enjoyed most of the rights of a province except direct representation in the General Chapter. The decree of 1484 erecting it into an independent province was revoked in 1491.

on the 15th August and here founded their first convent. This was in conformity with their policy, which had already made them choose the two most famous seats of learning in Europe, Bologna and Paris, as the centres of the Order. Before the coming of the Franciscans in 1224 they probably possessed only the two houses of Oxford and London. The comparative slowness of their expansion was probably due to their adherence to the constitution which required a minimum of twelve friars for a new convent. From 1226 the increase was so rapid as to suggest that the Dominicans may have imitated the methods of the Franciscans. Some fifteen houses were founded in the next ten years ; by 1300 the Dominican convents in England and Wales numbered forty-seven (including Berwick) : five more were added in the fourteenth century and one in the fifteenth, making a total of fifty-three.

The first provincial Chapter was held at Oxford in 1230. After this the Chapter was held every year in one of the principal towns. It was a model representative institution and may have influenced the growth of the representative principle in the English Church and State. The Chapter consisted of the provincial prior, the conventual priors, one elected representative of each convent, and the general preachers of the province. The assembled Chapter elected four of their number who with the provincial acted as *diffinitores*. This body had great executive powers ; they 'shall treat and decide all things'. All complaints, accusations, and questions brought up by the local representatives were decided by them ; they could punish or depose conventual priors, and punish or suspend the provincial prior. The election of a provincial prior was made in a special Chapter which consisted of the conventual priors and two elected representatives from each convent. The conventual priors were elected by the friars of the house. In all cases elections were decided by the majority of votes.

An important part of the work of the Chapter was to receive the reports of the visitors. The English province was divided into the four visitations of London, Oxford (or the March), Cambridge, and York. Four friars were elected each year by the provincial Chapter as visitors : they possessed certain powers of correcting abuses, and had to make a report to the next provincial Chapter on the state

of discipline and studies in the convents included in their
visitation.

The relations between the province and the General
Chapter, though carefully regulated, were not always har-
monious. The government of *studia generalia* and the
position of foreign students was the chief bone of contention. The long struggle between the English province and
the central authority of the Order, which began in 1372
and lasted well on into the fifteenth century, was a struggle
for control of university appointments. Though it had
nothing to do with the Great Schism, the latter event, which
split the Order into two, undoubtedly encouraged the
English province to maintain its assertion of independence.
The General Chapter of 1442 decreed that ' whereas the
English province has omitted to send to general chapters
for many years and has paid no attention to the acts of the
chapters nor sent any excuse, we will that those responsible
be punished '.

The Franciscan mission to England, which reached Dover
on September 10, 1224, under the leadership of Agnellus, consisted of four clerks and five laymen, with only one priest
among the nine. Within two months they had made
three settlements—at Canterbury, London, and Oxford, the
capitals of Church, commerce, and learning. Their proceedings were irregular, their needs few. When Brother Jordan
of Giano was asked in 1225 if he wanted a house built on the
plan of a cloister he replied (because he had never seen a
cloister in the Order) : ' I do not know what a cloister is ;
just build us a house near water, so that we can go
down and wash our feet.' A hired or borrowed house
or room, and two or three friars with perhaps a novice
as guardian, were enough to form a centre of spiritual
light. Within six years sixteen houses were established ;
in 1256 they numbered forty-nine in England and Scotland.
After this comparatively few were founded ; in 1300 there
were fifty-three (or fifty-four) Franciscan houses in England
and four (or five) in Scotland. In the fourteenth century four
more were added in England and two in Scotland. These
numbers remained unchanged until the era of Observan-
tine foundations in the latter half of the fifteenth century.

It is not true that the friars deliberately chose unhealthy

sites in neglected quarters of the towns. They took such sites as were offered them, and if these proved unhealthy they took pains to improve them or tried to move elsewhere. Their first settlements were generally within the walls ; as their numbers and needs increased they often migrated to more ample areas in the suburbs. In the narrow limits of a mediaeval town there was not room for an East End and a West End. Even in London prelates and nobles as well as the Friars Minor resided in or near 'Stinking Lane'.

FIG. 272. DRAWING OF A FRAN-CISCAN by Matthew Paris.

The government was in the hands of the minister and provincial chapter. The constitution of provincial chapters was not fixed by the Order but left to the provinces. As the records of the English province are lost, we cannot say definitely how the chapter was formed, but it probably resembled those of other provinces and consisted of the provincial minister, the custodians, some or all of the guardians, and one elected representative from each house. The minister was elected by the Chapter, which also elected every year four *diffinitores*, whose powers and functions were identical with those of the Dominican *diffinitores*. Custodians and guardians were not elected, but were appointed by the minister in provincial chapter with the counsel and consent of the *diffinitores*, after consultation with some friars of the custody or house. On the other hand custodians and guardians formally tendered their resignations every year at the provincial chapter. The Franciscans attached great importance to the temporary character of these offices, and held that 'frequent change of prelates keeps religious Orders in health'.

The custodian was head and permanent visitor of a group of houses known as a custody. The province of England was divided into the seven custodies of London, Oxford, Bristol, Cambridge, Worcester, York, and Newcastle.

The Carmelites were originally a group of hermits established in Palestine about the middle of the twelfth century, and living under an eremitical rule based on that of St. Basil. Wars and the growth of Turkish power made Palestine unsafe, and colonies of hermits migrated thence to Europe. Some of them were brought to England in 1240–1 and this country became for some time the centre of gravity of the Order. Their first houses were founded in thinly populated districts, but a change was made in the character of the Order by the General Chapter at Aylesford in 124? under Simon Stock. A revised Rule was obtained from Innocent IV which substituted the common life for the solitary life, allowed the friars to found houses elsewhere than *in eremo*, and to support themselves by begging, though they were still allowed to hold property in common. Houses were now founded in cities and especially the university towns, and the Order ranked as one of the Mendicant Orders. The change from the contemplative to the active life was not effected without serious opposition and temporary reactions, and perhaps the number of friars who lived as anchorites was larger in this Order than in the others. Traces also seem to have survived of the monastic *stabilitas loci*, or attachment of a brother to a particular house. But the general principles and methods of government were adopted from the Dominicans. The Order was in 132? divided into fifteen provinces, including those of Scotland and Ireland, which had till 1305 formed part of the province of England. There were thirty-eight Carmelite houses in England, divided for administrative and especially educational purposes into the four *distinctiones* of Oxford, London, York, and Norwich.

The Austin Friars are first heard of in England in 1249– seven years before the pope's efforts to unite the various

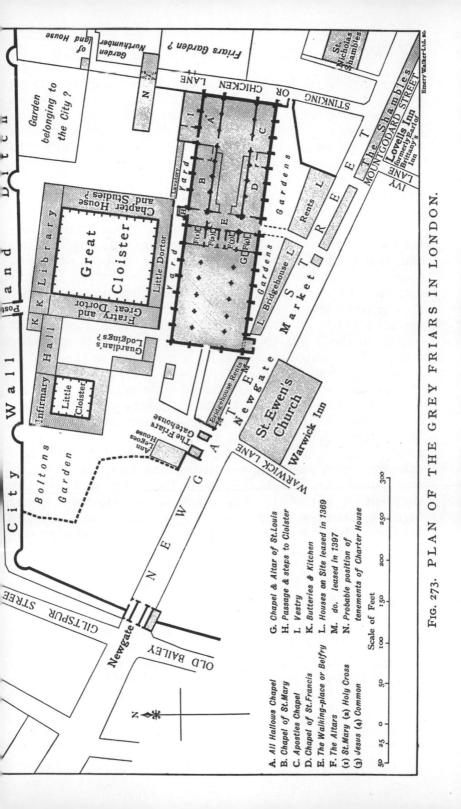

FIG. 273. PLAN OF THE GREY FRIARS IN LONDON.

A. All Hallows Chapel
B. Chapel of St. Mary
C. Apostles Chapel
D. Chapel of St. Francis
E. The Walking-place or Belfry
F. The Altars
(1) St. Mary (2) Holy Cross
(3) Jesus (4) Common

G. Chapel & Altar of St. Louis
H. Passage & steps to Cloister
I. Vestry
K. Butteries & Kitchen
L. Houses on Site leased in 1369
M. do.    leased in 1397
N. Probable position of
   tenements of Charter House

Scale of Feet

50  25  0   50    100   150   200   250   300

Emery Walker Ltd. sc.

congregations of hermits into one Order had met with partial success. Like the Carmelites they were from this time hermits only in name; they lived the common life in towns, performed pastoral duties, and enjoyed a form of government and possessed privileges similar to those of the other Orders. In England they had thirty-three houses divided for administrative purposes into the five *limites* of Oxford, Lincoln, Ludlow, Cambridge, and York.

All these friaries, with few exceptions, depended on voluntary alms. The most notable exception was the Dominican house of King's Langley, for the support of which considerable endowments were held in trust by the Dominican nuns of Dartford. Generally a house possessed only its site and a few acres of garden. The Franciscans claimed special sanctity on the ground that even their sites did not belong to them but to the community of the town or the donor. In practice there was little difference in this respect between the four Orders.

Life on these principles was possible only if needs were few or alms plentiful. During the first fifty years or so both conditions were fulfilled. 'At first', says Matthew Paris, 'the Preachers and Minorites lived a life of poverty and great sanctity . . . embracing voluntary poverty for God's sake, not even reserving for themselves food for the morrow'; and the first buildings of the friars were equally eloquent of poverty. The practical imitation of Christ fired all classes with enthusiasm; merchants and scholars flocked to the Orders, and all conditions of men and women—from the king to the seamstress—showed their admiration of the friars by giving of their wealth or poverty. Large houses, more or less on the monastic model,[1] were built to accommodate the increasing numbers of friars, and great churches—adorned in a manner befitting the worship of God; the gorgeous stained-glass windows of the Black Friars and Grey Friars Churches in London—each contributed by princes or city guilds or common alms—were the wonder of all beholders. But it was difficult to keep to the old simplicity of life in these surroundings. The maintenance of the

---

[1] See Mr. Kingsford's plan of the Grey Friars, London, reproduced in this volume (p. 389), and Mr. Clapham's plan of the Black Friars in *Archaeologia*, lxiii. 67–84.

buildings was a heavy drain; first enthusiasms cooled. The result was that the energy of the friars was more and more devoted to raising funds to maintain themselves and their houses, and diverted from purely spiritual work. The cares of poverty proved to the friars as exacting and distracting as the cares of property to the monks.

All the Orders suffered from the Black Death and the Great Schism. Efforts to revivify them and restore discipline by reforms from within were continually being made, especially from the end of the fourteenth century. These efforts had little effect on England. Towards the end of the fifteenth century several houses of the Franciscan Friars of the Strict Observance were founded under royal patronage, and some of the older houses adopted the reforms. The Observant Friars, by the austerity of their lives and their devotion to duty, won an influence altogether disproportionate to their numbers; and they alone of the Mendicant Orders offered a united resistance to the royal supremacy of Henry VIII.

### 3. *Relations to Secular Clergy.*

The introduction of new elements into the ecclesiastical system raised new questions and inevitably led to controversies. The bishops generally welcomed the friars and made great use of them, but naturally wanted to secure some control over them, and even claimed in some cases the right of appointing their officers. Against these episcopal claims Gregory IX in 1231 at the prayer of Agnellus issued the decretal *Nimis iniqua*, which declared the friars free from all episcopal jurisdiction, visitation, and taxation, and assured to them full rights of self-government.

If the Orders were independent of episcopal control, it was all the more necessary to define the relations of the friars to the parish priests. The controversies centred round three points—the right of the friars to preach, to hear confessions, and to bury in their churches persons not belonging to the Orders.

The parishes in England were not as a rule unwieldy in size or population, nor were the priests notoriously negligent or incompetent; a foreign observer in the thirteenth century singled out England (in contrast with other countries) as a country where the clergy lived as clergy should. But a higher ideal of pastoral duties was beginning to prevail, stimulated no doubt by the friars, and there was a greatly increased demand for sermons and popular instruction. It is possible that the decree of the fourth Lateran Council enjoining annual confession merely legalized a custom already in vogue, but it is certain that the practice of making frequent confessions was now becoming more general. Additional demands were thus being made upon the clergy, which they were generally not fitted to supply. There was scope for a highly trained and well-organized body of assistants like the friars.

The Rule of the Friars Minor and the Constitutions of the Friars Preachers forbade friars to preach in any diocese where the bishop refused his consent—unless the bishop's objection were overruled by the pope. Friars were licensed to preach only after examination and approval by the provincial and *diffinitores* of the provincial chapter. They organized missions throughout the country in Lent and other seasons with the encouragement and support of diocesan synods, which ordained ' that, since the preaching of these friars and their holy life are known to have produced no small fruit in the Church of God, they shall, when they pass through our diocese, everywhere be welcomed reverently and honourably'. A parson might refuse the friars admission to his church, but it was an unpopular proceeding. The parishioners of a Devon parish in 1301, when asked to report on its religious condition, stated that ' their vicar is an honest man, and preaches to them to the best of his ability, but inadequately, they think. They say also that his predecessors used to invite friars to instruct them on the salvation of the soul ; but he does not care for friars, and if they come, does not receive them or offer them hospitality ; hence they pray that he be corrected.' This extract is typical of the change which came over the relations of seculars and friars towards the end of the thirteenth century, but the change was not due to the preaching activities of the friars.

A more fruitful cause of enmity was the friars' right to hear confessions. The friars paid great attention to the theory and practice of the confessional, which was little understood at the beginning of the thirteenth century. In the confessional, even more than in the pulpit, they made a direct appeal to the individual conscience. Pecham at the beginning of his *Formula confessionum* makes the penitent decide for himself whether his act is sinful or not, insisting that he should confess 'only those sins of which his own conscience accuses him'. Grosseteste employed friars as confessors during his visitations. Many English bishops, especially those who were in closest contact with the friars, issued instructions on the confessional to their parish priests, and many handbooks on confession were produced by the friars in the thirteenth century. Instances occur of secular priests referring to friars questions which they found too difficult.

On the other hand protests against the demoralizing influence of the friar-confessors, which are first heard soon after the middle of the thirteenth century, grew in frequency and strength till they reached their climax in the attacks of Richard Fitzralph, Archbishop of Armagh, and Wyclif and his followers. The principal charges were : (1) the authority of the parish priest was undermined ; (2) confession to a wandering friar, whom the penitent might never see again, was more easy but far less morally efficacious than confession to a parish priest with whom he was in daily contact ; (3) the friars granted absolution on too easy terms, and thus the confessional was made an avenue to sin ; (4) alms which ought to go elsewhere were diverted to the houses of the friars.

All these charges were true : and the facts—apart from the inferences—were admitted by the friars. ' The clergy ', said Bonaventura, 'exaggerate their rights over their subjects, . . . and if we added to this by frightening them still more and magnifying the power of the clergy over them, we should further provoke the audacity of the clergy, and take the heart out of their timid subjects.' The friars' books of *exempla* are full of stories showing 'the evils that befall those who will not confess ' ; they also abound in stories which illustrate the virtue of light penances and inculcate the wisdom of imposing them. Stress was laid on confession and contrition rather than on punishment. It was better to impose a light penance which people would perform than a heavy one which they ignored to the peril of their souls. This view gained ground and became the general policy of the Church; it is embodied in Myrc's *Instructions for Parish Priests*:

> Better hyt ys wyth penaunce lutte
> Into purgatory a mon to putte
> Than wyth penaunce overmyche
> Sende hym to helle putte.

The objections to confessing to parish priests were so widespread and so well founded in the Middle Ages that it is safe to say that auricular confession could not have been universally enforced without the work of the friars.

Even more productive of ill will between the friars and the seculars was the papal privilege, which the Dominicans acquired in 1227 and the Franciscans in 1250, of burying in their churches or cemeteries persons not belonging to their Orders. Secular princes and nobles coveted the right to be buried in the churches of the friars, whose way of life they venerated and to whose prayers they ascribed extraordinary efficacy; it was probably in reply to their pressure that Innocent IV granted the privilege to the Franciscans in 1250. The Franciscans at any rate had hitherto refused to bury great men in their churches, 'from love of the clergy and desire to live in peace with them'. But when once the right was given the friars defended it with all their power, and the last quarter of the thirteenth century witnessed a series of sordid squabbles between friars and rectors of churches for the possession of corpses. The parish priests found themselves being deprived by interlopers, who professed to 'seek only spiritual things', of a valuable source of revenue; for burials involved not only fees, but generally gifts and bequests, payments for masses, anniversaries, and sometimes perpetual chantries, while further the connexion of powerful families with the parish church was weakened or destroyed. Thus the privilege turned out to be peculiarly and increasingly disastrous and demoralizing. The friars might well have prayed to be delivered from their friends.

Many papal bulls, embodying divergent policies, were issued between 1250 and 1300 to regulate the relations between friars and seculars. The two extremes are represented in the bulls *Etsi animarum* (1254) and *Ad fructus uberes* (1281). In the former Innocent IV decided the points at issue mainly against the friars; in the latter Martin IV gave the friars a free hand in the parishes and deprived the bishops of all control over them. A statesmanlike and lasting compromise was reached in the bull *Super Cathedram* issued by Boniface VIII in 1300. This provided that (1) the friars should have the right of preaching to clergy and people in their own churches and in public places, but should only preach in parish churches by invitation of the parish priest or command of the bishop ; (2) the friars should choose suitable persons from their members as confessors ; the persons so chosen should be presented by the provincials to the diocesan bishop and licensed by him— their numbers being regulated by the needs of the population; (3) the friars might bury in their churches those who desired it, but should give to the parish priest a quarter of all offerings and legacies.

### 4. *Schools and Learning.*

The rise of the friars coincided with the intellectual ferment which followed the rediscovery by the Western world of the philosophical works of Aristotle, and the friars soon became as famous for learning as for holiness. The Dominicans were from the first a learned Order, and no convent could be founded without a lecturer. The ultimate object was the training of preachers for the salvation of souls, and the curriculum was at first limited. The study of philosophy, the secular sciences, and liberal arts was forbidden. But the dispensing power was used freely, and it soon became clear that all sciences were necessary to the study of theology. A curious illustration is afforded by the famous *De proprietatibus rerum*, written by the Franciscan Bartholomew the Englishman, lecturer on theology in Germany, before 1250. Beginning as a commentary on animals, plants, &c., mentioned in the Bible, it grew into an encyclopaedia of knowledge and remained the most popular work on science through the Middle Ages.

The 'two Student Orders', as the Dominicans and Franciscans were often called, developed in England as in other provinces an elaborate system of schools of different grades. The essence of this organization was the combination of a number of convents into groups and the establishment of central schools for special studies in one or more convents of each group. The administrative divisions of the province—visitations and custodies—were made use of for this purpose.  Promising friars were sent from their convents to the special school of arts (or logic), then to the special school of natural philosophy, finally to the special school of theology, in their visitation or custody.  Sometimes these schools were united in one house.  The ablest students, after passing through these preliminary courses, were selected to study, teach, and take theological degrees in the universities.  Among the Dominicans the house at Langley Regis was designed as the chief training school for friars who were intended for the universities.

It is remarkable that the English Dominicans for many years resisted or ignored the decrees of the General Chapter ordering them to establish a *studium generale* in England. A *studium generale* was a place of study to which all the provinces had the right to send students—generally two students for each province.  The reasons of the resistance are not stated ; they may have been financial.  The maintenance of foreign students was a difficulty which occupied the General Chapters for many years, until by degrees the allocation of the expenses was regulated down to the minutest particulars.  In 1261 the General Chapter placed the *studium generale* at Oxford, punished and deposed the provincial prior and other obstructionists.  The new provincial was Robert Kilwardby, under whose rule the Oxford convent began its wider activities.

Oxford was the seat of the chief school of the province from the beginning ; it became a public school of the university when Robert Bacon, while regent master of theology, joined the Order and continued his lectures in the Dominican convent.  He was succeeded by Richard Fishacre, and these two, dying in 1248, left, in the opinion of Matthew Paris, no equals in theology and other sciences. The next master, Robert Kilwardby, successively master of the schools, provincial prior, Archbishop of Canterbury, and finally Cardinal, was the most distinguished of the Oxford Dominicans, and indeed the only one among them who can be placed in the front rank of scholastic philosophers. His treatise *De Ortu et Divisione Philosophiae* has been described as the most remarkable work of the Middle Ages on the classification of the sciences.  Though it shows the influence of Aristotle as well as of the Arabs, Kilwardby opposed the Aristotelian innovations of Thomas Aquinas, and as archbishop even secured the condemnation of some of his conclusions by the masters of the University of Oxford in 1277. The General Chapter at once took up the defence of their great doctor, ordered their friars to maintain his doctrines, and forbade them to teach anything contrary to them. From this time 'Thomism' became the official doctrine of the Dominicans at Oxford as elsewhere. This may partly account for the lack of originality among subsequent Dominican scholastics. They were distinguished as industrious compilers and commentators. Thus a number of 'student friars of England', at the head of whom was John of Darlington, compiled the concordances of the Bible known as *Concordantiae Anglicanae*. Nicholas Trevet, master of the Dominican school at Oxford in 1314, was perhaps better known in his own time for his voluminous commen-

FIG. 274. A DOMINICAN. From Queen's Coll. MS. 304.

taries on the Psalms, Augustine's *De Civitate Dei*, the works of Seneca and others, than for his history. Robert Holcot (*d.* 1349), the author of popular collections for the use of preachers and perhaps of the *Philobiblon*, was a theologian and philosopher of some note. And many others might be mentioned—such as Thomas Jorz and John Bromyard—who showed laborious industry but no originality. The two outstanding episodes in the history of the Dominicans

at Oxford were (1) the controversy with the University
(*c.* 1303–20), when the friars strove to deprive the secular
masters of any control over the conferment of degrees
on the regulars ; (2) the controversy (already mentioned)
between the Province and the Order, from *c.* 1372 to the
beginning of the fifteenth century, for the control of foreign
students and scholastic appointments.   Both involved constitutional and educational besides disciplinary and national
questions of some importance.

Oxford played a far more vital part in the history of the
Franciscans than in that of the Dominicans.   The Franciscan Order at its origin was the reverse of a learned Order,
and though circumstances, especially the entry of many
learned men, had modified its character before the coming of
the friars to England, there was yet no tradition of learning
and no educational organization.   This had to be built up
from the centre ; and the centre in England was Oxford and
to a less degree Cambridge.  The man who put the educational
system on a regular and permanent footing was William of
Nottingham, provincial minister 1240–54 ; he arranged for
the training of friars at the Universities who were to act as
lecturers in the various houses, and had, before his deposition,
supplied two-thirds of the houses with university teachers.

The fame of the Franciscan school at Oxford was due
to Robert Grosseteste, who, though already the most distinguished scholar of his time, accepted (*c.* 1230) the post
of lecturer to the poor friars.   For Grosseteste, unlike
St. Francis, saw in earnest study the surest means of preventing the friars degenerating like the earlier monastic
Orders.   His pupils 'in an incredibly short time made
such progress in philosophical questions and in the subtle
moralities suitable for preaching', that their services as
lecturers were in request in other provinces, and English
friars were soon teaching in France, Italy, and Germany.

Grosseteste impressed on the new school a peculiar
character.   The weakness of scholasticism was the divorce
of the form from the matter of knowledge.   The schoolmen
have been compared by an old writer to persons living in
populous towns who, having very little ground to build upon,
run their houses high up.   'So the schoolmen, lacking the
latitude of general learning and languages, thought to
enlarge their active minds by mounting up.'   It is Grosse-

teste's merit to have endeavoured (with partial success) to widen the bases of knowledge by the study of positive science and language. His work was carried on, on the same lines, by his immediate successors, notably by Friar Adam Marsh. The most famous disciple of the school was Roger Bacon. Most of the ideas which Bacon preached with such passionate insistence are to be found in embryo in the philosophical works of Grosseteste. The most far-reaching and fruitful of these is the idea that natural philosophy must be based on mathematics ; force is always subject to mathematical law, is 'multiplied' uniformly and regularly in space and time, and can consequently be expressed by ' lines, angles and figures '. The same thought is found in Grosseteste's short treatise *De lineis, angulis et figuris*, and Grosseteste, like Bacon, uses the science of optics to illustrate the principle. Bacon denounces, with more vigour than Grosseteste, the evil effects of reliance on authority in philosophy, expresses more clearly and epigrammatically the conception of progress in science ('quanto iuniores tanto perspicaciores'), insists more fully on the inadequacy of the deductive method and the necessity of ' verifying by experiment the conclusions arrived at by argument', but in all these respects he rightly claims to be the follower of Grosseteste. It is important to realize that the ideas which are generally associated with Roger Bacon were not merely those of a more or less isolated and suspected genius, but were taught to several generations of students in the Franciscan house at Oxford.

To Grosseteste's precepts and example is to be traced also Bacon's insistence on the study of languages—especially of Hebrew, Chaldaic, Greek, and Arabic. Bacon himself compiled a Greek grammar for the use of Western students. A slight knowledge of Greek is traceable among English Franciscans well on into the fourteenth century, and the Council of Vienne in 1314 ordered the foundation of salaried professorships in these four languages at Paris, Oxford, Bologna, and Salamanca.

Neither languages nor natural science were regarded as ends in themselves. A knowledge of languages was necessary to understand and establish a correct text of the Scriptures, to read and interpret the philosophers and to convert heathens and schismatics. So too the study of things seen was to lead to the study of things unseen and eternal ; philosophy, as Bacon understood it, was ' the endeavour to arrive at a knowledge of the Creator through knowledge of the created world '. But centuries of training in logic left the mediaeval mind very acute but impatient of careful observation ; ' thoughts ' were more tractable than ' things ', and Grosseteste's influence was unable to do more than shake, even among the Franciscans, the undisputed supremacy of dialectic.

Probably Richard of Middleton and Roger Marston, and certainly John Pecham, held an intermediate position and form links between Grosseteste's school and John Duns Scotus (c. 1270–1308). Duns Scotus was an extreme realist attributing to concepts of the mind a real or objective existence. He criticized most of his immediate predecessors and contemporaries—such as Bonaventura, Thomas Aquinas, Roger Bacon—and was the destroyer of systems. He attacked especially the system of Thomas Aquinas, which endeavoured to establish harmony between philosophy and theology, and showed the inadequacy of philosophical proofs of many theological doctrines. Two points in his philosophy may be noted as specially Franciscan : (1) his reassertion of the pre-eminence of the will and the good against the Dominican assertion of the pre-eminence of the intellect and the true ; (2) his theory that their participation in primal matter forms a bond of union between all created things, spiritual and corporeal. It is the philosophic expression of St. Francis's feeling of community with all nature. Primal matter, in Duns' poetical simile, is the root of the fair tree of the universe, which throws out leaves and branches and produces at last the flowers of the rational soul and the perfect fruits of the angelic nature : ' but the single power which directs and fashions the seedling—immediately or through creative creatures—is the hand of God '.

The ' realized abstractions ' of Duns Scotus were bound to lead to a reaction, and the leader of the opposition was also found among the Oxford Franciscans : William of Ockham was lecturing as B.D. at Oxford (c. 1320–4) when his academical career was suddenly cut short by a summons to Avignon to answer charges of heresy. While at Avignon 1324–8 he became interested in the controversy with the pope on Evangelical Poverty, in which the Franciscan Order was involved, escaped to the court of the emperor, and wrote the great series of treatises against the papal power. The charges of heresy in 1324 seem to have had no connexion with his (later) anti-papal attitude, and probably arose out of his nominalistic teaching.

According to Ockham, 'everything that exists, by the mere fact of its existence, is individual'. The universal is 'a mental concept signifying univocally several singulars', and has no reality beyond that of the mental act by which it is produced and that of the singulars of which it is predicated. Ockham distrusted abstractions and brought philosophy down from its speculative heights to common sense, direct observation, and induction. In this way he joins hands with Roger Bacon, and influenced profoundly all the leading minds of the next generations. On the other hand he follows and goes beyond Duns Scotus in proclaiming the divorce between theology and philosophy and maintaining that theological doctrines cannot be proved by reason. Neither he nor Duns thought of disputing the accepted faith, but their teaching promoted scepticism and heralded the fall of scholasticism.

After Ockham the intellectual leadership passed from the Mendicant Friars to the seculars. But for a century the Franciscan school at Oxford had exhibited an astonishing vigour, and the diversity of views represented by Roger Bacon, Duns Scotus, and William of Ockham is evidence of a spirit of liberty which tradition and authority were powerless to suppress.

The schools of the friars, not only in the Universities but elsewhere, were in the thirteenth century open to, and to some extent attended by, the secular clergy. Friars further were sent as theological lecturers to monasteries (e.g. to Canterbury) and to the schools of the secular cathedrals. Thus in 1377 the pope ordered the provincial chapter to place the Franciscan students at Cambridge on a level with those at Oxford in the matter of appointments to lectureships in cathedral churches. Many books for the education of the clergy and the training of preachers were composed by the friars : among these compilers may be mentioned the Franciscan John of Wales and the Dominicans Robert Holcot and John Bromyard.

## 5. *Popular Preaching.*

With the coming of the friars preaching acquired a new importance. The friars preached not only in churches but in market-places or recreation grounds (such as ' la Batail-place' at Lincoln) ; their own churches were designed on a new and simple plan, suitable rather for holding large congregations who came to hear sermons than for liturgical processions. A new style of preaching was evolved, designed especially to catch the attention and appeal to the feelings and intelligence of the uneducated, and to influence men's lives. The sermons were practical and moral rather than dogmatic, and interspersed with anec-dotes, often of a sensational type, and illustrations drawn from daily life. The method met with opposition and criticism (soon after the middle of the thirteenth century Thomas Aquinas had to defend the practice of making sermons interesting and attractive), and it was certainly liable to abuse ; both Dante and Wyclif denounced the friars for using the pulpit to amuse and not to edify. For good or evil, to go and hear a friar preach was one of the recognized forms of holiday entertainment in the merry England of the Middle Ages.

Popular sermons in the vernacular were delivered extempore, and no English friar seems to have had his sermons taken down in shorthand, as were those of St. Bernardino of Siena. Our information about their preaching is mainly derived from treatises for the general education of preachers (such as those of John of Wales), treatises on the art of preaching—often called *De modo dilatandi sermones* —model sermons written in Latin but probably not in the form in which they were, or were intended to be, preached, collections of *exempla*, which are sometimes given by them-selves, generally accompanied by moral and doctrinal matter, with references to suitable texts of Scripture. It must be remembered that *exempla* did not constitute the sermon ; they were, so to speak, the sweet given as a reward for taking the medicine, or the jam in which the powder was hidden.

St. Dominic is known to have made frequent use of *exempla*, or illustrative stories, but the practice was not confined to the friars. Two of the earliest collections extant

are those contained in or extracted from the sermons of
Jacques de Vitry and Odo of Cheriton.  The former (*d.* 1240)
was a regular canon, a famous preacher, as well as historian,
of the Crusades, and bishop of Acre, the latter a secular
priest who owned estates in Kent and died in 1247.  But
most collections of the kind were made by Mendicant Friars.

The earliest extant collection by an English friar is
one of edifying tales compiled by a Dominican, probably
of Cambridge, soon after 1250.[1]  The anecdotes are loosely
grouped according to their subject-matter, but there is not
much arrangement.  There are many local allusions and

FIG. 275. A FRIAR PREACHING.  (From Bodl. MS. 264, 14th cent.)

references to recent events, and the collection contains
fewer of the traditional stories than usual.  The *exempla*
deal with magic, transubstantiation, confession and penance,
observance of holy days, mercy, pilgrimages, almsgiving,
oppression of various kinds, usury, lawyers, drunkards,
priests' concubines, nepotism of bishops.  The next in
chronological order is a *Liber exemplorum*, compiled by an
English Franciscan in Ireland (*c.* 1275).  This is systematically arranged and divided into two parts : the first treats
of ' things above ', especially of the sacrament of the body
of Christ and the miracles of the Virgin ; the second of
' things below ' in alphabetical order.  Interspersed among
many old well-worn stories are some of extraordinary

[1] British Museum, MS. Royal, 7 D i.

interest, drawn from the personal experiences of the writer and his friends ; among them are *exempla* illustrating the power of faith, the duty of paying tithes, the efficacy of confession, the value of indulgences, even when transferred from one man to another for their cost price and a pot of beer. Some of the stories on the miracles and cult of the Virgin carry the implication that the performance of religious exercises compensates for an immoral life. The author occasionally points out that the obvious moral to be drawn from an *exemplum* is a bad one and advises the preachers to guard against this danger. Among other advice given to preachers is the warning that stories reflecting on the morals of clerks and monks should be altered for a lay audience.

The *Speculum Laicorum* was compiled about 1290, probably by a Franciscan, in answer to the request of a fellow friar who had asked the author to write something suitable for the instruction of the ignorant laity. The subjects are arranged alphabetically in eighty-seven chapters, each chapter containing (1) a definition and subdivisions of the subject, (2) quotations from authorities, (3) illustrative stories taken from legends and writings of the fathers, events in past and present times, and natural history.

More entertaining are *Les Contes moralisés de Nicole Bozon*, a Franciscan (*c.* 1320). This collection differs from the preceding in being written in French, in being arranged in no systematic order, and in the prominence given to analogies from natural history or ' the properties of things '. Another Franciscan compilation, written a few years later, is the *Fasciculus Morum* ; it is in the form of a treatise on the seven deadly sins and their counteracting virtues ; it is much more than a collection of *exempla* ; it contains short, pithy, moral discourses, suitable for direct use in sermons, and is particularly interesting from the number of English rhymes and of allusions to everyday life which it contains.

Among Dominican collections of the first half of the fourteenth century should be noticed the *Moralitates* of Robert Holcot and the moral discourses and moralized *exempla* known as *Convertimini*, probably by the same author. The former is specially remarkable, owing to the large use made of *exempla* derived from Greek and Roman history and mythology, and from classical and semi-classical authors—e. g. Ovid. Friar John of Wales made a collection of narratives about the great men of the ancient world ' for the benefit and instruction of rulers ', to whom the examples of Alexander, Caesar, Trajan, and so on were more likely to appeal than the examples of the Christian saints. The classical flavour in Holcot's *Moralitates* probably implies that they were intended for the upper classes of lay society.

All these collections are alike in their insistence on the efficacy of confession and the terrible results of neglecting it. They are alike too in their condemnation of oppression and injustice ; the virtue and duty of mercy and forgiveness is a favourite theme, and the story of the merciful knight who forgave his enemy is rarely omitted in any collection. The Franciscans, as one would expect, lay far more stress on the worship of the Virgin than the Dominicans ; and their style is generally adapted to less cultured audiences, and they draw illustrations more readily from the daily life of the common people.

A somewhat similar contrast might perhaps be made between the historical writers of the two Orders. On the one hand we have Thomas of Eccleston's charming and naïve story of the early years of his Order in England, telling of the men he had known and the events in which he had taken a humble part, and Richard of Durham's Chronicle (called of Lanercost)—inaccurate, irrelevant, biased, and very human ; both of these works partake of the nature of collections of *exempla*, written for direct edification. On the other hand we have the chronicle of Nicholas Trevet, sober, well arranged, accurate, objective —the work of a man who belonged to the administrative class and the aristocracy of learning, and was accustomed to take wide views. But in the paucity of evidence it would be unsafe to regard these three works as illustrating anything more than the personal idiosyncrasies of the authors.

The friars supplemented preaching by encouraging the formation of associations of persons pledged to lead a pious life. The most important of these were the congregations of the Third Order of St. Francis, i. e. groups of men and women living in their own homes and following their ordinary avocations, but bound to the performance of devotional exercises and works of charity and to simplicity of life ; each congregation was a religious gild under the spiritual direction of the Friars Minor.   The evidence so far collected as to the Third Order in England is scanty.   There is more evidence of another and less desirable practice—the granting of letters of fraternity to persons outside the Orders ;  here the stress was laid rather on the advantages to be derived from the prayers and masses of the friars than on the duty of leading a good and unselfish life.   The pecuniary value of letters of fraternity seems to have sunk very low before the dissolution of the friaries.

Popular sermons were naturally not concerned with the original function of the Dominicans—the defence of the faith against heretical attacks.   It is, however, probably not a mere coincidence that, a year after the Dominicans settled in Oxford, a deacon, who had forsworn his faith for love of a Jewess, was burned in Oxford.   The earliest mention of the Dominicans at Cambridge is connected with the trial of a heretic, and the Dominican prior of York had to be restrained from imprisoning heretics on his own responsibility.   The Dominicans were active in the efforts to convert Jews, and the *Domus conversorum* in London was under their charge.   It is right to remember that both Dominicans and Franciscans braved the fury of the mob and incurred hunger and obloquy to save the Jews accused of ritual murder in 1256.   The period from the expulsion of the Jews to the rise of the Lollards offered few opportunities for dogmatic controversy.   All the four Orders co-operated in opposition to the Lollard doctrines ; the Dominican provincial wrote *De adoratione imaginum*, but the leading part was taken by the Carmelite doctors.

The preaching of the Crusades was regularly entrusted to the Dominicans and Franciscans, and the whole country was mapped out into preaching areas and divided among the friars of each Order and convent.   The friars undertook this duty with the reservation that force could not take the place of argument, that Crusades were no substitute for missions.   English friars not only accompanied the crusading armies, but took part in missions to the Near and the Far East.   It is remarkable that the Carmelites, in spite of their eastern origin, seem to have had little interest in these expeditions. In their missionary activities the Dominicans and Franciscans co-operated, notwithstanding their frequent quarrels in Europe, and at some time in the fourteenth century formed the *Societas fratrum peregrinantium propter Christum*; the history of this institution is, however, obscure; there seems no reason for the traditional ascription of its foundation to 1252.

## 6. *Politics.*

The friars as organized communities seem to have taken little direct part in politics; individuals or groups are sometimes prominent; their indirect influence cannot be estimated. Nearly all the English kings from Henry III to Henry VI had Dominican confessors, while most of the queens chose Franciscans.[1] Friars were often sent as royal envoys not only to the pope but to secular princes. Their influence was not always exerted in favour of peace: thus at the beginning of the Great Schism a Franciscan advocated the invasion of France as the stronghold of the anti-pope. On the other hand Agnellus laboured to make peace between Henry III and Richard Marshal, and Pecham and John of Wales endeavoured without success to bring about peace between Edward I and Llewelyn. In general we may say that the Franciscans supported popular movements for constitutional liberty. The most striking instance is their adhesion to Simon de Montfort, whose canonization some of them advocated. The Dominicans seem to have held aloof or taken the royalist side, notwithstanding their close connexion with the house of Montfort; for the king's Dominican confessor, John of Darlington, was one of the king's representatives in the Provisions of Oxford, and it was the ingratitude of the Franciscans in opposing their benefactor, Henry III, which shocked the monk of Westminster.[2] The possible influence of the Dominican constitution in promoting the growth of representative institutions has already been alluded to; it is certainly noteworthy that in the period when Convocation acquired its definitive and semi-representative organization a Dominican and a Franciscan were successively archbishops of Canterbury.

[1] *Antiquary*, xxii. 114, 159, 262; xxiii. 24.
[2] *Flores Hist.* (R. S.), iii. 266.

In their struggle for self-government the townspeople sometimes found support among the Franciscans. But the political question which most persistently interested the friars, and especially the Franciscans, was the relation between Church and State. The temporal power of the pope, the endowments of clergy and monks, the jurisdiction of ecclesiastical courts, were hard to reconcile with the principle of Evangelical Poverty, and were frequently denounced by the friars from the fourteenth century to the sixteenth.

### Books for reference.

HEIMBUCHER, Die Orden und Kongregationen der katholischen Kirche, Paderborn, 1907.
DUGDALE, Monasticon Anglicanum, vol. vi, pt. iii, 1830.
Archiv für Literatur- und Kirchengeschichte des Mittelalters, vols. i and vi (ed. Denifle and Ehrle).
Monumenta Ordinis Praedicatorum Historica, ed. Reichert, Rome, 1896, et seq.
JARRETT, The English Dominicans, 1921.
BARKER, The Dominican Order and Convocation, Oxford, 1913.
Monumenta Franciscana (R.S.), i, ed. Brewer ; ii, ed. Howlett, 1858–82.
Tractatus Fratris Thomae [de Eccleston] de Adventu Fratrum Minorum in Angliam, ed. Little, Paris, 1909.
LITTLE, The Grey Friars in Oxford (Oxf. Hist. Soc.), 1892.
—— Studies in English Franciscan History, Manchester, 1917.
Monumenta Historica Carmelitana, ed. Zimmerman, Lérins, 1905.

Accounts of the various Dominican friaries are given by Father Palmer in the Reliquary, 1876–89 ; Archaeological Journal, 1880–4 ; and Archaeologia Cantiana, vol. xiii. See also articles on ' Friaries ' in Victoria County History, especially those on Oxford.

## § 3.　THE SECULAR CLERGY

### 1.　DIOCESES.

The rôle of the secular clergy in the Middle Ages does not at first sight seem so important as that of their regular brethren. Yet their organization, based as it was on the political divisions of the country and penetrating far more into the social life of the people, was in reality the stronger of the two. And even in the Middle Ages themselves there was a great change. The eleventh and twelfth centuries marked the hey-day of the monks and the thirteenth that of the friars, but in the fourteenth and fifteenth the secular clergy came into fashion again, as the rebuilding of parish churches on a larger scale and the foundation of collegiate churches and chantries show. Consequently, just when the mediaeval monastic system was declining, as is indicated

# DIOCESES, CATHEDRAL CHURCHES AND CHIEF COLLEGIATE CHURCHES OF ENGLAND IN THE MIDDLE AGES

SCOTLAND

THE NORTH SEA

To York

CARLISLE
Manchester
Chester-le-Street
DURHAM
Bishop Auckland
Barnard Castle
Staindrop

Ripon

THE IRISH SEA

YORK

Howden
Beverley

Manchester

Rotherham

BANGOR
St ASAPH
Chester-St-John
To Bangor
Southwell
LINCOLN
Tattersall

Stafford

Shrewsbury
Bridgnorth
LICHFIELD
Wolverhampton
COVENTRY
Leicester (Newark)
Fotheringhay
ELY
NORWICH
Thompson
Mettingham

CADIGAN BAY

To Bangor

Warwick
HEREFORD
WORCESTER
Higham Ferrers
Northill
Stoke by Clare
Sudbury
Pleshey

St Davids
Abergwili

Llandaff

Eton
Windsor
London
To Canterbury
ROCHESTER
CANTERBURY
Maidstone
Wye

BRISTOL CHANNEL

BATH
WELLS
Heytesbury
SALISBURY
Wimborne
Winchester
Chichester
Arundel
Hastings

Crediton
S. Teath
EXETER
Ottery St. Mary

Penryn
Penzance

THE ENGLISH CHANNEL

NOTE. The map represents the English dioceses after the foundation of the See of Ely by Henry I and before the creation of new sees by Henry VIII. The names of the Cathedral Cities are underlined. a single line for those cathedrals served by Secular Canons: a double line for those served by Monks or regular canons.

FIG. 276.

by the suppression of the Templars and then of the alien priories, the secular clergy were advancing. They were thus enabled to survive the storms of the sixteenth century with their organization but slightly impaired. The main system of the dioceses and parishes, the duties and status of bishops, deans, archdeacons, and parish priests, are in general the same nowadays as they were in the thirteenth century. Such changes as have occurred chiefly concern the organization and discipline of the Church courts ; they were the result either of eighteenth-century indifference or of the, often mistaken, reforms of the early Victorians.

*The diocesan system* of England in the Middle Ages was completed by the foundation of the see of Ely by Henry I in 1109, and it remained unchanged until Henry VIII undertook its partial reorganization. Of the two provinces into which the country was divided that of York contained but three sees, York, Durham, and Carlisle ; the remainder were included in that of Canterbury.[1] Mediaeval ideals required a bishop to be constantly resident in his diocese, feeding the hungry, clothing the poor, educating scholars. He was not expected to look a woman in the face or to allow his own sisters to kiss him.[2] But few dioceses were so lucky as to obtain such a chief. Just as the State nowadays tends to use the judges for all kinds of extra-judicial functions, so, in the Middle Ages, but to a vastly extended degree, did it use the bishops. It had long been customary to employ them as ministers of state or ambassadors ; in the later Middle Ages, when the Civil Service had become more highly developed, many of them were little more than departmental chiefs, paid, however, out of ecclesiastical and not out of public funds. Archbishop Kemp, who held the see of York from 1426 to 1452, was said to have been in his diocese no more than two or three weeks in ten or twelve years ; and it is for this reason that in times of social unrest bishops were generally selected by malcontents as fit subjects for attack. Even those who did reside more or less continuously had duties thrust on them from which their successors are free. They were responsible to the State for the collection of the taxes voted by the

---

[1] See map, p. 409.
[2] See the life of Bishop Robert Bethune of Hereford (1133-48) by his chaplain, William Wycombe, in Wharton, *Anglia Sacra* ; and that of St. Thomas of Cantelupe in the *Acta Sanctorum*, October 2.

clergy in Convocation, for the safe custody of clerical male-factors committed to their prisons, for the collection of debts proved in court against ecclesiastics. To them the king applied when he wanted a loan which it was difficult to extract from Parliament. Feudal duties and conflicts over jurisdiction occupied much of their time. So did travelling, for the ' palace' in the cathedral city was often little more than a ' court house', and the bishops lived chiefly in one or other of their scattered manors,[1] and also possessed ' inns' (which they sometimes let) to which they resorted when Convocation or Parliament summoned them to London. In these circumstances, and in view of the difficulty and length of communications (the diocese of Lincoln, for instance, was 150 miles long), it was impossible for even a stay-at-home bishop to carry out his episcopal duties efficiently. Take, for example, the Sacrament of Confirmation. Since it was conferred normally at three years from birth, confirmation classes were unnecessary, and the child was brought to the bishop, by the roadside if necessary, instead of, as nowadays, the bishop being brought to the child. Yet a prelate who rarely left his diocese [2] was forced to confess ' I know that large numbers of children have had to go without this sacrament, but pressure of business has prevented me from giving it '.

It became, therefore, the custom to employ *suffragan bishops* in increasing numbers to perform the strictly epis-copal acts of confirmation, ordination, and the reconciliation of churches after bloodshed. These were either English bishops of Welsh or Irish sees who found it more prudent to reside outside their dioceses than in them, or prelates who took their titles from places in Greece or Syria from which the Latins had been driven.[3] Towards the end of the Middle Ages a certain number of heads of religious houses were bishops with titles *in partibus* who acted as suffragans, while most of the bishops appointed under the Suffragans Act of 1534 had been abbots or priors of lately dissolved monasteries.

---

[1] Winchester had about fifty manors, of which Farnham was the chief.
[2] Richard Swinfield (Bishop of Hereford 1283–1317).
[3] Their commission was generally of a temporary nature, but there are instances of permanent suffragans. Thus in 1482 Bishop Myllyng of Hereford appointed one such, and got the Dean and Chapter to give him the mastership of St. Katharine's Hospital, Ledbury.

## 2. Administrative Divisions and Discipline of the Diocese.

The unit of administration was the parish.[1]  A group of parishes formed the rural deanery, the organization of which was fairly complete by the thirteenth century and which in area roughly corresponded to the hundred.[2]  The functions of the rural dean were both administrative and disciplinary. He inducted clergy, promulgated the bishop's citations and excommunications, and exercised small disciplinary powers, but his chief duty seems to have been to report serious cases of clerical or lay incontinence to the bishop's or archdeacon's court.  Above the rural deanery came the archdeaconry, which by the twelfth century usually corresponded to the shire; in this area the archdeacon was the bishop's delegate and exercised authority, particularly over the clergy in deacons' orders and below.  The bishop's consistory court, the highest ecclesiastical court of the diocese, was presided over by the bishop's representative or 'official', a general title, the diocesan chancellor being generally known as 'official principal'.  It is impossible here to give more than a bare outline of the jurisdiction of these courts.[3]  They concerned themselves with the property, dress, and conduct of the clergy from the gravest moral offences to small breaches of discipline, such as asserting oneself to be as learned as the Bishop of London.[4]  They dealt with all matrimonial and probate cases, and exercised corrective discipline over the laity, *pro salute animae*. Domestic scandals of all kinds, of which regular reports were compiled, came before them, while Sabbath breaking and attacks on the clergy were rigorously dealt with. 'John Johnson, a shoemaker, keepeth his bed upon the Sundays and other holy days at time of matins and mass, as it were a hound that should keep his kennel.'  'The host of the "Cock" inn (London Wall) says that the very sight of a clergyman makes him sick, and that he is only happy when he sees a clergyman in trouble.'[5]  The punish-

---

[1] For its organization see below, p. 414.
[2] The number varied according to the size of the shire; in Gloucestershire there were ten
[3] Full details will be found in Pollock and Maitland, *History of English Law*, ii. 543 ff.
[4] Cf. Archdeacon Hale's *Precedents*, p. 117.
[5] Cf. Hale's *Precedents, passim*.

ments inflicted were usually whipping or a fine, for it must be remembered that in the Middle Ages corporal punishment was normal and by no means confined to schoolboys. The most prominent layman of the district might render himself liable to be scourged round the parish church and market-place by the archdeacon. For clerical murderers and thieves handed over by the secular courts to the ecclesiastical authorities there was always the bishop's prison where they might be confined *in compedibus, collariis ferreis, armeboltis et neckcheynes*. The usual complaint, however, was that these instruments were not used enough : that the court to which the case was remitted scarcely ever gave a verdict of guilty and that, even if it did, the punishment was rarely more than a light fine. On the other hand, the clerical courts were unpopular with the clergy because of the excessive fees which were charged, and with the laity because of the spy system which they involved and the bribery which was prevalent. Dr. Gascoigne, writing in the middle of the fifteenth century, asserts that in his time instructions were given to the clergy not to give absolution unless the penitent paid so much towards the fabric fund of the cathedral church. Nevertheless, the system described above continued in full working order till the middle of the seventeenth century at least. But it was not uniform, and discipline was much weakened by the fact that much of the territory and many of the inhabitants of the diocese were not amenable to episcopal or archidiaconal jurisdiction. The number of exemptions was large. Thus the Cistercian and Premonstratensian orders and all four orders of friars were exempt from diocesan jurisdiction. Many also of the great Benedictine monasteries had escaped from what the Chronicle of Evesham calls the ' almost Egyptian servitude' of the bishop. Further there were the ' peculiars', either royal (like St. George's, Windsor) or ecclesiastical. Thus large tracts of Sussex were immediately subject to the Archbishop of Canterbury, and the Bishop of Chichester could not interfere in them.[1] To a considerable extent the jurisdiction of the Dean and Chapter also conflicted with the general administrative system of the diocese. We here refer to those cathedrals, nine English and four Welsh,[2] which were served

---

[1] The archbishop still has the patronage of the livings in his former peculiars.      [2] See map, p. 409.

by a dean and secular canons. In earliest times the episcopal and capitular estates were identical, but they had been separated soon after the Norman Conquest. The Chapter's share was thus subdivided into distinct estates or prebends, the number of which varied according to the wealth of the see (Hereford, a poor diocese, had twenty-eight). As time went on, and chiefly owing to the fact that there was only a small common fund, there was less and less temptation for the prebendaries to reside in the cathedral city ; they preferred their prebendal estates. By the fourteenth century practically only those resided who held diocesan offices, such as the Chancellor, in charge of the education of the diocese, the Penitentiar, the Treasurer, &c., notwithstanding numerous efforts on the part of ecclesiastical authorities to make the others do so. Even the mass pence—a fund which provided payment for each attendance at mass— failed to attract. The duties of the absentees were taken over by the vicars choral, two to each prebendary, who had the same relation to the latter as had perpetual vicars to rectors in 'appropriated' parishes.[1] The Dean and Chapter were exempt from archidiaconal, and did their best to be free from episcopal, visitation, and during the vacancy of the see they were in charge of the diocese. They conducted visitations of and exercised disciplinary powers in their own estates, which were sometimes very extensive. Thus from the twelfth century to the nineteenth the Peak district of Derbyshire was wholly exempt from the jurisdiction of the bishop and archdeacon because King John (while still Earl of Mortain) had given the district to the Bishops of Lichfield, who had transferred it to the Dean and Chapter.

### 3. THE PAROCHIAL SYSTEM.

The main body of the clergy in the latter part of the Middle Ages may be divided roughly into three groups : (1) the rectors, or richly beneficed ; (2) the perpetual vicars and chantry priests, or poorly beneficed ; (3) the

---

[1] See below. At Hereford traces of this system still survive in the titles of the vicars choral, De Lyra 1 and 2, and De Cormelliis 1 and 2. The explanation is that the abbots of Leire and Cormeilles, Norman abbeys which held large estates in Herefordshire, were *ex officio* prebendaries of the cathedral. The clearest account of the prebendal system will be found in Canon Capes' introduction to the *Charters and Records of Hereford*, published by the Cantelupe Society.

chaplains and other unbeneficed clergy, who went under the general designation of 'stipendiaries', though this term may also, though less correctly, be used for the members of the second group. The parochial system had grown up gradually during the Anglo-Saxon period. Great monasteries and landowners undertook the building of churches and the endowment of clergy in their estates, and by the time of the Norman Conquest the division of the country into parishes with definite areas and endowments, mainly from tithe and glebe, was practically completed. But just as the diocesan organization was soon to be broken into by the system of *exemptions*, so was the parochial by that of *appropriations*. In the period immediately following the Norman Conquest, and for the greater part of the twelfth century, fashionable generosity took the form of building and endowing monasteries : the secular clergy were more or less under a cloud, and were held to be inferior in learning and zeal to the regular. It was the fashion for owners of advowsons to transfer them to monasteries, just as they do nowadays to the bishop, in the belief that thus a better class of clergyman would be obtained. The monks were to appoint the incumbent, receiving in return a fixed sum by way of pension out of the income of the living. But if, as was later invariably the case, the tithe was given as well as the advowson, the monks would put in a chaplain at a small stipend to perform the spiritual duties of the parish, while the rest of the endowment went to them. This system was open to various objections. It tended to withdraw the parish from episcopal authority and to substitute for a resident rector a mere servant of the monks, dismissable at will. Consequently the bishops took up arms and a partial remedy was found in the *perpetual vicarage*. This institution was becoming usual at the end of the twelfth century and was definitely ordered by the Council of Westminster in 1200. It assured to the parish a clergyman with a fixed stipend [1] and tenure, duly instituted by the bishop of the diocese. Moreover, no further appropriations were to be effected without leave of the bishop and the Crown. In point of fact they did go on and to an increasing extent. It was difficult, in view of decreas-

[1] See below.

ing incomes, rising prices, and the diversion of fashionable charity to other objects, for the monasteries to remain solvent in any other way, and a heavy contribution on their part to the fabric fund of the cathedral was apt to make an otherwise unwilling bishop assent to the transaction. A recent writer [1] has said that but for the dissolution of the monasteries things in England would have become as bad as they actually did in France before the Revolution where ' the revenues of the Church were divided between a few privileged clergy and corporations and a multitude of ill-paid priests '.[2]

The *rector*, then, was the individual or corporation who received the whole of the income of the benefice, except where, as in the latter case, the *spiritual* duties were performed by the perpetual vicar. In the former the rector was personally responsible for them. The second Council of Lyons (1274) ordained that a rector must be twenty-five years of age at the least, that he must reside and take priest's orders within a year of his appointment. But here again exemptions came in and with them two great evils from which the mediaeval Church suffered (in a far greater degree than the Church in the eighteenth century), *non-residence and pluralities*. A living is vacant : the patron might appoint his younger son, a youth in his teens just received into minor orders (usually the sub-diaconate). The young man would then get the bishop's leave to go away for the purpose of study so long as the cure of souls was not neglected, i.e. provided that he put in a chaplain, or as we should say now a curate in charge. He would obtain one at the lowest possible salary [3] and let the rectory, perhaps, to a layman. Then he went to Oxford, Cambridge, or even Paris for one, three, or seven years, as the case might be, to waste his time or not as he chose.[4] He might get leave of absence for other reasons, to go on crusade or pilgrimage, to serve in the king's court (i.e. the Civil

---

[1] Dr. Watson in Ollard and Crosse, *Dictionary of English Church History*, article ' Tithe '.

[2] To do the monks justice they were not alone in the matter. Thus the Dean and Chapter of Hereford procured the ' appropriation ' of Shinfield, Berkshire, for the benefit of the fabric fund of the cathedral, while the Bishop of Hereford got the two churches of Bosbury and Ledbury appropriated to himself for the expenses of his table.  [3] See below, p. 417.

[4] Many rectors were weighed down all their lives by debts contracted to University tradesmen while studying under these conditions.

Service), or even if his parishioners had taken a dangerous dislike to him. He need not necessarily be rector of only one parish ; he might have several. And though the Church set its face against this practice and often tried to stop it, the force of public opinion in the matter was too weak and the pressure of private interests was too strong, and even the best men had no hesitation in being pluralists. Thus so pious a person as St. Thomas of Cantelupe held at the time of his accession to the see of Hereford the archdeaconry of Stafford, a canonry of Lichfield, the precentorship of York, prebends of St. Paul's and of Hereford, and nine rectories.

The *perpetual vicar* was, as has been said above, the resident clergyman in ' appropriated' parishes ; out of the income of the benefice he received a stipend which was supposed to give him a living wage.[1] This stipend was not proportionate to the total value of the benefice, and could vary greatly in this respect from one-third to a much smaller percentage. Thus in 1291 the vicar of Dymock, Gloucestershire, got six marks and the appropriators, the abbot and convent of Cormeilles in Normandy, got thirty-nine. The vicar's stipend was derived from the small tithes and altar offerings, and in addition the

FIG. 277. A PARISH PRIEST OF THE MIDDLE AGES.
William Goode, Rector of Dogmersfield ; once a Fellow of Merton College, Oxford. Died 1498. (From a Brass in Odiham Church.)

appropriators were obliged to provide accommodation, which could consist either of a separate vicarage or a portion of the rectory house, with a garden or a share of it. It is difficult to say how far the vicarial stipend *was* sufficient. The Oxford complaint of 1414[2] asserts that it was impossible for the vicars to keep themselves and

---

[1] Five marks was the *minimum* provided for by the Council of Oxford of 1222, 10 according to a decree of Convocation in 1429, the cost of living having practically doubled in the interval.
[2] Wilkins, *Concilia*, iii. 360 ff.

exercise hospitality on it, and also that the monks made a practice of making a vicar at his appointment swear that he would never ask for a larger one. It has been urged that a parish was better off under this system than under a non-resident rector with a curate in charge. But this does not seem to have been the view of contemporaries. Dr. Gascoigne, for instance, says that under the appropriation system the duty of hospitality was, *inter alia*, neglected. 'What', he says, 'do twenty monks do for a parish ? You may have a bad rector, but he may be succeeded by a good one : the parishioners have at least that hope, whereas in the case of the monks they can expect nothing.' Certainly the reports of episcopal visitations, especially those of the early sixteenth century, seem to show that the monks as a rule neglected their appropriated churches and often allowed both church (or rather chancel, for which they were responsible) and rectory house to fall into ruin.

We now come to a class of clergyman which though connected with the parochial system but loosely, if at all, yet ranked as beneficed, the *chantry priests and the canons of collegiate churches*, the endowment of whom was the favourite form of alms in the fourteenth and fifteenth centuries.

The primary purpose of the founder of a chantry was to secure in perpetuity the provision of a priest to say mass for his and his family's souls, and if many priests were provided the foundation was dignified by the name of a *college*, with a dean and chapter.[1] On the other hand, those who were too poor to found a chantry contented themselves with an *obit*, a mass said on the anniversary of the death of the founder, or with endowing a *light* to burn before the rood or the image of our Lady. The chantry was provided with a special chapel which might be situated in an outlying district, but was usually attached to the parish church in one form or another, as a separate structure, as an aisle, or as a second enclosure at the end of an aisle or between the pillars, in which case it was little more than a pew with an altar in it, the keys

---

[1] Thus the great Lancastrian foundation at Leicester, known as the Newark, had a dean, 12 prebendaries, 13 vicars choral, and 100 almsmen and women in the proportion of two-thirds to one-third.

of which were in the possession of the owner.[1]  The founder, having secured royal and episcopal permission, set aside property, generally lands or houses, to provide an endowment, the advowson of the chantry, i. e. the right of appointment of the chantry priest, remaining in his hands and passing to his successors in the ordinary way.  The chantry priest was therefore legally independent of the parson of the parish, and their interests often tended to clash.  Thus in 1385 we find that the inhabitants of Ledbury were in the habit of attending a short and early mass in the chantry of St. Anne (the south aisle of the parish church), and of spending the rest of Sunday morning in the public-houses discussing agricultural business and drinking more than was good for them, while the parish services were all but neglected.  The Bishop of Hereford was obliged to issue directions that the chantry services were not to begin until the Gospel had been reached in the High Mass at the parish altar.  The chantry priest was not, then, as he is often represented, an assistant to the parish priest in the sense that a 'curate' is nowadays, though most of the foundation charters insist on his being present in his surplice in the chancel of the parish church at the chief services.  In many cases, and especially in the small towns, he was also chaplain to an almshouse attached to the chantry, while in others he acted as schoolmaster, and a number of the smaller grammar schools of the country originated in this way.[2]  The history of the chantries has never been systematically investigated, and it is impossible to say how far they carried out the intentions of the founders, especially in regard to charity and education ; for pluralism reigned here as elsewhere, and the salaries were in any case small.[3]  Many of them remained vacant for years, while others lapsed.  The case of the *colleges* was generally worse, and the records of their visitations present an astonishing picture of disorder and indiscipline.[4]

[1] See *Plumpton Correspondence*, p. 189.  The chantry chapels of the Bishops of Winchester in that cathedral are good examples of the ' enclosed ' kind. A cathedral or large parish church would contain a considerable number of these.

[2] Thus at Henley-on-Thames the grammar school was originally situated in the churchyard, in a house which was also inhabited by the chantry priests.

[3] At St. Mary's, Reading, in 1547, the chantry priest had a salary of £16 ; he was also vicar of Hillingdon, Middlesex, and non-resident.

[4] See the *Visitations of Southwell Minster* (Camden Society).

A reformation of these foundations was sadly needed. The Act of 1547 which suppressed them and the chantries professed, while doing away with what it called 'superstitious' uses, an intention of preserving the educational provision and the payments for the poor; in fact, this was rarely done, and the money disappeared into the pockets of Edward VI's courtiers. 'In nine-tenths of the cases it was never done hereafter. In those cases in which it did come, it came only through the efforts of local people in particular cases.'[1]

Finally we have to notice the large class of *stipendiary priests* strictly so called, who answered to the assistant curates of to-day but in the Middle Ages were usually described as *chaplains*. The result of the prevalent pluralism was to create a large class of ill-paid and generally discontented clergy,[2] for whom, up to the middle of the fourteenth century, five marks was considered a sufficient wage. The increase in the cost of living which the Black Death of 1349 brought about caused the stipendiary clergy to charge more for their service. Archbishop Islip, after commenting acidly on the easy nature and irresponsibility of their work, grudgingly allowed an increase to six marks, a rate which a century later had gone up to nine. Employers and employed were forbidden by Archbishop Sudbury in 1378 to give or receive more. In the early part of the fourteenth century there existed an employers' federation among the beneficed clergy of London, 'one standing feature of which was a rule that, if a chaplain deserted his rector on any malicious pretext, he was not to be employed by any of the other confederates until he was reconciled'.[3] The chief duty of these clergy was to serve the parochial chapels in outlying districts, most of which have in comparatively recent times been constituted ecclesiastical parishes. They usually lived in a clergy house built in the churchyard of the parish church. Another large class was that of *private chaplains*. From the thirteenth century onwards it was a growing practice for the nobility and gentry to obtain episcopal leave to have private chapels

---

[1] Cf. A. F. Leach, *Early Yorkshire Schools*, ii. lvi ff.

[2] William Langland, the author of *The Vision of Piers Plowman*, was one of this class; so (probably) was John Ball, one of the chief leaders of the labour revolt of 1381.

[3] *Transactions of the Royal Historical Society*, 3rd series, vol. vi, p. 112.

in their houses ; these necessitated a private chaplain. But attendance at the parish church on Sundays and festivals was usually made a condition.[1] In a somewhat similar position were the chaplains attached to the numerous gilds in the towns ; some large town churches might have a dozen or more of such. Finally the parish clerk was in minor orders, and was therefore available to act as sub-deacon at a High Mass.

## 4. Training and Social Life of the Clergy.

The secular clergy were drawn from all ranks of society, from the younger sons of great houses destined for the Civil Service or for rich family livings to representatives of the villein class manumitted before ordination. But the greater number came from the ranks of the smaller freeholder and the lower middle class generally, to whom the clerical profession meant social advancement and escape from manual drudgery. The standard of education naturally varied greatly. It is probable that few but absentee rectors in minor orders obtained a university education, and even of these not many proceeded to the degree of Master of Arts.[2] That of the stipendiary clergy must have been confined to what they could pick up in the cathedral or chantry grammar schools (see above). Poor scholars were often given the office of parish clerk or *aquaebaiulus*, that they might continue their education with the aid of its perquisites. But the effect seems to have been poor, and Robert of Brunne says that everywhere the holy water clerk is ordained priest, though he has learned little in life. That the general standard of education was adequate or satisfied the authorities of the time cannot be asserted ; but it is well not to take too seriously the sneers of spiteful and superior critics like Roger Bacon, who amiably compared the country clergy to brutes. The huge number of ordinands seems to have escaped with no more than a perfunctory ordination examination, which probably amounted to an inquiry by the archdeacon into their physical and moral fitness.

[1] Thus we find a dispensation from Archbishop Laud (1640) to Sir J. and Lady Isabella Thynne to have an oratory in their house at Longleat, but they are to take the Sacrament at the parish church (*Third Report of Historical MSS. Commission*, p. 201).
[2] The term ' Sir ' John Smith on a clergyman's epitaph would imply that the deceased had held no higher degree than that of bachelor.

## 5. Everyday Life.

The houses of the clergy naturally varied in size and comfort according to circumstances.  As a rule they consisted of a large central hall extending to the roof with rooms and offices on either side and considerable stabling and garden.  A certain number of the mediaeval parsonage houses survive,[1] and have the appearance of large cottages.  Even so they would appear large for a bachelor clergyman had it not been for the obligation of hospitality, which means that the parsonage was intended to be used as an *inn* by the upper classes.  When the time came for a clergyman to retire he was either given a coadjutor or assigned a pension, part of which sometimes consisted of two or three rooms in the vicarage, surely a doubtful advantage for his successor.  The main income of the ordinary parish priest came from the produce of the glebe and from tithes, which up to the nineteenth century were paid in *kind*.  To quote an authority of the fifteenth century:[2]

> Every man hys teythynge shall paye
> Bothe of smale and of grete
> Of schep and swyne and other nete [horned cattle]
> Teythe of huyre and of honde [wages and handiwork]
> Gotte by costome of the londe;

while the balance of the income was made up by fees, offerings, obits, &c.

The duties of the parish priest were, of course, roughly the same as to-day.  In some ways his position was a more difficult one.  Thus the State expected him to act as a kind of Sunday newspaper and to read out from the pulpit official bulletins of victory or other intelligence.  Moreover, he was liable to military service for home defence.  The chronicler Knighton reports[3] (1360) that the clergy were ordered to be ready to serve, some as archers, some as men-at-arms, and formed according to a writ of Richard II in 1377[4] in battalions, companies, and platoons.[5]  The

---

[1] e.g. at West Dean and Alfriston near Eastbourne.
[2] John Myrc, *Instructions for Parish Priests*, ll. 351 ff.
[3] i. 110.                             [4] Wilkins, iii. 119, 120.
[5] In *Millenis, Centenis et Vintenis*.  In 1418 the Bishop of Hereford reported that the clergy of his diocese could furnish 41 men-at-arms and 200 archers from the archdeaconry of Hereford, and 36 and 233 respectively from that of Salop.

parish priest's main duties towards his parishioners were the preaching of the Word and the administration of the Sacraments.[1] Baptism was administered, except in case of necessity, only at Easter and Whitsuntide. Parents were responsible, on pain of excommunication, for bringing their children to the bishop for confirmation. As to the Sacrament of penance the position of the parish priest was legally unassailable. Not only were parishioners obliged to confess to him (once a year at least), but he was not allowed, except in cases of necessity, to hear the confessions of non-parishioners. The main exception to this rule was that the bishop could license special confessors or pardoners (generally friars).[2] As to the Sacrament of the Altar, the ordinary parish priest in a country parish would have sung or said the parish mass at nine,[3] preceded by matins and followed at two or three by vespers. But in the towns, as services became more numerous and complicated, partly as the result of the growing devotion to our Lord (in the Jesus mass) and our Lady, there would be a constant stream of masses from an early hour to midday. Sermons also became more elaborate and sought after, and there can be no doubt that the popular demand for preaching, which in the sixteenth and seventeenth centuries almost extirpated the spirit of worship, was rapidly growing in the fourteenth and fifteenth centuries, and numerous books of sermon-outlines, or ' sleep-wells ' as they were called,[4] were in circulation ; while the pulpit was the great medium of instruction, special stress being laid [5] on the teaching of children and adults the Lord's Prayer, Hail Mary,[6] Creed, ten Commandments, and how to cross themselves properly.

What, apart from his religious duties, occupied the

---

[1] Cf. Myrc's *Instructions* for details.

[2] For the difficulties which this involved, see chapter X, pp. 394–5. These rules still obtain in the Church of England, as a reference to the Book of Common Prayer will show, where confession is enjoined to the parish priest *or* to some other discreet and learned minister, i. e. authorized confessor ; but the licensing system has, unfortunately, broken down; see Pullan, *History of the Book of Common Prayer*, pp. 201 ff. For the rules of penance, see Myrc, *passim*.

[3] At North Cerney in Gloucestershire a bell is still rung on Sundays at nine, the old hour of the parish mass, though no service now takes place at that hour.

[4] i. e. because they enabled the clergy to sleep comfortably on Saturday nights with the knowledge that the Sunday sermon was safely prepared.

[5] Cf. Archbishop Neville's constitution of 1466 in Wilkins, iii. 599 ff.

[6] In its scriptural form. Cf. Myrc, ll. 422, 423.

ordinary parish priest's time ? Naturally the cultivation of his glebe and sometimes of other land as well, so as to make him a farmer on a sufficiently large scale ; others, for all that general and provincial councils could say, acted as tradesmen.[1] There was always a temptation to discard the clerical outdoor dress of cassock, gown, and hood (i. e. cape and head-piece) in favour of lay costume. The Oxford complaint of 1414 says that the clergy do this in the hope of being taken for country gentlemen. The sporting parson was far more conspicuous than he is nowadays. We are told of a Buckinghamshire chaplain who was so fond of football that it was his habit to say all his offices, including compline, early in the morning, so as to leave the rest of the day quite free. The punishment of a notorious clerical poacher at Ledbury in 1346 was that he should on our Lady's next birthday, during mass, sit or stand before the cross between clergy and people, habited in his surplice ; that he was not to leave the church till he had said through the whole of the Psalter, and that he must swear not to hunt again for three years.

The relations of the parish priest to his parishioners depended naturally to a great extent on his own tact and their disposition, or at any rate that of the chief of them. Assaults of the most painful nature were often made on unpopular clergymen, and cases of attacks on clergy were always ' reserved ' for the bishop's own court (see above). The squire was a grievous problem to the country clergyman.[2] The pew system began in the thirteenth and fourteenth centuries. By the fifteenth the squire was boxed up in a locked pew either in the chancel (in which the patrons of churches and their families had a right to sit) or in a chantry pew (see above, p. 418) ; nor did the service begin till he was in it.[3] The *pax*, or metal box, which was passed round the congregation during the gospel for the kiss of peace, had to be given in strict order of social

[1] Thus in 1399 the rector of Biggleswade was accused of living the life of an ordinary tradesman in his mother's house and letting the rectory go to ruin.

[2] The statement so often made by panegyrists of the Middle Ages that all were equal in the House of God is based on a complete misconception of the social conditions of the time.

[3] See the *Book of the Knight of La Tour Landry, passim.* J. Russell, *Book of Nurture* (c. 1460), p. 917, gives the arrangements as to pews of great men.

precedence or the disturbance was great. In 1496 a woman was accused in the Bishop of London's court of throwing the pax bread on the floor because another had kissed it before her.[1] The decline in church attendance was another worry for the clergy. 'People are deserting the church nowadays,' wrote Archbishop Islip in 1359,[2] and the author of *Dives et Pauper*, writing a century later, says that people would rather 'go to the tavern than to Holy Church . . . to hear a song of Robin Hood or of some ribaldry than to hear mass or matins'.[3] But 'attendance' is a relative term. Everything tended to make it good, and combined with convention and religious feeling was the fact that the churchwardens were bound to present shirkers. The mediaeval clergy were in other respects not exempt from the periodical panics which assail the clergy of all ages. The absence in most places of any building where secular business could be carried on gave rise to a tendency to use the churches as 'court houses' and the churchyards as fair grounds cumbered with booths. The efforts of the bishops to stop Sunday trading (including shaving) and the Sunday opening of public-houses were generally ineffectual. And the religious plays which the clergy encouraged tended to degenerate into purely secular amusements ;[4] while the sins of society were a perennial subject of alarm, and the dress and the behaviour of ladies at tournaments (the mediaeval race meeting) caused constant apprehension.[5] The fear of disendowment, too, was constantly before their eyes, and the ignorant politician of those days was equally persuaded with those of to-day that the Church was of Parliamentary origin.[6] From the end of the fourteenth century, at any rate, the fear of dissent was added to fear of the friars, and it passed the ordinary clergyman's understanding why the bishops were so remiss in dealing with the Lollards.

The secular clergy of the Middle Ages have suffered much at the hands of writers who have endeavoured for the purposes of ecclesiastical controversy to paint them *couleur de rose* or *couleur de noir* according to the respective

---

[1] Hale's *Precedents*, p. 192.    [2] Cf. Wilkins, iii. 43.
[3] Quoted in Coulton's *Mediaeval Studies*.
[4] See *Register of Bishop Trillek of Hereford* (1344–61), p. 141.
[5] Cf. Knighton, ii. 57.
[6] See the preamble to the Statutes of Provisors (1351–90).

tenets of the controversialist. They have suffered, too, from mediaeval controversialists, political or ecclesiastical, from disappointed clergymen like Langland, from writers like Gower or the authors of the pamphlets and songs which took the place of popular newspapers who were in search of literary sensation. The truth, of course, lies midway—the real colour was neither black nor white, but grey. The clergy could not fail to be affected by the faults of their own age, with its violence, its litigiousness, its want of discipline. We cannot imagine the present Archbishop of Canterbury putting London under an interdict so long as the Archbishop of York were in it, as Archbishop Reynolds did in 1317. The two great evils of pluralism and non-residence were too deep-seated for the means which the Church had at its disposal to extirpate. There were far too many clergy and far too many churches. Sir Thomas More says cynically that in 'Utopia' the clergy are exceeding holy, *for they are very few*; and the number of churches was too great to be kept up. At Winchester, for instance, there were forty-seven parish churches and three chapels in 1291, which at the accession of Bishop Fox in 1502 had been reduced to thirty, and by him were still further reduced to fifteen. Men lived nearer the sky then. Those who endowed the clergy anticipated the cultivation by them of the fields of Paradise, just as villeins cultivated their fields of Earth. And a church built here for God meant a mansion for its builder in God's heavenly kingdom. But the labourers might not be worthy of their hire, and succeeding generations might fail to keep the buildings in repair. Nevertheless, it would be well to keep one's eyes rather on the 'poor parson of the town' whom Chaucer has portrayed for us so enthusiastically. It was he and his like who were the real representatives of the parish clergy. And rapacious though kings and courtiers may have been in the sixteenth century, they never dared seriously to attack the secular clergy, for its interests were too much bound up with the interests of the people at large.

## Books for reference.

(1) *Original Sources.* The bishops' registers, which extend in most dioceses from the middle of the thirteenth century to the present day, are the official sources and record not only institutions, pensions, &c., but a crowd of details of parochial life. Unfortunately few of them are in print as a whole, though they are in slow process of publication by the Canterbury and York Society. The only diocese whose mediaeval registers have been so printed is that of Hereford (1275–1516) by the Cantelupe Society.

The decrees of provincial councils and the ' constitutions ' of bishops will be found in Wilkins's *Concilia Magnae Britanniae et Hiberniae* (3 vols.), 1737.

The best account of the everyday duties of the clergy is in J. Myrc, *Instructions for Parish Priests* (early fifteenth century), ed. E. Peacock, for the Early English Text Society (1865). The same society printed Robert of Brunne's *Handlyng Synne*, edited by F. J. Furnivall.

The works of Chaucer, Langland, Gower, and Wyclif give, of course, many sidelights on the condition of the clergy, but they must be read with the caution suggested on p. 426. So must Dr. Gascoigne's (†1458) Theological Dictionary, edited in part by J. E. T. Rogers as *Loci e Libro Veritatum* (1881).

(2) *Modern works:*

E. L. CUTTS, *Parish Priests and their People in the Middle Ages in England* (1898).

H. G. RICHARDSON, ' The Parish Clergy of the Thirteenth and Fourteenth Centuries ', in *Transactions of the Royal Historical Society*, 3rd series, vol. i (1912).

HUNT & STEPHENS, *History of the English Church*; cf. especially Canon Capes' *English Church in the Fourteenth and Fifteenth Centuries* (i. e. vol. iii), chapters 11–13.

G. G. COULTON, *Social Life in England in the Middle Ages*, 1920.

OLLARD & CROSSE, *Dictionary of English Church History* (especially the articles of Dr. Watson on Tithe, Archdeacon, &c.), 2nd ed., 1920.

The articles on ecclesiastical history in the *Victoria County Histories* are important for local conditions, and the diocesan histories published by the S. P. C. K. will be found useful.

ROBINSON, J. A., *The Times of St. Dunstan*, 1923.

BISHOP, EDMUND, *Liturgica Historica* (especially the essay on the Primer), 1918.

# XI

# LEARNING AND EDUCATION

## § 1. GENERAL SURVEY

### 1. *Anglo-Saxon and Norman Periods.*

WITH the Conversion of England begin the records of English learning and of English education. It does not enter into our province to deal directly with the history of literature ; but even an outline of the growth of learning and education cannot be written without reference to its familiar story. As in all departments of English history, so here, the first dividing line is produced by the twofold nature of the conversion to Christianity. The Celtic preachers, who taught the new faith in the north, brought with them an inefficient organization, both ecclesiastical and educational ; but, for that very reason, they did not employ the Latin of the Church to destroy at once the literary form of the vernacular tongue and the spirit of poetry which had produced the Germanic sagas. With the new teaching there came, rather, a new inspiration ; and hence there have descended to us the heathen song of Beowulf, softened here and there, as we possess it, by later Christian influence ; the deeply pious poems associated with the name of Cædmon, and the riddles erroneously attributed to Cynewulf. It was otherwise in the south of England, where the Roman Church established its organization and its ritual. Under the influence of St. Augustine there was more of actual teaching, and the instruction of youth was more systematically undertaken as the monastic system took deeper root on English soil. The result was that no English literature arose in the south of England, as in the Northumbrian kingdom.

The two influences met in the person of the Venerable Bede. Born in Northumbria, just after the Roman victory at the Synod of Whitby, and educated in the Benedictine monastery of Jarrow, he represents the conflict of the two opposing systems. It is significant of the result of that conflict that the works of Bede, which have come down to us, are written in Latin, and that we can just catch the echo of those snatches of English song for which Cuthbert watched so eagerly while his master lay dying. Not till the last traces of Northumbrian literature were disappearing did there arise a southern king to whom it was given to encourage and almost to create a school of English prose. One of Alfred's great services to England was the effort he made to promote learning and education. Latin and English alike were taught in English schools, and Alfred was able to rely upon the co-operation of the clergy in advancing his great projects for the education of his people. If modern criticism has rendered untenable the old faith in King Alfred as the founder of the University of Oxford, the legend itself may well stand for the fact that to Alfred is due the reawakening of intellectual life in the beginning of the ninth century. Alfred's successor as the patron of learning and education was the great Dunstan, the ' dear father Dunstan ', to whom, as Mr. Green has pointed out, the Canterbury schoolboys used to pray for protection.

Anglo-Saxon education was almost entirely dependent on the Church, and the earliest English school, the existence of which is known to us, was founded under the influence of St. Augustine at Canterbury. There were famous schools in such great ecclesiastical towns as Glastonbury and Abingdon, Winchester, Worcester, and York—the last mentioned rendered illustrious by its association with Alcuin. English prose, from the ninth century to the eleventh, proves the study of the vernacular ; but the chief subjects were those of the mediaeval *trivium*—grammar (i. e. the Latin classics), rhetoric, and logic. Of the *quadrivium*, which, including arithmetic, geometry, music, and astronomy, completed the list of the ' seven liberal arts ', only a portion was taught. Arithmetic was necessary for the computation of the Calendar, and music for the services of the Church. The great aim of education was a knowledge of grammar as a preparation for theology. Greek was introduced by Archbishop Theodore, and it had, for a short time, a vogue in England. Bede, writing of an exceptional state of things, tells us that, in his days, there were men ' as well versed in the Greek and Latin tongues as in their own ', while the records of Anglo-Saxon medicine indicate an acquaintance with Greek ideas.

A number of theological, philosophical, and scientific
treatises remain to us to testify to learning in England
before the Norman Conquest. Bede himself was learned
not only in history and in theology, but also in the science
of the age. His *De Temporum Ratione* attempted a scientific
account of the Calendar, and his *De Natura Rerum*, translated into Anglo-Saxon in the tenth century, made an
attempt to describe the constitution of the universe. In
the beginning of the eleventh century, Ælfric, who is known
best by his homilies, wrote upon astronomy. Other remains
of Anglo-Saxon science have been collected in the volumes
in the Rolls Series, entitled *Leechdoms, Wortcunning, and
Starcraft of Early England*, edited by Mr. Cockayne. In
philosophy no original treatise was produced ; King Alfred
translated the *De Consolatione Philosophiae* of Boethius,
but not till the coming of the Normans did any notable
philosopher write on English soil, although the Anglo-Saxon
race contributed to European thought so great a name as
that of Alcuin. In theology Anglo-Saxon literature is more
abundant. In addition to ecclesiastical history we have
collections of sermons in the *Blickling Homilies* (ed.
R. Morris, E. E. Text Soc.), the *Sermones Catholici* or
*Homilies* of Ælfric (ed. Thorpe), and the homilies of
Wulfstan, Bishop of York. A description of these writings
will be found in M. Jusserand's *Literary History of the
English People*, pp. 88–90. But Anglo-Saxon writers
reached their highest achievement in history. The Ecclesiastical History of Bede, the seven texts of the Anglo-Saxon
Chronicle, the various poems and legends of the saints,
represent a collection of historical material such as no other
primitive nation produced. There were hardly any students
of Roman law, and no great jurists, before the Norman
Conquest. Anglo-Saxon dooms and custumals are comparatively numerous, but they were never made part of
a great legal system.

Of the methods of Anglo-Saxon education we know but
little. A school-book has come down to us in the *Collo-
quium*, one of the manuscripts of which Mr. Cockayne has
printed in the preface to the first volume of his *Leechdoms*. It was an exercise in translation from English into
Latin, and certain glosses give evidence that Greek words
were taught, if no attempt was made to give instruction in

the language.   Bede tells us that, before the foundation of nunneries in England, the daughters of English parents were sent to be educated in the monasteries of the Franks or Gauls.   From the time of Alfred onwards there must have been a considerable number of grammar schools, connected with churches, cathedrals, and religious houses.

The immediate result of the Norman Conquest was to connect with England two great names in the history of European thought—Lanfranc, whose controversy with Berengar of Tours was one of the earliest results of the religious movement of the eleventh century, and St. Anselm, whose *Cur Deus Homo* has associated with the See of

FIG. 278.   A  S C H O O L.   (From Bodl. MS. 264, 14th cent.)

Canterbury one of the greatest of theological classics. With the literary products of Anglo-Norman writers we are not here concerned.   It is more important, for our purpose, that the Norman Conquest brought England into closer contact with continental thought and into more direct touch with continental life.   The reign of Edward the Confessor had helped to familiarize Englishmen with Norman ideas, and the Conquest brought about the introduction of many of these.   The Renaissance of the eleventh and twelfth centuries produced a new interest in law and in philosophy.   Thus we find English law systematized under Henry II, and stated by Glanvill, the first great English legist.   We find also an increase of interest in classical literature ; Anglo-Saxon text-books had been con-

cerned with medicine and practical science ; in the twelfth
century the boys were occupied with Priscian and Donatus,
the Aristotelian logic known chiefly through the Latin
rendering of Boethius, along with the writings of Cassiodorus
and Isidore of Seville. Through the great classical acquire-
ments of John of Salisbury, England may claim some share
in the brilliant, if brief, classical renaissance of the twelfth
century, and her part in the development of scholastic
theology is exemplified by the work of Robert Pullen, who
began to study in the schools of Oxford about 1133, and
who subsequently taught at Paris, and was known as one
of the greatest scholars of his day. His *Sententiarum theo-
logicarum Libri VIII* was a well-known text-book till the
appearance of the *Sentences* of Peter the Lombard.

## 2. *Origins of Mediaeval Schools and Universities.*

The mention of the schools of Oxford brings us to
perhaps the central question connected with the history
of learning in England—the origin of the oldest English
University. Until recent years the general belief has been
that the schools of Oxford arose in connexion with one
of the great religious houses—Oseney or St. Frideswide's.
Sir H. Maxwell Lyte and Dr. Rashdall have pointed out
the improbability of the origin of independent schools from
a monastic or capitular body, and that, in point of fact,
the schools of Oxford did not grow up around St. Frideswide's or Oseney, but around the parish church of St. Mary.
Dr. Rashdall has suggested a theory of their origin which
may be taken as the most probable explanation that has
yet appeared. He tells us that, where a University
originated spontaneously, it was usually in connexion
with a cathedral or collegiate church, and Oxford possessed neither ; and he proceeds to adduce some other
considerations which render it likely that the University
originated in one of the migrations which are frequent in
early academic history. Dr. Rashdall points out that
there are only three allusions to the existence of schools at
Oxford before the year 1167 : a certain Theobaldus
Stampensis, who had been a ' Doctor at Caen ', taught at
Oxford before 1117, and had under him ' sixty or a hundred
clerks, more or less ' ; Robert Pullen, already mentioned ;

and, perhaps, the Lombard jurist Vacarius. About the year 1167 we find more evidence for schools at Oxford, and Dr. Rashdall's theory is based on the coincidence in time between 'the sudden rise of Oxford into a *Studium Generale*' about 1167 and the issue of an ordinance by Henry II (then engaged in his quarrel with Becket), ordering all clerks possessing revenues in England and resident in France, where Philip II was aiding Becket, to return home within three months 'as they loved their revenues'. A very large proportion of clerks holding English benefices and residing in France must have consisted of students at the University of Paris. It is certain that many English scholars were forced to leave Paris in accordance with this ordinance. It is also certain that it was a usual practice in such cases to migrate and found another *Studium Generale*.

The commercial and strategic importance of Oxford, situated between Wessex and Mercia, and close to the Thames, rendered it easy of access for a large concourse of English students. A migration from Paris to Oxford is thus most probable, and the positive evidence consists in the fact that 'not merely in their number, but in their character, the allusions to Oxford schools after 1167 differ from the earlier notices'. One master, even if he enjoys a following of 'sixty or a hundred scholars, more or less', does not make a *Studium Generale*. After 1167 the notices are precisely of the kind which do point to the existence of a *Studium Generale* in the looser and earlier sense of the word, i. e. to the existence of schools in more than one Faculty, taught by many masters, attended by a numerous body of scholars, and by scholars from distant regions. Giraldus Cambrensis, who visited Oxford in 1184 or 1185, speaks of 'all the Doctors of the different Faculties' at Oxford, 'where the clergy in England chiefly flourished and excelled in clerkship'. A further piece of evidence is the document reproduced in Fig. 292. It is an early transfer of land in Catte Street, near St. Mary's Church, and 'among the parties or witnesses appear the names of one bookbinder, three illuminators, one writer, and two parchmenters'—an indication of the academic importance of the city. It may fairly be said that this theory offers the most adequate explanation of the whole circumstances.

The University of Cambridge, in like manner, originated through a migration from Oxford. In 1209 an Oxford townswoman was killed by a clerk ; whether accidentally or not, we do not know. King John, who was under sentence of excommunication, and so had no desire to protect the clergy, allowed the people of Oxford to have their revenge by putting two or three scholars to death. Their fellow students became alarmed, and began to migrate, some to Paris, some to Reading, and some to Cambridge. There is no evidence that Cambridge had

FIG. 279. A  S C R I B E.  From Paris MS. Fonds français 9198, fol. 19, written in 1456.

acquired any special pre-eminence as an educational centre before the beginning of the thirteenth century. No doubt it possessed one of the grammar schools which, by this time, were to be found in most English towns. The rise of Cambridge received a check from a return of scholars to Oxford in 1214, on John's reconciliation with the Church, but it had, some fifteen years later, an accession of strength from the dispersion of the scholars of Paris.

The distinguishing mark of the English Universities to-day is the collegiate system. Yet Paris, not Oxford, was the original home of the college as an academic institution. Colleges arose from a combination of two circumstances—

the existence of benevolent persons who wished to support poor students, and the custom of undergraduates living together under the lax rule of a head elected by themselves (latterly, but at first not necessarily, a Master of Arts). The provision of a hostel for the accommodation of students led to the enforcement of regulations for the conduct of its inmates. The beginnings of the college system in England belong to the thirteenth century. The thirteenth-century students congregated in self-governed Halls; these came into contact with the Chancellor of the University through giving him security for rent, and from this simple fact there developed the minute control subsequently exercised by the University. In the middle of the thirteenth century a Hall, known as Great University Hall, was endowed in accordance with a bequest of William of Durham, and this Hall became, about 1280, University College.

But between the first establishment of the Hall and the publication of the first code of statutes for

Fig. 280. AN ILLUMINATOR.
Dyson Perrins MS., c. 1524.

University College two important events had occurred. Between 1261 and 1266 Sir John de Balliol, father of the notorious John Balliol, did penance for an outrage upon the churches of Tynemouth and Durham by providing for the maintenance of some poor scholars at Oxford. There thus arose in Oxford the College subsequently developed by Devorguilla de Balliol, widow of the founder. The other event to which we referred was the foundation, in 1263–4, of Merton College. Its statutes were drawn up in 1264, and Walter de Merton was the first founder to provide suitable buildings and to make use of a magnificent church for his corporation. The quadrangle shape, now inseparably associated with a college, probably originated in the accidental circumstances which led to the formation of the Mob Quadrangle at Merton.

The movement for the endowment of colleges spread from Oxford to Cambridge, where Peterhouse arose about 1284. In Oxford and Cambridge alike, the rise of secular colleges was accompanied by the growth of monastic colleges, made for and by the Regulars of particular Orders. The Mendicants had, in both Universities, set the example of organized halls for their members. In 1289 Gloucester Hall or College (now represented by Worcester College) and Durham College (on the site of the modern Trinity) were founded at Oxford for the Benedictines. The fourteenth century witnessed important additions to the number of colleges in both Universities. At Cambridge, Clare was founded in 1326, Pembroke in 1347, Gonville in 1348, Trinity Hall in 1350, and in 1352

FIG. 281. The Chancellor of Oxford University receiving a Charter from Edward III. (From the Chancellor's book, *c.* 1375.)

Corpus Christi, where for the first time the design of a quadrangle was consciously adopted. At Oxford, Exeter dates from the year 1314, Oriel from 1326, Queen's from 1340, and in 1379 William of Wykeham founded his College of St. Mary of Winchester in Oxford, which soon became known as New College, in contradistinction to Merton, which had hitherto been pre-eminently *the* College.

The foundation of New College calls for some remark, because it may be taken as indicating the perfectly developed form of a collegiate foundation, and because its association with the sister college at Winchester requires some statement regarding the history of English schools from the Norman Conquest. In the course of the twelfth century the number of grammar schools was largely increased. Mr. A. F. Leach, in his *History of Winchester College*, quotes evidence for the re-foundation of the school of York in 1075 and its endowment in 1181. 'Warwick School', he says, 'is mentioned in a deed of 1123. . . . Bedford School is on record as existing . . . before 1120. . . . In London there were three grammar schools in 1137.' The twelfth-century revival of learning gave a great

FIG. 282. WINCHESTER COLLEGE, founded 1373.

impetus to the foundation of schools, and many arose in the thirteenth and fourteenth centuries, sometimes in dependence upon cathedrals and collegiate churches, and sometimes in connexion with hospitals, gilds, and chantries, while some came to exist without any such support. The place of monasteries in education seems to have been very greatly exaggerated. It is doubtful, says Mr. Leach, 'whether the monks ever affected even to keep a grammar school for any but their own novices, among whom outsiders were not admitted', and the contribution of monks to general education may be said to be confined to the early days of Christianity in England.

But, in spite of the increasing number of schools, there was a very considerable danger to the mediaeval Universities in the crowd of insufficiently educated youths who proceeded to the study of philosophy. When William of Wykeham founded a new college at Oxford, he determined to secure that his foundation should escape this danger, and, for this purpose, he conjoined with it the school of the College of St. Mary Winton near Winchester. There had long been in existence a high school or public grammar school at Winchester, but Wykeham did not employ it as the basis of his new foundation. He has frequently been credited with originating the public school system ; but it cannot be argued that he was the first to endow a grammar school. His work at Winchester is, in fact, precisely analogous to his work at Oxford : he did not invent the collegiate system, but he built a college on a grander scale than any of his predecessors, and in so complete a fashion that it became the model for almost all subsequent founders ; and, in like manner, at Winchester, he embodied the already existing idea of a public grammar school on a scale which made his work the type of what came to be the English public school. On October 20, 1382, he executed a deed of foundation for Winchester College, and on March 28, 1394, his society took possession of their magnificent home [Fig. 283]. It was, in spite of its association with New College, an independent corporation, the earliest corporation of ' warden and scholars ', except the colleges in the Universities. It was pre-eminently a school, and not (like the schools which had grown up in dependence upon cathedrals or chantries) an institution existing as a kind of parasite, preying upon a foundation made for another purpose.

Wykeham's great aim seems to have been to meet the new influences of the Lollard movement by enlisting learned men on the side of the Church. He founded Winchester because he knew that ' students, . . . through default of good and sufficient teaching in Latin, are deficient in grammar, and so fall into errors ' in studying philosophy, and, accordingly, he limited the membership of New College to boys educated at Winchester. From Winchester they were to go to the sister college to study arts or philosophy, and, subsequently, theology, or canon or civil law. In New College they found, not a mere convenient dwelling-place, but a great ecclesiastical house, equipped to meet all the wants of its inmates. It was not, in any sense, a monastic foundation ; any of Wykeham's scholars who entered a religious Order lost his position, for Wykeham was chiefly interested in the secular clergy. Its statutes exhibit a great development of the theory of college discipline which, in other foundations during the next two centuries, reduced the undergraduate to the level of a schoolboy, and made the birch no longer the symbol of the mere teacher of grammar. Wykeham, too, was the first to insist upon teaching within the college, which thus became the means of intellectual as well as of moral education, and, by forbidding any of his scholars to obtain from the University a 'grace' for their degree, he attempted to secure their fulfilment of all proper obligations.

FIG. 283. NEW COLLEGE AND ITS HUNDRED CLERKS (MS. New College 288).

His great collegiate building, with its chapel, its cloisters, and its garden, its separate establishment for the Warden, and its elaborate statutes, owed much to earlier foundations, and, more especially, to Merton, which it now superseded as the direct model for future colleges. The founder of Lincoln, the next Oxford college in point of date (1427), died without completing its foundation ; but the buildings bear a distinct resemblance, in arrangement, to those of New College. All Souls (1437) and Magdalen (1458) were founded by men who had been members of one or other of the St. Mary Winton Colleges, and they represent variations on Wykeham's plan. In 1441 a still more close imitation was devised by King Henry VI in the foundation of his two colleges—the King's College of St. Nicholas and Our Lady at Cambridge, and, in 1442, of the College of St. Mary at Eton. The foundations at Cambridge of Queens' College (1448), St. Catharine's (1475), and Jesus (1497) complete the list of purely mediaeval colleges. Before dealing with the effect of the Renaissance and the Reformation upon schools and universities, it is necessary to deal briefly with the subjects of mediaeval studies.

### 3. *Curricula in Mediaeval Schools and Universities.*

Of the teaching in mediaeval schools we know very little indeed. A distinction must be drawn between the mere Song Schools, which taught just sufficient Latin to enable boys to take part in the services of the Church, and the grammar schools, where a knowledge of the elements of Latin was assumed, and where preparation was given for the study of dialectic. The text-books in grammar were Donatus and Alexander de Villa Dei ; the Latin poets (especially Vergil) were read, and there were ' Disputations ' in grammar, similar to the philosophical disputations of the Universities. A knowledge of grammar was, of course, assumed in the Universities, where Latin was the language alike of lectures and of conversation, and where the only instruction in grammar was an analysis of the system of popular grammarians, based on the section *De barbarismo* in the *Ars Grammatica* of Aelius Donatus, a fourth-century grammarian, whose work became universally used throughout Europe. The Universities themselves were schools of philosophy, mental and physical. The attention of students in Arts was chiefly directed to the logic of Aristotle, and to his metaphysics, physics, and ethics. Up to the eleventh century Aristotle was known only through the translations into Latin of the sections of his *Organon*, entitled *De Interpretatione* and *Categoriae*, and through the logical works of the philosopher Boethius. The range of mediaeval

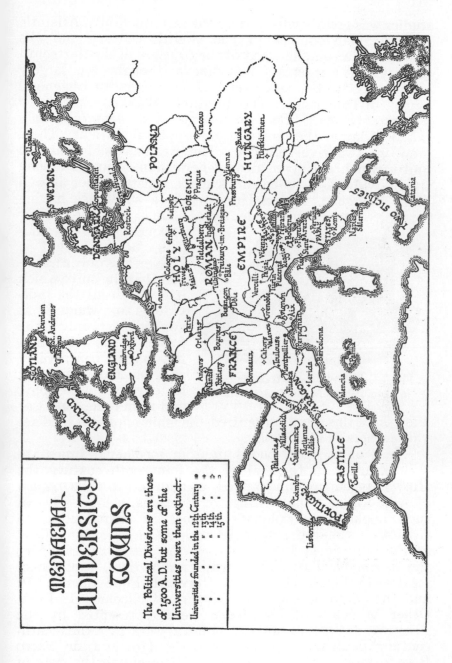

MEDIÆVAL
UNIVERSITY
TOWNS

The Political Divisions are those
of 1500 A.D. but some of the
Universities were then extinct.

Universities founded in the 12th Century
" " 13th "
" " 14th "
" " 15th "

studies was greatly enlarged by the introduction of Aristotle from Arabian sources in the twelfth century and the recovery of a complete text of the *Organon* in the thirteenth century.  The interest of mediaeval thought was largely connected with the controversy about the nature of general names, or Universals.  The questions, *What do we mean by a general name? Does it correspond to anything really existing?* lay at the centre of philosophical thought.  There grew up two rival schools.  The Realists held that the unity, which a Universal or general name implies among the individuals included in its scope, exists in fact as well as in thought ;  that a Universal is a substance having a real existence, independently of human thought.  Their opponents, the Nomina-lists, believed that a Universal is only a name, and that the unity which it gives to all the indi-viduals to whom it is applied exists only in the name.  A full account of this great controversy will be found in any history of philosophy, and round one aspect or another of this question centred the main efforts of mediae-val teachers of philosophy.

FIG. 284.  Old Schools, Oxford, built in 1439.  From Ingram's *Memorials*.

Most of the text-books used in mediaeval times are still extant.  In the end of the fourteenth century the University curriculum implied, in addition to the *Organon* of Aristotle and the writings of Boethius, a knowledge of such books as Porphyry's *Isagoge* or Introduction to Aristotle ;  the criticism of Aristotle's *Categories* by Gilbert of Poitiers (de la Porrée), known as the *Sex Principia* ; the *Summulae Logicales*, a semi-grammatical, semi-logical treatise by Petrus Hispanus (afterwards Pope John XXI), and the commentaries on Scripture of Nicolaus de Lyra. Other branches of knowledge were represented by the *Tractatus de Sphaera*, an astronomical work by a thirteenth-century Scotsman, John Holywood (Joannes de Sacro Bosco), and by the *Computus* for determining the date of Easter.  The method of teaching included the dictation of lectures, and the system of disputations, in accordance with which theses were selected to be attacked and defended (impugned and propugned) by different students as an exercise in dialectic. The main point is the supremacy of Aristotle as interpreted by the Schoolmen. *Absurdum est dicere Aristotelem errasse.* The works of Aristotle, as currently understood, served as a final authority on all questions, even in natural science. Greek was almost unknown, and the slight humanistic movement of the end of the twelfth century had been entirely crushed by the weight of scholastic philosophy.

The numbers of students in attendance at the mediaeval Universities cannot easily be estimated. The statements with regard to Oxford vary from 60,000 to 1,500. On a survey of the evidence, Dr. Rashdall concludes that, at Oxford, 'the numbers could at no time have exceeded 3,000, and were probably always much below it'; and the same may be said of Cambridge, where the numbers were still lower. No University, except Paris and Bologna, contained, at any time, more than 5,000 students.

Among Englishmen who, in the time of which we have been treating, became notable in the history of European learning, should be reckoned, in the twelfth century, John of Salisbury, the scholar and historian; Robert Pullen, whose *Sentences* we have already mentioned; the Latin versifier, Walter Map; and the historian Giraldus Cambrensis. In the following century we have the accomplished Robert Grosseteste; Alexander of Hales, the early Realist; Roger Bacon, the daring and original speculator; and to these succeeded Duns Scotus, the founder of the later Realism, and William of Ockham, the founder of the later Nominalism. The end of the fourteenth century and the beginning of the fifteenth witnessed the 'Oxford movement' connected with the name of John Wyclif, himself an Oxford man, as were also most of his preachers. But the accession of the House of Lancaster put an end to the importance of Lollardy, and the fifteenth century is notable for the 'Early Renaissance' which the late Bishop Creighton described in the Rede Lecture for 1895. The Maecenas of the age was Humphrey, Duke of Gloucester, with whose name we shall again meet in connexion with the Bodleian Library. Soon Aeneas Sylvius was able to write to an English scholar congratulating him that 'Latin style had penetrated into Britain'. The successor of

Gloucester in this respect was John Tiptoft, Earl of Worcester, who bought books in Florence, and himself wrote Latin.

FIG. 285.    J O H N   C O L E T   (the kneeling figure).    (From a MS. in Cambridge University Library, 1509, Dd. 7, 3.)

## 4. *The Renaissance and the Reformation.*

By the end of the fifteenth century the Renaissance was itself in full force, and the new learning soon found a place in the English Universities.    The main feature of this late fifteenth-century movement was the revival of the study of Greek and Roman literature.    The introduction of Greek into Oxford is traditionally attributed to Cornelio Vitello, who was made, about 1470, a Praelector in New College. To the same College belonged also William Grocyn, the most distinguished of Oxford humanists, the catalogue of whose remarkable library we still possess. Other famous names connected with Oxford learning of this period are Thomas Linacre, and his more famous pupil Thomas More, John Colet, and Desiderius Erasmus, whose great reputation shed fresh lustre over Oxford and Cambridge alike.

The revival of Humanism found further result in the foundation of colleges in both Universities. The first sixteenth-century college at Oxford is Brasenose (1509), a new foundation based upon the much older King's Hall. It followed closely the models of Merton and New College, and its statutes represent an advance in strictness of discipline. The new movement was more directly responsible for the foundation of Corpus Christi College in 1516 by Richard Foxe, Bishop of Winchester. The statutes of Corpus contain a provision for a Corpus Reader in Greek, who was to lecture to the whole University on Aristophanes, Theocritus, Euripides, Sophocles, Pindar, Hesiod, Demosthenes, Thucydides, Aristotle, or some similar author, along with Greek grammar and rhetoric. In like manner a Latin reader was appointed to lecture on Roman literature. The lists of Latin and Greek authors quoted in the statutes form a striking contrast to the mediaeval curriculum of the older colleges, and are evidence of Foxe's desire to unite the new interests with the faith of the Church. At Cambridge, Christ's College (1505), which included the older God's House (dating from 1441–2), owed its origin at once to the piety of the Lady Margaret, mother of Henry VII, and to the new learning, under the influence of Bishop Fisher. If his conservatism prevented either it or the subsequent foundation of St. John's College (1511), which was also initiated by the Lady Margaret, from representing quite so complete an acceptance of the new state of affairs as had been shown in the statutes of Bishop Foxe, both differ much from the older mediaeval colleges, and are unquestionably products of the Renaissance.

The last distinctively Renaissance College, founded by Wolsey in 1524 as ' Cardinal College ', became, under the name of Christ Church, the first Reformation College in Oxford. Wolsey had been educated at Magdalen while Oxford could claim Grocyn and More and Colet and Erasmus among its residents, and when he began the suppression of the smaller monasteries he seized the monastery of St. Frideswide's to form his new Cardinal College. It was incomplete at the time of his fall in 1529, and though Henry VIII gave it a charter, in his own name, in 1532, he afterwards suppressed it, and the actual foundation of Christ Church dates from 1546, when Henry removed to Oxford the new episcopal see, created at Oseney in 1542. The conjunction of an ecclesiastical and cathedral foundation with an academic institution is unique in history. To the religious changes introduced by Henry VIII Cambridge owes the largest of English colleges—' Trinity College within the town and University of Cambridge, of King Henry the Eighth's foundation', which arose on the ruins of the Franciscan buildings in 1546. Slightly older than Trinity is Magdalene College, in Cambridge ; its foundation had been attempted about 1519, but it actually dates from 1542, and, like Christ Church, possessed a charter from a king who was Supreme Head of the Church in England. Magdalene shares some of the peculiar interest attaching to two Oxford colleges—Trinity and St. John's. The statutes of Magdalene were not completed till 1554, and, when they were sanctioned, the sovereign of England was no longer Supreme Head of the Church. At Oxford, Trinity (1554) and St. John's (1555) belong to the same period of reaction, with which the founders of both seem to have sympathized. Under Queen Elizabeth originated the distinctively Protestant foundations of Jesus College, Oxford (1571), and Emmanuel (1584) and Sidney Sussex (1595) in Cambridge. With the sixteenth century the age of college-founding came to an end, and only four colleges arose between 1600 and quite recent times—Wadham (1612), Pembroke (1624), and Worcester (1714) at Oxford, and Downing (1800) at Cambridge.

The new learning, thus followed by an outburst of ecclesiastical and theological controversy, completely altered, in the course of the sixteenth century, the curriculum of a University education. We have seen that, at the beginning of it, Humanism had found a place in the statutes of Corpus Christi at Oxford, and Christ's and St. John's at Cambridge. As the century advanced there was added to the new love of literature a contempt for the ancient philosophical studies. At one time it appeared as if this contempt were

to involve the Universities in the destruction of the monasteries, and an Act was introduced into Parliament for the
dissolution of the colleges. But wiser counsels prevailed,
and Thomas Cromwell was satisfied with sending commissioners in 1535 to remodel academic institutions and
to expel the scholastic philosophy. There came a day
when the leaves of Duns Scotus—the ' dunce ' of Cromwell's
commissioners—were thrown to the winds in the great
quadrangle of New College, and, as they were blown here
and there, impressed strongly on the mind of at least one
on-looker the mutability of things human. Aristotle was
not totally neglected, but the mediaeval commentators
were disregarded. Plato found for the first time a worthy
place in the minds of Englishmen, and the classical historians
were read as well as the classical poets. The new religious
influences found an outcome in the professorships of Divinity,
and Hebrew began to be studied. Physics and mathematics,
released from bondage to Aristotle, attracted eager students
who prepared the way for the great advance of the next
century. The statutes of Pembroke College, Oxford, which,
though dating from 1624, represent fairly enough the conditions at the end of Elizabeth's reign, provide for a catecheti-
cal lecture in religious knowledge, and lectures in Natural
Philosophy, Logic, Rhetoric, and Greek, with Disputations
in Theology and Philosophy. The older terminology is
thus maintained to a considerable extent, but the facts
had altered, and the mediaeval student would have found
it difficult to recognize the ' Natural Philosophy ' or the
' Mathematics ' of 1600.

Renaissance and Reformation could not fail to modify
the condition of English schools as well as of the Universities. The new learning did not produce many important
foundations, although Colet's connexion with St. Paul's
and Wolsey's with Ipswich are important exceptions. Colet
attempted a compromise between the old and the new,
and prescribed St. Jerome and St. Augustine as classical
text-books, while Wolsey's scholars were to read Vergil
and Horace and Ovid. The Reformation brought about a
greater change in the numbers of English schools. In some
cases the change was for the better. Henry VIII maintained
and improved the cathedral schools, and in erecting new
cathedral and collegiate churches he made special provision
for education. But hospitals were included under the Act

for the Dissolution of the Monasteries, and the hospital schools fell with the hospitals. The Chantries Acts of Henry VIII and Edward VI were also in their results adverse to educational progress. The reputation of Edward VI as the founder of grammar schools has not survived recent historical criticism. Mr. Leach has shown that 'close on 200 grammar schools (and the schools of Winchester and Eton are included in the term grammar schools) existed in England before the reign of Edward VI, which were, for the most part, abolished or crippled under

In School.   From a sixteenth-century MS. in Lyons.

him'. The number 200 represents our definite knowledge; there must have been many others of which all traces have vanished. It is true that, from the Reformation onwards, the number and the importance of independent schools distinctly increased. Westminster owes its greatness to the Reformation; Shrewsbury takes its date from the reign of Edward VI, and the number of grammar schools which bear his name or are otherwise associated with him will suffice to indicate the importance of this development. Under Elizabeth the endowment of schools became a more generally recognized method of pious benefaction, and to John Lyon and Lawrence Sheriff Harrow and Rugby owe, respectively, their existence.

For whom were such endowed schools intended? Certain phrases in early statutes have led to considerable misapprehension in this connexion. Mr. Leach has pointed out how the expression *pauperes et indigentes*, as applied to Wykeham's schoolboys at Winchester, was necessitated by the legatine constitution forbidding the appropriation of churches except for the good of the poor. In order to carry out his schemes for the endowment of Winchester, it was necessary for the founder to speak of his scholars as *pauperes* : but, in point of fact, they might possess what was, in those days, the considerable income of five marks annually. Similarly, there can be little doubt that, at its foundation, Eton was not intended for others than the conventionally ' poor' students, and there is a clause in the original statutes forbidding the reception of the sons of villeins into college. The free grammar schools of the towns, in like manner, were intended for the free tuition of some or all of the boys of the neigh-bourhood, i. e. largely for the class which now uses them, and not for *pau-peres et indigentes* in the modern sense. The ob-vious meaning of the word ' free' is the correct one, and the ingenious expla-nations that have been derived for it may be safely disregarded. Alike in regard to Winchester, Eton, and Rugby, and with respect to humbler foundations, there is much exaggeration in the statement, sometimes

Out of School. Lyons MS.

made, that they are really ' charity hospitals ', whose reve-nues have been misapplied for the advantage of higher classes than those whom they were originally intended to benefit. Christ's Hospital is the most important instance of a foundation for the poor in the modern sense of the word.

In conclusion, something must be said with regard to the educational theories of the sixteenth century, as com-pared with those of mediaeval days. The *plagosus Orbilius* was certainly not less in evidence at the end of the reign of Queen Elizabeth than in the days when the scholars of Canterbury cried for protection to sweet Father Dunstan, although in the interval Sir Thomas Elyot and Roger Ascham had attempted to convince Englishmen that learning might be instilled otherwise than by means of the rod. The method of teaching was thoroughly mechanical : Elyot's remarks in *The Governour* on the wisdom of adapting instruction to particular cases, and his desire to substitute love of literature for slavish adherence to grammatical niceties, go to show the condition of education in which such suggestions were novelties. *The Governour* was published in 1531, but when Ascham wrote his *Scholemaster* in 1570 he had to plead for precisely the same views, and with just the same result. His method of teaching Latin grammar has frequently been stated. It was based on translation, and it attempted to make use of the bond of association of ideas, thus saving the childish mind from the effort of mastering a long series of disconnected facts. He argued that the learner might begin with a piece of Latin prose, for example, a letter of Cicero. After its general meaning was explained, it should be translated, word by word, with all due attention to the attainment of the proper equivalent. It was then to be translated into proper English, and, after an interval, re-translated into Latin, and the new version compared with the original. Ascham's method did not appeal to sixteenth-century schoolmasters, who preferred the retention of the mediaeval plan of forcing upon the minds of their pupils long lists of grammatical intricacies, and the reform of educational method was reserved for a later day.

## Books for reference.

COCKAYNE, *Leechdoms, Wortcunning, and Starcraft of Early England* (Rolls Series), 1864–6.

WRIGHT, *Popular Treatises on Science*, 1841.

KER, W. P., *English Literature : Medieval* (Home University Library), 1912.

MAITLAND, S. R., *The Dark Ages*, 1844.

POOLE, *Illustrations of Mediaeval Thought*, 2nd edition, 1920.

MULLINGER, *The Schools of Charles the Great*, 1877.

—— *History of the University of Cambridge*, 1873.

RASHDALL, *The Universities of Europe in the Middle Ages*, 1895.

MAXWELL-LYTE, *History of the University of Oxford*, 1886.

BRODRICK, *History of the University of Oxford*, 1886.

The relevant sections of *Social England*, edited by TRAILL, 1892–6, and histories of individual Universities, Colleges, and Schools.

LEACH, (1) *The Schools of Mediaeval England*, 2nd edition, 1916 ; (2) *English Schools at the Reformation*, 1896 ; (3) ' St. Paul's School before Colet ', in *Archaeologia*, vol. lxii, Part I (1910).

## § 2. HANDWRITING

### 1. *Introduction.*

For the study of mediaeval British handwriting it is not necessary to go farther back than to the old Roman *Square Capitals*. These are surprisingly like the present capitals of ordinary roman type, excluding J, U or V, W, as printers still do in book-signatures. Only one of them will not fit into a square frame, namely, Q, with its peculiar tag. The pure capital is chiefly found in Roman inscriptions, and in a very few existing MSS., such as the fragmentary Virgil at St. Gall in Switzerland. The first declension in style is the *Rustic Capital* (centt. i–ix A.D.), which is much less rare in MSS. Here the letters have suffered lateral compression, so that, for instance, T is hardly distinguishable from I, especially as the ceriphs of the letters are slightly exaggerated, so that (to take another example) F and E approximate in shape [see Fig. 287]. In *Uncials* (centt. iv–viii) we first find clear evidence of the two natural feelings which account for almost all changes in writing: the desire to save time and trouble (consider how the four-stroke E can become the two-stroke ϵ or the one-stroke e); and the countercheck, the absolute necessity in good writing to preserve clearness (observe the differentiation of I and J, when their functions became different; and the dotting of the i to avoid confusion in such a word as *minimum* [1]). In Uncial A D E H M Q lose their square character and become ᴀ ᵭ ϵ h ɷ q [see Fig. 287]: the general aspect of the hand is, however, still capital. In *Half-uncial* (centt. vi–viii) all pretence to a capital style is gone: only F and N retain their shape: the rest approximate to modern forms (see the example of fine Irish Half-uncial in Fig. 286). All the preceding styles may be called majuscule, and all that succeed minuscule.

Two general remarks may be made here which affect all writing. First, each style has its own characteristic periods of growth (with alternative forms struggling for existence), perfection, and decay (with feebler imitative strokes). Next, side by side with the calligraphic writing

[1] f in Half-uncial and thereafter up to the nineteenth century is a good example of both tendencies. f was simplified *too far*, to ſ, which collided with l: so the former was deliberately differentiated by a mark affixed to the left side of the stem.

used for permanent records, such as literary works, chronicles, and liturgies (*book-hand*), there is always the common running hand of private use, in accounts, familiar letters, diaries, and the like (*cursive*) ; and this latter hand is usually much more difficult to read and tends to influence for the worse the contemporary book-hand.

When St. Patrick landed in Ireland, about A.D. 450, he brought with him beyond doubt some Half-uncial MSS., which became the foundation of the national hands of the British Isles until the Conquest ; and in the blaze and heat of religious and literary activity which ensued on the conversion of Ireland to Christianity, the handwriting and illumination were wrought to a perfection which is the admiration and despair of succeeding ages. All the earliest specimens have perished, and the Cathach Psalter, attributed to St. Columba's own hand (*d.* 597) but probably of the seventh century, is among the earliest which have survived. To this century also belongs the wonderful Book of Kells, of which a fragment is shown in Fig. 286. Characteristic forms are ᚱ (r), Ꮙ (s), and especially ᚹ (g).[1] In the eighth century a pointed style (in which for instance r becomes ᚹᚹ) is developed, and the two styles characterize all native Irish writing. It is the latter which ultimately survived and is still represented in Irish printing.

The religious fervour of the Irish could not be confined within the borders of Ireland, and Irish missionaries poured northward and eastward to evangelize Scotland and England, carrying with them MSS. in the Irish script. St. Columba, who founded the first Scottish monastery on the island of Iona, died in 597, the year of the arrival of St. Augustine in Kent. Then in 635 the Irish influence reached England from Iona, when St. Aidan founded Lindisfarne Abbey on Holy Island, on the Northumbrian coast. From this year two rival scripts struggled for the conquest of England, for Augustine introduced into Canterbury the Roman Half-uncial as normally developed in Italy. It is not a great stretch of fancy to say that at the Council of Whitby in 664, when the Irish Christianity of the north and the Roman Christianity of the south met to decide questions of ritual, the rival scripts were also,

[1] These Irish forms of r and s will be found in Fig. 288.

in a sense, on their trial. But whereas the victory in ritual rested with Rome, it was the Irish hand which won ascendancy over its rival. We have volumes like the Lindisfarne and Macregol Gospels which can hardly be distinguished from Hibernian script, and both in church writings and in charters the Hiberno-Saxon (or, as it is now called, the Insular) hand is overwhelmingly predominant, the Roman being confined to a few great centres like Canterbury and Winchester. In the Charters of the Anglo-Saxon period, the earliest of which are of the close of the seventh century, are found both the Roman hand (especially for Latin deeds) and the round and pointed Insular hand where Old English is the language.

But from the tenth century onward a great and increasing vogue was given to foreign writing, not only by the weakening of English monasticism in face of the Danish invasions (centt. viii fin.–xi init.), but also by the invasion of the *Carolingian Minuscule*, which at last broke down all opposition at the time of the Norman Conquest, and flooded the land. This new and fine minuscule was the creation of Charles the Great. It was needed, for in the

FIG. 286. FINE EARLY IRISH HAND. The Book of Kells. The finest Irish writing based on Roman half-uncial. Transcr. *& crucifixerun[t eu] | m | Et erat tit[ulus . . . | scriptu[s . . .] | cum eo . . . [la] | trones |*, &c. Vulgate of Mark xv. 25–8. MS. in Trin.Coll., Dublin.

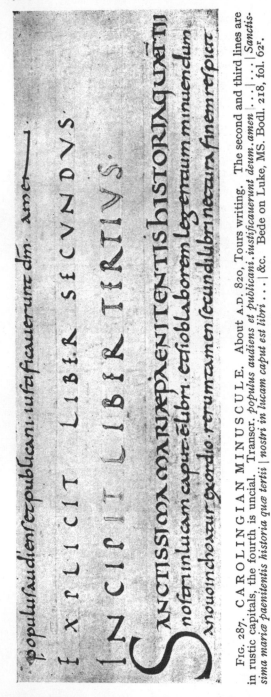

FIG. 287. CAROLINGIAN MINUSCULE. About A.D. 820, Tours writing. The second and third lines are in rustic capitals, the fourth is uncial. Transcr. *populus audiens et publicani*.*iustificauerunt deum*.*amen* . . . | *Sanctissima maria paenitentis historia quae tertii* | *nostri in lucam caput est libri* . . . | &c. Bede on Luke, MS. Bodl. 218, fol. 62ᵛ.

seventh and eighth centuries the Half-uncial hand on the Continent had developed into three chief national hands, marking the effect of the inroads of the Barbarians on the Roman Empire: namely, the Merovingian hand in France (650–1150), the Beneventan in Italy (centt. viii–xii), and the Visigothic in Spain (centt. viii–xi). These styles mark a great declension from clearness, and Charles the Great, who had set Alcuin of York at the head of his famous school of Tours in 796, took in hand the reform of writing, and with rare taste and rarer opportunities of success secured for his script [1] throughout the empire a regular and clear style based on old and pure forms, to the exclusion of the contorted handwritings which it superseded. The Carolingian Minuscule

[1] *Qui facit per alium facit per se.* Charles the Great personally read and wrote with difficulty, but his was the master mind.

is at the base of all the mediaeval European hands, and
approximates to the ordinary 'lower-case' roman type of
our modern printing.  It saved Europe from a welter of
unhistorical and misshapen characters.  Its earliest shape can
be well studied in Fig. 287, derived from a manuscript declared
by Ludwig Traube to be written at Tours about 820.  As will
be seen, if the i's were dotted, if the perpendicular stroke
of the t were continued upward, and if the long ſ were
reduced to s, every letter could be easily read at once.
Fortunate would it have been for researchers if this high
standard had been maintained in the thirteenth, fourteenth,
and fifteenth centuries.

## 2. *The Norman Conquest.*

In general terms it may be said that, from the point
of view of literature, both the English language and the

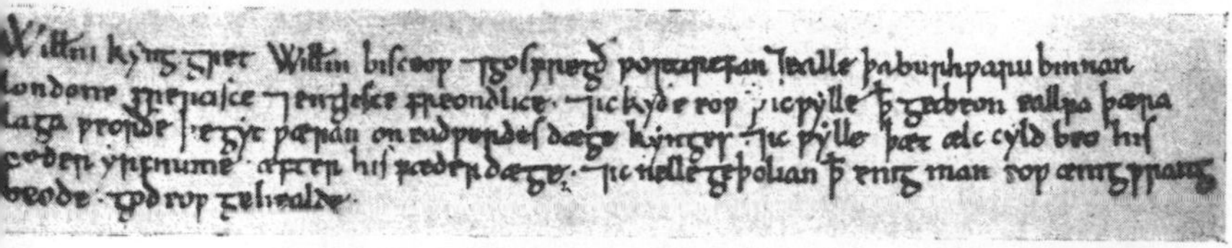

FIG. 288.  ENGLISH HAND OF 1066.  First charter of
London.  (A.D. 1066, in Old English, written in insular script.  Transcr.
*William Kyng gret William bisceop & gosfregth porterefan & ealle tha burhwaru
binnan | Londone frencisce & englisce freondlice.  & ic kythe eow that ic
wylle that get beon eallra thæra | laga weorthe the gyt wæran on eadwardes dæge
kynges . . . | &c.  MS. in the Guildhall, London.)*

English writing sank out of sight in the second half of the
eleventh century.  We know that neither actually died,
but Norman-French (or Latin) and the continental style
of writing took their place for all public and most private
purposes.  The going and the coming styles could not be
better represented than in Figs. 288, 289.  In the English
Charter to London, granted soon after the battle of Hastings
(1066), the king wisely allows the writing (and the language)
to be English, and the three distinctive Insular letter-
forms of f, g, r, though moribund, all occur even in the first
line.  In the Latin extract from Domesday (1086) we find
the Carolingian minuscule, as modified from its earliest
form, and without a trace of English influence.  Yet the
persistence of the four genuine Old-English letters shows

clearly that the national hand was only, as it were, pressed beneath the surface. Those four are

ᵽ = w (wen)　　Died out about A.D. 1300; rare in the thirteenth century.

þ = th (thorn)　Survived till the fifteenth century, and was printed as y (in ẏ = the).

ð = th (barred *d*)　Survived till the fifteenth century.

ȝ = gh　　　　Existed side by side with the continental g till about A.D. 1100, and was then differentiated, as the *gh* in such a word as *night*; and as such lasted till the fifteenth century.

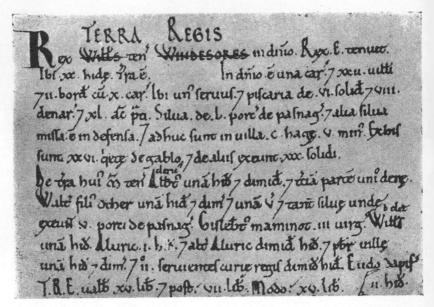

FIG. 289. DOMESDAY BOOK, WINDSOR. A.D. 1085: a general survey of England, in the Continental Minuscule, but written in England. Transcr. *Rex Willelmus tenet Windesores in dominio* [demesne]. *Rex E[dwardus] tenuit.* | *Ibi xx hidæ. Terra est. In dominio est una caruca et xxii uillani* | *& ii bordarii cum x carucis. Ibi unus seruus & piscaria de vi solidis & viii* | *denariis.* .... MS. in Public Record Office, London.

### 3. *The Twelfth Century.*

In the twelfth century English handwriting reaches its high-water mark. It exhibits the best form attainable by the Carolingian Minuscule, and is distinguished by size,

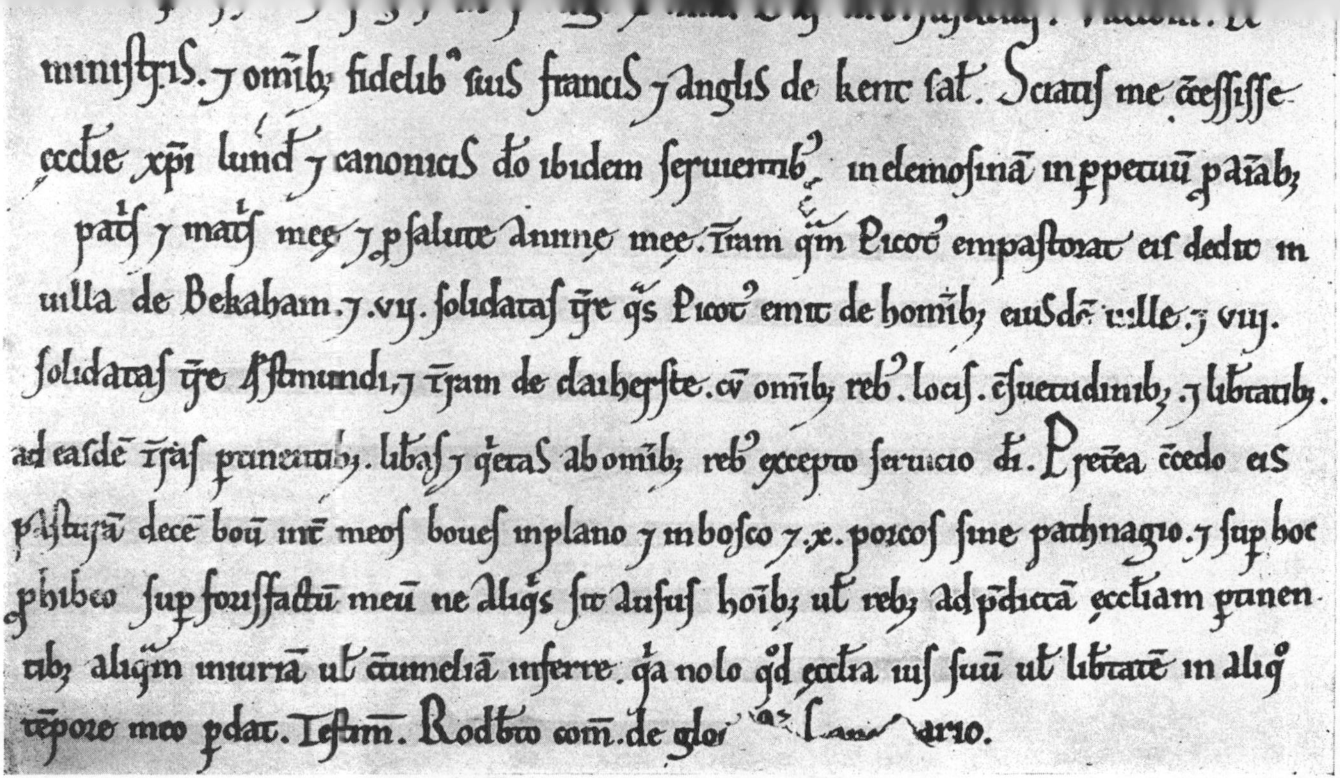

FIG. 290. FINE ENGLISH TWELFTH-CENTURY HAND. A.D. 1141. Grant by the Empress Maud to Christ Church, London. Transcr. M[atildæ] imperatrix H[enrici] regis filia & anglorum domina Baronibus Justiciariis Vicecomitibus et ministris et omnibus fidelibus suis francis & anglis de kent sal[utem] Sciatis me concessisse | &c. MS. in Public Record Office, London.

boldness, firmness of stroke, roundness of outline, and elegance : there is hardly an unnecessary stroke and hardly an ambiguous one. Fig. 290 gives an example of this hand, with a few modifications showing the beginnings of *Court-hand*, the name given to the legal script so soon as it diverged from the literary. On the Continent it is found as early as the ninth century, but in England hardly occurs before the late eleventh. If we remove the long *s* (∫), and the lower half of the long *r*, and straighten the part of *p* and *q* below the line, a good idea may be gained of the ordinary hand from Fig. 290.

The central position of this fine hand may be brought out by a few sets of comparative tendencies, which being stated in very general terms are subject to exceptions in detail.

| *Before.* | *XII.* | *After.* |
|---|---|---|
| Roundness. | — | Angularity. |
| Archaistic roughness, want of uniformity. | Care and method. | Decadent carelessness about essentials. |
| Varieties of size. | Large size in general use for the last time. | General use of minute characters. |
| Court-hand forming itself. | — | Developed court-hand of special difficulty. |

It is not the twelfth-century hand, but the influences under which it deteriorated in the next four centuries which cause difficulty to the researcher. Those influences were the change from a rounded to an angular script (which obliterated all differences between *minimum* and *munimini*, for instance) ; the effect of the court-hand, which has always delighted in artificial forms ; the increase of abbreviations ; and most of all a general carelessness about the essential parts of each letter (i.e. the history and *differentia* of each shape were not considered), coupled with the growing need of writing rapidly rather than clearly. The difficulties connected with abbreviations are so insistent, that even in this brief survey it is necessary to classify them and present them in a clear order to our readers (see pp. 466–9).

## 4. *The Thirteenth Century.*

The multiplication of records and the greater demand
for books caused a smaller hand to be used, with many
contractions and with letters written more closely together.
In fact the minute Latin bibles of this period are almost
pocket volumes, so small (but careful) is the script. The
chief characteristic is the angularity of the elements (for
example) which make up *i, m, n, u,* no longer $\iota$ but $\iota$.
The *i*'s are therefore usually marked with a stroke above,

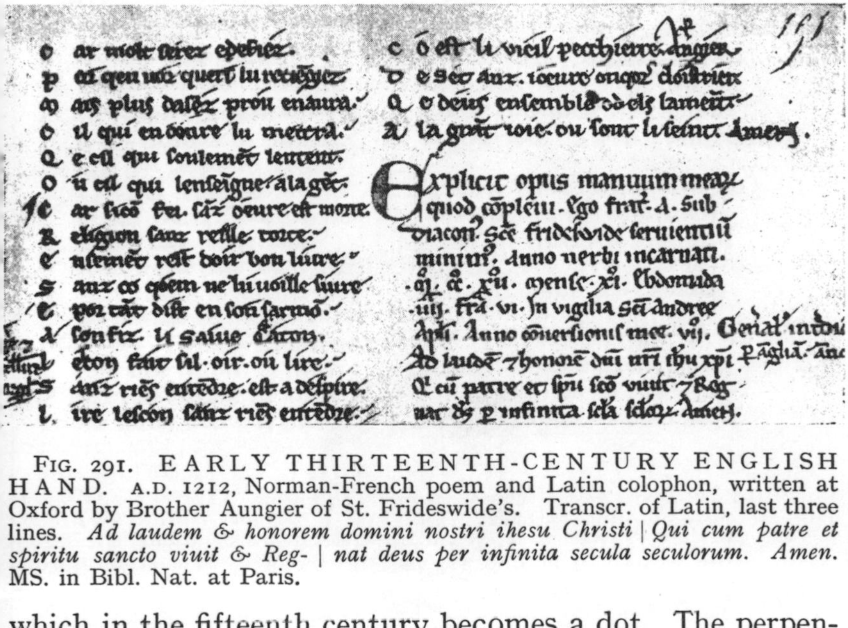

FIG. 291. EARLY THIRTEENTH-CENTURY ENGLISH
HAND. A.D. 1212, Norman-French poem and Latin colophon, written at
Oxford by Brother Aungier of St. Frideswide's. Transcr. of Latin, last three
lines. *Ad laudem & honorem domini nostri ihesu Christi | Qui cum patre et
spiritu sancto viuit & Reg- | nat deus per infinita secula seculorum.* Amen.
MS. in Bibl. Nat. at Paris.

which in the fifteenth century becomes a dot. The perpendicular stroke in a *t* (τ) now first (about 1250) begins to
appear above the horizontal stroke, reaching the height
of the modern letter in the second half of the fifteenth
century. The upper bow of the *a* (a) tends to close on to
the top of the lower, by about 1275 ; *u* and *v* initial begin
to be distinguished. There are still traces of the clearer
twelfth-century style, but the *facilis descensus* has begun.
In court-hand *b, h,* and *l,* there is a fine form characteristic
of English writing, in which the upper loop of the stem
is duplicated on the left-hand side (φ). Dateless deeds are
usual before 1300, and never found after. See Figs. 291–3.

## 5. *The Fourteenth Century.*

Nearly all simplicity of writing is gone, the forms become more artificial, and the letters more difficult to

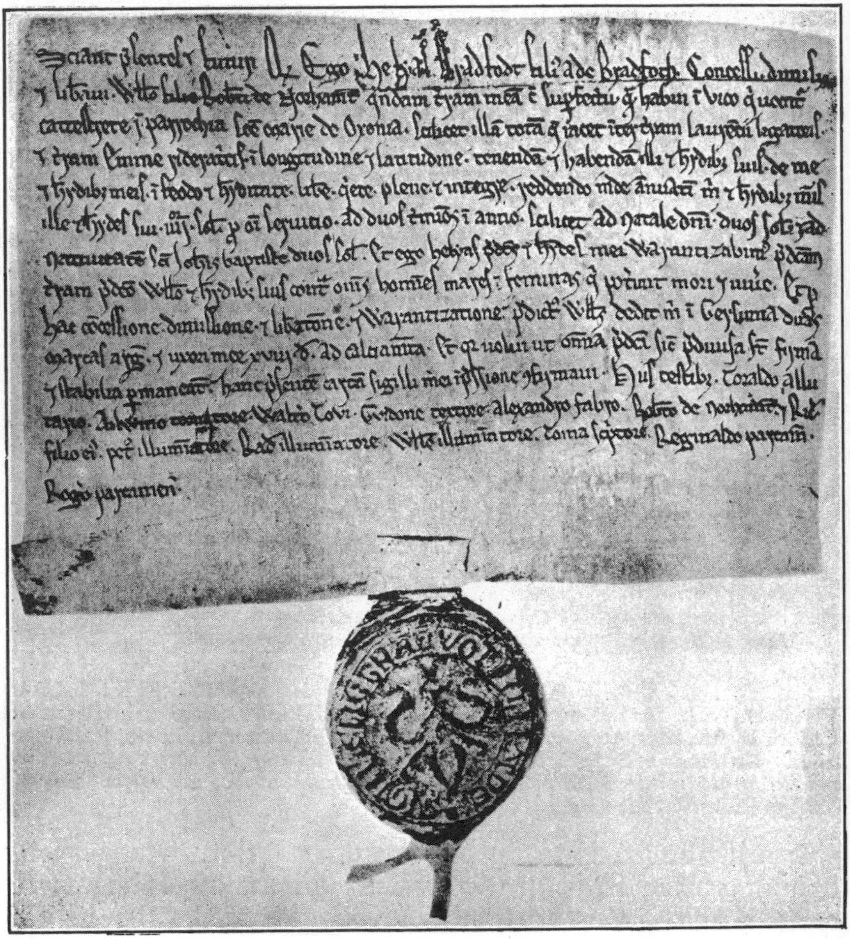

FIG. 292. THIRTEENTH-CENTURY ENGLISH COURT-HAND. About 1220. Complete grant written at Oxford in Latin. Transcr. *Sciant presentes & futuri Quod ego helyas Bradfodt filius Ade Bradfoth Concessi dimisi | & liberaui Willelmo filio Roberti de Norhamton quandam terram meam cum superfectu quam habui in vico qui vocatur | &c.* MS. in Oxford University Archives.

read. The exception is liturgical books, in which a large and clear hand was absolutely necessary. In them the shapes of letters are the stiff small hand enlarged, but by now, for instance, the upper bow of *a* is heavily closed, and the

letter looks almost like an angular 8. The formality and
extravagance of the capitals of the court-hand are fully
developed, and can hardly be said to have any obvious
connexion with the earlier forms. For instance, C may be
⊕, E ⊕, G ⊕, S ⊕ or ⊖. In short a student can only study
Wright's *Court Hand Restored*, or deal with the capitals

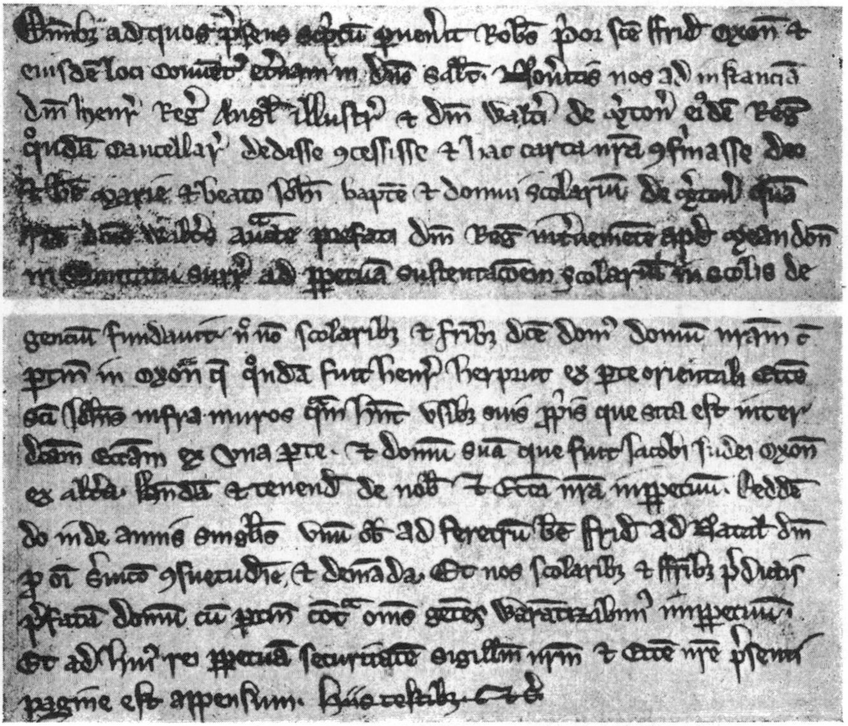

FIG. 293. THIRTEENTH-CENTURY ENGLISH HAND.
About 1310–20. Grant from St. Frideswide's to Merton College, Oxford.
Transcr. *Omnibus ad quos presens scriptum peruenerit Robertus Prior sancte
Frid[eswide] Oxon[ie] &* | *eiusdem loci conuentus eternam in domino salutem.
Noueritis nos ad instanciam* | &c. MS. at Corpus Christi College, Oxford.

as if they were a cryptogram, but when once proficient he
will trace the ancient forms in their new disguise, and in
the ordinary book-hand he will recognize some merit,
since the numerous abbreviations are not used at random
and the changes of form exhibit evolution.

## 6. *The Fifteenth Century.*

The accelerated writing, now imperatively needed, was
not counterbalanced by any proper sense of its inevitable

defects. If the eyes and temper of mankind were to be saved, it was high time for printing to come in. Europe may be said to have passed in many cases from book-hand to cursive, the scribble hand which is older than book-hand, and has had some effect on almost all styles, but had never before dominated any. Unless we are dealing with legal documents, which were more carefully but not more clearly written than the common hand, or with luxurious liturgical or other volumes, the study of handwriting becomes a task of increasing difficulty. The more elaborate letters, especially in their capital form, have, as it were, fallen to pieces (see Figs. 294–6) ; the marks of abbreviation are irregular in shape ; and the alteration of shapes of letters meaningless. The principles and rules of palaeography can therefore no longer be stated shortly, and nothing will supersede a close attention to facsimiles or originals.

The prospect is not, however, without some redeeming features. The most striking is the course of events which on the Continent developed the roman type of the printing-press. The saving power of Charles the Great has been referred to on pp. 453–5 ; but who could have foreseen that Niccolo de' Niccoli at Florence (a little before 1430) would have selected the best twelfth-century form of the Carolingian minuscule for a new *scrittura umanistica* or *rotonda* which should provide Italian nobles with clear and pure writing, and incidentally supply to the early printers their roman type in 1467 ? The writing itself, however, did not reach England till the sixteenth century ; see below. And again, the beauty of the illuminations, which increased through this period and produced a careful script to correspond, makes some fifteenth-century MSS. the most splendid known.

After the Reformation we reach the period of modern English writing, which is best studied in connexion with the seventeenth century. The wide spread of printing tended to restrict the use of handwriting to dispatches, letters, and formal records ; and palaeography loses much of its importance. The interesting point about it is that the new 'Italian hand' described above is found side by side with the angular or 'Gothic' hand, from about 1540 onwards, and many persons in the public service could write in either hand, according to the subject-matter.

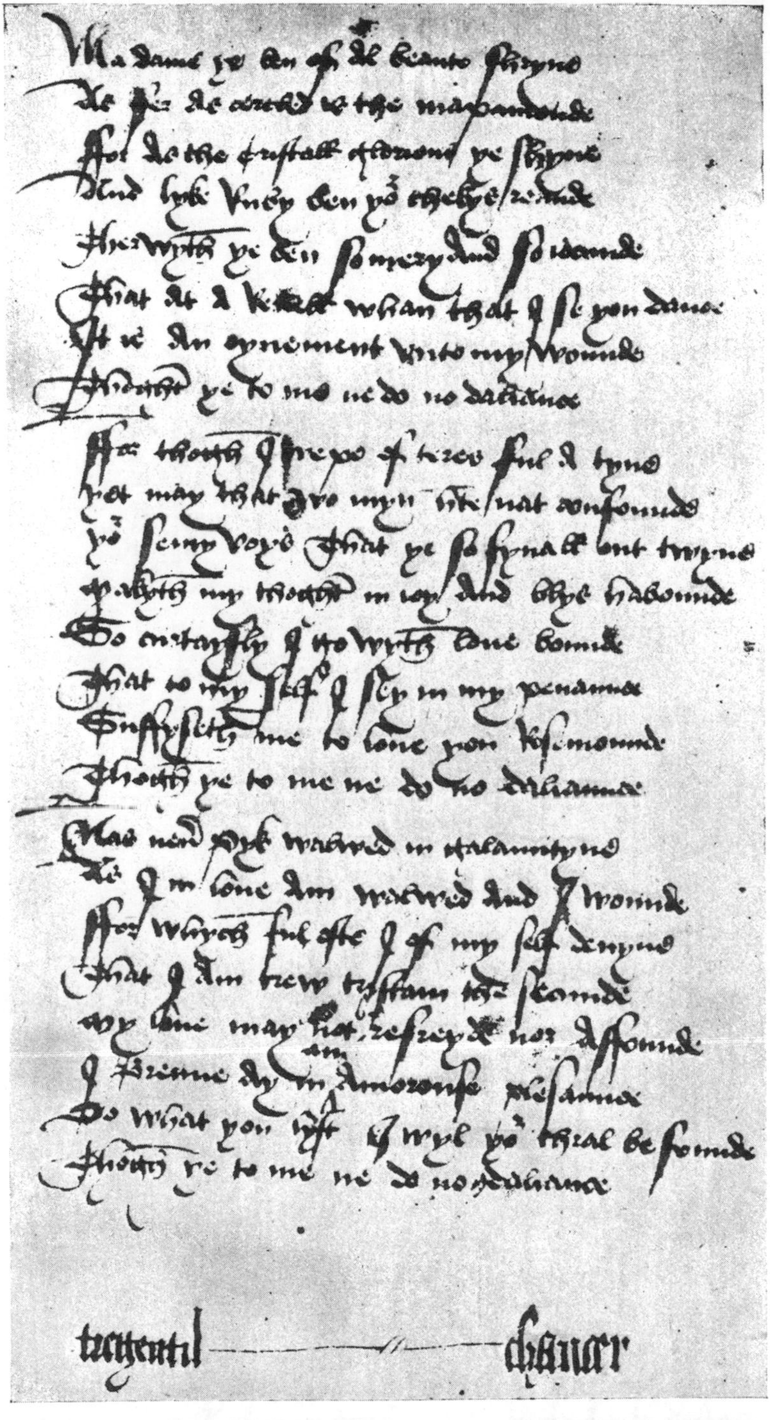

FIG. 294. ENGLISH FIFTEENTH-CENTURY HAND. About 1450. Poem by Chaucer. Transcr. *Madame ye ben of al beaute shryne* | *As fer as cercled is the mapamonde* [mappa mundi] | *For as the Cristalle glorious ye shyne* | &c. Bodl. MS. Rawl. Poet. 163, fol. 114ʳ.

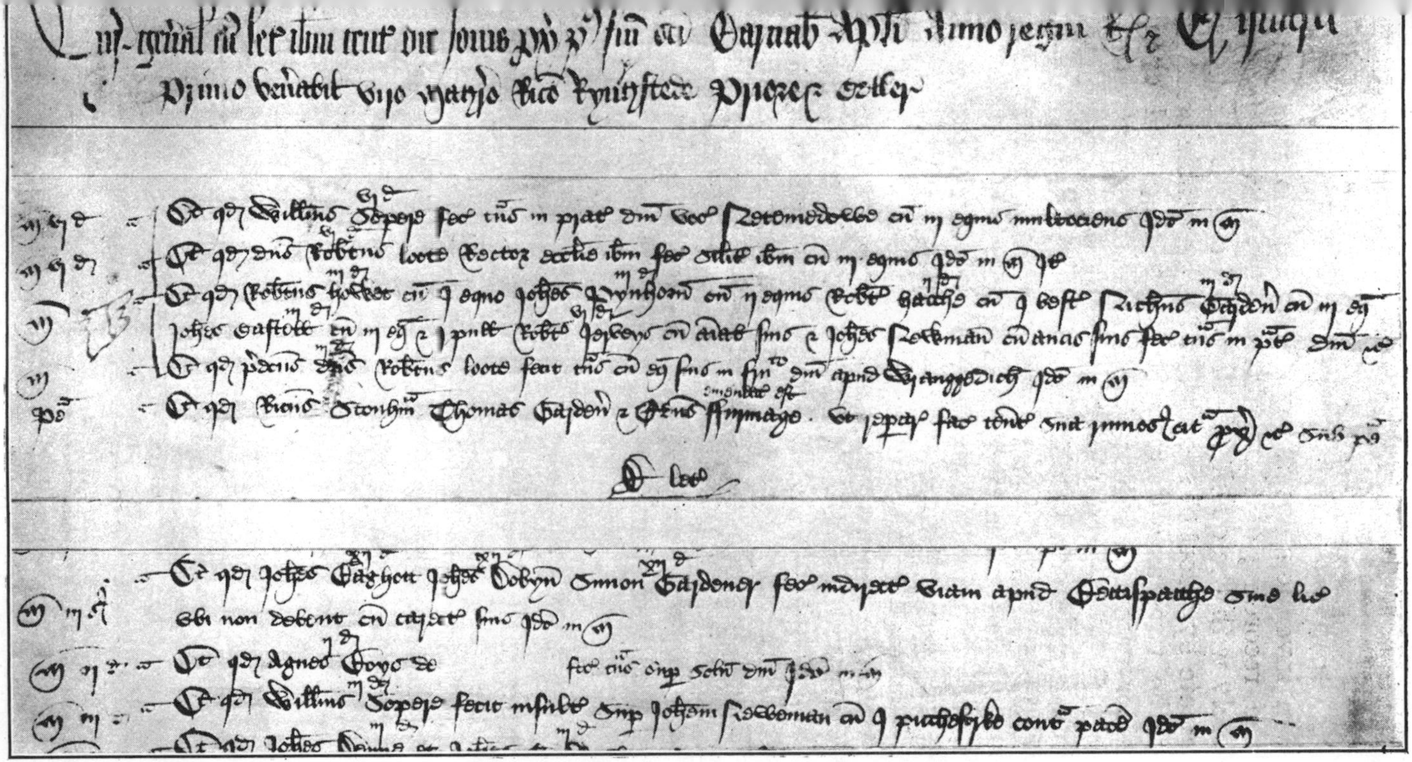

FIG. 296. ENGLISH FIFTEENTH-CENTURY COURT-HAND. A.D. 1461, a Little Barton [Suffolk] Court Roll. Transcr. *Curia generalis cum leta ibidem tenta die Iouis* [Thursday] *proximo post festum Barnabe Apostoli. Anno regni Regis E[dwardi] quarti* | *Primo venerabili viro Magistro Ricardo Ryngstede Priore & cellerario* | &c. 7th line *Et* [dicunt] *quod predictus dominus Robertus loote fecit transgressionem cum equis suis in fruticeto domini apud Wranggediche. Ideo in miseri-cordia* | penult. line: *Et quod Willelmus Sopere fecit insultum super Johannem Neweman cum J* [=una] *piccheforke* &c. | Bodl. MS. Suffolk Rolls I.

## 7. *Abbreviations*.

Human invention has always been on the stretch to enable the recording of thought to correspond more and more closely with the quickness of thought itself. It seeks to abbreviate by a sort of shorthand the inevitable interval between the two, and thereby it saves time and even expense, for parchment has always been expensive. But there was fortunately a check to extreme abbreviation in the imperious necessity of being legible. The mediaeval system of abbreviation, like its writing (see p. 451), was a compromise between the two opposing forces.

There are two, and only two, systems of abbreviation found in European writing.

Abbreviation by *Suspension* is the older. Instead of a word we write the first part only, or the first letter or letters of each part, and omit all else. .Test. would stand for Testamentum (Will), .Nt. for Noster. But this gives no indication whatever of the termination, and so (like all abbreviation) could only be used in well-known expressions or words where mistake was hardly possible. This system was employed especially by the old Roman jurists, who used recurring formulae of law, but it has left traces of itself throughout mediaeval palaeography, as will be seen.

The other system is Abbreviation by *Contraction*. In this we write the first letter or letters and the last letter of a word, often with one striking letter from the middle of the word. Thus dñs is dominus, n̄r noster, a superposed line invariably marking an abbreviated word. This system was first used in Hebrew, from a reluctance to write the divine names in full ; it thence passed through hellenizing Jews to the Greeks, and from them, about A.D. 300, to Rome. Even then the system was at first strictly confined to five *Nomina Sacra*, d̄s (Deus), īh̄s (Jesus), x̄p̄s (Christus), s̄p̄s (Spiritus), and dñs (Dominus) ; the Greek origin is clear, from the H in Jesus and X and P in Christus, which are Greek letters. From its convenience and from the fact that it gave some hint of the termination, the new system gradually gained ground, and reached Ireland and England in the eighth century.

The groundwork of the following scheme is therefore

Abbreviation by Contraction, with traces of Abbreviation by Suspension.

## (A) Abbreviation by Abbreviated Signs.

Nine were in common use in the Middle Ages.

| No. | Form. | Position. | Value. | Example. |
|---|---|---|---|---|
| i. | –  ~ | above preceding letter | -m or -n | Fig. 290, ll. 6, 11 |
| ii. | ካ  ʃ | do. | er, re, ir, ri (or, r) | Fig. 293, ll. 1, 2 |
| iii. | ⁊ | above, but following, preceding letter | -us (or, os) | Fig. 290, ll. 1, 5 |
| iv. | ᴎ  ⁊ | above preceding letter | -ur | |
| v. | ᴐ  ꝯ | on the line | con-, com- | Fig. 293, l. 4 |
| vi. | :, later ;, then ꝫ | on line | -(q)ue, -(b)us, et, -m | Fig. 290, l. 2 |
| vii. | ꝰ | on line | -rum | Fig. 290, l. 1 |
| viii. | ꝑ | on line | -is or -es, as a termination (e.g. regꝑ = regis or reges) | |
| ix. | { – , | above preceding letter⎫ above, but following, preceding letter ⎬ | a general sign indicating suspension (e.g. -n̄, -ñ, -n') | Fig. 290, l. 11 |

Of the above, some are Tironian notes or Notae Iuris (see p. 468) from classical times. No. vi is an early general note of Suspension, curiously restricted in later times to -que and -bus. *Et* seems to have been drawn in by the *que*. The symbol happens to collide with a careless dropping form of *m*. We still use the mark in ' viz.', i.e. v̄ꝫ. (videlicet). In No. vii the 2 is an old form of r, and the bar is a mark of suspension. No. ix is a common sign, convenient for scribes who were shaky in their Latin, for Oxō would stand for Oxonia, Oxonienses, Oxoniensibus, &c.·

## (B) Abbreviation by Position of Letters.

x. Vowels superposed on the letter preceding indicate the omission of an *r* before or after the vowel, e.g. c̊men = crimen ; ůbi = uerbi, not ubi ; g̊ue = graue ; fig̊at = figurat, not figat.

xi. *q*—which is invariably followed by *u*—may have any vowel superposed except *u*, and then the *u* may be omitted (e.g. q̊ = quo ; aq̊ = aqua ; q̇ = qui.

Also, xii, *p* is modified in three ways with definite meanings : p̄ = pre ; p͜ = per ; ꝓ = pro.

## (C) Abbreviation by Contraction.

xiii. This, as has been explained on p. 466, is subject to three conditions : the word must be in common use ; the first letter at least and the termination must be preserved, as well as (often) one significant letter from the middle ; and the result should not be ambiguous. A horizontal line over the word indicates contraction. Examples are e̅p̅s̅ = episcopus, o̅e̅ = omne, o̅m̅ = obiectum, si̅r = similiter.

Some of the commonest of these contractions which follow general rules are next given, and then some special ones of an irregular type.

xiv. Common *regular* contractions (which can be carried through all the cases of the noun).

-a̅o̅ = -atio ; -a̅o̅e̅m = -ationem, &c., but r̅o̅ = ratio, r̅o̅e̅ = ratione. So -o̅e̅, -o̅i̅s̅ = -ione, -ionis.

bi̅s̅ = beatus ; d̅c̅s̅ = dictus, s̅c̅o̅ = sancto.

fr̅ = frater (so p̅r̅ = pater) ; fr̅e̅m = fratrem, but fm̅ = festum ; fc̅um = factum (fc̅o̅ = facto, &c.) ; fto = falso.

hr̅e = habere ; ħendum = habendum, &c.

lr̅e = litere.

m̅a̅ = materia ; m̅i̅a̅ = misericordia *or* miseria, m̅r̅ = mater *or* martyr.

n̅r̅ = noster ; u̅r̅ = uester, u̅r̅i̅ = uestri, &c.

q̅m̅ = *not* quum, but quoniam.

q̅n̅ = quando (abbreviation by suspension).

ẝ : the long s (ſ) so modified represents ser ; ẝm is used for secundum (' according to ', *not* ' second ').

t̅m̅ = tantum.

t̅n̅ = tamen.

### Special Forms.

xv. g̓ = igitur ; g̊ = ergo ; ·i· = id est ; l̵ = uel (*not* lege) ; ·N· = enim ; ·s· = scilicet ; ∻ = est ; ↄ = eius ; 7 = &. Several of these are Tironian notes or Notae Iuris, i.e. either short-hand of Cicero's time, or used by early Roman jurists.

The normal arabic numerals (in use from the fourteenth century onwards) are :

*0, 1, 7, 3, 8, ᛃ, 6, ᚠ, 8, 9*

The foregoing minimum of principles and facts about writing and abbreviation will, with the plates, give a student a fair chance of starting for himself on a mediaeval document. And the following brief list of books of reference will assist him when further information is needed.

### Books for reference.

MAUNDE THOMPSON, *Greek and Latin Palaeography*, 1912.
—— ' English Handwriting ' (*Bibliogr. Soc. Transactions*, 1899, 1901).
WRIGHT, *Courthand Restored*, edited by Martin, 1912.
JOHNSON, C. & JENKINSON, H., *English Court Hand*, 1066 to 1500 A.D., 1915.
MARTIN, *Record Interpreter*, 1910.
MADAN, *Books in Manuscript*, 1920.
*Facsimiles of National MSS.* England, 1865–8.
Ibid. Ireland, 1874–84.
Ibid. Scotland, 1867–71.
Palaeographical Society, *Facsimiles*.
For lists of Abbreviations use Chassant (1876) or Cappelli (1912); in court-hand, Jenkinson, as above.
The British Museum has issued Facsimiles of Ancient Charters, 1873–8 and Notable Autographs, 1896–1900.
KELLER, W., *Angelsächsische Palaeographie*, Berlin, 1906.

## § 3. PRINTED BOOKS, THE BOOK-TRADE, AND LIBRARIES

### 1. *Printing*.

The introducer of printing into England, William Caxton, was born in Kent about the year 1420. Most of his life was spent in business on the Continent, where he became Governor of the English Nation in the Low Countries.[1] By the year 1469 he had also entered the service of the Duchess of Burgundy, for whom he made various translations. His work proved popular, but the task of copying becoming burdensome he decided to multiply copies of his translations by the novel art of printing. Caxton seems to have learnt this in Cologne, but it was at Bruges that he printed, with the assistance of Colard Mansion, in 1475, the *Recuyell of the Historyes of Troye,* the first book printed in the English language. The year following Caxton returned to England, and set up a printing press at Westminster. In 1477 his first dated book, the *Dictes or Sayengis of the Philosophers*, appeared. From that date to 1491

---

[1] The Governor was an official of the association of Merchant Adventurers; he was elected by the members who resided in the Low Countries. His headquarters were at Bruges. He acted as an arbitrator in disputes between English merchants and represented them in correspondence with the home government.

Caxton printed ninety-six separate books, the most notable being Chaucer's *Canterbury Tales*, Malory's *Morte d' Arthur*, and the *Golden Legend*.

Caxton died in 1491 and left all his materials to his apprentice, Wynkyn de Worde, who printed over one hundred books in the fifteenth century, the majority being works of a popular character in English. In 1500 De Worde moved from Westminster to London, where he continued printing until 1534, by which time he had produced from 700 to 800 books. The other fifteenth-century printers of Westminster and London were Julian Notary, John Lettou, William de Machlinia, and Richard Pynson.

Oxford was the first provincial town in which a press was set up. Its earliest production was Rufinus's *Expositio in simbolum Apostolorum*, which, although dated ' MCCCCLXVIII ', was almost certainly printed in 1478, the figure X having accidentally dropped out of the date. The name of the printer is not given, but it is generally assumed that he was Theodoric Rood of Cologne, whose name appears in 1481 as printer of the Oxford edition of Alexander de Hales's commentary on the *De Anima* of Aristotle. Four years later Rood is found associated in his business with Thomas Hunte, a University stationer. Seventeen books are assigned to the fifteenth-century Oxford press, but some of them are known only from fragments.

St. Albans had a printing press in 1480 ; the printer's name is unknown. He is generally called the Schoolmaster Printer, because of a reference to him by Wynkyn de Worde, who states in one of his books that it had also been printed by one sometime ' scole master of saynt Albons '. The most notable production of the press is the famous *Boke of St. Albans*, which treats of hawking, hunting, and heraldry. Eight books are known to have issued from this press, which ceased working, with the Oxford press, in 1486.

In London alone was there any continuity of printing ; Wynkyn de Worde, Pynson, and Notary carried on their work into the sixteenth century, Copland, Faques, Redman, Berthelet, and Rastell being the more notable of their contemporaries or successors. The Oxford press resumed work from 1517 to 1519, and then broke off again till 1585. St. Albans also had a press working from 1534 to 1538. Other towns at which books were printed before 1550 were York

(1509), Cambridge (1521), Tavistock (1525), Abingdon (1528), Ipswich (1547), Worcester (1549), and Canterbury (1549). Printing was introduced into Scotland by Andrew Myllar, who issued in 1508 a few poetical tracts. The most important work of this printer is the Aberdeen *Breviary* of 1510. No press existed in Ireland before 1551, in which year Humphrey Powell printed an edition of the Book of Common Prayer in Dublin.

It is a significant fact that the first book printed in England was in the vernacular. In no other European country

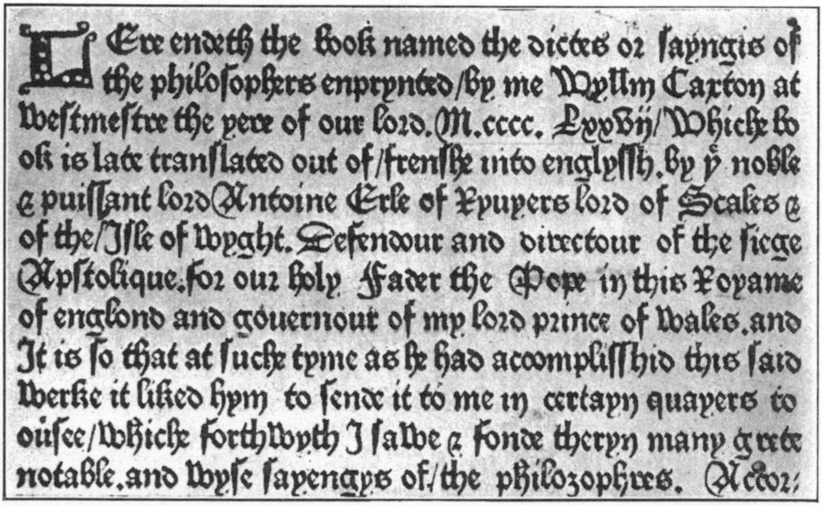
Here endeth the book named the dictes or sayngis of
the philosophers enprynted/by me Wyllm Caxton at
Westmestre the yere of our lord. M.cccc. Lxxvij/Whiche bo
ok is late translated out of/frenshe into englysshe. by ye noble
& puissant lord Antoine Erle of Ryuyers lord of Scales &
of the/Isle of Wyght. Defendour and directour of the siege
Apstolique. for our holy Fader the Pope in this Royame
of englond and gouernour of my lord prince of Wales. and
It is so that at suche tyme as he had acomplisshid this said
werke it liked hym to sende it to me in certayn quayers to
ousee/Whiche forthwyth I sawe & fonde therin many grete
notable. and wyse sayengys of/the philozophres. Accor:

Fig. 297. FROM DICTES OF THE PHILOSOPHERS.
Printed by Caxton, '1477' [*c.* 1490].

where printing was practised in the fifteenth century was such the case. The majority of books printed by Caxton were in English, many being of a popular character. His successor, De Worde, also issued a large number of small popular poems and tracts. Besides this popular literature, service books, law treatises, and minor theological and scholastic books were printed in considerable numbers by the earlier English printers, but for editions of the Bible, Latin and Greek classical texts, and works of scholarship generally, England was dependent on the Continent.

The first classical text published in England is an edition of Cicero's *Pro Milone* printed by Theodoric Rood of Oxford about 1480. The earliest specimen of Greek movable type is found in a motto on the title-page of a book printed by Siberch at Cambridge in 1521. De Worde had previously used a few Greek words in some of his books, but they had been printed from wood-blocks. A Chrysostom printed by Wolfe of London in 1543 is the earliest Greek text printed in England.

The *editio princeps* of the English Bible was printed on the Continent in 1535 at some place unknown. This was Coverdale's translation. The first Bible actually printed in England was produced by James Nicholson of Southwark in 1537. In the same year appeared 'Matthew's Bible', another Continental printed version. This was followed by the 'Great Bible' of 1539, printed partly in France and partly in England. In 1560 the Geneva version was published. This, the first popular edition of the Bible, is noteworthy for its small size, the use of Roman type, and the division of chapters into verses. The next important versions were the 'Bishops' Bible' (1568) and the Authorized Version (1611).

The press used by printers of the fifteenth century was made of wood, and of similar construction to the small platen presses of to-day. Two men sufficed to work it, one operating the lever of the press, the other inking the type with ink-balls.

Very many books printed in the fifteenth century are without name of printer, place of printing, or date. When these are given they are usually found in the colophon, that is, a paragraph at the end of the book giving details about its production. Sometimes the printer's device occurs. It is a curious fact that Caxton first used his device in the *Sarum Missal* of 1487, which was not printed by him but for him by W. Maynyal of Paris. Title-pages are uncommon; the earliest English book with a title-page is the *Treatise of the Pestilence*, printed by Machlinia about 1486.

In the lower margin of certain leaves in a printed book will generally be found a series of letters or numbers recurring at regular intervals. These are called 'signatures', and are intended to guide the binder when he 'gathers up' the sheets of the book he is about to bind. The first printer in England to use signatures was Theodoric Rood of Oxford. When a sheet is folded once it forms two leaves (a folio or

funt partim cū ad rhedam pugnari viderent et dño fuc,
crecere phibentur:Milonemq3 occisum ex ipso Clodio
audirent/et ita esse putarent:fecerunt id(dicam eni nõ
deriuandi criminis causa sed vt factum est)Neq3 impe,
rante/neq3 sciente/neq3 presente domino qd suos quisq3
seruos in tali re facere voluisset. hec sicut exposui/ita ges
ta sunt iudices:insidiator superatus:vi victa vis/vel po,
tius oppressa virtute audacia est. Nichil dico quid Res
pub. consecuta sit:Nichil quid vos/Nichil quid omnes
boni.Nichil sane id profit Miloni : qui hoc fato natus
est/vt ne si quidem seruare potuerit/qm̄ vna Rem pu/
vosq3 seruaret.Si id iure non possit:Nichil habeo quod
defendat.Sin hoc & ratio doctis/et necessitas barbaris/
& mos gentibus et feris natura ipsa prescripsit:vt om,
nem semp vim quacūq3 ope possent/a corpore/a capite
de vita sua ppulsarent:Non poteftis hoc facinus impbū
iudicare:qm̄ simul iudicetis ommbue/qui in latrones in,
ciderint:aut illor telis/aut vestris sentencijs esse peun,
dum.Quod si ista putasset:certe optabilius miloni fuit/

FIG. 297A.  CICERO, PRO MILONE.  [Oxford,
c. 1480.]  The first classic printed in England.

# The new testament.

The gospell of S.Mathew.
The gospell of S.Marke.
The gospell of S.Luke.
The gospell of S. Jhon.
The Actes of the Apostles

## The epistles of S. Paul.

The epistle vnto the Romaynes.
The first and seconde epistle to the Corinthians
The epistle to the Galathians.
The epistle to the Ephesians.
The epistle to the Philippians.
The epistle to the Colossians.
The first and secöde epistle to the Tessalonians
The first and seconde epistle vnto Tymothy.
The epistle vnto Titus.
The epistle vnto philemon.

The first and seconde epistle of S.peter.
The thre epistles of S. Jhon.
The epistle vnto the Hebrues.
The epistle of S. James.
The epistle of S. Jude.
The Reuelacion of S. Jhon.

FIG. 297 B.  COVERDALE'S BIBLE, 1535.  Title-page of
the New Testament.

fol.) ; when twice, four leaves (a quarto or 4to) ; when thrice, eight leaves (an octavo or 8vo). These are the normal sizes of early printed books. Julian Notary, however, in 1500, published a minute book made up of sheets folded six times, thus making 64 leaves in a ' gathering '.

## 2. *Binding.*

Leather has always been the usual covering for books in Western Europe, although in early times manuscripts were sometimes cased in precious metals decorated with jewels. The earliest extant English leather binding is on a copy of the Gospel of St. John at Stonyhurst, and is supposed to be tenth-century work. The bindings produced at Durham and Winchester in the twelfth century are remarkable for the beauty of the dies used to stamp the leather. Fifteenth-century bindings have very distinct characteristics, and it is possible to identify a considerable number of them by means of the dies used for their decoration. The use of small stamps was continued until the beginning of the sixteenth century when a large stamp, called a ' panel', came into general use. This was succeeded by a tool of wheel shape called a ' roll', which by revolution could reproduce indefinitely the design cut upon it. The use of gold on bindings was popularized in England by the King's Printer, Thomas Berthelet (died 1555), who produced some very fine bindings in leather and velvet.

## 3. *Book Trade.*

Before the introduction of printing into England our knowledge of the production and selling of books depends largely on isolated facts gathered together from a variety of documents. The transcription and binding of manuscripts were carried on at most monastic foundations, while at literary centres such as Oxford, scribes, illuminators, binders, and parchment-sellers are found in considerable numbers from the twelfth century onwards.

Although it was an Englishman who introduced printing into England, yet it must not be assumed that Englishmen at first held any important place in the book-trade in England. Caxton is, in fact, the only known native fifteenth-century printer in England ; De Worde, Lettou, Machlinia, Notary, and Rood were all foreigners. And so it was with the book-trade generally. From 1476 to 1535 it is estimated that two-thirds of those engaged in the book-trade in England were foreigners. This influx of aliens was largely due to an Act of 1484 which allowed 'any artificer, or merchant stranger of what nation or country he be . . . or any scrivener, alluminor [illuminator], binder, or printer' to exercise their trade and to reside in England.

These foreign stationers not only had books printed for them on the Continent for sale in England, but established themselves at literary centres and attended fairs where any considerable trade in books was likely to be done. An account-book of John Dorne, an early sixteenth-century Oxford stationer, is still preserved, and shows that a large part of his trade was done at the Oxford book-fairs, and that he made periodical visits to the Continent to replenish his stock of books.

The book-trade flourished in England from the passing of the Act of 1484 until 1534, when another Act was passed, placing severe restrictions on foreign printers and stationers, and on the importation of ready-bound books. The Act was ostensibly for the protection of native workmen ; it was, however, also directed against the importation of prohibited books, for which there was a great demand. The number, for instance, of copies of Tyndale's New Testament printed on the Continent from 1525 to 1528 has been estimated at 18,000. From 1535 the book-trade in England rapidly declined and did not permanently revive until the reign of Elizabeth.

### 4. *Libraries.*

References to collections of books in the British Isles are frequent from the seventh century, but there is little information about the manner in which the earliest collections were stored. We read, for instance, of manuscripts at Canterbury in the age of St. Augustine, and of a library belonging to Alcuin at York in 778. In the twelfth century there were more than 300 works at Durham Priory and over 200 volumes at Christ Church, Canterbury. In the latter collection were works by Cicero, Plato, Terence, Sallust, Vergil, Horace, Lucan, Statius, Juvenal, Persius, Cato, and Ovid. These collections were probably kept in presses in the cloisters. where they were also read. In the cloisters of Gloucester Cathedral may be seen little alcoves, called carrells, where the monks of the Benedictine Abbey of St. Peter pursued their studies. Later, when monastic collections increased in size, special book-rooms were provided. In the book-room of Christ Church, Canterbury, at the end of the thirteenth century, the books were arranged in two *demonstrationes* (large general divisions), and then into *distinctiones* (probably book-cases), each *distinctio* having a certain number of *gradus* (shelves). The books

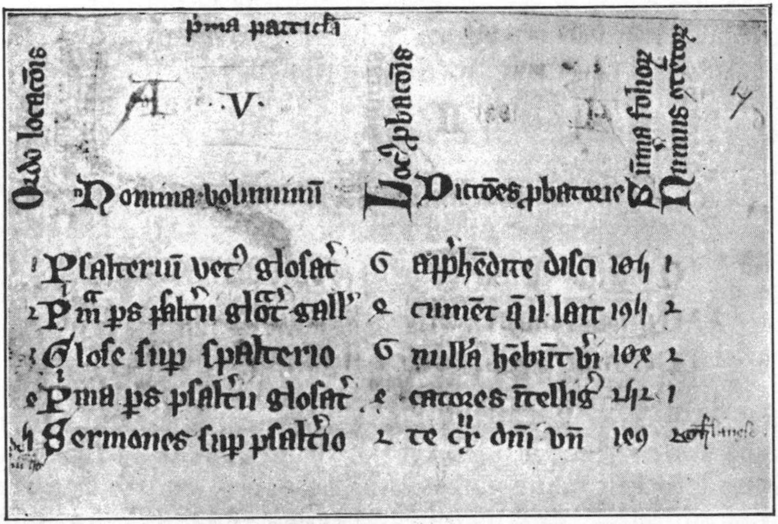

FIG. 298. FROM THE CATALOGUE OF DOVER PRIORY, 1389. MS. Bodl. 920.

were classified under groups such as Theology, History, Philosophy, Music, Medicine.

A considerable amount of information about the arrangement and classification of books in monastic libraries can be derived from their catalogues, of which several are extant. The illustration shows a portion of the catalogue of the Priory of St. Martin, Dover, compiled in 1389. This Library was divided into nine *distinctiones*, designated by the nine first letters of the alphabet, each being divided into seven *gradus* numbered with Roman figures. Each entry in the catalogue has six divisions (see Fig. 298): the first gives the shelf-mark A. v. 1 (Case A, shelf v, book 1); the second the book (an old glossed Psalter); the third, the leaf on which certain opening words, selected for the identification of the volume, occur (i. e. on leaf 6); the fourth, the two first words on that leaf (*apprehendite disci*); the fifth, the number of leaves in the volume (i. e. 105); and the sixth, the number of works contained in the volume (viz. one).

The provision of a special building for a library seems not to be found before the fourteenth century. The aspect favoured by the early builder of collegiate libraries was one with the walls facing east and west, so that advantage might be taken of the morning sun, light rather than warmth being essential to the student. With the decline of asceticism and a greater desire for physical comfort a warmer aspect was often chosen. The lighting of the building was secured by lancet windows placed closely together.

The earliest libraries were probably fitted up with book-cases in the shape of lecterns, to which the books were chained on either side. When books and readers were few this was convenient enough, but, when they multiplied, the lecterns became crowded and one reader hindered another. The development of the lectern was a case (still having counters on either side) with a flat top, above which two or three shelves were fixed. Along the shelves ran a rod, to which were attached chains, the other ends of which were secured to the manuscripts. This system, which has been styled the stall-system, naturally accommodated a much larger number of books and left the counters free for those actually in use. The practice of fitting cases against the walls of a library and carrying them from floor to ceiling is in England a late development of library economy. The Arts End (1612) of the Bodleian Library at Oxford is the earliest example of the style in this country.

No example of the lectern system any longer exists in England, but the cases in Queens' College Library, Cambridge, show traces of having been converted from lecterns, and there is documentary evidence to prove that Pembroke College Library, Cambridge, was fitted with lecterns until 1617. Apparently the only surviving example of the style is the Library of the Church of SS. Peter and Walburga at Zutphen, in the Netherlands.

Several excellent examples of the stall system still survive. One of the finest is the west wing of the Library of

Merton College, Oxford, the best example of a mediaeval library in England. The bookcases, each with four shelves on either side, are placed in the intervals between

FIG. 299. THE WEST WING OF MERTON COLLEGE LIBRARY, OXFORD.

the windows. On each side of a case are sloping counters, and between each pair of cases is a thick wooden bench. The building itself dates from about 1380, but there is reason to believe that the existing bookcases are of later date. Other good examples of the stall-system are the libraries of Corpus Christi College (1517) and St. John's

(1597–1636) at Oxford, and the Old Reading-room of the Bodleian Library (1602).

Of the two great English University Libraries that of Oxford has priority of foundation, while that of Cambridge can claim a longer continuous history. The University of Cambridge received its first important gift of books in 1424. Its earliest library was on the first floor of the west side of the Schools' Quadrangle, but the room seems to have been employed for the purpose for no great length of time. The chief Library (*Libraria communis*) was built in 1470 on the south side of the Quadrangle ; five years later another library was erected on the east side by the Chancellor of the University, Archbishop Rotherham. This smaller room was reserved for the archbishop's own library and the more valuable books possessed by the University. In the sixteenth century the fortunes of the Library declined to such an extent that the *Libraria communis* was disfurnished in 1547. When, however, the University received large gifts of books from Archbishop Parker and others towards the close of the century, the Library was restored to its former use.

Some idea of the routine of a mediaeval library may be gained by reciting some of the statutes framed for the Library (*Libraria communis*) of the University of Oxford, which was founded by Thomas Cobham, Bishop of Worcester, between the years 1320 and 1327. The Library, which was built above the Congregation House adjoining St. Mary's Church, was to be in the charge of two chaplains, one of whom was to be on duty before dinner, the other after. The books were to be secured by chains, and no one was to be admitted unless one of the chaplains was present. It was the duty of the chaplains to see that no reader entered the Library in wet clothes, or having pen, ink, or knife ; if notes had to be taken they were to be made in pencil.

Bishop Cobham died in 1327 heavily in debt, and there was some delay in securing the use of the Library for the University, but by 1337 its history may be said to begin, and by the beginning of the fifteenth century it was fully established. In 1412 a new code of statutes was formulated. It provided that the librarian, who in addition to his ordinary library duties said masses in St. Mary's Church for the souls of benefactors, should be subjected to a

FIG. 300.  LIBRARY OF WELLS CATHEDRAL.

yearly visitation by the Chancellor and Proctors. The librarian's salary was fixed at £5 6s. 8d. a year, to be paid half-yearly. In addition he might also claim a robe from every beneficed scholar at graduation. Should he desire to resign his office, a month's notice was required. Admission to the Library was restricted to students who had studied in the Schools for eight years, an exception being made in the case of the sons of lords who had seats in Parliament. Each reader on admission had to take an oath that he would not injure any book maliciously by erasing or by detaching sections and leaves ; theft of a whole volume was unlikely as the books were chained. The Library was to be open from 9 till 11 and from 2 till 4, except on Sundays and the greater festivals, when it was entirely closed. In the Long Vacation the librarian was allowed one month's holiday. All books used during the day were to be closed at night, and all the windows fastened.

The Library received, a few years later, munificent gifts from Humphrey, Duke of Gloucester. About 1485 the books from Cobham's Library were removed to the new building ('Duke Humphrey's Library') which had been erected above the Divinity School. In 1550 all the books were swept away by the Commissioners of Edward VI, and six years later the bookcases were sold as no longer necessary. In 1598 Sir Thomas Bodley refurnished Duke Humphrey's Library, which, in 1602, again became the library of the University, and is now not only one of the earliest public libraries in Europe, but the largest University library in the world.

## Books for reference.

CLARK, J. W., The Care of Books, 2nd edition, 1909.
DUFF, E. G., The Printers, Stationers, and Bookbinders of Westminster and London, 1906.
—— The English Provincial Printers, Stationers, and Bookbinders, 1912.
—— A Century of the English Book Trade, 1457–1557. 1905.
DARLOW, T. H., & MOULE, H. F., Historical Catalogue of the Printed Editions of Holy Scripture in the Library of the Bible Society, vol. i, 1903.
JAMES, M. R., The Ancient Libraries of Canterbury and Dover, 1903.
MACRAY, W. D., Annals of the Bodleian Library, 2nd edition, 1890.
MADAN, F., Oxford Books, 2 vols., 1912.
Munimenta Academica (Rolls Series), 2 vols., 1868.
SAVAGE, E. A., Old English Libraries, 1911.
SAYLE, C., Annals of the Cambridge University Library, 1916.

# XII

# ART

## 1. *Anglo-Saxon Art.*

JUST as the Roman occupation had almost entirely
ousted Celtic art from Roman Britain, so Roman art disappeared in its turn before the
English invasion. The conquest
did not in itself produce any new
artistic impulse, for the invaders
were less civilized than the conquered Britons. But it marks the
beginning of an epoch in which
various circumstances combined
to produce a definite artistic style
which may be described as Anglo-
Saxon. It was derived from two
sources, one coming from continental Europe, the other from
Ireland, where Celtic art had
taken refuge and developed independently. Both were intimately
connected with the Christian
Church.

With the coming of Augustine
and the Italian missionaries (597)
Southern England was once more
brought directly into connexion
with the traditional art of the
lands which had belonged to the
Roman Empire. That art, in its
home in Italy, was in a debased

FIG. 301. THE CROSS
OF ACCA. Middle of the
eighth century. Face and sides.
The back is covered with the
inscription. Sandstone. Nearly
14 ft. high when perfect. The
head is lost.

state at this period, but in two respects it was superior to
anything then existing in the British Isles. The first was
architecture. Celtic and Anglo-Saxon buildings were of
the most elementary character when of stone, and were
generally constructed only in wood. Italy had inherited

the tradition of classical architecture, though in a degraded form, and was beginning to develop out of this a distinctive style—the earliest Romanesque. Again, in the representation of the human figure, whether in sculpture or in

FIG. 302. THE ORMSIDE BOWL (outside view), *c.* 700. Diameter 5½ inches. Notice on the sides design of fanciful creatures and trees, of classical origin ; on the base, interlacing of Northern origin. Imitation jewels of coloured glass.

painting, the classical tradition gave to continental art a superiority over the style which had been developed out of the late-Celtic art in the Irish monasteries, though in decorative perfection it was far inferior.

It is more than half a century after the death of Augustine before we get any definite traces of Italian influence. Bishop Wilfrid and Benedict Biscop were the first to introduce into England builders and artists from Gaul and Italy. Of Wilfrid's church at Hexham (*c.* 672) we still possess fragments of scenes in bas-relief, and portions of a string-course representing in relief the baluster shafts [Fig. 6], which were a characteristic ornament of these buildings, and apparently of local origin. Baluster shafts employed in windows and doorways have also survived from Biscop's churches at Monkwearmouth (*c.* 675)

FIG. 303. FRONT OF THE FRANKS CASKET, eighth century. Length 9 inches. Left: Weland's revenge for his imprisonment by King Nithhad. At his anvil he fashions into a goblet the skull of one of the king's sons, whose body lies at his feet. The king's daughter with attendant brings a jewel to be mended. Behind them Egil, Weland's brother, catches birds from which Weland made himself wings. Right: the Wise Men bring their gifts to Christ in Mary's lap on a throne. Above, their name *Magi* and the star; below, a bird. The inscription reads: 'Whale's bone. The flood lifted the fish on to the steep shore; the ocean became turbid where he swam aground on the shingle.'

and Jarrow (685). But the finest examples of the decorative work of this period are to be found in the stone crosses mostly existing in the north of England. The perfection of both design and execution in the earliest specimens shows that they must be the work of foreign artists such as those brought over by Wilfrid and Benedict. They are in fact superior to any contemporary Italian carving that has survived. Two characteristics of that work are interlaced patterns and bands of conventional foliage.

These, combined with representations of the human figure and simple scenes in relief, are precisely the features of the 'Anglian' crosses. The earliest is that at Bewcastle (Cumberland), the Runic inscription on which, mentioning Alchfrith and his brother Ecgfrith, King of Northumbria, suggests a date about 670. The masterly design of its conventionalized vine-foliage, together with the dignity of pose and effective drapery of the figures which occupy one of the faces, give a high idea of the powers of the sculptor. There is a similar cross not far away at Ruthwell (Dumfries: cast in the Victoria and Albert Museum). To a later generation belongs the sepulchral cross of Acca, Bishop of Hexham (*d.* 740), preserved in the cathedral library at Durham [Fig. 301], on which the interlacing vine-scrolls are designed with even greater decorative skill than in the earlier examples. A unique example in metal-work of the art of this style and period is the bowl of silver lined with copper (both gilt) from Ormside (Westmorland), now in the York Museum [Fig. 302], the sides

FIG. 304. FONT AT DEER-HURST, eleventh or twelfth century. Local oolite stone. The bowl is 21 inches high. The base, decorated with similar spirals, and also interlacing, was found separately.

of which are decorated in *repoussé* with a fine design of conventional foliage, including fanciful birds and beasts. The early inspiration of this school of Anglian art was not maintained, and surviving examples show deterioration ending in positive barbarism. Here may be mentioned the fragments of the wooden coffin in which the body of St. Cuthbert was deposited in 698 (Cathedral Library, Durham), decorated with figures of saints and angels drawn in incised lines. They are elementary in character, and mainly interesting as showing their classical origin. A carved whale-bone casket in the British Museum (eighth century), interesting for its sacred, classical, and Norse subjects, with Runic inscriptions in the Northumbrian dialect, is rude in style [Fig. 303]. The font in Deerhurst church (Glos.),

FIG. 305. FONT AT BRIDEKIRK, *c.* 1150. Red freestone. On the band between the two lower scrolls is inscribed in North-English (Runic letters) : ' Richard, he me wrought, and to this beauty carefully me brought.'

probably not older than the eleventh or even twelfth century, illustrates a late survival of the characteristic Celtic design of the divergent spiral, bordered by bands of scroll-work of Italian (i.e. classical) derivation [Fig. 304].

Later, with the arrival of the Norsemen, an element of Scandinavian art was introduced into the district. Stories from the Edda appear on crosses, of which that at Gosforth (Cumberland: *c.* 900: cast in the V. and A. Museum) is the most notable instance. This so-called 'Viking' art is distinguished by an absence of the classical scroll-work, by peculiar forms of interlacing, and by the characteristic dragon monsters. The latter appear on the font at Bridekirk (Cumberland: cast in the V. and A. Museum) [Fig. 305], a late survival (*c.* 1150).

FIG. 306. DAVID PLAYING ON THE LYRE, early eighth century. Cotton MS. Vespasian A. i. David on his throne plays on a rote or lyre: the scribe on the left holds a roll, the one on the right writing tablets; both have a stilus. Below, two men dancing between four blowing horns. The chief colours are red, blue, green, and brown, with a sparing use of silver and gold.

Just as the two streams of missionary influence, the Irish and the Italian, met and coalesced in the north of England (Synod of Whitby, 664), so we find subsequent to that event a combination of the artistic elements which each side brought with it, the southern, however, tending always to predominate. The Irish influence is most noticeable in illuminated manuscripts. Thus the Durham Book or Lindisfarne Gospels (*c.* 700: British Museum) must be the work of some artist who, while thoroughly at home in the typical Irish ornament, copied with more or less success figure-subjects (the four Evangelists) from some South Italian MS. which had, perhaps, been brought to England by one of the companions of Archbishop Theodore (668–90). The Psalter of St. Augustine's Abbey, Canterbury (British Museum), of not much• later date and similar character, shows that this tendency to combine the best features in the two styles, Celtic ornament and Italian figure-subjects, spread to the south of England [Fig. 306].

Out of these elements there grew up in England an Anglo-Saxon art. The imported foreign culture took root, and by the time of Charles the Great the English mon-asteries (especially in the north) form centres of learning and art superior to anything in Western Europe out-side of Italy. Through Alcuin of York (735–804), the organizer of Charles's revival of learning, the Anglo-Celtic style influenced the Carolingian schools of manuscripts gener-ally. But we possess hardly any remains of this first period of Anglo-Saxon art. It came to an end with the ruin caused by the Danish invasions in the ninth century, and after this time the northern school (repre-sented by York and Lindisfarne) ceases to be important.

FIG. 307. THE VISIT OF THE THREE KINGS from the Bene-dictional of Æthelwold ; c. 970. Mary, seated under an arch (the star above) has a gold dress and red mantle ; the Child is in gold and violet. The kings have gold crowns, and garments of blue, green, red, and purple. The offering of the first seems to be a crown. The conventional clouds above are pink and white. The frame is gold with foliated ornaments in colours.

When Alfred (871–99) restored security a revival took place, but now the inspiration has to come once more from the continent, and the chief art centre is Winchester. The most important monuments of the later Anglo-Saxon period which have come down to us are the illuminated manu-scripts; and in these the influence of the Carolingian style, in which many artistic elements, eastern and western, united to enrich the old classical tradition, is apparent. The Benedictional of Æthelwold, Bishop of Winchester (963–84), in the Duke of Devonshire's library at Chats-

FIG. 308. LAZARUS RELIEF, CHICHESTER, eleventh century. Caen stone: about 3½ feet square. Mary and Martha receive Christ and the Apostles at the door of their house. The eyes are drilled for the insertion of artificial eye-balls. For zigzag edges of drapery folds compare Fig. 309. Notice the ancient classical design of the border above.

worth, shows what magnificent results were produced. Fine drawing of the figures with drapery of many folds in the classical style is combined with rich decoration in gold and colour [Fig. 307]. The conventional foliage of the borders is also mainly due to classical inspiration. In the course of the

tenth century a style
which, though of con-
tinental origin (e.g. the
Utrecht Psalter, ninth
century), became
characteristic of
Anglo-Saxon manu-
scripts, was developed
in the outline illustra-
tions having small
elongated figures, in
rather conventional
attitudes and with
fluttering drapery, but
far from contemptible
in drawing. The ulti-
mate source of inspira-
tion, as before, is to
be found in the classi-
cal style.

The Anglo-Saxon
coinage again, though
the designs are de-
rived from continental
models, shows a high
level of excellence.
The coins of Offa, King
of Mercia (755–96),
have been described
as the best drawn and
executed of Western
Europe between 750
and 1000. Of the rare
examples of finer
metal-work which
have come down to us
the most important is
the so-called 'Alfred
jewel' (Ashmolean
Museum, Oxford:
found in the Isle of
Athelney)—a human
figure (perhaps Christ)

FIG. 309. ANGLO-SAXON CARV-
ING: ADORATION OF THE MAGI,
c. 1000. 14 inches high. The child holds a
book, and Mary a flower. To the right of her
feet a small palm with dates. Above the kings
is the star. On the roof of the house or canopy
are an owl and a small human figure. The base
has a scene of wild life: a centaur with bow,
and two lions attacking a bear and a boar.

in coloured enamels enclosed in an elaborate gold setting with an inscription stating that ' Alfred commanded me to be made '. The peculiar and elementary drawing of the figure as well as the ornamental gold work recall certain forms of Irish art. An *ouche* or brooch of similar style, in which the crowned head of a man in enamel is framed in a border of gold

FIG. 310. ST. PAUL SHAKING OFF THE VIPER. Wall-painting: Canterbury, *c.* 1100. About 3 ft. 6 in. by 3 ft. 4 in. St. Paul has a pale red mantle over a white tunic. Blue background with greenish border; the conventional clouds above are shaded with red.

filigree work (British Museum : the Roach-Smith Jewel ; found in London), shows that the Alfred jewel was not unique. These pieces give a high idea of the skill of the Anglo-Saxon goldsmiths.

The sculpture of the later Anglo-Saxon period is rare, and there is an element of uncertainty in its identification. The 'Monks' Stone' in Peterborough Cathedral, a tomb recalling an ancient sarcophagus, with saints under arcades on its sides, may belong to the eleventh century. In Chichester Cathedral are two reliefs (the story of Lazarus : casts in the V. and A. Museum) which may be as old as 1000 [Fig. 308]. The ornamental border of one of them is almost identical with the design on the frame of a relief of the Crucifixion in Stepney Church, London. An important whale-bone carving in the Victoria and Albert Museum, representing the adoration of the Magi [Fig. 309], seems to belong to the same school.

## 2. *The Norman Period and Twelfth-Century Art.*

Though the Normans cannot be said to have introduced a new style into England, the Conquest marks an epoch in the history of English art owing to their great capacities as architects. The very frequent remains of Norman work in churches all over England show an immense architectural activity during the first century after the Conquest. In the later examples the capitals of the pillars are sometimes elaborately carved with conventional foliage or scroll-work (a fine series in St. Peter's, Northampton), and occasionally figure-subjects (e.g. at Romsey, Southwell, and in the crypt of Canterbury. Some figure-capitals from Westminster Hall may also be seen in the V. and A. Museum). The ordinary sculpture appears chiefly in the decoration of fonts [Fig. 305], and in the somewhat barbaric but vigorous reliefs over church doors (the tympanum). The later developments are illustrated by the elaborate carvings (belonging to different schools) of the west front of Lincoln Cathedral (*c.* 1160), the south porch of Malmesbury Abbey (*c.* 1160), the well-known door-

FIG. 311. DAVID PLAYING ON THE HARP. British Museum : Royal MS. 2 A. xxii. *c.* 1180. David wears a brown mantle lined with ermine over a violet tunic with gold jewelled borders ; white under-garment. Yellow harp. Back of throne blue. Gold background. Notice the bells hanging from the canopy. Frame salmon pink.

ways of Ely (*c.* 1150) and Rochester (*c.* 1180) Cathedrals, and the churches of Kilpeck (Herefordshire, *c.* 1150), Iffley (Oxon., *c.* 1160) [Fig. 9], and Barfreston (Kent, *c.* 1170).

The large wall-surfaces and simple vaulting or flat ceilings of the Norman churches gave an opportunity for pictorial decoration, the earliest paintings of the kind of which we have any remains in England. Those in Canterbury Cathedral were specially famous. To this series probably belonged the paintings still existing in St. Gabriel's chapel in the crypt, which represent Christ enthroned, and scenes (e. g. the Annunciation) in which the archangel Gabriel plays a part. They are drawn in strong outlines,

FIG. 312. THE CONVERSION OF THE HEATHEN. From a window in the north aisle of the choir, Canterbury Cathedral, end of the twelfth century.

The heathen (in white, green, red, yellow), in spite of the efforts of a devil (dull red, green wings) in the air, desert a temple containing an idol (pale blue against red background) behind an altar (gold, blue top) and follow Christ (red cross-nimbus, pink mantle) mounting the steps (green) of a church (red roof) with its altar (gold, white top) and font (purple). Blue background. The picture, as the texts above and below show, is a pendant to one of the Magi leaving Herod to visit Christ.

the colours being afterwards filled in. It need scarcely be said that the pose and elaborate drapery of the figures show their derivation from the ' classical ' style. Important as these pictures are in the history of English painting, they are careful rather than great works of art. Far finer is the (probably contemporary) figure of St. Paul in the chapel of St. Anselm in the upper church, a noble figure,

with finely drawn head and classical drapery, against a blue
background [Fig. 310]. The small church of Kempley
(Gloucestershire) has also preserved the original decoration
of its chancel (early twelfth century), which, for its scale,
is a singularly complete example of the wall-painting of
this period. And here we must not omit to notice (for
such things have rarely survived) the decoration in colour

FIG. 313. ANGEL, LINCOLN CATHEDRAL,
*c*. 1270. Angel of Judgement, holding scales. Seen from below,
the distortion of the left arm is corrected by perspective.

applied to the carved stonework (capitals, mouldings, &c.)
of the chancel-arch. Of about the same date are the notable
remains of paintings in Hardham church (Sussex).

The illuminated MSS. of the twelfth century belong to
a period of transition. An important feature are the
decorated initial letters, which now are often ' historiated ',
i. e. filled with figure-subjects. They may be illustrated by
the Bibles executed at Winchester, perhaps under Bishop
Henry of Blois (1129–71), one in the Cathedral Library,
the other in the British Museum ; and also by a roll with
medallion outline illustrations of the life of St. Guthlac
(British Museum : probably done at Crowland Abbey).
Later, signs of the impending change to a new style become
apparent. In a typical MS. of the end of the century (the
Westminster Psalter : British Museum) [Fig. 311] the

drapery is no longer of the classical type, clinging to the limbs and with many strongly marked folds, but lies broadly upon the figure. These tendencies may be safely attributed to the closer connexion of England with the continent since the Conquest.

It is in this period that we first come across any remains of stained or painted glass in England (Canterbury Cathedral). Circular or rectangular panels with small figures of the classical type [Fig. 312] are set in conventional foliage and scroll-work, the whole in deep and rich colours. A rare and splendid example of twelfth-century metal-work is a candlestick given to Gloucester Abbey about 1110, now in the Victoria and Albert Museum.

### 3. *The Thirteenth Century and the Rise of Gothic Art.*

Hitherto, ever since the restoration of England to its share in the culture of Western Christendom, we have seen that English art and architecture have been dominated by the classical tradition, i.e. that system of design which can be traced back to the art of the late Roman Empire (hence often called ' Romanesque '), two prominent characteristics being the round arch, and the treatment of the human figure with its drapery, derived from models in sculpture. With the thirteenth century we reach a great artistic revolution—the creation of ' Gothic ' art. Its leading features are the pointed arch, a larger use of naturalistic as opposed to conventional ornament, and in figure-subjects, whether in sculpture or in painting, greater freedom, truth, and originality of treatment. Though the origin of this movement is to be sought in France, yet from this time onwards English art becomes increasingly independent and individual. The artistic impulse which was expressed by this independence and casting aside of traditional forms produced work of a very high order, especially in the thirteenth and early fourteenth centuries, when the inspiration was still fresh and pure.

This is not the place for tracing in detail the development of Gothic architecture, but we may remark that its earliest form (Early English), with its richly moulded pointed arches and slender shafts (sometimes of Purbeck marble) crowned by exquisitely designed capitals of free though conventional foliage [Figs. 13, 18], produces an effect of combined strength and beauty which is perhaps not equalled in any other style. The elaborate design of prominent portions of the exteriors, such as the west and transept fronts, gave an opportunity for the introduction of sculpture in the form of single figures or of groups. The sculpture of this period was never surpassed in England. Preserving much of the severity of form, dignity in attitude, and treatment of drapery, derived indirectly from classical models, it shows at the same time a freedom and originality and sometimes a grandeur of style, which give it a high place in the history of art. We may select as examples the sculptures in the west front of Wells Cathedral (1220–50), the most complete collection in England ; the grand figure of Christ in Judgement, from the south-east door (cast of the unrestored figure in the V. and A. Museum), with the graceful figures of angels in the spandrels of the arches in the Angel Choir of Lincoln Cathedral (c. 1270) [Fig. 313] ; and those in similar spaces in the transepts of Westminster Abbey (c. 1250).

In the thirteenth century the sepulchral effigy, which made its appearance in the second half of the preceding century, becomes important as a form of sculpture. The figures are generally those of warriors and ecclesiastics ; and the close-fitting mail of the former as well as the dignified drapery of the latter gave an opportunity for much grace and nobility of treatment. One of the most perfect monuments is the tomb of Archbishop Walter de Gray (d. 1255) in York Minster (cast in the V. and A. Museum), where the fine effigy is combined with the graceful architecture and decorative sculpture of the period. Attention may also be called to the earliest royal effigy in England, that of King John in Worcester Cathedral (perhaps not earlier than c. 1240 : cast in the V. and A. Museum), and to the knights (c. 1225–60) in the Temple Church, London. The cathedrals of Exeter, Hereford, Salisbury, Wells, and Worcester contain notable collections of effigies. The earlier ones are of the hard Purbeck marble : later, the use of stone allowed more freedom of treatment. In spite of the recumbent position, they are often represented in action—the bishop giving his blessing, and the knight sometimes drawing or sheathing his sword ; but in the latter part

of the century they tend to be represented in repose. A peculiarly English motive, introduced about the middle of the thirteenth century, was the representation of the recumbent warrior with the legs crossed [Figs. 213, 214], a natural attitude of repose. The practice, which, it may be added, had no connexion with the Crusades, and also appears in the seated kings of the west fronts of Exeter (see below: *c.* 1345) and Lincoln (*c.* 1380), lasted for about a century and gradually disappeared with the introduction of plate armour, for which the posture is as unfitted as it is appropriate for the easy-fitting and yielding chain-mail. Effigies, it may be noted, were painted and gilt,

FIG. 314. FROM PAINTED CHAMBER WESTMINSTER. Gentleness subduing Anger. *c.* 1262. Gentleness (Débonnaireté) wears a mail hauberk over light green tunic (her rod is of the same colour), and purple surcoat. Gold crown. Shield, slung by strap over right shoulder, has gold lions and bars on a red field. Anger wears a purple mantle over light blue tunic. Blue background. In the border the arms of England alternate with those of Edward the Confessor and Edmund of East Anglia.

FIG. 315. ST. ANNE TEACHING THE VIRGIN
TO READ. Bodleian Library: MS. Douce 231. Last quarter
of the thirteenth century. Anne wears a pink mantle lined with
fur over a pale brown dress. Her nimbus and the dress of Mary
are light red. The lozenges of the diaper background are gold and
blue, the latter picked out with red and white. The border is pink
and pale green with gold leaves.

ornamental details being sometimes moulded or stamped on
a coating of plaster ('gesso'). A De Lucy effigy (1320–40)
from Lesnes Abbey, Kent, now in the Victoria and Albert
Museum, retains some of its original decoration.

It was about the middle of the thirteenth century that English art blossomed out into its first stage of perfection. Important was the impulse derived from royal patronage. The records reveal great activity in the decoration of the royal residences, mainly by native artists. The most remarkable of these works were the mural paintings by ' Master Walter ' (from 1262) in ' the King's Great Chamber ' in the palace of Westminster, which came in consequence to be known as ' the Painted Chamber '. Early in the next century they are referred to by travellers as being a well-known sight [Fig. 314]. The pictures, which we only know from copies made in 1819 by C. A. Stothard from the surviving fragments, were arranged on the walls of the room in six bands or tiers, increasing in breadth as they were farther removed from the eye. The subjects (mainly the Old Testament history) were represented in brilliant colours with a rather sparing use of gold, on blue (occasionally red or green) backgrounds. The figures wear the costume and armour of the time. The action is clearly and directly expressed, and the crowded battle-scenes especially are full of vigour and movement. It is possible that Master Walter was also responsible for a retable, probably for the high altar, belonging to Westminster Abbey, which Mr. Lethaby has described as ' the most beautiful thirteenth-century painting in England '. The source of designs such as those of the Painted Chamber is perhaps suggested by an order of the king to the Master of the Temple to lend a French MS. to one of the royal painters, for use in decorating rooms in the Tower and at Westminster. It must be remembered that the style of French and English illuminations of this period is closely allied. In the course of the thirteenth century that style became definitely ' Gothic '. Characteristic features are the elegant figures of the miniatures with their diapered or gold backgrounds [Fig. 315], and the elaborated initial letters and border designs. It may be noted that in the twelfth and thirteenth centuries two favourite forms of illustrated books were the Apocalypse and the manuals of natural history known as Bestiaries [Fig. 316].

At the end of Henry's long reign, by a curious invasion of foreign taste, the pavement before the high altar (1268), and the basement of Edward the Confessor's shrine (finished

officium habeant. Amphi enim grece utrunq; dr. i
q̃ inaquis ꞇintris uiuiunt. ut boce. cocodrilli ypota
mu. h̄. eʒt equi fluctuales. ✝ De balena.

ᵗt belua inmari q̃ grece aspido delone dr̃. latine ũ
aspido testudo. lece i dicta. ob immanitatem coꝛ
poꝛis. e̅. enim si̅c ille qui excepit ionam. cuius aluus
tante magnitudinis fuit ut putareꞇ infernus diceꞇ

FIG. 316.   PAGE   FROM   BESTIARY.   THE   WHALE.
Bodleian Library.  MS. Ashmole 1511, c. 1200.  Sailors are about to moor
their ship to a whale, which they mistake for an island.  The whale emits
a pleasant odour which attracts fish.  Its colour is bluish-grey in a dark
green sea.  The ship and sailors are treated realistically, the sail being dull
pink.  Gold background.

1279), with the surrounding pavement in the new choir of
Westminster Abbey, were executed by artists from Rome
in the characteristic mosaic and inlaid marble work con-

FIG. 317. TOMB OF HENRY III, WESTMIN-
STER ABBEY. 1291. South side. The large oblong slab
in the upper part of the tomb is red porphyry. Gold is freely used
in the mosaic work of the borders, twisted shafts, &c. It has been
suggested that the three cavities in the base, once closed by grilles,
and marked with mosaic crosses at the back, held reliquaries;
but this is unlikely.

nected with the Roman family called Cosmati. The king's
tomb close by is another example of this exotic art. On
the other hand, the gilt metal effigies of Henry (1291) and
of Queen Eleanor of Castile (d. 1290) are the work of an
English goldsmith, William Torel, and display the severe

dignity and grace of the sculpture of the time [Fig. 317].
Notable examples of the later monumental and decorative
sculpture of the age are the surviving ' Eleanor Crosses ',
erected by Edward I (c. 1290–5) to the memory of his
queen, at Geddington (Northants.), Northampton, and Wal-
tham (Herts. : reconstructed). The portrait statues of the
last were carved by Alexander of Abingdon.

The earliest English seals belong to the beginning of
the twelfth century, but it was in the thirteenth and early
fourteenth that they reached their highest level of vigour
and refinement. The severely beautiful seal executed for
Henry III at the beginning of his reign by Walter de Ripa,
and that of Queen Philippa (1328), may be instanced.

The painted glass is merely a development of that of
the previous century, and may be illustrated by the rose
window in the north transept of Lincoln Cathedral (first
half of the thirteenth century), and by the remains of the
original glazing in Salisbury Cathedral (c. 1250).

### 4. *The Fourteenth Century and the Perfection of English Art.*

It was in the latter half of the thirteenth century that
the new style was developed, and it continued for about
a hundred years. In this period, art as a whole reached
its greatest perfection in mediaeval England. A prominent
architectural feature is the traceried window [Figs. 21–4],
which gave quite a new character to buildings. Noticeable
also is the carved foliage, often imitating natural
forms (the oak-leaf, vine, &c.), though arranged in a conventional and decorative way [Fig. 26]. The enrichment
of all the architectural members by mouldings or carved
ornaments is carried to the extreme allowed by a sense of
good taste and proportion [Figs. 22, 27]. Moreover, the
woodwork of screens and canopied stalls (notable are those
in the choir of Winchester Cathedral), which from the
nature of the material demands a certain elaboration for
purposes of effect, and had therefore hitherto been unimportant owing to the simplicity of the prevailing style, now
attains its proper development, following the lines of the
architecture. The choir and nave of Exeter Cathedral
(1280–1345) contain fine examples of the decorative and

FIG. 318. VIRGIN AND CHILD, WIN-
CHESTER COLLEGE, *c.* 1390. About life-
size. Bere stone (much used for the finer work in the
original college buildings). The object held by the child
was a bird.

figure sculpture of the period, notably the statues of kings (c. 1345) in the lower part of the west front (the apostles and prophets above are of the fifteenth century). A statue of the Virgin and Child over the outer gateway of Winchester College (c. 1390), though its architectural setting belongs to the next period, is a masterpiece of fourteenth-century art [Fig. 318].

The canopied tombs, which now become an important feature in churches, give a good idea of the decorative qualities of the style. The upper portion is of two forms ; either an arch under a gable, or an erection of open tabernacle-work in several tiers. Examples of the former, elaborately decorated with the beautiful foliage of the period, are the tomb of Aymer de Valence (d. 1324) at Westminster and the Percy tomb (c. 1345) in Beverley Minster [Fig. 319]. The tabernacle-work of the other form does not give such scope for ornament ; but its grace, light-ness, and proportion have great merit, though the second of these qualities is sometimes carried to an extreme scarcely appropriate to the material. The tombs of Edward II (d. 1327) at Gloucester [Fig. 320], and of Hugh le Despenser (d. 1349) and Sir Guy de Brien (d. 1390 : erected in his lifetime) at Tewkesbury, are good examples. The recum-bent effigies, as works of art, are scarcely equal to their magnificent setting. The attempts at portraiture, though more marked than in the preceding period, are still ele-mentary : the features are flat, and the posture is stiff and uninteresting, an effect often due to the armour. But the use of the comparatively soft alabaster for the figure that of Edward II at Gloucester is one of the earliest instances— gave greater scope for freedom in the pose, and a richer treatment of drapery and other details. Another material occasionally used for effigies, especially in the earlier part of this period, was oak. By the middle of the century the attitude of repose with the hands joined in prayer is almost invariable.

The fragments from St. Stephen's Chapel, Westminster (c. 1356), now in the British Museum, give an idea of the high standard attained in painting at this period. So far as any comparison is possible, they show an advance on the works in the Painted Chamber. They consist of small scenes from the stories of Job and Tobit, which occupied

Fig. 319.  PERCY TOMB, BEVERLEY MIN-
STER, *c.* 1345.  South face of freestone canopy over grey
marble tomb, inlaid with metal effigy (lost) of Lady Eleanor
Percy (*d.* 1328).  In the spandrels of the cusps of the ogee arch
are the shields, held by knights, of (right) Edward III (after 1340),
and of her family, viz. FitzAlan, (left) De Warenne, and the
lordship of Clun (held by a lady.  See Hope's *Grammar of English
Heraldry,* Fig. 103).  Below the finial, Christ seated holds the
soul in a cloth supported by angels.  The larger angels, like those
on the other face, may have held Passion emblems.

FIG. 320. TOMB OF EDWARD II, GLOUCESTER
CATHEDRAL, c. 1337. Stone. The bracket projecting
from the tomb may have supported a light, or a box for offerings,
or, perhaps, the votive gold ship given by Edward III in 1337 for
his preservation at sea.

the lower part of the lights in the side-windows of the chapel, treated with considerable freedom and originality. The faces and attitudes are natural and expressive, and the execution is almost of miniature finish. The backgrounds are of gesso, stamped with patterns and gilt. Other paintings in the chapel are known to us from drawings and tracings made in 1805. The most important were a series of portraits of Edward III and his family, which are of more conventional character and analogous to the better

FIG. 321. PAINTINGS FROM ST. STEPHEN'S CHAPEL, WESTMINSTER. Between 1350 and 1360. The angels were about 5 ft. high. The stories of Job and Tobit were immediately above the row of shields with the arms of contemporary lords and knights.

work in stained glass, and standing figures of angels holding up brocaded draperies, which occupied the background of the arcade below the windows [Fig. 321]. We learn from the accounts of payments made for the work that the artists employed, whether in painting, glass, or sculpture, were Englishmen. This chapel after its restoration by Edward III (c. 1330–60) must have formed a monument of the finest English art of the period. We may add that this king's gold coinage is unsurpassed both for design and execution.

Meanwhile the emancipation from the old traditions, which resulted from the new artistic impulse of the thirteenth century, had been making itself felt in the manuscript illuminations. The initial letter and the border were developed till in the fourteenth century they became the most important features of manuscript decoration, while the illustrations are remarkable for freedom and delicacy of drawing. The finest work was produced in the earlier part of the century. The exquisite drawings of Biblical and other subjects in the MS. known from its later owner as Queen Mary's Psalter (British Museum) [Fig. 322] are of exceptional merit, and confirm the high opinion which the remains of mural decoration would lead us to form about fourteenth-century painting in England. Hardly less important are the works of the East Anglian school, which also belong to the early part of the century. Their chief characteristics are the splendid decorative treatment, and the marginal borders rich with the most spirited representations derived from life, legend, and imagination. Some of the best specimens are in foreign

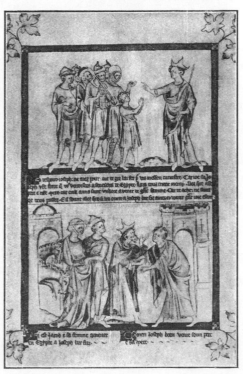

FIG. 322. FROM QUEEN MARY'S PSALTER. Brit. Mus. Roy. MS. 2 B. vii. Early fourteenth century. Top, Joseph makes himself known to his brethren. Bottom, Joseph receives Jacob and his wife in Egypt. The scenes are delicately tinted in green, brown, and violet. Backgrounds uncoloured. Red borders. Texts in French. Given to Queen Mary in 1553.

or private libraries, but the Arundel Psalter (c. 1310), in the British Museum, and the Norwich or Ormesby Psalter, in the Bodleian [Fig. 323], are representative. One centre of production seems to have been at Gorleston, near Yarmouth. The disappearance of this school after 1350 is, perhaps, an instance of the effects of the Black Death.

FIG. 323. PAGE FROM THE ORMESBY PSALTER. MS. Douce 366. *c.* 1290. The text has the end of a collect, followed by Ps. xxxix (*Dixi custodiam*). 1–6. In the initial D (blue and gold; pink background) is Christ before the high priest. In the bottom border is the story of the unicorn (symbol of the Incarnation) which loses its fierceness in the lap of a virgin. Notice the knight's armour and ailettes. The main design of the border is in blue and gold, with details in pink and green. The human and grotesque figures, &c., are treated realistically.

Fig. 324. FROM RETABLE, NORWICH
CATHEDRAL: the Resurrection. c. 1382. 2 ft. 10½ in.
by 1 ft. 3½ in. On oak boards. Christ has a purple-pink robe,
lined with blue ; green crown of thorns and cross-staff with white
pennon and red cross. The soldier to left has bascinet and camail,
blue jupon, and small red target. The other has a red jupon.
The one behind, in hat-helmet with pole-axe, has a green cloak.
Inside of alabaster tomb and canopy red. Shields with emblems
of the Passion hang from two gilt eagles.

At the end of the century some splendid manuscripts (e.g. the great Bible in the British Museum, perhaps executed for Richard II) show a new style, which has been explained by the foreign art influences accompanying the arrival in England (1382) of Anne of Bohemia, queen of Richard II. Characteristics are softness of treatment, especially in the well-modelled faces, and warmth of colour. One artist of this school, John Siferwas, a Dominican friar, the chief illuminator of the Missal of Sherborne Abbey (c. 1396–1407: now at Alnwick Castle), has left remarkable portraits of himself and his patron, Lord Lovel, in the large miniature of a Lectionary in the British Museum.

A few paintings on panel survive from the end of the period, but there is considerable uncertainty about their origin. The (mutilated) retable in Norwich Cathedral, with Passion scenes on gold backgrounds stamped with patterns (c. 1382: facsimile in the V. and A. Museum), does not suggest any immediate foreign source [Fig. 324]. The diptych at Wilton House, representing Richard II with his patron saints kneeling before the Virgin and Child, is of Italian derivation, and almost certainly by a foreign artist.

FIG. 325. LIGHT FROM GLOUCESTER EAST WINDOW. c. 1350. St. Peter holding the keys and a church. His nimbus is light blue, the diapered background dark blue. The rest is carried out in white and yellow stain. (Photograph by S. A. Pitcher.)

More may be said for an English origin of the fine portrait of the king enthroned, which hangs in the choir of Westminster Abbey, though it has been ascribed to a French or German painter. At any rate it seems to share the characteristics of the contemporary illuminations mentioned above. The suggestion of melancholy in the face gives an impression of true portraiture, while the carefully modelled forms, the well-arranged drapery, and the soft rich tones show an artist of no mean capacity.

With the great increase of window-space the stained glass of this period makes a considerable advance. In the earlier instances the small figures in the traditional attitudes, set in fields of patterned quarries or trailing foliage, recall the older style; but the subjects are now often framed under architectural cano-

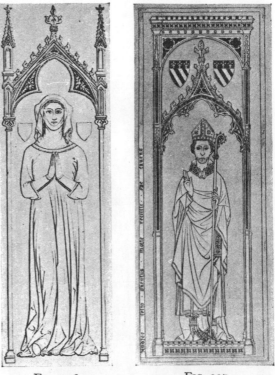

FIG. 326.        FIG. 327.

FIG. 326. BRASS OF LADY DE COB-HAM. c. 1320. Cobham Church, Kent. Joan, first wife of Sir John de Cobham. The buttoned sleeves of her kirtle appear within those of the cote-hardi or over-tunic. A veil or kerchief covers her head, with wimple over chin and throat. The gable-canopy is the oldest English surviving example. The marginal text (lost, like the arms on either side of the head) was in Lombardic letters and Norman-French.

FIG. 327. BRASS OF BISHOP TRIL-LECK. 1360. Hereford Cathedral, choir. In pontifical mass-vestments (the tunicle invisible). Under an ogee canopy, with embattled super-canopy. Shields of the bishop's personal arms.

pies. The windows of Merton College Chapel (c. 1300), and the north windows of the Latin Chapel in Oxford Cathedral (c. 1350), may be mentioned. The meagreness of effect

FIG. 328. FELBRIGG BRASS, 1416. Felbrigg Church, Norfolk. Sir Simon Felbrygge, K.G., and his wife Margaret (cousin to Anne of Bohemia) who died 1416, when the brass was made, the spaces for the date of his death being left blank. He is represented as standard-bearer to Richard II. Notice his palettes bearing St. George's cross, and the garter on his left leg. She wears kirtle, mantle, and crespine head-dress, and has a pet dog at her feet. Above are the arms of Richard II and his queen, and on the middle pinnacle those of Sir Simon and his wife, with his badge, a fetterlock, repeated. Richard II's badge, a white hart, forms the corbel from which the arches spring.

with the increased glass-space led to the introduction of large figures under canopies taking up the whole of each of the lights. An example on a grand scale is the east window of Gloucester Cathedral (c. 1350) [Fig. 325]. Fourteenth-century glass-painting reflects the tendencies of the pictorial and decorative art of the time. Figures become more natural in pose and proportion, and the ornamental foliage is derived from natural forms. The range of colour is also greater, and its tones are clearer and brighter than before, a result to which the discovery of the yellow silver-stain contributed. Characteristic examples of fourteenth-century glass are the seven windows in the choir and apse of Tewkesbury. The nave of York Minster is also rich in glass of this period.

The fourteenth century is also the great age of the brass, a form of monument in which the figure, with a framework of more or less architectural design, is incised on a plate of metal embedded in a slab forming part of the floor of the church. In English brasses the parts of the design are usually let into the stone separately. The earliest specimens that have survived belong to the last quarter of the thirteenth century, and for boldness and precision of drawing, which was of course favoured by the material, these early brasses are unequalled. In the fourteenth century the treatment both in design and in drawing becomes more elaborate. Shading is introduced, and the folds of drapery are more complicated. The canopies and ornamental adjuncts are also considerably developed. Nor must we omit to notice the part which the admirable lettering of the inscriptions often has in the general

FIG. 329. GRANDISSON TRIPTYCH. c. 1350. Above, the Coronation of Mary; below, the Crucifixion. The saints on the side leaves are Peter, Paul, Stephen, and Thomas of Canterbury. In the lower inner spandrels are the personal arms of the bishop: paly of six arg. and az. on a bend gu. a mitre between two eaglets or. The roses in the other spandrels are an English characteristic.

decorative effect [Figs. 326, 327, 328]. No English work, however, approaches in completeness and magnificence Flemish examples such as those commemorating the Walsoken and Braunche families in St. Margaret's Church, King's Lynn, which are the most splendid brasses in England. Like most branches of art, in the next period brasses, though very numerous, degenerate in both design and execution.

The fourteenth century was the golden age of carving

in ivory, a refined form of art which had its centre in France. These delicate reliefs of figures or simple scriptural scenes under architectural canopies were usually combined in triptychs or diptychs, and generally picked out with colour or gilding. The English specimens of this work are distinguished from the French by the same differences which appear in the contemporary sculpture. The excessive grace and sentimentality of the French work is contrasted with comparative severity and seriousness of expression accompanied by less finished workmanship in the English. A triptych in the British Museum, which belonged to Bishop Grandisson of Exeter (1327–69), is characteristic [Fig. 329].

Among the minor forms in which English art of the best period manifested itself we must not omit to mention embroidery. English embroidery had always been famous, but in the latter part of the thirteenth century the invention of a new method brought it into still greater favour on the continent. This was described as *opus Anglicanum* or English work, and its merit was that the treatment of the figures (wrought in a kind of chain stitch) produced the effect of low relief. The finest example is the Syon Cope (V. and A. Museum) [Fig. 330]. The surface, which is entirely covered with stitches, is treated with a pattern of intersecting quatrefoils which enclose single figures and scenes from the Gospel history. The effect is broadly decorative ; rich, yet never crowded. The border is noticed on p. 211. We may call attention to a cope in the same collection as a fine example of English embroidery of a rather later date (early fourteenth century). On a red silk ground a trailing vine delicately covers the surface and forms a Tree of Jesse, enclosing the figures in circles of its foliage. Like most other branches of English art, embroidery deteriorated in the fifteenth century, both design and workmanship becoming comparatively coarse and formal.

## 5. *The Fifteenth Century and the Period of Decline.*

Towards the end of the fourteenth century it begins to be evident that a period of decline in art was setting in. It is not that there was any cessation of activity in building and decorating : on the contrary, the fifteenth century was

Fig. 330. THE SYON COPE. End of the thirteenth century. Worked in silk and gold thread on linen. The quatrefoils have red grounds, the intervening spaces (with angels) green. The lower part has been curtailed, and an heraldic border and orphrey (of about the same date) added. Once belonged to the Bridgetine convent of Syon (Isleworth, Middlesex), founded in 1415.

the most busy of any age since the Norman, and has left its mark on nearly every ecclesiastical building in England. But Gothic art lost much of its freshness, and true artistic feeling gave way to formality and mechanical ornamentation. It is, perhaps, significant that the first indications of decline appear after the Black Death (1349).

On the other hand, this tendency was favourable in some respects to the carved woodwork of choir-stalls, canopies, and the richer pieces of domestic furniture. The chancel or rood-screens were an important decorative feature in English fifteenth-century churches [Fig. 331]. They were completely coloured and gilt, and in the eastern counties were sometimes decorated with fine gilt gesso work (e. g. at Southwold, Suffolk). A considerable number have survived (especially in Devonshire, Somerset, and Norfolk), and give an idea of the brightness and warmth of colour which was the aim of the church decoration of the fifteenth century. The effect was often aided by the encaustic floor-tiles (occasionally, as at Great Malvern, used also for wall-decoration), though the finer designs (especially figure-subjects) date from the earlier periods (e. g. the Chertsey tiles of c. 1270 : specimens in the British Museum). Rare instances of a large extent of tiling *in situ* exist in the Chapter House, Westminster Abbey (c. 1255), and the presbytery of Gloucester Cathedral (c. 1450).

The multiplication of niches and the abundance of elaborate tombs gave great opportunity for sculpture, but in the treatment of the human figure it is rare in this period to find results of any great artistic merit. The numerous images of the chantry chapel of Henry V in Westminster Abbey (c. 1440–50) are favourable examples, but the finest are the statues of saints in Henry VII's Chapel, Westminster (c. 1510), where the splendid bronze screen with its images, enclosing the tomb, is also, probably, the work of English craftsmen, though the royal effigies were made by Pietro Torrigiano of Florence. Heraldic sculpture flourished in this period, ' supporters ' especially being treated with skill and vigour (e. g. in King's College Chapel, Cambridge).

Characteristic products of English fifteenth-century art are the alabaster tables (the earliest are c. 1350), i. e. panels with sacred figures or subjects in relief, coloured and gilt,

FIG. 331. FIFTEENTH-CENTURY SCREEN IN BISHOP'S LYDIARD CHURCH, SOMERSETSHIRE. The Apostles' Creed is carved on the narrow middle band of the cornice or beam.

generally framed in sets for reredoses [Fig. 332]. A minor form were the devotional tablets known as 'St. John's Heads' (examples in the British, Victoria and Albert, and Ashmolean Museums). Nottingham, which supplied a sculptured alabaster retable for the high altar of St. George's Chapel, Windsor, in 1367, seems to have been the centre of the manufacture of these tables, which were widely diffused over England, and largely exported to the continent. They are to be found in France, Spain, Italy, North Germany, the Scandinavian countries, and even Iceland.

Alabaster was also the favourite material at this time for tombs and effigies. While the details of dress and armour are rendered with elaborate care, the figures are mostly conventional, and lack variety. A more splendid form of effigy in gilt metal (laton or latten) was sometimes used for royal and illustrious personages. The effigy of the Black Prince (1376) at Canterbury is a favourable specimen, but the monument (c. 1450) of Richard Beauchamp, Earl of Warwick (d. 1439), is the most impressive example. The effigy, with its elaborate armour, is thought to have been derived from a foreign (German) model. The small figures ('weepers', i.e. mourners) round the tomb exhibit a grace and variety in the drapery unusual in the ordinary works of this period. The contracts for the chapel at Warwick in which the tomb stands give some information about the craftsmen of the period. The chief contractor for the monument was John Essex, a London 'marbler'; the effigy and other images were made by William Austen, 'citizen and founder of London'; Bartholomew Lambespring, 'Dutchman and goldsmith of London', was to polish and gild the figures, and make the 'scutcheons of arms'; and the marble tomb was the work of John Bourde of Corfe Castle, 'marbler'. The stall-work, painting, and glass in the chapel were also due to London artists.

More freshness and power is shown in wood-carving, especially in the Eastern and Western counties, the angels of the roofs of some Norfolk churches (e. g. March and Knapton), and the bench-ends of Cornwall and Devonshire, being remarkable. Some of the best work is to be seen in the carvings of the 'misericords' or brackets under choir seats (a continuous series from the first quarter of the thirteenth century at Christchurch, Hants, down to those

Fig. 332. ALABASTER RETABLE, Victoria and Albert Museum. Second half of the fifteenth century. Length 7 ft. The seven alabaster panels are framed in an oak triptych, painted and decorated with bands of gilt and gesso ornament. The subjects are (from left to right): John the Baptist, the Annunciation, the Offering of the Magi, the Trinity (the dove is lost), the Ascension, the Assumption and Coronation of Mary, John the Evangelist.

in Henry VII's Chapel, Westminster, *c.* 1520), with their vivacious scenes of everyday life, or mythical and symbolical subjects.

The most important artistic product of the period in England was the painted glass. The great size of the windows with their regular forms [Fig. 31] gave wide scope for the display of large single figures or of scenes in very light and transparent colours, the clearness and brightness of the effect being increased by a liberal use of white or yellow (silver-stain) glass. The drawing, though it seldom reaches a very high level, shows a great advance. The pose of the figures becomes natural, and they are given a proper relief and roundness. The general effect is extraordinarily successful, and it is hardly too much to say that the highest capacities of stained glass have never been more nearly attained than in the best fifteenth-century English windows.

Fine early examples of this work may be seen in the windows of the ante-chapel, New College, Oxford (*c.* 1385). The full-length figures of saints and prophets have still much of the ' Decorated ' character. The effect is flat, the heads are large, the attitudes sometimes clumsy, and the drawing generally is indifferent. But great advance is shown in brightness and transparency of effect by the use of very light glass in the canopies and of delicate half-tints (especially greens and pinks) in the drapery. The progress of the art is well illustrated in the churches and Minster at York, where the east window of the choir and the north and south windows of the eastern transepts are specially important from their great size, and cover the period from 1405 to about 1430. Very fine examples of the work of the latter half of the century may be seen in the Priory Church, Great Malvern [Fig. 333], the latest window being of 1501–2. The numerous fragments still remaining in churches show how large was the production of painted glass in this period, and it even appeared in houses of the best class. The names of some of the makers are known, e. g. John Thornton of Coventry, whose contract for the great east window of York Minster in 1405 is preserved ; and we have no reason to doubt that they were mainly English, though the designs they used seem often to have been derived from the great centres of Northern Continental art between the Rhine and the Channel. One source may have been the numerous series of popular illustrations of Scripture history (e. g. the so-called 'Block Books'), which were produced in Europe from the middle of the fifteenth century onwards. At the beginning of the sixteenth century the influence of the Renaissance is apparent. The exceptionally perfect windows of Fairford Church (Glos.), though probably made in London (*c.* 1500), reproduce Flemish or German designs. The most splendid examples of this influence are the windows of King's College Chapel, Cambridge (1515–31), the four earliest of which were made by Barnard Flower 'the king's glazier', a naturalized German (*d.* 1517 : *Notes and Queries*, 1917, p. 436), who had probably executed the glass for Henry VII's Chapel, Westminster, very little of which has survived.

The remains of painting

FIG. 333. LIGHT FROM A WINDOW in the north clerestory of the choir, Great Malvern, *c.* 1460–70. St. Wulfstan, Bishop of Worcester (1062–95), in white and gold vestments, with red dalmatic and apparels. Black and white checker pavement. The canopy is in white and yellow stain. Blue background for the figure, red for the canopy. (Photo by S. A. Pitcher.)

in England at this period are fairly copious, but the general impression which they convey is that pictorial art had not passed beyond the stage of mere illustration and decoration. The mural paintings are the most numerous.  Just as every church at this time that could afford it had its windows filled with the clear and brilliant glass of the period, so the walls were covered with painted scenes.  Having been white-washed over at the time of the Reformation many of these have been preserved, in a more or less damaged state.  Un-fortunately they nearly always belong to the ordinary parish churches, where we could not expect to find the finer work. In facial expression, action, and composition, they are usually elementary and popular ; while, even when we take into account the difference of the medium, there is nothing analogous to the brilliant effects achieved in glass. Examples of the better work are the ' Unbelief of Thomas ' in the north transept of St. Albans Cathedral (c. 1425); the Apocalypse scenes in the Chapter House, Westminster Abbey (c. 1475); and the 'Miracles of the Virgin', in Eton College Chapel (1479–88).

Paintings on panel are rarer, partly owing to destruc-tion ; but apparently the painted retable was not common in England (an example with figures of saints in Romsey Church, Hants).  In the Eastern Counties and in Devonshire a certain number of screens have survived, the lower panels of which contain figures of saints.  Those in the Eastern Counties are older and generally superior to those in the West.  In no case, however, do they reach a high level as works of art.  Some panels from a screen erected in St. John Maddermarket, Norwich, in 1451 may be seen in the Victoria and Albert Museum.  A late retable (probably near to 1550) in Gloucester Cathedral represents the Last Judgement.  The art is still Gothic, though Renaissance details occur, and gold is freely used.  The heads and features are coarse, and the figures short and clumsy. The inscriptions (texts) are in English, and there are no definite traces of foreign origin in the picture [Fig. 334].

There is little to be said about English illuminated manuscripts in the fifteenth century.  Good work was still being done at its beginning, but the growth of a taste, first for French and later for Flemish manuscripts, seems to have been fatal to the native art.  It is significant that the exquisite drawings of a family record such as the 'Pageant of Richard Beauchamp Earl of Warwick' (*c.* 1485–90 : British Museum) appear to be the work of a Flemish artist.

From Richard II onwards we have a continuous series of English royal portraits, which may be regarded as the

FIG. 334. RETABLE, GLOUCESTER CATHEDRAL. *c.* 1550. 7 ft. 7 in. by 9 ft. 10 in. Painted on boards covered with gesso. Christ the Judge, with emblems of justice and mercy, attended by angels holding the instruments of the Passion, and the Apostles. Below, the resurrection. Left, the gate of heaven ; right, the mouth of hell. The upper central group has a gold background.

work of English artists, though in their present state they mostly date from the Tudor period. Examples may be seen in the National Portrait Gallery. It should be noted that the king's serjeant painters (the first in 1511) appear to have been craftsmen and decorators, not artists proper. The court generally patronized foreign portrait-painters.

The residence and work in London (1525-9, 1531-43) of Hans Holbein cannot have been without influence on English portraiture, though he seems to have had no direct pupils, and founded no school. Later, royal patronage was transferred to the portrait-painters of the Franco-Flemish school, which flourished at the court of Francis I of France. The names of English painters begin to emerge about the middle of the century. In the National Gallery is a remarkable portrait of Edmund Butts (1545) by John Bettes. Some of them were also ' limners ' or painters of miniature portraits, an art which originated in illuminated manuscripts, and had been carried to perfection by Holbein. Before the end of the century two miniaturists, Nicholas Hilliard (1547-1619) and his pupil, Isaac Oliver (c. 1556-1617: of French origin), attained a high level of excellence.

FIG. 335. FOUNDRESS'S CUP, CHRIST'S COLLEGE, CAM-BRIDGE. c. 1430-40. On the ' print ' are the arms of Humphrey, Duke of Gloucester, impaling those of his second wife, Eleanor Cobham. Given to the College by Margaret, Countess of Richmond.

Mediaeval English plate is rare. The civil wars in the fifteenth century were as fatal to precious objects of this kind in great houses as the religious changes of the sixteenth were to those in monasteries and churches. Of the ecclesiastical plate which has survived, the late-Gothic chalices and patens form the largest class. Of exceptional importance are the magnificent silver-gilt censer (second half of the 14th cent.) which may have belonged to Ramsey Abbey (Hunts.), now in the Victoria and Albert Museum, and the crozier of William of Wykeham belonging to New College, Oxford, one of the most elaborate examples in existence. Of the various kinds of secular or domestic plate, some, such as the mazer-bowls, from the simplicity of their form, scarcely admit of high artistic treatment. From the latter point of view the most important are the vessels for holding salt, and the tall covered cups. A number of these belong to corporate bodies, which have been better able to preserve them than private or even royal owners. The gracefully shaped 'Foundress's Cup' (about 1440) at Christ's College, Cambridge, is of purely Gothic design, and is ornamented with diagonal bands of beautiful foliage in *repoussé* work [Fig. 335]. More magnificent is the Salt (about 1490) given by Bishop Fox to Corpus Christi College, Oxford, on which all the resources of the goldsmith's art of the time have been lavished. Reproductions of other important pieces may be seen in the Victoria and Albert Museum. Beautiful objects of this kind were produced in the Elizabethan age after the influence of the Renaissance had superseded the Gothic tradition. Though modelled on foreign types (especially

FIG. 336. STANDING CUP, CORPUS CHRISTI COLLEGE, CAMBRIDGE. 1570. London hall-marks of 1569–70, the year in which Parker gave it to the College.

Italian and German) in form and ornament, they are nevertheless, like the architecture of the period, distinctively English. A notable example is the covered cup given by Archbishop Parker to Corpus Christi College, Cambridge [Fig. 336].

FIG. 337. MARNEY TOMB, LAYER MARNEY. *c.* 1525.
The decorative work of the tomb is in terra-cotta. The effigy (in armour and Garter robes) with its slab is of black marble.

## 6. *The Influence of the Italian Renaissance.*

With the sixteenth century the forms of the Italian Renaissance began to make their way into England, at first only in ornamental details and subsidiary construction. The tomb-chapel of Margaret, Countess of Salisbury, at Christchurch (Hants : finished before her death in 1541),

FIG. 338. ELIZABETHAN TOMBS OF PEYTON FAMILY, ISLEHAM CHURCH, CAMBRIDGE. The canopied tomb on the left is that of Sir Robert Peyton (*d.* 1590) ; that on the right of his son, Sir John Peyton (*d.* 1616). Stone, painted and gilded. Alabaster effigies. In front, on right, fourteenth-century effigy of Sir Gilbert Barnard. Background, centre : tomb of Sir William Barnard (*d.* 1293).

and the monument of Henry, Lord Marney (*d.* 1523), in Layer Marney Church (Essex) [Fig. 337], illustrate this. The Gothic feeling was far too deeply rooted in England to be easily eradicated, and it was not till well into the seventeenth century that an English architect could be found capable of producing works wholly classical in style.

Meanwhile there was a long period of transition. A distinction may be made between the earlier and purer work, of direct Italian inspiration (Henry VIII–Mary : e.g. a Dormer monument of 1552 in Wing Church, Bucks., is strictly classical in style) and the later Elizabethan or Jacobean decoration, produced under Dutch or German influence—a distinction which partly reflects the religious changes of the times. The Reformation brought to a close the series of great ecclesiastical buildings ; but, on the other hand, domestic architecture, whether in the form of great houses or of colleges, had wide scope. While parts, such as the windows, and the timber roofs of the great hall, retain at least a Gothic outline, the ornamental features, and also furniture, display the forms of Renaissance art [Fig. 74]. A style was thus developed peculiarly suited to domestic buildings, and at the same time quite individual and national in character. Its most characteristic products are the monumental doorways and chimney-pieces, the plaster ceilings, and the woodwork of panelling, screens, and staircases [Fig. 70]. Sculpture in stone (often coloured and gilt when used internally) is also common, but it does not attain a high level of art. Better results were obtained in the portrait-effigies on monuments, the heads being sometimes well moulded and expressive. The canopied tombs are often elaborate and characteristic [Fig. 338].

It is not our business here to follow the later fortunes of art in England, and a few words must suffice to indicate the course of events. For a moment it seemed possible that a school of English art might have grown up under royal patronage. Charles I, commanding the services of a foreign painter (Van Dyck) and an English architect (Inigo Jones), both brought up in the great traditions of their respective arts, with a gallery of Italian masterpieces and a magnificent palace in which to house them, might under happier political conditions have provided the starting-point for a school of English art. But his pictures were scattered, and the new Whitehall was never built. The result was that native painting never achieved independence or distinction till the eighteenth century, when Hogarth suddenly appeared with his scenes from English life, while portrait painting received a new impulse under Reynolds, and a characteristic English landscape style (especially in water-colours) had its origin. Architecture, on the other hand, was more fortunate in maintaining a continuous tradition, at a high level, from Inigo Jones onwards. Here too the national feeling asserted itself, and a definite English Palladian style was produced.

Looking back over the whole period, it cannot be said that England has ever been the home of a great art, though at times English artists have produced work of the highest class. But, though again and again the impulse has come from without, the results have always been marked by independence and individuality. And among the countries of Europe the art of England holds a distinguished place, with, on the one hand, its perception of beauty, and on the other, its dislike of sentimentality and exaggeration.

*Books for reference.*

SIR W. ARMSTRONG, *Art in Great Britain and Ireland*, 1909.
W. S. CALVERLEY & W. G. COLLINGWOOD, *Notes on the Early Sculptured Crosses in the Diocese of Carlisle*, 1899.
W. GREENWELL & F. J. HAVERFIELD, *Catalogue of the Inscribed and Sculptured Stones in the Chapter Library, Durham*, 1899.
E. S. PRIOR & A. GARDNER, *An Account of Medieval Figure-Sculpture in England*, 1912.
E. S. PRIOR, *Eight Chapters on English Medieval Art*, Cambridge, 1922.
A. HARTSHORNE, *Portraiture in Recumbent Effigies* (Exeter, Pollard, 1899).
W. R. LETHABY, *Westminster Abbey and the Kings' Craftsmen*, 1906.
F. H. CROSSLEY, *English Church Monuments, 1150–1550* (London, 1921). Includes illustrations of several of the monuments mentioned in this chapter.
SIR E. MAUNDE THOMPSON, *English Illuminated Manuscripts*, 1895.
J. A. HERBERT, *Illuminated Manuscripts* (The Connoisseur's Library), 1911.
British Museum. *Reproductions from Illuminated Manuscripts*. Series i (1910) and iii (1908) contain illustrations from several of the MSS. mentioned in this chapter.
C. WINSTON, *Inquiry into the Difference of Style observable in Ancient Glass Paintings*, 2nd edition, 2 vols., 1867.
P. NELSON, *Ancient Painted Glass in England* (The Antiquary's Books), 1913.
H. WALPOLE, *Anecdotes of Painting in England* (ed. R. N. Wornum, London, 1876).
C. E. KEYSER, *List of buildings having mural decorations.*
—— *List of Norman tympana and lintels* (1904).
Monographs on Church Art in England, by F. BOND (fully illustrated) :
    *Fonts and Font Covers*, 1908.
    *Screens and Galleries in English Churches*, 1908.
    *Wood Carvings in English Churches* : I, *Misericords ;* II, *Stalls and Tabernacle Work*, 1910.
J. C. COX, *Bench-ends in English Churches*, 1916.
C. J. JACKSON, *Illustrated History of English Plate*, 2 vols., 1911.
MOLLET, *Illustrated Dictionary of Words used in Art and Archaeology*, 1883.

(For other works see under Sections I, II, V.)

# XIII

# COINAGE

## 1. *The Anglo-Saxon Period.*

THE most primitive form of trade, the direct exchange of one commodity for another, had at the beginning of the fifth century long been supplanted in this country by purchase through the medium of coinage. The use of coinage was introduced to the British in the third or early second century B.C. through the distant wandering, in the course of trade, of the gold staters of Philip II of Macedon and their imitations. By the end of the second century the British were striking coins imitative of this Greek prototype, and the native currency was supplemented in the next two centuries, and gradually supplanted, by Roman coins. A mint at London, opened by Carausius and closed forty years later, was reopened by Valentinian in 368 under the name of Augusta or Londinium Augusta and was active under Magnus Maximus but closed at his death in 388. During the fifth century the currency of Britain consisted mainly of silver coins of the later emperors, which are called 'siliquae' and 'minutuli' and weighed approximately 30–35 and 15–20 grains respectively; they are found in large hoards in Mendip and the neighbouring country. Roman coins still in circulation and the new Merovingian gold were presumably the medium of exchange in this country in the sixth century, at the close of which a new native coinage was inspired by the intercourse of trade with the Franks under the Merovingian kings.

This development of a native coinage subsequent to the long period of the Roman currency in Britain seems to have taken place during the hegemony of Kent under Æthelberht. His marriage with Bertha, daughter of the king of Paris, brought to England Merovingian craftsmen, and one, Eusebius by name, struck at Canterbury the gold coin bearing the name of the mint 'Dorovernis Civitas' which is illustrated in Fig. 339, *a*. The name of Abbo, possibly the Abbo who worked at Châlons and

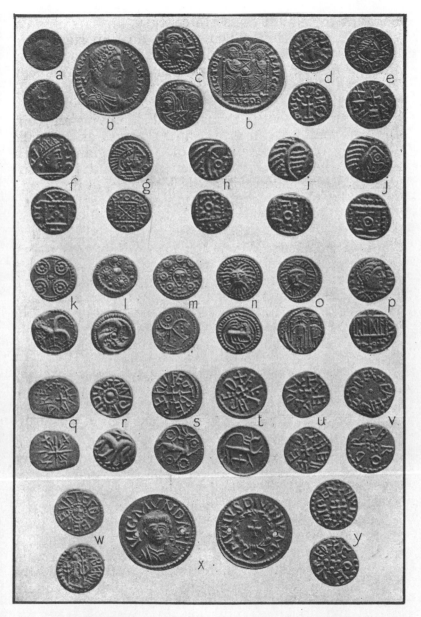

FIG. 339. ANGLO-SAXON COINS. Thrymsa, Sceat, and Styca Coinages.

Limoges at the end of the sixth century, appears on a coin of ruder workmanship which was in an important hoard found at Crondale in Hampshire in 1828. In this find were two Anglo-Saxon gold chains with jewelled ornaments, and 100 gold coins, some of which were Merovingian trientes but the greater part imitations—evidently of British work—of both Roman and Merovingian coins. In Fig. 339 may be seen a triens, or thrymsa as it is called in the laws, of Roman (c) and of Merovingian type (e); b and d in the same Figure show the parent types on a solidus of Magnus Maximus and a Merovingian triens; the reverse design of d was copied from gold coins of Tiberius II (578–82). Blundered legends in Roman script are usually found on these coins, occasionally a mint is indicated—Londinium and Venta (Winchester ?); on Fig. 339, e, may be seen a Runic inscription of uncertain meaning which is attributed on palaeographical grounds to the middle of the seventh century. The weight of the thrymsa averages about 20 grains.

Commercial intercourse and the passing of gold coins into this country in the course of trade with the continent had thus produced at the beginning of the seventh century the first efforts of native craftsmen since the period of Roman occupation. But it was not long before this currency of gold was supplemented by, or gradually reduced to, a silver coinage. At the time of the Anglo-Saxon invasions both the invading and the conquered peoples had for many years been accustomed to use silver as the chief medium of currency. The rising power of the Franks under the Merovingian kings in the sixth and seventh centuries influenced them for the adoption of gold, but the gold coinage was probably not continued for long; for the gold types do not show extensive degradation. It was, however, probably still in issue when the similar silver coinage began. This, too, was a coinage imitative of both Roman and Merovingian types, but it is better regarded as a development from the thrymsa coinage which explains the apparent imitation in silver of types from a gold original. A few of the coins are made of an alloy of gold and silver, a sort of electrum; some, on the other hand, are of debased silver.

This is the 'Sceat' coinage, valued at $4\frac{1}{6}$ to the Mercian shilling or 250 to the pound. It began presumably about the middle of the seventh century and continued to nearly the end of the eighth. The evolution of types on these coins is of considerable interest; in Fig. 339 is illustrated the gradual development of a bird from a profile head (*f* to *j*), and a similar series is shown in the same Figure, *k* to *o*. A few coins bear in Runic lettering the legends ' PADA ' (Fig. 339, *p*) and ' ÆTHILRAED ' which identify them as coins of the Mercian kings Peada (655–7) and Æthelred (675–704). ' Lundonia ' and uncertain inscriptions in Roman and in Runic scripts are found on the sceat series. The weight of the coins seems to range from 15 to 20 grains. A base metal coin bearing in Runic lettering the name Beonna, which is attributed to Beorn of East Anglia (*c.* 760 ?), is perhaps the latest southern sceat before the introduction of the Penny [Fig. 341, *e*].

In Northumbria there was a similar coinage, but it differed in being made, though occasionally of silver, more commonly of brass or copper, while the sceat of the rest of England was usually of silver but occasionally debased. This was probably due to the scarcity in the north of silver, which in the south was obtainable from the mines of south-west England. The earliest named coins are of Ecgfrith (670–85) and Aldfrith (685–705), which are illustrated in Fig. 339, *q*, *r*.

These Northumbrian coins are commonly known as ' Stycas ', a term not found in the Laws but used to translate λεπτόν, the widow's ' mite ', in the Gospel. A comparison of the earlier coins [Fig. 339, *r*, *s*, *t*, Aldfrith, Eadberht, Alchred] with some of the sceat series [Fig. 339, reverses of *k*, *l*, *m*] shows a close resemblance in design and technique. They should no doubt be regarded not as a copper but as a debased silver coinage, and we should probably be right in giving the name Sceat to the northern as well as the southern issues, though it is convenient to retain Styca as a distinctive title for the Northumbrian coins. Large finds of Stycas have been unearthed in the north, especially in York and the neighbourhood. From Eardulf (796–806) onwards the type is simplified to a small cross, circle, or pellet design, and the name of the moneyer is placed on the reverse [Fig. 339, *u*, *v*, Eardulf and Eanred]. The names of the archbishops of York from Ecgberht (734–66) to Wulfhere

(854–900 ?) are found on coins struck by them in their own rights [Fig. 339, *w*, *y*, Ecgberht and Wigmund] ; we do not know when the privilege was first granted to them. The Styca issue continued till the Viking invasions of the ninth century. The coin illustrated in Fig. 339, *x* is a gold solidus of Archbishop Wigmund. It is of Roman style, and bears, like some solidi of Louis le Pieux, the reverse legend ' Munus Divinum ', to which no satisfactory meaning has yet been attached ; perhaps, like *Salus Mundi* on late Roman and Byzantine coins, it refers to the cross which forms the central feature of the type.

Towards the close of the eighth century there was a large circulation of Arab coins in Europe ; the Scandinavian and North German countries were still true to their preference for silver currency, and consequently the large hoards of Arab coins found in the Baltic regions are always composed of silver ' Dirhems ' ; in Southern and Western Europe, however, the gold ' Dinar ' was prevalent. In the British Museum there is a most interesting coin [see Fig. 340, *a*] which imitates closely an Arab dinar of the year 774, but bears on the reverse the title OFFA REX inserted upside down in the Arabic inscription. That the title of Offa was worked in the die and not counterstruck on the coin is sufficient proof that the dinar was copied in this country ; in addition, the errors in the Arabic legends prove that the dies were not made by Arab workmen. It is interesting to note that three similar dinars are known of the same date which have the same errors but have no Roman inscription added ; these also are doubtless either Frankish or Anglo-Saxon copies. Marseilles was the port of landing for Eastern trade and the intercourse between the Carolingian Emperors and the Abassid Caliphs was marked by frequent embassies. It was through France that the dinar was known to England.

It must have been at about the same time as the copying of Arab dinars occurred that a very important change took place in the coinage of this country. This was the replacement of the Sceat by the Penny, in respect of value a small matter—240 pennies as against 250 sceatta were the equivalent of the pound—but historically the birth of a coin that has continued in use to the present day. The rise of the house of Heristal had seen in France a replace-

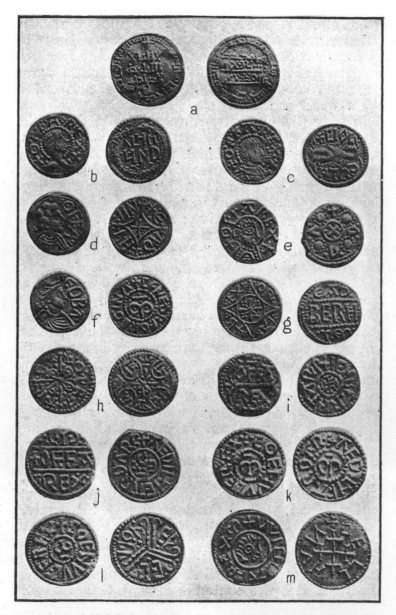

FIG. 340. ANGLO-SAXON COINS. Kings of Mercia.

ment of gold by silver, and had introduced the penny,
which was standardized in 781 by a decree of Charlemagne.
When first introduced into England the penny seems to have
averaged rather less than 20 grains, and it only reached its
full weight of 22½ grains at the end of the ninth century,
though some coins of Alfred, Edward the Elder, and
Æthelstan weigh as much as 24 grains.

The penny was evidently introduced about the middle
of the reign of Offa ; his earliest pennies were struck, it
seems, in Kent, and therefore after the battle of Otford (774).
In form the penny was broader and thinner than the sceat,
and in this respect only did it reflect its parent coinage of
the Carolings.  The art on the pennies of Offa [see *b* to *h*
in Fig. 340] is essentially native ; some of the designs throw
back to sceat types [cf. reverses of *e* and *h* in Fig. 340
with obverses of Fig. 399, *l* and *k*, respectively] ; some types,
especially the serpent wreaths, spirals, and the boss
and pellet pattern [Fig. 340, *b*, *c*, *e*], may be compared with
illustrated manuscripts of contemporary Anglo-Saxon and
Irish work.  The high sense of artistic composition and the
skill of the die-engraving are remarkable ; the execution of
the portrait is curious rather than artistic, but shows more
life than any English coin-portrait before 1503, when
Alexander of Brussels engraved the dies of Henry VII.
By no means all the pennies of Offa display this artistic
merit, some [see, for example, the obverse of *e* in Fig. 340]
are of the poorest execution.  The name of the moneyer,
the officer responsible for the coin, now forms the reverse
legend ; at a later period the name of the mint is added.
This precaution against forgery was, later at least, very
ineffectual.

At this period, with the introduction of the penny, we
see for the first time the privilege of coinage being exercised
by the archbishops of Canterbury.  In what circumstances
and in whose archbishopric the privilege was granted is,
as at York, uncertain ; the earliest name found on
coins is Jænberht, the contemporary of Offa, and on all
his coins the name of Offa appears as king [see Fig. 340, *i*].
It is interesting to find at the same time coins of Eadberht,
Bishop of London [Fig. 340, *g*], and also, if we may accept
a rather doubtful attribution, one of Higberht, the Bishop
of Lichfield, for whom after much controversy Offa secured

archiepiscopal rank [Fig. 340, *h*]. Jænberht died in 790–1 and was succeeded by Æthilheard, who struck coins under both Offa and Cœnwulf [Fig. 340, *j*, *k*].

A coinage of Cynethrith, the wife of Offa [Fig. 340, *f*], must have been struck during Offa's life and may perhaps be regarded as a complimentary issue. Cœnwulf, the successor of Offa, struck pennies of various types and made use of the mint of Canterbury [Fig. 340, *l*, has the tribrach, or pall, of Canterbury]; in his reign the coinage falls into a conventional style which continues under Ceolwulf, Beornwulf, Ludican, and Wiglaf. Wiglaf [Fig. 340, *m*] was defeated at Ellandune and deposed by Ecgberht of Wessex, who struck coins at London and adopted the title King of the Mercians.

Though we can without doubt assign the introduction of the penny to the time of Offa, it is not certain that it was introduced by him. There is every reason to believe that it was in the first instance a Kentish coinage, and it may have been introduced by Ecgberht of Kent, but unfortunately the evidence of this Ecgberht's existence depends only on the coins and some charters of doubtful authenticity. It is difficult to place the coins assigned to him as late as the death of Offa, and that is required for his identification with the Ecgberht who later became king of Wessex [see *a* in Fig. 341]. Coins are known of Eadberht Praen [Fig. 341, *b*], who was deposed by Cœnwulf of Mercia in 798, of Cuthred, the Mercian nominee [Fig. 341, *c*], and of Baldred, who was expelled by Ecgberht of Wessex in 825 [Fig. 341, *d*]. It will be noticed that Cuthred and Baldred use the title ' Rex Cant[iae] '.

In East Anglia the Beonna coin mentioned above (p. 535) is followed by an interesting coin of pure Roman type [Fig. 341, *f*] which is attributed to Æthelberht, the king of East Anglia who was murdered by Offa at the instigation of Cynethrith in 793/4 ; the obverse legend, which is partly in Runic letters, joins the name Æthilberht with that of Lul (the moneyer), the title Rex being placed on the reverse. Coins of Eadwald [Fig. 341, *g*] were also struck before 825, but this king is not known to history.

The year 825 marks an epoch in the history of the coinage no less than in political history. After the battle of Ellandune Ecgberht became master of the whole of

England south of the Humber ; but this did not bring to an end the coinages of all the tributary states. In Mercia the coins of Wiglaf, who was deposed in 825 and restored in 830, were probably struck in his first reign, but his successors Berhtwulf and Burgred still exercised the privilege. A coin of Burgred is shown in Fig. 341, *h* ; his coins are the last struck by an independent Mercian king ; in 874 he was driven out by the Danes, who set up the puppet king Ceolwulf II. The East Anglian kings, of whom little is known, continued a coinage till the death of (St.) Edmund [Fig. 341, *i*, is a penny of Edmund] and his death was followed by an issue of memorial pennies [Fig. 343, *c*]. Kent was more definitely merged into the kingdom of Wessex ; the Kentish title was held by the King of Wessex or his heir and the independent coinage ceased. The archbishopric of Canterbury was at this time held by Wulfred, whose coins are the earliest that bear a tonsured bust, and the first to use the monogram of Dorobernia as the reverse type [see Fig. 341, *j*]. The officers of the Canterbury mint, at which doubtless were struck the issues both of the kings of Kent and of the archbishops of Canterbury, seem to have adopted a temporizing policy after the battle of Ellandune, while the future position of the kings and archbishops remained uncertain ; for we find a curious double series of coins on which no royal or episcopal title appears, some have a diademed bust in profile [Fig. 341, *k*], others a facing bust with tonsure, both bearing on obverse the moneyer's name and on reverse ' Dorobernia Civitas ' ; the moneyers are known to us as moneyers of Baldred and Wulfred. The probable explanation of these coins is that the royal and episcopal moneyers in the uncertainty of the political position thus continued their work at the mint, without binding themselves to a Kentish or Wessex overlord. Wulfred for a time wavered in allegiance between Baldred and Ecgberht, but did not, like his predecessor, put the name of an overlord on his coins. His successor, Ceolnoth (833–70), also exercised the privilege of coining [see *l* in Fig. 341] and in the same Figure are pennies of Archbishop Æthered (870–89) and Plegmund (890–914).

The supremacy of Wessex, which dates from the battle of Ellandune (825), produced for the first time a series of

FIG. 341. ANGLO-SAXON COINS. Kings of Kent
and Archbishops of Canterbury.

coins of the kings of Wessex. The earliest were probably struck at Canterbury, the mint of the defeated Kentish kings, for some of the coins of Ecgberht bear the Dorobernia monogram on the reverse. A coin reading 'Londonia Civitas' [Fig. 342, a] must have been struck at the Mercian mint after the expulsion of Wiglaf in 829. Another reverse legend found on coins of Ecgberht, ' S[an]C[tu]S Andreas ', may no doubt be interpreted as St. Andrew of Rochester [Fig. 342, b]. Ecgberht sometimes adopted on his coins the titles ' Rex M[erciorum]' [see Fig. 342, a] and ' Rex Saxonio- rum '. His successor Æthelwulf added ' Occidentalium ' to Saxonum or Saxoniorum [both forms are found in the latinity of the die-engraver ; see Fig. 342, c]. He also took the monogram of Cantiae as an obverse design, thus assuming the title Rex Cantiae, in conjunction with the Dorobernia monogram on the reverse. It is not, however, possible to assign these Kentish coins to the period of his Kentish title during the lifetime of his father, for no similar coins are known of his younger brother Æthelstan, who followed him as sub-king of Kent. Probably the crown of Kent did not carry with it the privilege of striking coins. New mints in the West of England came into use in the reign of Alfred ; the names of Bath, Exeter [Fig. 342, e], Gloucester, Winchester, and Oxford, as well as Canterbury, are inscribed on his coins, and London [Fig. 342, d] and Lincoln occur in monogram form. This practice of mono- gram signature has up to the present only been found in the monograms of Dorobernia and Cantiae ; the former was introduced by Archbishop Wulfred, who derived the style from the coins of the Carolingian kings. Its revival and common use in the reign of Alfred comes again from the same original source, but this time through the inter- mediate step of the Viking coinages, of which the early issues are essentially Frankish in style and design. The monogram of London appears to have been first used by Halfdan and was presumably adopted by Alfred when he rebuilt the city in 886. The very frequent blundered and barbarous pennies of Alfred were struck by the Danes or during the troublous times of Danish invasions. Alfred coined halfpence as well as pennies ; in this matter also he probably followed an example set by the Viking.

FIG. 342. ANGLO-SAXON COINS. Kings of Wessex.

## 2. The Danish Invasions.

At the end of the eighth century the Viking settlements on the coast of Ireland began, and from these settlements came the earliest raids on the English coasts. A hoard of English pennies was found in 1874 at Delgany near Wicklow, which comprised issues of kings of Mercia and Kent, of archbishops of Canterbury, and a few of Ecgberht of Wessex, the latest in date of issue being the anonymous Canterbury pennies attributed above to the year 825 ; this hoard of coins must have formed part of the plunder carried back by the Vikings to their Irish homes after a raid such as that on Sheppey which took place in 834. The first definite settlement in Thanet seems to have come in 850/1, after the defeat of Rorik at Ockley. In 867/8 the Great Army, marching from East Anglia, defeated and killed the Northumbrian kings Osberht and Ælla, and from this date the so-called ' Styca ' currency came to an end. The army then went south to Nottingham, but after sustaining siege by Burgred, who was supported by Æthelwulf and Alfred, withdrew to the north. In 870 the Vikings again invaded East Anglia and murdered (St.) Edmund, who, we have already seen, was commemorated on an issue of coins after his death [Fig. 343, c]. After Ashdown in the following year Halfdan alone of the leaders escaped to Reading ; in 874 he had returned to Mercia and, deposing Burgred, set up the puppet king Ceolwulf II [see b in Fig. 343]. Halfdan was now presumably in possession of London, and at this time (872–5) struck the interesting coin shown in Fig. 343, a, which for its obverse type reverts to the design of the solidus of Magnus Maximus and on its reverse introduces the new London monogram which comes into common use on the coins of Alfred. In 875–6 Halfdan marched north and seized the southern half of Northumbria, including York, leaving the northern part under its own kings as tributaries. The remainder of the army, under Guthrum, continued the attack on Wessex, and, after his decisive defeat at Æthandune and the partition of the Wessex and Mercian kingdoms by which he held possession of the part north of the Thames and east of Watling Street, he settled there in 880 under the name of Æthelstan II.

The coinages of the Viking invasions form an interesting group. The earliest coin of the series seems to be the London penny of Halfdan to which attention has already been drawn. Halfdan also struck a halfpenny without name of mint, which from its resemblance to halfpence of Alfred appears to belong to the south of England. A penny of Ceolwulf II of Mercia is illustrated in Fig. 343, *b*; another is similar to, and no doubt copied from, the London penny of Halfdan. In East Anglia the memorial coinage of St. Eadmund is followed or accompanied by a coinage of Guthrum-Æthelstan, and to the Danes or to the disordered conditions consequent upon their invasions may be attributed the many blundered imitations of St. Eadmund, Alfred, and Plegmund. There is also at this period a coinage of Lincoln dedicated to St. Martin, and rather later a very large and apparently prolonged issue of St. Peter at York [Fig. 343, *d*].

Halfdan was expelled from Northumbria in 878 (?) and, after an interval of five years, a new king, Guthred or Cnut, was set up at York and reigned from 883 to 894; of this king are known both pennies and halfpennies entitled Cnut Rex and bearing on the reverse the mint signature 'Ebraice Civitas' [Fig. 343, *e*]. Some of his coins bear the Scriptural legends 'Dns Ds Re' (Dominus Deus Rex) or 'Mirabilia Fecit' in place of the mint name. One penny is known which couples the title of Alfred on the one side with that of Guthred-Cnut on the other, but it is hardly safe to read in this coin evidence of an acknowledgement by Guthred of Alfred as overlord, for its barbarous workmanship classes it rather with the many blundered imitations of the time; a close parallel for such a 'muling' of types may be found in a penny that combines the St. Eadmund legend with an obverse of Alfred, and another bears the St. Eadmund legend on obverse and the signature of the mint of York on reverse. Siefred, who followed Guthred at York in 894 and brought an army south to help Hasting in his attacks on Wessex in 893–6, struck coins similar to those of Guthred, and used the same varieties of legend on the reverse [Fig. 343, *f*]. Closely connected with the Cnut and Siefred coinages is a penny which bears the name 'Alwaldus' and the reverse legend 'Dns Ds REX' [see *g* in Fig. 343]; it has been attributed to Æthelweald, who made an attempt to seize the throne on the death of Alfred and was acknowledged king by the Danes in Northumbria and East Anglia ; this coin was found in the Cuerdale hoard, and the attribution is therefore possible in point of date. A coin, illustrated in Fig. 343, *h*, which bears the title ' Sitric Comes ' and on the reverse the name of the moneyer Gundibert and the mint ' Sceldfor ' (Shelford in Nottinghamshire ?), was also in the Cuerdale hoard, but its attribution is uncertain ; in type it resembles the Oxford pennies of Alfred.

It is chiefly from the hoard of coins which was found at Cuerdale in Lancashire in 1840 that we derive our knowledge of the Viking issues ; the hoard contained nearly 7,000 coins, including as many as 900 of Alfred and only 51 of Edward the Elder, whence the deposit may be dated shortly after the death of Alfred. In addition to the Danish issues already described there were a few Oriental and more than 1,000 French, German, and Italian coins, mostly of the Carolingian emperors, the latest being of Berengar. The coins of Guthred-Cnut numbered over 2,500, of Siefred nearly 250, and those of St. Edmund over 1,800 ; there were in the hoard more than 50 pennies of Archbishop Plegmund, and only one each of Ceolnoth and Æthered. It was therefore essentially a Viking hoard, and thoroughly illustrative of the currency of this country in the second half of the ninth century. The constant incursions of the Vikings into France are illustrated not only by the large number of Frankish coins in the hoard which were probably brought by the Danes and used as currency here, but also by the large number of pennies that bear the name of the Frankish mint Quentovic ; others bearing the name Cunnetti have not been attributed with certainty ; Condé has been suggested, or a blundered form of Quentovic. The style and designs, notably the monogram devices, of the Viking coins struck in England in the ninth century are of Frankish origin, and the majority of the moneyers of the St. Edmund coinage have Frankish names.

At the beginning of the tenth century the Danes in Northumbria were in close touch with the Danes in Ireland, and the kings of York, who were constantly at the head of risings in Northumbria, were mostly of the family of

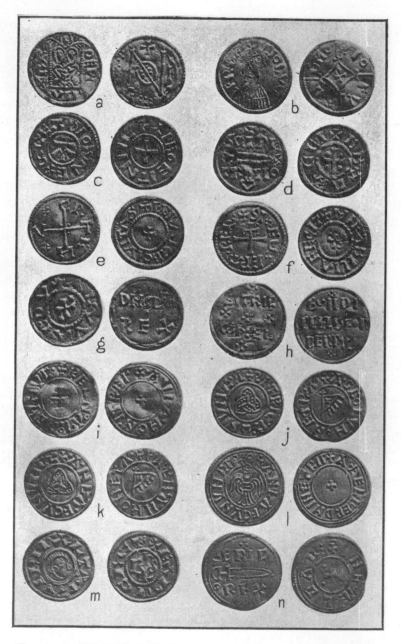

FIG. 343. COINS OF THE DANISH INVASIONS.

Ingwar. Regnald, grandson of Ingwar, after invading Scotland as far as Dunblane, seized York in 919, and was one of the kings who did homage to Edward in the year 921. He seems to have remained as king at York till his death in 921 or 924, when he was succeeded by Sihtric Caoch, who did homage to Æthelstan in 925 and married his sister ; he died in 926. To these two kings, as we shall see later, may with certainty be assigned some pennies which derive their types both from Danish designs and from English coin-types ; but similar pennies bearing the name Anlaf present considerable difficulty owing to the scanty information available of the two Anlafs, Quaran and Guthrethsson, who, at various times in the second quarter of the tenth century, were in possession of the throne of York.

There are two types of Regnald, one is illustrated in Fig. 343, *i*, and the other (known from a fragment only) is the type used by his successor, Sihtric, bearing on one side a Danish shield and on the other a Danish standard or pennon. Sihtric has this one type only [Fig. 343, *j*]. Anlaf's coins form two distinct groups, the earlier being clearly distinguished by the neater style of the coins and also by the spelling of the name which is always 'Anlaf' on the earlier and 'Onlaf' on the later coins. Of the earlier group there are five types ; these include both the types used by Regnald, and on that which Sihtric also used [Fig. 343, *k*] the moneyer of Regnald appears again as moneyer of Anlaf ; there is another distinct Danish type, the Raven with wings displayed [Fig. 343, *l*], and two English types, one of which closely follows a floral design used by Edward the Elder, and the other, which was struck at Derby, is on a coin identical but for the king's title with a coin of Æthelstan. The later group is of one type only, with the sword as obverse design, and this appears again on coins of Eric [Fig. 343, *m*].

It would seem reasonable to conclude that the earlier group, the 'Anlaf' coins, were struck within limits of a few years before and after 930 ; the coin with the floral ornament follows so closely that of Edward not only in design but also in style that it cannot have been struck many years after his death ; the type of Æthelstan that is copied on another coin belongs to an early period of his reign, and may perhaps be the type which followed the monetary edicts of the Council of Greatley (928) ; in addition, the close relation of the other coins of this group to those of Regnald and Sihtric prevents a long interval being placed between the death of Sihtric and their issue. The later group is in close alliance with the coins of Eric, and falls naturally into the years 942–54 when Anlaf Quaran and Eric Blothox were taking turn and turn about on the throne of York. On the death of Sihtric in 926 we hear of Æthelstan driving out Sihtric's son Guthfrith and annexing York, and coins struck by Æthelstan at York might well belong to this date. In 933 Anlaf Quaran contracted his alliance with Constantine III of Scotland with a view, it is said, to designs on York, and in 937 he was one of the allied kings who were defeated by Æthelstan at Brunanburgh. But, if we may judge from the coins, it would appear that Anlaf came into possession of York after the expulsion of Guthfrith by Æthelstan and was already accepted as king by the Danes when he allied himself with Constantine and married his daughter ; the York coins of Æthelstan would in this case be placed after the battle of Brunanburgh (937–9).

It does not seem possible to attribute any coins to Anlaf Guthfrithsson, who joined Quaran in the rising of 940 and died in 942. At his death Anlaf Quaran was again sole king of York, and was engaged in a conflict with Regnald, brother of Guthfrithsson, who may well be the ' Rainaut ' or ' Raienalt ' of some pennies that bear the mint signature of York [Fig. 343, *m*] ; both were expelled by Edmund in 944. Eric Blothox was on the throne in 947-8, Anlaf from 949 to 952, and Eric again from 952 to 954. Thus the ' Onlaf ' group may be attributed without difficulty to the period of Anlaf's reign between 942 and 952, the see-saw between him and Eric being illustrated by the close connexion already noticed in their coins. With the expulsion of Eric in 952 the separate kingdom of Northumbria comes to an end.

Before returning to the coinages of the kings of Wessex a coin deserves mention which is known to us from one specimen only, now in the British Museum [Fig. 342, *i*]. It is of the common English type of this period but bears the title ' Howael Rex ' and the name of the moneyer

Gillys. The date of the coin, *tempore* Edmund, assigns it without doubt to Howel Dda, who is best known for his code of laws ; he was king of South Wales for about thirty-five years and died in 948 or 950. He was one of the kings who did homage to Æthelstan in the north in 926, and is said to have been among the kings defeated at Brunanburgh. The coin seems, from its resemblance to pennies of Edmund, to have been struck towards the close of Howel's reign, after the death of Æthelstan. It was possibly struck at Chester, as the uncommon name Gillys is found on Chester coins of Edred and Edgar.

The progress of culture which became possible once more after the peace of Wedmore had a marked influence on the coinage of Edward the Elder. The pennies of his reign owe their elegance not only to the greater care with which they were struck and to the better finish with which the dies were engraved, but to an entirely new development of artistic composition in the workmanship of the die-engravers. The portrait, when it appears, though still of a conventional form which fails to attain the lively realism of the portrait of Offa, is more carefully engraved and ceases to be a mere outline drawing. But the chief feature of this reign is the original work shown in the elaborate and carefully executed designs which now appear on the coins ; floral ornamentation especially [see Fig. 342, *f*] is most artistically treated, and other new designs, such as the Hand of Providence and representations of buildings, are a welcome relief from the cross and pellet patterns which were previously the limits of the engraver's imagination. The walled buildings which appear on some coins [see Fig. 342, *g*] have been supposed to be a type commemorative of the burgs that were erected by Edward and Æthelflæd in their successful warfare against the Danes. This artistic level is not long maintained ; the coins of Æthelstan, with a few exceptions, revert to the small cross as the central design with the names of mint and moneyer forming a circular inscription, or the arrangement of the moneyer's name in two or three lines across the field of the coin, but good style is shown in the neatness of the engraver's work and the striking of the coins is still very carefully done ; a portrait occurs only on a few types, but it shows in some cases an improvement on that of Edward ; a jewelled crown, instead of the Roman diadem, is for the first time depicted [see Fig. 342, *h*]. The edicts of the Council of Greatley (928) contain the earliest surviving ordinances in which mention is made of the mints ; coins were not to be struck except within a town, and each town was to have one moneyer with certain specified exceptions among which were London with eight moneyers, Winchester with six, and Canterbury with seven—four for the king, two for the bishop, and one for the abbot. The names of Chester, Derby, and Nottingham on the coins of Æthelstan illustrate the progress made by him and his father against the Danes ; reference has already been made to his coinage at the mint of York; the title 'Rex Totius Britanniae' which he commonly adopts on his coins, like similar titles used in his signature to charters, marks his own appreciation of his military achievements.

The end of the Danish kingdom in Northumbria is marked by the appearance of the name of York on coins of Edwig [Fig. 342, *j*]; no York coins are yet known of Edred by whom the kingdom was finally reduced. About this time, perhaps in consequence of the edicts of Greatley, it had become the regular, instead of occasional, practice to put the name of the mint as well as that of the moneyer on the coins. The number of mints now increases rapidly until, under the stress of work occasioned by the payments of tribute to the Danes in the reign of Æthelred, there were more than seventy in operation. The very large and frequent hoards of Æthelred's pennies that have been found in Scandinavia prove that the payments to the Danes must, in some cases at least, have been conveyed in coin to Denmark ; the very large collection of these coins in the museum at Stockholm is evidence of the great extent of their exportation. The pennies of Æthelred were commonly imitated for the currencies of the Danish kings of Denmark and Ireland. From this period the king's likeness, which was hitherto only occasionally used, is always placed on the obverse of the coins. There is one exception, a curious issue of the latter part of Æthelred's reign, on which the Agnus Dei on the obverse is joined with the Dove on the reverse ; the coins bear the names of English mints, and one cut halfpenny of this issue is known.

The later Anglo-Saxon coins call for little comment.

The portrait forms the obverse design and the reverse is usually, but not always, a cross variously ornamented. The chief object seems to have been a clear differentiation of the types, and there does not appear to be adequate reason for attempting to attach a political significance to the Hand of Providence on coins of Æthelred [Fig. 342, *k*], to the use of the word Pax on coins of Cnut, Edward Confessor, and Harold II [Fig. 342, *n*], or to other particular devices; they are probably religious rather than political in their origin. On some coins of Cnut and the Confessor the king is shown wearing a helmet with high peak such as may be seen on the Bayeux Tapestry [Fig. 342, *l*]. The type of Edward the Confessor shown in Fig. 342, *m*, represents the full figure of the king enthroned, and on the reverse a martlet is placed in each angle of the cross.

### 3. *From the Norman Conquest to the Middle of the Fourteenth Century.*

The coinage of William the Conqueror is illustrative of his political principle of adopting the native institutions and adapting them, when necessary, to suit his purpose. Therefore we find after the Norman Conquest a continuance of the denomination, standard, value, and design of the Anglo-Saxon coinage; two of the eight types issued by the Conqueror are illustrated in Fig. 344, *a, b*. The number of mints in operation in both the Conqueror's and the Confessor's reigns is approximately seventy, and many of the same moneyers continued in office after the Conquest. Mention of moneyers occurs occasionally in Domesday, whence we learn that the office was one of importance and that the men who held it were men of substance. From the same source we learn that the moneyers made a payment when the type of the coinage was changed (*quando moneta vertebatur*), from which we may conclude that the periodical change of type was a source of revenue to the king, though probably its primary object was a control similar to the later Trial of the Pyx (see below, p. 559), a tax being collected on delivery of the new dies. Assaying was certainly understood at this time, for payments in Domesday are sometimes 'blanched', i.e. assayed and compensated. In France the privilege of coinage was made a considerable source of profit to the feudal lords by means of its debasement ; in Normandy William had instituted a triennial hearth-tax in place of this source of revenue, but it had led to failure owing to his better coins being driven out by the more debased deniers of the neighbouring feudal states. The dies for the coinage throughout the country were, with few exceptions, made at London, where, Domesday tells us, the moneyers made their payments on receipt of their new dies. The pennies of Rufus do not bear any marks of difference from those of his father, but it is possible, on the cumulative evidence of the grouping of types by the hoards in which they have been found, the ' muling' of types (i.e. the combination of the obverse die of one type with the reverse of another), the over-striking of coins (coins are not infrequently found which were restruck with a pair of dies of a later type than that which originally struck the coin), and from the forms of lettering employed on the coins, to arrange in their order the thirteen types which bear the name of William, and, by a proportionate distribution, to assign the first eight to the Conqueror and the remaining five to Rufus ; the second of the five types of William II is illustrated in Fig. 344, c. The style of the coins shows a great deterioration under Rufus, which is progressive throughout the reign.

The Coronation Charter of Henry I removed the *Monetagium*, which was probably identical with the payments *de moneta* mentioned above : ' Monetagium commune quod capiebatur per civitates et comitatus, quod non fuit tempore regis Eadwardi, hoc ne amodo sit, omnino defendo.' His ordinance *de moneta falsa et cambiatoribus* fixed the penalty of mutilation for forgery and forbade the moneyers to exercise their rights of exchange outside their own *comitatus* and any but the moneyers to hold exchange ; this charter is assigned to 1100–1 or 1103. Nevertheless, forgery or debasement by the moneyers was rife in his reign, and the Anglo-Saxon Chronicle records that in the year 1125 Bishop Roger of Salisbury summoned all the moneyers to Winchester and had them all mutilated in accordance with the king's instructions, ' and that was all with great justice ', says the chronicler, ' because they had foredone all the land with their great quantity of false money' ; the Winton Annals say that all the moneyers of England except three of Winchester were mutilated,

and the Margam Annals give the number mutilated as
ninety-four. A more curious monetary difficulty is noted
in the summary of Henry's character by William of Malmesbury ; curious, too, is the homoeopathic remedy which was
applied : ' Cum nummos fractos, licet boni argenti, a ven-
ditoribus non recipi audisset, omnes vel frangi vel incidi
praecepit.' This seems to mean that the traders made
a practice of incising or snicking the coins for the
purpose of testing their quality and that pennies so dis-
figured were being refused for ordinary circulation ; Henry,
to meet the difficulty, ordered all coins to be snicked at the
mints before issue. The evidence of the coins agrees with
this interpretation ; such an incision is found in all the
coins of Henry I from his seventh to his twelfth type
inclusive (see *d* in Fig. 344, which shows the snick through
the N of ' Henricus ' and between A and L of the
mint-name Wall[ingford]), the order being presumably
withdrawn under the reorganization following the examination and punishment of the moneyers in 1125. It is interesting at this period to observe the proportion of the types
to the length of the reign ; Edward Confessor issued
ten or eleven types in twenty-four years, the two Williams
thirteen types in thirty-four years, Henry fifteen types in
thirty-five years ; this rather points to the conclusion that
each type had a regular duration of two or three years.
Two types of Henry I, his twelfth and fifteenth, are shown
in Fig. 344, *d, e.*

The civil wars of the reign of Stephen produced a great
variety of interesting coins, though some are as yet of
uncertain attribution. The normal issues of the king
do not require special comment, but their rarity gives them
a special value for collectors ; his first and last types only
are, by the discovery of hoards in Hertfordshire and
Hampshire, known to us in any number. A coin of the first
type is illustrated in Fig. 344, *f.* The Angevin party had a
coinage struck at mints in the west of England in the name
of Matildis Imperatrix or Comitissa [Fig. 344, *i*, struck at
Oxford], and, after her retirement in favour of her son,
in the name of Henricus or Henricus Rex. A series of
coins, on which the type is identical with Stephen's first
issue, but the king's name is replaced by the inscription
' P(or W ?)ereric ' or ' P(or W ?)ereric M ', may perhaps be

explained as a temporary issue of the period of the king's captivity (1141), the engravers, who presumably prepared the dies at London, having clumsily endeavoured to introduce the name of the Empress (Empereriz) Matilda in place of that of Stephen. To the same period seem to belong pennies having on the obverse two full-length figures, male and female, holding between them a long sceptre, with the king's title as inscription but ornaments in place of a reverse legend [Fig. 344, g] ; the two figures are probably Queen Matilda and Stephen, signifying the attempt of Matilda to support her husband's cause during his captivity. Coins of Eustace FitzJohn [Fig. 344, k, l] and Robert de Stuteville [Fig. 344, j], two northern barons of whom little is known, of Henry, Bishop of Winchester and brother of the king [Fig. 344, h], and of Brian FitzCount (?), who took an active part on the Angevin side and was three times besieged in his castle at Wallingford, show either a freedom in granting the privilege of coining or its frequent usurpation during these troublous times.

In the reign of Henry II the periodical changing of types was abandoned, perhaps with a view to decreasing forgery, and the first type of his reign continued to be struck until 1180 [Fig. 344, m]. The money was then in a wretched condition through the incompetence of the moneyers ; and the king decided to issue a new type and to obtain the services of a foreigner, Philip Aymery of Tours, to supervise the new coinage ; the foreigner is said to have quickly fallen a victim to the profitable abuses that were still rife among the moneyers and to have been dismissed from the country for conniving with them. The various abuses that were practised on the coinage were too profitable to be amenable to the most severe penalties, and, though there seems to have been some further action taken against the moneyers in 1205, the abuses continued. In 1247 Henry III, in the hope of putting an end to the clipping of the coins, made another change in the type. In the meantime the type of 1180, which is commonly known as the Short-cross type [Fig. 344, n], had remained unchanged through the reigns of Richard and John, who omitted even to replace the name Henricus by their own names on the pennies issued during their reigns. The new coinage of 1247 was somewhat similar to that of the previous issue.

but on the reverse the voided cross was continued to the edge of the coin, and an order was issued that no coin should pass current on which the ends of the cross were not visible [see Fig. 344, *o*].

From the death of Plegmund (914) and Wulfhere (900 ?) the archbishops ceased to place their names on their coins, and we are therefore unable to distinguish in the issues of the Canterbury and York mints the royal from the ecclesiastical pennies, except in certain cases where a moneyer is known from the Pipe Rolls or other sources to have been employed in the king's or the archbishop's service ; but in the reign of Edward I and in subsequent reigns, a quatrefoil in the centre of the reverse differentiates the coins of the Archbishop of York. The palatinate bishops of Durham had, from some early date which we cannot determine, the right of coinage ; the earliest Durham coin at present known is of the last type of William I. In the foundation charter of the Abbey of Reading (1125) Henry I granted to the abbey a mint and a moneyer at Reading, which was soon exchanged for the use of one of the moneyers at the London mint. But a grant of greater importance to the student of coins is that to the Abbot of St. Edmund ; charters of renewal only are extant and the date of the original grant is not known, but, apart from the memorial coinage at the end of the ninth century, the earliest coins attributed to the mint of Bury St. Edmunds are of the Confessor's reign. The coinage of the Abbey of St. Edmund is of value in determining the chronological arrangement of coins of the twelfth and thirteenth centuries owing to the limitation of the grant to one moneyer and to the use of one pair of dies which had apparently to be returned before a new pair was obtained. The coinage of the bishops of Durham is even more valuable as a guide to the classification of groups of coins ; from about the end of the thirteenth century, except during the reigns of Richard II and Henry IV and V, it was customary for the bishops to place on their coins personal symbols which are therefore absent from coins struck at periods when the temporalities of the see were in the hands of the king's receiver through the suspension or death of the bishop.

These ecclesiastical issues have been the chief means of arriving at a classification of the long series of pennies

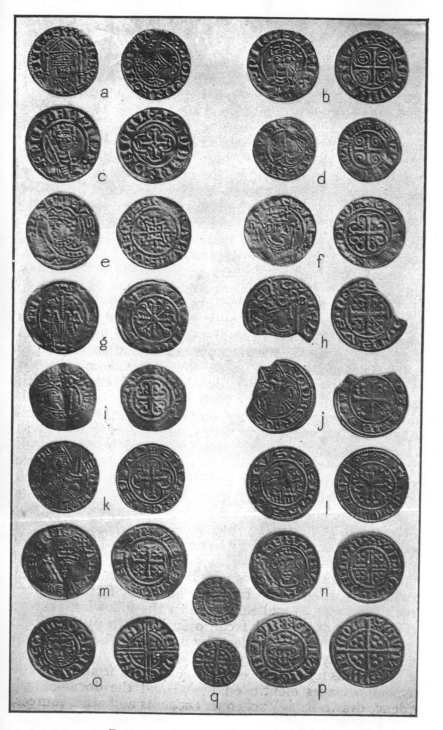

FIG. 344. ENGLISH COINS.

bearing the name of Edward, which were substituted in 1279 for the 'Long-cross' pennies and continued to the end of the reign of Edward III without any change except a very slight variety of style ; they remained, in respect of type, unchanged till the reign of Henry VII. The crowned head of the king is the obverse design and the reverse a long cross with three pellets in each angle. Fig. 344, *p*, shows one of these pennies bearing, at the beginning of the inscription on both sides, the cross moline of Anthony Bek (1283–1311) ; his successor, Kellawe, used a crozier as his badge, and Beaumont a lion rampant.

With the introduction of the new coinage of Edward I the custom of placing the moneyer's name on the coin disappears, but there is a curious survival in the occurrence, on some pennies struck in and shortly after 1280, of the name Robert de Hadley. The name of the mint is omitted, but from documentary evidence we know Robert de Hadley to have been the moneyer of St. Edmund. There was a mint at Berwick in use by the English kings at this time ; most of the dies were made locally and consequently the coins are of somewhat barbarous workmanship.

The striking of halfpennies at the end of the ninth century and beginning of the tenth has already been noticed, but subsequently the penny only was coined and small change was provided by cutting the penny into halves and quarters ; this cutting was facilitated by the use of a voided or plain cross in the reverse design. We have documentary evidence of an order for halfpence to be struck in the reign of Henry III, and also the evidence of the chroniclers for an order to strike round halfpence as early as the reign of Henry I ; but none have yet been found earlier than the reign of Edward I and, as discoveries of cut halfpence in finds of this period show that the old method still continued, it is possible that the order was not previously carried out. In 1279, however, farthings were struck [Fig. 344, *q*] and halfpence in the following year.

The coins of Edward I can only be distinguished from those of his son and grandson by arranging the coins upon a close scrutiny of their style and lettering and applying to the series thus formed the evidence available from the ecclesiastical coinages mentioned above and the documentary evidence drawn from Exchequer accounts and other sources.

The appendix to the chronicle of John de Oxenedes gives a long account of a trial of the money which was held in the thirty-second year of the reign of Henry III. A mandamus was issued to the mayor and citizens of London to summon twelve ' de discretioribus et legalioribus hominibus ' and twelve good goldsmiths to present themselves before the barons of the Exchequer at Westminster, and there to examine both the old and the new coinage and to propose measures for its improvement. An assay by fire was accordingly made both of the old money (i.e. the 1180 issue of ' short-cross ' pennies) and of the new money (i.e. the 1247 issue of ' long-cross ' pennies) ; the new money was found up to standard but the short-cross pennies were below standard. For future use it was decided to keep two proof-pieces, one of pure silver and the other of standard silver, in the treasury at Westminster, and similar proof-pieces were sent to each of the mints. An order follows for the appointment of officers of mints other than London and Canterbury, the mints numbering sixteen, excluding Durham and Bury St. Edmunds ; a few years later the provincial mints were closed, only the mints of London, Canterbury, Durham, and Bury St. Edmunds remaining in operation. About the year 1300 the mints of Chester, Newcastle, Kingston-on-Hull, and Exeter were opened for a short time ; Bristol was working towards the beginning and the end of the reign of Edward I, and Calais in 1363–4.

## 4. *The Coinage of the English Possessions in France.*

The coins issued for circulation in the English possessions in France, though properly regarded from the numismatic point of view as belonging to the French series, have considerable interest as illustrating the history of this country in its relations with France from the middle of the twelfth century to the middle of the fifteenth. The issues of the Calais mint are not included in this section ; Calais was regarded as an English mint and issued English coins under indentures identical with those for the mints in England ; it was often under the same Master as the mint of London.

The earliest of the coins are deniers and oboles struck by Henry II for Aquitaine, which came to him by his marriage with Eleanor ; they are of a simple form, inscribed on one side ' Henricus (or Enricus) Rex ' and on the other ' Aquitanie '. In 1168 he ceded the province to his son Richard, who continued the coinage in his own name without the title Rex until his father's death, when he resigned Aquitaine to Eleanor ; after his accession he struck similar coins for Poitou and a rare denier of Issoudun (Exolduni) which must have been struck after the treaty of 1196. After the death of Eleanor (1204) the French king confiscated John's possessions, and neither he nor Henry III is known to have struck coins for French circulation. In 1252 Henry III ceded such rights as he had in France to his son Edward, who struck during this period deniers and oboles of lion type with the title ' Edwardus Filius Henrici Regis Angliae '. A coinage without name of mint struck by Edward for Ponthieu (*Moneta Potivi*), which fell to Eleanor of Castille in 1279 and was confirmed by the treaty of Amiens, and some coins struck at Abbeville were followed by a coinage for Guienne (1286–93), part of which bears the mark of Bordeaux.

The interest of these early issues is purely historical ; the spasmodic issues of coins by the English kings show the varying security of the tenure of their French possessions, and the coins of Richard and Edward struck before their accession to the English throne illustrate the principle of ceding the French territories to the heir apparent, which culminated in the creation of the principality of Aquitaine in favour of the Black Prince. In the reign of Edward III the Anglo-Gallic coins assume a much wider interest. The adoption of a gold coinage and the addition of the groat to the silver series are important innovations in this coinage, both of which, if we overlook the abortive attempt of Henry III to introduce gold, preceded similar innovations in the English currency. There is also at this time a great artistic interest in the study of the Anglo-Gallic gold coins. The artistic imagination of the engravers is given ample scope in this series ; it is not, as in the English coinage, limited by the political or financial necessity of adhering so long as possible to a single type. The *écu*, *léopard*, and *guiennois* of Edward III, and the *pavillon* and *hardi* of the Black Prince, are fine examples of the application of Gothic art to the limited medium at the disposal of the die-engraver. The short-lived English Florin series and the earliest Nobles are, as we shall see later, not inferior to these ; but, as no new designs were introduced for a century and a quarter, the Noble with its half and quarter, which were the only gold currency of this country, very quickly assumed the spiritless style that differentiates the work of the copyist from that of the original artist.

It is not possible to assign a date to the first gold coinage of Edward—the gold florin struck for Aquitaine— but it was certainly struck before 1337. It is one of the many close imitations of the famous *Fiorino d'oro* which was first struck at Florence in 1252 ; on the obverse is the *fiore*, or lily, and on the reverse the standing figure and the name of S. Iohannes Baptista. The obverse is inscribed ' Dux Aquitanie ', the name of Edward does not appear [Fig. 345, *a*]. The *écu* or *chaise d'or*, imitated not long after 1337 from the coinage of the King of France where it first appeared in 1336, represented the king enthroned holding a sword and the shield of France. This was soon superseded by a coin of original design, named, from its obverse type, the *léopard*, which continued till after the treaty of Brétigny when Edward gave up the use of the title ' Rex Franciae '. Between 1360 and 1362 was struck for Guienne a new coin of the same value as the *léopard*, which was the first gold coin to be marked with mint initials ; the letters of Bordeaux, Limoges, Poitiers, Rochelle, and Figeac are found. The king is represented on the *guiennois* standing in full armour under a portal of Gothic style ; a specimen from the Rochelle mint is illustrated [Fig. 345, *b*]. The reverse legends of these coins are Scriptural : ' Christus vincit, Christus regnat, Christus imperat ' appears on both *écu* and *léopard ;* ' Gloria in excelsis deo et in terra pax hominibus ' on the *guiennois* has a special reference to the peace following the treaty of Brétigny. The florin had a currency value of three shillings ; the *écu*, *léopard*, and *guiennois* were equivalent to the half-noble, or 3s. 4d.

The alliance of Edward III with Flanders and Brabant in 1339 was the source of the introduction of the Groat into the Anglo-Gallic coinage. The *gros* of the Lion type was the ' monnoye commune, bonne et loyale, qui aura son cours dans les deux pays ' under the treaty of the same year between the Count of Flanders and the Duke of Brabant, and the same coin was included in the French coinage of Edward III, presumably at the same time. He also struck a *gros tournois* which was the original type of groat introduced into the French coinage by Louis IX in 1266. A sterling, copied from the English penny but having a crown in place of the three pellets in each angle of the cross on the reverse, was struck for Aquitaine. After 1360 a half-length figure of the king was placed on the obverse of the groat and sterling, and the ' Gloria in excelsis' legend took the place of ' Benedictum sit Nomen Domini' on the groat.

A very extensive coinage was issued by the Black Prince during the few years of his tenure of the Principality (1362–72). During the first year he continued the issue at Bordeaux of *léopards* and *guiennois* of the type previously issued by his father. Fig. 345, *d*, is a *léopard* struck by the Black Prince at Bordeaux. After July 1363, when he arrived in France, he struck the *écu* or *chaise d'or* at Bordeaux, Limoges, and Rochelle. In the following year he is said to have turned his attention to the coinage after returning from his tour of the principality, and to have issued the new gold coin called the *pavillon* or *royal* ; the prince is represented seated under a Gothic pavilion, robed, and wearing a wreath of roses, his right arm resting on a shield and holding a sword ; his feet rest on two leopards couchant and in the field are four feathers, two at either side of the prince ; the reverse, which has feathers inserted in the highly ornamental design, bears the legend ' Dominus adiutor et protector meus et in ipso speravit cor meum' [Fig. 345, *c*]. The mint-marks of Bordeaux, Limoges, Poitiers, and Rochelle are found on the pavilion. Another gold coin was issued after the prince's return from his Spanish expedition in 1368, called the *hardi d'or*, of much simpler design ; the obverse has a three-quarter figure of the prince facing, holding a sword, the reverse a floriate cross with leopard and lis in alternate angles and the inscription ' Auxilium meum a Domino' ; it was issued at Bordeaux, Limoges, and Rochelle [Fig. 345, *e*, struck at Limoges]. In silver there were regular issues of *gros* and sterlings, the sterling being superseded by a *hardi d'argent* with three-quarter length figure at the same time as the *hardi d'or* was introduced. In billon,

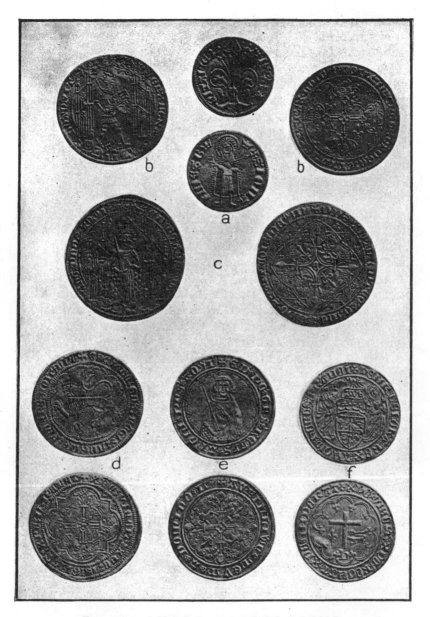

FIG. 345. ANGLO-GALLIC COINS.

or base metal, he struck *Doubles* and *Deniers*. The style adopted by the Black Prince on his coins was 'Edwardus Primogenitus Regis Angliae Princeps Aquitaniae'.

Henry of Lancaster in 1347 was granted the town of Bergerac with the right of coinage ; between 1347 and 1352 he struck *gros* and *demi-gros* with the title 'Henricus Comes Lancastriae Dominus Bragairacii', and after 1352, as 'Dux Lancastriae', *demi-gros* and sterlings. On his death in 1361 Bergerac reverted to the crown, and in the following year became part of the principality of the Black Prince, who granted it in 1370, with rights of coinage, to John of Gaunt.

In addition to the right of coinage at Bergerac, John of Gaunt was granted by Edward III coinage at Bayonne and Guiche in 1377, and at Bayonne and D'Ax by Richard II in 1380. In 1390 he became Duke of Aquitaine with privilege of coining. Nevertheless, we have no coins bearing his name, but it is possible that a Bordeaux *double* and *denier* bearing the title 'Edwardus Rex Angliae' and a *denier* of D'Ax reading 'Dux Aquitaniae' without a name were struck by him under the grant of 1377.

Richard II and Henry IV continued the gold and silver issues of the *hardi* type and a billon *denier* similar to those of the Black Prince. In the latter reign the planta genista takes the place of the fleur-de-lis on the silver coin.

At the accession of Henry V the scene of English activity in France is removed from Aquitaine in consequence of the strife for the French throne. Henry's offer to forgo his claim to the crown of France in virtue of certain concessions was rejected and, war being declared, he landed at Harfleur in 1415 but gained nothing beyond the moral effect of the victory of Agincourt. In 1417 he took Caen, and there issued a curious and very rare *demi-gros* of French type. After the capture of Rouen (January 1419), he established a mint there and struck the *gros d'argent* and *mouton d'or*. The *mouton*, or *agneau*, was a type introduced into the French coinage in 1311 ; on the obverse is the Paschal Lamb with banner and the legend 'Agnus dei qui tollis peccata mundi miserere nobis', the king's title in abbreviated form being below the lamb. The reverse has the usual ornate design with floriate cross and the legend 'Christus vincit, &c.' In the following

April another mint was opened at St. Lô.  By the treaty of Troyes (May 1420) Henry acquired the regency during the lifetime of Charles and the succession at his death, and in the following month he issued an order for the inscription ' Henricus Francorum Rex ' on his coins to be changed to ' H Rex Anglie et Heres Francie '.  In November 1421, to remedy the loss consequent upon his fine coinage being undervalued in comparison with the poorer coins issued by the Dauphin, a new coinage was ordered.  The new gold coin was the *salute*, which represents on the obverse the Annunciation with the crowned shield of England and France quarterly between the Angel and the Virgin ; on the reverse it has a plain cross between a lis and a leopard, with the letter H below, and the *Christus Vincit* legend [Fig. 345, *f*].

On the death of Charles, in October 1422, Henry VI became, in virtue of the treaty of Troyes, *de facto* King of France.  He issued an extensive French coinage, which was no longer a currency struck by an English king for feudal possessions in France, or, as in the reign of Henry V, in virtue of tenure by force of conquest, but the French coinage struck by the King of France.

## 5.  *The Introduction of Gold.*

With the exception of a very few isolated instances of the striking of gold coins, such as the gold dinar of Offa, the solidus of Archbishop Wigmund, and gold pennies of Æthelred II and Edward the Confessor, the coinage of this country had been confined to silver from the beginning of the eighth century.  The tendency towards the adoption of a gold currency, which was the outcome of the increase of trade in the thirteenth century and which produced in Italy the Florin in 1252 and the Sequin in 1284, made its appearance also in England in the attempt of Henry III to bring a gold penny into circulation.  This coin [Fig. 346, *a*] was struck, under an order of the year 1257, of the weight of two sterlings, or silver pennies, of pure gold, and was proclaimed in the same year at the value of 20 pence, raised later to 24 pence.  It is of neat and careful workmanship but of meagre design ; on the obverse is a figure of the king enthroned holding sceptre and orb ; on the reverse, as on the silver pennies of the same period, a long cross voided, but with the addition of a rose between the three pellets in each angle. It was very unfavourably received by the public, and a protest from the city of London resulted in the withdrawal of the obligation to accept it in payment. Its issue seems to have been discontinued about 1270 ; the unpopularity of the coin was probably due to the low ratio which the gold held to the silver coinage.

No further attempt was made to establish a gold coinage until the end of the year 1343, when an indenture was issued ordering the first English gold coinage of Edward III, which was put into currency by a proclamation of January 1344. This was the famous *florin* series, consisting of a *florin*, or two-leopard piece, a *léopard*, or half-florin, and a *helm*, or quarter-florin, weighing 108, 54, and 27 grains and current for 6, 3, and 1½ shillings respectively ; the standard gold of which they were made was 23 carats 3½ grains fine and ½ grain alloy. The use of the name *florin* was inappropriate ; its value was double that of the continental florin and the florin type was not adopted on any of the three coins. In type the *florin* was somewhat similar to the *pavillon* of the Black Prince ; on the obverse the king is represented in royal robes seated under a Gothic canopy ; the *léopard*, or half-florin, and the *helm*, or quarter, take their names from their obverse designs, the one a crowned leopard with a banner bearing the arms of England and France fastened to its neck, the other a crested helm ; the obverse fields of the florin and quarter are sown with fleurs-de-lis. The reverse of each has an ornamental design with a floriate cross as its main feature [Fig. 346, *b, c, d*]. Scriptural mottoes are taken as reverse legends : ' Iesus transiens per medium illorum ibat ' on the *florin* is supposed to have reference to the activity of the king's ship at the battle of Sluys ; on the half is ' Domine ne in furore tuo arguas me ', and on the quarter ' Exaltabitur in gloria '.

These coins are the finest in the English series ; they are beautifully designed and most carefully executed. The issue did not, however, obtain a favourable reception ; the gold was too highly valued in proportion to the silver ; after six months the acceptance of the gold coins was made optional, and they were almost immediately withdrawn

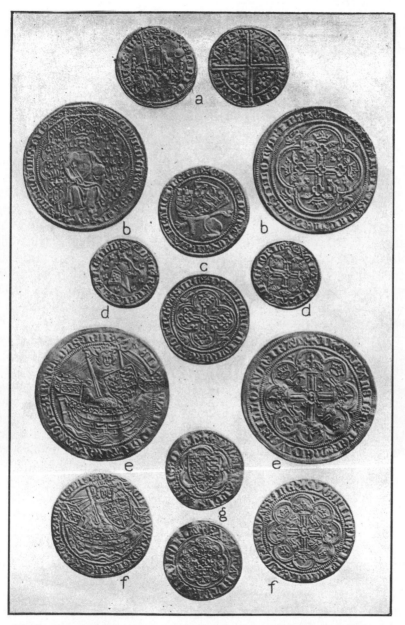

FIG. 346. EARLY GOLD COINS. Gold penny; Florin and Noble Issues.

and a new gold coinage issued. The *noble*, with its half and quarter, was proclaimed in August 1344, at the value of 80 pence and weighing $138\frac{6}{13}$ grains, and the weight of the penny was reduced to $20\frac{1}{4}$ grains. The proportion between gold and silver still caused trouble, the gold being now slightly undervalued, in addition to the difficulty of retaining in currency a coinage that was very extensively imitated on the Continent. After an intermediate step in 1346, the ratio between standard gold and silver was fixed in 1351 at 12 to 1 by reducing the noble to 120 and the penny to 18 grains. The name of the noble is assumed to refer to its metal, signifying the standard coin of gold as opposed to the sterling of silver. Its design, the king standing in a ship and holding shield and sword, is thought to refer to the naval power of Edward and his victory at Sluys. The half-noble is of the same type as the noble ; the obverse design of the quarter is a shield of arms. The reverse legends and types are similar to those of the florin series. The noble, half-noble, and quarter-noble of the issue of 1346–51 are illustrated in Fig. 346, *e, f, g*.

Another innovation of the reign of Edward III was the introduction in 1351 of the groat into the silver coinage [Fig. 347, *a*]. It was of the value and weight of four pence and bore on the reverse a double legend in two concentric circles, the inner being the name of the mint, ' Civitas London.', &c., and the outer scriptural, ' Posui Deum Adiutorem Meum ' ; on the obverse is the king's bust facing, crowned, within a fleured tressure. The treaty of Brétigny and its rupture caused the obverse legends of the coins to be changed in 1360 by the omission of the French title and in 1369 by its restoration.

The mint of Calais was at this time in active operation, coining both gold and silver, as an English mint. The Calais nobles and half-nobles of the earlier issues are distinguished from those of the London mint by the use of the letter C in place of the king's initial in the centre of the reverse, and on later coins by a flag at the stern of the ship on the obverse. The mark of differentiation on the quarter-nobles is not known ; the silver coins bear on the reverse the inscription ' Villa Calisie '.

In 1411 parliament ordered a reduction in the weight of the coins, the noble from 120 to 108 grains and the penny from 18 to 15 grains, ' because of the great scarcity of money at this time within the realm of England, and because of other mischiefs and causes manifest'; the other causes are not now manifest, but probably the removal of English coins and importation of foreign coins of poorer quality is implied, as this had in recent years been a matter of grave concern to parliament. It appears that the king's revenues were considerably increased both by the reduction of weight in the coinage and by the seizure of forfeited money, presumably foreign coins and imitations that were not legal tender. With this exception the coinage remained unchanged in value, quality, and design from the time of Edward III until Edward IV came to the throne. In the reign of Henry VI the issues are for the first time clearly marked by the insertion of certain marks of difference, such as roses, pine-cones, leaves, annulets, and mascles between the words of the inscriptions, and in later reigns the initial cross of the legends is superseded by a similar differentiating mark; but it is not at present possible to assign a definite period of duration to a particular mark. The mark in place of the initial cross is commonly called the mint-mark; but this is an unsuitable name, as the mark serves various purposes at different periods and only very occasionally denotes the place of issue. At first, as we have already seen, it marks the issues of all mints of certain periods; in the reign of Henry VII the London coins were thus differentiated at yearly intervals, though the Trial of the Pyx was then held quarterly. At the end of the reign of Henry VIII it seems to be used as a mark of the mint, the monograms of WS and TC being the marks of William Sharrington and Thomas Chamberlain, the masters of the Bristol mint. Under Charles I, as we know from documentary evidence, it was the privy mark differentiating the issues for the Trials of the Pyx, which were then held annually.

In 1464 the weight of the silver coins was reduced, the penny being struck at 12 instead of 15 grains; the gold coins were not reduced in weight but were increased proportionately in value, the noble being proclaimed at the value of 100 instead of 80 pence. In the following year a new gold coin, called the *Rose Noble* or *Ryal*, was issued weighing 120 grains and having a value of ten shillings, and another, called the *Angel*, of the weight of 80 grains, took the value of the old noble of 80 pence. The ryal issue continued the types and legends of the noble issue, but on the reverse a rose upon a radiate sun was imposed upon the centre of the floriate cross, and on the obverse of the ryal and half-ryal a rose was placed on the side of the ship and a banner bearing the king's initial set in the stern [Fig. 347, *b*]. For the angel a new type was introduced from which it took its name, the archangel transfixing the dragon ; on the reverse is a ship which has a cross set in front of the mast with a shield of arms below it and the king's initial and a rose at either side [Fig. 347, *c*] ; 'Per Crucem Tuam Salva Nos Christe Redemptor' is used in slightly abbreviated form as the reverse legend of this coin. There was a very large output of the new coinage, and to meet the increase of work mints were opened at Bristol, Coventry, Norwich, and York for the coining of both gold and silver ; the gold coins of these mints are differentiated by an initial placed on or below the side of the ship ; a Bristol ryal is shown in Fig. 347, *b*. The extensive recoinage was soon effected and the extra mints closed down.

During the short period of his restoration (1470–1) Henry VI struck a very large coinage of the light standard introduced by Edward IV ; in gold he struck angels and half-angels only, the issue of the ryal having been previously discontinued by Edward IV. The type of the angel remained the same but for the substitution of the letter H and a fleur-de-lis for Edward's E and rose on the reverse. The ryal coinage was revived by Henry VII with a new reverse design which covers the field with an exquisitely moulded Tudor rose bearing in its centre a shield with the arms of France [Fig. 348, *a*].

The reign of Henry VII brought two important changes in the coinage. The first, which took place quite early in the reign, was the issue of the *Sovereign*, a gold coin weighing 240 grains and having a current value of twenty shillings. It was a large thin coin, about 1½ inches in diameter [Fig. 347, *d*]. The king is seated on a throne of elaborate design which fills the field of the obverse ; the reverse type is the same which he adopted for the ryal [Fig. 348, *a*], but usually the work is more crowded, a fleured tressure

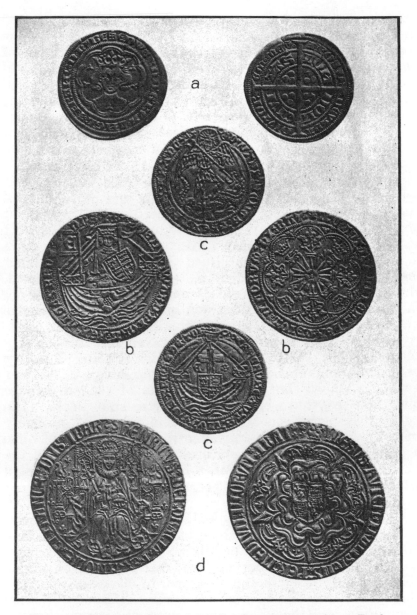

FIG. 347.  ENGLISH COINS.  Groat, Rose Noble or Ryal,
Angel, and Sovereign.

being added round the rose, and lions and fleurs inserted
in the small intervening spaces.  The coin, in spite of the
somewhat restless effect produced by the massing of
detailed ornamentation on the reverse, is a wonderful
creation of Tudor art ;  the composition of the throned
figure, adapted most skilfully to the circular field, and the
powerful handling of perspective to defeat the limitations
of the shallow relief which was necessary in the engraving of
dies for striking so thin a flan, show a complete mastery of
technique combined with the highest artistic inspiration.

The other noteworthy change in the coinage during this
reign was the removal from the groats and half-groats of
the conventional bust which was used with very slight
change from the time of their introduction by Edward III
to the end of the fifteenth century.  In the year 1503/4
a new type of groat was issued [Fig. 348, b] ;  the inner
legend which contained the name of the mint was removed,
the scriptural legend 'Posui Deum', &c., being retained ;
in the field a shield of arms was imposed upon the centre
of the long cross which divided the legend into four parts.
A new portrait in profile was engraved for this coinage
by a foreigner, Alexander of Brussels.  A piece of twelve
pence, 144 grains in weight, of the same design as the new
groat, is known, but no record exists of such a coinage
and these may have been struck only as trial pieces.  The
type of the penny was also changed in this reign, probably
in 1489 when the sovereign was introduced ;  on the obverse
a seated figure takes the place of the king's bust, and the
new reverse type, a shield on a long cross, was the design
which was adopted fifteen years later for the new groat
coinage.

The early coins of Henry VIII were similar to the latest
of the previous reign.  In the groat series he even used the
portrait of Henry VII, though he changed the numeral
in the title ;  his own portrait was first engraved in profile
[Fig. 348, c] in 1526 and changed to a facing portrait
[Fig. 348, d] in 1542.  In 1526 a warrant was issued to Wolsey
appointing him the king's agent with full powers for the
purpose of the coinage ;  this irregular system was regular-
ized in 1530 by a warrant to the new chancellor, Sir Thomas
More, and the usual indentures with the master-workers
of the mint.  The warrant to Wolsey ordered him to carry

into effect the king's design of reducing his money to the standard of foreign coins. ' Owing ', a proclamation of the same year informs us, ' to the enhancement of value abroad, money was carried out of this realm by secret means.' Wolsey, acting on the advice of a committee of goldsmiths, ordered a new standard of gold of 22 carats fine gold alloyed with 2 carats sterling silver (known as crown gold) to be introduced, of which a *Crown* of 5s. was struck and its half, bearing a double rose crowned on the obverse and a crowned shield on the reverse (the Half-crown is shown in Fig. 348, *e*) ; this coin superseded a crown of 4s. 6d., called the Crown of the Rose, which had been issued three months previously. The sovereign, valued at 22s. 6d., the angel (7s. 6d.), ryal (11s. 3d.), and a new coin called the *George Noble* [Fig. 348, *f*] of the value of 6s. 8d. were still struck of the old standard gold. The silver coinage remained at the old standard of 11 dwt. 2 gr. fine. It was during the period 1530–40 that the privilege of coinage was removed from the archbishops of Canterbury and York and the bishops of Durham. In the articles issued against Wolsey in 1529 there was included the charge that he had ' enterprised to join and imprint the cardinal's hat under your [the king's] arms in your coin of groats, made at your city of York ' ; one of these groats struck by Wolsey may be seen in Fig. 348, *c*. The crime was not, as would appear, the use of the cardinal's hat as his privy mark, but the appropriation of the groat, which was the king's coin ; the archbishops' privilege included only the half-groat, penny, and half-penny, and the coinage of the bishops of Durham was limited to the penny.

The issue of crown gold, though its object seems to have been to prevent the coinage being removed from the country, was the beginning of the debasement for which the reign of Henry VIII is notorious. The gold of the sovereign and angel series was reduced to 23 carat in 1542, 22 carat in 1545, and 20 carat (including crown gold) in 1546 ; the silver went to 10 oz. fine in 1542, 9 oz. in 1544, 6 oz. in 1545, and 4 oz. in 1546. In the following reign, though the debased coinage continued, there was evidently an intention to reform it, for we find Henry's name on all the early coins issued by Edward, and his portrait also on the early groats ; further, the inscription, ' Redde cuique

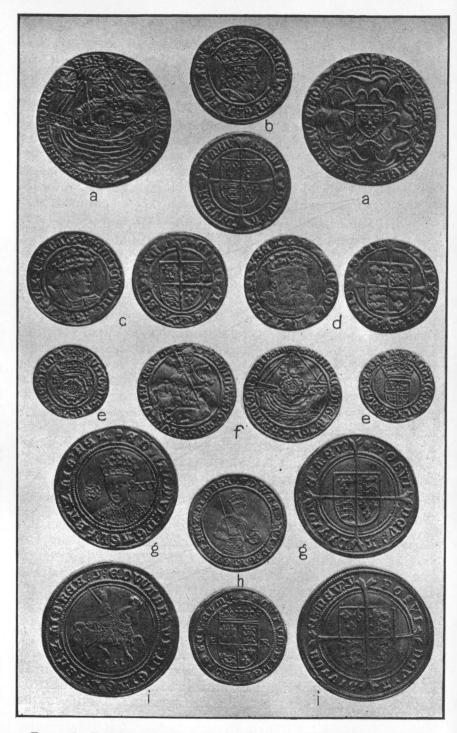

FIG. 348. ENGLISH COINS. Ryal, Groats, Half-Crown, George Noble, Shilling, Gold Crown, Silver Half-Crown.

quod suum est ', which may be interpreted (in conjunction with the use of Henry's name) 'Give the devil his due', is found on base silver coins struck at a mint which was opened at Durham House, Strand, for about a year in 1548-9. The restoration of the coinage was a long and difficult business, and for a time coinages of two standards were being issued together. Edward's last issue consisted of a sovereign of thirty shillings and angel of ten shillings of standard gold, a sovereign of twenty shillings, and crown of five shillings of 22 carat gold, and a crown, half-crown, shilling, and sixpence of silver of 11 oz. 1 dwt. fine. The shilling [g] and the gold crown [h] and silver half-crown [i] of Edward VI are illustrated in Fig. 348. The use of both standard and crown gold continued to the time of the Commonwealth, when the angel, which was the last surviving coin of old standard gold and had a peculiar connexion with royalty through its use in the ceremony of touching for the king's evil, disappeared from the coinage. Twenty-two carat gold has remained ever since as the standard for the gold coinage. The restoration of the silver to the old standard of 11 oz. 2 dwt. was completed by Elizabeth, to whom is also due the less fortunate distinction of having taken, by the introduction of the screw press, the first step towards the elimination of art by modern machinery.

## Books for reference.

N.B.—The works mentioned in the section for general reference, with the exception of the *Dialogus*, must be used with caution ; they are out of date and consequently inaccurate and incomplete. For the special periods it is only possible to mention a few out of the many articles that have been published, mostly by the Royal Numismatic Society and the British Numismatic Society ; those of a more comprehensive nature have therefore been selected, and they will usually be found to contain reference to other papers of detail. In order to make a serious study of the subject a careful search must be made through the journals of these two societies, the *Numismatic Chronicle* and the *British Numismatic Journal*, which are referred to below as *N. C.* and *B. N. J.* respectively. Sale catalogues, especially the illustrated catalogues of large collections, are useful for reference. Close and Patent Rolls, Pipe Rolls, Exchequer Accounts, and other State papers must be in constant use.

### General.

RUDING, R., *Annals of the Coinage* (3rd edition), 3 vols., 1840.
MADOX, T., *History of the Exchequer*, 2 vols., 1769.
*Dialogus de Scaccario*, ed. A. Hughes, C. G. Crump, and C. Johnson, 1902.
GRUEBER, H. A., *Handbook of Coins of Great Britain and Ireland*, 1899.
KENYON, R. Ll., *Gold Coins of England*, 1884.
HAWKINS, E., *Silver Coins of England* (3rd edition), 1887.

### Anglo-Saxon Period.

KEARY, C. F., & GRUEBER, H. A., *Catalogue of English Coins in the British Museum, Anglo-Saxon Series*, 2 vols., 1887 and 1893.

HILDEBRAND, B. E. *Anglo-Saxon Coins in the Royal Swedish Cabinet of Medals at Stockholm*, 1881.

KEARY, C. F., *The Coinages of Western Europe; from the Fall of the Western Empire till the Accession of Charlemagne*, 1879 (reprinted from *N. C.*)

DIRKS, J., *Les Anglo-Saxons et leurs Petits Deniers dits Sceattas*, 1870.

LOCKETT, R. C., ' The Coinage of Offa ', *N. C.*, 1920, p. 57.

HOWORTH, H. H., ' Ecgberht and his son Athelstan ', *N. C.*, 1900, p. 66 ; 1908, p. 222.

CARLYON-BRITTON, P. W. P., ' Howel Dda ', *B. N. J.*, ii. 31.

——— ' Eadward the Confessor and his Coins ', *N. C.*, 1905, p. 179.

PARSONS, H. A., 'The Coin-types of Æthelred II', *N. C.*, 1910, pp. 251, 370, 381.

——— ' The Coins of Harold I ', *B. N. J.*, xv. 1.

——— ' The Anglo-Saxon Coins of Harthacnut ', *B. N. J.*, xi. 21.

### Norman Conquest to the Introduction of Gold.

BROOKE, G. C., *Catalogue of English Coins in the British Museum, Norman Kings*, 2 vols., 1916.

CARLYON-BRITTON, P. W. P., ' Numismatic History of the Reigns of William I and II ', *B. N. J.*, vols. ii ff. (not yet completed).

——— ' Historical Notes on the First Coinage of Henry II ', *B. N. J.*, ii. 185.

ANDREW, W. J., ' Numismatic History of the Reign of Stephen ', *B. N. J.*, vols. vi ff. (not yet completed).

LAWRENCE, L. A., ' First Coinage of Henry II ', *B. N. J.*, xiv. 13

——— ' The Short-Cross Coinage ', *B. N. J.*, xi. 59.

——— ' The Long-Cross Coinage ', *B. N. J.*, ix. 145 ; x. 69 ; xi. 101.

Fox, E., & J. S., ' Numismatic History of the Reigns of Edward I, II, and III ', *B. N. J.*, vols. vi ff. (not yet completed).

CRUMP, C. G., & JOHNSON, C., ' Tables of Bullion Coined under Edward I, II, and III ', *N. C.*, 1913, p. 200.

### Anglo-Gallic.

HEWLETT, L. M., *Anglo-Gallic Coins*, 1920, reprinted from *N. C.*, 1905 ff.

DE SAULCY, F., *Histoire numismatique de Henri V et Henri VI, Rois d'Angleterre*, 1878.

### The Introduction of Gold to Edward VI.

EVANS, J., ' The First Gold Coins of England ', *N. C.*, 1900, p. 218.

BROOKE, G. C., ' East Raynham Find ' (gold coinage of Edward III), *N. C.*, 1911, p. 291.

LAWRENCE, L. A., ' The Coinage of Henry IV ', *N. C.*, 1905, p. 83.

——— ' A Find of Late Plantagenet Groats ', *B. N. J.*, viii. 149.

——— ' The Coinage of Henry VII ', *N. C.*, 1918, p. 205.

WALTERS, F. A., ' The Coinage of Henry V ', *N. C.*, 1906, p. 172.

——— ' Gold Coinage of the Reign of Henry VI ', *N. C.*, 1903, p. 286.

——— ' Silver Coinage of the Reign of Henry VI ', *N. C.*, 1902, p. 224.

——— 'Stamford Find '(supplementary to coinage of Henry VI), *N.C.*, 1911, p.153.

——— 'The Coinage of Edward IV', *N. C.*, 1909, p. 132; 1910, p. 117; 1914, p. 330.

——— ' The Coinage of Richard II ', *N. C.*, 1904, p. 326.

——— ' The Coinage of Henry IV ', *N. C.*, 1905, p. 247.

MONTAGU, H., ' The Coinage of Edward V ', *N. C.*, 1895, p. 117.

SYMONDS, H., ' Documentary Evidence for the English Royal Coinages of Henry VII and Henry VIII ', *B. N. J.*, x. 127.

——— ' The English Coinages of Edward VI ' (documentary), *B. N. J.*, xi. 123.

EVANS, J., ' The Debased Coinage bearing the name of Henry VIII ', *N. C.*, 1886, p. 114.

MORRIESON, H. W., ' The Silver Coins of Edward VI ', *B. N. J.*, xii. 137.

# XIV

# TRADE AND COMMERCE

### 1. *General Sketch to* 1300.

THE earliest information that we have as to foreign commerce after the Anglo-Saxon invasion and the general disappearance of Roman civilization associates trade with the service of religion. We learn from Bede that Benedict Biscop, in the year 675, went to Gaul to engage masons and glass-makers to build and glaze the windows of his church at Wearmouth. In 678 he paid a fourth visit to Rome to procure books, vestments, images, and pictures, of which he imported a large store. So thoroughly was the art of embroidery domesticated here, that at the time of the Norman Conquest it was exported to Italy under the name of ' English work '. English merchants frequented the French fairs, and an English merchant was living at Marseilles early in the eighth century. In 796 Charles the Great, in a letter to Offa, King of Mercia, gave assurances of protection to English merchants within his dominions, and solicited it for his subjects trading in Offa's territory. We also hear at this time of a trade in slaves, perhaps a relic of the Roman occupation. At the time of the Conquest, and a century later, slaves were regularly exported to Ireland. The invasions of the Danes opened up new directions for English commerce. An extraordinary number of early English coins have been found in Scandinavia. From their settlements in Dublin and along the southern coasts of Ireland, the Danes carried on an active intercourse with Chester and Bristol. The trade with Iceland, a frequent source of dispute and bloodshed during the Middle Ages, dates from this period. With the Norman Conquest began a systematic connexion with the continent. Internal trade was now recruited by the immigration of foreign artisans. Henry I settled a number of Flemish weavers at Ross, Tenby, and Haverfordwest, and another colony at the mouth of the Tweed. In the twelfth century, we hear of weavers' gilds in London, York, Nottingham, Lincoln, Huntingdon, Winchester, and Oxford. Many of these were aliens, enjoying a special royal protection. An immense impulse was given by the Conquest to the building of churches and castles. For this purpose large quantities of stone were imported from Caen during the eleventh, twelfth, and thirteenth centuries. Architects and masons flocked into England from both Normandy and the Low Countries.

Besides these scattered bodies of foreign artisans there were organized bodies of foreign merchants. The men of the Emperor (*homines Imperatoris*) had been established in a settlement in London as early as the time of Æthelred the Redeless (978–1016). It was a characteristic of the mediaeval merchant that he travelled with his merchandise. Protection was, therefore, necessary for both his goods and his person. Royal letters of privilege were not enough to ensure safety from the jealousies of native traders. A more effective guarantee of security was obtained by a common dwelling within a fortified inclosure, corresponding to the English 'factories' in India in the seventeenth century. The generic name given by the English to these trading associations was 'Hanse'. The first hanse of which we hear was that of Cologne. In 1157 Henry II granted it extensive privileges. The merchants of this hanse received, besides protection to their goods and their house in London, a concession to sell their wines subject to the same tolls as French wines. When Richard I passed through Cologne on his way home in 1194, these rights were largely augmented. Merchants of the Cologne Hanse were granted freedom from all tolls and customs in the city of London, and were at liberty to trade at fairs throughout the country.

Early in the thirteenth century another hanse was formed, known as the Flemish Hanse of London. It comprised as many as thirty-four towns of Flanders and of the north of France engaged in the manufacture of cloth, for which purpose they were exporters of wool from England. But the greatest hanse of all was the German or Teutonic Hanse. The origin of this hanse was the reluctance of Cologne to admit to its privileges the rising town of Lübeck. Lübeck and Hamburg accordingly joined together in 1266, under a licence from Henry III, to form an organization of their own. Their house was called the Steelyard, from the fact that their weighing machine stood there, the use of which, instead of that of the city, was a standing grievance to the Londoners. By the middle of the thirteenth century their importance was rapidly increasing. They were joined by all the German towns engaged in the Baltic trade. As early as 1271 they had already formed an affiliated society at Lynn, and not only there but also at Boston, York, Hull, Bristol, Norwich, Ipswich, and Yarmouth they subsequently built hanse houses.

Trade with the Latin nations, like the trade with Germany, was at first inter-municipal, not international in the modern sense. Before the formation of the Flemish Hanse, at least as early as 1237, an agreement had been entered into between the city of London and the towns of Corbie, Nesle, and Amiens, the last of which towns afterwards joined that hanse. The rights purchased by these towns were, after protracted disputes, settled by a treaty of 1334. Its contents illustrate the points of controversy between the citizens of an English town and 'foreigners', in which term were included even English born, not free of the town. By the agreement of 1334 the citizens of the three towns were entitled to unload and store their woad, garlic, and onions in the city, to sell anything but wine and corn, as well to strangers as to citizens of London, a valuable right. They might keep inns for the reception of their townsmen, though not for longer than a year. They were to have a voice in the appointment of the officials authorized to supervise the measurement and sale of the woad. The mayor of London was pledged to aid them to recover debts due to them. They were to enjoy the right of meeting. They were to be free from taxes for the repair of the city walls.

The rest of the English foreign trade in the thirteenth century was less in the hands of trading corporations. The French wine trade had been in existence since before the Conquest. In the twelfth century it was chiefly carried on by the merchants of Rouen. With a view not only to its encouragement, but also to the conciliation of his French provinces, Edward I, in 1275, granted a charter of privileges to the Gascon merchants, which the citizens of London resisted. Italian wool-buyers travelled through the country, and probably suffered less than other aliens from the hostility of the people to foreigners, because many of them bore a semi-sacred character as the agents employed by the popes for the collection of their revenues. We hear of firms from Piacenza, Florence, and Lucca, engaged in the export of wool to Italy. They contracted with the religious houses for yearly supplies of wool. Lists of these houses, nearly two hundred in number, still exist, belonging to the thirteenth and fourteenth centuries. They include most of the counties of England and Wales. The Jews appeared in England in the eleventh century. They were held to be the bondmen of the king, and as such enjoyed the royal protection. As bondmen they could only acquire for their

Fig. 349. A DISPENSARY. From a twelfth-century dispensary. MS. Trinity College, Cambridge, O. 1, 20.

master's profit. Upon this legal doctrine was based the system of royal exactions, by submission to which they purchased toleration. They maintained themselves in isolated communities in the towns, abstained alike from agriculture and handicraft, and confined themselves to money-lending at high rates of interest. For this pursuit the field was left open to them by the prohibition to Christians of lending upon interest laid down by the canon law. The kings found connivance more profitable than repression. Edward I, however, endeavoured to compel the Jews to practise trades recognized as legitimate. Failing in this, he limited their right to interest to 42 per cent., perhaps not an excessive rate in view of the scarcity of capital and the risks incurred. He further decreed that not more than the principal sum lent and three years' interest should be recoverable by them.  But these restrictions failed to quench the general animosity felt against them.  In 1290 fifteen or sixteen thousand were compelled to leave the country. This was followed by a more complete measure of expulsion in 1358, and from that time, although Jewish names are occasionally found, the Jews as a body disappeared from England, until their recall by Cromwell in the seventeenth century.  Many of their bonds are still preserved in the original presses in the ancient Star Chamber of Westminster Abbey.

As an importer of articles of luxury, which could not be manufactured at home, the foreign merchant was welcome

Fig. 350.  A P A W N B R O K E R ' S  S H O P.  From a fifteenth-century MS. in the British Museum.  Add. MSS. 27,695.

to the king, the nobles, and the wealthy clergy.  Upon this point both the parties to the Great Charter were agreed.  At the beginning of his reign John, discerning that a liberal treatment of importers was the most profitable policy for the Exchequer, forbade the practice of exacting capricious and unreasonable duties.  By the forty-first and forty-second articles of the Great Charter, security for persons and goods, together with freedom of trade in time of peace, were guaranteed to all merchants.  They were to be exempt from all ' evil tolls ' (*sine omnibus malis toltis*).  The extension of this provision to all merchants, as well English as foreign, was intended to reconcile the towns to the facilities afforded to their alien competitors.  But the interpretation of the term ' evil tolls ' remained a subject of dispute down to the reign of Edward III, when it was finally held to mean all tolls exacted without authority of Parliament.

Notwithstanding the charter, the great towns constantly asserted a right to subject 'foreign' merchants, that is, all not free of their privileges, whether English or alien born, to their own by-laws. In the early part of the thirteenth century the *Liber Custumarum* of the city of London systematized the supervision exercised over the transactions of the foreign merchant. He was bound to take up his abode in the house of a citizen : he might not sell any wares by retail ; he might not buy cloth in an unfinished stage of manufacture with a view to finishing it himself ; he might only buy of freemen of the city ; he might not buy to sell again within the city ; he might only sell to persons not free of the city on three days of the week ; he might only sell within a circuit of three miles ; he might not bid against a freeman of the city ; he might only remain in the city forty days, at the end of that time he must forfeit all his wares remaining unsold. There is reason for believing that some of these restrictions dated from the days before the Conquest. This jealous care for the profit of the citizen was not confined to London ; it existed, in varying degrees of rigour, in all the great towns, and it was not less prevalent on the continent than in England. It was justified upon exactly the same ground as that insisted upon by modern Protectionism, that the citizens had special burdens to bear, from which foreigners were exempt. During the reign of Henry III foreign merchants, encouraged by the king, swarmed into England. The citizens of London complained that foreign merchants, especially those from Italy and Provence, had ceased to observe the regulations prescribing their lodgement, and were building themselves dwelling-houses, in which they stored their goods. But the city, being in alliance with the opposition, received little favour from Henry, beyond the destruction of the alien's private weights and measures. In 1266 he nominated Prince Edward protector of the foreign merchants in England. Edward's liberal treatment of foreigners, to whom he granted special trading privileges by licences issued by royal prerogative, increased the hostility of the city. In 1285 he seized its liberties. Under his administration the grossest abuses of its privileges were suppressed. He put an end to a vexatious system of hindering the unloading of merchant's goods.  He tolerated no delays of justice, but insisted that the sheriffs should give daily audience to foreign complainants ;  he made it easy for them to acquire the freedom of the city, with its consequent privileges.  But the expulsion of the Jews had whetted the national antipathy to foreigners.  The Commons complained that the foreign merchants lorded it in the city (*dominantur in civitate*).  In 1298, when the city's charter was restored, the city at once enforced its vexatious ordinances.  Edward retorted in

1303 by the *Carta Mercatoria*, a charter of privilege to all alien merchants trading throughout the kingdom.  They in return consented to an increase of duties, which an assembly of English merchants had refused to grant.  This tariff was long known as the New Custom (*Nova Custuma*).  Its most important item was an increase of fifty per cent. upon exported wool and leather.

The importance of this charter lay in the fact that it elevated to the rank of a national question a dispute which had hitherto ranged round the limited area of the privileges of the towns respectively concerned, and that it established

FIG. 351.  A Jew of Colchester, from a forest roll of Essex, in the Record Office, fourteenth century.

a policy for the kings who were to follow.  Edward pledged both himself and his successors to accord peace and security to all alien merchants.  He conceded to them the right to sell their wares wholesale to all, whether citizens or strangers.  No check was to be put on exports, provided the duties were paid, so that the vexatious prohibition to re-export imported but unsold goods was abolished, except as regards wine, in the case of which a royal licence was to be procured ; restrictions upon lodging, sojourn, and storing of goods were abolished ;  in actions at law in which aliens were parties at issue with Englishmen, half the jury was to consist of members of the alien party's nationality ;  a special tribunal was erected for aliens, to which appeal lay against delays of justice by the mayor and sheriffs. In return for these concessions the alien merchants agreed to the 'New Custom', with the proviso that no duty was to be levied on the sale by them of wool to other aliens within the kingdom. The pledges given by the Great Charter were now made a reality.

## 2. *General Sketch* (*continued*) : 1300–1485.

The first struggle between the trading and aristocratic classes regarding the rights of aliens had ended in favour of the king and nobles. In the Parliament of 1309 the Commons complained of the rise of prices, attributing them to the new duties. The barons, eager to buy wine and foreign cloth cheap, supported and obtained the abolition of the new duties. In 1311, after a prolonged struggle, the new allies succeeded in procuring the repeal of the principal clauses of the *Carta Mercatoria* as infringing the Great Charter.

Edward III, upon his accession, was in no condition to resist the pressure of the towns. The national jealousy of foreigners, lately directed against the Jews, was now transferred to the Italians. Of these the Florentines were the most successful. They enjoyed a practical monopoly of the tin of Devon and Cornwall. The Cornish had complained to Parliament in 1315 that they beat down prices and starved the tinners. They were dominant in the wool trade. One John Van, with his Lombard partners, farmed the Exchange. They made large advances to the Crown ; but a competing class of English capitalists was arising, with aims more ambitious than those of hampering alien merchants in the transaction of their business. William de la Pole, of Edward I's recently founded town of Kingston-upon-Hull, was amassing an enormous fortune by speculation in wool, and by the farm of the wool tax. Newcastle was becoming prosperous by its coal trade, London by its shipping, Gloucestershire by its cloth trade. The mercers, the drapers, the pepperers were already known as wealthy gilds. The year of the outbreak of the Hundred Years' War, 1338, was marked by an act which showed Edward's determination to dispense henceforth with the assistance of foreign capitalists. He ordered the arrest of all the Italian merchants in the kingdom, with the exception of certain

Florentines, to whom he was specially indebted. In 1339, being pressed for ready money, he first offered to the English merchants the purchase of the great subsidy of 30,000 sacks of wool voted by Parliament. There was some difficulty on the part of the merchants in completing this transaction ; but after 1345, when Edward repudiated his debts to the Italians, an English combination of capitalist merchants appeared, who succeeded to their business, and styled themselves 'the king's merchants'.

Notwithstanding these transfers of the finance of the State in great measure to English capitalists, Edward III had no intention to discourage foreign trade. On the contrary, from 1351 to 1354, he passed a number of statutes in favour of alien merchants. He abolished the principle of corporate liability for crime or debt, by which members of a whole nationality were exposed to the arrest and the seizure of their goods for the default of one of their number. He allowed sales on board ships in harbour, which checked the rapacity of municipal officers. He laid upon the Chancellor and Treasurer the duty of hearing complaints by alien merchants. He allowed their oath to be taken by the Customers as to the contents of their imported cargoes. He relieved them from the exactions of the royal purveyors. With the object of improving the prosperity of the English staple towns, he took, in 1353, the extraordinary step of prohibiting the export of wool by Englishmen, so that foreign merchants might be attracted to the country.

Royal favour to the alien had now reached high water-mark, and the ebb forthwith set in. But it was not until the close of Edward III's reign that the change showed itself. In 1376 the rights of keeping lodgings, of acting as broker, and of retail trading were taken away from aliens. A petition to limit their sojourn and restrict their trading with each other was rejected. On the accession of Richard II the Londoners demanded the confirmation of their charters, any statutes to the contrary notwithstanding. But again complaint was made in Parliament that prices were rising. In 1378, therefore, Parliament passed a statute of which the preamble inveighs against ' the great damages and outrageous grievances ' caused by the discouragement of merchant strangers. The privileges of the towns were for the most part swept away. Alien merchants were to be free to come and abide within the realm, and to buy and sell in gross and by retail provisions and small wares. Wines and a few specified manufactures, not including cloth, they must sell in gross only. In 1381 came the rebellion of Wat Tyler, whose following massacred the Flemish bankers and weavers. Richard II, grateful for the city's aid, confirmed its privileges. On the eve of his dethronement, in 1398, he renewed those of all the towns of the realm. But his usurping successor, Henry IV, was no less anxious to conciliate the city. In 1404 he passed an Act which opened the door to every abuse. It provided that the treatment of 'merchant strangers' should be regulated by that in use abroad. This vague legislation practically placed the foreigner at the mercy of the municipal authorities. By another Act of the same year merchant strangers were compelled to sell their merchandise within a quarter of a year ; they were forbidden to trade with one another ; and lastly, the old regulation that they should be lodged with assigned hosts was re-enacted. Whether designedly or not, the restrictions imposed by this Act extended to all 'strangers', and were interpreted by the citizens of London to exclude all dealings between aliens and English traders not free of the city. Within a year the complaints of the country cloth-dealers at the injury to their trade had become audible. In 1406 a fresh Act was passed, admitting them to trade directly with alien merchants, the franchises of the city notwithstanding.

But the Crown held in reserve a power which nullified, at its will, the operation of Acts of Parliament. Dispensations from the statutes were for centuries lavishly granted in favour of the foreign merchant. On the accession of Henry VI the Commons voted the tax called Tonnage on the express condition that the Acts against restricting the dealings of foreign merchants should not be enforced. But the Chancellor, Beaufort, Bishop of Winchester, who was largely involved in trading enterprises with the Netherlands, so favoured aliens, especially Flemings, that in 1425 an insurrection took place in the city. In 1436 the city's complaints took shape in the well-known poem called *The Libelle of Englyshe Polycye*. This was followed by a reaction in opinion among the governing classes, the expression of which was an Act of 1439, enforcing the existing restrictions and placing foreign merchants under the most rigorous supervision of English hosts. But the excessive severity of its provisions defeated the object of the Act. It drove the foreign merchants, especially the Italians, out of the towns into the country, where they traded directly with the producer. At its expiration, after eight years, it was not renewed. During the rest of the reign of Henry VI the towns did not cease their complaints. All the satisfaction they obtained was the raising of the customs duties and the imposition of a poll tax upon foreigners. With the advent to power of the House of York in 1461 a change in policy at once appeared. The Yorkists enjoyed the support of the towns. In return they studied the towns'

Fig. 352. A BAKER'S SHOP. From MS. Bodl. 264.

interests. Edward IV made the first systematic endeavour to bring within the existing municipal organizations those bodies of foreign workmen, such as the weavers, who had up till then maintained an independence. In 1463 he checked the growing activity of the Italian wool-buyers by prohibiting purchases of wool by aliens altogether— a measure in response to the complaints of the English cloth-workers. He was also the first to adopt a strongly protectionist policy. Still more anxious was Richard III to conciliate the commercial classes. In the first year of his reign (1484) he passed a remarkable Act 'touching the merchants of Italy'. The preamble set forth that the Italians and Catalans kept households in London and other cities, wherein they stored their merchandise until the price had risen ; that they freely sold and bought, both by wholesale and by retail, all over the country ; that they violated the laws on the subject of exchange ; that they acted as hosts for their fellow countrymen ; that they employed cloth-workers to make cloth to suit their own taste, these cloth-workers being also aliens ; and that these proceedings were the cause of the increasing decay of the towns. The Act, therefore, provided that Italian merchants should thereafter sell their wares within eight months of landing them, to English subjects and in gross. Two months further were allowed them within which to carry away the goods remaining unsold. With the proceeds of sale they were to buy English goods. Merchant strangers were not to act as hosts or guests to one another, unless they were of the same nation. No non-naturalized alien was to act as middleman between English subjects in the purchase and sale of wool or of woollen cloth. None such should employ workmen in the manufacture of cloth. But the most important provision of all was that which forbade any Italian merchant, unless naturalized, to sell wool or woollen cloth bought within the realm, or to employ work-men to make cloth. The statute was, in fact, a great measure for the protection not only of the town, but also of the country industries, now important enough to make themselves heard. The restrictions imposed by the ordin-ances of the towns had brought them into being. To these, and not to the merchant strangers, were imputable that ' greate poverte and dekay ' of the towns complained of in the preamble. Another Act, passed in the same session, regulating the cloth manufacture, contained a clause directed against the Italians, forbidding them to export selected wool, ' but that the same wool be as it is shorn '. The policy of keeping the fine wools for the home manufacture was habitually advocated by the party of protection to native industry.

### 3.  *General Sketch* (*continued*) :  1485–1600.

A complete reversal of this policy, so far as Italian merchants were concerned, marked the accession of Henry VII (1485). This was, perhaps, partly a return for financial assistance towards the invasion of England derived from the Italians, who had always supported the House of Lancaster. But it was also probably due to the perception

FIG. 353. CALCULATING WITH JETTONS ON A COUNTER-TABLE (right); ciphering with Hindu-Arabic figures (left). From Reisch's *Margarita Philosophica*, 1503.

of the English class which was essentially Lancastrian, the country gentry, that restrictions upon purchasers were not favourable to the price of their produce.   On the other hand, Henry sought to conciliate the country cloth-workers by renewing an Act of 1465, which prohibited the purchase of wool before clipping.   A right of pre-emption was reserved to the cloth-workers in the first place, and after them to English merchants.   This Act was not renewed on its expiration in 1499.   It was revived in 1531, and again, four years after its expiration, in 1545.   But its effectiveness was always paralysed by royal letters of licence.   When in 1552 Parliament passed a similar measure, it incorporated in it the unusual clause that the Act should be revocable by royal proclamation, a large concession to prerogative.

The general policy of Henry VII was one of lavish encouragement to foreigners by the issue of letters of licence, profitable alike to him and to them, dispensing them from the obligations imposed by the various restrictive statutes in nominal force.   National indignation waxed high.   In 1514, after the accession of Henry VIII, the trading companies of the whole kingdom, supported by the handicrafts, joined in a petition to the king.   They affirmed that the multitude of immigrant aliens was such as to exclude Englishmen from all kinds of occupation.   They recounted the former restrictive statutes.   But they did not venture upon any higher demand than the suppression of retail dealing by aliens in the towns.   Even this minimum of demand was not granted.   Among the handicrafts the pent-up ill feeling disclosed itself in 1517, in the riot against alien artificers long known as 'Evil May Day'.   But Wolsey's government held on its course.   In 1525 a treaty was concluded with France giving full freedom of trade to French merchants.   It contained, it is true, a customary clause in favour of existing restrictions, but these remained unenforced.   The value of such clauses in foreign treaties was that of a weapon held in reserve in case of emergency. Aided by the exercise of the royal prerogative, alien merchants had succeeded in rendering these restrictions obsolete. But the government was now beginning to substitute its own control for the ineffective supervision of municipal authorities.

A series of documents has been printed, extending from

the accession of Henry VII to the end of the next century, which sets forth the grievances felt by alien merchants against the restrictions imposed on their trade in this country. Their complaints range themselves under three heads—complaints against English commercial law, such as the Navigation Acts, &c. ; complaints against the customs duties ; and complaints against officials, both those of the Crown and of the city of London. These complaints against the city become louder towards the close of the period, but, subject to specific changes effected by statute, the general tenor of grievances was the same throughout. Of all the grievances complained of, especially by the French, the principal was the grievance of the Navigation Acts.

With all foreign merchants it remained, throughout the whole period included in this retrospect, a common grievance that they were compelled to take English goods in exchange for their imports. Not that they conceived the accumulation of the precious metals to be the object of trade. This, the ' mercantile theory ', was not yet developed. But it would have been a far more profitable transaction for them to have received money and exchanged it with the Hanse for tin and hides than to be compelled to submit to the exorbitant additions to the cost of production made by the monopoly of the staplers. This compulsion to take English goods in exchange rested upon statutes of 1402, 1404, 1423, 1465, and 1478, of which the object was rather to secure the country against a depletion of the precious metals than to enrich it by an accumulation of them.

Since, with the exception of cloth, England's exports were raw material, her imports, had trade been unfettered, would naturally have been manufactured articles. To counteract this tendency statutes were passed, especially by the Yorkist sovereigns, protecting English finished products. It must be remembered of mediaeval protectionist Acts that a counterpoise to their natural operation of raising prices was held in reserve by municipal authorities and the legislature. This was the power of fixing prices constantly exercised in the case of commodities in general demand. To the foreign merchant there was no compensation. He could import such commodities as spices, which enjoyed no protection, or such articles of apparel and luxury as escaped the meshes of the protectionist statutes. Such included finer kinds of cloth than the English manufacturer could produce, and silks. Or he could import victuals, except so far as checked by the protectionist corn law passed by Edward IV in 1463, excluding corn when the price in the home market was below 6s. 8d. a quarter. But the natural market was London, and the merchant who brought in foodstuffs at once came into collision with the city's privileges. London, like other towns, enjoyed the right of fixing the prices of victuals. The assessments, it can well be believed, did not always give satisfaction to the seller, who was denied the alternative of removing his goods to another market. As security against this, the practice in London was for a city officer to preside over the sales, and to retain the money received until the whole stock had been disposed of. Though by custom the mayor was empowered to fix prices for all such importers, as well native as foreign, the alien merchants constantly complained that Englishmen selling victuals in the same market were not subjected to interference. Worse than this, the rights of purveyance were exercised, and the imported victuals seised as for the king until the English merchants had concluded their sales. Having thus reserved to his countrymen the advantages of a monopoly market, the mayor raised the arrest and availed himself of his powers of assessment for the benefit of the consumer.

In addition to all these obstacles to freedom of trade, an infinite multiplicity of petty exactions was devised, alike by the officers of the king and by those of the municipalities. Some four-and-twenty of these occur in the numerous complaints of the fifteenth and sixteenth centuries. 'Capitage', or head-money, charges by the searchers for searching the ships for wares contrary to statute, charges by the customers upon the bonds taken for the payment of customs and for the purchase of English goods in exchange for the cargo, charges for the entries on the customs' rolls, charges for taking declarations of the merchandise, for permits to discharge, for anchorage, for 'groundage', for lighterage, which was compulsory, for boat hire—all these had to be met before the cargo could be landed. Everywhere there were market tolls. In the city of London there was a special exaction, called 'scavage', before goods could be exposed for sale. Wharfage, carriage, and package, the last in the case of goods for export, were also levied. The foreign exporter from the port of London further paid a local duty called ' water-bailage'. Two other exactions were called ' cranage' and ' cocket money', the last being a fee for the customer's certificate of payment of export duties. Decade after decade the complaints of these exactions were renewed. According to the complainants, who from time to time laid their case before the Privy Council, the exactions were either new or enhanced. The common form of defence was that they dated from time immemorial. In 1505 the city of London resorted to forgery to establish this contention. The forgery being manifest, Bishop Foxe, as President of the Council, ordered the erasure of thirteen articles in dispute. But the citizens only awaited a favourable opportunity to renew their demands.

### 4. *The Hanse.*

The foundation of the German or Teutonic Hanse has already been mentioned. Its special privileges may be said to date from the *Carta Mercatoria* of 1303, since for more than two centuries the Hanse was the only body of alien merchants that was able to insist on its observance. Edward II granted it a most important privilege, abolishing in its favour the principle of corporate liability for debt, the debtor himself and his sureties alone to be answerable. Under Edward III and Richard II constant attempts were made to invade its privileges, especially on the ground of the alleged ill treatment of English subjects in the Hanse towns. The secret of its successful resistance to kings and parliaments was the fact that it was the dominant naval Power in the northern seas, from which the men-of-war of the Hanseatic League could have excluded English merchants altogether. Henry IV raised the customs duties against the Hanse, but Henry V's financial exigencies compelled him to confirm it in its ancient privileges. The accession of Edward IV with a strong nationalist policy was followed by some vexatious pecuniary exactions, and limitations of the Hanse privileges would undoubtedly have been undertaken but for the occurrence of an extraordinary crisis in domestic politics. In the autumn of 1470 a sudden rising replaced Henry VI upon the throne, and Edward IV was driven to the continent. In his extremity he applied for succour to the Hanse. Aided by its men and money he succeeded in regaining his kingdom in the following year. For this service the Hanse reaped its reward. The Treaty of Utrecht, negotiated in 1473, and ratified by Edward in February 1474, not only renewed its ancient privileges, but granted them considerable extension. By this treaty the Hanse was promised the king's protection against the unauthorized exactions of the customers and port officials, and against the competing privileges of the city of London. Two judges were to be specially nominated for the hearing of causes in which it was involved. This was, in fact, a ratification and extension of a right which had been conceded to it by the city as early as 1282. It was to be allowed a weigher and cloth measurer of its own. It was to be exempt from certain internal tolls, and to enjoy the right of selling Rhenish wine by retail, &c. In return, the English were to trade freely in the territories of the Hanse and to be protected against new imposts. The Hanse had now reached the zenith of its prosperity in this country.

The advantages enjoyed by the Hanse in the matter of customs were very remarkable. The ' custom ' on the piece of undyed cloth was, for English exporters 1s. 2d., for the Hanse 1s., for other aliens 2s. 9d. On dyed cloth, for English 2s. 4d., for the Hanse 2s., for other aliens 5s. 6d. For other than staple wares English exporters paid 1s. in the pound *ad valorem* as subsidy, aliens generally the same, besides a ' custom ' of 3d. in the pound *ad valorem*, but the Hanse only this last item. It imported into England bacon, copper, steel, silver plate, wax, linen, materials for shipping, wine, and beer. Even the protectionist *Libelle of Englyshe Polycye* approved of this part of its trade. It carried out cloth undyed, and in the early stages of manufacture, to be finished abroad. At the close of the reign of Henry VIII, during which great attention had been given to shipping, it still exported 22 per cent. of the cloth, imported 97 per cent. of the wax, and enjoyed 6 per cent. of the trade in other commodities.

In 1467, four years before the Hanse had, by aiding his restoration, earned the gratitude of Edward IV, he had passed a protectionist measure adverse to its interest prohibiting the export of unfulled cloth and of woollen yarn. This was, in fact, a re-enactment of a statute of 1376, which, however, does not seem to have been enforced against the Hanse. Although by the subsequent Treaty of Utrecht all its privileges were conserved, Henry VII, in 1487, passed an Act extending that of 1467, by the requirement that exported cloths should first have gone through the processes of being ' barbed, rowed, and shorn '. The law was set in motion against the Hanse. The Hanse claimed exemption upon the ground of the first article of the *Carta Mercatoria* permitting, in general terms, the export of commodities purchased in England. It similarly claimed exemption from another Act of 1487, renewing Acts of many previous sovereigns, compelling foreign merchants to exchange the money received for their goods for English commodities. It complained, too, that the inhabitants of Hull, in accordance with the terms of the Act, insisted that the exchange should take place in the port of import. A consequence of insistence by the provincial ports upon this right was to drive their trade to London, since that was by far the best market in which to purchase English commodities. The accounts of the port of London show that while the duties there paid averaged 49·5 per cent. of the whole kingdom in the reign of Henry VII, they had risen to 66·1 per cent. in that of Henry VIII, while the percentage of all other ports had fallen. By 1582 London had monopolized 86·4 per cent. of the whole foreign trade of the country. Not content with these measures, Henry VII, who never forgave the Hanse for its alliance with the Yorkists, devised a blow which threatened the very foundations of its prosperity. The Hanse towns were the carriers of Europe. Their imports were brought from Russia, Hungary, Bohemia, Flanders, Brabant, Germany, and France. Among the privileges granted them by Edward III was that of entering English ports *cum mercandisis suis quibuscunque, de muragio, pontagio et pavagio liberi et quieti*. It was now contended by the English lawyers that by the word *suis* was intended only such products as were actually native to the territories of the Hanse. Against such an interpretation, conflicting with the usage of more than a century, the Hanse vehemently protested. To them it was a point of vital consequence ;

and, as such, was utilized by the English as a weapon to extort the right for English merchants to trade freely within the territory of Danzig. The appearance of Perkin Warbeck, who, with the support of the Hanse, would have proved a formidable enemy, disposed Henry to acquiesce in the *status quo*, and an agreement was made at Antwerp in 1491 confirming in general terms the Treaty of Utrecht. This was followed by a brisk revival in the Hanse trade with England. Owing, also, to the patronage of Perkin Warbeck by Margaret, Duchess of Burgundy, direct commercial intercourse between England and the Netherlands ceased. The Hanse at once stepped in and took up the trade. English merchants were compelled to stand by and see the Hansards fill the shops of London with Flemish goods. In 1492 a riot ensued, which led to an unsuccessful attack on the Steelyard. Considerations of popularity, as well as of policy, henceforth united in urging Henry to carry forward at the first favourable opportunity his measures against the Hanse. He compelled them to enter into a bond of £20,000 to abstain from trading between England and the duchess's territories. The terms of the bond were wide, ' from this time forth' (*exnunc*), with no clause rendering the bond void in the event of the restoration of amicable relations. Upon this omission, doubtless intentional, hung the future fortunes of the Hanse. Henry, meanwhile, was sensible of the danger of forcing the Hanse into an active alliance with the duchess, and, after the attempt of Perkin Warbeck had failed, an agreement was arrived at, negotiated by Archbishop Warham, renewing the *status quo ante* till 1501, a term subsequently extended to 1504. The political dangers still surrounding Henry were then such as to induce him to pass an Act ' for the Stillyard' confirming the Hanse in all its privileges, though with an important proviso for those of the city of London.

The rapid increase of trade in the country, consequent upon the cessation of the Wars of the Roses, and the growing activity of English shipping in the northern seas, supplied plentiful occasions of friction with the Hanse during the succeeding years. Wolsey revived against them the whole category of ingenious chicane which had been set in motion by Henry VII. A congress for the settlement of reciprocal complaints was held at Bruges in 1520. The

Hanse maintained that the Treaty of Utrecht was an absolute engagement by the English kings for themselves and their successors, the English that it was conditional on good behaviour, and had, in fact, been forfeited by the Hansards' infractions of various commercial statutes. But in the critical condition of foreign affairs Wolsey had no desire to provoke the Hanse to desperation. They, on their part, were solicitous to retain as much as possible of their lucrative trade. A compromise was, therefore, agreed to in 1522 upon the basis of the *status quo* which, in effect, conceded to the English most of their demands, until a new convention could be arranged.

Notwithstanding the animosity of the commercial classes to the Hanse, Henry VIII did not deem it prudent, after his rupture with the Papacy, to alienate a power whose alliance would have been invaluable in the event of a general combination against him. The Hanse, on their part, were forward to conciliate the court and ministry. When, in 1546, a famine occurred in England, the Hanse, by their promptitude in furnishing supplies, earned the acknowledgements of the Privy Council. But this very action had the effect of hastening their downfall. The quarter of wheat fell in 1547 to 4s. 11d., whereas in 1545 it had stood at 15s. 6¾d. No doubt this was due, in the main, to abundant harvests. By the agricultural classes it was ascribed to excessive foreign importations. Hitherto, despite the jealousies of the commercial classes, the landed proprietors had stood by the Hanse. When, at the accession of Henry VIII, the Commons had voted a subsidy, imposing it upon Hansards as upon other aliens, the Lords had inserted a proviso for their exemption. When Bills regulating commerce came before them, the Lords persistently inserted like exempting clauses. But with a plethora of wheat deluging the country the hand of every man of the influential classes had joined against the Hanse. Their ruin was but a question of means. In 1551 the Hanse were cited before the Privy Council at the suit of the Merchant Adventurers. The chief gravamen against them was the alleged violation of the terms of their charter, *cum mercandisis suis*. 'This yeare (1551) . . . in October, the liberties of the Stiliard were seazed into the kinges handes.' For some time longer the Hanse merchants were permitted to trade upon the basis of the traditional customs duties by royal licences confining them to traffic in their own (*suis*) commodities. With the accession of Mary came a turn in the tide of their fortunes. The decline of the Hanse was prejudicial to the Spanish provinces of the Netherlands. The negotiations for the Spanish marriage were already on foot. It was, therefore, an act of policy to revoke the confiscatory degree of 1551. On October 24, 1553, the privileges of the Hanse, subject to the English lawyers' interpretation of *cum mercandisis suis*, were restored.

The commercial classes were at once in arms. In December 1554, a long information against the malpractices of the ' Easterlings ' was lodged with the Privy Council by a number of merchants. In February 1555, the Merchant Adventurers presented a petition to the same effect. The city of London added complaints of its own. The case came before the Privy Council in 1556. By a decree of March 23, 1557, the Hanse were found guilty of an abuse of their privileges in the export of cloths, and a diet for the settlement of disputes was fixed for the following year. The Hanse alleged that the summons to the diet was made at too short notice. They failed to appear, but in September held a diet of their own at Lübeck and published a formal protest to the queen. They demanded a rescission of certain decrees of the Privy Council restrictive of their trade, and a restoration of the *status quo ante*, with a view to a conference. The queen replied (October 6, 1557) setting forth the English complaints, and maintaining that the decree of Edward VI repealing their privileges was not annulled, but only suspended. The Hanse towns retorted by boycotting English goods in their ports and ill treating English merchants. Elizabeth, uncertain of the security of her throne, was long unwilling to break with a power which would prove a valuable ally against a papal confederation. For twenty years she kept them in suspense as to her ultimate intentions. At last, in 1578, she prohibited them, in common with other foreigners, to export wool, her object being to encourage the new settlements of Flemish weavers. The Hanse retaliated by levying a duty of $7\frac{3}{4}$ per cent. on English imports into their territories. Elizabeth replied with a like duty upon all their exports and imports. In 1589 she seized in the Tagus sixty cargoes of munitions and provisions shipped by the Hanse to the Spanish Government. Angry remonstrances followed. These proving fruitless, the Hanse procured the expulsion of the Merchant Adventurers from Germany. Elizabeth, thereupon, in 1597, forfeited their privileges, closed the Steelyard, and expelled them the kingdom.

## 5. *The Staple and the Merchant Adventurers.*

The trading corporation, styled the Merchant Adventurers, which fought this battle against the foreigner to a successful issue, had come into existence some time in the thirteenth century. It claimed a charter from John, Duke of Brabant, dated 1216, constituting it an organization analogous to the Hanse, for the purpose of trade in the Netherlands. A corresponding organization was established in England under the name of the Brotherhood of St. Thomas of Canterbury. From this, in the reign of Edward III, sprang the Mercers' Company, and in 1407 an offshoot of the Company received its final form as the Company of Merchant Adventurers, and was granted a house or factory at Antwerp. As the cloth industry grew, this Company increased in wealth and importance. The Merchant Adventurers were the exporters of manufactured goods ; their elder rivals, the Merchants of the Staple, of raw materials. London was the head-quarters of the Merchant Adventurers, but they had branches at Exeter, Newcastle, and elsewhere. So great were the advantages secured for them by their organization in the Netherlands, that with the development of mercantile enterprise after the Wars of the Roses, they found their ranks overcrowded. To enhance their monopoly, they imposed heavy fines, amounting to as much as £20 (about £240 of our money in value), upon new members when they entered the Company. In 1496, therefore, an Act was passed restricting the sum to ten marks (£6 13s. 4d.). In order to equalize among themselves the profits of the trade, they imposed a ' stint ', or maximum limit, to the number of cloths which it was permissible to a member to export to any of the four great annual marts at which their goods were disposed of in the Netherlands.

The causes which added to the prosperity of the Merchant Adventurers involved a corresponding decline in the fortunes of their rivals, the Merchants of the Staple. The Staple was the earliest governmental organization of English commerce. Its origin is lost in obscurity, but probabilities point to its formation, for fiscal purposes, by Edward I. Its object was to insure the collection of the royal customs by defining the channels of export for the staple produce of the country, wool, hides, and tin. A patent of 1313 dwells on the mischiefs arising from allowing merchants, whether native or alien, to ship wool to any port at choice, and orders 'the mayor and communaltie of merchants of

FIG. 354. A WALLED TOWN.
An early plan of Hull.

the realm' to fix on a town in the Low Countries as a Staple to which all wool should be carried. Staple towns were also appointed for this country, where the wool could be collected, weighed, and customed. By the statute of Northampton in 1328, all Staples both at home and abroad were abolished. Nevertheless, the Staple existed in Flanders in 1343, probably on account of the convenience experienced in retaining a centre for trade. The Merchants of the Staple as an organized body came into existence in the reign of Edward III.

In 1353 Edward III made a new departure in policy. He removed the Staple from Bruges, where it then was, to England. The object of this was to avoid the restrictive regulations, harassing to trade, imposed by the men of Bruges, and to attract foreigners to this country. Newcastle, York, Lincoln, Norwich, Westminster, Canterbury, Chichester, Winchester, Exeter, and Bristol were named Staple towns for England. The export of Staple goods was exclusively reserved for aliens, Englishmen being forbidden to engage in it. But the decay of the English mercantile marine, and therefore of the reserve of the royal navy, was soon discerned as the consequence. The Staple was removed from England to Calais, to Middle-

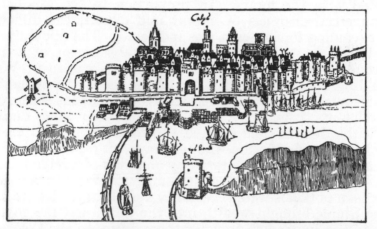

FIG. 355.   CALAIS TOWN AND HARBOUR.
(Cott. MS. Aug. I. ii. 70.)

burgh, to Calais, to England and to Calais again, according to the aspect of foreign affairs. It was finally fixed at Calais in the reign of Richard II. An elaborate system was devised to ensure that all Staple goods should be consigned to that port, except wool and tin allowed by the king's special licence to alien merchants to be transported ' beyond the straits of Morocco ', that is, as a rule, to Italy. Certain ports in England were assigned as ports of shipment for wool, and the shippers compelled to find security that the cargo should be discharged at Calais. The king's ' customer ' at Calais then delivered to the shipper a certificate of the cargo, thus keeping a check upon the collectors of customs at the exporting ports, who were likewise compelled to return a register to the exchequer. By this supervision at the ports alike of shipment and discharge some check was put on smuggling, and this was only possible where the port of discharge was in English hands. But the final and determining reasons for fixing the Staple at Calais were, no doubt, political and military. There were also financial considerations in its favour. Successive governments had long endeavoured to check the displacement of English money by foreign coin of inferior weight and standard. For this end royal exchanges had existed since the reign of Henry I, and in towns where coins were struck, as London and York, these exchanges were associated with the mints. In proportion to the number of commercial channels of import and export, the difficulty of excluding foreign coin was increased. The appointment of Calais as sole Staple was the establishment of a neck through which the bulk of trade necessarily passed. When the English stapler sold his wool, he received payment in English money, exchanged at the Calais Mint for the foreign purchaser's coin. By this exchange the king derived a double benefit : he secured the commission paid on the exchange and averted the expense of recoinage, which would have been necessitated by an influx of foreign money. Lastly, the expenses of maintaining the fortifications and garrison of Calais were necessarily very heavy. Its creation as a Staple brought wealth into the town, and the government was enabled to transfer these duties to the Company of the Staple whom its measures had enriched.

The Merchants of the Staple appear to have originally consisted of those traders in Staple goods who naturally resorted to the Staple towns, whether in England or abroad. By the organizing statute of 1353 they were sworn to submit to the jurisdiction of the mayor and constables of the Staple. At Calais the court of the Staple consisted of the mayor and aldermen. In it was administered the Law Merchant, with an appeal to the King's Court at Westminster.

The great impairers of the fortunes of the Staple during the fifteenth century were the kings themselves. It was a frequent practice with them to grant licences for export to other ports of Western Europe than Calais. Parliament made constant remonstrances, and in 1485 the legality of these licences was tried in the courts, the judges giving judgement for the Crown. An Act of 1449, complaining of the practice, states that the customs of Calais had stood at £68,000 a year in the reign of Edward III, and were then reduced to £12,000. In the time of Henry V the duties on wool were said to have exceeded 50 per cent. of the whole revenue. In the reign of Henry VII they averaged no more than 36 per cent. It was not until 1557 that the Government, by a change in the tariff, showed its recognition of the fact which had long been patent, that the staple trade of England had ceased to be raw material, and was then become the manufacture of cloth. In 1558, on the loss of Calais, the Staple was removed to Bruges, and in 1561 a new charter was granted, confirming the former privileges. But the trade of the Staple declined, owing to the superior concessions enjoyed by the Merchant Adventurers in the Netherlands.

While the cloth industry flourished, the worsted industry fell off. It had been established in Norfolk in the fourteenth century, having been imported from Flanders. Norwich, its centre, had become through it one of the wealthiest cities in the kingdom. But in the fifteenth century this industry was already failing. The cause was alleged to be fraudulent manufacture, impairing its reputation abroad. To check this, an elaborate Act regulating the manufacture was passed by Edward IV in 1467. Still the trade decayed, and in 1495 an Act was passed improving the training of apprentices, and repealing a statute of 1407, which limited their supply by imposing a pecuniary qualification upon the parents. For a while after this, as we learn from the preamble of a regulative Act of 1523, the trade prospered throughout the county of Norfolk. An Act of 1534 prohibited the exportation of worsted cloths in any unfinished state. It is possible that the Government's prescriptions for manufacture did not suit the demand abroad, for in 1542 we hear a complaint that the regrators were buying up worsted yarn and exporting it to France and Flanders, there to be made into worsted cloth. The export of yarn was accordingly forbidden. But the decline continued. The average export fell from 6,000 pieces for the first nineteen years of Henry VIII to 1,600 pieces for the last nine years. Meanwhile, the rival industry in the Netherlands flourished, and Norwich suffered, until in 1565 the barbarities of Alva and of the Inquisition were followed by the immigration of a thousand Flemish weavers.

From the twelfth century, when Richard I issued an Assize of Cloth, that manufacture was deemed by Government of sufficient importance to be dealt with by general legislation, rather than by the caprice of municipal authorities. The Assize of Cloth was enforced by *Magna Carta*. To promote the manufacture, the Oxford Parliament in 1258 prohibited the export of wool. But the finer cloths were at this time imported from Flanders. Edward III, therefore, favoured by the disturbed state of affairs in the Netherlands, invited Flemish weavers to England. He abolished in their interest the standard measurements, and ensured them a supply of raw material by again prohibiting for a while the export of wool. By the end of the century cloth was a common article of sale at all fairs, Cloth Fair, held near St. Bartholomew's, Smithfield, being the most celebrated. The traders in cloth, the Mercers and Drapers, were already in the fourteenth century the chief of the trading companies of London and other towns. The tide of commerce began to turn. Instead of suffering from a flow of cloth from the Netherlands to England, the cloth of this country threatened that of the Netherlands, so that in 1434 the importation of English cloth into the Netherlands was entirely forbidden. After many vicissitudes of diplomacy, the treaty called in England *Intercursus Magnus*, but nicknamed in the Netherlands *Intercursus Malus*, was secured by Henry VII, in 1496, allowing free entry into Flanders of English cloth.

In the fifteenth century the cloth industry spread from the towns to the country, where it was exempt from the vexatious regulations of the gilds. In the country it was carried on by the system known as domestic industry. The clothier delivered the material at the various stages of the manufacture to the several classes of artisans, supervised their work upon it, and sold it to the draper. In the sixteenth century we find the beginnings of a factory system, the celebrated Jack of Newbury having a hundred looms in his own house. This development was suppressed by the Weavers' Act of 1555, the design of which was to protect the handicraftsmen against the oppressions of capitalist employers. A new method of cloth manufacture began in the reign of Henry VIII, and continued through that of Elizabeth. The refugees from religious persecution in the Netherlands brought with them the ' new draperies ', slighter stuffs called ' bays and says '.   They settled principally in Norwich and in the south-eastern counties.

The minor industries, though in the fifteenth century the central government frequently interfered in their regulation, were for the most part controlled by gilds, to whose history they therefore properly belong.

The success of the Merchant Adventurers suggested them as a model for other trading companies.   In 1554 the Muscovy Company was incorporated by Mary, with exclusive trading rights to Russia.   The Eastland Company, with like rights to Scandinavia, Poland, Prussia, and Finland, was chartered by Elizabeth in 1579.   The Turkey Company obtained a revocable charter in 1581, for seven years, which was finally made perpetual in 1605.   Another such charter was granted to the Guinea Company in 1588.

## 6.  *The Currency.*

From very early times the issue and control of the currency was a royal prerogative.   But it was the practice of the earlier kings before the Conquest to grant the right of coinage to great persons.   By a law of Æthelstan bishops were authorized to possess mints in various towns.   The king received a seignorage, as we know from Domesday, upon change of dies.   The highest unit of value at the time of the Conquest was the pound, that is, the pound of silver. There were three different divisions of the pound prevailing in various parts of England.   They were (*a*) twenty shillings of twelve pence each, (*b*) forty-eight shillings of five pence each, (*c*) sixteen ounces of sixteen pence each.   A fourth division, used in Wales, was twelve ounces of twenty pence each.   Payment by weight was common till late in the Middle Ages, owing to the imperfect state of the coinage.

For a century and a half after the Conquest the coinage was, on the whole, inferior in quality to that of the earlier kings.   The centralizing policy of Henry II embraced this department of administration, and minting became chiefly confined to London.   As the export trade in wool increased, foreign money poured into the realm until Edward I undertook a reorganization of the currency.   Search was to be made of all merchants and ships entering English ports, and foreign to be delivered up in exchange for English money. King's exchangers were appointed for this duty. With the troubled times of Edward II the evil of a debased coinage reappeared. In conformity with the generalization from experience known as Gresham's law, that over-valued money drives under-valued money out of circulation, the bad foreign coins were expelling the improved English coinage of Edward I. To provide material for a fresh coinage an Act was passed in 1340 requiring exporters of wool to import bullion to the value of 13s. 4d. for every sack exported. A gold coinage was also struck for currency in both England and Flanders, and the export of any other coin prohibited. These measures proving unsuccessful, in

FIG. 356. OFFICERS RECEIVING AND WEIGHING COIN AT THE EXCHEQUER, A.D. 1130–74. (MS. Trin. Coll., Camb., R. 17. 1.)

1351 an entirely new coinage of gold and of silver was issued, of the same fineness but of less weight, so that the new coins approximated to the old coins in value. Nevertheless, the scarcity of the precious metals was still felt in England, as elsewhere in Europe. An Act of Richard II, in 1381, complains that 'there is scarcely any gold or silver left'. Its exportation in any shape was forbidden. Where money was due abroad, exchange was to be effected by merchants in England with the king's licence, both for the persons from whom the payments were due and for the exchangers. These last were further sworn not to send any gold or silver abroad under cover of exchange. From the accounts of the king's exchangers, preserved in the Record Office, it appears that the charge for letters of exchange was a little more than 3½ per cent. The *Libelle of Englyshe Polycye* states it at 1s. in the pound, or 5 per cent.

In 1421 Henry V projected a scheme of recoinage. To encourage the holders to bring their coins to the mint he provided, firstly, that they should there be exchanged for

*A Part of the STANDARD of Weights and Measures in the Exchequer.*
*Anno 12 Henrici Septimi.*

*From the Original Table, formerly in the Treasury of the King's Exchequer*

FIG. 357.

new coins at their nominal value ; secondly, that payments between private persons should be by weight, and not by tale. The enforcement of this provision by creditors would naturally be an inducement to debtors to offer payment in the new coinage. These attractions, perhaps, caused too speedy a drain of the Government's store of bullion, for by a later statute of the same year a seignorage was charged of 5s. on the Tower pound of gold, and 15d. on that of silver.

The Acts of Henry VI show that, in the opinion of the Government, the prohibitions to export the precious metals were ineffective. In 1423 a statute was passed compelling alien merchants to give security in Chancery, ' every Company for them of their Company', for their observance of the regulations. This proving inadequate, Edward IV, in 1478, took the extraordinary step of making the export of gold or silver without licence a felony, that is, a capital offence. The dearth of money was increased by the hoarding of Henry VII to such a degree that private tokens did duty for silver coinage. In 1504 an Act was passed for the recoinage of silver, and Irish money was forbidden currency in England.

The extravagant penalty of the Act of 1478 had clearly failed in its object. The Act was renewed for twenty years in 1510, the punishment for exporting bullion being reduced to a forfeiture of double the value exported. Complaints were still made of the scarcity of money, which was thought to be due to export under cover of letters of exchange. A proclamation was, therefore, issued in 1530 forbidding exchanges. But the remonstrances of the merchants, and their assurances that this prohibition would certainly cause the evil it was designed to check, caused the Government to abstain from enforcement of the law. At last, in 1539, public opinion became enlightened. A royal proclamation gave a general dispensation from the statutes restraining foreign exchange. Shortly after this, in 1543, took place the first great debasement of the coinage. Precedents had occurred, but they had been confined to reductions of the weight of the coins. In 1300 Edward I coined the pound of silver into 243 pence. Under Edward III, in 1344, these had increased to 266, and in 1352 to 360 pence. Edward IV, in 1465, raised the number to 450 pence. In 1526 Henry VIII substituted the French pound troy, weighing ¾ oz. more, for the Tower pound as the unit of weight, but he further reduced the weight of the silver penny, coining 540 pence out of the new pound, equal to 506¼ out of the old. He was the first king to lower the standard of fineness. Instead of 18 dwt. of alloy in 12 oz. of silver, the debasement increased the alloy to 2 oz. in twelve. In 1545 the alloy in the silver coinage was increased to 6 oz. in twelve ; in 1546 to 8 oz. in twelve. Under Edward VI, in 1551, it rose to

9 oz. The shilling now contained only $2\frac{3}{4}d.$ worth of silver, the worst money ever coined in England. Proclamations and statutes proving ineffective to control the consequent rise in prices, the disturbance of trade, and the exportation of the good coin, some improvement in the standard was made in 1552. In 1560 Elizabeth restored the standard to its old fineness, and reduced the number of pence in the pound of silver to 720, whereas in 1550 a pound of metal, of which three ounces only were silver, had been coined into 864 pence. In 1600 the number was fixed at 744 pence for the pound of silver, and at this it remained so long as silver continued to be the standard, that is, till 1816.

### 7. *The Road System and the Water-Ways.*

At the time of the Anglo-Saxon invasion Britain was covered with a network of Roman roads. Of these the four principal are still known as 'the four Roman ways'. The most famous of them is Watling Street. It ran from Dover to London, and from London zigzag through Chester and York, thence by two branches to Carlisle and the neighbourhood of Newcastle. The Fosse Way ran from Bath by way of Cirencester, Leamington, and Leicester to the great Roman settlement of Lincoln. The Ermin Street ran direct from London to Lincoln, and thence to Doncaster and York. Icknield Street, or the Ikenild Way, joined Southampton with Norwich through Silchester, Dunstable, and Newmarket. These main highways, so called because their construction raised them above the level of the contiguous soil, were connected by intersecting roads all over the country. The great junctions were Carlisle, Chester, Manchester, York, Doncaster, Lincoln, Caerleon, Silchester, Winchester, London, Dunstable, Colchester, and Canterbury. From the eighth century onwards the maintenance of these roads and of the bridges belonging to them formed one of the divisions of the *trinoda necessitas* then imposed on grantees of land. The peace of the four highways (*quatuor chimini*) was maintained by a special fine in the laws of Edward the Confessor. Under the Normans the general maintenance of highways was the duty of the manorial tenants, that of main road bridges of the hundred, that of smaller bridges of the tithings. In chartered towns care of the roads and bridges fell upon the municipality.

But these duties were so frequently neglected that the Church encouraged the undertaking of them as pious works meriting indulgences. Accordingly, gilds came into existence with this object, like that of the Holy Cross at Birmingham in the reign of Richard II, which was reported by the commissioners of Edward VI as keeping in good repair two great stone bridges and divers foul and dangerous highways near the town. The duty of building and maintaining bridges and roads also continued after the Conquest to be attached to grants of land. The grantee was sometimes entitled to take *pontagium*, or bridge-toll. In some places, as at Huntingdon, bridge repairs were provided for by the voluntary offerings of passers-by. Sometimes, as at London and Rochester, a trust fund was provided by endowments of land for the bridge. In 1281 Edward I ordered the bishops to allow royal collectors to address ' pious exhortations' to the people for the repair of London Bridge. Complaints of the ruinous state of bridges are frequently found in the Rolls of Parliament. Conflicting jurisdictions constantly rendered doubtful the onus of the liability to make repairs. In such cases the Court of Chancery issued commissions for inquiry. Upon default proved, information lay in the King's Bench. The way-wardens in the courts of manors and the sheriffs in the counties were both bound to hold inquests of roads and bridges.

In 1285 Edward I took up the improvement of roads as a general measure of police. Highways to market towns were ordered to be enlarged and cleared of underwood for a space of two hundred feet on each side, so as to prevent ambuscades of highway robbers. But in the next century civil distractions, the scarcity of labour following the great pestilences, and the expenditure upon Edward III's wars, caused a general decay of highways and bridges. Parliaments were adjourned in 1331, 1339, and 1380, because the state of the roads prevented sufficient attendance. In 1344 and 1353 Edward III ordered the repair of the road near London, and a collection of tolls for horses and carts. Other provincial towns established turnpikes at their approaches for this purpose. In 1406 a complaint was made to Parliament that the sheriffs of various counties were enforcing unreasonable fines upon the religious houses and the secular clergy for the repair of highways. According to the complainants the highways were, as a matter of fact, kept in sufficient repair. It was necessary for Henry IV to maintain good relations with the clergy. The reply of the Crown, therefore, was a caution to the sheriffs against excessive zeal, rather than a censure upon those guilty of dereliction of duty. Nevertheless, commissions for the repair of causeways and bridges were from time to time issued by this king and his successors.

The rapid growth of internal trade, after the cessation of the Wars of the Roses, soon demanded the attention of the legislature to the state of the roads. At first public opinion seems to have been unprepared to revive the method of Edward I, by the adoption of a general measure for the whole country. In 1523 Parliament passed an Act to encourage landowners in the weald of Kent to make new roads, and this Act was extended to Sussex two years later. In 1530 a general Act was passed dealing with bridges. This empowered the Justices of the Peace, in cases where the liability to repair was doubtful, to rate the inhabitants of counties and of corporate towns for the repair of bridges and of the highways within three hundred feet of either end of them. To these magistrates was thenceforth entrusted the care of their maintenance. In the case of Chester provision was made, by an Act of 1545, for a permanent highway overseer of two miles and a half of road leading to that city. Acts were passed for paving the streets of London and Westminster and the neighbourhood in 1533, 1534, 1540, and 1543. All of their preambles describe the perilousness and noisomeness of the roads. At last, in 1555, a general Act was passed for roads upon the model of the Bridge Act of 1530. Every parish was bound to elect two road surveyors at Easter, and the parishioners to give four days' labour before midsummer for their maintenance and repair. This measure was doubtless rendered urgent by the dissolution of the monasteries, of which the wealthier had maintained the roads as a pious work. A succession of Acts followed under Elizabeth enlarging the provisions of the Act of 1555.

More useful than the roads to internal trade were the water-ways. The forests attracted rain, and brooks, of which the courses have now silted up till the stream is both shallow and narrow, are recorded in Domesday to have been navigable by vessels. The trade backwards and forwards with the continent was carried inland by water. Hence inland towns, such as York and Doncaster, are spoken of by chroniclers as 'ports', and enjoyed rights of 'wrecks at sea'. This use of rivers checked the number of bridges, as being obstacles to navigation, and made fords and ferries of importance. Traders and riverside dwellers were constantly on the alert to oppose hindrances to free passage. It was of importance, therefore, to thriving towns to secure grants giving them the control of the water-ways on which they were situate. By a charter of Richard I the citizens of London obtained the right of putting down all weirs on the Thames, and a general authority over its waters. The twenty-third article of *Magna Carta* is a general prohibition of weirs in rivers. Under Henry III these prohibitions were enforced ; but in the stormy days of Edward II a general disregard for law showed itself. In 1314 the merchants of Bristol complained to Parliament of the hindrance to their trade with Hereford caused by the weirs on the Wye. About the same date the merchants of London trading with Oxford complained of like obstructions on the Thames, Richard I's charter notwithstanding. In 1351 Edward III resolved on a strong measure. He passed an Act for the removal of all obstructions placed in rivers since the time of Edward I. As that king had strenuously enforced the law, this retrospective limit probably covered the Thames case. But the interests of the manufacturing industry continued to assert themselves, and weirs and mills were presently constructed. Parliament, therefore, in 1371 attached the great penalty of a hundred marks (£66 13s. 4d.) to this offence. Still the Commons complained, though now only of the obstructions erected prior to the reign of Edward I, which shows that the measures of the Government had proved effectual. Commissions were accordingly issued in 1398 to Justices of the Peace to destroy all of them which were a nuisance to navigation. These measures were enforced by Henry IV in Acts of 1399 and 1402. But in 1423 complaints were made that the law was ineffectively executed in Kent, Surrey, and Essex, and fresh commissions were issued. The conflict of interests, however, was now becoming more equal, for in 1464 Edward IV, who solicitously courted the favour of the manufacturers, refused a petition of the Commons to enforce the statutes of 1351 and 1371 in the case of the Severn and its tributaries. Nevertheless, in 1472, after his restoration, the shipping and mercantile interests prevailed. Appeal was made to *Magna Carta*, offenders ordered to destroy obstructions themselves, and a fine of a hundred marks imposed upon defaulters. Special Acts were passed for Southampton Water in 1495 and 1523, and for the Ouse and Humber in 1532. These measures do not prove that the Government confined the enforcement of the law to the more important water-ways, for the *Domestic State Papers* show that throughout Henry VIII's reign the policy of suppression of obstructions was everywhere rigorously maintained, especially under Thomas

FIG. 358. A COUNTRY CART. From the Luttrell Psalter, fourteenth century.

Cromwell, himself of the merchant class. On the other side was an industry rapidly acquiring a paramount importance, the cloth manufacture. An Act of 1555 sets forth the injury done to the city of Hereford by the destruction of two fulling mills and two corn mills on the Wye in 1528. The Dean and Chapter were now authorized to rebuild them. The change had set in. After this time the prohibitory statutes were suffered to fall into desuetude.

The constant use of the water-ways, disclosed by the history of these measures, accounts for a remarkable economic fact, the cheapness of land transport. Thorold Rogers has been inclined to infer from it that, before the dissolution of the monasteries, the roads were really well kept, an inference not warranted by the language of the Rolls of Parliament. Land-carriage was chiefly on horseback or sumpter mules. Rude two-wheeled carts were constructed in the villages from very early times. They are represented in manuscripts as boxes of planks on wheels studded with great nails. The cost of carriage naturally varied with the nature of the article. From the thirteenth century to the fifteenth we know, from Rogers's investigations, that twopence a ton per mile was the average charge for carrying heavy goods in the thirteenth century, and a little more than a penny a mile from the fourteenth century till the rise in prices in the fifteenth century. Even wine, a most perishable and cumbersome article, was carried at no more than about twopence a mile per ton weight in 1264 and 1298, and a penny a mile in 1406. The average cost of cart hire in the fifteenth century was 1s. 3½d. a day. Water-carriage, it is to be noted, was extraordinarily cheap —about one-sixth of the cost of land-carriage. A ship with its complement of sailors, chartered to carry munitions from Bristol to Carnarvon Castle, was hired in 1297 at less than 2s. a day. Corn could be carried on the Thames, from Henley to London, at between two and three pence a quarter. Valuable articles and money were carried at an extra rate for insurance. Inns were numerous, though the traveller, as still in the East, was expected to supply his own provisions, fuel, and bedding.

FIG. 359. A FORGE. MS. Bodl. 264, fourteenth century.

## Books for reference.

JOHN SMITH, *Memoirs of Wool*, 2nd ed., 1756.
*Statutes of the Realm*, Record Commission, 1810–28.
*Rolls of Parliament, 1278–1503*, 6 vols., 1832.
MACPHERSON, *Annals of Commerce*, &c., 4 vols., 1805.
RUDING, *Annals of the Coinage*, 3 vols., 1840.
THOROLD ROGERS, *History of Agriculture and Prices in England*, 6 vols., 1866–87.
—— *Six Centuries of Work and Wages*, 2 vols., 1884–90.
—— *The Economic Interpretation of History*, 2nd ed., 1891.
JUSSERAND, *English Wayfaring Life in the Middle Ages*, translated by L. TOULMIN SMITH, 1892.
OCHENKOWSKI, *Englands wirthschaftliche Entwickelung am Ausgange des Mittelalters*, 1879.
SCHANZ, *Englische Handelspolitik gegen Ende des Mittelalters*, 1881.
ASHLEY, *Introduction to English Economic History*, 2 vols., 1888–94.
CUNNINGHAM, *The Growth of English Industry and Commerce during the Early and Middle Ages*, 3rd ed., 1896.
ZIMMERN, *The Hanse Towns*, 1889.
BARNARD, F. P., *The Casting-Counter and the Counting-Board*, 1917.

# GLOSSARY

*Abacus*, the square, uppermost part of a capital. (Arch.)

*Ad valorem duty*, a duty levied upon, and varying with, the value of a commodity.

*Ailettes*, ' little wings '. (Armour.)

*Alb*, a kind of surplice, with close sleeves.

*Amice*, a square of white linen, folded diagonally, worn by the celebrant priest, on the head or about the neck and shoulders.

*Anchoret*, M.E. *ancre*, a hermit, or recluse (L.L. *anachoreta*, fr. Gk. ἀναχωρητής, one who has withdrawn from the world).

*Anelace*, a heavy, broad-bladed, sharp-pointed, double-edged knife.

*Apparels*, small rectangular pieces of embroidered stuff, used as ornaments to the alb and amice.

*Arquebus*, an improved hand-gun, either match-lock or wheel-lock.

*Articulated*, or *Laminated*, constructed with overlapping plates. (Armour.)

*Aumbry*, a cupboard in a church in which to lock up sacred vessels, &c. (O.F. *armarie*; L.L. *armaria, -um*, a cupboard, originally for arms).

*Aventaille*, or *Ventail*, vizor (*avant-taille*).

*Axial line*, the central line round which, or in common relation to which, the parts of a building are arranged. (Arch.)

*Badge*, an emblematic figure, especially placed on some prominent part of the clothing of servants and retainers, such as the breast, back, sleeve, &c., to show to what household they belonged; found also on flags, buildings, &c.

*Baluster*, a short shaft, such as is used in balustrades, usually thicker in the middle than at the ends.

*Barbed, rowed, and shorn*, three finishing processes in the manufacture of cloth.

*Bar-tracery*, so called from its resemblance to iron bars bent to the forms required. (Arch.)

*Bastille*, redoubt or outwork. (Mil. Arch.)

*Bavier*, chin-piece; so called from its resemblance to a bib. (Armour.)

*Bay*, a constituent portion or compartment of a building, complete in itself and corresponding to other portions.

*Bell-capital*, Fig. 18.

*Bolting-house*, a place where bran is bolted (i. e. sifted) from flour.

*Bombasted*, stuffed with cotton, hair, &c. (Costume.)

*Breche*, breeches.

*Brigandine*, metal splints sewed upon canvas, linen, or leather and covered with similar materials; a material used in making light armour. A *pair of brigandines* is a body-coat of this material, in two pieces.

*Burel cloth*, coarse woollen cloth.

*Burgonet*, a steel cap with chin-piece; a feature of sixteenth-century armour.

*Buttery*, M.E. *botelerie*; store room for beer, wine, and the like.

*Byrnie*, a mail shirt, the precursor of the *hauberk*.

*Cabasset*, a steel cap resembling the *morion* (q.v.).

*Cadency, marks of*, marks by which the coats of arms of all kinsfolk by blood, other than that of the head of the family, were distinguished therefrom and from each other. ' Difference ' is often loosely used in this sense.

*Cadre*, skeleton of a regiment or other military unit.

*Caliver*, or *arquebus de calibre*, so called from its bore being of a prescribed size as a matter of convenience in the supply of bullets; whereas before, the bore of arquebuses varied according to the individual discretion of captains of bands.

*Camail*, fr. Prov. *cap-malh* (*cap-mail*), i. e. head mail or armour.

*Capitular*, of or pertaining to an ecclesiastical chapter.

*Caput baroniae*, chief seat of a gentle family.

*Carabine*, rifled-barrelled matchlock.

*Cellarer*, steward, or bursar, of a monastery.

*Chamfer*, a surface formed by paring off an angle. (Arch.)

*Chasuble*, a sleeveless mantle, worn over the alb and stole by a celebrant priest.

*Chausses*, breeches of mail or other pliant armour. In civilian costume = drawers.

*Ciclaton*, a kind of silk. A Persian word = scarlet.

*Cingulum*, the military belt of a knight or gentleman.

*Cinquecento*, Italian art of the sixteenth century.

*Cocket*, or *coket*, a document drawn up by the customer from the declarations of merchants exporting goods. It was the duty of the searcher in the port of export to search the goods when on ship-board, and verify by aid of the cocket the consignor's declarations.

*Collateral shields.* Before marshalling came into use, subsidiary coats of arms were often placed on separate shields by the side of, or round, the chief coat or ' coat of name '.

*Cope*, a semicircular piece of silk or other cloth, worn by ecclesiastical persons in processions, at vespers and on other occasions.

*Corked shoes*, shoes with cork pads inserted on which the wearer's heels were raised.

*Corporation sole*, a corporation composed of a single member, as contrasted with a ' corporation aggregate ', such as a dean and chapter, a mayor and commonalty, &c.

*Coute*, or *coudière*, elbow-piece. (Armour.)

*Cranage*, a charge for the use of a crane for loading or discharging a vessel.

*Crocket*, lit. a little crook or bend (Arch.).

*Cross Flory*, Fig. 202.

*Cross-œuillet*, cross-shaped loopholes, with the end of each arm enlarged into a circle to facilitate the use of firearms.

*Cuir-bouilli*, leather boiled in oil to render it easier to mould into shapes.

*Cuirie*, a body-defence of leather, a cuirass (which, as its derivation shows, was originally of that material).

*Cuisses*, thigh-armour.

*Curtains*, those portions of a fortified wall which connect adjacent flanking-towers.

*Cushion-capital*, Fig. 7.

*Customers*, officials who levied import and export duties.

*Cyclas*, a species of military surcoat.

*Dagged*, jagged.

*Dalmatic*, a wide-sleeved vestment, slit on each side of the skirt, and marked with two stripes. Worn by deacons and bishops ; also by kings and emperors at their coronation. Originally used in the province of Dalmatia.

*Dead angle*, an angle, the ground contained by which cannot be seen by the defenders, and is therefore indefensible. (Mil. Arch.)

*Dead pays*, introduced from the land service, in which the custom existed certainly as early as the reign of Henry VII. They were extra allowances, the pay of fictitious men, of which a certain number were permitted to be borne on the muster-roll of each company of soldiers or ship, for the purpose of increasing the pay of the officers. They were divided among the officers on some complex system not easy to determine.

*Debruised*, said of an animal charged on a shield and surmounted by an ordinary or other charge ; Fig. 225.

*Demi-jambes*, greaves. (Armour.)

*Diaper*, a repeated ornament that varies what would otherwise be a plain surface. (O.F. *diaspre*, varied, and so like *jasper*.)

*Difference*, an addition to, or a modification of, a coat of arms that, while it was often such as to indicate alliance with or dependence upon the bearer of that coat, also served as a distinguishing mark.

*Diptych*, a folding tablet of two leaves, joined together by strings or by hinges.

*Dorter*, a dormitory.

*Dripstone*, a projecting moulding above the heads of doors, windows, and other openings, primarily intended to throw off rain, but also found as an ornament in interior work.

*Easterlings*, the inhabitants of the eastern shores of the Baltic, and so generally those of the Hanse towns, whose ' easterling ' became our ' sterling ' money.

*Enamel*, a vitreous glaze applied by fusion to metallic surfaces.

*Enfeoffment*, investiture with dignities or possessions.

*Entablature*, that part of the superstructure of a classical building which is supported by the columns.

*Exchange.* The exchange of English and foreign coins was a royal prerogative. A royal exchange was first set up by Henry I. Exchanges were established by Edward I at various trading centres, as York, Dover, Canterbury, with tables of rates. After the fourteenth century there was one at Calais. The central exchange office was in the Tower of London. The exchange was farmed out to capitalists ; that is, the right to receive the profits arising from the exchange during a fixed period was sold by the Crown. The accounts of the exchangers are extant.

*Fibula*, a brooch.

*Franchises of the City of London*, the rights granted to the citizens by royal charters, viz. of Wm. I, Hen. I, Stephen,

Hen. II, Rich. I, John, Ed. I and III, Rich. II, Hen. IV and V, &c. These charters were confirmed by succeeding sovereigns, and allowed the citizens to elect their own mayor and sheriffs, to hold their own law courts, to levy their own taxation, to impose their own tolls, and generally to act independently of royal officers in their internal administration.

*Frater*, refectory. (Monastic.)

*Freeman of a city, town*, &c., a person entitled, either by birth, privileged admission, or admission by payment, to enter a craft gild or merchant gild of a town, and freely practise a craft or buy and sell within the town.

*Fret*, a network for confining the hair.

*Gadlings*, spikes, or knobs, on the knuckles of gauntlets.

*Gambeson*, a close-fitting, quilted tunic of defence, stuffed with wool, tow, rags, &c.

*Gesso*, an Italian term for plaster of Paris, especially when used as a ground for painting or a material for decorative mouldings.

*Gorget*, a steel collar, used in fifteenth-century armour.

*Greek cross*, a plain cross, the four limbs of which are of equal length.

*Groining*, the angular edges formed by the intersection of vaults in a ceiling.

*Groundage*, also called *strandage*. 'Every great vessel that grounds shall pay twopence for strandage. For a small vessel with oarlocks that grounds, one penny. For a boat that grounds, one half-penny' (*Liber Albus*, tr. Riley, 208). In 1545 fourpence was charged for every ship. Ships of freemen of the city were exempt.

*Guige*, the strap by which a shield was hung round the neck.

*Gypcière*, a hanging purse or pouch, from Fr. *gibecière*, a game-pouch, because originally used in hawking.

*Habergeon*, a short, light hauberk, of which the word is a diminutive; usually therefore of mail, but sometimes merely a small plate for the defence of the throat and breast.

*Haketon*, a variety of gambeson, said to have been of buckskin stuffed with cotton.

*Hall for hynds*, servants' hall. Cp. Shak. *As You Like It*, i. 1. 20.

*Hanse*: (1) The entrance fee of a trading gild. (2) Any mercantile exaction, e. g. a toll paid by non-gildsmen for the privilege of trading in a town. (3) A synonym of the *gilda mercatoria*, the merchant gild of a town. (4) From this sometimes extended to a craft gild. (5) A society of merchants trading abroad. (6) A society of foreign merchants trading in England. (7) The confederation of North German States known as the Hanseatic League.

*Hauberk*, a tunic of iron rings interlinked.

*Heater-shaped shield*, a triangular shield with curved sides, shaped like a flat-iron heater.

*Helm*, from the end of the twelfth century the word was confined to the great close casque which then came into use; e. g. Figs. 151, 171.

*Helmet*, diminutive of *helm*, than which it was lighter, and originally a vizorless defence. The helm was often worn over it.

*Herring-bone pattern*, the placing of stones aslant in a wall so that each two rows form a succession of angles resembling the backbone of a herring.

*Hobilar, -er*, a light cavalry soldier. Perhaps so called from his wearing a *hobille*, i. e. a quilted jack, or gambeson, instead of metal armour; more probably from his riding a 'hobby', or small horse.

*Hose-stocks*, or *upper-stocks*, short breeches; 'nether-stocks' were hose.

*Impale*, to divide a shield vertically into halves, and charge a coat of arms on each half; Fig. 223, c.

*Incunabula*, early printed books, especially those printed before A.D. 1500.

*Jack*, a general term for a coat of defence, whether wadded or of mail; but also especially used for the inexpensive body-garment of the ordinary soldier, formed of small pieces of metal secured between two folds of leather, canvas, or some quilted stuff.

*Jambes*, shin and calf plates. (Armour.)

*Jazerine*, light armour of small plates, or splints, of metal, riveted together or to some strong material.

*Jupon*, a tight, short surcoat.

*Kirtle*, tunic.

*Lamboys*, steel skirts, a feature of sixteenth-century armour.

*Lantern*, or *Louvre*, a small open turret placed on a roof as an outlet for smoke.

*Lanzknecht*, a German pikeman, billman, or halberdier.

*Latten*, an alloy of copper and zinc, also known as *Cullen plate*, from Cologne, where it was principally fabricated, of which monumental brasses, seal-dies, candlesticks, crosses, &c., were largely made in the Middle Ages. It is what is now called ' cock-brass ', a specially hard mixed metal used for the cocks of casks and cisterns.

*Launder*, a person (of either sex) who washes linen.

*Law merchant*, the law common to mercantile transactions in England and abroad, declared in contested cases at fairs and markets by the assembled merchants, or before the King's Bench upon a summons from the Chief Justice issued to twelve merchants.

*Lighterage*, a duty levied on the discharge of cargo by foreign ships in mid stream from their own boats, when they did not make use of English lighters ; also the charge for the use of the latter.

*Lights*, the spaces between the mullions of a window. (Arch.)

*Locket*, a metal or leather band on a scabbard.

*Luce*, the heraldic term for the pike (fish, Lat. *lucius*).

*Mazer*, a wooden drinking bowl, usually mounted with an engraved and inscribed silver band.

*Members*, mouldings, or subordinate parts of a building generally.

*Millrind*, the iron fixed to the centre of a millstone.

*Misericord* (Lat. *misericordia* = mercy, pity, compassion). (1) A special apartment in a monastery, for the use of monks receiving special indulgences in respect of diet and discipline ; (2) a long, narrow dagger used for giving the *coup de grâce* ; (3) a bracket on the under-side of a choir-seat, which, when the seat is turned up, gives some support to a person standing.

*Morion*, a steel cap, with curved brim and high comb.

*Mullet*, a five-pointed spur-rowel. (Heraldry.)

*Mullions*, the vertical divisions of stone or wood between the lights of windows.

*Murage*, a port-due levied by authority of the Crown for the repair of the walls of seaport towns.

*Nasal*, the vertical nose-bar of a helmet.

*Newel*, the column round which a circular staircase winds.

*Nimbus*, a bright or golden disk, surrounding the head of a divine or canonized person.

*Obedientiary*, the holder of any office in a monastery under the abbot.

*Ogee*, an arch formed of a double curve,

the lower convex, the upper concave : e. g. Fig. 32.

*Orle*, a decorated wreath, worn round the bascinet in fifteenth-century armour.

*Orlop, Overlop*, Du. *overloop*. In the early sixteenth century the word was applied to either of a vessel's two decks. Late in the reign of Elizabeth, a partial deck was introduced below the two usual ones for the carriage of stores and cables, and this was called a ' false orlop '. Later this deck was extended to the whole length of the ship, was always below the water-line, and was called, distinctively, the orlop.

*Orphrey*, gold or other rich embroidery applied either to ecclesiastical vestments or to articles of lay attire.

*Pallets*, plates that protect the armpits. They superseded the mail gusset.

*Parmenter*, a maker of short coats, or vestments, of skin with the fur on, or of well-dressed skins embroidered.

*Passant gardant*, walking past, but turning the head so as to show the full face. (Heraldry.)

*Pavage*, a duty levied on foreign merchants by way of contribution to the paving of the city (*Liber Albus*, tr. Riley, 126).

*Petronel*, a firearm discharged from the chest (*poitrine*) ; in size midway between the pistol and the arquebus.

*Pier*, the mass of masonry between arches and other openings.

*Pilaster*, a square or rectangular pillar, engaged in, and projecting slightly from, a wall.

*Pinched*, plaited. (Costume.)

*Points*, ties, laces. (Costume.)

*Poleyns*, overlapping foot-plates. (Armour.)

*Pomander*, a scent-box.

*Pontage*, used in the threefold sense of a duty levied for the repair of a bridge, and for the passing under or over it.

*Postern*, a private or subsidiary entrance ; lit. a back-door. (Mil. Arch.)

*Pourpoint*, double stuff, padded or quilted (*perpunctum*). (Armour.)

*Pretence, in*, by way of claim (*prétendre*). (Heraldry.)

*Protection*, the policy of encouraging certain selected home industries by the discouragement or exclusion, by means of import duties, of competing commodities manufactured abroad.

*Quainted*, made stylish by dagging or scalloping. (Costume.)

*Quarrel*, a bolt with a four-sided pyramidal head. (Arms.)

*Quarter*, to arrange coats of arms in

sequence on a shield in accordance with the laws of armory.

*Quoins*, dressed corner-stones. (Arch.)

*Rampant sinister*, rampant, but facing to the left side of the shield, Fig. 210.

*Regrators*, purchasers who bought to sell again at an enhanced price. The word originally applied to purchasers by wholesale to sell by retail, but by the sixteenth century it had generally come to mean purchasers buying to sell at an enhanced price in the same market or fair, or within five miles thereof, which was a statutory offence. But on p. 603 it is used as equivalent to 'engrossers', or purchasers on a wholesale scale.

*Reiters*, or *Pistoliers*, light cavalry whose special weapons were a pair of wheel-lock pistols.

*Repoussé*, ornamentation in relief on metal, hammered out from behind.

*Retable* (Reredos), a piece of sculptured or painted decoration behind and above an altar.

*Runes*, inscriptions in ancient Scandinavian characters.

*Scavage*. 'Be it known that Scavage is so called as being a "shewing", because it behoves the merchants that they shew unto the Sheriffs the merchandise for which the custom is to be taken, before that any of it be sold.' Hence, the name for a duty levied on articles exposed to sale by persons not free of the city or corporate town. (See *Liber Albus*, tr. Riley, 196-9.)

*Sepulchre, Easter*, a recess, or structure, on the north side of a chancel, used at Easter in the setting up of a representation of the burial of Christ; but often merely a temporary wooden erection.

*Sewery*, a store-room for provisions, linen, and other table-furniture.

*Shingles*, wooden tiles.

*Sinister quarter*, a quarter (Fig. 188, N) on the sinister or left side of a shield. (Heraldry.)

*Spandrels*, the two triangular spaces above the curves of an arch that is enclosed within a square moulding; e. g. Fig. 19.

*Splayed*. A window, or other opening, of which the sides are expanded by being slanted, is said to be splayed : a contracted form of 'displayed'.

*Staple wares*. 'Staple signifieth this or that towne or citie whither the merchants of England by common order or commandement did carrie their woolles, wool-fels, cloathes, leade and tinne [staple wares] and such like commodoties of our land for the utterance [sale] of them by the great [wholesale].'

*String*, or *String-course*, a horizontal line of projecting mouldings carried along a building.

*Supportasses*, wire supports for the ruff. (Costume.)

*Supporters*, usually two in number, and generally animals. They appear to support a shield, but had their origin in the fancy of early seal engravers, who thus filled up the unoccupied space in armorial seals. (Heraldry.)

*Tabard*, a loose, wide-sleeved surcoat, richly figured on back, front, and sleeves.

*Tassets*, steel hip-bands, a feature of fifteenth-century armour. Also called *taces*.

*Tokens*, coins of copper, lead, tin, and occasionally even of leather, issued by private persons, often by tradesmen. Licences were sometimes issued for their coinage. When the royal currency was scarce, they obtained considerable circulation.

*Tonnage*, or *Tunnage*, a tax, originally of 2s., afterwards of 3s., per tun, or ton, of 252 gallons of wine, first imposed by agreement with the merchants in 1347 for the purpose of paying the wage of ships of war acting as convoys to merchant vessels. At the same time a tax was imposed called poundage, at first 6d. and after 1406 1s. in the £, levied on exports and imports except wool and skins. These two taxes were from 1373 regularly granted by Parliament under the name of Tunnage and Poundage.

*Transom*, a thwart-bar of wood or stone extending across a window. A corruption of the Lat. *transtrum*.

*Trick*, to indicate the tinctures of a coat of arms by letters ; from the Dutch *trekken*, to delineate.

*Triptych*, a folding tablet of three panels, of which the two outer form doors that fold over the central panel (cp. *Diptych*).

*Trussed*, tied. (Costume.)

*Tuilles*, plates suspended from the tassets ; Fr. *tuile* = tile, Lat. *tegula*. (Armour.)

*Tympanum*, the semicircular or triangular space above a square-topped door which has an arch over it. Found commonly in Norman work, and usually filled with sculpture.

*Umbo*, the boss of a shield.
*Ungentle*, not befitting a gentleman.

*Vert*, green. (Heraldry.)

*Waterbailage, Ballivagium*, a duty levied by the City of London upon goods there shipped on foreign vessels for export.
*Were*, protect.
*Wharfage.* ' It is reasonable, considering the wharfes be repared at the cost of the private inhabitants of the same, and it is equitye, that the shippes approching theim and with their weight putting theim to stresse, ther shuld be made a recompence to the partye ' (*Instructions of Henry VIII to his plenipotentiaries in the Netherlands* 19 *April* 1532).
*Wimple*, a covering for the head, gathered round it and pleated under the chin.

# INDEX

# INDEX